CLINICAL ANTHOLOGY
READINGS FOR
LIVE-CLIENT CLINCIS

ANDERSON'S
Law School Publications

Administrative Law Anthology
Thomas O. Sargentich

Administrative Law: Cases and Materials
Daniel J. Gifford

Alternative Dispute Resolution: Strategies for Law and Business
E. Wendy Trachte-Huber and Stephen K. Huber

American Legal Systems: A Resource and Reference Guide
Toni M. Fine

An Admiralty Law Anthology
Robert M. Jarvis

Analytic Jurisprudence Anthology
Anthony D'Amato

An Antitrust Anthology
Andrew I. Gavil

Appellate Advocacy: Principles and Practice: Cases and Materials, Second Edition
Ursula Bentele and Eve Cary

Basic Accounting Principles for Lawyers: With Present Value and Expected Value
C. Steven Bradford and Gary A. Ames

A Capital Punishment Anthology (and Electronic Caselaw Appendix)
Victor L. Streib

Cases and Problems in Criminal Law, Third Edition
Myron Moskovitz

The Citation Workbook
Maria L. Ciampi, Rivka Widerman, and Vicki Lutz

Civil Procedure: Cases, Materials, and Questions
Richard D. Freer and Wendy C. Perdue

Clinical Anthology: Readings for Live-Client Clinics
Alex J. Hurder, Frank S. Bloch, Susan L. Brooks, and Susan L. Kay

Commercial Transactions: Problems and Materials
Louis F. Del Duca, Egon Guttman, Alphonse M. Squillante, Fred H. Miller, and Peter Winship
    Vol. 1: Secured Transactions Under the UCC
    Vol. 2: Sales Under the UCC and the CISG
    Vol. 3: Negotiable Instruments Under the UCC and the CIBN

Communications Law: Media, Entertainment, and Regulation
Donald E. Lively, Allen S. Hammond, IV, Blake D. Morant, and Russell L. Weaver

A Conflict-of-Laws Anthology
Gene R. Shreve

A Constitutional Law Anthology
Michael J. Glennon

Constitutional Conflicts, Part I
Derrick A. Bell, Jr.

Constitutional Law: Cases, History, and Dialogues
Donald E. Lively, Phoebe A. Haddon, Dorothy E. Roberts, and Russell L. Weaver

The Constitutional Law of the European Union
James D. Dinnage and John F. Murphy

The Constitutional Law of the European Union: Documentary Supplement
James D. Dinnage and John F. Murphy

Constitutional Torts
Sheldon H. Nahmod, Michael L. Wells, and Thomas A. Eaton

Contracts
Contemporary Cases, Comments, and Problems
Michael L. Closen, Richard M. Perlmutter, and Jeffrey D. Wittenberg

A Contracts Anthology, Second Edition
Peter Linzer

A Corporate Law Anthology
Franklin A. Gevurtz

Corporate and White Collar Crime: An Anthology
Leonard Orland

A Criminal Law Anthology
Arnold H. Loewy

Criminal Law: Cases and Materials
Arnold H. Loewy

A Criminal Procedure Anthology
Silas J. Wasserstrom and Christie L. Snyder

Criminal Procedure: Arrest and Investigation
Arnold H. Loewy and Arthur B. LaFrance

Criminal Procedure: Trial and Sentencing
Arthur B. LaFrance and Arnold H. Loewy

Economic Regulation: Cases and Materials
Richard J. Pierce, Jr.

Elements of Law
Eva H. Hanks, Michael E. Herz, and Steven S. Nemerson

Ending It: Dispute Resolution in America
Descriptions, Examples, Cases and Questions
Susan M. Leeson and Bryan M. Johnston

Environmental Law, Second Edition
Jackson B. Battle, Robert L. Fischman, Maxine I. Lipeles, and Mark S. Squillace
    Vol. 1: Environmental Decisionmaking: NEPA and the Endangered Species Act
    Vol. 2: Water Pollution
    Vol. 3: Air Pollution
    Vol. 4: Hazardous Waste

An Environmental Law Anthology
Robert L. Fischman, Maxine I. Lipeles, and Mark S. Squillace

Environmental Protection and Justice
Readings and Commentary on Environmental Law and Practice
Kenneth A. Manaster

An Evidence Anthology
Edward J. Imwinkelried and Glen Weissenberger

Federal Evidence Courtroom Manual
Glen Weissenberger

Federal Income Tax Anthology
Paul L. Caron, Karen C. Burke, and Grayson M.P. McCouch

Federal Rules of Evidence, 1996-97 Edition
Rules, Legislative History, Commentary and Authority
Glen Weissenberger

Federal Rules of Evidence Handbook, 1996-97 Edition
Publisher's Staff

First Amendment Anthology
Donald E. Lively, Dorothy E. Roberts, and Russell L. Weaver

International Environmental Law Anthology
Anthony D'Amato and Kirsten Engel

International Human Rights: Law, Policy and Process, Second Edition
Frank C. Newman and David Weissbrodt

**Selected International Human Rights Instruments and
Bibliography For Research on International Human Rights Law, Second Edition**
Frank C. Newman and David Weissbrodt

International Intellectual Property Anthology
Anthony D'Amato and Doris Estelle Long

International Law Anthology
Anthony D'Amato

International Law Coursebook
Anthony D'Amato

Introduction to The Study of Law: Cases and Materials
John Makdisi

Judicial Externships: The Clinic Inside The Courthouse
Rebecca A. Cochran

Justice and the Legal System
A Coursebook
Anthony D'Amato and Arthur J. Jacobson

The Law of Disability Discrimination
Ruth Colker

ADA Handbook
Statutes, Regulations and Related Materials
Publisher's Staff

The Law of Modern Payment Systems and Notes
Fred H. Miller and Alvin C. Harrell

Lawyers and Fundamental Moral Responsibility
Daniel R. Coquillette

Microeconomic Predicates to Law and Economics
Mark Seidenfeld

Patients, Psychiatrists and Lawyers Law and the Mental Health System, Second Edition
Raymond L. Spring, Roy B. Lacoursiere, M.D., and Glen Weissenberger

Principles of Evidence, Third Edition
Irving Younger, Michael Goldsmith, and David A. Sonenshein

Problems and Simulations in Evidence, Second Edition
Thomas F. Guernsey

A Products Liability Anthology
Anita Bernstein

Professional Responsibility Anthology
Thomas B. Metzloff

A Property Anthology
Richard H. Chused

Public Choice and Public Law: Readings and Commentary
Maxwell L. Stearns

Preventive Law: Materials on a Non Adversarial Legal Process
Robert M. Hardaway

The Regulation of Banking
Cases and Materials on Depository Institutions and Their Regulators
Michael P. Malloy

Science in Evidence
David H. Kaye

A Section 1983 Civil Rights Anthology
Sheldon H. Nahmod

Sports Law: Cases and Materials, Third Edition
Ray L. Yasser, James R. McCurdy, and C. Peter Goplerud

A Torts Anthology
Lawrence C. Levine, Julie A. Davies, and Edward J. Kionka

Trial Practice
Lawrence A. Dubin and Thomas F. Guernsey

Trial Practice Problems and Case Files
Edward R. Stein and Lawrence A. Dubin

Trial Practice and Case Files with *Video* Presentation
Edward R. Stein and Lawrence A. Dubin

Unincorporated Business Entities
Larry E. Ribstein

FORTHCOMING PUBLICATIONS

A Civil Procedure Anthology
David I. Levine, Donald L. Doernberg, and Melissa L. Nelken

A Constitutional Law Anthology, Second Edition
Donald E. Lively, Michael J. Glennon, Phoebe A. Haddon, Dorothy E. Roberts, and Russell L. Weaver

Antitrust Law: Cases and Materials
Daniel J. Gifford and Leo J. Raskind

A Property Law Anthology, Second Edition
Richard H. Chused

Citation Workbook, Second Edition
Maria L. Ciampi, Rivka Widerman, and Vicki Lutz

Constitutional Conflicts, Part II
Derrick A. Bell, Jr.

Contract Law and Practice: Cases and Materials
Michael L. Closen, Gerald E. Berendt, Doris Estelle Long, Marie A. Monahan, Robert J. Nye, and John H. Scheid

European Union Law Anthology
Anthony D'Amato and Karen V. Kole

Family Law Anthology
Frances E. Olsen

Law and Economics: An Anthology
Kenneth G. Dau-Schmidt and Thomas S. Ulen

CLINICAL ANTHOLOGY
READINGS FOR
LIVE-CLIENT CLINCIS

EDITED BY

ALEX J. HURDER

Associate Professor of the Practice of Law
Vanderbilt University School of Law

FRANK S. BLOCH

Professor of Law and Director of Clinical Education
Vanderbilt University School of Law

SUSAN L. BROOKS

Assistant Professor of the Practice of Law
Vanderbilt University School of Law

SUSAN L. KAY

Professor of the Practice of Law
Vanderbilt University School of Law

ANDERSON PUBLISHING CO.
CINCINNATI, OHIO

CLINICAL ANTHOLOGY: READINGS FOR LIVE-CLIENT CLINICS
EDITED BY: ALEX J. HURDER, FRANK S. BLOCH, SUSAN L. BROOKS, SUSAN L. KAY

© 1997 by Anderson Publishing Co.

Anderson Publishing Co.
2035 Reading Road / Cincinnati, Ohio 45202
800-582-7295 / e-mail andpubco@aol.com / Fax 513-562-5430

ISBN: 0-87084-352-4

To Mary Winifred Wrasman. A.J.H.

To the memory of my mother. F.S.B.

To my parents. S.L.B.

To my parents, Sanford and Micki Kay. S.L.K.

Contents

Preface

The CLINICAL ANTHOLOGY grew out of our four-year search for readings to use in the classroom component of the live-client clinic at Vanderbilt Law School. We each supervise students who represent clients in areas of our separate specialties, including civil, criminal and juvenile law matters. The classroom sessions include all of our students and are intended to help them reflect more generally on their clinical practice experience.

Our search for reading materials required us to identify issues that we wanted all of our students to recognize and to consider in the context of their clinical practice. We were also guided by our view that the classroom component of a live-client clinic is secondary to students' learning through representation of clients. Our goal was to identify a set of materials that raise certain issues that arise consistently in clinical practice, as well as others that constitute a core set of topics about the lawyering process. Given this orientation, we decided not to include materials that focus on particular practice skills. Rather, the readings in this anthology reflect the growing body of scholarship about the issues and dilemmas that lawyers confront in practice. This new body of clinical scholarship, when read and discussed in conjunction with actual casework in the clinic, can make a law student's first exposure to the world of law practice a richer learning experience.

The time available for classroom teaching and discussion in a live-client clinic limits the topics that can be taken up in the classroom. Although there is a coherence to the set of readings as a whole, instructors can select readings from the anthology that will meet the needs of their particular courses and that address the problems of their students' caseload. In our view, classroom sessions for a particular clinical course should focus to a significant degree on the types of cases handled in the clinic and even on current developments in individual cases. Accordingly, the anthology is designed to allow flexibility in assignments. Classroom discussion based on readings can incorporate illustrations and problems from on-going cases.

The organization of the readings in the anthology reflects a suggested order that topics might be taken up in the classroom. The excerpts in the first chapter offer different views of what law students can and should learn in clinical courses and explain methods of clinical teaching and learning. The next four chapters explore issues of lawyer-client relations and relations with other parties and court systems that are likely to arise as a case progresses in a student's clinical practice. The final chapter examines the lawyer's obligation to pursue justice and to ensure access to the courts.

The four middle chapters focus specifically on issues that arise in practice and begin with Chapter II on professional ethics and values. The topic of professional ethics and values is taken up at the beginning for two reasons. First, law students must be aware that their conduct is governed by rules of ethics before they take on responsibility for clients. Second, law students should be aware of the breadth of professional responsibility issues. Every aspect of the practice of law, from how one communicates with clients to how one negotiates with an adversary, has ethical implications. As the readings throughout this anthology illustrate, learning to practice law includes not only skills training but also developing standards of ethical and moral conduct.

Chapter III emphasizes issues that arise when lawyers relate to clients, including how lawyers communicate with clients and the nature of the lawyer-client relationship. Chapter IV explores how lawyers and clients work together to frame the story of a case, to make decisions, and to gather information about relevant facts.

Chapter V focuses on the lawyer's role as an advocate. It examines the respective roles of lawyers and clients when their goal is to persuade an adversary or to convince a court.

The final chapter raises broad issues about the justice mission of lawyers and the duty of lawyers to guarantee access to the courts. The excerpts reflect the unique role of live-client clinics, most of which provide free legal services to persons who could not otherwise afford legal representation.

The excerpts selected for the anthology reflect current discussions and debates in legal education generally and in the field of clinical legal education in particular. They represent a wide range of viewpoints; inclusion of an excerpt in the anthology does not constitute an endorsement of its point of view.

Most of the excerpts selected for the anthology are only small portions of the articles from which they are taken. We encourage readers to refer to the complete article for a full explanation of the author's point of view. We have omitted footnotes whenever possible in order to focus attention on the points made in the text. Asterisks indicate omissions from the text. We have also corrected minor typographical errors.

We wish to thank those who helped us prepare this book. Linda Williams deserves special recognition for her contribution to the CLINICAL ANTHOLOGY. She prepared the entire manuscript and coordinated the task of requesting copyright permissions and the work of the proofreaders. The project would have stalled without her dedication and commitment. We are grateful to Professors Anthony V. Alfieri, Paul Bergman, Naomi Cahn, Clark D. Cunningham, Peter T. Hoffman, Carol Bensinger Liebman, Peter Margulies, Elliott S. Milstein,

Dean Rivkin, Paul Tremblay, and Roy T. Stuckey for their comments and suggestions. Many Vanderbilt law students helped with research, screening and proofreading. We are particularly indebted to Paige Black, Shalini Gopalakrishnan, Mark Helm, Caroline Memnon, Neil Morholt, Michelle Morseman, Hugh Ray, Amber St. John, Miguel Soto, and Christine Wohar.

A.J.H.
F.S.B.
S.L.B.
S.L.K.
Nashville, Tennessee
March, 1997

Chapter 1

LIVE-CLIENT CLINICS

A. Clinics and the Law School Curriculum

Casebook-based law teaching dominated legal education almost without exception for nearly a century preceding the widespread introduction of clinical programs in the late 1960s, with few persons of stature in law schools or the legal profession questioning the dominant approach throughout that period. One exception was Professor, later Judge, Jerome Frank who tried to start a dialogue in the 1930s on the value of practice-based training for law students. The following excerpt is from his classic article in which he sets up and answers what now seems to be an obvious question: why not a clinical lawyer-school?

Jerome Frank, *Why Not a Clinical Lawyer-School?*, 81 U. PA. L. REV. 907 (1933)*

The method of teaching still used in some university law schools (and accepted by them as more or less sacrosanct) is founded upon the ideas of Christopher Columbus Langdell. It may be said, indeed, to be the expression of that man's peculiar temperament.

Langdell unequivocally stated as the fundamental tenet of his system of teaching *"that all the available materials . . . are contained in printed books"*. The printed opinions of judges are, he maintained, the *exclusive* repositories of the wisdom which law students must acquire to make them lawyers.

Now it is important to observe the manner of man who impressed those notions on American legal pedagogy for more than half a century:

When Langdell was himself a law student he was almost constantly in the law library. His fellow students said of him that he slept on the library table. At that time he served for several years as an assistant librarian. One of his friends found him one day in an alcove of the library absorbed in a black-letter folio, one of the year books. "As he drew near", we are told, "Langdell looked up and said, in a tone of mingled exhilaration and regret, and with an emphatic gesture, 'Oh, if only I could have lived in the time of the Plantaganets!'"

He practiced law in New York City for sixteen years. But he seldom tried a case. He spent most of his time in the library of the New York Law Institute. He led a peculiarly secluded life. His biographer says of him: *"In the almost inaccessible retirement of his office, and in the library of the Law Institute, he did the greater part of his work. He went little into company."* His clients were mostly other lawyers for whom, after much lucubration, he wrote briefs or prepared pleadings.

Is it any wonder that such a man had an obsessive and almost exclusive interest in books? The raw material of law, he devoutly believed, was to be discovered in a library and nowhere else; it consisted, as he himself said, solely of what could be found in the pages of law reports. One of his biographers praises him because he sought *"the living founts"* of law in the works on the library shelves! Practicing law to Langdell meant the writing of briefs, examination of printed authorities. The lawyer-client relation, the numerous non-rational factors involved in persuasion of a judge at a trial, the face-to-face appeals to the emotions of juries, the elements that go to make up what is loosely known as the "atmosphere" of a case—everything that is undisclosed in judicial opinions—was virtually unknown (and was therefore meaningless) to Langdell. A great part of the realities of the life of the average lawyer was unreal to him.

* * *

A brief outline of the history of legal education in American universities is helpful as a preliminary to some tentative suggestions for changes.

It began with the apprentice system. The prospective lawyer "read law" in the office of a practicing lawyer. He saw daily what courts were doing. The first American law school, founded by Judge Reeves, in the 1780's was merely the apprentice system on a group basis. The students were still in intimate daily contact with the courts. Then (about 1830) came the college law school with teaching on the college pattern of lectures and text-books. This step is ordinarily pictured as progress. For the student now devoted full time to his books and lectures and the distractions of office and court work were removed. A more unpleasant story could be told: The student was cloistered; he learned of court doings from books and lectures only; the *false* aspects of theory could no longer be compared by him with the actualities of practice.

There followed the period when the leading law schools were dominated by the great systematic text-book writers, the makers of so-called (American) "substantive law", substantive law which was divorced and living apart from procedure. The rift widened between theory and practice.

Then came Langdell. Noting his plea for induction, his efforts to avoid the glib generalities of text-books, one cannot help feeling that he was seeking obliquely and fumblingly to return to some limited extent to court-room actualities. But he was patently thinking of the lawyer as brief-writer and nothing more. Consequently, the material on which he based his so-called "induction" was hopelessly limited.

Ostensibly, the students were to study cases. But they did not and *they do not study cases.* They do not even study the printed records of cases (although that would be little enough), let alone cases as living processes. Their attention is restricted to judicial *opinions. But an opinion is not a decision.* A decision is a specific judgment, or order or decree entered after a trial of a specific lawsuit between specific litigants. There are a multitude of factors which induce a jury to return a verdict, or a judge to enter a decree. Of those numerous factors, but few are set forth in judicial opinions. And those factors, not expressed in the opinions, frequently are the most important in the real causal explanation of the decisions.

* * *

For the practicing lawyer and his client, the specific decisions of actual specific cases are ultimates. Decisions, not opinions. What the lawyer and his client want are concrete judgments and decrees—regardless of the presence or absence of concomitant opinions, irrespective of the contents of the opinions, if there are any. Since the opinions—and the works of those commentators who discuss opinions—are emasculated explanations of decisions, they are of limited assistance to the practicing lawyer. Not only do they disclose merely a fractional part of how decisions come into being, but, if the lawyer takes them as adequate explanations of how decisions are reached, he will act with a treacherously false sense of certainty in advising clients, drafting instruments, writing briefs—or any other work he has to perform.

* * *

The trouble with much law school teaching is that, confining its attention to a study of upper court opinions, it is hopelessly oversimplified. Something important and of immense worth was given up when the legal apprentice system was abandoned as the basis of teaching in the leading American law schools. This does not mean that we should return to the old system in its old form, that we want mere apprentice-trained lawyers or law schools which are merely "expanded law offices". But is it not plain that, without giving up entirely the case-book system or the growing and valuable alliance with the so-called social sciences, the law schools should once more get in intimate contact with what clients need and with what courts and lawyers actually do? Must we not execute an about-face and return to Judge Reeves' 18th century apprentice method, but on a higher, more sophisticated level?

II

To be more specific, the following ideas are recommended for consideration:

* * *

4. And now we come to a point which the writer considers of major importance. It was stated above that law schools could learn much from the medical schools. The parallel cannot be carried too far. But a brief scrutiny of medical education suggests the use of a device which may be employed as an adequate method of obtaining apprentice work for law students:

Medical schools rely to a very large extent on the free medical clinics and dispensaries. * * *

Suppose, however, that there were in each law school a legal clinic or dispensary. As before indicated, a considerable part of the teaching staff of a law school should consist of lawyers who already had varied experience in practice. * * *

The work of these clinics would be done for little or no charge. The teacher-clinicians would devote their full time to their teaching, including such clinical work, and would not engage in private practice.

* * *

In this way, the students would learn to observe the true relation between the contents of upper court opinions and the work of the practicing lawyers and the courts. *The student would be made to see, among other things, the human side of the administration of justice*, including the following:

(a) How juries decide cases. The factors that count in jury trials. The slight effect of the judges' instructions on verdicts. The hazards of a jury trial.

(b) The uncertain character of the "facts" of a case when it is "contested", *i.e.*, when conflicting testimony is introduced. The difference between what actually happened between the parties to the suit and the way those actual happenings can be made to appear to a judge or jury. The transcendent importance of the "facts" of a case. The inherent subjectivity of those "facts" in "contested cases". The inability to guess future decisions (even when the "legal rules" seem clear) because it is impossible to guess, before a suit has been begun, whether there will be an issue of fact, and, if so, whether conflicting testimony will be introduced, what judge or jury will try the case and what the reaction of that unknown judge or jury will be to that unknown testimony.

The student should learn that "legal rights and duties" are inextricably intertwined with litigation—that, for instance, there is no such thing as "the law of torts" as distinguished from decisions in lawsuits, and that the so-called rules and principles of torts are only some among the many implements employed by lawyers in their efforts to win lawsuits.

(c) How legal rights often turn on the faulty memory of witnesses, the bias of witnesses, the perjury of witnesses.

(d) The effects of fatigue, alertness, political pull, graft, laziness, conscientiousness, patience, impatience, prejudice and open-mindedness of judges. How legal rights may vary with the judge who tries the case and with that judge's varying and often unpredictable reactions to various kinds of cases and divers kinds of witnesses.

(e) The methods used in negotiating contracts and settlements of controversies.

(f) The nature of draftsmanship: How the lawyer tries to translate the wishes of a client (often inadequately expressed by the client) into wills, contracts or corporate instruments.

What is intended is not that (as a scoffing neo-Langdellian recently suggested) the student should in his law-school days learn "the way to the post-office" or "the mechanics of the short-trial list". What is intended is that, almost at the beginning of and during his law-school days, the student should learn the very limited (although real) importance in the actual legal world of so-called substantive law and of so-called legal rules and principles. He should learn that "legal rights" and "duties" mean merely what may some day happen at the end of specific lawsuits. And that all so-called legal rules—including the so-called rules of substantive law—are "procedural"; *i.e.*, among the many implements to be used in the kind of fight, conducted in a court room, which we call "litigation". He should learn that judges are fallible human beings and that legal rights often depend on the unpredictable reactions of those fallible human beings to a multitude of stimuli, including the rules, but also including the fallible testimony of other human beings called witnesses. The student should become aware of the slippery character of "the facts" of a case, when there is conflicting testimony, and of the marked importance of what happens in trial courts.

* * *

Jerome Frank's vision of a clinical lawyer-school began to take hold in the 1960s and 1970s as persistent cries went out for relevance—social and professional—in legal education. The going was slow, however, and there remained deep resistance among traditionalists in law schools and in the legal profession. In the following excerpt, Anthony G. Amsterdam looks back at a resilient status quo while charting the future for clinical legal education.

Anthony G. Amsterdam, *Clinical Legal Education—A 21st Century Perspective*, 34 J. LEGAL EDUC. 612 (1984)*

I. Introduction

Since the theme of this conference is "Approaching the 21st Century," I mean to talk about legal education in the twenty-first century, not the twentieth. This will permit me to do two things I very much want to do.

Initially, I can put behind us certain debates that badly bedeviled legal education at the end of the twentieth century. These debates had to do with so-called skills training and clinical legal education—what they were all about and whether they should be taught in law school. The debates particularly flourished in the period between the late 1970s and 1995 or so. But now that we are in the enlightened twenty-first century, I can happily assume that they have been resolved (and, naturally, in keeping with my own desires).

Also, I can now say some things that it would have been politically unwise for me to say back at the end of the twentieth century. Please recall always that I speak for twenty-first century ears, not twentieth.

II. Summary of Points

First, I want to specify one of the principal ways in which legal education at the end of the twentieth century was too narrow. In those days the criticism was often voiced that legal education was too narrow because it failed to teach students how to practice law, failed to develop in them practical skills necessary for the competent

---

*   Reprinted with permission.

performance of lawyers' work. We now realize that this criticism—while valid to some extent—concealed a deeper, more important one. Legal education in those days was too narrow because it failed to develop in students ways of thinking within and about the role of lawyers—methods of critical analysis, planning, and decision-making which are not themselves practical skills but rather the conceptual foundations for practical skills and for much else, just as case reading and doctrinal analysis are foundations for practical skills and for much else.

Second, I want to identify an even more basic shortcoming of legal education back at the end of the twentieth century. This was the assumption that the job of law schools was to impart to students a self-contained body of instruction in the law. In the twenty-first century we realize, of course, that a major function of law schools is to give students systematic training in effective techniques for learning law from the experience of practicing law.

Third, I want to describe briefly a pedagogic method—sometimes called the clinical method of legal instruction—which was developed in the last quarter of the twentieth century to broaden legal education in all of these dimensions.

Fourth, I want to point out—and this is what would have been political dynamite at the end of the twentieth century—that the only way in which the law schools could have afforded to utilize this new technique of legal instruction effectively was to cut back substantially on teaching what they used to teach in the way they used to teach it.

III. Discussion
Point One: Divers Analytic Modes

The best way to develop my first point is to itemize three kinds of analytic thinking that were traditionally taught in law schools and three that were not.

1. *Case reading and interpretation.* Law schools traditionally taught students how to interpret judicial opinions, to examine their implications and the limits of their implications, to reason from them and predict their applications in other hypothesized factual situations. (This involves comprehension of the basic *stare decisis* principle, such concepts as "holdings" and "dicta" and notions of why and how the procedural posture of litigation frames the "issues" for decision, the idea of "distinctions" and "analogies," and how and when distinctions and analogies can be drawn.) Through this mode of reasoning, a student or a lawyer can predict or argue that a decided case will or will not, should or should not, control legal consequences in different factual situations subsequently arising.

2. *Doctrinal analysis and application.* Law schools traditionally taught students how to synthesize whole bodies of decided cases, how to discern patterns in them, identify and reconcile potential contradictions, isolate and compose the strands of reasoning reflected in them, so as to distill principles or rules or doctrines which can then be applied to predict or argue the legal consequences that will or should attach to given fact situations. In this mode of reasoning, techniques of classification and characterization are developed which are the lawyer's (and the judge's) tools for determining whether, for example, one precedent or another more strongly attracts a given situation.

3. *Logical conceptualization and criticism.* Law schools traditionally taught students—to some extent—how to array legal authorities and principles in some sort of logical system, so as to criticize the symmetry or asymmetry of its parts, trace out their relationships, and discern or propose explanatory principles that might account for the whole system, improve its harmony, perhaps increase its serviceability for one or another purpose.

These are three of perhaps six or seven kinds of reasoning which were traditionally taught in law schools. Now let me itemize three of perhaps fifteen or twenty that were not:

1. *Ends-means thinking.* This is the process by which one starts with a factual situation presenting a problem or an opportunity and figures out the ways in which the problem might be solved or the opportunity might be realized. What is involved is making a thorough, systematic, and creative canvass of all of the possible goals or objectives in the situation—the "end points" to which movement from the present state of affairs might be made—then making an equally systematic and creative inventory of the possible means or routes to each goal, then analyzing the ways in which and the extent to which the various means and goals are compatible or incompatible with one another, seeking means to reconcile them or to prioritize them to the extent that they are irreconcilable. This includes estimating the probabilities that certain means will lead to certain goals: it may utilize such analytic techniques as best-case/worst-case analyses, and such strategic principles as keeping options open. In any event, by reasoning backward from goals, by mapping the various roads that might be taken to each goal, by proceeding backward step by step along each road and asking what steps have to be taken before each following step can be taken, one comes at last to have some well-advised basis for answering the question "how on earth do I get started in dealing with this situation? (What are the implications of the various first steps that I could take?)" You might consider whether, during your three years of law school, you ever once received any training or experience in this kind of reasoning. I know I didn't.

2. *Hypothesis formulation and testing in information acquisition.* This is a matter of devising methods for acquiring the information needed to make decisions when one starts with less than all of the necessary information. It is seldom practicable and almost never efficient to begin to deal with any situation by gathering every piece of information that might conceivably be remotely relevant. Hypotheses about what is really relevant are the precondition of effective information gathering. The trouble is that these hypotheses must necessarily be framed before the acquisition of information that could generate alternative and perhaps better hypotheses. Are there modes of thinking that enable one to select better rather than worse initial hypotheses for the purpose of guiding one's information gathering, then to test and to modify or refine the hypotheses progressively as additional information is acquired? Certainly there are. Were you ever exposed to any of them in three years of law school back in the twentieth century? I wasn't.

3. *Decisionmaking in situations where options involve differing and often uncertain degrees of risks and promises of different sorts.* When I was in law school, I spent virtually all of my time learning analytic techniques for predicting or arguing

what was the legal result, or what should be the legal result, *in a given fact situation*. Since I got out of law school, I have spent virtually all of my time dealing with situations in which the facts were not given, in which there were options as to what fact situation should be created—situations in which I had the choice whether to present evidence on certain aspects of the facts in a litigation or to leave the record silent on those aspects, whether to draft a contract or a release that was more or less specific on a particular subject, whether to counsel a client to follow one or another course of conduct. In these situations, the real question concerned the relative probability that various legal results would obtain under alternative states of facts; the task was to decide which state of facts should be created in view of the relative costs and benefits of each including the comparative risks of the best, worst, and intermediate legal results that might obtain under each state of facts. To perform this task, it was not enough to identify each state of facts and ask "what result?" or even to recognize that, for many states of facts, the result was uncertain. It was necessary to specify and compare degrees of uncertainty, and to identify the considerations that made particular degrees of uncertainty less acceptable in the case of some legal results than in the case of others. I will not ask you whether you ever examined modes for this kind of thinking when you went to law school back in the twentieth century.

I have described these six kinds of analytic thinking to make a single basic point. By no means all of us so-called clinical teachers who began in the twentieth century to teach such things as counseling and negotiation and trial advocacy thought of ourselves as doing something properly described as skills training. We thought that what we were doing was no more or less skills training than what traditional classroom teachers of contracts and torts and criminal law had done when they taught students to read and interpret cases and to analyze legal doctrines. Case reading seemed to us to be skills training in the double sense that it required certain skills and was the precondition of still other skills. In exactly the same sense we were doing skills training when we taught ends-means thinking, information-acquisition analyses, contingency planning, comparative risk evaluation in decisionmaking, and the like. These subjects seemed to us no less conceptual or academically rigorous than case reading and doctrinal analysis. We therefore could not see the issue of the 1970s and 1980s as being whether the law schools should go on teaching legal analysis or should conduct skills training. We rather saw the issue as *which* legal analyses and skills the law schools should teach, and *how much* of each.

Here, we did differ from some of the traditionalists. Looking back on our own student days, we felt that we had spent too much time on too few legal analyses and skills. We had learned case reading and doctrinal analysis *sub nom.* torts, contracts, criminal law, property, civil procedure, admiralty, antitrust, and twenty-two other substantive titles. The substantive law we learned in these courses was interesting, but it was nothing that we could not have learned equally well, to the extent we wanted or needed it, by independent reading in law school or on-the-job research after we got out. Having learned to interpret cases and to analyze doctrine in a half a dozen courses, we had no trouble at all reading cases and analyzing doctrine in any new substantive area we encountered. What we did have trouble learning was all of the legal analyses and skills that had not been touched upon at all—such analyses and skills as ends-means thinking, information acquisition, contingency planning, and the rest.

Point Two: Learning to Learn From Experience

When we were students, law school did absolutely nothing to prepare us to learn from our experience in practice after graduation. Law school was conceived as a wholly self-contained and terminal educational episode. Practice after graduation was either ignored as a potential source of education or viewed as an entirely different kind of education—the school of hard knocks—having no institutional affiliation or functional connection with the school of law.

In the twenty-first century we realize what a misguided and pedagogically unproductive view that was. We realize that law schools cannot hope to begin to teach their students "law" in a scant three years. The students who spend three years in law school will spend the next thirty or fifty years in practice. These thirty or fifty years in practice will provide by far the major part of the student's legal education, whether the law schools like it or not. They can be a purblind, blundering, inefficient, hit-or-miss learning experience in the school of hard knocks. Or they can be a reflective, organized, systematic learning experience—*if* the law schools undertake as a part of their curricula to teach students effective techniques of learning from experience.

Point Three: The Method of Clinical Legal Instruction

Toward the end of the twentieth century, techniques of legal education became widespread which were designed precisely to teach students how to learn systematically from experience, and simultaneously to educate them in a broader range of legal analyses and skills than had theretofore been taught in law schools.

This development was called "clinical legal education." It took numerous forms, but the basic technique was this:

1. Students were confronted with problem situations of the sort that lawyers encounter in practice. The situations might be simulated—role-playing exercises in which some students played the role of legal counselors and others played the role of clients, for example—or they might be real—students might be assigned to represent actual clients and to counsel those clients under the close supervision of clinical faculty members, for example.

2. The problem situations were: (a) concrete, that is, textured by specific factual detail; (b) complex, that is, they required the consideration of interacting factors in a number of dimensions—legal, practical, institutional, personal; and (c) unrefined, that is, they were not predigested for the student through the medium of appellate opinions or coursebooks, but were unstructured, requiring the student to identify "the problem[s]" or "the issue[s]."

3. The students dealt with the problem *in role*. They bore the responsibility for decision and action to solve the problem. They had to: (a) identify the problem; (b) analyze it; (c) consider, formulate, and evaluate possible responses to it; (d) plan a course of action; and (e) execute that course of action. In all of these activities, the students were required to interact with other people. They were thus required to work through the relationships between legal analysis, communication, and interpersonal dynamics.

4. The students' performance was subjected to intensive and rigorous *post mortem* critical review. With faculty and other students, the performing students sat down, re-created, and criticized every step of their planning, decisionmaking, and action. Sometimes this was done by replaying videotapes or audiotapes of their performance, sometimes by reviewing notes and memoranda that they had made during the performance stage, often by both. The students' own thinking and behavior in role were thus made the central subject of study, just as, in a traditional classroom course, a judicial opinion or a statute would have been the subject of study.

5. This critical review focused upon the development of models of analysis for understanding past experience and for predicting and planning future conduct. It identified and explored the questions to be asked following any experience—a meeting with a client, a negotiation with another lawyer, a conference with a government official, a trial, the closure of a case—in order to draw from that experience the maximum of learning it can provide. The students learned to ask, for example: "What were my objectives in that performance? How did I define them? Might I have defined them differently? Why did I define them as I did? What were the means available to me to achieve my objectives? Did I consider the full range of them? If not, why not? What modes of thinking would have broadened by options? How did I expect other people to behave? How did they behave? Might I have anticipated their behavior—their goals, their needs, their expectations, their reactions to me—more accurately than I did? What clues to these things did I overlook, and why did I overlook them? Through what kind of thinking, analysis, planning, perceptivity, might I see them better next time?" These questions are, of course, the points of entry to examination of the kinds of reasoning I've mentioned—ends-means thinking, contingency planning, and the rest. They are also the beginning of the students' development of conscious, rigorous self-evaluative methodologies for learning from experience—the kind of learning that makes law school the beginning, not the end, of a lawyer's legal education.

Point Four: Paying for Clinical Legal Education

By 1983 or 1984, the teaching methods I have just described were fairly well developed, and were operational on a small scale in a number of law schools. But how did it come about that, between then and the twenty-first century, these methods became widespread? Because they are highly individualized, clinical teaching methods require very low student-teacher ratios and are therefore relatively expensive. In an era of economic pinch, where did the resources come from for their expansion?

* * *

* * * By * * * [the mid-nineties], clinical methods—although still used only on a small scale—had gained sufficient exposure so that their values could be realistically assessed in comparison with the values of the law schools' traditional commitment of the overwhelming bulk of teaching resources to the multiplication of classroom courses in a wide variety of substantive subject matters. People began to ask *why* do we need to teach case reading and doctrinal analysis to the same students

twenty-nine times *sub nom.* torts, contracts, criminal law, admiralty, antitrust, civil rights, corporations, commercial law, conflict of laws, trusts, securities regulation, and so forth? Given the substantive proliferation, complexity, and fast-paced growth of modern law, it had been impossible to teach students the *corpus juris*, in any meaningful sense, long before the 1980s. At best, the law schools could convey to students a very small and rapidly outdated portion of all the substantive law there was, or even that any one lawyer was likely to need.

Was it not therefore a wiser deployment of scarce teaching resources to devote some of them to giving students a broader range of legal analytic methods and skills, which would enable the students more effectively to acquire, understand, and use the substantive law, as they needed it, after they got out of law school? True scholarship—the critical examination of law as an intellectual discipline and of legal institutions as components of the social order—had to continue in the law schools, of course. Indeed, it had to be increased and intensified. But the vast mass of large-class doctrinal teaching had never involved true scholarship or pretended to. It was this vast mass that came to be perceived as seriously redundant when the question was asked why a modest portion of it should not be redeployed into clinical methods of teaching (and another modest portion, I might add, redeployed into true scholarly teaching).

The redeployment was very difficult to achieve politically because—again—it involved a large amount of remotivation of law teachers, and even a very small amount of retraining. But happily, from our twenty-first century perspective, we can now see that the gains were well worth the difficulties.

The most recent major assessment of clinical legal education is contained in a 1992 report of a task force of the American Bar Association's Section of Legal Education and Admissions to the Bar, popularly known as the MacCrate Report. The task force examined the profession and sought to identify the fundamental professional needs of a new practicing lawyer. The centerpiece of the task force's work is its statement of skills and values fundamental to the practice of law and its admonition that training in those fundamental skills and values should take place in an "educational continuum" from law school through practice. The following brief excerpts from this wide-ranging report introduces these two themes.

AMERICAN BAR ASSOCIATION, SECTION OF LEGAL EDUCATION AND ADMISSIONS TO THE BAR, LEGAL EDUCATION AND PROFESSIONAL DEVELOPMENT—AN EDUCATIONAL CONTINUUM, REPORT OF THE TASK FORCE ON LAW SCHOOLS AND THE PROFESSION: NARROWING THE GAP (1992) [THE MACCRATE REPORT]*

* * *

Chapter Four
Formulating a Statement of Skills
and Values

* * *

A. Reasons for a Statement

When the Task Force began to consider how the preparation of lawyers for practice could be improved, it felt the need to develop a conception of the object of this preparation, in the form of a compendium of the skills and values that are desirable for practitioners to have. * * * After the Task Force had reviewed prior writings on the subject and examined the range and complexity of lawyers' work * * *, two points became quite apparent:

First, the Task Force itself could not hope to write a comprehensive statement of skills and values that all members of the profession would—or could reasonably be expected to—accept as definitive. * * *

Second, for precisely this reason, there was considerable value in putting together the best comprehensive statement which the Task Force itself could develop, so as to begin a process through which, in the years ahead, discussion in all sectors of the profession could be focused on questions about the nature of the skills and values that are central to the role and functioning of lawyers in practice. By hammering out this kind of a statement, the Task Force would refine and guide its own analysis of immediate steps that might be taken to enhance the quality of lawyers' preparation for practice; by disseminating the statement, the Task Force would encourage the profession to examine it critically and to improve upon the thinking that went into it.

B. Focus of the Statement

An analysis of skills and values necessarily must take account of the phenomena of specialization and of division of labor within law firms. * * * These developments are not inconsistent, however, with the traditional vision of law as a unitary profession whose members share a common calling. Regardless of their particular fields of practice or specialties, lawyers are united by their pursuit of certain values, which this Statement terms the "fundamental values of the profession." These values inform and shape the lawyer's use of professional skills. * * *

---

*   Reprinted by permission of the American Bar Association.

Moreover, notwithstanding the increasing demand for specialized knowledge and skills, competent representation of a client still requires a well-trained generalist—one who has a broad range of knowledge of legal institutions and who is proficient at a number of diverse tasks. This is so because any problem presented by a client (or other entity employing a lawyer's services) may be amenable to a variety of types of solutions of differing degrees of efficacy; a lawyer cannot competently represent or advise the client or other entity unless he or she has the breadth of knowledge and skill necessary to perceive, evaluate, and begin to pursue each of the options. Indeed, the lawyer is not even in a position to diagnose the client's problem adequately unless the lawyer has the range of knowledge and skill necessary to look beyond the client's definition of the problem and identify aspects of the problem and related problems which the client has not perceived.

The focus of this Statement is on the skills and values with which a well-trained generalist should be familiar before assuming ultimate responsibility for a client. Different lawyers will emphasize different skills, and practitioners will often be concerned with matters outside the scope of the Statement, such as attracting and retaining clients. The Statement is concerned with what it takes to practice law competently and professionally.

* * *

Chapter Five
The Statement of Fundamental
Lawyering Skills and Professional Values

* * *

A. Organization of the Statement

The Statement first analyzes the fundamental lawyering skills essential for competent representation. It begins with two analytical skills that are conceptual foundations for virtually all aspects of legal practice: problem solving (Skill § 1) and legal analysis (Skill § 2). It then examines five skills that are essential throughout a wide range of kinds of legal practice: legal research (Skill § 3), factual investigation (Skill § 4), communication (Skill § 5), counseling (Skill § 6), and negotiation (Skill § 7). The Statement next focuses upon the skills required to employ, or to advise a client about, the options of litigation and alternative dispute resolution (Skill § 8). Although there are many lawyers who do not engage in litigation or make use of alternative dispute resolution mechanisms, even these lawyers are frequently in a position of having to consider litigation or alternative dispute resolution as possible solutions to a client's problem, or to counsel a client about these options, or to factor the options into planning for negotiation. To accomplish these tasks, a lawyer needs to have at least a basic familiarity with the aspects of litigation and alternative dispute resolution described in Skill § 8. Skill § 9 identifies the administrative skills necessary to organize and manage legal work effectively. This section reflects the perception that adequate practice management skills are an essential precondition for competent representation of clients. Finally, Skill § 10 analyzes the skills involved in recognizing and resolving ethical dilemmas.

The analysis of professional values recognizes that "training in professional responsibility" should involve more than "just the specifics of the Code of Professional Responsibility and the Model Rules of Professional Conduct"; it should encompass "the values of the profession," including "the obligations and accountability of a professional dealing with the lives and affairs of clients." McKay, [*What Law Schools Can and Should Do (and Sometimes Do)*, 30 N.Y. L. SCH. L. REV. 491], at 509-10 [(1985)]. Value § 1 examines the value of competent representation, analyzing the ideals to which a lawyer should be committed as a member of a profession dedicated to the service of clients. Value § 2 considers the value of striving to promote justice, fairness, and morality; it examines the ideals to which a lawyer should be committed as a member of a profession that bears "special responsibilit[ies] for the quality of justice" (Model Rules, Preamble). Value § 3 addresses the value of striving to improve the profession; it explores the ideals to which a lawyer should be committed as a member of a "self-governing" profession (*ibid.*). Finally, Value § 4 examines the value of professional self-development, analyzing the ideals to which a lawyer should be committed as a member of a "learned profession" (*ibid.*).

* * *

The skills and values in this Statement are analyzed separately in order to promote clarity in examining the components of each one. However, the vision of legal practice underlying the Statement recognizes that individual skills and values cannot be neatly compartmentalized. There are numerous relationships between individual skills. Thus, for example, the formulations of the skills of counseling (Skill § 6), negotiation (Skill § 7), and litigation (Skill § 8) explain that these skills may require the application of the skills of legal analysis, legal research, and factual investigation (*see, e.g.,* Skill §§ 6.2(a)-(b), 7.1(b), 8.1(c), 8.3(d)); the analysis of the skill of negotiation explains that counseling skills are ordinarily employed to help a client decide whether to accept or reject the best terms obtained from the other side in a negotiation session (Skill § 7.3(a)); and the skill of problem solving typically requires that a lawyer employ interviewing skills to gather the facts needed to identify and diagnose the client's problem (*see* Skill § 1.1). Similarly, there are relationships between individual values. For example, both the value of competent representation (Value § 1) and the value of professional self-development (Value § 4) call for a commitment to continuing study, although the former section conceives of such study as a means of maintaining competence while the latter treats it as a means of attaining excellence.

Moreover, there is a relationship between the skills and the values. As Value § 1 explains, the specific skills examined in Skill §§ 1-10, together with the more general skill of self-appraisal (which is discussed in the text and Commentary of Skill § 1) are essential means by which a lawyer fulfills his or her responsibilities to a client and simultaneously realizes the ideal of competent representation. The process of preparing to represent clients competently is a matter both of accepting certain professional values and of acquiring the skills necessary to promote these values.

These relationships between skills and values were taken into account in deciding the order in which to present the various skills and values. Thus, for example, the Statement analyzes skills before values because familiarity with Skill §§ 1-10 is essential for understanding the ideal of competent representation which is discussed in Value § 1. General foundational skills such as problem solving (Skill § 1) and legal analysis (Skill § 2) are addressed before other skills that build upon them, just as the value of continuing study for the purpose of maintaining competence (Value § 1) is addressed before the value of continuing study for the purpose of attaining excellence (Value § 4). Otherwise, the order in which skills or values are presented does not reflect any views about their relative importance in the practice of law or in the process of preparing for practice.

The arrangement of skills is also not descriptive of the sequence in which they may be used in handling a client's legal problem. Effective lawyering is rarely, if ever, a linear, step-by-step process. * * *

B. Overview of the Skills and Values Analyzed

Fundamental Lawyering Skills

Skill § 1: *Problem Solving*

In order to develop and evaluate strategies for solving a problem or accomplishing an objective, a lawyer should be familiar with the skills and concepts involved in:

1.1   Identifying and Diagnosing the Problem;
1.2   Generating Alternative Solutions and Strategies;
1.3   Developing a Plan of Action;
1.4   Implementing the Plan;
1.5   Keeping the Planning Process Open to New Information and New Ideas.

Skill § 2: *Legal Analysis and Reasoning*

In order to analyze and apply legal rules and principles, a lawyer should be familiar with the skills and concepts involved in:

2.1   Identifying and Formulating Legal Issues;
2.2   Formulating Relevant Legal Theories;
2.3   Elaborating Legal Theory;
2.4   Evaluating Legal Theory;
2.5   Criticizing and Synthesizing Legal Argumentation.

Skill § 3: *Legal Research*

In order to identify legal issues and to research them thoroughly and efficiently, a lawyer should have:

3.1   Knowledge of the Nature of Legal Rules and Institutions;
3.2   Knowledge of and Ability to Use the Most Fundamental Tools of Legal Research;
3.3   Understanding of the Process of Devising and Implementing a Coherent and Effective Research Design.

Skill § 4: *Factual Investigation*

In order to plan, direct, and (where applicable) participate in factual investigation, a lawyer should be familiar with the skills and concepts involved in:

4.1   Determining the Need for Factual Investigation;
4.2   Planning a Factual Investigation;
4.3   Implementing the Investigative Strategy;
4.4   Memorializing and Organizing Information in an Accessible Form;
4.5   Deciding Whether to Conclude the Process of Fact-Gathering;
4.6   Evaluating the Information That Has Been Gathered.

Skill § 5: *Communication*

In order to communicate effectively, whether orally or in writing, a lawyer should be familiar with the skills and concepts involved in:

5.1   Assessing the Perspective of the Recipient of the Communication;
5.2   Using Effective Methods of Communication.

Skill § 6: *Counseling*

In order to counsel clients about decisions or courses of action, a lawyer should be familiar with the skills and concepts involved in:

6.1   Establishing a Counseling Relationship That Respects the Nature and Bounds of a Lawyer's Role;
6.2   Gathering Information Relevant to the Decision to Be Made;
6.3   Analyzing the Decision to Be Made;
6.4   Counseling the Client About the Decision to Be Made;
6.5   Ascertaining and Implementing the Client's Decision.

Skill § 7: *Negotiation*

In order to negotiate in either a dispute-resolution or transactional context, a lawyer should be familiar with the skills and concepts involved in:

7.1   Preparing for Negotiation;
7.2   Conducting a Negotiation Session;
7.3   Counseling the Client About the Terms Obtained From the Other Side in the Negotiation and Implementing the Client's Decision.

Skill § 8: *Litigation and Alternative Dispute-Resolution Procedures*

In order to employ—or to advise a client about—the options of litigation and alternative dispute resolution, a lawyer should understand the potential functions and consequences of these processes and should have a working knowledge of the fundamentals of:

8.1   Litigation at the Trial-Court Level;
8.2   Litigation at the Appellate Level;
8.3   Advocacy in Administrative and Executive Forums;
8.4   Proceedings in Other Dispute-Resolution Forums.

Skill § 9: *Organization and Management of Legal Work*

In order to practice effectively, a lawyer should be familiar with the skills and concepts required for efficient management, including:

9.1   Formulating Goals and Principles for Effective Practice Management;

9.2   Developing Systems and Procedures to Ensure that Time, Effort, and Resources Are Allocated Efficiently;

9.3   Developing Systems and Procedures to Ensure that Work is Performed and Completed at the Appropriate Time;

9.4   Developing Systems and Procedures for Effectively Working with Other People;

9.5   Developing Systems and Procedures for Efficiently Administering a Law Office.

Skill § 10: *Recognizing and Resolving Ethical Dilemmas*

In order to represent a client consistently with applicable ethical standards, a lawyer should be familiar with:

10.1 The Nature and Sources of Ethical Standards;

10.2 The Means by Which Ethical Standards are Enforced;

10.3 The Processes for Recognizing and Resolving Ethical Dilemmas.

Fundamental Values of the Profession

Value § 1: *Provision of Competent Representation*

As a member of a profession dedicated to the service of clients, a lawyer should be committed to the values of:

1.1   Attaining a Level of Competence in One's Own Field of Practice;

1.2   Maintaining a Level of Competence in One's Own Field of Practice;

1.3   Representing Clients in a Competent Manner.

Value § 2: *Striving to Promote Justice, Fairness, and Morality*

As a member of a profession that bears special responsibilities for the quality of justice, a lawyer should be committed to the values of:

2.1   Promoting Justice, Fairness, and Morality in One's Own Daily Practice;

2.2   Contributing to the Profession's Fulfillment of its Responsibility to Ensure that Adequate Legal Services Are Provided to Those Who Cannot Afford to Pay for Them;

2.3   Contributing to the Profession's Fulfillment of its Responsibility to Enhance the Capacity of Law and Legal Institutions to Do Justice.

Value § 3: *Striving to Improve the Profession*

As a member of a self-governing profession, a lawyer should be committed to the values of:

3.1   Participating in Activities Designed to Improve the Profession;

3.2   Assisting in the Training and Preparation of New Lawyers;

3.3   Striving to Rid the Profession of Bias Based on Race, Religion, Ethnic Origin, Gender, Sexual Orientation, or Disability, and to Rectify the Effects of These Biases.

Value § 4: *Professional Self-Development*

As a member of a learned profession, a lawyer should be committed to the values of:

4.1   Seeking Out and Taking Advantage of Opportunities to Increase His or Her Knowledge and Improve His or Her Skills;

4.2   Selecting and Maintaining Employment That Will Allow the Lawyer to Develop As a Professional and to Pursue His or Her Professional and Personal Goals.

* * *

Chapter Seven
Professional Development
During Law School

* * *

A. The Law School's Role in Professional Development

* * *

While * * * law schools and the practicing bar should participate jointly in the professional development of lawyers, it is important for legal educators and practicing lawyers to recognize that they have different capacities and opportunities to impart these skills and values to future lawyers.

Specifically, law schools should continue to emphasize the teaching of "legal analysis and reasoning," and "legal research," as described in the Statement. Indeed, the unfortunate tendency to define "skills instruction" as dealing with skills other than legal analysis and research has obscured the obvious fact that appellate-case analysis—the technique for teaching traditional courses—involves the teaching of important professional skills. Moreover, it is now apparent that a well-structured clinical program also provides an important vehicle for the development of the skills of legal analysis and research. These skills can no longer be viewed as teachable only in the traditional classroom setting.

* * *

Law schools also have an important, and varied, role to play in developing the skill of "recognizing and resolving ethical dilemmas." Although the teaching of professional responsibility in law schools has been criticized for being too rule-oriented, this criticism ignores the opportunity that clinical programs provide for sensitizing students to ethical issues. * * *

* * * [L]aw schools can help students to recognize ethical dilemmas and can provide the rudiments of training for resolving them. It must be emphasized, however, that the exposure of students to these issues in law school clinical programs, or in the

classroom, is very limited compared to the variety and complexity of the ethical dilemmas that students confront in practice. * * *

In a similar vein, a well-structured clinical program, particularly in the live-client context, can help students understand the importance of the skill of "organization and management of legal work," but it remains for the first employer, or mentor, to translate this awareness into a functioning reality. * * *

Turning to the "fundamental values of the profession," as set forth in the Statement of Skills and Values, law schools, from which the vast majority of lawyers enter the profession, have a responsibility to stress that these values are at least as important as the substance of courses or the skills of practice. Students must be made aware of the fundamental professional values of "competent representation," of "striving to improve the profession," and of "professional self-development." Law schools can, and should, teach these values in clinical and traditional courses and should instill in students the desire to achieve them in the course of their professional careers. The efforts of law schools, however, will mean little if the practicing bar shuns its own responsibilities for inculcating professional values. Practicing lawyers can teach by the power of example. Practicing lawyers influence students during their law school years, through contact in part-time work or through summer jobs. Later, in a young lawyer's early years of practice, partners, associates, other mentors, and adversaries may be more significant than law teachers in teaching those professional values.

Finally, the Statement of Skills and Values identifies, as a fundamental professional value, the need to "promote justice, fairness, and morality." * * * Too often, the Socratic method of teaching emphasizes qualities that have little to do with justice, fairness, and morality in daily practice. Students too easily gain the impression that wit, sharp responses, and dazzling performance are more important than the personal moral values that lawyers must possess and that the profession must espouse. * * *

* * *

B. Assessing Current Instruction in Skills and Values

* * *

* * * The great majority of law schools now offer a variety of skills courses spread over the entire three year curriculum. Many of these schools have advanced beyond simply offering a broad blend of skills courses and have begun implementing sequences of courses. In either case, there is an increased probability that skills instruction is available in the full spectrum of professional skills outlined in the Statement of Skills and Values. * * *

* * *

Clinics have made, and continue to make, an invaluable contribution to the entire legal education enterprise. They are a key component in the development and advancement of skills and values throughout the profession. Their role in the curricular mix of courses is vital. Much of the research leading to the advancement of knowledge about lawyering, the legal profession and its institutions is found in the work of clinicians, and many are recognized to be among the most dedicated and talented teachers in law schools. Clinics provide students with the opportunity to integrate, in an actual practice setting, all of the fundamental lawyering skills. In clinic courses, students sharpen their understanding of professional responsibility and deepen their appreciation for their own values as well as those of the profession as a whole.

* * *

Predictably, the MacCrate Report's Statement of Fundamental Skills and Values has drawn some fire. Some see the Statement as overwhelming and believe that law schools cannot undertake skills and values training of such magnitude. Others fear that the Statement's listing of skills and values may serve to constrain more broadly defined professional training. As the following excerpt demonstrates, the Report has certainly raised important issues, and it has served to stimulate valuable discussion on the subject.

Jonathan Rose, *The MacCrate Report's Restatement of Legal Education: The Need for Reflection and Horse Sense*, 44 J. LEGAL EDUC. 548 (1994)*

* * *

Assessing the Report

* * *

The Report's Positive Contributions

The report's most significant contribution is to publicize the "common enterprise—the education and professional development of the members of a great profession," a subject whose importance should not be underestimated. * * *

* * *

A second significant contribution is that the report's authors gathered a great deal of important current information and statistical data. * * *

Finally, the report's discussion of professional development after law school is important. It confirms that professional development occurs throughout a continuum and dispels the conventional notion of a gap between law school and development thereafter. * * *

Criticisms of the Report
Identification of the Necessary Skills

The logical starting point for any criticism of the MacCrate Report is its identification of the necessary skills, the Statement of Fundamental Skills and Values; it is the first step in dealing with "the gap between expectation and reality." The existence of this "gap"—that many law school graduates are unable to do competently

---

*   Reprinted with permission.

what is expected of them in practice—raises a fundamental question: What is the reasonable, appropriate expectation of the lawyering skills and professional values that a law school graduate should possess? Unfortunately, the report does not attempt a careful answer. It merely identifies the ten critical skills and four values and says that law schools should provide instruction in all of them. It is not clear whether the skills should be possessed upon graduation, or when a lawyer assumes the ultimate or unsupervised responsibility for a client. Certainly the gist of the report is that most of the skills should be acquired, although not necessarily mastered, in law school. The report recommends that, at a minimum, law schools should provide exposure to all these skills and values.

Here the report overlooks several important issues. For example, some skills may be more important or fundamental than others. And it seems that there should be some logical order in which skills should be mastered. Arguably, there is a core that all graduates should have, with mastery of other skills coming later and depending on varying practice needs. There is also the question of the most effective time for instruction in each skill: one skill might best be taught at an early stage, and another later on. The report gives that question little attention.

Finally, the proficiency of beginning lawyers is surely an empirical matter. While the report's conclusion about the competency of recent graduates may have some validity, it seems to be based on impressions and assumptions rather than facts. Recommendations as dramatic and costly as the report's require better corroborating data. Indeed, one recent empirical study appears to provide only limited support for the report's recommendations that law schools increase instruction in lawyering skills; it supports increased instruction in a limited subset of core skills, but not more broadly in the ten fundamental lawyering skills.

Another criticism involves the report's concept of the legal profession: it is concerned that the diversity of practice settings and differentiation of legal work present a substantial threat to "the unitary concept of being a lawyer." The report's identification of fundamental lawyering skills and values is a response to this threat; the skills and values are those with which "a well-trained generalist" should be familiar. The report assumes that "maintaining the unitary concept of lawyer" is a realistic and appropriate objective.

Again, the report overlooks important issues. It is not clear that a "unitary concept" exists in our day of varied practice settings and highly differentiated work. Many forms of practice require highly developed skills in certain areas and little proficiency in others. The pervasive de facto specialization makes one doubt the image of the profession as populated by "well-trained generalists," and specialization is clearly increasing, not diminishing. It may not be possible, necessary, or appropriate for all lawyers to possess, even minimally, all ten fundamental lawyering skills. Complete proficiency in all of them seems both unrealistic and inefficient, but maybe all lawyers, no matter what they do, need a limited subset. So we return to the fundamental issue: Is there a core of skills that all lawyers need for practice and should largely have when they graduate from law school? And how will societal and institutional change affect the skills that lawyers will need in the future? The report does little to address that question.

Instruction in the Fundamental Skills

The report's discussion of instruction in the identified skills also presents some problems. The first is the report's treatment of the basic model of legal education. If, as the report says, beginning lawyers are inadequately trained in the necessary skills and values, the first question should be whether the existing model is adequate: can it accomplish the desired result? Unfortunately, the report simply accepts law schools and legal education as they are and concludes that the primary increase in skills/values training should occur in law school. Even though law schools are teaching skills and values and increasing their emphasis on such instruction, the report says they need to do more. The report does recognize that law schools cannot produce mastery without some help from the bar. Nevertheless, by putting the main responsibility on the law schools, the report seems to be asking the legal education model to produce many of the results of the very different medical education model—a model traditionally rejected by the legal profession. And there is substantial doubt whether legal education is up to the task. The issues have to do with comparative advantage, instructional sequencing, resources, and opportunity costs: When should certain skills be taught and who should teach them? Of the skills and values that beginning lawyers need, which ones should be taught first? Which ones can best be taught by law professors and which by the practicing bar? And, of course, what are the financial and curricular implications of increased skills/values instruction in law school?

These questions point to the second problem. The report's primary focus on the law schools as the place for increased instruction seems too narrow, somewhat misdirected, and a bit superficial. The focus is too narrow because it is directed almost exclusively at skills other than problem-solving, legal analysis and reasoning, and legal writing and research. The report has no real discussion of student proficiency in these more traditional aspects of legal education. Concentrating its attention on clinical and related forms of instruction, the report seems to assume that instruction in law school in these other areas, with the possible exception of writing, is adequate. From my experience with students' classroom and written work, I am skeptical. It is certainly arguable that some, or even many, students do not demonstrate the proficiency in the traditional skills that they should achieve in law school, and that more instruction is needed, particularly in statutory interpretation, organized and analytical writing, and more-than-elementary legal research. Practitioners frequently complain about the writing ability of recent graduates.

* * *

* * * By emphasizing law schools, the report gives insufficient attention to the transition period and subsequent professional development. By focusing primarily on the deficiencies of recent law school graduates, the report overlooks the question whether many transition and post-transition lawyers may also be deficient and in need of further skills training (as is suggested by the report's recommendations for CLE). On the other hand, many of these lawyers are quite competent. More data about these lawyers and about the ways some of them have achieved competence would bear on any proposed remedy for the deficiencies of beginning lawyers. In all likelihood, such information would suggest that the post-law school stage of the continuum is where improvement is needed and where significant efforts ought to be directed. The more extensive and difficult problems in skills training are there, especially in the transition period.

* * *

The MacCrate Report is the latest volley in what has been a persistent debate in the legal profession over the nature of legal education. Although the report focuses on an important issue, it provides the wrong answers, or at least ones that need much more evaluation and reflection. It does a better job in raising issues than in offering solutions. It provides a place to start, but not to end. More study and refinement are needed to identify "the fundamental skills and values that every lawyer should acquire before assuming responsibility for the handling of a legal matter" and "to recommend how the legal education community and the practicing bar can join together to fulfill their respective responsibilities to the profession and the consuming public."

While legal education is certainly not perfect and law schools ought constantly to engage in self-evaluation, reformers should focus on the post-law school period for any increase in skills/values instruction. The real challenge for the "common enterprise" is to continue effective professional training after law school—to pick up where law school leaves off. * * *

Skills and values training has expanded from an exciting concept to an indispensable element of legal education. There remain, however, significant differences about the proper scope of a clinical curriculum. The following excerpt lays out a model curriculum from the perspective of the in-house, live-client approach to clinical teaching.

Association of American Law Schools, Section on Clinical Legal Education, Report of the Committee on the Future of the In-House Clinic, 42 J. LEGAL EDUC. 511 (1992)*

* * *

I. A Definition of In-House, Live-Client Clinical Education

* * * Clinical education is first and foremost a method of teaching. Among the principal aspects of that method are these features: students are confronted with problem situations of the sort that lawyers confront in practice; the students deal with the problem in role; the students are required to interact with others in attempts to identify and solve the problem; and, perhaps most critically, the student performance is subjected to intensive critical review.

If these characteristics define clinical teaching, then the live-client clinic adds to the definition the requirement that at least some of the interaction in role be in real

---

*   Reprinted with permission.

situations rather than in make-believe ones. That is, the interaction with others in role occurs with real clients and participants in the legal system rather than with other students and actors. The nature of the real issues and cases in the live-client clinic provides both concreteness and complexity to the student's learning experience.

* * *

II. The Principal Goals of In-House, Live-Client Clinics

With the above concepts in mind, the Committee has identified nine teaching goals present, to a greater or lesser degree, in most clinics.

A. Developing Modes of Planning and Analysis for Dealing with Unstructured Situations

Anthony Amsterdam has described these modes of learning as "conceptual foundations for practical skills" and analogized them to the foundations provided by case reading and doctrinal analysis taught in first-year classes.[1] These analytical methods differ from case reading and doctrinal analysis, among other reasons, because they are prospective as well as retrospective, and because their context is not bound by the pre-digested world of the appellate case.

One of the modes of planning and analysis that Amsterdam has identified is "ends-means thinking." That skill involves starting with a fact situation presenting a problem or opportunity and figuring out the ways in which the problem might be solved. The skill requires a thorough canvass of one's goals and an equally thorough study of the ways in which those goals might be accomplished.

A second kind of analytical mode requires structuring and applying doctrine to situations where the facts are unclear or developing. Thus, while in the classroom doctrinal analysis is usually confined to analysis of what will happen in a given fact situation, the student in a clinical program is required to grapple with the impact of doctrine when there is no "given" fact situation.

The clinic is an ideal vehicle for imparting these skills. First, the problems presented to students have all the difficulty, texture, and chance that occur in the world of practice. Students must consider this range of issues while problem solving. Second, the in-house clinic possesses the resources to develop these skills. Many clinical teachers who convey these skills begin with lecture and simulation discussing problem-solving models. Most then follow with intensive discussion during student supervision. While time-consuming, that individual supervision is a powerful means to focus student attention on these skills.

In sum, this critical goal of clinical education aims to teach students how to be "reflective practitioners."

B. Providing Professional Skills Instruction

This goal is so well established that, as noted above, it is often taken as a synonym for clinical education. For years, clinics have been providing training in interviewing, counseling, fact investigation, oral advocacy, and brief-writing. For many

---

1   Anthony G. Amsterdam, Clinical Legal Education—A 21st Century Perspective, 34 J. Legal Educ. 612, 612 (1984).

clinicians, a critical component of that teaching is to provide models for the exercise of these skills, rather than simply focusing on how-to-do-it. At present, there is no serious dispute within the academy that law schools must provide opportunities for such instruction. Indeed, ABA accreditation standards require law schools to offer courses in professional skills instruction. The Committee recognizes that this goal of clinical education may be conveyed efficiently by simulation. Indeed, most clinicians recognize the utility of simulations by using them to teach lawyering skills in their classroom components, complementing that instruction with the one-on-one supervision in actual cases. Even so, there may be some unique advantages to skills instruction in the live-client setting. Clinics require students to apply practice skills in situations of unpredictability and stress that are unlikely to occur in the same way in simulated performance. Moreover, the live-client experience provides strong motivation for students to learn and apply their nascent professional skills.

C. Teaching Means of Learning from Experience

One of the primary goals in teaching modes of analysis and professional skills is to provide means by which students can learn from experience. Most of us recognize that most of our learning about the law occurred after graduation. Law school cannot possibly teach even most of the "law" in three years. For better or worse, that learning will occur in practice. Because the student's performance in role is the heart of the clinical experience, many clinicians recognize as an explicit goal the inculcation of methods by which the student can learn from experience. By critiquing student performance and by encouraging students to engage in self- and peer-critique, clinicians seek to provide their students with the tools to enable them to engage in analysis of their performance when they are in practice. To that end, most clinicians not only engage in extensive postperformance critique, but do so with the use of analysis or models that can be adapted by the student for use in future performance.

D. Instructing Students in Professional Responsibility

For many years, clinicians have been attempting to use live-client instruction as a vehicle to train students in professional responsibility and professional self-awareness. By professional responsibility, we refer to more than an awareness of the rules of the Code of Professional Responsibility. For many clinicians, the teaching of professional responsibility also includes the development of the student's ethical understanding. That understanding requires that the individual interpret her performance in light of the rules and values of the profession. As David Barnhizer has written, this notion of professional responsibility comprehends

> a series of judgments and value orientations that become both an explicit and implicit part of the individual's decision making and professional behavior. The achieving of this level of understanding demands education experiences that are capable of providing a source and kind of involvement penetrating enough to cultivate the clarification of values, and flexible enough to allow the instructor to guide the experience into a functional structure. This level of understanding is developed not in sole relation to

intellectual theories of ethical behavior, but in response to the kinds of actual forces that will confront, challenge, and tend to seduce the person as a lawyer.[6]

Most clinicians believe that it is part of their charge to teach this kind of professional responsibility. In the clinic, students are provided with firsthand exposure to the actual mores of the profession. They are also required to respond in role to ethical dilemmas, with real-life consequences attached to their decisions. Students are able to judge their ethical standards not just by their ideals, but by their actual deeds. All of us have had the experience of student behavior diverging radically from not only the norm the student may have been taught, but the norm the student actually articulated prior to the performance. The in-house aspect of clinics is critical to this goal, because it allows student performance to be observed and critiqued by a faculty member on the scene. Moreover, the students are able to observe the faculty member modeling how she would address the professional responsibility issue in question, and to learn that competent professionals take ethical responsibilities seriously.

E. Exposing Students to the Demands and Methods of Acting in Role

Clinics also may have as a goal the analysis of role-based behavior. While related to the professional responsibility concerns just discussed, the analysis of role implicates the interpersonal side of lawyering and can have foci beyond ethics or responsibility. Mark Spiegel[7] and Carrie Menkel-Meadow[8] have identified two different dimensions of inquiry.

First, because lawyers do their work through others, lawyering can be conceptualized according to the psychological aspects of the transaction. Clinical work may use theories developed in social psychology to explain lawyering behavior. Thus, students may attempt to analyze the effects of partisan role on behavior and the effects of role in communicating with persons who have different interests.

A second component is sociological in nature and looks to the impact of socially generated role-expectations on behavior. Thus, a student may use the clinical experience as data for determining "what is expected" in a given situation. That analysis, in turn, can provide insight into issues such as problems of authority relationships, lawyer dominance of clients, and relationships with adversaries. This inquiry, as Menkel-Meadow has argued, can be "simultaneously procedural, instrumental, and evaluative."

In-house clinics thus provide students with an opportunity to learn about critical relationships, such as the lawyer-client relationship, from a variety of perspectives that can inform their understanding of the legal system and their role within it.

---

6   David R. Barnhizer, Clinical Education at the Crossroads: The Need for Direction, 1977 B.Y.U. L. Rev. 1025, 1035.

7   Mark Spiegel, Theory and Practice in Legal Education: An Essay on Clinical Education, 34 UCLA L. Rev. 577, 592-94 (1987).

8   Carrie Menkel-Meadow, The Legacy of Clinical Education: Theories About Lawyering, 29 Clev. St. L. Rev. 555, 565-67 (1980).

F. Providing Opportunities for Collaborative Learning

Although related to a number of goals already discussed, an additional feature of the in-house clinic is the opportunity it provides to engage in collaborative learning. Most of law school learning is intensely individual. Legal practice, in contrast, is replete with situations in which preparation and performance occur in a collaborative environment. The in-house clinic provides a setting where this collaborative learning can occur. Moreover, in many clinics, an examination of the process of student-student or student-faculty interaction is an explicit focus of the experience.

G. Imparting the Obligation for Service to Indigent Clients, Information About How to Engage in Such Representation, and Knowledge Concerning the Impact of the Legal System on Poor People

In addition to providing the opportunity for students to engage in service, clinics may seek to teach students how to accomplish such representation and to expose students to the effect of our legal system on poor people. This goal, somewhat de-emphasized in recent years, was one of the original justifications for clinical education and has recently been rearticulated by Gary Palm, who urged clinical education to provide students with instruction that

> they will never otherwise receive. This instruction includes learning about poverty. . . . They should confront the failure of our government to provide equal justice and fair legal procedures for the poor. We should help them structure their careers to include pro bono work through community group representation, litigation and legislative advocacy.[10]

Nurturing the student's ability to engage in representation of indigent clients ought to be an important part of the training of ethical lawyers. The clinic can provide both the experience of representing indigent clients and the opportunity for reflection on and discussion of such representation.

H. Providing the Opportunity for Examining the Impact of Doctrine in Real Life and Providing a Laboratory in which Students and Faculty Study Particular Areas of the Law

Stephen Wizner and Dennis Curtis described the purpose of their clinical teaching as attempting "through a sustained and comprehensive combination of practice and research to develop a profound understanding of the legal theory, economic implications and social dynamics of a given segment of the legal system."[11] This goal of the in-house clinic can be analogized to a "seminar plus." Many of our nonclinical colleagues frequently offer seminars in which students engage in a thorough examination of an area of law or of legal institutions. In-house clinical programs can

---

10   Gary H. Palm, Message from the Chair, AALS Section on Clinical Legal Education Newsletter, Nov. 1986, at 2.

11   Stephen Wizner & Dennis Curtis, "Here's What We Do": Some Notes on Clinical Legal Education, 29 Clev. St. L. Rev. 673, 678-79 (1980).

provide all of what seminars provide and a good deal more. By examining and understanding the impact of doctrine on individual lives, students deepen their understanding of that doctrine. That understanding may also lead to sophisticated student involvement in law reform efforts infrequently attempted by seminars. Thus, clinical students may involve themselves in presenting comments to administrative agencies, filing amicus curiae briefs, or even presenting testimony before legislative agencies.

I. Critiquing the Capacities and Limitations of Lawyers and the Legal System

This critique is intertwined with and builds upon the goals already discussed. Robert Condlin has described the critique of lawyering as requiring

> analyzing and evaluating the patterns and theories immanent in the methods lawyers use to perform and think about skill practices against conceptions of what would be better, for the purpose of resolving perceived contradictions between theory and practice. This analysis presupposes a critical theory, which in turn presupposes worked-out views on the nature of a fair and just legal system and the role of lawyer practices in operating and improving it.[12]

In addition to analyzing legal practices, clinical programs can provide the opportunity for examining the functioning of legal institutions as a whole, analyzing how such institutions are operating currently and how they might be changed to work more effectively. While a clinic alone probably cannot accomplish this function, it is a critical complement to other areas of the curriculum in which such issues are or ought to be addressed. The clinic provides data about the reality of practice and the legal system that the student cannot obtain in class. The clinic further requires the student to examine her own performance in light of this data. Finally, the clinic provides an opportunity for dialogue on these questions that is difficult to achieve in the classroom, even in those classes organized in seminar fashion.

J. Conclusion: Integration, or The Whole Is Greater than the Sum of Its Parts

Clinics provide the best opportunity in the curriculum to integrate these manifold teaching goals. The goals, of course, state educational objectives. We believe they also state lawyering qualities that we would like ourselves and our students to possess. Many of us would like to have the opportunity to teach our students all of the goals listed above. All of us would also hope that we and our students possessed the qualities that would result from taking those goals to heart—analytical planning abilities, proficient legal performance skills, an understanding of the rules of professional responsibility and the implication of ethical issues, an ability to learn from experience, a deep understanding of role and the impact of doctrine, a commitment

---

12   [Robert J.] Condlin, ["Tastes Great, Less Filling": The Law School Clinic and Political Critique, 36 J. Legal Educ. 45] at 48-49 [(1986)].

to and knowledge about service, and an ability to challenge prevailing notions of acceptable lawyer behavior and legitimate institutional functioning.

None of us can be perfect exemplars of all of these qualities, and none can teach all of these goals in our clinic with perfect emphasis. But the Committee believes that the in-house clinic provides the optimal means of integrating the theoretical, analytical, skills, and ethical goals we have identified. Moreover, an important concomitant of the development of these goals is the opportunity for personal growth that the clinic affords to students. No other learning experience in law school combines the extraordinarily varied and dramatic context of real cases and problems with the opportunity for intensive teaching, supervision, growth, and reflection.

* * *

Proponents of live-client clinical teaching regularly extol the richness of experience as teaching material. In the following excerpt, Ann Shalleck illustrates the range of learning opportunities that can be developed in supervised clinical practice.

Ann Shalleck, *Clinical Contexts: Theory and Practice in Law and Supervision*, 21 N.Y.U. Rev. L. & Soc. Change, Vol. 21:1, pp. 109-82 (1993-1994)*

* * *

Introduction: Genesis and Method

Nowhere is the intersection of legal theory and legal practice more intense than in supervising students representing real clients on real cases. Supervision is an ongoing dialogue between student and teacher about that representation. The teacher gives shape to the dialogue through each decision about what to include in, and how to conduct, the discussion. The student's practice is the focus of the supervisory discussion, but the teacher frames how that practice is understood. In shaping the dialogue, the teacher conveys both explicitly and implicitly a vision of law, legal institutions, and lawyering. * * *

* * *

I

The Jessica Green Case

This case has been assigned to a team of two students who are in the midst of their clinic experience; they have worked together on other cases and have established a relationship with their Supervisor. As part of their participation in the clinic, they have been attending, with the other students in the clinic, weekly classes

---

*   Reprinted by permission of the New York University Review of Law & Social Change.

that examine the lawyering process and weekly case analysis meetings that focus on developments in their cases. They are familiar with casework and clinical methodology but are still uncertain when working on their cases. The students' only prior contact with the Supervisor about the Green case occurred when the Supervisor gave the students the client's name and telephone number. The clinic had received this information from an organization that regularly refers domestic violence cases. * * *

* * *

Scene 1: Supervisory Session—Planning

Supervisor:	The memo you did yesterday shows a lot of progress since the beginning of the year. I saw that there are six things that you would like to talk about. Where do you want to start?
Amelia:	We'd like to begin with drafting the petition. We are not sure how much of the history of abuse we should include in the petition.
Supervisor:	Why you are concerned about that?
Amelia:	Well, how much of the history is relevant to getting a CPO[12] now?
Supervisor:	Why are you worried about the history? Is it important to your theory of the case?
Susan:	You can't really understand the seriousness of the present abuse unless you look at what our client has been through. The recent incident doesn't seem so bad by itself.
Supervisor:	What are the legal consequences of the recent incident not seeming so bad?
Susan:	The judge could refuse to issue a CPO, even though I think that what Mr. Green did most recently qualifies as an intrafamily offense. The real problem is getting an eviction.
Amelia:	Why should the seriousness of the abuse be linked to the relief? Once you've got an intrafamily offense, isn't the full range of statutory relief available? There aren't any limits in the statute.
Supervisor:	What do you think?
Susan:	The alternatives for relief are probably meant to let the judge fit the relief to specific circumstances.
Supervisor:	Think back to what you know about remedies from other classes. The argument you just made is certainly consistent with the idea that the judge has discretion to fashion a remedy to fit the particular harm in a given case. What else might influence the relief you can get?
Amelia:	Perhaps the more serious the abuse, the more drastic a remedy.
Supervisor:	Be more specific about the relationship of the eviction to the seriousness of the abuse. Why is an eviction order important to your client?
Amelia:	Because she feels like her life is in danger. She believes that her husband could be really violent—choke her again or even worse. It ter-

---

12   Civil protection order.

rifies her to have him in the same house with her. She doesn't know what will happen at any minute.

Susan: Also, she's worried about the children—not that he'll do anything to them, but that they'll be exposed to his unpredictable behavior—especially Kyle, since he's now old enough to know what's going on.

Supervisor: So your theory is that the respondent's potential dangerousness to your client and her children makes an eviction necessary. To demonstrate his present dangerousness, the history of his unpredictable and sometimes quite violent actions needs to be brought out. Now what?

* * *

Supervisor: What do you think the judge might think about the issues you're raising?

Amelia: The judge might be concerned about fairness and about a right to a hearing. But he probably feels pressured. After all, the judge did not create the situation.

Supervisor: So the judge is caught between processing cases efficiently to comply with bureaucratic imperatives and ensuring fairness and justice in a particular case. Given the conflict that you've identified, how can you appeal to the values that help your client?

Susan: Perhaps by directly addressing the conflict as a preliminary matter.

Supervisor: How can you do that?

Amelia: After the parties have introduced themselves we can say that our case will take some time—tell the judge the number of witnesses that we'll have.

Susan: We could include in our opening an explanation of why the witnesses are important and how much time each may take.

Supervisor: Of the witnesses you listed in your memo, do you have a sense of which are the most important for your case theory?

Amelia: No. It's hard to tell at this point. We need to talk to them first—find out how much information they have and how they'll come across when they testify.

Susan: We also need to think about the story we're telling. We'll have to be economical. Maybe not so complete or dramatic.

Supervisor: I think you're right. You have hard choices to make about how to structure your case—how to pick witnesses and structure each direct examination. It may be too early to know exactly what trade-offs to make. As you do your investigation, keep these strategy questions in mind. Remember our class discussion about investigation and its relation to case theory. Think about how each piece fits with the story you're telling. When we meet next time, let's talk about other ideas you may have and what you've decided to do. Let's move on to the second issue in your memo. You said that Mrs. Green wants a support

	order because that's the only way that she can afford to stay in the house. She has no source of income. Is that right?
Amelia:	Yes.
Supervisor:	Given the discussion we just had about eviction orders, what problems can you anticipate in getting a temporary support order?
Amelia:	Well, obviously, asking for a temporary support order could add to the time.
Supervisor:	What problems are different from those raised by the eviction order?

* * *

Scene 2: Trial

Clerk:	All rise! This court is now in session. All those having business in the Superior Court before the Honorable Jeffrey Albert draw nigh and give your attention. God save the United States and this honorable court.
Judge:	Good afternoon.
All:	Good afternoon, your honor.

[Everyone sits.]

Judge:	[To the clerk] Please call the next case.
Clerk:	Jessica Green v. Roger Green, I.F. 123 - 87.

[Amelia, Supervisor, Jessica Green, opposing counsel, and Roger Green all take their places at counsel table.]

Clerk:	Will counsel and the parties please identify themselves.
Amelia:	Good afternoon, your honor. My name is Amelia Durenmatt, and I'm a certified law student. I'm here with my supervisor, Ms. Brooks. We represent the petitioner, Jessica Green [*indicates Mrs. Green*].
Judge:	Good afternoon.
Dana:	Dana Brinkley for the Respondent, Roger Green [*indicates Mr. Green*].
Judge:	Are we ready to proceed?
Amelia:	Yes, your honor.
Judge:	Call your first witness.

[Amelia turns quickly to Supervisor with a questioning look. The two briefly confer in whispers as others at counsel table take their seats.]

Amelia:	Umm, your honor, if it please the court, I have a brief opening statement.
Judge:	Very well counsel, but make it brief.
Amelia:	Yes, your honor. We are here today to seek a civil protection order for Jessica Green against her husband, Roger Green. There has been a long history of abuse in this case, including one incident requiring Mrs. Green's hospitalization. Because her husband is unpredictable and sometimes quite violent, Mrs. Green feels that her life is in danger. Therefore, Mrs. Green is asking that the court order her husband not to threaten or abuse her, to leave the family home, and tem-

porarily to make support payments, which will allow her and her two children to remain in the family home. In addition, Mrs. Green is requesting temporary custody of her two children. Because of the . . . .

Judge: Excuse me, Ms. Durenmatt, how many witnesses do you intend to call?

Amelia: Three. I was just . . . .

Judge: And you, Ms. Brinkley?

Dana: Only one.

Judge: What's your estimate on time?

Dana: Fifteen minutes, at the most, your honor.

Judge: Ms. Durenmatt?

Amelia: Yes, your honor?

Judge: How much time will your case take?

Amelia: Approximately one and a half to two hours.

Judge: Counsel, have you attempted settlement in this matter?

Dana: Yes, we have, your honor. The parties were unable to come to any agreement, especially regarding support.

Judge: Support? I'm not going to hear any support matters at this time. This is a CPO hearing, counsel, not a support hearing.

[Supervisor taps on Amelia's arm to get attention. Amelia bends down to listen and immediately straightens up to ask question.]

Amelia: With the court's indulgence?

Judge: *[Looking directly at the supervising attorney.]* Ms. Brooks, you know the court's position on the matter of support in these hearings. It is inappropriate to bring it up, it's outside the scope of the statute, and I have ten other cases to dispose of this afternoon and can't spend two hours on one case.

Supervisor: *[Supervisor rises and addresses the judge.]* Your honor, Ms. Durenmatt is prepared to argue the necessity of support in this particular situation. We ask the court for an opportunity to do so.

Judge: Very well, Ms. Brooks, you have two minutes to put this on the record.

Supervisor: Your honor, Ms. Durenmatt will present the argument.

Judge: Whoever, let's just get on with it!

Amelia: Your honor, there's great danger that past serious abuse will be repeated. Mr. Green has recently made specific threats to that effect. In addition, Mr. Green has abused his wife in front of the children. Therefore, the court should order Mr. Green to leave the family home. Mrs. Green, however, is totally dependent on Mr. Green financially. She left her job as a school teacher after the birth of their first child. Without a temporary support order, she would be forced to live in the same house with Mr. Green. This result would not be an effective resolution of this violent situation as contemplated by the statute 16 - 1005(10).

* * *

Judge:	Ms. Durenmatt, call your first witness, and we'll see how this goes. If I find that you've proved your case as to abuse, I'll reconsider your argument about support.
Amelia:	Thank you, your honor. I'd like to call Mrs. Jessica Green.

[Jessica Green walks to witness stand.]

* * *

Amelia:	Mrs. Green, please describe in detail what happened on Monday, May 11, 1987.
Jessica:	My husband, who's an economist with the Department of Commerce, was getting ready to go to Canada for a three-week business trip. I was on the phone with my friend, Sharon Winston. My husband got upset and accused me of going out with other men. When I didn't get off the phone right away, he got mad and ripped the phone out of the wall. He pulled my hair and grabbed me and said if I went out of the house while he was gone, he would mess me up so badly no one would ever want me. He said the last time he sent me to the hospital was nothing compared to what he would do now.
Amelia:	When was the last time your husband sent you to the hospital?
Dana:	Objection, your honor. What is the time frame? The question may be irrelevant.
Judge:	Ms. Durenmatt?
Amelia:	Your honor, the question is relevant and clarifies Mrs. Green's last answer. You need to know about the past incident to understand the significance of the current threat to Mrs. Green.
Judge:	How remote is the last hospitalization, Ms. Durenmatt?
Amelia:	June 1984.
Judge:	Ms. Brinkley?
Dana:	I still object. It's over three years ago—that's remote in time and irrelevant to the current situation, your honor.
Amelia:	Your honor, it is extremely relevant. *[Whispers with supervisor.]*
Judge:	Ahem, Ms. Durenmatt, anything that occurred three years ago is not relevant to granting a civil protection order now. Objection sustained.
Amelia:	With the court's indulgence. *[Whispers again to supervisor.]* Mrs. Green, what did it mean to you when your husband threatened you last Tuesday?
Jessica:	It really frightened me. It meant that if I did anything to displease him while he was away, he would choke me like he did the last time.
Dana:	Objection. Your honor has already ruled. Move to strike.
Judge:	Ms. Durenmatt?

Amelia: Your honor, this is relevant to Mrs. Green's current fears from her husband's threats. They relate directly to what physical abuse, in addition to hair pulling, she can expect from him right now.

Judge: Ms. Durenmatt, it is a bit remote, isn't it?

Amelia: Somewhat, your honor, but it is still relevant.

[Supervisor taps student on arm. Amelia looks down and then speaks.]

Amelia: With the court's indulgence. *[Whispers to supervisor.]* Your honor, we'll tie this up with other instances of abuse that will show that our client has a reasonable fear of harm from this man based on his past actions.

Judge: On that basis, I'll allow the question and answer to stand.

* * *

Amelia: In addition to the incidents on May 19 of this year and in April 1986, which you have described, have there been any other incidents of violence?

Dana: Objection, your honor.

Judge: Ms. Durenmatt?

Amelia: Your honor, we are talking about a series of major incidents in Mrs. Green's life with Mr. Green. They are the foundation of her present fear. These will help the court understand the nature of the abuse and the protection needed.

Judge: I've gotten the picture, counsel. Can we move on?

Amelia: Your honor, one more major incident is relevant to the recent abuse, if I may proceed?

Judge: Very well, counsel, but hurry it up please.

* * *

Scene 3: Supervision Session—Critique

The judge granted the CPO, ordered Mr. Green to vacate the parties' home and to maintain the mortgage payments for ninety days. The judge refused to order support for Mrs. Green and the children. When Amelia began to argue with this aspect of his ruling, the judge lost his temper, cut the student off, and snapped, "I've already ruled, Ms. Durenmatt. Please prepare an appropriate order." The supervisor and the two students met shortly after the hearing and had the following discussion.

Supervisor: You've had some time to think about the hearing. I have some thoughts, but first, what would you like to talk about?

Amelia: Susan and I talked a lot about the hearing. There are a number of things we'd like to go over with you.

Supervisor: Let's identify them first and then go back to them one by one.

Amelia: Although the client is happy, we both feel as though we lost because the judge didn't order support payments.

Susan: We've tried to figure out how we could have strengthened our arguments, and what things might have influenced the judge. Maybe the judge was less sympathetic because Jessica was well-dressed, middle class, and college-educated. How could we have made her more sympathetic?

Amelia: We also thought that the judge wanted to compromise—to find a middle ground. He refused to do all that was needed.

Susan: And how far should we have pushed him? Did we go far enough in fighting for what we wanted? Amelia really fought hard, and it seemed to make a difference on the issue of eviction. But on the support issue, it didn't get us very far.

* * *

Supervisor: The points you raise are excellent. They show how much understanding you've gained. In addition to the five things you've mentioned, I'd like to talk about the judge's critique. What a judge says can be very powerful, and it's important to look at his comments critically. Also, I'd like to talk about your client. You say she's "happy", but I'd like to find out more about what this decision means to her and how it's been to work with her. Let's begin with your feeling about having lost.

Amelia: I really believed in our theory of the case—that support was basic to the client's safety.

Supervisor: Step back for a minute and think about what your client's goals were in the case.

Susan: Jessica's first priority was being protected from her husband's violence and having a safe place for herself and her children to stay.

Amelia: We did get the CPO, the eviction, and custody. So she is safe, and she and her children are together at home.

Susan: You could say we were partially successful on support. The judge did order her husband to keep up the mortgage payments for ninety days.

Amelia: Jessica seemed relieved and happy. I sensed that she could figure out a way to make ends meet for a short time if the mortgage were paid.

Supervisor: So although the judge may not have accepted the support part of your case theory, you got your client what she most wanted—at least for the short term. And you gained some time to work out a more viable long-term solution.

Amelia: I guess that's right. But I still think the judge should have heard testimony about support. He said he would, if we proved our case on abuse. When he started making his findings, everything happened so fast. I didn't even get a chance to argue. When I tried, he got mad and cut me off. Maybe I should have tried again.

Supervisor: Thinking back now, what else could you have said to change his mind?

Susan: I don't think Amelia could have said anything else. It seemed that the judge had already made up his mind.

Amelia: Maybe I could have woven support issues into the client's testimony—so that it didn't seem so tacked on at the end. That would have made support seem more basic.

Supervisor:	That is a very sophisticated point; your case theory does get played out in each of the details of the testimony. But what were the dangers of intricately building support into the client's story?
Susan:	It might have detracted from the issue of physical danger to the client. It was hard enough getting the judge to listen to the history of violence. We could have lost the whole thing. The judge was pretty annoyed.
Supervisor:	Should you worry about annoying the judge?
Susan:	He's human, too, and he might change his mind if you anger him.
Amelia:	He was annoyed when I kept arguing about the prior incidents. But finally he changed his mind and let them in. If I hadn't kept arguing, we might not have gotten the eviction.
Supervisor:	I thought you did a great job of not backing off. It's often hard to decide when to hang in there and when to let go.
Susan:	Given the number of decisions a judge has to make in the course of a hearing, you can't argue with him about every adverse decision. You have to decide which are the most important.
Supervisor:	How do you decide?
Amelia:	You have to think about what your client cares about and whether the point is essential to your case.
Susan:	Also, you might need to make a record on a particular issue.
Supervisor:	Good points. Given your client's goals and the strategy you chose of emphasizing the danger to Jessica, do you think your decision to fight harder on the history of abuse than on the client's financial condition was a good one?
Amelia:	When put that way, I think it was.
Supervisor:	Are there things that might have annoyed the judge less?
Amelia:	The judge became irritated when I got flustered or wasn't really following what was happening. It's incredibly hard to listen to what's happening, remember where you're trying to go, and decide how to respond, especially when you're nervous. It all goes so fast.
Supervisor:	You're exactly right. You have to both be well prepared—as you both were—and be able to adapt to each of the changes that occurs. What seems like a little thing—like having your questions out of order—can really throw you off. But you were able to recover, and that's an important skill. How about some coffee? Then we can finish our discussion of the hearing and move on to what to do next.

II

Three Supervisory Decisions in Context

* * *

Students in clinical courses have a unique opportunity to combine analysis of their own experience with critical, systemic analysis. Seeing, participating in, and, most importantly, reflecting upon the law in action provides the student with an opportunity for engaging in self-conscious critical analysis of legal institutions, rules, and procedures that is rooted in, yet transcends, the student's own experience. At the same time that they engage in critical, systemic analysis, however, the students act as advocates for a particular client. They are learning to confront another person's desires, fears, and idiosyncracies while undertaking strategic action on that person's behalf. They must master the modes of thought and skills necessary for those tasks.

* * *

III

A VISION OF SUPERVISION

* * * The issues that the teacher frames as the most important for supervision (the decisions) and the ways that she chooses to view those issues (the contexts) create a complex and constantly shifting scheme requiring the teacher's constant attention to the fundamental assumptions underlying each choice she makes. This scheme permits the supervisor to shift "back and forth between the concrete and the abstract, the practical and the reflective, the specific and the general." By engaging in this process, the teacher constructs a concept of supervision out of the material presented by the cases and the students, the dynamics of the educational enterprise, and the self-conscious application of critical perspectives to daily work in the clinic.

The particular characteristics of supervision will, therefore, constantly change. Identifying these characteristics at any particular time helps us to see the themes and concerns we have made central to the supervisory project. In this analysis of the Green case, at least eight characteristics of supervision emerge. First, the teacher is very active in defining the content and structure of the supervisory experience. Although a student may be very involved in shaping a particular dialogue, the teacher initiates and directs the inquiries into particular topics. In the Green case, there was no discussion with the students about any of the teacher's three decisions. The teacher did not consult the students about whether to have a supervisory meeting prior to the interview. Similarly, although the students had prepared a proposed agenda for the supervision meeting that did not include case theory, the teacher did not discuss with them her decision to focus on case theory. Through the discussion of case theory, the teacher addressed many of the students' concerns, but the decision to proceed through case theory was hers. The teacher also introduced the possibilities of institutional critique and strategic action. In these three decisions, the teacher structured the intellectual inquiry. Within that inquiry, the students were active participants in particular discussions, but the teacher defined the educational project.

Second, the teacher engages in a very self-conscious decision-making process in shaping supervision. From the moment of the initial referral in the Green case, the teacher began a continuing evaluation of how best to structure supervision to accomplish her educational project. In making each decision, she looked to the overall structure of the clinical course, the flow of case-related experiences, the knowledge developed through case activities, the relationship between the students and their client, the particular qualities of individual students, and the dynamics of the relationship between the students and herself. While any given interaction between teacher and student may have become very nondirective—either in the sense of being very free flowing, without a structured or predefined agenda, or in the sense of not leading to a particular answer or way of looking at things—the teacher was nonetheless both defining the educational agenda and making decisions in a self-conscious, directed manner.

Third, revealing the teacher's understanding of the supervisory process can be an important part of supervision. Although the teacher actively defines the educational project, the students have access to that process of definition. Demystification can either advance discussion of a particular issue or enable students to question or challenge the teacher's project. For example, in setting the agenda for the critique in the Green case, the teacher first let the students know the process she wanted to follow. She then elicited their concerns, identified her own, and went back to address the students' issues. Although the teacher was directing the agenda, the students could see what she was doing and had opportunities to challenge and change the direction.

Fourth, supervision requires the teacher to engage in different kinds of dialogue. In some instances, the dialogue is directive with the teacher raising issues and structuring discussion. Sometimes, she may even seek to achieve a particular result. In other instances, the dialogue is open-ended, designed to explore different possibilities or provide opportunities for students to develop their own interpretations of events. In the Green case, the discussions of case theory and institutional analysis were both quite directive. In the case theory discussion, the teacher did not define the content of the case theory, but she carefully directed its development. Similarly, she did not tell the students how to analyze the court's treatment of intrafamily offense cases, but she led them to analyze that treatment and to use that analysis to obtain an adequate hearing for their client. However, the teacher was much less directive in her handling of planning. The students planned the interview without any prior direction. When they planned further actions at the close of the first supervision, she intervened at only two points, directing them to consider the client in their planning and to set priorities among the identified tasks.

Fifth, the students' actions on cases and the knowledge gained from those activities form the organizing principle for the intellectual inquiry in supervision. Students examine lawyering theories, skills, social theories, institutional critique, and personal feelings within the framework of their cases. The material presented in the other components of the course is tested and modified through case experiences. Casework reveals the students' characteristics and capacities. The relationship between the students and clients takes shape through the case. Supervisory inquiry focuses upon the case.

Sixth, the student-client relationship mediates the teacher's concern for the client. Therefore, the teacher expresses her responsibility for and commitment to the client in two ways. First, the teacher intervenes in the students' construction of a relationship with a client. The intervention may be minor or major, exploratory or directive, but the students have the opportunity to construct a relationship with the client. The teacher does not become the lawyer. Rather, the teacher acts to ensure that the students adequately fulfill their responsibility to the client. Through intervention, the teacher discharges her duty to protect the client from harm. Second, the teacher repeatedly directs the students to examine their actions in relationship to the client. In the Green case, in constructing a case theory, planning an interview, and evaluating a result, the students were taught to look through the client's eyes. Seeing the world in this way required the students to understand who their client was and how their client viewed the situation before they could decide upon action.

Seventh, supervision requires an inquiry into the institutional structures within which a case arises and the social and political forces that shape the development of the case. In the Green case, exploring the court system's structure for handling domestic violence cases shaped the litigation strategy. Understanding the dynamics of abuse against women aided in the development of a case theory about dangerousness. Teaching students to be lawyers included analyzing the meaning of gender in the client's and the students' experience, in the student-client relationship, in the court system, and in the other institutions of society.

Eighth, all supervisory action is intervention. Intervention is not just acting when something has gone wrong or is about to go wrong. The students' experience with the case and the client exists within the supervisory framework, and the many different sorts of interactions with the teacher shape those experiences. Although the teacher in the Green case had no direct contact with the client and did not take over the hearing when the student was making mistakes, her participation in the planning meetings and critique sessions altered the students' representation of and relationship with their client.

* * *

A fully exploited clinical curriculum can offer unique insight not only into the workings of the legal profession, but also into the workings and practices of lawyers. The following exploration of lawyer expertise is but one example of the world of lawyering open to the inquiring clinic student.

Gary Blasi, *What Lawyers Know: Lawyering Expertise, Cognitive Science, and the Functions of Theory*, 45 J. LEGAL EDUC. 313 (1995)*

* * *

I. Introduction

What do experienced lawyers know? How do they know it? What *is* an expert attorney? Why do some lawyers grow more expert with experience, while others seem only to grow older? How do the novices produced by law schools become experienced, expert attorneys? What might law schools do to increase the efficiency with which students extract expertise from their later experiences in practice? * * *

---

*   Reprinted with permission.

* * *

A Continuing Context:
Ned, Oscar, Ellen, and Clyde v. Def Records

I begin with an imaginary tale, to which I shall often return, of a simple decision in a simple case.

Ned is fresh out of law school, a newly hired associate in a small firm with a general practice. In his first week, he has been assigned a handful of small research projects and one "real" case: a contract dispute between the firm's client Clyde, a computer programmer, and Def Records, the small corporation that now refuses to pay for the accounting software Clyde wrote for the company, on grounds that the software does not do what Clyde said it would do. Because the amount in controversy in the case is too small for the firm's busy partners, they assign it to Ned with instructions to "evaluate this one for summary judgment." To Ned, this is a pretty straightforward matter. He remembers the basics about summary judgment from his civil procedure class in law school and can easily find some cases about warranties and custom software. His reading of the contract's warranty waivers and a couple of recent appellate decisions makes fairly straightforward the recommendation Ned puts in his memo to the partner on the case: Ned should prepare a motion for summary judgment to get Clyde out of the case. Simple. Or so it seems to Ned. Ned is a novice.

Ned looks for an older, and presumably wiser, lawyer with whom to check his tentative decision. In the hallway he runs into Oscar, now a rainmaking partner with twenty years of experience, five of them as an active litigator. Ned lays out the situation and his assessment. Oscar responds, "Sounds right to me. We want to keep our reputation as an aggressive lean-and-mean firm, and summary judgment will get Clyde out of the case in a hurry. Litigation is like tennis: Go for the winning shot." Oscar has experience.

Ned feels more confident but decides to consult Ellen, the senior litigator in the firm, before commencing work on the summary judgment papers. Ellen has some twenty years of litigation experience. She listens to Ned's presentation, goes over the file with him briefly, and then quickly responds: the firm will not recommend to Clyde that they move for summary judgment. While it is true that Clyde has a strong case because of the clear language in the warranty waiver, other considerations compel Ellen's decision. First, Def Records is represented by a sole practitioner named Frank Oster. So far, the *Clyde* case has been pending for a year and Oster has not served any discovery. There is still about a year to go before trial. If Clyde moves for summary judgment, Oster will be forced to actually think about the case and the need to do discovery. If Oster does conduct discovery, he may uncover a series of letters about the software's promised performance that will, at the very least, muddy the water on the warranty waiver issue and will certainly provoke Oster to take depositions he might otherwise not take.

Second, Ellen explains, she finds it unlikely that any judge, including Judge Mathers, before whom this motion will come, will want to decide this case for Clyde on a technicality if Clyde really did mislead Def Records in some way. Although attitudes toward summary judgment vary by judge and by court system, a good many judges are hostile to summary judgment motions, and some of that hostility may carry over to lawyers who bring weak ones. Since the judge in this case will also be the trial judge, we do not want him to think that we are wasting his time and ours.

Third, she says, preparing and arguing the motion will actually take about as much time as a trial in a case like this. Thus, if the motion loses, Clyde will be paying nearly twice as much in attorney fees. Since the amount in dispute is not all that large, this is a significant factor.

Finally, Ellen argues, if Clyde wins on summary judgment, Def Records is likely to appeal. On appeal from a summary judgment, all presumptions will be against Clyde; on the other hand, if he wins at trial, all presumptions on appeal will be in his favor. Thus, even if they could persuade Judge Mathers to grant summary judgment, the firm might have to try the case anyway—after exposing their case to Frank Oster and after Clyde has spent several thousand more dollars. There are many other factors to consider, Ellen explains, and on balance they weigh against moving for summary judgment at this time. Ellen is an expert.

* * *

II. Expertise at What? Lawyering as Problem-Solving

One intuitive notion of an expert lawyer is a lawyer with deep knowledge of the substantive and procedural rules of law in a particular area (say, federal income tax, bankruptcy, or family law). Clearly, however, something more is involved than the mere quantity of knowledge of detailed law and procedure. For the purposes of this exploration, the notion of legal expertise is predicated on the assumption that there are some capacities that are central to the expertise of experienced attorneys, without regard to the nature of their practices, and that those capacities go beyond a more detailed knowledge of a particular set of legal doctrines. This assumption, in turn, rests on certain conceptions of what lawyers actually *do*.

* * *

A. Prototypical Lawyering in Cultural Context

Our legal education system is predicated on unstated and generally unexamined assumptions about what lawyers do. For each of us, including lawyers and law professors, the concept of "lawyer" draws upon a prototypical lawyer engaged in a prototypically lawyerly endeavor. Although the content of such prototypes might be explored as an empirical matter, there are as yet no reported empirical studies. For most of the public, the results would likely be as heavily influenced by depictions of lawyers on television programs as by personal experiences, presumably placing a trial lawyer more centrally than a specialist in tax-exempt real estate exchanges.

Even in more sophisticated circles, including law schools, people have central notions about lawyering: a lawyer is a litigator, very likely a trial lawyer, knowledgeable about both legal doctrine and procedure, and able to put that knowledge to use on behalf of an individual client, generally in a fairly simple dispute with another party, in order to achieve a desired result. One need only examine the casebooks and teaching materials of law schools to confirm the assumed centrality of these features.

In disproportionately rare instances (compared to the distribution of actual legal work), one finds in these materials examples of lawyers working as members of teams, representing large organizations in multiparty transactions and disputes, but only rarely going to court. It is still the rare law school text that mentions what lawyers (as opposed to judges) actually do (unless to suggest implicitly that most lawyers spend their time analyzing appellate opinions for consistency and hidden policy implications).

B. Lawyering as a Collection of Competencies

More sophisticated notions about what lawyers do have been motivated by the desire to better define and conceptualize the various "competencies" a lawyer should have, in order to improve legal education or to judge attorney competence. This has been the focus of recurrent efforts both by the American Bar Association and by legal educators to address perceived deficiencies in legal education as preparation for the practice of law. The most recent and formidable example of this approach to lawyering is found in the MacCrate Report. A separate effort by the General Practice Section of the ABA produced an inventory of capacities required of general practice attorneys.[19] In all these approaches, lawyering is viewed as the bundle of skills and abilities a "good lawyer" should possess. Whether the contents of the requisite bundle of skills are arrived at by the subjective judgment of accomplished lawyers and scholars or by surveying the opinions of a larger number of practicing lawyers, behind the explicit enumeration of important abilities are implicit notions of what lawyers do. But there is often little to suggest any sense of priority among competencies or the nature of the knowledge that the competencies reflect.

Several scholars, however, have conducted systematic surveys of practicing lawyers to ascertain their opinions on the relative importance of various skills to the practice of law. Taken together, they cast some light on what practicing lawyers think are the important aspects of lawyering. One common theme in these studies is the importance of a lawyer's ability to integrate factual and legal knowledge and to exercise good judgment in light of that integrated understanding.

The most recent study of this kind found that practitioners (in this case, young Chicago lawyers) believed most important three qualities not unique to lawyers: "oral communication," "written communication," and "instilling others' confidence in you." After these, the skills or areas of knowledge considered most important were, in order, "ability in legal analysis and legal reasoning," "drafting legal documents," and "ability to diagnose and plan solutions for legal problems."[20] This survey replicated the 1980 survey of Chicago lawyers by Zemans and Rosenblum, which found the skills and areas of knowledge ranked most important by practitioners to be "fact gathering" and "capacity to marshal facts and order them so that concepts can be

---

19   The Section of General Practice Report on Lawyer Competencies is an Appendix to Steven C. Bahls, Preparing General Practice Attorneys: Context-Based Lawyer Competencies, 16 J. Legal Prof. 63, 79-93 (1991).

20   [Bryant G.] Garth & [Joanne] Martin, [Law Schools and the Construction of Competence, 43 J. Legal Educ. 469] at 473 [(1993)].

applied."[21] Similarly, in a survey of the alumni of six "representative" law schools, the skill viewed as most important was "ability to analyze and synthesize law/facts."[22] The skills most often rated as essential by California practitioners in 1972 were "analyzing cases/legal research" and "investigating facts of client's case."[23] A study of Montana lawyers ranked as most important "the trait of judgment" and "capacity to analyze."[24]

C. Clinical Legal Education and Lawyering as Problem-Solving

Surveys like those reported above help elucidate in rough form the kinds of skills practitioners judge important, notwithstanding fairly severe methodological problems. They offer only a general and unstructured suggestion, however, of practitioners' conceptions of practice. The effort to develop a more coherent and systematic understanding of lawyering practice was an early goal of the clinical movement in legal education. As Carrie Menkel-Meadow wrote in 1980, "The developing clinical legal education movement has been concerned with the central question: 'What is it that lawyers do?'"[26] Menkel-Meadow identified in the contemporary clinical literature studies defining the central work of the lawyer as "decision-maker, advisor, fact developer, advocate, friend, investigator, and organizer." The clinical education movement provided both the incentives and the means by which to study systematically the question, "What is it that lawyers do?" But more than a decade later, clinical scholars have produced little in the way of empirical answers to the question. They have, however, produced some illuminating ideas and hypotheses, drawing primarily on personal experiences.

For example, Jerry Lopez's essay, "Lay Lawyering," begins: "Lawyering means problem-solving. Problem-solving involves perceiving that the world we would like varies from the world as it is and trying to move the world in the desired direction."[28] This probably remains the dominant notion within the clinical education community of what a lawyer is and does. In their widely used clinical text, David Binder, Paul Bergman, and Susan Price advise future lawyers: "But no matter who the client, what the substantive legal issues or whether the situation involves litigation or planning, your principal role as lawyer will almost always be the same—to help clients achieve effective solutions to their problems."[29]

---

21   [Frances Kahn] Zemans & [Victor G.] Rosenblum, [The Making of a Public Profession (Chicago, 1981)] at 123-125.

22   Leonard L. Baird, A Survey of the Relevance of Legal Training to Law School Graduates, 29 J. Legal Educ. 264, 273 (1978).

23   Robert A. D. Schwartz, The Relative Importance of Skills Used by Attorneys, 3 Golden Gate L. Rev. 321, 325 (1973).

24   [John O.] Mudd & [John W.] LaTrielle, [Professional Competence: A Study of New Lawyers, 49 Mont. L. Rev. 11] at 18 [(1988)].

26   [Carrie R. Menkle-Meadow,] The Legacy of Clinical Education: Theories About Lawyering, 29 Clev. St. L. Rev. 555, 555 (1980).

28   Gerald P. Lopez, Lay Lawyering, 32 UCLA L. Rev. 1, 2 (1984).

29   Lawyers as Counselors: A Client-Centered Approach 3 (St. Paul, 1991).

Perhaps owing to the significant participation of clinicians in the recent ABA task force, this perspective also appears prominently in the MacCrate Report. Indeed, "problem solving" is the "fundamental lawyering skill" listed first among those skills the task force deems important. It is described as follows:

Skill 1: Problem Solving

In order to develop and evaluate strategies for solving a problem or accomplishing an objective, a lawyer should be familiar with the skills and concepts involved in:

1.1   Identifying and Diagnosing the Problem;
1.2   Generating Alternative Solutions and Strategies;
1.3   Developing a Plan of Action;
1.4   Implementing the Plan;
1.5   Keeping the Planning Process Open to New Information and New Ideas.

In this formulation, the emphasis is on the conscious consideration of alternatives, and the planning function in problem-solving, at a level of abstraction that does not add much to the aphorism "Think before you act." Despite this focus and the initial goals of the task force, there is not much indication as to how the "fundamental lawyering skill" of problem-solving is, or should be, acquired. Instead, the MacCrate Report cites the brief account of problem-solving as a generic activity in the 1984 work of task force member Anthony G. Amsterdam.[32]

Similarly, although legal scholars have often conceived of lawyering and legal education as somehow involving problem-solving, they have rarely tapped the enormous literature on the topic outside the law journals. There are at least two strains of research and scholarship outside the legal journals that are worth considering in the context of expert problem-solving by lawyers.

III. The Expert as Decision-Maker and Problem-Solver: Decision Theory and Cognitive Science

In our rough formulation thus far, a more expert lawyer will recommend the wiser course, make or suggest better decisions, and have a better chance of helping the client move toward the desired resolution. Reframed in the terms of the dominant legal culture: in an adversary setting, given a fair contest between an expert lawyer and a novice lawyer, the expert will generally win. Other things being equal, we expect that in litigation the expert Ellen will trounce the novice Ned. We expect not only that Ellen will make better individual decisions than Ned about such things as whether or not to file a particular motion, but also that she will have a better chance of solving the overall problem the client Clyde has brought to the firm. Lawyers are, of course, not the only professionals concerned with making decisions and solving problems: those processes are at the core of every profession. In the legal academy, however, such matters are generally relegated to the "art" of practice, of which the less said the better.

---

[32]   Clinical Legal Education—A 21st-Century Perspective, 34 J. Legal Educ. 612 (1984) * * * .

By contrast, professionals in other domains have drawn on more elaborated theories of decision-making and problem-solving. There are two dominant paradigms. The decision-theoretic paradigm takes as the central issue the optimal making of individual decisions, some of which may be critical to outcomes in particular problems. There is also now a large body of scholarship describing and explaining how people actually *do* make decisions, much of it devoted to documenting ways in which people systematically depart from the ideals of statistical rationality. By contrast, the cognitive science paradigm of problem-solving takes as its focus the entire process of problem-solving, which may include the making of sequences of interrelated decisions, no single one of which is likely to be determinative of the outcome.

Lawyering may include "problems" better fitted to one paradigm than the other. A decision whether to file a case, or whether to accept a particular offer of settlement, might best be informed by a decision-theoretic approach. Sophisticated lawyers and clients with the necessary informational resources (e.g., insurance companies) evaluate the settlement value of injury cases, for example, by considering the outcomes of large numbers of similar past cases. In our example, the conversation between Ned and Ellen might be changed abruptly if they learned that Judge Mathers has granted only one of the 115 summary judgment motions submitted to him. Although lawyers may occasionally draw on decision-theoretic techniques, particularly in making "big" decisions, even those lawyers trained in statistical decision theory only rarely apply it. The solving of client problems does entail the making of decisions, but in the main these are smaller decisions embedded in a web of evaluation, decision-making, and implementation—the whole of which constitutes the problem-solving process. This process is typically informed not by decision-theoretic principles at each juncture, but by "judgment" or "experience."

The decision-theoretic paradigm is enormously attractive as a normative matter: leaving aside the initial (and often unspoken or ignored) decisions about which factors should be taken into account, statistical decision theory offers a demonstrably superior approach to decision-making under conditions of uncertainty. But there is an enormous amount of evidence that human beings—experts and novices alike—do not conform to the decision-theoretic ideal. Nor is this surprising. In a world that goes forward in real time, even the statistically sophisticated are able to apply decision theory to only a tiny fraction of the decisions they confront. In the context of the thousands of decisions required in problem-solving in any but the most trivial areas, human beings simply lack the necessary internal computational power (or the interpretive power required to translate for machines with greater computational power) to conform to the normative ideal. This is not to say that lawyers ought not to try to take advantage of the work in decision theory over the past three decades in making or recommending the "big" decisions. To the contrary, several recent works illustrate the potential value of decision theory to practitioners who must decide which cases to accept, whether to settle or go to trial, and so on. But decision theory neither accurately describes how expert problem-solvers make decisions nor provides a feasible model for problem-solving in the real world of complex problems.

The cognitive science paradigm takes a wider view than decision theory. Rather than focusing on optimal methods of making individual decisions, cognitive science conceives problem-solving as a process that entails a sequence of decisions and actions, no single one of which is likely to be determinative. A problem is defined broadly as any situation in which the current state of affairs varies from the desired state of affairs, when there is no obvious way to reach the desired state. In this paradigm, problem-solving entails the making of decisions at various critical junctures, each of which may constrain choices in the future. The focus is not on one or a few critical decisions, but on the entire sequence and pattern of decisions.

The original conceptualization of problem-solving in cognitive science described problem-solving as a search through the web of possible paths from the current situation to the desired outcome or solution, or a search through a "problem space." Problem-solving involved traversing this network of possible paths to a solution, entailing decisions at intersections or nodes in the network, but focusing on the overall sequence of decisions and the connections between interrelated decision-points. Expertise in problem-solving in the cognitivist paradigm thus entailed the ability to make the best individual or "local" decisions at the nodes of the network, *together* with a superior ability to consider the "global" effects of potential "local" decisions as their consequences are carried forward through time and in interconnection with other decisions. In the context of the often used example of chess, masters make better individual moves, and they do so in a way that ultimately serves important strategic goals. Factoring into a "local" decision the consequences that may emerge much later in the process requires a more global sense of the situation and an overall plan for solving the problem, a characteristic of expertise. We observe that not only do novices often seem too much distracted by the trees to see the forest; sometimes they are completely absorbed by a single leaf.

In our example, Ned sees no further than the decision by the trial court on the motion for summary judgment. By contrast, Ellen has considered the likelihood of reversal on appeal and the cost of further proceedings on remand to the trial court. Experience and conventional wisdom counsel that a long chain of seemingly brilliant individual, localized decisions can lead to ultimate failure, if the individual decisions are made solely on the basis of "local" consequences and without regard to their context and effect on the overall problem-solving plan. Put more simply, without some sense of the problem-solving plan and a more global perspective, it is often difficult to tell whether a given "local" decision contributes to an eventual victory or a defeat. In our idealized model of expert problem-solving, then, expertise results from superior decision-making in the local and near term, but the superiority of decisions can be evaluated only as they affect the global and long term. Looking at the matter from the decision-theoretic perspective, expertise would thus seem nearly impossible: the complex web of individual decisions, many of them contingent on the outcomes of other decisions and on the evolving context for the problem, seems simply to overwhelm the tools offered by decision theory. And yet people obviously do become expert at solving problems. Cognitive science has provided convincing explanations of some of the processes that make problem-solving expertise possible.

* * *

X. Conclusions: Some Implications and Opportunities

* * *

A. Implications for Curriculum

At the outset, we recognize the obvious: that formal legal education can provide only the foundation for the later acquisition of lawyering expertise. And, if one conceives of lawyering as entailing mainly the analysis of appellate cases, and legal education as the process by which one acquires the requisite conceptual apparatus, the Langdellian approach still followed in nearly every American law school is both entirely adequate and consistent with the cognitivist paradigm. We have a system quite well designed to produce judicial clerks and appellate advocates, notwithstanding that very few law graduates ever play those roles. It is clear that expertise in learning to "read cases" and extract and apply legal rules by analogy to new situations can be acquired by doing just that, and that some infusion of jurisprudential theory may improve the efficiency and depth of doctrinal learning. Further, it is not difficult to reframe the learning of doctrine and legal reasoning in cognitivist terms. Indeed, there have been some successes at modeling doctrinal expertise in computer expert systems, at least in limited doctrinal areas.

But if one conceives of lawyering as problem-solving in a much broader range of activities, more is required. In every other human endeavor, expertise in problem-solving is acquired by solving problems. There may be better and worse ways to learn to solve problems, but there appears to be no substitute for context. Legal education has completely internalized the lesson that in order to learn to solve problems of doctrinal analysis, one must actually engage in solving doctrinal problems. But the lesson has not been everywhere extended to the other areas of lawyering. We often teach civil procedure as if one can learn about making decisions in litigation by reading about how a few such decisions were made. This seems no more likely a possibility than that we could learn how to solve doctrinal problems by reading *The Paper Chase*.

Similar insights have led other professions, as well as some academics, to consider creating a problem-based pedagogy, essentially abandoning the doctrinal case method of the Harvard Law School for the more holistic, problem-based case method of the Harvard Business School. Indeed, the call of the MacCrate Report for legal education to emphasize problem-solving derives from Anthony Amsterdam's perceptive 1984 essay. And what used to be called the clinical education "movement" is clearly animated in large part by these concerns. But what does all this mean, as it were, in practice? Where would these movements lead, if they were fully informed by the insights of cognitive science?

First, one might reconceive traditional, *non*clinical legal education. At the outset, the goal would be to replicate in hypothetical "problems" as closely as possible the complexities and nuances of a situation that might arise in practice, including the ever present background noise of only potentially relevant detail. * * *

There is, of course, no equivalent need to reconceive *clinical* legal education along similar lines. Or is there? Despite the emphasis at the origins of clinical legal education on problem-solving, much of clinical education today appears aimed at the task of adding to the student's tool kit a few discrete skills beyond the ability to do doctrinal analysis: a little interviewing here, some negotiations there, drafting some interrogatories. There are, to be sure, legal clinics in which the appearance of real clients with genuine, complex problems requires a broader and more coherent problem-based approach. In most law school clinics the limitation is not one of dimensionality of the problems (unless some dimensions are ignored by the faculty), but one of scale. The prototypical problem confronted in a law school clinic is the seemingly small, single-client case: one client, one problem, one student. Much can be learned in this context, but much cannot. A good many lawyering abilities required in the context of small cases simply do not "scale up" to work on larger problems involving multiple parties, many attorneys and other legal workers, and large quantities of information. Given time constraints, it may not be possible for law students to grapple with larger-scale problems from start to finish, but students may be able to perform the kind of situated problem-solving required by work on discrete pieces of larger problems, while still keeping the larger problem in view.

Such an ambition is realizable to the degree that we can supply students with methods of modeling complexity, with problem and solution schemas that can be described, with some sense of the architectures that mental models of legal problems might take, with "theory" as I have defined it. In fact, it is the very existence of such theory that raises the possibility of teaching problem-solving lawyering skills to *all* law students, not merely to those lucky enough to spend extended time in individual mentoring situations. Some of what experienced lawyers know seems capable of transmission to younger lawyers only through the process of individual mentoring or apprenticeship. But to the extent that some of that knowledge can be generalized and communicated * * *, it can be learned in less mentor-intensive settings. * * *

This is not to suggest that we should merely replace one kind of talk with another kind of talk in the classroom. * * * [W]e ought to be teaching students how to go about constructing in the novel domains they will encounter in practice their own theories and models. We should be teaching future lawyers, among other things, how to scavenge other disciplines and professions for methods, models, and analogs. In other words, though we should teach more "theory" of the kinds I have mentioned, we ought mainly to be teaching students *to be* theoreticians, both grounded in their own experience and making as much of it as possible for future use. * * *

* * *

B. The Clinical Method

Much of the value of clinical legal education comes directly from the exposure of law students to clinical practice. Clinical teachers must guide and help consolidate this powerful experiential learning opportunity without undercutting the strength of the experience by falling back on traditional norms of student-teacher interactions. In the following excerpt, Frank S. Bloch proposes a model for clinical law teaching based on theories of adult learning.

Frank S. Bloch, *The Andragogical Basis of Clinical Legal Education,*
35 Vand. L. Rev. 321 (1982)*

* * *

II. Andragogy

In a seminal work that was published in 1970, Malcolm S. Knowles introduced the concept of andragogy to modern education theory to separate the concerns that are peculiar to adult education from those theretofore addressed in traditional education literature.[16] In coining the new term, which is derived by substituting the Greek stem *andr*, meaning adult, for the stem *paid*, meaning child, as the latter is used in the term pedagogy, Knowles intended to communicate that andragogy is "the art and science of helping adults learn." Knowles felt that a distinction between andragogy and traditional pedagogy was necessary because, as the dominant use of the term pedagogy in education literature implies, "most teachers of adults have only known how to teach adults as if they were children."

* * *

A. *Underlying Assumptions of Andragogy*

Knowles' theory of andragogy is premised on four underlying assumptions about the characteristics of adult learners that are drawn largely from the work of clinical psychologists such as Abraham H. Maslow and Carl R. Rogers.[23] These assumptions relate to how self-concept, the role of experience in learning, readiness to learn, and orientation of learning change from childhood to adulthood; they lead to the conclusion that adults are substantially different from children in these respects and that a theory of instruction that takes into account the self-concept of adults, the role of experience in adult learning, adults' readiness to learn, and their orientation to learning will of necessity differ from a theory based on traditional pedagogy.

The first assumption which Knowles makes is that adults see themselves as self-directing personalities, unlike children who expect the will of adults to be imposed on them. Adults' self-concept is such that they expect to make their own decisions, face the consequences of their decisions, and manage their own lives. Indeed, Knowles asserts that one becomes an adult psychologically only when one perceives of oneself as wholly self-directing.

The second assumption underlying the theory of andragogy is that adults accumulate a greater amount and variety of experience than children, and, as a result, their experience becomes a greater resource for learning. In addition, Knowles argues that this difference of quantity and quality of experience is heightened by a difference

---

    16   M. Knowles, The Modern Practice of Adult Education (1970). * * *

    23   * * * Knowles seems to have relied particularly on A. Maslow, Motivation And Personality (1954), and C. Rogers, Client-Centered Therapy (1951).

between children and adults as to the importance of their experiences to them. According to Knowles, while children take note of their experiences, "to an adult, his experience *is* him. He defines who he is, establishes his self-identity, in terms of his accumulation of a unique set of experiences."

The third assumption is based on the concept of "developmental tasks." Developmental tasks are those tasks that must be dealt with at various stages in life if one is to pass from one phase of personal development to the next. Educators have found that children demonstrate a heightened readiness to learn those tasks that are appropriate for them to master at a given phase of their development. Knowles assumes from this finding that adults also will have a heightened readiness to learn those developmental tasks that are appropriate for them. Adult developmental tasks are keyed primarily to the various social roles that adults must fulfill. Thus, as adults' social roles change, their developmental tasks change, and their readiness to learn any particular subject matter or skill changes with each change in appropriate developmental tasks.

Knowles' final assumption is that adults seek to apply learning immediately, while children tend to see acquired knowledge solely as a future benefit. Since education to children is the accumulation of knowledge for future use, children study in a subject-centered frame of mind. By contrast, adults "engage in learning largely in response to pressures they feel from their current life situation. . . . They tend, therefore, to enter an educational activity in a *problem-centered* frame of mind."

B. *Methodological Implications of the Underlying Assumptions of Andragogy*

Each of the four underlying assumptions of andragogy led Knowles to a set of related "technological implications" for the education of adults. These implications in turn can serve as a guide for an andragogical methodology for legal education in general and for clinical legal education in particular. Before applying this methodology, however, Knowles' implications for each of the assumptions of andragogy must be examined in some detail.

1. Self-Concept

Knowles considers the change in self-concept—from the dependent child to the self-directing adult—to be the most important difference between children and adults as learners. The methodological implications of this change for teachers of adults reach into the climate of the learning environment to be established and the relationship between learner and teacher in planning, conducting, and evaluating the course of study.

According to Knowles, the most important aspect of the adult learning environment is the psychological climate, which "should be one which causes adults to feel accepted, respected, and supported; in which there exists a spirit of mutuality between teachers and students as joint inquirers." Knowles believes that andragogical methodology requires teachers to show interest in and respect for their students by listening to them and making use of their contributions; educators should not view their students as "receiving sets for [the teacher's] transmissions of wisdom."

Knowles also argues that this "climate of adultness" is most effective when extended beyond individual classes to the institution as a whole.

Knowles discusses two aspects of course planning in the context of the self-concept of adults and andragogical methodology. The first of these aspects is that self-directing adults can be expected to be more deeply motivated when they are learning what they think they need to learn and when they participate in the planning of their course of study. Accordingly, students in an andragogically sound educational setting are required to participate both in the diagnosis of their learning needs and in the planning of how and when they are to be taught.

The second aspect relates to the actual process of teaching and to the evaluation of learning for self-directing adults, and follows the same theme. Knowles argues that the attitudes underlying traditional pedagogical practice—in which the teacher alone takes responsibility for teaching and learning, as well as for evaluating the students' progress and performance—conflict with the self-concept of self-directing adults. To correct this conflict, andragogical practice calls for dividing responsibility equally between teacher and student for the execution of the teaching process and the evaluation of learning.

2. Role of Experience

Andragogical methodology favors participatory, experiential learning techniques—for example, exercises, role playing, field work, seminars, and counseling—to reinforce the important role of experience in the lives and learning of adults. The assumption is that "the more active the learner's role in the process, the more he is probably learning." Because of the importance that adults place on experiences, they naturally want to learn from experience; indeed, they may even resent learning situations in which their experience is not being used. For this reason, adults' experiences are included in andragogical methodology both by encouraging the use of students' life experiences as illustrations and examples for learning, and by planning for students to use what they learn in their daily lives.

3. Readiness to Learn

Concerning adults' readiness to learn, Knowles presents two methodological implications that he derives from applying the concept of developmental tasks to adult education. First, Knowles believes that because adults' developmental tasks parallel their social roles, adult students should be taught matters that relate to existing or changing social roles appropriate to their personal development. Thus, the curriculum must be timed to coordinate the teaching of subjects or skills with the developmental tasks facing the students at that time. Second, Knowles argues that students who must deal with similar developmental tasks, that is, those with similar social roles, should be grouped together so the course of instruction can focus on their shared interests in learning.

4. Orientation to Learning

The major element of andragogical methodology that is related to adults' orientation to learning is based on the change in adults from a subject-centered to a problem-centered frame of mind. Thus, andragogical methodology calls for a shift in emphasis from teaching the traditional subject areas to teaching material likely to assist students in dealing with problems they will encounter. A proper andragogical approach would teach about problem areas that the students will deal with at or close to the time of learning, rather than offer broad coverage of general subjects that have little or no relation to the students' relatively short-term goals and ambitions.

* * *

III. ANDRAGOGY AND CLINICAL LEGAL EDUCATION

As with any general theory based largely on a single idea, a danger of tautology exists when one attempts to explain and apply the theory of andragogy at a practical level through numerous examples. Although Knowles and those following him have elaborated upon and expanded the four basic assumptions of andragogy and the methodological implications based on those assumptions, the important elements of each andragogical assumption can be reduced to a single methodological point. These points can be presented, in declining order of importance, as follows: (1) Learning should be through mutual inquiry by teacher and student (adults' self-concept as self-directing); (2) emphasis should be on active, experiential learning (role of experience in adult leaning [sic]); (3) learning should relate to concurrent changes in the students' social roles (readiness to learn); and (4) learning should be presented in the context of problems that students are likely to face (orientation to learning).

These four central elements of andragogy and their related methodological implications provide a theoretical framework for examining the appropriateness of the methods by which law is taught to adult law students both in clinical programs and throughout legal education. This theoretical framework offers legal educators the opportunity to plan a course of law study that is fully consistent with the capabilities and aspirations of adult law students. * * *

* * *

B. Andragogy and Clinical Legal Education
* * *

1. Learning Through Mutual Inquiry by Teacher and Student

The recognition of adults as self-directing learners is the most important source of the departures from traditional pedagogy that are contained in Knowles' andragogy. The key methodological implication that follows from this recognition is the creation of a learning climate which includes what Knowles calls "a spirit of mutuality between teachers and students as joint inquirers." The idea is that teachers and their adult students, by working together, can create a setting in which the students are both acting consistently with their self-concept and benefiting from the teaching of their co-inquirer/teacher.

The clinical method of legal instruction applies this aspect of andragogical methodology in a way that is otherwise unavailable in the traditional law school curriculum. Gary Bellow and Earl Johnson describe the unique "two-way street" of the clinical experience and its contrast with traditional law teaching as follows:

> While the combative nature of the socratic method tends to substitute spar-
> ring for learning, in a setting in which faculty and students find themselves
> in a shared enterprise, and in which inquiry is concerned with emotional
> reaction as well as analysis, the classroom, although rigorous, becomes a
> mutual search for solutions and knowledge. The instructor receives direct
> feedback indicating the relevance of his conceptual approach, and is
> thereby forced to rethink his approaches and perceptions in light of the
> experiences of those whom he is teaching. If such a dynamic is implicit in
> the clinical methodology, this may be its most pervasive contribution to
> legal education.[65]

The sharing of responsibility for clinic cases creates the proper atmosphere for an
optimum andragogical learning experience, which takes place when the teacher
uses a shared experience to point out and convey to the student points of law, methods of practice, and elements of the legal process. In this setting all learning does not
have to come directly from the teacher; indeed, when a case is so novel or complex
that the clinical teacher really must struggle together with the student, the answer may
be that there is no answer, and the student both experiences and learns this limit of
the rules of law.

Knowles and other educators working in the field of andragogy have found that
the adult students for whom a self-directed learning setting is designed do not necessarily welcome this type of environment. When first placed in the position of having to participate actively in the planning and execution of a learning experience,
students can be skeptical and even resentful before coming to realize the benefits of
this aspect of andragogical methodology. Michael Meltsner and Philip Schrag also
noted this problem in general terms when they experimented with various clinical
models at Columbia Law School and moved toward a policy of requiring students to
assume a more active role in representing clients. They noted that this change in
approach affected both students and faculty: "Students and faculty had to come to
terms with the passivity of the student role, and the implicit assumption of much legal
education that the faculty is solely responsible for whether learning takes place."[69]
Writing a few years later on their experiences with the clinical program that they
eventually developed following earlier experimentation with various clinical models,
Meltsner and Schrag reported instances in which students initially would be confused
and even actively hostile when given responsibility for handling and administering
their cases—that is, for planning and executing their clinical experience.[70]

---

65   Bellow & Johnson, [*Reflections on the University of Southern California Clinical Semester*,
44 S. Cal. L. Rev. 664,] at 694 [(1971)]. * * *

69   Meltsner & Schrag, [*Report From a CLEPR Colony*, 76 Colum. L. Rev. 581,] at 626 [(1976)].
* * *

70   Meltsner & Schrag, *Scenes From a Clinic*, 127 U. Pa. L. Rev. 1, 32-33 (1978). Meltsner &
Schrag stated,
  Such [non-directive] encounters [between teacher and student] can go very badly if the participants do not take into account the norms of the law school. The intern who asks a supervisor which witnesses he or she should call and hears the supervisor say, "Do you want me to

2. Active, Experiential Learning

Experiential learning has been promoted, of course, outside of the context of andragogical theory. In fact, experiential learning is a part of any professional education program that has a clinical component. An obvious example is medical training, which often is cited as a model for law schools to consider when designing a program of clinical legal education. The use of experiential learning in clinical programs ties the clinical method of legal instruction into the second key element of andragogical theory.

Clinical legal education is experiential learning both in terms of what the students bring to the learning setting and in terms of the experiences that the students work through in the clinical program itself. Law students, like any other adults, have their experiences in life to draw upon in learning. Perhaps more important, second year and particularly third year students often have law-related experience that they can use—and that they expect to use—in their last two years in law school. Finally, the experience of actual representation is available to the law student in the clinic. In sum, there is a role for experience in law teaching, and that role is best developed through the clinical method.

The range of experiences that are available to students in clinical education programs encompasses more than the normal lawyering skills of interviewing, counseling, negotiation, and trial and appellate advocacy. To the extent that broader human relations skills are a desirable subject of learning in law school, clinical legal education—with its emphasis on experiential learning—offers the opportunity to teach those skills. As Alan Stone stated, "[T]he student's experience with human problems in the legal clinic always has the potential of being emotionally real. The student is directly involved in a case and can explore its social and psychological implications in as great a depth as his motivation allows."[77]

Since clinical legal education provides law students with the opportunity to relate their own experiences, as well as their new lawyering experiences presented to them in clinical practice, to whatever is being taught in the clinical program, supervised practice can achieve the optimal level of educational meaning and impact. Preble Stolz perhaps summarized this notion best when he stated that

> attitudes towards the world—morals to use an older term—especially insofar as they influence behavior, probably come more from classmates and experience than anything that happens in the classroom. Perhaps including clinical exposure in legal education will improve the law

---

answer that question now?" may understand the dialogue in terms of a previous experience with law teachers who hide the ball and never really answer questions. If we are to succeed in the supervisory role, we must demonstrate that we have much to give and that we will give it; but that it is the interns' responsibility to decide when, where, and how to get it.
Id. at 22-23.

* * *

77   Stone, Legal Education on the Couch, 85 HARV. L. REV. 392, 429 (1971). * * *

school's capacity to reach the deeper motivations of its students and thus to influence their careers.[78]

Gary Bellow and Earl Johnson found that students handling cases in their clinic "began to be far more interested in their own experiences as a source of theoretical generalization, and far more concerned with theory as a tool for defining and understanding experience, than they were when they first started."[79] When students use the experiences that they obtain in the clinic as a tool for learning, "[t]he clinical process radically alters the usual relationship of faculty to student. The students have, at last, a body of their own experience which they can compare to the faculty's assertions and statements."

3. Learning, Students' Social Roles, and Problem Solving

The final two elements of Knowles' andragogy—students' changing social roles and their readiness to learn, and students' focus on problem solving and their orientation to learning—also fit the clinical method of legal instruction. These elements, however, are perhaps less uniquely suited to clinical legal education than learning through mutual inquiry and active experiential learning. Since law students are about to make one of the major social role changes of their lives—becoming a lawyer—they are naturally ready to learn about law and lawyering. Regardless of the method of instruction, they will view whatever they learn as some form of preparation for solving problems that they will face in their professional careers. One need not enter into the debate over the quality and relevance of every part of the law school curriculum to recognize that—at least to some extent—legal education generally is andragogically sound in the categories of readiness to learn and orientation to learning.

Nevertheless, the clinical method of legal instruction does apply andragogical methodology in these areas more directly and regularly than does traditional legal education. When a student who is about to become a lawyer enters a clinical learning environment and is taught through actual representation of a client in a legal dispute, optimal compliance with the andragogically dictated sensitivity to the student's readiness to learn is attained. Thus, one commentator has observed that "[t]he student response to the challenge of situations of 'professional responsibility' while participating in the clinic depends on his thinking of himself as a lawyer." Similarly, notwithstanding the recent appearance of some innovative problem-oriented law school casebooks, clinical legal education epitomizes andragogy's problem-centered methodology. Not only are issues and material presented as problems, but also "legal training is immediately useful. The student *must learn* or he will be embarrassed before real clients, lawyers and judges."

---

[78]   Stolz, *Clinical Experience in American Legal Education: Why Has it Failed?*, in [CLINICAL EDUCATION AND THE] LAW SCHOOL OF THE FUTURE 138, at 54, 76 [U. of Chicago Law School Conference Series No. 20) (E. Kitch ed. 1970)].

[79]   Bellow & Johnson, supra note [65], at 693.

C. Toward An Andragogically Based Model for Clinical Legal Education

As previously discussed, proponents of clinical legal education usually have supported their case by emphasizing the new areas of study that can be introduced into the law school curriculum. Most critics of the clinical method also have focused on the substantive content, arguing that what is taught in clinical programs need not or should not be taught in law school at all.[87] Only recently have clinicians begun to go beyond the debate over the value of the substantive content of clinical programs to look critically at their own methodology and its implementation. These efforts differ fundamentally from the literature on effective models for clinical instruction, which are concerned primarily with questions of technique, and from guidelines for clinical legal education, which seek to establish the characteristics that clinical programs should have without any particular reference to a theory of learning.

Andragogy can be extremely useful in this critical examination of clinical methodology because it can provide the coherent, theoretical framework of a methodology-based justification for clinical education that has been missing in the attempts to establish various content-based justifications. As discussed above, andragogy has become established as a significant theory of instruction for adult learners, and its methodology is consistent with the general methods used to implement clinical programs. When viewed as an educational basis for clinical legal education, andragogy can be useful to clinicians in their attempts to improve the clinical method of law teaching, to take full advantage of a clinical setting for legal instruction, and to establish clinical legal education as an essential element of professional legal education.

Andragogical theory need not provide a single, definitive model for clinical legal education to be useful. Indeed, uncritical reliance on the principles of andragogy is unwarranted if for no other reason than because andragogy is still a developing field. Nonetheless, the four central elements of andragogy suggest the beginnings of a model for clinical legal education that addresses the three major issues which legal educators have debated in this field: The use of actual clients rather than simulations, the method and extent of supervision by clinical faculty, and the types of cases to be handled in a clinical program.

1. Actual Client Representation

An andragogically based model for clinical legal education should rely heavily on actual client representation.[95] A relationship based on shared, mutual inquiry simply cannot be established through the alternative technique of simulation. An effective, competent simulation must be pre-planned so that even if the instructor participates in the simulation, the law student knows that there is nothing like shared

---

87   This type of criticism is levelled most often at the teaching of lawyering skills, which is an area in which traditional law teachers seem to have tremendous faith in post-formal education, on-the-job training. * * *

95   This proposition means that *all* students would be engaged *primarily* in the representation of actual clients, but it is not meant to denigrate the value of simulations as a *supplemental* method of instruction. Simulations can be particularly valuable in a clinical program when they are used to help prepare students for interviewing, taking depositions, and certain other aspects of trial work.

inquiry or a co-counsel relationship between student and teacher. In fact, it is likely that the instructor would not participate at all in the simulation and instead let the student work through the problem alone. In an actual client setting, on the other hand, the student and teacher are forced to work together at every step in the case because crucial decisions may have to be made at any time that could be critical to the client's claim or defense. As a result, a co-counsel relationship develops between the student and the teacher that continues throughout the student's involvement in the case and offers the student opportunities for valuable learning experiences both at expected and unexpected moments during representation. The differences between the use of actual clients and the use of simulations in establishing an atmosphere of mutual inquiry can be seen perhaps most clearly in the area of decisions on case strategy. Such decisions are so important in actual client representation that the clinical instructor must examine and participate in the student's analysis and judgments. In a simulation setting, it is most likely that the instructor would not participate in any case strategy at all, and the advantages of such an experience would be lost.

Although an actual client representation setting makes it possible for the student and the teacher to establish a continuous co-counsel relationship, the proposition does not follow that the teacher and the student should work together on every aspect of all the student's cases. The optimal andragogical setting is one in which students are given the opportunity to learn through their own initiative by working together with—rather than being dominated by—the teacher. When students and teachers work together on actual cases, a true "climate of adultness" consistent with the self-concept of law students is maintained because the students practice together with their instructors in a setting in which their participation means something not only to themselves, but also to the instructors with whom they work. A teacher representing an actual client in conjunction with a student relies heavily on the student's work and, therefore, is deeply concerned with how the student performs during the representation. In such a setting, even though the instructors are set apart because of the knowledge that they can convey to students who are working with them, they are not removed entirely from the process of learning, as tends to be the case with simulations. Instructors thus are far less likely to engage in the type of one-way transmittal of knowledge that is antithetical to andragogy.

Actual client representation is also necessary to involve law students in andragogically sound active, experiential learning. Although role playing is a type of experiential learning, law students must be allowed to practice law on behalf of real clients if a clinical program is to take full advantage of the role of experience in adult learning. Actual client representation is real and, therefore, andragogically effective. Simulations, on the other hand, are recognized as imaginary and thus are less effective as learning experiences, since law students may not be willing to relate what they were taught in simulations to other lawyering experiences that they have had or will have outside of law school.

Similarly, while clinical legal education possesses the potential to take full advantage of law students' readiness to learn, the lack of reality inherent in simulations can undermine that potential. When representing actual clients, law students are in fact lawyers; accordingly, they are fully aware that what they are learning relates to what they came to law school to learn. In a simulation setting, however, students can become unsure about the relationship between the simulation and actual practice of law, and, consequently, they can become less interested in what the teacher is trying to teach.

2. Close Supervision by Clinical Faculty

Proper implementation of andragogical methodology in a law school clinical setting requires that clinical faculty supervise students closely and directly. Probably the most important element of an andragogically sound model for clinical supervision is the establishment of a co-counsel relationship between the student and the teacher. This method of supervision allows students to learn through mutual inquiry, which is consistent with andragogical theory, and to make the most of the learning opportunities that are available through actual client representation. Placing students outside of a law school controlled setting in which they are likely either to work unattended or to be limited to observing the "real lawyers" in the office would dilute the educational value of having students represent actual clients. Both of these circumstances are totally at odds with the type of shared responsibility for learning that andragogical theory envisions.

Clinical faculty, however, must do more than just work together with students on cases. Clinical instructors must be willing and able to teach their students once a proper andragogical setting is established. Although the teacher and the student working together as co-counsel create Knowles' "spirit of the mutuality," the teacher is largely responsible for taking advantage of this setting and turning it into an effective learning opportunity. A law teacher working on a case with a law student must be able to guide the student toward learning whatever lawyering skills or substantive material the student needs to know to participate effectively in handling the case. This guidance can be provided without undermining the co-counsel relationship between the teacher and the student or sacrificing the teacher's responsibility to teach, particularly if the teacher follows the andragogical prescriptions of being sensitive to the student's role as a self-directed learner in planning the learning experience and of giving the student the opportunity to choose how to make the most of the learning opportunity. Thus, the teacher and student should share the assignment of responsibilities in a particular case.

Since clinical teachers are still teachers and their co-counsel are still their students, the possibility always exists that mutual inquiry will be forsaken and that the teacher will take control of the representation by lecturing to the student and directing him or her to do what the teacher knows—or has determined—must be done. An andragogical model would specifically discourage this type of supervision, except to the extent that it is necessary to ensure competent representation in a particular case. Instead of extensive lecturing and excessive direction, students should be encouraged to decide when to ask questions and when to explore for answers on their own. In other words, the student should help the teacher decide when the teacher needs to direct and teach, and when the student can be left alone. Close supervision, therefore, does not mean a constant faculty presence.

* * *

The following brief excerpt picks up and develops further the educational opportunities presented by the collaborative setting in which clinic students and faculty work. Gary Palm argues that collaboration is more than a structure for teaching; collaboration goes to the heart of effective lawyering and can stimulate clinical-based scholarship as well.

Gary Palm, *Reconceptualizing Clinical Scholarship as Clinical Instruction*, 1 CLINICAL L. REV. 127 (1994)*

* * *

One of the great strengths of clinical education is that clinical teachers and students collaborate on every matter that emerges from the clinic. For most students, it is the only point in legal education where they can work together with a law teacher on a joint project, for which student and teacher share responsibility. This is not the type of brief criticism which a teacher may provide to a student on a law review draft or a paper submitted for a seminar. When students work together with their teachers on cases in a clinic, the student and the professor share responsibility for the client and are both liable as practitioners. Indeed, the student is not permitted to proceed and take action on behalf of clients without the ongoing direct supervision and acquiescence of the supervising attorney.

At the University of Chicago's Mandel Legal Aid Clinic, for example, every case, project and activity must be the *joint responsibility* of an attorney and a student. No matter how complex or important a case or project may be, the clinical teacher collaborates with the students on all aspects of the case or project. This does not mean that in every situation the student will perform the lawyering function in public. What it does mean is that the student will be fully integrated into the work that goes on. The student and teacher discuss the alternative strategies available and prepare together for each lawyering activity. Often the attorney may write the final version of parts of the brief or deliver an oral argument, but the student plays an integral part in preparing for that activity and critiquing the result.

The essential functions and effects of collaborative work in clinical education are explained by Frank S. Bloch in his article on the andragogical basis of clinical education.[2] "Probably the most important element of an andragogically sound model for clinical supervision," he observes, "is the establishment of a co-counsel relationship between the student and the teacher." He goes on to indicate that students

---

*   Reprinted with permission.

2   Frank S. Bloch, *The Andragogical Basis of Clinical Legal Education*, 35 VAND. L. REV. 321 (1982).

learn through this process of mutual effort and inquiry with the teacher. Bloch also identifies other attributes of excellent clinical teaching, but he maintains that the collaborative process is central to andragogical theory.

Noting that "the possibility always exists that mutual inquiry will be forsaken and that the teacher will take control of the representation by lecturing to the student and directing him or her to do what the teacher knows—or has determined—must be done," Bloch emphasizes that "an andragogical model would specifically discourage this type of supervision." Yet, the question of when, and how much, to intervene, is a very difficult one. Sometimes a clinical teacher takes on too much control and in other situations does not take on enough. It is an ongoing struggle for each clinical teacher to intervene appropriately with each student based upon the student's competence and responsibility.

To be sure, the clinical teacher's function does not end with collaboration, nor is it magically made easy by a collaborative relationship. Indeed, collaborating with an inexperienced law student can often be difficult and time consuming. Nonetheless, the co-counsel approach provides a particularly effective means for accomplishing the clinical teacher's dual goals of supervising and instructing. As Kenneth Kreiling has observed,[6] clinical supervision requires genuine congruence between the supervisor and the student, which is possible only when the supervisor has unconditional positive regard for the student. These aspects of supervision are made easier by a collaborative relationship between supervisor and student.

Not only is collaboration an essential aspect of effective clinical instruction, it may also be an appropriate subject for law school teaching. In an innovative article, Susan Bryant shows the need for training law students in how to be effective collaborators when they go into practice.[7] Observing that collaborative practice is widespread, she points out that

> collaborative work methods cannot improve the work of lawyers unless they approach their work with an understanding of the value and the limits of collaboration and with good collaborative skills. Law students are unlikely to achieve such understanding and skills unless law schools and practicing lawyers make serious attempts to teach them. . . . Moreover, collaboration provides students with valuable insights into clinical judgment and the attorney client relationship.

As Bryant demonstrates, there are teaching methods that can be used to teach collaboration effectively. In the future, clinical teachers will no doubt be taught at AALS conferences and workshops how to teach collaborative practice effectively and how to structure learning arrangements in a clinical law office and classroom to best accomplish this goal.

---

6   Kenneth Kreiling, *Clinical Education and Lawyer Competency: The Process of Learning to Learn Through Properly Structured Clinical Supervision*, 40 MD. L. REV. 284, 302 (1981).

7   Susan J. Bryant, *Collaboration in Law Practice: A Satisfying and Productive Process for a Diverse Profession*, 17 VT. L. REV. 459 (1993).

* * *

I would urge clinical teachers to experiment with collaborative scholarship with students. Many analytic research and writing skills could be taught through collaborative scholarship. Moreover, collaborative scholarship may be a useful tool for helping students understand the theoretical foundations of lawyering. Others have pointed out that effective use of lawyering skills requires an awareness of the theoretical dimensions of these skills and an appreciation of what is an effective performance. It may be possible to teach lessons such as these by means of collaborative scholarship.

* * *

———————————

There must also be direction in clinical teaching. In the next excerpt Robert Condlin questions whether the instruction that actually takes place during clinical practice is as progressive and innovative as it purports to be, or could be.

Robert Condlin, *"Tastes Great, Less Filling": The Law School Clinic and Political Critique*, 36 J. LEGAL EDUC. 45 (1986)*

* * *

The Purpose of Clinical Practice Instruction

Our starting point must be an understanding of what clinical practice instruction tries to accomplish. Over the years the most popular objectives have been training in the motor dimensions of lawyer practice skills (skills training); teaching ethics, both the development of character and informing about relevant codes and rules (ethics); internalizing the tacit norms and lore of law practice (socialization); inspecting particular types of lawyer work prior to job selection (placement); increasing self-awareness of dispositions and values likely to affect performances as lawyers (self-awareness); teaching doctrine and analysis in an engaging fashion (pedagogy); and understanding and criticizing standard ways of performing lawyer practice skills for their contributions, both in specific instances and in the aggregate, to the legal system and the outcomes it produces (critique). Usually, clinical teachers have favorites among these objectives and shape their programs to emphasize one or two in a sustained and systematic way. But this narrowing of focus can create problems if the teachers choose unwisely, for the objectives exist in a hierarchy, and critique is at the top. This fact has consequences for all the decisions involved in constructing a clinical program and in teaching a clinical course.

———————————

*   Reprinted with permission.

Clinical critique takes as its subject the skill practices (and the theories on which they are based) lawyers use to give effect to legal rules and is concerned with understanding and evaluating the manner in which such practices contribute to the justice of the legal system. These practices are important because they make up the low-visibility ways in which lawyers amend, abrogate, and enforce the law, and in the process, determine much of law's meaning for persons who come in contact with it. The practices are amenable to theoretical elaboration, support multiple research agendas, and can be divided, categorized, and sequenced conceptually for purposes of instruction. In addition, they provide a distinct and relatively unexplored vantage point on the operation of the legal system from which new critical insights about law may be produced, and these insights in turn will have implications for the ways in which statutes are drafted and doctrines elaborated. One can have normative theories about the proper performance of lawyer practices, and theories about how lawyer practices contribute to the justice of the legal system as a whole. While clinical thinking in each of these areas is far from developed, the work to be done is familiar and manageable. In studying lawyer-skill practices, teachers and students come to see how the individual actions of lawyers constitute and reconstitute legal rules, and how the legal system's kantian (rule/policy) and aristotelian (lawyer dispositional) halves fit together.

Critique consists of analyzing and evaluating the patterns and theories immanent in the methods lawyers use to perform and think about skill practices against conceptions of what would be better, for the purpose of resolving perceived contradictions between theory and practice. This analysis presupposes a critical theory, which in turn presupposes worked-out views on the nature of a fair and just legal system and the role of lawyer practices in operating and improving it. This theory can be a psychology of law practice, in which individual lawyer behavior is viewed as relatively discrete and self-contained action and the principles that explain its operation are identified and categorized, or a kind of legal sociology (or economics), in which principles of individual action are replaced by equivalent principles about legal institutions and systems, and lawyer behavior is explained by the incentives and constraints of the social matrix in which it occurs. A psychology or sociology is not critical, however, until it challenges prevailing conceptions of good behavior and identifies (even if only implicitly) better ways of thinking about and performing in lawyer role. To make judgments about what would be better, principles of individual action and social organization must be linked to a theory of society or theory of justice, a theory of the way in which lawyers and legal institutions ought to operate in order that fair and just states of affairs be produced. These theories can be incomplete, tentative, or not wholly (or even in major part) original, as long as they are also coherent, intelligent, and genuinely open to further development. Clinical teachers do not have to be original political thinkers, but they should have a political dimension to their conception of the clinical subject.

Political critique is the most important clinical objective for several reasons. To begin with, it is the objective most adapted to the university setting in which legal instruction occurs. Critique is a university's reason for being, its identifying characteristic, and the only one of its multiple functions it fails to perform at the price of being a university. Stripped of its critical role, the university is a mere socializing agent, an instrument of prevailing orthodoxy, engaged only in legitimation and control. One might be skeptical about the modern university's commitment to critique and this would be fair. Day-to-day university activity is often mundane; critique is rare, and socialization and control are commonplace. But critique is the university's highest function, its aspiration, the source of its greatest potential and its occasional achievement and it remains the strongest basis of the argument for the university's existence.

The critical task is particularly important to the university law school. The ability to judge day-to-day law practice against objective standards of justice and fairness is an essential quality of a good citizen and a good lawyer. Yet legal work settings make this kind of deliberation difficult. Lawyer tasks have predefined instrumental ends and lawyer roles come with a full complement of powerfully felt self-interests, and the combination of the two often distorts critical thinking and sometimes corrupts it. For most, law school provides the last unrestricted opportunity to take a larger view, where "work" itself obliges one to develop a conception of lawyer behavior that serves more than selfish ends. In an important sense, the obligation to pursue critique is heightened not diminished by the fact that law school is the last step on a journey into a profession.

In addition, in the legal system's educational division of labor critique of lawyer practices is the special domain of the clinical law teacher. Students learn about law practice from many directions and sources. Expert practitioners develop skills, law firms socialize, psychologists increase self-awareness, placement officers find jobs, traditional law professors teach about doctrine and analysis, and philosophers develop ethical sophistication. These processes occur in clinics, but good instruction depends upon both format and expertise, and in most of these subjects clinical teachers are not expert, at least not in comparison with persons who work with the subject full time. For some of these subjects, skills training is the best example, clinicians are additionally disabled because unlike practitioners, they do not work with students for a long enough period of time for the instruction to take hold. (Skills are based on habit and habit takes longer than a semester to develop.) Clinicians have time and opportunity to analyze lawyer skill practices, however, they can develop the necessary expertise and they are likely to be the only person in the students' educational process concerned principally with this topic. Not to pursue the subject is to fail to deliver on the clinical teacher's implied promise to teach about lawyer practices as a critical perspective on law.

Moreover, critique is the foundation on which the other clinical objectives rest. Even skills training presupposes critical judgments about what skills ought to be learned, in what order, and in what form, and these judgments in turn presuppose a conception of a fair and just legal system and the role of lawyer practices in operating and improving it. One cannot say, for example, what kind of rhetorical and strategic maneuvering is proper in influencing an adversary to settle until one has worked out a moral and political view about how dispute negotiation ought to proceed. For example, we do not call a person who fabricates evidence and obtains a favorable settlement as a result, skillful; we call him dishonest. And a person who curses an adverse negotiator because he knows the adversary will be upset and bargain badly is often thought of as abusive not skillful, even when the tactic succeeds. The concept of skill has no meaning outside an ever-changing and controversial normative context and it must be studied in that context to be understood. Political critique is a necessary not just interesting part of the study of skill, therefore, and those who fail to engage in it are forever at the mercy of the prevailing "wisdom" of their environments and the tacit biases imbedded in their personal beliefs. The subordination of skills training to critique does not preclude clinical courses emphasizing skills. But such training ought not to come first, it ought not to be pervasive, and even when pursued for its own sake it ought not to ignore altogether the critical background questions temporarily bracketed.

In suggesting that clinical study ought to engage in critique of lawyer practices I make no judgments about the outcome of that critique. Many standard conceptions of and methods for performing lawyer practices could be improved, but I do not assume at the outset that these conceptions or methods are corrupt, or that they systematically deny justice to a substantial part of the legal client population. In fact, I would not be surprised to learn that, as the end products of a complicated set of necessary trade-offs and accommodations to practical realities, such practices reflect a kind of Burkean equilibrium that makes radical reform inadvisable. The opposite also probably will sometimes be true. My present argument is only that clinicians ought to determine for themselves the extent to which each such situation exists.

In the end, critique of lawyer practices is pursued for its contribution to the development of the individual—not to be unknowingly captive to received wisdom is to be more fully autonomous—because it is an essential element of a law trained person's completed world view, and as a foundation for reform of the incentive structures within which lawyer behavior operates. When it is present and done well, clinical instruction is successful and the simultaneous pursuit of other objectives makes the instruction that much better, but when it is absent, no amount of training in motor skill, socialization, or self-awareness can wag the dog. It is the only element of clinical study that is both a necessary and sufficient condition of good instruction.

II. Two Problems with the Conventional Clinic

Two features of the conventional clinic inhibit effective critique. I shall discuss the first as a problem of design, and the second as a problem of resources.

A. *Design*

The conventional clinic purports to be both law school and law office, and its supervising attorneys both law teachers and lawyers, who both produce data and evaluate it. These dimensions cross-pollinate, clinicians claim, to create in the clinic the best of both worlds, a critical practice and an informed and relevant critique. Perhaps this is correct and certainly it is worth exploring, but there are reasons for dividing the labor of lawyering from the labor of critique that arguments for the conventional clinic do not take into account.

To begin with, to conceive of a clinical teacher as both lawyer and professor, or as both data and critic, is to build into the role a conflict of interest. There is an emotional stake in a personal work product that makes it difficult to see weaknesses let alone criticize them with others, particularly when one is viewed as an "expert" and not expected to make mistakes. In evaluating his own efforts a clinical teacher will pull analytical punches, no matter how large his reservoir of earnestness and good will, and be oblivious to this fact. If I am paternalistic in my relations with clients, for example, and evidence this by shielding them from unpleasant information, either by withholding it or presenting it in its "best" (i.e., inaccurate) light, but paternalism is not consistent with my image of myself or my conception of good lawyering, the insight that I am paternalistic is one I typically would screen out. Either I would not notice the behavior manifesting this pattern, or I would interpret it as showing concern for the client. Yet to teach from the behavior I would have to recognize and acknowledge the paternalism. Otherwise, I would teach about the wrong issue, and perhaps fail to understand the issue at all.

The negative effect of this screening process on student learning is often extreme. Not only will clinical teachers miss problematic patterns in their practice behavior, but they will miss patterns likely to be the most educationally interesting because they are also likely to be the most threatening. In an ideal world this would not happen. There, a clinician would be as critical of his own work as that of others, and most accounts of clinical study assume this ideal. But experience teaches that this is an optimistic assumption most of the time because it does not take into account the finely developed mechanisms all of us possess to shield ourselves from information about how far we have fallen short. We may listen to such information under the right conditions, but it is the rare one among us who is willing or able to be the messenger at the same time. This is not pathological. Defenses are adaptive mechanisms that perform necessary functions in life. But one thing they do not do is allow one to know oneself by oneself.

To this it might be argued that in the conventional clinic the student's work is criticized and not the professor's. As a description of what typically occurs that is no doubt true, but as a claim about what ought to occur it is not. Practice instruction is the study of lawyer behavior and in this study student behavior is a small and often not very interesting part. Behavior of experienced and skilled lawyers, even if only a little more experience and skilled, must be added to the hopper if the study is to prove comprehensive and rich, and the supervising attorney's behavior is the logical candidate. Clinical teachers can suppress discussion of their own efforts, of course, and many do, but at the cost of greatly restricting the scope and sophistication of their study.

It is also difficult in a clinical setting to separate student from supervisor work. Student decisions typically are reviewed in advance and students believe teachers have ratified important strategic choices before actions affecting client interests are taken. Students say as much in after-the-fact discussions if the teacher is critical ("you told me it was all right," or "why didn't you tell me not to do it"). These are legitimate protests. Protecting client interests is more important than allowing students to learn from mistakes and when student choices jeopardize such interests it is irresponsible for teachers not to intervene. When teachers are implicated in even this secondary sense, as all conventional clinicians are, their defenses are likely to be mobilized and their analytical punches are likely to be pulled. At a minimum, valuable time will be wasted resolving the not very important question of whether the teacher said that the choice was all right. Clinical students should review work in advance—I do not suggest the opposite—but postperformance analysis is likely to be more probing if the professor is not already on record (even arguably) as having approved of the work.

Clinical students are not good critics of their professors' work because students and professors are not true colleagues within the social and political structure of law school. The two groups have different levels of experience, status, perspective, and formal authority, and in each of these categories teachers have the upper hand, and often use it to suppress nonconforming views. Clinicians sometimes pretend that they are no different from their students, but this usually appears patronizing or silly, and is the opposite of what the students bargained for in paying tuition. When clinicians report that students are effective critics, it is usually because they (the clinicians) have a unduly narrow sense of what can be said about their work, or because the student has learned what the professor would like to hear.

Additionally, when the attorney and professor are one and the same there is increased pressure to avoid critique. For example, an attorney/professor often will want to use clients for instructional ends when the needs of the client conflict, usually in the interest of student education rather than out of a disrespect for client autonomy. (The opposite problem can occur as well. A clinician who sees himself more as an attorney than professor may want to use students to perform routine representational tasks with little or no instructional benefit.) Thus, he might schedule extra discovery, hearings on motions, bargaining sessions, or the like so that students can try their hands at prized but infrequent tasks. Sometimes such procedures benefit clients, and other times they do not, but they are always costly, even to those who do not pay their lawyers (e.g., delay, extended uncertainty, unpleasantness), and the decision of whether the game is worth the candle is for the client to make based on client considerations. Since the student and attorney/professor describe the choices that must be made, and provide much of the information on which such decisions are based, the potential for loading the deck in the direction of educational ends is high. And because the same persons are also responsible for detecting self-interested action after the fact, the likelihood of discovery is low.

Lawyer-client conflicts occur in all practice settings, of course, but they are particularly pronounced in the monopoly conditions experienced by most clinics. Poor persons will not want to jeopardize their chance for legal redress by seeming "uncooperative" or "ungrateful," and will be susceptible to "suggestions" or "hints" that additional work needs to be done. A genuine desire to avoid controlling the choice on the part of the clinician does not make this risk any less real. In fact, because his motives are noble he may be less likely to engage in it, or to have interests different from those of his client. And a clinic, because it is large and relatively undisciplined, may be less able to monitor closely all the interactions in which such problems are likely to arise. This is a variation on a familiar point, discussed in the early clinical literature as the conflict between service and education, and dismissed there by the assertion that work generated for educational purposes invariably improved the quality of the client's representation. The argument was powerful at the time because the way in which clinical practitioner interests could differ from those of their clients or clients could wish to avoid procedures that provided instrumental benefits was not widely apparent. Now it is evident that the argument is too simple.

This conflict between service and education is exacerbated by limitations of time. In even a moderately busy clinic, preparation of client cases must receive the highest priority, looked at from the perspective of both lawyer and teacher (because giving client interests the highest priority is itself an important teaching message), and preparing cases thoroughly, as a law school clinic should, will expand to fill the available time. This priority is reflected in all aspects of the clinic's operation, but is perhaps most apparent in the patterns that appear in conversations between teachers and students. Most of these conversations consist of requests by students for information to fill gaps in their experience, or to help them make strategic judgments in their cases (what do I do next? where do I find a form for that?), and clinical teacher responses that answer these requests. The underlying assumptions are that there are set ways, known to experts, of performing lawyer tasks, and that a novice's best course is to ask an expert about them. Since few clinical teachers espouse these assumptions, it is ironic that in answering student questions they convey the opposite message. Other discussion, often sophisticated, is about the manipulation of rules, procedures, and institutions for the purpose of gaining an instrumental advantage against an adversary. This "ends-means" thinking, as Anthony Amsterdam calls it,[36] like any puzzle-solving, can be complicated and challenging, but it need not be critical political thinking, and usually it is not. The assumption in "puzzle solving" is that the structure of the puzzle is legitimate, so much so that awareness of the underlying question of legitimacy recedes into unconsciousness.

The foregoing is what one would expect of law office conversation. It is reasonable for students, as novices, to be preoccupied with impending instrumental tasks, particularly if client interests are at stake, the tasks are unfamiliar, and the students' role is defined as performing them successfully. The first objective in any environment is survival (though students do not always appreciate that this represents relative rather than absolute success). And it is only slightly less understandable that clinicians, as supervising lawyers, would answer student questions to prevent client interests from being sacrificed, office resources from being wasted, and student effort from coming to a standstill. This illustrates not so much the failure of individual clinical teachers and students as the inadequacy of the metaphor of the teaching law office. Law offices represent rather than teach, and when they try to do both it is the teaching that suffers, as it should.

Clinical participants will usually be satisfied with using legal rules and institutions cleverly on behalf of disadvantaged groups (a good thing in itself), and accept rather than criticize the premises of the system they so skillfully manipulate.

---

36   *See* [Anthony] Amsterdam, [Clinical Legal Education: A 21st Century Perspective, 34 J. Legal Educ. 612,] at 614 [(1984)].

In a world where real client interests are in jeopardy, obligations are numerous and pressing, and time is limited, understanding for understanding's sake will not be given a high priority, and reasonably so.[39] In such a world questions about the justice of individual outcomes will sometimes be examined, though often only implicitly, but questions about the justice of systemic or institutional arrangements or standard practice methodologies will usually go begging. Ends-means thinking makes it difficult to see the forest for the trees and undercuts a lawyer's capacity for utopian thinking, an attribute one ordinarily would think desirable in a social engineer.

The conflict-of-interest problem is built deeply into the structure of the conventional clinic. It is not a cosmetic defect or a failure of execution, and it is not going to go away on its own as clinics and clinicians mature. If anything, it will become more serious as clinical practice slips into the routinized patterns of day-to-day law practice generally, as it has in many places. Even exceptionally able teachers, who are genuinely interested in critique, will find it difficult to pursue that process in such an environment and this brings us to the second problem. A disproportionate number of clinical teachers seem uninterested in critique, so much so that even if the problem of design were corrected, critique would not necessarily become the central objective of the conventional clinic. This is the problem of resources.

* * *

In the following excerpt, Kenney Hegland both responds to and builds on Robert Condlin's criticism of live-client clinical teaching.

Kenney Hegland, *Condlin's Critique of Conventional Clinics: The Case of the Missing Case*, 36 J. LEGAL EDUC. 427 (1986)*

In an important and controversial article Professor Robert Condlin dismisses the crown jewel of clinical legal education, the "in house" clinic, with, of all things, a beer slogan: "Tastes Great, Less Filling."[1] Incredible feat.

In-house clinics, in which clinical professors supervise students handling real-life cases, are "less filling" because they cannot provide for a meaningful critique of the practice of law, a critique that is the chief, perhaps the only, justification for clinical education. Not skills training, not client representation, but critique is Job One.

---

39   The problem may be more serious than lack of time. Lawyer thinking differs radically from critical reflection. It starts from a narrower focus, looks at evidence from a more instrumental perspective, and is more manipulative in the manner it thinks of and expresses its conclusions. In a sense, legal and critical thinking are the work of different people, and a shift from one perspective to the other is a shift in personas. Most of us do not embody two such equally developed personas, and as a result, would find such a shift difficult to make.

*   Reprinted with permission.

1   Robert J. Condlin, 'Tastes Great, Less Filling': The Law School Clinic and Political Critique, 36 J. Legal Educ. 45 (1986).

Condlin favors the "placement model," in which students, supervised by practicing lawyers in private firms and governmental agencies, periodically return to the law school to discuss their experiences with clinical instructors. Placement programs, he feels, are more conducive to the critique of practice.

Thus Condlin challenges the received wisdom of the clinical world—that only in-house clinics are the "real thing." * * *

Condlin begins by urging clinicians to challenge the "prevailing conceptions of good behavior and indentif[y] . . . better ways of thinking about and performing in lawyer roles." We should do so, not necessarily to transform the world of practice (because we cannot be sure where critique will take us), but rather to contribute "to the development of the individual—not to be unknowingly captive to received wisdom is to be more fully autonomous. . . ."

* * *

Condlin argues that in-house clinics don't and can't provide critique. Clinical instructors, he feels, are too close to their subject matter; for reasons of ego and professional pride, a clinical professor cannot be both "data and critic." * * *

The critique of "prevailing conceptions of good behavior" should not be simply the critique of what almost everyone agrees is bad behavior—lawyer paternalism, lying, and bullying. The critique must also question what is considered good behavior, such as "Never ask 'Why?' on cross." Challenging "good" techniques of client interviewing, negotiation, and trial practice might best be accomplished "in house," right after the student has "successfully" completed the task.

* * *

Even if in-house clinics do generate sufficient data for critique, Condlin argues that critique will not happen; their focus is elsewhere, on client representation. In that intellectual climate, critique is doomed.

> Lawyer thinking differs radically from critical reflection. It starts from a narrower focus, looks at evidence from a more instrumental perspective, and is more manipulative in the manner it thinks of and expresses its conclusions. In a sense, legal and critical thinking are the work of different people, and a shift from one perspective to the other is a shift in personas. Most of us do not embody two such equally developed personas, and as a result, would find such a shift difficult to make.

If this is true, our boat is sunk. Theory and practice will forever remain apart; practitioners will always remain slaves of received wisdom while theoreticians will float freely but irrelevantly among the abstractions.

Fortunately, Condlin is wrong. While it is easy to get carried away in the nitty-gritty of client representation, it is possible to step back and say "Just what does my nondisclosure of that fact have to do with achieving justice?"

Although we can shift personas, perhaps those currently engaged in clinical teaching just don't want to do so. Condlin asserts that most clinicians are not interested in critique, that they are practitioners more than scholars and that they "measure success more by how students imitate [prevailing methods for performing lawyer practices] than by how they analyze them." Of course, if this is true, a simple change of structure will not do. But is it true?

* * * I don't know and I doubt if Condlin knows either. But the empirical question is not important; as long as critique is structurally possible in in-house clinics, as I have demonstrated it is, Condlin's case against them has failed.

I believe, however, that there is a major limitation on the ability of in-house clinics to do the kind of critique I think must be done. That drawback stems, ironically, from what is touted as the chief advantage of the in-house clinic: that it provides an "ideal" situation in which students can develop the "right" techniques for the practice of law. Whether or not in-house clinics are exemplars of ideal practice, the fact remains that they are artificial—students do not experience the dynamics of the hurly-burly of a real law office, they are not supervised by lawyers who face the pressure of making a living practicing law—in short, they are not thrown into the rough and tumble of the everyday. I find this to be a fundamental limitation.

Like Condlin, I would have our students be anthropologists. They should reflect on the following questions:

1. Do lawyers adequately represent their clients? Do they have the skill and do they take the time required to do a good job?
2. Who are the most effective lawyers and why? Do they win cases others would lose? If so, what are the implications for our system of justice? What does it mean to be a "good" lawyer? How do lawyers measure success?
3. Is too much of society's limited pool of talent devoted to the law? What would lawyers be doing if they did not practice?
4. Do lawyers consider themselves hired guns or do they share their client's goals? Are lawyers too adversarial or do they sacrifice their clients in order to go along with societal or professional pressure?
5. How important is legal doctrine? Does it control legal behavior or is it indeterminate?
6. How important, in terms of judicial outcomes, are the social, racial, and economic backgrounds of the client? Of the lawyer?
7. Are lawyers content? Are there better, more satisfying, ways, to spend one's time?

* * *

Both in-house and placement programs can engage in meaningful critique while helping students master some of the techniques of lawyering. Obviously, there remains the difficult question of the proper mix between critique and skills training. Like Condlin, I would fault any program that takes its mission to be solely skills training, and in the case of in-house clinics, solely client representation. On the other hand, I see a danger in too great an emphasis on critique. I believe we have an obligation to help our students master the legal skills. Further, I fear that, in the name of "critique," clinical education will be turned into a ponderous exploration of the "received wisdom" of other disciplines—sociology, anthropology, and moral and political philosophy.

* * * My fear * * * is that instructors will feel pressured to assign lengthy academic readings (as opposed to those dealing with skills acquisition) at the outset, and will then approach those readings hypothetically rather than in the context of real life experiences.

* * *

Even if we could gracefully mesh academic readings with triggering field events, we still pay a price. We may be teaching our students that they are incompetent to challenge received wisdom on their own; that they need others to make their cases for them, and that before they can say anything intelligent about lying, they must read [Sissela Bok, *Lying: Moral Choice in Public and Private Life*]. Although suggested readings can often expand and deepen analysis, the most effective way to encourage our students to think reflectively is to encourage them to ask tough questions about routine matters and then to struggle with their own answers—"What's wrong with clients lying if it will help their case?" As we encourage our students to think of thinking for themselves, we must take care not to cow them with citations.

_____

Another important focus of clinical law teaching is the supervisory relationship. In the following excerpt, Peter Toll Hoffman notes the dynamic nature of the relationship between clinical teachers and their students and proposes a staged model of clinical supervision. The lawyering and learning roles of both student and teacher must change over time to accommodate the evolution of the clinic student's professional competence and identity.

Peter Toll Hoffman, *The Stages of the Clinical Supervisory Relationship*, 4 ANTIOCH L.J. 301 (1986)*

* * *

Supervision is at the core of effective clinical teaching. It is through supervision that the clinical teacher responds to the individualized learning needs of the students and the requirements of the cases. Despite the recognized importance of supervision in the success of clinical education, we know very little about what is effective supervision, what are the characteristics of the effective supervisor, or how the supervisory process can be improved.

The difficulty in answering these questions is that the dynamics of supervision and of the supervisory relationship elude precise definition. Supervision varies not only in the types of encounters that may take place between teacher and student, but also in the types of teaching that may occur in the encounters. The form of the encounter may range from a spontaneous, brief meeting where the teacher answers

_____

*   Reprinted with permission.

a question about a case, to a formal, structured conference where the student's cases and actions are explored in depth. * * *

The supervisory relationship also varies through time. What may be effective supervision at one point may result in undesirable learning consequences at a later point. A close, structured form of supervision at the beginning of the course may, for instance, become stifling and overly restrictive by the end of the semester. * * *

* * *

The mutual nature of learning causes the relationship between student and teacher to be constantly changing. The changes in the relationship reflect not only the student's increasing knowledge and understanding of the process of learning, but also the teacher's adaptation of his or her supervisory techniques to the changing needs of the student.

I. BEGINNING STAGE

* * *

Functioning as a lawyer requires not only knowledge of the substantive and procedural rules applicable in the legal system and in the particular type of practice in which the lawyer is operating, but also knowledge of how to apply these rules. In addition, the lawyer must possess a panoply of lawyering skills, such as the ability to interview and counsel clients, engage in factual investigation, negotiate, draft pleadings and documents, develop case strategies, and present cases in court. While traditional legal education ably teaches rules and analysis, most courses ignore the practical application of the rules.

As a result, in the initial stages of a clinical course, most students do not possess the knowledge necessary to make appropriate decisions about what course of action to follow in a case, or how to implement a plan of action. If forced to make decisions beyond their capabilities, students often become overwhelmed with anxiety and frustration. Every task, no matter how simple to the experienced lawyer, assumes insurmountable proportions to the neophyte. With no base to build on, the student may not even be able to recognize which questions need to be addressed.

* * *

In this initial stage of developing skills and knowledge, students need vast amounts of specific information, e.g., whether there is an applicable statute, what is the filing fee in district court, and what is the time limit for filing an appeal. To force students to seek out this information when their knowledge is so limited will only result in wasting endless, frustrating hours in the library or on the telephone. This, in turn, can only exacerbate the students' initial feeling of inadequacy.

To avoid these types of reactions, initial decisions in cases must be made by the supervisor, and preliminary information must be given to the students, rather than left for them to discover on their own. Specific instructions must be given by the supervisor stating explicitly what must be done in each case, and how to carry out directions given. * * *

* * *

In addition to all of the other uncertainties confronting them in a clinical course, students face uncertainty surrounding the issue of how to respond to the supervisor. Are they to ask questions? Should they obtain the supervisor's approval before taking action in a case? Answers to many of these questions can be provided through specific responses by the supervisor in the form of an orientation lecture, office manual, or both. Since students are far more likely to rely on their experiences than on what they are told, it is important that the supervisor reinforce the desired supervisory model through example and encouragement. The supervisory relationship developed in the initial stage of the course will establish the contours for the way student and teacher interact during the remainder of the course. Starting with the desired supervisory model in the beginning will avoid many problems at the later stages of the course.

* * *

II. MIDDLE STAGE

In the middle stage of the course, students become capable of taking more responsibility and initiative for their cases. At this point, instead of merely following the supervisor's directions as to the next step to be taken, students can approach cases as a collaborative experience involving both student and supervisor. Through joint discussion, as between partners in a law firm, the two can determine the definition of the legal problem to be solved, develop procedures for solving the problem, evaluate the effectiveness of the solution, and implement it. The discussions need not be confined to the intermediate demands of the caseload, but may also extend to such matters as questions of ethics, the lawyer's role, standards of professionalism, individual and group dynamics, and the functioning of legal institutions.

In contrast to the initial stage of the course when the supervisor's role was didactic and directive, the supervisor in the middle stage serves to stimulate and guide the students in interpreting, analyzing, applying, synthesizing and evaluating the students' clinical experiences. The supervisor must still provide information and direction as needed, but this function is now subordinate to the role of serving as a sounding board and corrective for the student's efforts, and as a prod coaxing and encouraging the student to objectively and critically examine actions and purposes.

Instead of relying on the supervisor to determine what must be done and how to do it, students begin to make these decisions themselves; instead of having the reasons for a particular strategy explained to them, students begin to analyze and develop the reasons themselves; instead of merely acquiring the rudiments of skills, students begin to improve and polish skills. The supervision process becomes progressively more an exploration of the supervisor's solution and less of an imposition of the supervisor's solution on the students. The supervisor shifts from the role of senior partner working with a new associate to that of a co-equal assisting and critiquing the student's work.

During the middle stage, greater emphasis is placed on analysis of why things are done and how to improve the student's skills performance. There is more exploring and clarifying of issues. The interaction between student and supervisor changes from one in which the teacher provided instruction and information and the student asked questions and related data, into one in which the student takes the initiative and actively participates in discussions.

* * *

The mix of interactions between student and supervisor will vary with the situation, but the identifying feature of this middle stage of the course is the co-equal exchange of ideas and information between the two. Each has something to contribute to the lawyering process and from their interchanges, the student learns how to be an effective lawyer.

The transition from the initial stage to the middle stage is not as abrupt as the term "stage" might suggest. In fact, the process in each stage is a progression along a continuum. In the middle stage, for instance, the amount of control and direction by the supervisor will be greatest at the beginning and will slowly diminish as the student becomes more comfortable with the new responsibilities being assumed.

III. FINAL STAGE

In the final stage, the students are sufficiently secure and competent to act, in effect, as lawyers in their own right. This does not mean they have progressed as far as they will in their careers, but it does mean that they are now capable of acting without close supervision, and that they are now, at least, minimally competent. At this stage, the supervisor should defer to the student's analyses and decisions in cases where reasonable lawyers might differ. Of course, where the student is appearing under the sponsorship of the supervisor under the applicable local student practice rule, the supervisor has an ethical obligation to prevent incompetent representation. But when, as with most decisions in a case, there is more than one correct solution to a problem, the supervisor should defer to the student's decision. The supervisor's role, in this final stage, is that of a confirmer and guider; a safeguard against serious error.

* * *

In this last stage, the supervisor should be checking the student's decisions for soundness. Has the student checked all aspects of an idea? Has the student correctly analyzed the facts and law? Is the student missing a step in the proper procedure? The supervisor has become more like a safety net preventing error on the part of the student, but the initiative and the decisions are now coming from the student.

The clinical supervisor must adapt his or her teaching techniques and styles to the students' rate of development, or the result will be frustration for both student and teacher, and a failed learning experience. This is particularly true of the amount of supervisory control exerted over the students actions. Several studies have indicated that students' perceived need for freedom in the supervisory relationship increases during the course of the relationship. As students progress toward the goals of competence and professionalism, they expect to be treated as professionals. They expect and require more freedom and less structure in the later stages of the course. If the supervisor persists in holding the reins too tightly, the result will be dependency and rebellion among the students. Under such conditions, a more serious consequence is that students may fail to internalize the standards of conduct being taught.

* * *

Another difficulty arises in assisting students to make the transition from one stage to the next. If students are not made aware of the progression of the course through the several stages, they will develop the expectation that the beginning stage represents the expected student-supervisor relationship for the entire course. While student resentment might develop because of the restrictions the first stage places on the students, few students will do anything to change the relationship because of the inherently authoritarian nature of the relationship between student and supervisor. The problem, then, is how to move students into subsequent stages and how to make them aware of the progression they are expected to follow.

The best approach is to make the sequence of expected student development explicit at the outset of the course. In the orientation process, students should be told what will be expected of them at each stage of the course. Similarly, when a student is judged ready to move into the next stage, the student should be told this, and informed of the expectations that he or she will encounter.

* * *

IV. CONCLUSION

The task of the clinical supervisor is to help students through the process of experiential learning, in acquiring the knowledge and skills necessary to become capable and effective lawyers. Students will pass through several predictable stages while engaging in this process. The challenge to the supervisor is to maximize the opportunities presented by this progression so as to make the students' learning as efficient and beneficial as possible. What has been presented is a model for accomplishing these ends.

———————————

The truly unique feature of clinical education is its ability to put students in their professional role. It is the starting point of the clinical method of law teaching in a live-client setting; it sets up the opportunity for students to learn in role. In this final excerpt, Minna J. Kotkin explores the relative values of role-modeling—and role-assumption-based clinical instruction.

Minna J. Kotkin, *Reconsidering Role Assumption in Clinical Education*, 19 N. Mex. L. Rev. 185 (1989)*

* * *

IV. THE VARIATIONS IN THE SUCCESS OF THE ROLE ASSUMPTION MODEL

Most clinicians would agree that there is a large variation in how much students learn from a clinical experience premised on role-assumption, regardless of how broad or narrow the goals of the program, or how talented the students may be. * * * There are always some "good" and motivated students who fail to make much progress either in skills development or towards the broader goals of achieving an analytical and self-critical perspective on the lawyering process.

Clinicians tend to diagnose the problem for these students as revolving around the feedback process. It is assumed that something in the interaction between student and teacher is amiss. My experience in supervision suggests, however, that for some students it is the very concept of role assumption that inhibits their learning.

A typical learning difficulty arises in the context of interviewing a client. In the best of all worlds, the learning process might begin with the student reading about a model of interviewing, such as Binder and Price's work, which offers both skills guidance (for example, the use of open-ended questions to elicit the broadest factual chronology) and theory (the value of client-centered decision-making).[39] Supervisor and student then would discuss the student's plan for the interview, perhaps rehearse a portion of it, and possibly watch and critique a videotape of another interview. All of this pre-performance guidance is designed to insure that the student has a basic comprehension of the skills dimension and at least understands the justification for the model and the values underlying it. Thus, a student should understand the differences between asking, "The light at the intersection was green, wasn't it?", "So you went through a red light?", and "Can you tell me what happened when you approached the intersection?", in terms of the interviewer's ability to gain a full factual picture, and to actively involve the client in the process of representation.

After the interview, the supervisor reviews a tape of the session, and finds to his surprise that it sounds more like a cross-examination, filled with narrow questions, value-laden responses, and directive advice. In the post-performance analysis with the student, the supervisor explores how successfully the previously articulated goals of the interview were accomplished. Through the use of a non-directive approach, the supervisor elicits from the student a self-reflective critique of the interview, which enables the student to learn very efficiently the basics of this skill from one experience. For most students, the second interview shows a vast improvement. This teaching methodology substantially compacts the learning curve for any particular

---

*   Reprinted with permission.

39   D. Binder & S. Price, Legal Interviewing and Counseling: A Client Centered Approach (1979). * * *

skill. It replaces the years of trial and error through which practicing lawyers developed skills before the advent of clinical teaching.

For some students, however, the methodology simply does not work. Despite the students' ability to articulate interviewing theory and identify shortfalls in their own performance, the second interview is no more skillful than the first. In these circumstances, the supervisor may fall back on more directive feedback, which only succeeds in decreasing the students' ability to engage in self-reflection, undermines the self-confidence and further inhibits experiential learning. I have found that the only way to break out of this cycle is through modeling by the supervisor: what, in essence, amounts to role reversal. The supervisor takes on the lawyer's role, the student plays the client. This technique has substantial pedagogical drawbacks, which will be discussed below, but it does seem to lead to a sometimes dramatic improvement in a student's ability to translate thinking into effective performance, as compared to directive feedback, which takes the form of the teacher pronouncing what is good and what is bad.

These admittedly anecdotal experiences have led me to question whether it is the feedback process that is creating the learning difficulty, or whether it is the process of role assumption itself that stands in the way of some students' mastery of skills.

V. THE THEORETICAL BASIS FOR
QUESTIONING ROLE ASSUMPTION

The hypothesis that not all students learn well through role assumption finds support in the study of learning theory. * * * [W]hen clinical teaching came under increased scrutiny, learning theory was used to justify the role assumption methodology already in place, which was derived from a service orientation. Thus, role assumption was legitimized under the general theory of experiential learning.

In the experiential learning model, learning is viewed as a four-stage cycle. The learner first must immerse herself in immediate, concrete experience. The experience then forms a basis for the learner's reflection and self-observation. From this process emerges the formulation of abstract concepts, hypotheses, and generalizations. Finally, the learner tests the implications of the deduced theories in new experiential situations.

The basic progression of experiential learning is easily understood, and its applicability as a theoretical framework for clinical legal education is apparent. It exactly describes the methodology that many clinicians instinctively developed, and forms a strong foundation for the assumption that "in role" performance is an indispensable starting point for clinical programs.

Learning theorists have begun to explore the experiential learning cycle in more depth, however, examining the effect of individual differences on a person's ability to profit from teaching methods constructed on this model. The work of David Kolb has been particularly influential.[42] Kolb notes that in experiential learning situations,

---

42   *See* D. KOLB & R. FRY, *Towards an Applied Theory of Experiential Learning*, in THEORIES OF GROUP PROCESSES, 33-57 (G. Cooper, ed. 1975). * * *

the student must possess an unusually broad range of different skills, which he calls concrete experience abilities, reflective observation abilities, abstract conceptualization abilities, and active experimentation abilities. Moreover, this learning mode requires the utilization of skills that are polar opposites, concreteness and abstraction; the learner must continually choose which set of learning abilities she will rely on in any given situation. Most people resolve this conflict in characteristic ways: "Some people develop minds that excel at assimilating disparate facts into coherent theories, yet these same people are incapable or uninterested in deducing hypotheses from their theory; others are logical geniuses, but find it impossible to involve and surrender themselves to an experience, and so on," Kolb notes.

Kolb has developed a questionnaire known as the Learning Style Inventory, which identifies a person's strengths and weaknesses in the four skills required for experiential learning. According to his research based on the inventory, there are four dominant types of learning styles. The "converger" excels at abstract conceptualization and active experimentation: she can effectively apply ideas to concrete situations. The "diverger" has the opposite skills, and is most comfortable with concrete experience and reflective observation. The "assimilator" relies on abstract conceptualization and reflective observation: he is best at creating theoretical models, and has most difficulty with practical application. The "accommodator's" strengths lie in concrete experience and active experimentation; he is likely to disregard theory when faced with facts.

Applying Kolb's research to the typical law school clinical experience, some conclusions emerge that are consistent with questioning the utility of role assumption as the starting point for every student. The converger will have difficulty with the beginning stages of the experiential learning cycle: performing in role and reflecting on the experience. While the student-teacher interaction can promote increased reflection, the student's difficulties in getting into role will limit the effectiveness of the process. The assimilator may have more pronounced problems with the clinical methodology. His weaknesses lie in both the immersion and the application phases, while his strengths replicate what clinical teachers typically see as their function, encouraging reflection and generalization. The diverger will profit from a teacher's efforts to promote generalization from experience, but may have problems putting theory into practice. The typical clinical teaching methodology is probably best suited to the accommodator. The teacher's guidance in developing reflection and abstraction skills will provide the missing link to enable her to learn from experience.

The Kolb learning style analysis may explain the sense of frustration clinicians experience when a well-executed feedback process does not result in improved student performance. It suggests that teachers can improve the learning process for some students by facilitating their ability to function in role, rather than concentrating only on the reflection and abstraction stages of the experiential cycle.

* * *

VII. ROLE MODELING AS AN
ALTERNATIVE TO ROLE ASSUMPTION

Before clinical education took hold in the law school curriculum, law graduates learned skills largely by watching the performance of other lawyers, and analyzing the good and the bad in what they observed as best they could. The luck of the draw in choosing a role model was the controlling factor in defining the young lawyer's norms of practice. Clinical methodology rejects role modeling as an inefficient and unsystematic learning technique. Clinicians, when they find themselves in pre- or post-performance sessions demonstrating a particular skill at length, conclude that they have gone astray from the goals of clinical pedagogy, because they perceive the technique as inhibiting the student's self-reflection and critical thinking. A teacher's performance leads the student to half-hearted attempts at mimicry.

Learning theory suggests, however, that for students who have difficulty immersing themselves in an experience, opportunities to observe others "in role" provide an important bridge to the acquisition of skills. The problem with utilizing modeling may be that clinicians do too little of it rather than too much, and that they do it without attention to the other aspects of experiential learning. The modeling is considered the end, rather than the beginning of the interaction between student and teacher.

Modeling, as now utilized in clinical programs, is narrowly focused on the rudimentary skills elements of lawyering. Thus, a clinician may offer for analysis an alternative approach to beginning an interview or using non-leading questions in a direct examination. Rarely do we try to model the more complex aspects of case preparation such as ends-means thinking, legal and factual theory development, and strategic judgment. The demonstration of these skills is difficult to contemplate, perhaps because norms of effective performance are more elusive even to the most analytical clinicians. If we cannot ourselves completely define these processes, we are naturally reluctant to offer our approach.

Even at the basic skills level, our modeling generally only addresses a small segment of the task, because of the time constraints under which we all operate. Thus, a student might be able to provide an adequate opening to an interview after observing the supervisor's example, but flounders through the rest of the meeting. Finally, our approach to modeling necessarily creates in the student's mind a right-wrong dichotomy. It is unrealistic to expect a student to reflect critically on a sequence performed by a supervisor, particularly when it comes after a prolonged attempt at using less directive methods to improve performance. The student acknowledges that he has seen the light and the teacher breathes a sigh of relief. How much real experiential learning that can be translated to other contexts, has taken place, is open to question, however.

* * *

Clinical programs can utilize modeling in a more honest, rigorous, methodical and analytical manner, however. To surmount modeling's significant drawbacks, clinicians must demonstrate the full range of lawyering skills, as well as the process of

experiential learning, by engaging in real or simulated client representation. In partnership with the student, the supervisor acts in role, reflects, generalizes, and applies.
Thus, we ask of ourselves the same that we ask of our students.

In practical application, this theory of clinical teaching could operate in at least
three ways. The first application would be structured so that there was a gradual shifting of lawyer role from supervisor to student over the course of the clinical experience. The student's observation and participation in critique not only would build his
confidence and break down existing but unproductive patterns of interaction, but
would also help him to internalize the sense of advocacy that poor role assumers seem
to lack. This application is not intended to replicate the apprenticeship or law clerk
system, which may be successful over the long term in teaching skills, but does little to teach the ability to learn from experience. The difference is in the scope of the
observation and in the process that occurs thereafter. Modeling requires, in addition
to skills demonstration, the exposing of the analysis that goes into every decision and
judgment; the supervisor must think out loud. The supervisor must then remove herself from the task at hand and consider her choice of actions, reflecting on its effectiveness and conformity to normative models and previously defined goals. She
must engage the student in the effort, opening herself to the same kind of critical
examination that the student is expected to develop from his own performance in traditional clinical experiences.

This application basically calls on us to practice what we preach. The process
of critique breaks down the right-wrong dichotomy that makes modeling so flawed.
It teaches what many clinicians acknowledge as a central goal: that learning from
experience requires a methodology that extends through one's entire career. If we
cannot analyze how our thinking and performance as lawyers can be improved, we
can hardly expect our students to reflect upon their own performance, particularly
given their very limited basis of comparison in relation to our presumably more substantial scope of experience.

There are obvious practical drawbacks, however, to the notion of shifting roles.
Particularly in a live client clinic, when client representation begins with the teacher
rather than the student in role, the dynamic of authority established in the minds of
the client, adversary, and court, may be irrevocable. Because of the perceptions of
these other actors, the student may never be able to fully assume the lawyer's role.

A second alternative that addresses this difficulty is for student and teacher to
assume different roles in different cases. The teacher would be primarily responsible
for the lawyering in one matter, to which the student was assigned also, along with
the student's normal caseload. The student could then immediately put into practice
the learning derived from the experience in observation, critique and reflection on the
"co-counselled" matter.

A potential disadvantage of both the shifting role and the co-counsel concepts
is the time investment that they require on the part of the supervisor. Clinicians are
already consumed with the everyday demands of individual supervision, and now
increasingly add to their commitments classroom teaching and scholarship. An
expectation of practice in addition would be viewed by many as simply too much. I
suggest, however, that the practice aspect of these methodologies may ultimately

relieve some of the frustration of clinical teaching and have a liberating effect. The use of non-directive feedback requires constant attention to restraint and self-control. Our own lawyering can serve as a release from that restraint and thereby reinvigorate our teaching.

* * *

VIII. CONCLUSION

Extended role modeling combined with critical examination, as an alternative or supplement to the role assumption format of clinical education, surely presents a number of troubling questions. It requires a discomforting degree of self-exposure and revelation on the part of the teacher. But this is exactly what clinical teachers ask of their students, and it is on the students' ability to comply with this request that clinical teachers judge them. Furthermore, for role-modeling to be of value, the students must be able to break down the hierarchy inherent in the academic setting so they can objectively and without inhibition critique the performance of those in the position of authority. The solution here depends on the clinician's leading the way through honest self-reflection, which also accomplishes the function of creating a model for the students' process of self-reflection. * * *

Chapter 2

PROFESSIONALISM: ETHICS AND VALUES

A. Identifying Ethical Issues

Ethical issues pervade the practice of law and, consequently, arise almost daily in clinical casework. In the following excerpt, the students face several ethical dilemmas, some that they anticipated and others that arose unexpectedly.

Robert D. Dinerstein, *A Meditation on the Theoretics of Practice*, 43 HASTINGS L.J. 971 (1992)*

* * *

I. The Story of the Case

I teach a criminal justice clinic in which third-year students, under faculty supervision, represent indigent defendants charged with misdemeanors, and some felonies, in a local suburban jurisdiction outside Washington, D.C. Last semester, two of my students represented a client whom I will call Mrs. Smith. The State had charged Mrs. Smith, a black immigrant from a West African country, with one count of common-law battery against each of two sisters. The sisters were African-Americans from a lower-class background. The prosecution claimed that our client had hit one of the sisters with a tennis racket for no apparent reason, and then hit the other sister when she tried to intervene.

The jurisdiction in question has a two-tiered trial court system. Mrs. Smith, represented by the local public defender's office, went to trial before a judge in the lower court, testified in her own defense, and was convicted on both counts of battery. The court sentenced her to concurrent suspended sentences and imposed a fine; she appealed. Under the procedures of the jurisdiction, she was entitled to a trial de novo, with the right to trial by jury in the second court. Our clinic received the case from the local public defender's office after the defendant filed notice of her appeal, and we assigned the case to one of our student teams. Trial was scheduled to occur in less than four weeks.

As is our clinic's practice, I did not accompany the students when they interviewed the client. Our first supervision meeting after the initial client interview made it clear that this case was not going to be easy. The students reported that the client was adamant about going to trial because she "wanted to tell her story." Mrs. Smith's articulation of her goal was striking because of our focus during the semester on the importance of client story-telling. It was as if Mrs. Smith was a simulated client whose "client instructions" had directed her to state this as her goal. Her story, interestingly enough, did not differ greatly from the story the prosecution had told in the first trial. She admitted that she had swung at and hit the first sister with the tennis racket, although she described the second battery as more of a wrestling scuffle than an unprovoked battery. What she did dispute, however, were her motivations. The client indicated that prior to the initial battery the complainant had waved to her with an outstretched palm, which, she told us, was a sign of disrespect in her culture. Faced with this provocation, Mrs. Smith felt justified in swinging her tennis racket at the complainant.

So far, the story was an intriguing one. But while recognizing various defenses to battery, our jurisdiction did not accept disrespectful words or gestures as justifications for the offense. Nevertheless, our client insisted that she wanted to go to trial. She told the students that she was unhappy with the assistant public defender who had handled her case because he had strongly urged her to accept a negotiated resolution. Although she faced the prospect of being incarcerated if she went to trial and lost, Mrs. Smith stated on a number of occasions that it this was the price of "telling her story" it was a price she was willing to pay.

As the students continued to meet with the client over the next two weeks, it became apparent that her situation was more complex than we had initially perceived. For example, she stated that the complainants were harassing her by reading her mail and listening in on her telephone conversations. As Mrs. Smith reiterated and elaborated upon this claim, the students and I became more and more concerned about her emotional state. Whatever psychiatric problems she might have had, however, did not appear to interfere with her ability to assist us in defending her. Nor was her desire to go to trial, even without a legally cognizable defense, so irrational or unusual that we could conclude that we should override the client's choice of trial over a plea. We teach the theory of client-centered decisionmaking in our clinic, and we try to take it seriously in our practice. If client-centered decisionmaking means anything, it means that, so long as we counsel the client thoroughly about her options and predict the legal consequences of her choice as accurately as we can, the decision ultimately is for the client to make. Thus, we told Mrs. Smith that, based on our research, the likely result of a trial was that she would be convicted. Nonetheless, she wanted to go to trial, and we prepared to do so.

Yet as the trial date loomed, the students and I had to deal with the practical realities facing our client. She was a mother of three young children, the oldest seven years old. If she went to trial and took the witness stand—which seemed necessary if she was truly to "tell her story"—she ran the risk not only of another conviction, but of receiving jail time. In theory, of course, trial judges are not supposed to penalize a defendant for exercising her constitutional right to trial. But in the real world, judges sometimes do just that, especially if the defendant testifies and the court concludes that the jury's finding of guilt implies the defendant must have lied. Moreover, we suspected the judge would wonder why we were taking a case to trial when the client's story was not exculpatory. Judges sometimes are critical of clinical programs because they think the students' inexperience may hurt their clients. Here, we thought, the judge might well conclude that "real lawyers" would have persuaded the client that a trial was not in her interest.

On the eve of trial, before the students were to review Mrs. Smith's testimony with her for the next day, I discussed the situation with them. I sometimes worry that when students counsel clients about the likelihood of success at trial they are prone to say unhelpful things like "you have a fifty-fifty chance."[12] So I emphasized to the students the importance of telling Mrs. Smith that if she told the story she had told us all along we would be happy to represent her at trial, but our best legal judgment was that the story would result in a conviction on one or both counts of the charging document. In theory, providing this information to the client is not only consistent with, but required by, even the most client-centered approaches to legal counseling. But I had to question whether, here, our timing might not be a subtle attempt to convince the client to change her mind, while maintaining the illusion that she was making the decision herself.

We also discussed another option: the client could go to trial, but not testify; if she were convicted, the sentencing hearing would provide her an opportunity to tell her story. Though this option would serve some of her interests, it would provide a less satisfactory way to present her story. Moreover, it probably would not provide any greater likelihood of success on the merits, as our case theory would be reduced to attempting to poke holes in the State's case by suggesting the complaining witness might have been mistaken (or might have lied) about whether Mrs. Smith hit her.

Furthermore, we discussed whether our theory of the case could or should include an argument that Mrs. Smith was psychiatrically disabled in some manner that caused her to misinterpret some of the things that had happened to her. I was skeptical that she would agree to this theory, but a full examination of the options seemed to argue for at least exploring this alternative. We had to recognize, however, that even tentatively floating this theory would risk whatever fragile rapport the students had developed with her. The students approached the problem by inquiring whether Mrs. Smith would be interested in attending a counseling program if the state insisted on it as part of a negotiated disposition. Her sharp insistence that she would

---

12   This may be because the students do not have sufficient experience on which to base such a judgment or because they are uncomfortable making predictions on which the client might rely. I have found that students who are averse to trial may understate the chances of success for that reason. Conversely, it is at least possible that students who wish to gain trial experience will overstate the chances of success in order to influence a client to select the trial option. These misjudgments, of course, are not unique to student lawyers.

not attend a program because there was nothing wrong with her seemed to indicate an unwillingness to admit to any psychiatric problems or to proffer a psychiatrically-based defense.

We had not been able to unearth any authority that would support a defense to battery based on Mrs. Smith's perception of the complainant's insulting behavior towards her. Were the students being creative and thorough enough in their research and in thinking about the case? Was I pushing them hard enough to look at the case creatively? Was there some social or political theory underlying the criminal justice system's treatment of Mrs. Smith that could explain her actions and be used to fashion a defense? Would it be appropriate to focus on a seemingly fanciful theory of legitimate provocation at the expense of other preparations we knew we needed to make? Was it possible to consider all sides of the case given the comparatively short period of time we had for trial preparation? What were—and what should have been—our priorities? By listening to our client's story and trying to incorporate it into the existing legal context, we implicitly answered these questions. But I wish we had had the time to be more explicit about choosing the more conventional approach over possibly more creative options. In any event, the students completed their preparation and counseling of Mrs. Smith, and she remained committed both to going to trial and to testifying on her own behalf. We were ready for trial.

The morning of the trial, we waited in the courtroom to learn whether our case actually would go to trial that day or whether it would be postponed because not enough judges were available. Eventually, the clerk called our case. The judge questioned us sharply on why we were taking the case to trial, wondering why he had to impanel a jury on this simple battery charge.[15] Of course, we could not say anything about whether we thought the client had a good defense or why she wanted to go forward. We merely indicated that we had counseled the client thoroughly and carefully and were persuaded that her informed decision was to go to trial.

In many ways, the trial is the least important part of this story. The State presented three witnesses, the two complainants and their sister. The students cross-examined them, doing a good job of raising questions about the alleged battery against the second sister. After the court denied our motion for judgment of acquittal, we prepared to present our case. Once again, we consulted Mrs. Smith about the wisdom of her testifying in light of her inculpatory story. She reiterated her intention to testify and we called her to the stand. She testified that one sister had waved to her with splayed fingers and that she took this as an insult. Unfortunately, she also testified to the sisters' practice of reading her mail and tapping her phone, and to their generally knowing her unexpressed thoughts. True to her concern, the client told her story. We rested our case after our one witness, and after a very brief rebuttal by the State we adjourned for lunch.

---

15   Here again, theory and practice in lower criminal courts diverge sharply. In theory, defendants choose whether to go to trial or accept a plea offer. * * * In practice, judges often assume that experienced lawyers will be able to persuade their clients to accept what the lawyer believes is in their best interest, and that such persuasion is both appropriate and necessary. In the jurisdiction in question, the circuit court judges frequently dislike hearing cases that begin in district court, believing that trials de novo are frequently a waste of time and resources.

While in the cafeteria line, the judge came up to me and whispered that he now thought he understood why we had gone forward with the trial. I took his comment to mean not that he thought we had a good defense, but rather that he believed the client was mentally disturbed and had left us little choice but to proceed. His comment made me feel ambivalent. I was pleased the judge recognized that we were not just "kids" playing at having a trial in the face of the client's contrary interest in a plea bargain. But I was uncomfortable with the suggestion that the client's case was a loser and that she was somehow out of control. My dual loyalty as a lawyer was thus engaged; even as the judge—the embodiment of the legal system—vindicated our judgment, he served notice that, after all, it was and always would be the professionals against the lay people. So much for the power of client narratives.

After lunch, the court instructed the jury and both sides presented their closing arguments. One of the student-attorneys gave an excellent closing, and the court submitted the case to the jury. We commenced to wait, as they say. While we waited, Mrs. Smith and the students had a heated discussion. Mrs. Smith felt we had not presented her case as forcefully as we might have. In particular, she thought we should have argued more vociferously for her version of the key interaction with the complainants and should have emphasized their interference with her mail, telephone, and thought processes. She repeatedly pointed out that in her country lawyers do whatever their clients want and said we had not lived up to this standard. The conversation ended uneasily and unsatisfactorily for all concerned.

The jury was out for over two hours, which, in the time-honored fashion of the criminal defense bar, we took as at least a moral victory. Finally, the jury returned a verdict. It found Mrs. Smith guilty on one count of battery (against the first sister) but not guilty on the second count.

For a moment—a long moment—we were elated. Here was a client who despite all odds had done better at this second trial than at the first one. The jury had either believed our argument that the physical contact with the second sister was at best ambiguous, or had had at least a reasonable doubt that the battery was intentional. I expected the court to leave Mrs. Smith out on bond pending sentencing, which I expected would occur in about four to six weeks.

Then all hell broke loose. As the judge began to address the students, Mrs. Smith suddenly interrupted the colloquy and began to complain that the complainants—who had returned to the courtroom to hear the jury render its verdict—were continuing to bother her and that the conviction was unfair. She grew increasingly agitated, yelling "Excuse me, excuse me," whenever the judge tried to get a word in. Though we tried, there was little we could do to control her. The judge, faced with Mrs. Smith's outburst and undoubtedly thinking back to her testimony regarding the sisters' alleged nefarious spying, decided that she was in psychiatric distress. He ordered the sheriffs to place her in handcuffs and directed that she be transported to a local emergency room for psychiatric evaluation.

One of the students argued that our client would be prepared to seek treatment voluntarily pending sentencing and that commitment was therefore unnecessary. Though improbable, the argument demonstrated that the student was doing his utmost to be an advocate under extremely difficult circumstances. Unfortunately, to bolster the argument he told the judge that Mrs. Smith could not be committed because to do so would leave her three young children with no one to care for them. When the judge asked who was caring for the children that day, the student answered that no one was. Mrs. Smith apparently had left her children unattended, and her husband would not return home from work until around 9:00 p.m. The judge, outraged at our client's conduct and apparently concerned for her children's welfare, directed the clerk to call protective services. We could only hope Mrs. Smith would not lose custody of her children, in addition to her liberty.

This was the first that I knew of the client's decision to leave her children home alone that day. To the student, this disclosure undoubtedly had seemed the best available means to forestall the harm of an involuntary emergency civil commitment. On reflection, of course, it put the client in even greater jeopardy. Despite all our case supervision meetings, the student's revelation in response to the unpredictable turn of events highlighted for me the contingent nature of clinical supervision and provided fresh evidence that it is never possible to anticipate every issue that may arise in representing real clients with real cases. As the sheriffs took Mrs. Smith away, the judge indicated that his office would contact us regarding the sentencing. We left the courtroom in something of a daze, truly having experienced defeat pulled from the jaws of at least partial victory.

It took a while to track down Mrs. Smith, but we later learned that she was committed for observation and then sent to the local mental institution, where she stayed for over two weeks. The students spoke to her near the end of her commitment. Happily, the children had not been removed from the home. Mrs. Smith was calm and looking forward to her imminent release. She thanked the students for representing her. The students indicated that they would contact her when the court set a sentencing date. Although we later learned that our client was in fact released from the hospital, we never heard from her again.

The court scheduled the sentencing for approximately three weeks after our last contact with Mrs. Smith. A week prior to the sentencing, the students called her apartment, but the phone was disconnected with no forwarding number. They visited the apartment complex, but the resident manager reported she had moved out a few days before. At the sentencing, we stated that our client was not present. In light of our knowledge that Mrs. Smith had moved, we could not represent that she merely might be delayed. We awaited the inevitable set piece: the prosecutor would ask for a bench warrant; the court would grant (perhaps after fulminating against ungrateful defendants); and we would return to our office with one more experience to debrief in our supervision session.

But a curious thing happened on the way to the case's inexorable conclusion. The judge said that he had only been trying to help Mrs. Smith when he committed her and that he hoped he had not unduly complicated her situation. After going on for a few moments about how difficult a case it was, he looked out at us and the prosecutor and asked what he should do. Amazingly, there was silence. The prosecutor was not asking for a bench warrant. The judge was not offering to issue one. And we, of course, were not about to volunteer our conclusion that a bench warrant probably was in order.

Finally, the judge pierced the silence. He supposed that he could not sentence the defendant *in absentia* and that he appeared to have no choice but to issue a bench warrant. As he signed the order, though, he leaned over to the clerk and told her to tell the sheriffs not to look too hard for the defendant. The judge said he hoped Mrs. Smith would find help, observed to the students that the case had certainly turned out differently from what they must have expected, and thanked us. We left the courtroom. The case was over, the story of the trial complete—at least for now. Of course, the story was not really over. We do not know what had happened to Mrs. Smith, and for all we know she may yet be picked up on the bench warrant. Nor do we know how our client felt about the ultimate turn of events. However much we might have hoped for a tidy resolution, we have not gotten one.

* * *

Beyond the Model Rules of Professional Conduct and the Model Code of Professional Responsibility lie the standards to which each person holds himself or herself. The Rules or Code often set the minimum standard by which one governs his or her conduct. In the following excerpt, Amy D. Ronner points out that a lawyer's moral and ethical sense may set rules that exceed those minima.

Amy D. Ronner, *Some In-House Appellate Litigation Clinic's Lessons in Professional Responsibility: Musical Stories of Candor and the Sandbag*, 45 AM. U. L. REV. 859 (1996)*

* * *

II. TWO STORIES OF PROFESSIONAL RESPONSIBILITY

Professional responsibility is an expansive domain, one which Professor David Barnhizer has described as including

> judgments and value orientations that become both an explicit and implicit part of the individual's decisionmaking and professional behavior. The achieving of this level of understanding demands educational experiences that are capable of providing a source and kind of involvement penetrating enough to cultivate the clarification of values, and flexible enough to allow the instructor to guide the experience into a functional structure. This level of understanding is developed not in sole relation to intellectual theories of ethical behavior, but in response to the kinds of actual forces that will confront, challenge, and tend to seduce the person as a lawyer.[62]

---

*   Reprinted with permission.

62   David R. Barnhizer, *Clinical Education at the Crossroads: The Need for Direction*, 1977 B.Y.U. L. REV. 1025, 1035.

A clinic lends itself to the training of professional responsibility because it is elastic: it brings all kinds of experiences to the students that inevitably force them to explore their own judgments and values, the very ones that percolate within the decisions they do and must make as lawyers.

In an appellate clinic, professional responsibility training cannot be isolated into a lesson unto itself, but pervades all of the clinic's educational objectives. Specifically, it breathes within appellate practice and procedure and is inextricable from the clinic's journey into the artistry of legal writing and oral advocacy. Professional responsibility, also, comprehends the students' interactions with each other and the clients, trial counsel, and the courts.

What emerges in the clinical context is an incipient integration of the students' identities as lawyers with their identities as human beings. They come to feel and even articulate that the ethical and moral dilemmas they face while in their "legal" personae have a meaningful nexus to the choices they make and will always make about how they want to live their lives as people.

* * *

A. The Candor

The story of candor was born in what appeared at first to be a near certain loser. Our client was a juvenile who the trial court had adjudicated delinquent for violating a criminal statute that proscribed a child's use of BB-guns, air or gas-operated guns, electric weapons or devices, or firearms.

Defense counsel had moved to dismiss the charge in the court below on the ground that the penalty portion of the statute provides for the punishment of only the parent or guardian of the minor child who had used one of the specified weapons. After a hearing, the trial court rejected the defense's motion and interpreted the penalty provision of the statute as applicable to the child himself.

On appeal, we sought a reversal of the trial court's order denying the motion to dismiss and the adjudication of delinquency. When I accepted the appeal for the appellate litigation clinic, I was aware of the fact that there was only one decision, *In re W.O.C.*,[75] interpreting the penalty provision of the statute. Although *W.O.C.* was decided in another jurisdiction, the decision was squarely against us. In fact, an outside criminal defense attorney tactfully suggested that we might ultimately decide to file an *Anders* brief, which is the procedure for a criminal appeal that lacks a meritorious issue.

In *W.O.C.*, the State had charged a child with violating the same statute and the appellate court had said point blank that the statute created "a criminal offense, subjecting juvenile offenders to arrest and prosecution." Lamentably, the situation in *W.O.C.* was indistinguishable from that in our case. In handing the appeal over to the students, however, I was resolved not to mention this decisional blemish.

---

[75]   *In re W.O.C.*, 318 So. 2d 148 (Fla. Dist. Ct. App. 1975).

Not unexpectedly, a group of students rushed forthwith into my office as if they were in the throes of a life-or-death emergency with copies of *W.O.C.* flapping in their hands. At first, they tried to convince me that we should simply "throw in the towel" and take another case—one we could win. Alas, they informed me that the Fourth District Court of Appeals had killed their argument and they wanted me to understand that this was indeed one of those rare funereal moments where they simply could not distinguish the unfavorable precedent.

While the discussion of the crisis desultorily progressed, one student, mentioning in a near whisper that she had actually consulted the Rules of Professional Conduct, pointed out that the Rules did not *require* us to disclose that bad case. Specifically, the Rules mandated disclosure "to the tribunal legal authority in the *controlling* jurisdiction" and we were not before the very district court that, as my student put it, "did us dirt."

At this juncture, I made a valiant effort to repress what was almost a reflexive impulse to express repulsion. Instead, we modulated into a hashing over of the sort of things that could happen if we simply concealed *W.O.C.* from our tribunal. The students' prognostications ranged from us winning the case to us losing and being sanctioned. The students, in fact, even envisioned us having to submit to a public flogging. Most of the initial predictions did not appear to ensue from any moral or ethical twinges, but rather from purely cerebral theories about what would be the best strategy on appeal or what approach could bring us the victory trophy.

The turning point, however, came when a student, who appeared quite troubled, inquired, "Professor Ronner, you wouldn't *make* us hide the case? Because I just don't think I could be that kind of person." After assuring them that I would not *make* anybody do anything that made them feel uncomfortable about themselves as people, we embarked on a hypothetical, one which contained a caricatured portrait of a partner with whom I, as a new lawyer, had actually once worked.

I quoted Mr. Partner verbatim—"Don't put the bad case in the initial brief because the court might not find it and the dolts on the other side probably won't either." From there, the students considered and even fought over how one might and should handle such a directive from a superior. The motif that ultimately surfaced, however, left the Rules of Professional Conduct and even our case far behind: it issued forth in the form of the students' consensus about a need to not bifurcate our lawyer identity from how we define ourselves as people.

Because so few contemporary stories have happy endings, I would like to relate that the "bad" case became the very hub of our initial brief. We did not merely present *W.O.C.* to the court, but built our argument around the reasons why the decision in *W.O.C.* was wrong and in the end, our court actually agreed with us.

B. The Sandbag

The sandbag story was born when our client, Mr. Gibson, was sitting on a milk crate in front of a grocery store. Mr. Gibson is black and many black people resided in the neighborhood where Mr. Gibson was sitting.

When a police officer received an anonymous tip that a black man was selling drugs in the area, he drove up to Mr. Gibson in his marked police car. When Mr. Gibson got up and walked away, the officer drove right in front of Mr. Gibson and blocked his path. The officer later ordered Mr. Gibson to stop and Mr. Gibson stopped. The officer told Mr. Gibson to place his hands on the police car and Mr. Gibson again complied. When the officer told Mr. Gibson to spread his legs, Mr. Gibson did that as well.

The officer then conducted a pat down of Mr. Gibson and pulled a small brown bag out of his right pocket. The bag contained what was later identified as crack cocaine. As a result, the officer arrested Mr. Gibson and the State charged him with possession of cocaine.

Mr. Gibson's defense counsel had filed a motion to suppress the evidence and after conducting an evidentiary hearing, the trial court deemed the search to be illegal and granted the motion. An Assistant Attorney General, acting on behalf of the State, appealed the decision and our clinic represented Mr. Gibson, the appellee.

On the morning of the oral argument, we were waiting in the lawyer's lounge in the courthouse when an Assistant Attorney General glided in and plunked down on our table a "Notice of Supplemental Authority" with a case, *Minnesota v. Dickerson*,[82] appended to it. The Assistant, however, made a point of informing us that because she was filing the notice at "the last minute," she would neither argue it nor mention it during the oral argument. Almost automatically, we agreed that we would not discuss it either.

After this seemingly innocuous encounter, Jeff, the one presenting the oral argument, and I read and discussed the *Dickerson* decision. Jeff correctly pointed out that the circumstances in *Dickerson* did not materially differ from those in the many cases that we had already addressed and distinguished in our brief.

Also, as Jeff saw it, the distinction between *Dickerson* and our case actually supported *our* position—not the State's. Specifically, in *Dickerson*, the United States Supreme Court reiterated the language in *Terry v. Ohio*, which allows officers to conduct a pat down search "'to determine whether the person is in fact carrying a weapon'" when that officer justifiably believes that "the individual whose suspicious behavior he is investigating at close range is armed and presently dangerous." Under *Dickerson*, when officers are conducting such a protective *Terry* search and they discover "nonthreatening contraband," they may lawfully seize it.

As Jeff analyzed it, our case did not even arguably fall into that *Terry-Dickerson* exception because the officer who stopped Mr. Gibson had testified that he did not believe that Mr. Gibson had a weapon or that Mr. Gibson was dangerous. This was, in fact, something that the students had already underscored in their brief.

At first, the oral argument was rather uneventful. The Assistant Attorney General went first because the State was the appellant, and even the purblind could see that the panel was not inclined to reverse. When Jeff stood up at the podium, all went quite well and the court's questions were quite friendly to our position. Because the Assistant Attorney General had set aside a minute or two for rebuttal, the State, of course, had the final word. As her final word, the Assistant Attorney General, appear-

---

82   113 S. Ct. 2130 (1993).

ing somewhat flushed and suddenly ironically stammering like a Billy Budd, uttered *Dickerson* and argued that her supplemental authority mandated a reversal.

Interestingly, while most assistants in the Attorney General's Office tend to be quite cordial and usually make a point of stopping to compliment the law students with a hearty handshake at the end of the argument, this particular Assistant Attorney General dashed out of the courthouse. We, however, huddled together in the heat of the Miami parking lot to discuss our story, a pow-wow which continued into the next class meeting. By then, some students had scrutinized the deific Rules of Professional Conduct and were somewhat miffed to discover that no provision precisely covered our event.

The students' reactions to the incident spanned the gamut of the rational to the emotional. In articulating even some spiritual concerns, the students referred to both heaven and karma. They, of course, dwelled on what they thought it meant to be a lawyer, but a truly sentient nugget, the one that is most memorable for me, is one student's remark, "Gee, it must suck to *be* her."

* * *

In the story of candor, the decision that the students ultimately made sprung from a consensus about the way the students wished to conduct their lives. This, in essence, fueled their incentive to make an act of candor conspire with—not against—zealous advocacy. In the story of the sandbag, a seemingly minuscule event, which to the students magnified itself into a monstrous betrayal, led to an insight into what certain choices can harvest. Part of that realization was a sentiment that the most insidiously toxic aftermath of certain decisions does not take the form of a bad result in a case or the sting of disciplinary proceedings or some olympian lightning bolt striking us down, but rather issues forth as a subtle yet solemn sentence to simply keep marching through life as oneself.

In an in-house appellate clinic, what we denominate "professional responsibility" lessons become inseparable from the lessons in appellate practice and procedure. That is, the "forces that will [and do] confront, challenge, and tend to seduce the person as a lawyer," erupt while reading the appellate rules, reviewing the record, writing the briefs, doing the oral argument and while communicating with clients, opposing counsel, and each other. Such a clinic is one of the few contexts in which variegated goals become a complete amalgam.

* * *

A lawyer's actions are guided by those values codified in the Model Rules of Professional Conduct and the Model Code of Professional Responsibility, by the traditions of the legal profession, and by the habits of other lawyers in the community. In the next excerpt, Geoffrey Hazard contends that the lawyer must also be guided by his or her own fundamental values.

Geoffrey Hazard, *Personal Values and Professional Ethics*, 40 CLEVELAND ST. L. REV. 133 (1992)*

* * *

My purpose on this occasion is to urge reexamination of personal values as a fundamental resource of professional ethics. The essential point is that rules of ethics, such as those embodied in the profession's ethical codes, are insufficient guides to making the choices of action that a professional must make in practice. I will suggest that the same is true of professional tradition and conventional ways of practice. This is not to say that rules of ethics and traditions are irrelevant. Rules of professional ethics frame the ethical problems that are encountered in a lawyer's life throughout practice. Moreover, professional tradition provides an idealized portrait of a professional that serves as a model for action in real world situations. However, framing an ethical problem is one thing, resolving such a problem is something else. Oliver Wendell Holmes remarked about the judicial function that "[g]eneral propositions do not decide concrete cases." The same point supports ethical choices that must be made by lawyers in conducting their practice. So also an idealized conception of what a professional should be, as portrayed in professional tradition, does not determine what a professional should do in the nonideal world of actual practice.

I. PROFESSIONAL ETHICS

The term "professional ethics" can be understood to refer to at least three different but related normative sources: first, the profession's rules of ethics; second, ethical tradition including professional myths, lore and narrative; and, third, the standards of conduct that an observing anthropologist would describe as the profession's conventions of actual practice. The last source may also be captured by the term "habit" which at one time was used to describe a group's regular pattern of conduct. The term "professional" simply denotes that these normative sources function within a specific subgroup in society, in our case the American legal profession.

II. RULES, TRADITIONS AND PRACTICE

The rules of ethics of the American legal profession are constituted in the Rules of Professional Conduct, previously in the Code of Professional Responsibility and before that in the American Bar Association Canons of Professional Ethics. Various subsections of these codes incorporate rules of general law that govern the citizenry at large. For example, the profession's ethical codes require a lawyer to refrain from violating the general criminal law and from committing civil fraud in his own conduct. The codes also permit a lawyer to use the process of the courts only for lawful purposes.

Our professional tradition is another source of ethical guidance. That tradition includes such articles of faith as "equal justice under law," "a lawyer knows no duty

---

*   Reprinted by permission of Geoffrey C. Hazard.

other than to his client," "every client with a just cause has a right to a lawyer's assistance," and "due process of law is a fundamental right."[7] In contemporary discourse about the legal profession, the profession's espoused tradition or mythology (I use the term in the anthropological sense) is often referred to as its narrative.

The legal profession's practice conventions or "habits"—its ways of actually doing things as observable by an anthropologist—are what we learn after we get out of law school. One example is the practice of using a form book whenever possible even when the specific form is not completely appropriate to the task. A legal form embodies precedent and precedent usually produces better results for a busy practitioner, rather than thinking a problem through de novo. Another professional "habit" consists of putting off any less urgent matter in favor of a more urgent matter. In general, this is a sensible scheduling principle in our work, which mostly consists of dealing with one emergency after another. However, in practice this habit often translates into doing all tasks at the last minute.

The relationship among these normative sources—rules, traditions and "habits of practice" is dynamic and complex. Lawyers are ever mindful of the central principles in the rules of ethics even if most lawyers do not know the letter of the ethical codes, let alone follow the rules to the letter. Our profession's traditions hover in the back of every lawyer's mind, helping us to interpret, justify and give higher meaning to our work. The idealized conception of the lawyer's vocation is that we are in the service of justice and the protection of the oppressed, including oppressed corporate clients. Without such an idealization the work often would be too tedious and frustrating.

The habits of lawyers' work, as observed by an anthropologist, tend to contradict the idealized version expressed in professional narrative. Moreover, some conventions of practice violate the rules prescribed in the ethical codes. Lawyers violate the rules and fail to fulfill their own professional ideals because, like everyone else, they are subject to the constraints of economics, politics and human frailty. The contradiction between the ideal and the legal, on the one hand, and actual practice, on the other, does not prove that lawyers are indifferent to their ethical obligations. It proves only that practicing law according to the rules, let alone according to idealization, is not easy.

III. OBJECTIVITY AND SUBJECTIVITY

Practice as it is actually performed is an outward and observable activity that is guided by inner and invisible norms. These norms are given expression in our codes and the traditions about our profession. The codes are promulgated as public law. The traditions are transmitted by recitations, for example, in the forms of stories about lawyers such as *Anatomy of a Murder* and *To Kill a Mockingbird*. We also hold periodic recitations in the form of bar association speeches and of lectures given to law students by professional elders. In these forms the codes and traditions take on shared meaning.

---

7   Many of these articles of faith are expressed in the Ethical Considerations of the Code of Professional Responsibility. * * *

Because the rules of professional ethics and professional narratives can be shared in this way, they are "objective" in an important sense. The rules are objective in the same sense that all legal rules are objective in an important way. The professional narratives similarly convey a commonly understood meaning within the legal community. Thus, "we" lawyers are able to say such things to each other as "during cross examination, never ask a question unless you already know the answer," and "there is nothing as insecure as an unsecured creditor."

The codes and narratives are objective in the further sense that they refer to patterns of conduct that can be observed and proved through evidence. For example, the rules prohibiting conflict of interest refer to specific observable situations where a lawyer has more than one client. Accordingly, it is possible to observe in a specific case whether a lawyer in fact has more than one client and whether the relationships are such that there is an adverse interest among the clients as defined in the rules. For further example, the rules requiring that a fee be reasonable refer to the legal services market as a standard of reasonableness. It is possible to observe in a specific case whether the fee meets this standard. Again, the rules requiring candor to the court make a comparison between facts that the lawyer may be inferred to know and the account of such facts that the lawyer has given to the tribunal.

The same is true, in a less rigorous sense, of professional tradition. A narrative or tradition is a story shared among a group in terms of which the group defines its place in the world and proclaims its identity to itself and others. We tell these stories to make vivid in our minds the ways we are supposed to act. Thus, the tradition that a lawyer knows no duty other than to his client is the counterpart of the rule that a lawyer must avoid impermissible conflicts of interest. The image projected in such a story can then be compared to practice in a real world situation. Professional narratives, myths, ideals—call them what we will—are media of interpersonal communication. In this sense they too are objective like the codes or rules.

And, of course, actual practice is objective in the sense that it can be observed, described and compared with other kinds of activity. To be sure, the help of an external observer is often necessary to see what a group actually does as distinct from what it professes to do. However, the most acute observers of law practice are those newly admitted young lawyers who are learning their trade. No learning curve is as steep as that in the first few months of practice. Every beginning lawyer is something of an on-the-job anthropologist. As Yogi Berra has said, "You can observe a lot by watching."

But what is going on in the minds of the people who engage in this thing called the practice of law?

IV. THE LAWYER'S SUBJECTIVE WORLD

From the outside, a lawyer's thoughts, her state of mind at any given moment, cannot be observed. The observer can only make inferences, perhaps nothing more than guesses, about the mental pathway by which a lawyer gets from dilemma to resolution every day and every moment of actual practice. That pathway runs through the realm of the individual lawyer's subjective reality. The pathway actually chosen is not revealed to others except through circumstantial evidence. It is the silent world of personal consciousness. Yet this is the world in which each of us as lawyers must make decisions about what to do in concrete situations encountered in practice. This is the realm that I now want to address.

Lawyers do many different kinds of things. Most of these tasks are variations of three basic functions: first, interviewing and giving advice to clients; second, negotiating contracts, settlements and other arrangements with third parties; and third, presenting evidence and legal argument before the courts. In each of these tasks the lawyer confronts an external reality, consisting of the client, the opposing parties, the court, and the world at large. But the lawyer experiences this world through the process of her own consciousness.

It is through the lawyer's own consciousness that all the relevant variables come into view and proceed into motion. Although law practice starts with having a client, a person who enters the lawyer's immediate environment becomes a "client" only through the lawyer's awareness and interpretation. Law practice involved encounters with other third parties such as opposing parties in litigation or negotiation only through the lawyer's interpretation of that party's interests. It is familiar lore that parties formally aligned on opposite sides of litigation may have essential common interests. It also holds true that parties formally on the same side may have fundamentally conflicting interests.

Similar awareness and interpretation is required in determining the strategy and tactics to be followed in carrying out a representation. It is a familiar rule of ethics that a lawyer may not offer false evidence such as perjured testimony. How does a lawyer go about determining whether a specific item of evidence falls within this prohibited category? Awareness and interpretation is required in order to apply this rule. It is an equally familiar rule that a lawyer may offer evidence whose authenticity is dubious. But how does a lawyer arrive at the conclusion that a specific item of evidence is merely dubious rather than fabricated? Whatever conclusion is reached in this respect, how does a lawyer decide whether it would be strategically imprudent to offer evidence that is not fabricated but which is dubious? There is lawyers' lore, not to be disregarded, that a jury might think that dubious evidence is fabrication, and infer from that the same is true of the case as a whole.

I will give another case, a true war story. A lawyer represented the seller of real property under a contract that required the seller to disclose all adverse facts known to the seller but which otherwise imposed on the buyer the burden of *caveat emptor*. In the course of representing another client in an unrelated matter, the lawyer discovered a serious legal impediment to the development of the property that very likely would abort the deal if the fact was made known to the buyer. The lawyer therefore confronted the following question: Should she apprise her client (the seller) of this impediment, thus putting the seller under the obligation to transmit the information to the buyer? Or should the lawyer treat the information as a matter not to be revealed to the client? Nondisclosure would subject the client to the risk that the transaction, if allowed to go forward, could later be attacked on the ground of mutual mistake or perhaps fraud. Six million dollars in damages for the client and a possible malpractice suit for the lawyer could turn on the lawyer's pathway of thought in resolving that dilemma.

The point to be made through these anecdotes is that the precise knowledge upon which the lawyer must proceed is known only to the lawyer. This is because the lawyer's private knowledge is by necessity the lawyer's personal, subjective awareness and interpretation of the situation before him. The lawyer cannot seek a declaratory ruling from the court as to what the facts are and what ethical judgment should be made in light of the facts. Shortage of time and urgency of circumstances will not permit the lawyer to obtain such authoritative determination of reality. Indeed shortage of time and urgency of circumstances may not even permit consultation with a colleague, or seeking an answer from an ethics committee or a bar association "hot line." Solo practitioners usually have to resolve these problems without anyone to consult, and law firm lawyers often must proceed in the same isolation. Even a lawyer who has taken consultation ultimately has to make a personal decision as to what to do.

V. Personal Values In Professional Ethics

It is in this lonely subjective world that a lawyer is required to "call the shots" in ethical dilemmas. In this lonely world the rules of ethics usually appear as merely vacuous generalizations. The rules say that evidence may not be offered if the lawyer knows it is fabricated, but of what avail is that guidance? The rules do not and cannot say whether specific evidence is fabricated. A court may eventually make a finding on the issue one way or another, but such a finding will be long after the event and even then the court might be wrong. Before that event comes about the lawyer has to resolve the question through irreversible action by deciding whether to use the evidence. Similarly, the rules say that nondisclosure of a material fact in a financial transaction may constitute fraud, but so what? The rules do not and cannot say whether a specific financial datum is material or even whether it is a fact. Perhaps the datum is merely the figment of some anxious accountant's hypercautiousness. Perhaps, however, it is a fact. The lawyer has to resolve the question, sometimes in an instant.

How does a lawyer decide such issues? None of our standard professional techniques are of much help in such situations. Professional technique in the interpretation of rules would permit us to determine whether the rules prohibit introduction of fabricated evidence in litigation or require disclosure of material facts in a transaction. The difficult ethical problem in such cases is not, however, what the rule says but whether the factual conditions have arisen that call the rule into operation. The technique for interpreting the rules therefore has no application unless merely for the purpose of reaching the self-deceptive conclusion that the rule does not mean what it says. Professional technique in the proof of facts would enable us to make an evidentiary showing to someone else as to whether the evidence is fabricated or whether the facts are material. But the professional techniques for proving facts to others are insufficient for the purpose of deciding facts for ourselves. Surely it is nonsense to speak of establishing a prima facie case to one's self.

Likewise, professional narrative and tradition do not provide means of resolving issues of this kind. Professional narrative speaks in terms of concrete cases, not in the abstract generalizations of the ethical codes. However, the concrete cases incorporated in professional tradition are either historical or apocryphal. Either way, they do not replicate the concrete case that the lawyer must resolve. An example is the story of Abe Lincoln's successful use of the Farmer's Almanac to demolish the testimony of a lying witness. Such a concrete case presents a model for action in a present ethical dilemma, but only if the facts of the present dilemma correspond to those in the model case. If there are differences in the facts, the model indeed can be misleading. For example, a lawyer who supposes that his only duty is to his client is in for an unpleasant surprise if the client is seeking help in concealing the evidence of a crime.

The limited utility of professional narrative resembles the limited utility of the case method of judicial reasoning. A prior case that is on point may indeed be a binding authority. However, it is always an open question whether a prior case is on point. A prior decision becomes binding when we conclude that it is on point, but there is nothing about a prior decision that binds us to first test the prior case on point.

Conventions of practice have similar limited utility in the lawyer's subject realm. Studying what lawyers do in their practice does not tell us what is going on in their minds. As to that we can only make educated guesses. Indeed, on this matter Yogi Berra may have further wisdom from which we can benefit. He said that "You can't think and hit at the same time." A successful batter is in some sense unconscious in the moment of choice when he swings the bat. I also believe that a lawyer is in some sense unconscious in the moment of choice when he resolves an ethical dilemma.

In the literature of professional ethics, remarkably little attention is given to this matter. The rules of professional ethics differentiate various states of mind as the predicates of various kinds of ethical decisions. Thus, the rules differentiate between "believing," "knowing" and "reasonably believing." However, these rules are designed to guide decision-makers such as grievance committees in resolving issues of circumstantial evidence as to a particular lawyer's state of mind on a particular occasion. By extension, these rules also tell a lawyer how a tribunal may be inclined to assess the lawyer's conduct after the fact. At most, therefore, these rules inform the lawyer how others in the future will think about what the lawyer is now thinking. The rules governing others in assessing a lawyer's state of mind do not provide insight to the lawyer about his own state of mind.

VI. CONCLUSION

There is of course more to be said on this problem. When all has been said, however, the fact will remain that a lawyer's ethical deliberations are a process of personal thought and action. That process is guided by the rules of the ethical codes, by professional tradition, and by prevailing standards of practice. According to these normative sources, a lawyer in litigation is well advised not to offer in evidence material that the lawyer thinks is fabricated and that he should know would be found to be so by a moderately sensible trier of fact. Similarly, a lawyer in a transaction is well advised to make disclosure of a fact that the lawyer thinks is material and which he should know would be found to be so by a moderately sensible trier of fact.

The practical judgments necessary to these tasks are essentially the same as those made by people in ordinary life. They are personal judgments. As such, they incorporate an unavoidable element of personal value, just as an element of value is incorporated in how we treat our friends, members of our family, professional colleagues, rivals, and the people who live across the street. Thus, it is not true—no matter what they say—that in becoming a lawyer one ceases to be a person.

The question remains of what kind of person one wants to be.

David Luban and Michael Millemann discuss the history of lawyer regulation, from the Canons of Professional Ethics to the Code of Professional Responsibility and finally to the Rules of Professional Conduct. They trace the transition from the aspirational values encompassed in the Code's ethical considerations to the more black letter approach adopted in the Rules.

David Luban and Michael Milleman, *Good Judgment: Ethics Teaching in Dark Times*, 9 GEO. J. LEGAL ETHICS 31 (1995)*

* * *

A. THE DEVOLUTION OF THE ETHICS CODES

The very idea of professional self-regulation—of embodying professional ethics in an official code formulated by the profession itself—rests upon two assumptions. These two assumptions are seldom stated or defended. Instead, they are presupposed as truisms, and we will refer to them as the Two Truisms.

> *First Truism*: There is a subject of "professional ethics." More precisely, there is a set of professional rights and responsibilities unique enough to be worth differentiating from ethics in general, subtle enough to require explicit articulation, and determinate enough to be embodied in rules.

Since these rights and responsibilities are assumed to exist even before they are codified, it seems appropriate to refer to them as the natural law of the profession. Thus, in the case of legal ethics the first assumption underlying the project of self-regulation is that something like a *natural law of lawyering* exists.

> *Second Truism*: Members of the profession itself are uniquely well-situated to articulate the natural law of lawyering, and to determine the application of its rules to concrete cases.

The Two Truisms imply what one might grandly call the "Fundamental Theorem of Self-Regulation," that the profession itself should write and enforce its own rules. This makes professional governance something of an anomaly, since the default assumption in the theory of regulation is that interest groups should never be trusted to regulate themselves, and that the capture of a regulatory agency by the industry it

---

*   Reprinted with permission.

regulates poses a perennial danger of self-preference at the expense of the public. Because of this default assumption, the Fundamental Theorem of Self-Regulation follows only if the Two Truisms are right. In logical terms, the Two Truisms are thus necessary and sufficient conditions for the Fundamental Theorem.

The history of the official legal ethics codes is well-enough known that only a brief summary should be necessary here. The precursors of the codes were David Hoffman's 1836 *Rules of Professional Deportment*, a catechism that a lawyer was supposed to read "twice every year, during my professional life,"[42] and the influential 1854 lectures of George Sharswood, a Pennsylvania judge. The latter formed the model for the Alabama code of ethics of 1887, which became in turn a template for the ABA's first essay into the area, the *1908 Canons of Professional Ethics (1908 Canons)*. The immediate impetus for the *1908 Canons* was a speech by President Theodore Roosevelt at Harvard, excoriating the corporate bar for its tenacious opposition to Progressive legislation. The bar, thus provoked, established a committee that in 1906 reported on the need for a code of ethics. The *1908 Canons* were the work of that committee. As the product of a private organization, the *1908 Canons* had no legally binding force, and unlike the later codes, they were never promulgated as court rules by state supreme courts. Instead, they functioned primarily as quasi-official guidance to courts in cases of professional malfeasance.

The first genuinely authoritative code was the 1969 ABA *Model Code of Professional Responsibility (Model Code)*, which with minor modifications was given force of law by the courts of all the states except California, which maintains its own rules. The *Model Code* has an unusual format. Its provisions are organized under nine Canons, or "axiomatic norms," which on the printed page appear to be chapter titles, but which read like rules. Canon 9, for example, reads: "A Lawyer Shall Avoid Even the Appearance of Professional Impropriety." Under the Canons are subsections of two kinds: Ethical Considerations (ECs) and Disciplinary Rules (DRs). As the prefatory material to the *Model Code* explains, the DRs are mandatory rules, violation of which subjects a lawyer to discipline, while the ECs are "aspirational" in character. The idea was that the ECs would formulate professional ideals and set the ceiling of professional behavior, while the DRs set the floor.

The move from the *Canons* to the *Model Code* was a watershed event, because the DRs marked the first time that legal ethics was regulated by hard law. Because of the anomaly of the *Model Code's* Canons and Ethical Considerations, however, the legal force of which was unclear, the ABA's transition to hard law was not complete until it adopted the *Model Rules of Professional Conduct (Model Rules)* in 1983. The *Model Rules* adopted a rule-and-comment format that had become wholly familiar in the Uniform Commercial Code, the Model Penal Code and the various Restatements. Although several states (including California and New York) have resisted adopting a version of *the Model Rules*, it has provided the dominant paradigm for the regulation of professional ethics.

The very titles of the documents indicate the change:

---

[42]   DAVID HOFFMAN, *Rules of Professional Deportment, Resolution 50, in* 2 A COURSE OF LEGAL STUDY 775 (1836). * * *

Canons of Professional Ethics;
Code of Professional Responsibility;
Rules of Professional Conduct.

The term "canon" derives initially from biblical studies, where "the canon" referred to those sacred texts officially included in the Bible (the antonym was "apocrypha"). The *Canons of Professional Ethics* were those sacred principles officially endorsed by the ABA. As the 1906 ABA report put it, the idea was to replace the "rope of sand of moral suasion" with a

> "thus it is written" of an American Bar Association code of ethics that should prove a beacon light on the mountain of high resolve to lead the young practitioner safely through the snares and pitfalls of his early practice up to and along the straight and narrow path of high and honorable professional achievement.[49]

"Thus it is written!" Evidently the word "canons" was not lightly chosen. By 1969, however, the ABA had decided to descend from Sinai and create a code. The term "ethics" dropped out of the title, to be replaced by the more technical-sounding "professional responsibility." Finally, the *Model Rules* announced itself as nothing more than an effort to regulate conduct. The de-moralization of the ethics rules was complete.

Geoffrey Hazard's views of the transformation are particularly significant, because, as the Kutak Commission's reporter who drafted the *Model Rules*, he occupies the dual role of chronicler and prime mover of the final stage of the transition. The guiding vision of Hazard's effort to legalize and de-moralize the ethics codes is this: "It is time that lawyers and the organized bar came to understand that they are governed by law, bound by law, and answerable before the law, like other people."[51] To Hazard, this ideal seems to have meant several things. First, the ethics codes themselves should walk like law and quack like law—if lawyers are to be sanctioned for violating ethics rules, the rules should be drafted with meticulous craftsmanship in a lawyerly manner, and should be readily interpretable by anyone with legal training. Hence, no more anomalies like Canons and Ethical Considerations. Second, the rules should "track" obligations imposed on lawyers through other laws. This the *Model Rules* did by modeling its own provisions on decisional or other law, to avoid a conflict of legal obligations. Third, in cases of conflict the rules should defer to other sources of legal obligation. A continuing theme of Hazard's writing has been that professional self-regulation does not permit lawyers to exempt themselves from other law, and that it is a persistent professional self-delusion to believe otherwise.

Hazard's distaste for the Ethical Considerations of the *Model Code* seems to have been visceral. He dismisses the ECs as "exhortations and idealisms echoing the

---

49   *Report [of the Committee on [the] Code of Professional Ethics*, 1906 A.B.A. Rep. 600], at 64 * * *.

51   Hazard, *[Rule of Legal Ethics: The] Drafting Task*, [36 Rec. Bar City N.Y. 77], at 84 [(March 1981)].

Victorian antecedents," and appears to believe that they were intended to concern mere "matters of etiquette or personal taste." He also argued ingeniously that the split-level format was technically incoherent, because instead of expanding lawyers' moral horizons, the ECs and Canons would actually narrow the DRs: under the principle of *expressio unius*, elaborations of DRs appearing in the ECs would not be mandatory, and would therefore serve to pre-empt broad, penumbral interpretations of the DRs.

This argument sounds like a devastating objection, but for two points. First, Hazard's *expressio unius* analysis was not how courts actually construed the *Model Code*. Invariably, they invoked the ECs to underline and emphasize the DRs, as the *Code's* drafters surely intended, and not to narrow them. Second, Hazard's analysis begged the question at a deep level. *Expressio unius* is a principle of statutory construction—but why think of the *Model Code*, with its idiosyncratic split-level structure, as a statute? If it is not, then it is beside the point that applying a principle of statutory construction to it generates absurd results. Evidently, Hazard analyzed the *Model Code* like a statute because he had concluded that the ethics code should be a statute. In effect, he argued for replacing the *Code's* format with the *Model Rules'* format because the *Code* was a second-rate statute. Defenders of the *Code*—and it continues to have admirers—dislike the *Model Rules* format because they regard it as a second-rate non-statutory or semi-statutory statement of the profession's aspirations.

The real problem with the Ethical Considerations in the *Model Code* was not their format but their content. Some of them contain no aspiration at all, but rather the debatable conclusions of a potted legal philosophy. Others are transparently self-serving, such as EC 2-16, "The legal profession cannot remain a viable force in fulfilling its role in our society unless its members receive adequate compensation for services rendered." Still others contain requirements that should have been Disciplinary Rules, such as EC 5-5: "A lawyer should not suggest to his client that a gift be made to himself or for his benefit." It is hard to see refraining from soliciting gifts from clients as an aspiration, the sort of surpassing lawyerly excellence that many strive for but few attain. The numerous vacuities in the ECs provided ample reason for replacing them, but that does not settle the issue of whether the ethics codes should state aspirational ideals. That issue is worth pursuing a bit further.

In a recent lecture, Hazard argued that "rules of ethics are insufficient guides to making the choices of action that a professional must make in practice."[60] Partly, this is for reasons very similar to Kant's argument about the necessity of judgment: "The rules say that evidence may not be offered if the lawyer knows it is fabricated, but of what avail is that guidance? The rules do not and cannot say whether specific evidence is fabricated." By itself, of course, the argument shows only that the rules (like all law) cannot be self-interpreting. But Hazard takes away from the argument a broader conclusion: that the rightful guide of a lawyer's actions is not rules but "practical judgments" that "are personal judgments. As such, they incorporate an unavoidable element of personal value. The question remains of what kind of person

---

[60] Geoffrey C. Hazard, Jr., *Personal Values and Professional Ethics*, 40 CLEV. ST. L. REV. 133, 133 (1992) [hereinafter Hazard, *Personal Values*].

one wants to be." If we read him aright, Hazard's basic objection to incorporating aspirational ideals in the ethics codes is that it involves a fundamental moral confusion, a conflation of personal value with positive law.

Understood in this way, Hazard's position is very close to H.L.A. Hart's, in his famous debate with Lon Fuller.[64] Hart insisted on the separation of law and morality. In the most powerful portion of his paper, Hart criticized the German philosopher Gustav Radbruch, who had recanted his pre-World-War II legal positivism because he thought that positivism had disarmed the German judiciary in the face of the Nazis. According to Radbruch, that is, the German judges had blindly enforced Hitler's monstrous decrees because they believed that law is law regardless of its moral content. Instead, Radbruch argued, they should have realized that monstrously immoral law is no law at all and therefore they did not need to enforce it.

Though he admired Radbruch's sincerity, Hart argued tellingly that Radbruch seems to have only "half digested the spiritual message of liberalism." By this Hart meant that Radbruch's journey through Hell had taught him that individual conscience is free to assert itself against immoral law. That is the spiritual message of liberalism. But Radbruch could bring himself to believe that conscientious disobedience was the right path only by convincing himself that the law was no law at all. That is, in the end he *still* did not fully understand the liberty of conscience to reject the law, and that is why he had only half digested the message of liberalism.

By analogy, Hazard's distaste for the Ethical Considerations seems to arise at bottom from the sense that a profession that needs to codify its aspirations to supplement the "rope of sand of moral suasion" has only half digested the spiritual message not only of liberalism, but of adult living. "When all has been said, however, the fact will remain that a lawyer's ethical deliberations are a process of personal thought and action."[70]

This is a respectable and thoughtful position, but it is not the only respectable and thoughtful position. Fuller provided the counter-argument in his rebuttal of Hart.[71] Judges, he argued, have a special obligation of fidelity toward law, and an honorable judge will experience a strong commitment to the law. Is it reasonable or realistic, Fuller asked, to expect judges to jump the rails of their sworn obligation and issue rulings that they believe defy the law? His answer was no, and as an empirical matter there seems little doubt that he was right. Of course, this by itself is no refutation of Hart's philosophical positivism, and Fuller did not regard it as one. (For that, he employed other arguments.) But it is a powerful argument against an overly optimistic or overly idealistic faith in the unfortified liberal conscience. There is nothing especially farfetched in the idea that a jurist's conscience will function better when it is buttressed by legal authority. Plainly, the drafters of the *Model Code* were following Fuller's side of the famous controversy.

---

64   Hart's side of the debate is given in H.L.A. Hart, *Positivism and the Separation of Law and Morals*, 71 HARV. L. REV 593 (1958).

70   Hazard, *Personal Values, supra* note 60, at 140.

71   Lon L. Fuller, *Positivism and Fidelity to Law — A Reply to Professor Hart*, 71 HARV. L. REV. 630, 655, 658-60 (1958).

An example will illustrate what is lost in a de-moralized code of conduct. Consider *Model Code* EC 2-27's proposition that "a lawyer should not decline representation because a client or a cause is unpopular or community reaction is adverse," together with EC 2-28's reminder that "the personal preference of a lawyer to avoid adversary alignment against judges, other lawyers, public officials, or influential members of the community does not justify his rejection of tendered employment." These aspirations simply vanish from the *Model Rules*, which replace them with a rule stating that a lawyer "shall not seek to avoid appointment by a tribunal to represent a person except for good cause." Not only is the latter rule narrower than the ECs, it omits any tincture of the *Code's* suggestion that professional honor takes guts, that lawyers may sometimes have to stand up against the community and the establishment. These are properly aspirations rather than duties, since it is too much to require every lawyer to have the courage and steadfastness of Atticus Finch; but it is one property of an aspiration that we properly feel ashamed of ourselves for not living up to it. The *Model Rules*, by contrast, don't offer the slightest suggestion that a lawyer should feel ashamed of turning away a client out of a lack of nerve. The Comment to Rule 6.2 says that a lawyer fulfills the responsibility to perform pro bono service "by accepting a fair share of unpopular matters or indigent or unpopular clients," but it carefully refrains from saying that a lawyer fails to fulfill any responsibility by *not* accepting that fair share.

Fuller's argument, applied to this example, is that rules such as EC 2-27 and EC 2-28 can fortify a lawyer's conscience. If a lawyer has "other lawyers, public officials, or influential members of the community" telling her that if she knows what is good for her, she will stop fighting so hard for her client, it is not only her courage but her confidence in her own judgment that is likely to need fortification. Can she really be sure that she is right when the mandarins of the local bar, the bureaucrats of city hall, and business leaders who have sent work her way in the past are all telling her that she's upsetting the apple-cart on behalf of a client who is not good enough for her in the first place? It is in a crisis like this that it might help to have an official statement of the profession's aspirations—an official statement that she can read to the president of the city bar, who happens to be representing her client's adversary, shortly before telling him to take a hike. Or so a Fullerian would argue.

Whatever the ultimate merits of the argument—and the Hart-Fuller controversy had no clear victor—Hazard's impetus toward legalizing and de-moralizing the codes has triumphed in the field of professional regulation. Indeed, the next giant step—the American Law Institute (ALI) *Restatement of the Law Governing Lawyers* that now exists in draft—brings professional rules into full parity with the other departments of the law. What seems to have been overlooked, however, is that this triumph has gone a long way toward undermining the whole enterprise of lawyer self-regulation.

After all, if all of the moral content has been squeezed out of the professional codes; if, moreover, the codes have been drafted to track exogenous legal obligations; if the motivation of the enterprise is to bring the bar to heel, by getting lawyers at last to "understand that they are governed by law, bound by law, and answerable before the law, like other people;"[80] and if, finally, the commercialization of the bar is proceeding toward a point where lawyers will be indistinguishable from other business advisors and entrepreneurial consultants—then what remains of the Twin Truisms of self-regulation, the assumptions 1) that there is a natural law of lawyering, and 2) that lawyers are uniquely suited to give it determinate form?

As to the First Truism, there is little sense in the *Model Rules* that they are based on a natural law of lawyering. How could they be, if their self-conscious aim is to track exogenous law that applies to lawyers because it applies to everyone? Hazard's own views on the subject are somewhat difficult to discern. In a 1992 lecture, Hazard has argued that the seemingly unique obligations of lawyers have commonsensical analogues in lay life—which, if true, undercuts the contrast between common morality and a special role morality of lawyers.[81] Elsewhere, in a paper entitled *My Station as a Lawyer*,[82] Hazard defends a version of the unique-role-morality thesis—the nineteenth-century British philosopher F.H. Bradley's theory of "my station and its duties," according to which the ethical life consists not in following universalistic prescriptions, but rather in doing the duties of one's own station. Hazard points out that "[i]n ordinary life, all of us have such special stations." Ergo, universalistic moral prescriptions are uselessly abstract and are relevant only in the classroom or the church, where we are insulated from the need to act on them.

This argument is too conclusory to persuade anyone who entertains doubts about either the justness of their station or the defensibility of its duties. Significantly, Hazard neglects to add that Bradley himself rejected "my station and its duties" for its unreflective deference to the community's pre-existing social structure. "My station and its duties" presupposes the status quo. For our purposes, the important point is that, in Hazard's view, so does the enterprise of professional ethics, and with this presupposition in hand, he argues for something like a natural law of lawyering: "By definition, professional ethics concerns a subset, or norms specifically governing some subset, of people who have a specific station in life, a particular vocation."

How those norms are discovered, however, and (more importantly) who is in the best position to discover them, are questions that Hazard does not really address. This takes us to the Second Truism, that lawyers themselves are uniquely positioned to articulate the duties of their station. Ironically, the drafter of the *Model Rules* defined the drafting task in such a way as to suggest that this truism is untrue. Hazard's stern dictum that lawyers must be made to understand that they are answerable before the law, like other people, suggests that lawyers habitually misunderstand this point, and seems like an effort to break through the profession's shield of self-proclaimed and self-serving superiority. But then why should lawyers be allowed to regulate themselves? Isn't that a case of the fox guarding the henhouse? If it is true that "public law has come to define the profession's duties and responsibilities," then why shouldn't the public take that part of the lawmaking process out of the profession's hands?

---

80   Hazard, *Drafting Task*, *supra* note [51], at 84.

81   Geoffrey C. Hazard, Jr., *Doing the Right Thing*, 70 WASH. U. L.Q. 691, 695-700 (1992).

82   Geoffrey C. Hazard, Jr., *My Station as a Lawyer*, 6 GA. ST. U. L. REV. 1 (1989). * * *

B. THE REGULATORY REVOLUTION

As a matter of fact, that is precisely what has been happening. Within the past two decades, it has become abundantly clear that the ethics codes are just one piece of the law governing lawyers, and not necessarily the most important. To take a few examples:

Item: The domain of professional regulation of lawyer advertising and solicitation has eroded steadily in the face of constitutional decisions over the twenty years since *Bates*.

Item: Rule 11 sanctions of the Federal Rules of Civil Procedure have been orders of magnitude more important for regulating frivolous or harassing litigation than the Rule's ethical counterparts, whose language Rule 11 more or less replicates.

Item: The enormous explosion in legal malpractice has become the most prominent feature of the contemporary landscape of lawyer behavior. In the 1960s, malpractice liability insurance was largely unavailable on the domestic market, because the claims were so few. By contrast, some contemporary estimates suggest that as many as ten percent of lawyers face malpractice charges. Multi-million dollar malpractice settlements arising from the savings and loan collapses have sent a massive shudder through the large-firm bar, and may well change the way such firms structure themselves and practice law.

Item: Over the vigorous protests of the criminal defense bar, lawyers' fees were brought under the fee-forfeiture provisions of the Racketeer Influenced and Corrupt Organizations Act (RICO) and the Continuing Criminal Enterprises Act.

Item: In the wake of notorious attorney participation in the 1989 savings and loan debacle, Congress enacted the Financial Institutional Reform, Recovery, and Enforcement Act of 1989 (FIRREA), which explicitly includes lawyers among the "institution-affiliated parties" who are subject to stiff penalties for "causing, bringing about, participating in, counseling, or aiding and abetting a violation" of a broadly drawn banking law.

Item: The Department of Justice (DOJ) has aggressively asserted the power to preempt state ethical regulation of federal prosecutors, who have challenged efforts to discipline them for violations of state no-contact rules and state ethics rules discouraging subpoenas of defense lawyers.

Item: The legal profession is subject to antitrust legislation. Law firms are subject to Title VII strictures in promotion decisions. Constitutional principles governing labor unions apply to mandatory bar associations as well. Internal Revenue Service (IRS) disclosure provisions for large cash transactions apply to lawyers' fees, and IRS rules include lawyers among the tax-preparers who are subject to civil fines for taking hyper-aggressive positions without flagging them.

The list could go on. In fifty years, we may come to regard the by-then-defunct *Model Rules* as merely an unstable halfway-point between robust self-regulation and fully external regulation of lawyers. Hazard and the Kutak Commission may come to be seen as moles within the enterprise of self- regulation.

* * *

B. Lawyer Roles and Responsibilities

In the following excerpt, Joseph Allegretti uses George Orwell's self-description in his essay "Shooting an Elephant" as a metaphor for lawyers' behavior. Regardless whether one agrees that lawyers generally respond in the manner Alegretti suggests, one might wish to be cautious to ensure that reactions to clients are not borne of the emotional quandaries faced by Orwell.

Joseph Allegretti, *Shooting Elephants, Serving Clients: An Essay on George Orwell and the Lawyer-Client Relationship*, 27 CREIGHTON L. REV. 1 (1993)*

"I perceived in this moment that when the white man turns tyrant it is his own freedom that he destroys. . . . He wears a mask, and his face grows to fit it."[1]

"The recognition of complicity is the beginning of innocence."[2]

In Moulmein, Lower Burma, while serving as sub-divisional police officer, George Orwell shot an elephant. Years later he wrote a celebrated essay on the incident. The shooting raises two questions for lawyers. The first, Why did Orwell shoot the elephant? The second, Why should we care?

I. WHY ORWELL SHOT THE ELEPHANT

Orwell begins his essay by describing the intense hatred of the Burmese for their European masters. "In Moulmein, in Lower Burma, I was hated by large numbers of people—the only time in my life that I have been important enough for this to happen to me." Europeans were spit at, jeered at, and insulted. "As a police officer I was an obvious target and was baited whenever it seemed safe to do so."

The petty humiliations were especially "perplexing and upsetting" to Orwell because he secretly agreed with the Burmese that British rule was a terrible evil. In

---

*   Reprinted from Creighton Law Review by permission. Copyright © 1993 by Creighton University.

1   George Orwell, *Shooting an Elephant, in* THE COLLECTED ESSAYS, JOURNALISM, AND LETTERS OF GEORGE ORWELL I 235, 239 (1968) [hereinafter ORWELL].

2   Thomas L. Shaffer, *The Legal Ethics of the Two Kingdoms*, 17 VAL. U.L. REV. 3, 34 (1983) (*quoting* ROBERT PENN WARREN, BROTHER TO DRAGONS 213-15 (1953)).

his job as a police officer he saw "the dirty work of the Empire at close quarters." He knew first hand about the imprisonments, the floggings, the injustices.

Thus, his unspoken sympathies were all on the side of the Burmese, and against the British. He hated his work and found himself overwhelmed by an intolerable sense of guilt. He already had decided to leave his post, but he was young and confused, and uncertain how to proceed.

Yet, he hated not only his job, but those who hated him for doing his job. Orwell stated that "[a]ll I knew was that I was stuck between my hatred of the empire I served and my rage against the evil-spirited little beasts who tried to make my job impossible." One part of him condemned the Empire as morally bankrupt, while another part "thought that the greatest joy in the world would be to drive a bayonet into a Buddhist priest's guts." His sympathy for the cause of the Burmese existed side by side with a deep and savage anger at their mistreatment of him.

One day an incident took place that revealed to Orwell the "real nature of imperialism—the real motives for which despotic governments act." It happened that a tame elephant ran amok, destroying property and animals, and eventually killing a man. Orwell was called upon to subdue the animal. Armed with a rifle, he tracked down the elephant, only to find it grazing peacefully, looking "no more dangerous than a cow."

Orwell had no intention of killing the elephant. Already its madness had worn off. It was only necessary to keep an eye on the animal until its handler came and caught him. Orwell "decided that I would watch him for a little while to make sure that he did not turn savage again, and then go home."

And so it might have ended, if Orwell had been alone. But as he started out on his search for the elephant, the inhabitants of the area "flocked out of their houses and followed me. They had seen the rifle and were all shouting excitedly that I was going to shoot the elephant."

As he stood before the elephant, Orwell glanced back at the crowd that had followed him. It had grown to several thousand, and Orwell looked out at a throng of "faces all happy and excited over this bit of fun, all certain that the elephant was going to be shot."

At that moment, Orwell realized that he had no choice but to kill the elephant, for that was what the people expected of him, and he felt powerless to defy those expectations. He could not run the risk of exposing the Empire he represented to the ridicule of its subjects:

> And suddenly I realized that I should have to shoot the elephant after all. The people expected it of me and I had got to do it; I could feel their two thousand wills pressing me forward, irresistibly. And it was at this moment, as I stood there with the rifle in my hands, that I first grasped the hollowness, the futility of the white man's dominion in the East. Here was I, the white man with his gun, standing in front of the unarmed native crowd—seemingly the leading actor of the piece; but in reality I was only an absurd puppet pushed to and fro by the will of those yellow faces behind. I perceived in this moment that when the white man turns tyrant

it his own freedom that he destroys. He becomes a sort of hollow, posing dummy, the conventionalized figure of a sahib. For it is the condition of his rule that he shall spend his life in trying to impress the 'natives,' and so in every crisis he has got to do what the 'natives' expect of him. He wears a mask, and his face grows to fit it.

Orwell had to shoot the elephant. He felt that "[a] sahib has got to act like a sahib; he has got to appear resolute, to know his own mind and to do definite things." If he did not carry through with the shooting, then the crowd would feel cheated and might laugh at him. That could not be tolerated, for "my whole life, every white man's life in the East, was one long struggle not to be laughed at." His authority and British rule depended upon a display of might and competence. As long as the Burmese acquiesced in Britain's pretensions, the Empire could stand proud; but if the Burmese withdrew their tacit support—if they laughed at Orwell!—the hollowness at the center of the Empire would stand revealed.

So, Orwell had to kill the elephant. He was a poor shot, and he knew there was a risk that he would be killed by the animal. However, his thoughts were not on his own safety, but on the crowd watching him. If he had been alone, he would have been scared, but now his only concern was to kill the elephant cleanly, and give the crowd no cause for laughter.

When he shot the elephant, Orwell heard the "devilish roar of glee that went up from the crowd." The animal did not die easily. Even after Orwell had shot him several times, and the animal had crashed to the ground, he would not die. His breath came in "long rattling gasps." Blood poured from him. Orwell fired shot after shot, trying to put the poor animal out of his misery, but the death agony continued. Orwell recalled that "[t]he tortured gasps continued as steadily as the ticking of a clock."

Eventually, Orwell could take it no longer. He left the animal to the crowd, who waited patiently for its death, and then stripped the meat from the carcass.

Later, there were discussions among the Europeans about whether Orwell had done the right thing. Some thought it was right to kill the elephant; others thought it was foolish to shoot a valuable animal for killing a mere "coolie." Orwell stated that "afterwards I was very glad that the coolie had been killed; it put me legally in the right and gave me a sufficient pretext for shooting the elephant."

Why had he killed the elephant? Orwell's own answer was simple: "I often wondered whether any of the others grasped that I had done it solely to avoid looking like a fool."

The incident taught Orwell the dirty truth that those who hold power over others may in their own way be just as enslaved as those they purport to rule. As Orwell's biographer puts it: "It is easy enough to see how imperialism enslaves its subjects, but the great lesson that Orwell learned in Burma is that the system also has endless ways of enslaving its masters."[26]

---

26   SHELDEN, [ORWELL, THE AUTHORIZED BIOGRAPHY] at 106 [(1991)].

II. WHY LAWYERS SHOULD CARE

My claim is that Orwell's essay can help illuminate the relationship between lawyers and clients. It can help us to see more clearly and truthfully what is really going on when lawyers encounter clients. It can do so in at least two ways. First, Orwell's essay can help us better understand the *resentment* that lawyers frequently feel towards their clients. Second, it can enlighten us about the *roles* that lawyers and clients play, and the ways these roles can be an obstacle to forging a relationship of mutual trust and dialogue. I will address each in turn.

A. RESENTMENT

"[T]he greatest joy in the world would be to drive a bayonet into a Buddhist priest's guts."

Orwell arrived in Burma at a time when tensions were on the rise between the local people and their British rulers. Although there was little risk of violence, a "general atmosphere of hostility" confronted the British stationed there.[30]

Orwell was forced to endure the insults and hatred of the Burmese. His response was to return the hostility. He found himself resenting the very people that he was duty-bound to protect as a colonial police officer. The animosity he encountered is one simple and obvious explanation for Orwell's anger towards the Burmese.

But there is another, more complex, reason for Orwell's anger. It was his own ambivalence about his job and self that fueled his resentment of the Burmese.

Orwell had "already made up my mind that imperialism was an evil thing. . . . Theoretically—and secretly, of course—I was all for the Burmese and all against their oppressors, the British." But although Orwell hated the Empire, he continued to serve as an instrument of its rule. He continued to participate in the very evils he silently opposed. From the vantage point of the Burmese, Orwell was just another imperialist.

As a result, Orwell was plagued by gnawing pangs of self-doubt and self-loathing over the role he played. He felt himself a cog in a terrible machine. The prisoners and the floggings and the injustices "oppressed me with an intolerable sense of guilt." He hated what he was doing and hated himself for doing it.

The problem was that Orwell had no way to confront openly these feelings of guilt and self-hatred. As he admitted, he "could get nothing into perspective. I was young and ill-educated and I had to think out my problems in the utter silence that is imposed on every Englishman in the East."

Lacking the resources to cope with his self-doubts, Orwell projected his negative feelings about himself onto the Burmese. Projection can be defined as "the mechanism whereby painful or objectionable feelings or ideas are perceived as if they originated from persons or things in the environment and thus are not seen as belonging to the self."[34] Thomas Shaffer and James Elkins explain the phenomenon as fol-

---

30   CRICK, [GEORGE ORWELL: A LIFE] at 81 [(1980)]. * * *

34   ANDREW S. WATSON, PSYCHIATRY FOR LAWYERS 161 (Rev. ed. 1978). * * *

lows: "One way to live with ourselves, and those aspects of self that we find unacceptable, is to see in others what we cannot see in ourselves. Unable to tolerate the possibility of our own weakness, vulnerability, fear, we see those things in others."[35]

An understanding of projection can help explain the wildly conflicting emotions that beset Orwell. The anger he felt at himself for serving the Empire, and the guilt he felt for not actively supporting the Burmese, were turned outward: He came to hate not only his job and himself for doing it, but the Burmese people whose cause he secretly supported. At the same time that he thought of the British Empire as an "unbreakable tyranny," he could not help but feel "that the greatest joy in the world would be to drive a bayonet into a Buddhist priest's guts."

My purpose in introducing psychoanalytical theory is not to present a crudely reductionist portrait of Orwell, but to make the point that his resentment towards the Burmese can plausibly be explained in part as a projection of certain negative feelings he held for himself as the agent of (in his mind) an evil imperialist Empire.

How is this relevant to lawyers? We are not imperial officers; we serve no Raj; and our clients are not our subjects, but our employers.

Despite such obvious differences, I suggest that Orwell's experience with the Burmese can help to explain the resentment that attorneys often feel towards their clients. Few writers on legal ethics or lawyer-client relationships explore this issue, although anyone who has spent any time around lawyers knows that they often harbor strongly negative feelings about their clients. This animosity may be expressed in crude jokes about clients, sarcastic comments about client dress or appearance, frustration at client "stupidity," wistful comments about how enjoyable it would be to practice law if only there were no clients, a reluctance to return client phone calls, a tendency to postpone or neglect the work of "difficult" clients, an unwillingness to treat some clients as autonomous adults, and so on.

What lies at the root of this resentment and anger? Some of it, no doubt, is a response to the unreasoning demands of clients, who are often unfamiliar with the legal system and the kind of work that lawyers do. Some of it springs from the inevitable tensions and uncertainties that accompany any relationship in which one person serves as the agent of another. Some of it results from the inherent conflict of interest that underlies all lawyer-client relationships in which money is involved. Some of it may be a response to a gradual shift in the balance of power between lawyers and clients—away from the paternalistic model of the past, where the lawyer was unquestionably in charge, to a more participatory model where lawyers and clients share decisionmaking authority.

Furthermore, some degree of projection can be expected in a lawyer's dealings with her clients. Indeed, the natural human tendency toward projection is intensified in the lawyer-client relation because lawyers often deal with their clients in a face-to-face, long-term, and intensely personal relationship. Such an intimate personal relationship can generate the psychological phenomenon known as transference, which is the projection onto another of irrational feelings that derive from the pro-

---

35 THOMAS L. SHAFFER & JAMES ELKINS, LEGAL INTERVIEWING AND COUNSELING 106-07 (2d ed. 1987). * * *

jecting party's dealings with important persons in his or her life. Transference is not limited to clients. Thus a lawyer's hostility toward a client or fear of a client or sexual attraction toward a client might stem from the lawyer's past dealings with her family members or other influential persons. The lawyer may be "reliving an emotional relationship from the past," and forcing the client to "stand in for an important person in the [lawyer's] life."

Under such circumstances, a lawyer may unconsciously frustrate or sabotage (sic) her relationship with her client. Robert Bastress and Joseph Harbaugh provide a fictional example.[45] Attorney Frank Adams represented Sherm Clayton, a prominent local businessman. Clayton was handsome, athletic, and self-confident; in contrast, Adams was "slightly built, nasal, and rather dull . . . more of a plodder than a dynamo." Adams grew increasingly reticent and hostile toward his client, for no apparent reason. The real reason, unknown to the parties, lay in the attorney's past life. Adams subconsciously associated Clayton with his older brother, who always had been more successful in school, athletics, and social relations. "So when Clayton's appearance and success sprung a subconscious association in Frank's mind with his brother, Frank also transferred his fraternal resentment to Clayton, which eventually destroyed the attorney-client relationship."

Similarly, a lawyer with legitimate grievances against a client may exaggerate them out of proportion because of her unconscious projections. A client is late paying a fee or makes excuses to avoid paying. A client places unreasonable demands upon a lawyer. A client insists on calling daily just to "check up" on the progress of a case. A client is sullen and grudging in disclosing information that the lawyer needs. Instead of feeling mild annoyance, the attorney may feel extreme hostility, even hatred, of the client. Perhaps for a moment the attorney even feels that "the greatest joy in the world would be to drive a bayonet into the guts" of the troublesome, client. Such anger at a client—particularly such unreasoning, extreme anger—is a signal that something is going on deep in the lawyer's own personality.

All of this is true, and yet . . . There can be something more to this resentment, a moral dimension, that is easily overlooked, but which Orwell alerts us to in his essay. As we have seen, Orwell's hostility towards the Burmese masked deep self-doubts about the morality of his actions. The same can be true of the hostility that lawyers feel towards their clients.

Sometimes lawyers do not like what they are doing for a client. They are troubled by the character of their client or by the ends they are seeking for the client. They feel uncomfortable about helping a corporation evade environmental regulations or a landlord evict a penniless family or a "guilty" criminal defendant avoid punishment.

Sometimes lawyers do not like the means they feel compelled to use to accomplish their client's ends. They experience a moral queaziness at using discovery or delay to frustrate an opponent, or cross-examining a truthful witness to make him or her look like a liar, or preparing a witness to testify in a way that will be truthful but misleading.

---

45   BASTRESS & HARBAUGH, [INTERVIEWING, COUNSELING AND NEGOTIATION], at 296 [(1990)].

When these moral doubts arise, the lawyer may have the legal authority to withdraw from the case. Assuming however that the lawyer will not violate a professional rule of conduct or other law, she will probably continue with the representation. Most lawyers will not withdraw from a case simply because they have some moral doubts about the matter or the client. And as long as the attorney remains in the case, she is expected to do all that she can to achieve the client's objectives. As Professor Murray Schwartz puts it: "When acting as an advocate, a lawyer must, within the established constraints upon professional behavior, maximize the likelihood that the client will prevail."[50] For many lawyers, the bottom line is simple and straightforward: When you're in, you're in—all the way in.

When a lawyer continues to represent a client under such circumstances, she may attempt to put her moral doubts behind her and get on with the business of zealously representing her client. This strategy allows the lawyer to bypass the messy business of openly confronting her client with her moral misgivings. It lets the lawyer avoid the unpleasantness of entering into a moral dialogue with her client in which each of the parties will be challenged by the other.

In short, by bracketing her moral doubts, a lawyer can concentrate on winning her case and can ignore the troubling questions of whether the case should be won and whether it should be won in a certain way. This is a psychologically attractive approach. It makes the attorney's moral world "a simpler, less complicated, and less ambiguous world" than it would be if moral issues were confronted openly. Indeed, if a lawyer ignores or represses her moral doubts, over time it is likely that those doubts will lessen or disappear.

Lawyers who adopt such a tack come to see themselves not as moral agents, but as "amoral technicians." Like the proverbial hired gun, they envision themselves as the zealous partisan of their client, detached from personal moral judgments. "Like the hired gun, the lawyer passes no judgment on the client's goals but strives to effectuate them." This is one option—perhaps the most common—for dealing with the moral discomfort that lawyers often experience.

There is another possibility. The attorney may not succeed in bracketing or jettisoning her moral scruples. Instead, she may continue with the representation, yet at the same time be plagued by a nagging sense of guilt or anxiety about her work. There may be an undercurrent of disquiet that barely rises to the level of consciousness, yet which affects her approach to her job and colors her relationship with her client.

Like Orwell, the lawyer may not like what she is doing and may not like herself very much doing it. She may feel a stifling sense of being trapped in her role with no way out. Yet rather than face these doubts openly, the lawyer's moral paralysis may be transmuted into anger at others, and so she many find herself experiencing the same sort of unreasoning hostility towards her clients that Orwell felt towards the Burmese people he was sent to serve. Resentment of a client can plausibly be

---

50   Schwartz calls this the principle of professionalism. Murray L. Schwartz, *The Professionalism and Accountability of Lawyers*, 66 CAL. L. REV. 669, 673 (1978). He argues that the standard vision of the advocate's role consists of this principle and what he calls the principle of accountability: "[A] lawyer is neither legally, professionally, nor morally accountable for the means used or the ends achieved." *Id.* * * *

explained, at least in part, as the lawyer's unconscious projection of guilt and self-loathing, stemming from her moral discomfort with the client or the case.

Furthermore, I suspect that this projected resentment lies at the root of much of the paternalism and manipulation that so often infect lawyers in their dealings with clients. We do not inevitably manipulate and dominate those we resent, but unconscious resentment certainly makes it easier to treat a client "more like an object than a human being, more like a child than an adult."

If I am right, then what should be the response of lawyers who find themselves experiencing unreasoning anger and resentment at their clients?

Projections are, by definition, unconscious. Like bad dreams, they disappear in the light of day. Thus the first step in reducing the power that projections hold over us is to recognize their existence. This apparently happened with Orwell, at least eventually, for in his essay, written a decade after the shooting, he acknowledges that his resentment of the Burmese was fueled by a certain self-loathing. Unfortunately, at the time of the shooting, Orwell was still inclined to blame the Burmese for much of the guilt and self-hatred he was experiencing.

If lawyers are to escape the hold of unreasonable projections, then they must first acknowledge that these projections underlie much of their hostility towards clients:

> The mere acknowledgment of the possibility of such unconscious reactions permits the participants to look more objectively at their relationships and to question causes. The capacity to accept the possibility that one's feelings about another may be due to unconscious and unrealistic coloring rather than to the other's real traits is a major step towards understanding. Without awareness of transference phenomena, people are over- or under-convinced by their own emotional responses, and have no opportunity to work out any understanding of them.

This requires that attorneys break free of the hired gun model, which seduces them into bracketing moral concerns and concentrating solely on achieving the ends of their clients by all legally available means. Instead, they must come to see themselves as moral agents involved in a relationship with clients in which morals matter, both the morals of the client and the morals of the lawyer.

Above all, this means that lawyers must be honest with their clients. They must be willing to explore their feelings of anger and resentment. Rather than choosing the safe and comfortable route of ignoring or repressing their moral doubts, they must be willing to express these moral qualms openly to their clients. If a lawyer believes that her client's objectives are immoral or can be obtained only by morally questionable means, she should not shirk from raising her concerns. Lawyers must feel free to say to a client, "Yes, you can do that, but do you really want to?"

As part of this openness and honesty, lawyers also must be willing to listen to their clients and be prepared to reexamine their own views after exploring the matter fully. What may seem a morally dubious undertaking may look much different after the lawyer listens carefully and respectfully to a client tell her story. I am arguing for the freedom of lawyers to bring their moral doubts into the open, but I acknowledge that these doubts may well be dispelled by a frank and sensitive discussion with the client. "[T]he assumption of moral discourse is that each of the discoursers is open to change."[65] Lawyers and clients are not autonomous and isolated agents: For better or for worse, they are in it together, each influencing the other.

When lawyers fail to confront their unconscious projections, the projections fester, contaminating their relations with their clients. The moral doubts that they repress do not disappear but reemerge in the guise of resentment and hostility towards clients. This is the important insight that Orwell offers to lawyers.

It is never easy to confront our projections. When it comes to lawyers in their dealings with clients, however, there is an additional difficulty. The problem stems from the differing roles that lawyers and clients are expected to play in the relationship, for these roles often stand in the way of greater honesty and self-disclosure, and obscure the delicate and complex way in which lawyers and clients influence each other. It is to this issue that I now turn.

B. ROLES

"A sahib has got to act like a sahib. . . ."

Orwell's essay can be read as an exploration and critique of the ways in which certain roles can blind persons to the moral consequences of their actions. Orwell's personal moral values condemned the needless shooting of the elephant. Left to his own devices, he would have stood watch over the elephant until its handler came and recaptured it. But the role he was playing—colonial policeman, symbol of the British Empire—made certain choices unthinkable and others unavoidable. Viewed in this way, Orwell's essay is especially relevant for lawyers, who often act for clients in ways that conflict with their own moral values.

Indeed, the standard complaint about lawyers is that they are too disposed to substitute role morality for ordinary morality. They do things that ordinary morality condemns, yet defend their actions on the grounds that their role as a zealous advocate justifies or even demands such actions.

As Richard Wasserstrom puts it:

> Conventional wisdom has it that where the attorney-client relationship exists, the point of view of the attorney is properly different—and appreciably so—from that which would be appropriate in the absence of the attorney-client relationship. For where the attorney-client relationship exists, it is often appropriate and many times even obligatory for the attorney to do things that, all other things being equal, an ordinary person need not, and should not do. What is characteristic of this role of a lawyer is the lawyer's required indifference to a wide variety of ends and consequences that in other contexts would be of undeniable moral significance. Once a lawyer represents a client, the lawyer has a duty to make his or her expertise fully available in the realization of the end sought by the client, irrespective, for the most part, of the moral worth to which the end will be put or the character of the client who seeks to utilize it. Provided that the

---

65   THOMAS L. SHAFFER, ON BEING A CHRISTIAN AND A LAWYER 28 (1981).

end sought is not illegal, the lawyer is, in essence, an amoral technician whose peculiar skills and knowledge in respect to the law are available to those with whom the relationship of client is established.[70]

For those who accept this way of thinking, it is morally appropriate to cross-examine a truthful witness to make the witness appear to be lying. True, ordinary non-lawyer morality would condemn this misrepresentation. But in the context of a judicial proceeding, in which both sides are represented by attorneys, and in which a neutral and impartial decisionmaker will evaluate the evidence and render judgment, it is morally proper to act zealously on behalf of a client, as long as no laws or professional rules are violated.

The role-differentiated behavior of lawyers has come under increasing attack in recent years, with many scholars arguing that lawyers should not see themselves as "amoral technicians," but should take moral responsibility for the means they employ and the ends they achieve:

> [L]awyers should not be able to hide behind the mask of the hired gun, the detached partisan, the amoral technician. Instead, like other persons, they must assume the burdens of the moral life, and take responsibility for their actions. We would all be better off if lawyers came to see themselves as subject to the demands of ordinary morality.

Orwell's essay can be read usefully as a study of the dangers of role-differentiated behavior. Rather than taking personal moral responsibility for his actions, which would have meant resisting the unreasoning clamor of the crowd, Orwell retreated into his role and did what he felt he had to do as a representative of the British Empire. His moral doubts gave way to the duties of his role.

I want to suggest, however, that there is much more to Orwell's essay than simply a critique of role-differentiated behavior. Its true significance for the debate over lawyers' roles lies elsewhere. In a way that few others have done, Orwell brings to light the conspiracy of silence that binds lawyers and clients, impeding the prospects for moral dialogue and growth between the parties.

We find this conspiracy of silence at work in the relationship between Orwell and the Burmese. Orwell describes a relationship of unequal power. As a colonial policeman, a representative of the British Empire, Orwell held a position of power over the Burmese. Yet, as he perceptively suggests, in relationships of unequal power a subtle dance takes place in which the parties take their cues from and jointly shape the actions of each other. In Orwell's essay, all of the participants find themselves moving along certain appointed pathways. A "magnetic field" grabs ruler and subject alike.

Thus in Orwell's essay there is an inevitability about the shooting. As his biographers put it:

> By the time [Orwell] arrives, the elephant has subsided in his fury and in due course is discovered standing in a field, calmly eating grass, appar-

---

    70   Wasserstrom, [*Lawyers as Professionals: Some Moral Issues,*] 5 HUM. RTS. Q. [1] at 5-6 [1975].

ently no longer a danger to anyone. It is now that the tyranny of the Institution—with its power to impose "roles"—begins to function. A kind of ritual ceremony is set in motion, which continues until the elephant has been killed and its carcass stripped. One feels that nothing can alter it: their roles have taken over the lives of the people who play them. The Burmese, virtually all the inhabitants of the quarter, will behave as the Institution expects them to behave; so, in his fashion, will [Orwell].[76]

All of the participants in the "ritual ceremony" perform according to the roles they are playing. The Burmese demand a killing; Orwell shoots the elephant. No one ever questions openly whether the elephant should be shot. There is no dialogue, no give-and-take, between the parties. Everyone acts "as the Institution expects."

Lawyers and clients, too, have their assigned roles to play. According to the traditional paradigm of lawyer-client relationships, clients are expected to be docile and passive. They are to trust their lawyers to act in their best interests. They are not to ask too many questions. On most matters they are expected to defer to the judgments of their lawyers.

In contrast, lawyers are expected to be aggressive, decisive, and competent. As one commentator notes, "The traditional idea is that both parties are best served by the professional's assuming broad control over solutions to the problems brought by the client."[81] Despite the conventional wisdom that decisions about "ends" are for clients and "means" for lawyers, there remains the persistent complaint that lawyers paternalistically dominate the relationship.

The reasons for this lawyer dominance are not hard to imagine. Clients are often vulnerable, troubled persons. They lack understanding of the language or the nuances of the law. They are strangers in the strange land of the courts. They have little choice but to trust in the competence of their lawyer. At the same time, lawyers have been acculturated to see themselves as "members of an elite . . . different from and somewhat better" than those they are paid to serve.

The result is that:

> [I]t is inevitable in the course of a professional relationship that the 'helper' will feel strong or subtle pressure to take command of the situation and wield power over the client. . . . In the relationship of lawyer and client, the lawyer is pushed from many directions, internal (psychological) and external (social, political, and cultural) to take charge and be in control.

Yet such dominance is purchased at a price. In Orwell's case, for example, his power to control events was limited by the expectations of those he governed. Certain decisions that were theoretically within his prerogative—for example, the decision to let the elephant live—were actually not his to make at all, for his freedom to act was circumscribed by the obligations of his role. And so he could write later of "the hollowness, the futility" of British rule in the East.

---

76   *Id.* [PETER STANSKY & WILLIAM ABRAHAMS, THE UNKNOWN ORWELL] at 202 [(1972)].
81   ROSENTHAL, [LAWYER AND CLIENT: WHO'S IN CHARGE?], at 7 [(1974)].

Likewise, the power of lawyers over their clients is more limited and fragile than it first appears. Like Orwell, the lawyer may find herself "forced" to act in ways counter to her best judgment because of her perceptions of what her client wants. Like Orwell, she may feel herself pushed "to and fro" by the will of her clients. What Orwell said of imperialists and subjects is no less true of lawyers and clients: "For it is the condition of his rule that he spend his life in trying to impress the 'natives,' and so in every case he has got to do what the 'natives' expect of him."

In effect, the lawyer says to her client, "I am the expert. I know what to do. Trust me. I am in charge." The client accedes, but in an unwritten deal insists that the lawyer fulfill her grossly exaggerated claims. As a consequence, the lawyer cannot let her expertise be questioned. She cannot admit that she has made a mistake. She cannot risk revealing her ignorance, imperfections, and weaknesses. She cannot permit her client to glimpse "the hollowness, the futility" at the heart of her rule, or else the whole fragile structure of her dominance would crumble.

This helps to explain the shell game that is often played out between lawyers and clients, whereby a lawyer tells her clients just enough about what is going on to convince them that *something* is going on, proposes only those options she herself would choose, politely asks for authority to do what she has already done, uses arcane legal language to comfort and to mystify, or generates much sound and fury and paperwork to assure her bewildered clients that everything that could be done on their behalf is being done. These and other strategies are meant to project an image of lawyer competence, and to make second-guessing by clients impossible. Orwell's words are apt: "I often wondered whether any of the others grasped that I had done it solely to avoid looking like a fool."

This conspiracy of silence extends to moral issues as well. Orwell was convinced that his unstable position of dominance over his subjects could only be maintained by ignoring his moral doubts and shooting the elephant. So too the attorney feels that it would be a fatal sign of "weakness" to raise moral doubts about a client's ends or the means needed to achieve those ends. As Orwell wrote, "[a] sahib has got to act like a sahib; he has got to appear resolute, to know his own mind, and to do definite things."

Because the client takes her cues from the lawyer, the lawyer's reluctance to discuss moral questions and explore moral doubts speaks loudly about the irrelevance of morals and moral discourse to the legal process. Thus, neither party in the symbiotic relationship assumes responsibility for raising moral issues. The lawyer sees herself as an "amoral technician" whose job is to maximize the client's objectives within the constraints of the law. At the same time, the lawyer remains aloof and detached both from her own moral values and from her client as well. The client is ultimately in charge, yet as a practical matter defers to the decisions of the lawyer, decisions often based upon a cramped and inaccurate perception of the client's values. It is as if the parties have agreed that certain messy matters are better left unmentioned. As a result, the moral doubts of lawyer and client are left to fester, and to engender unconscious hostility.

Such a vision of the lawyer-client relationship encourages the illusion that the parties are locked in rigid roles, separate and isolated, with nothing to contribute to the moral universe of the other. It sees the relationship as a zero sum game: Someone must win and someone lose, someone must be on top and someone on the bottom.

No doubt there is an inequality inherent in the lawyer-client relationship. The real problem however is not so much the existence of inequality, as it is the conspiracy of silence that excludes certain matters from discussion. Again, Orwell's essay is instructive. Orwell thought that he had no choice but to kill the elephant. He did not even consider another possibility: He could have talked to the Burmese. He could have confronted their expectations of him. He could have developed a real relationship of mutuality and dialogue. Or at least he could have tried.

Likewise, lawyers are free to refuse to join with their clients in a conspiracy of silence. They can speak openly about their fears and resentments. They can discuss their moral doubts. They can admit that they are just as troubled and fallible as the next person. They can move beyond roles and resentments to forge a new relationship of mutual respect and dialogue in which both sides participate as moral actors and both sides seek to find the best in each other. Moral interdependence can take the place of moral isolation. As theologian Karl Barth put it, "He who takes the risk of counseling must be prepared to be counseled in turn by his brother if there is need of it."[101]

Lawyers may fear that discussing their moral doubts will compromise the adequacy of the representation they provide. They may believe that as a hired gun they cannot question the need to shoot. Yet, in the long run, a lawyer cannot adequately represent a client if she is cut off from her own moral values and concerns. "Moral arguments have their rightful place in law, but someone who has been trained to ignore moral values can hardly be expected to have the resources at hand to make moral arguments on behalf of clients." When lawyers join with their clients in a conspiracy of silence, they necessarily diminish the quality of their representation.

* * * * * * *

Orwell claimed that the masks we wear come to dominate us. The tyrant "wears a mask, and his face grows to fit it." Lawyers wear a mask, too, a "legal persona," which shapes how they think and talk and act. Like any mask, the legal persona narrows the scope of vision. The lawyer comes to believe that she is an "amoral technician," that her feelings are off-limits, that she has a job to do and should do it, that moral doubts must be repressed or ignored, that "a sahib has got to act like a sahib." As Robert Bastress puts it, "[t]he professional mask chills the lawyer-client relationship. The lawyer acts out a role and cordons himself off from his and the client's feelings."[108]

The risk of wearing a mask is that the I, the self behind the mask, will be lost. In the end, there can be only one cure for the lawyer whose face has grown to fit the legal mask—she must find the courage and the trust to take off the mask and meet the other face to face.

---

[101] KARL BARTH, THE HUMANITY OF GOD 86-87 (1960), *quoted in* Thomas L. Shaffer, *Advocacy as Moral Discourse*, 57 N.C. L. REV. 647, 652 (1979).

[108] Robert M. Bastress, *Client Centered Counseling and Moral Accountability for Lawyers*, 10 J. LEGAL PROF. 97, 127 (1985).

As the following excerpt demonstrates, clinic faculty, as well as students, often face professional choices. The faculty member's decision whether to intervene in the student's representation of a client is guided by many factors, including the rules of professional conduct and the faculty member's relationship with both the student and the client. At the core of the faculty member's balancing of these factors lies the role conflict faced by the faculty member who must simultaneously be both a lawyer and a teacher.

George Critchlow, *Professional Responsibility, Student Practice, and the Clinical Teacher's Duty to Intervene*, 26 Gonz. L. Rev. 415 (1990/1991)*

* * *

The live client clinic * * * is a special hybrid, presenting pedagogical and ethical concerns not encountered in other law school settings. The clinical teacher will face role confusion and professional conflict when his or her assessment of what is educationally productive for the student collides with the teacher's assessment of professional obligations owed to the client. This conflict may turn generally on the teacher's sense that the client's interests are not being zealously served and protected by the student advocate. It might stem from a perception that the student is committing violations of more specific ethical rules (*e.g.*, making a false statement of material fact to a tribunal) or committing errors or omissions which would constitute professional negligence. The clinical teacher may also have a particular moral sensibility about the specific case, or about conflict resolution in general, which differs from that of the student and which suggests responsibilities or constraints beyond those dictated by the applicable ethical code.

Such conflict raises the prospect of the clinical teacher's intervening directly between the student and client to safeguard the client's interests or to promote some other moral objective. But the very act of direct intervention disturbs the student-teacher and student-client relationships in ways that can produce undesired and unintended consequences. The student may feel his or her judgment has been unnecessarily impugned. Intervention may cause the student to feel demoralized and inadequate and to become overly dependent on the clinical teacher. The student-client relationship is at risk of being undermined. The client may infer that he or she is receiving inept or second-rate legal services and may be more circumspect in further dealings with the student. The resulting mix of emotions and uncertain expectations injects instability and distrust into the problem-solving process which can hinder fur-

---

*   Reprinted with permission.

ther work on the client's case. Thus the act of clinical intervention, while motivated by ethical propriety and professional responsibility, can result in an unsatisfactory educational experience for the student, an anxious legal experience for the client—regardless of the objective legal result—and serious role conflict for the clinical teacher.

* * *

I. What is Meant by Intervention by the Clinical Teacher

The term "intervention" in this article is used to describe the act of a clinical teacher directly engaging the client, adversary party, or adjudicative process in a manner which replaces the teacher's authority and judgment for that of the student. The clinical teacher's assumption of direct responsibility brings a dynamic new factor into a case. It may be good or bad, but it changes the experience for all concerned. Client, adversary party, and court may all manifest new expectations and unpredictable responses when the established student-client relationship is disrupted.

I do not use intervention to mean the one-on-one supervision of the student by the clinical teacher. The teacher is routinely called upon to communicate information to the student. The teaching mode may be expository, dialectic, evaluative or demonstrative—depending on the teacher's objective—but effective skills training and the student's development of reflective self-criticism could not be accomplished without regular teacher involvement. I also do not use the term intervention to encompass aggressive criticism or outright disapproval of a student's written work product, problem-solving strategy, interviewing skills, trial tactics, legal analysis, or the like. Directive supervision and criticism may detrimentally affect the learning process by transferring responsibility for making decisions from student to teacher. It may also suggest a need for reflection on the part of the clinical teacher as to teaching style, interpersonal communication, and the way people learn. But unless the criticism is palpable to the client, it is not intervention in the sense that the clinic teacher has directly assumed responsibility for performing the lawyering activity in question.

* * *

II. Developing Criteria for Intervention

* * *

B. *Beyond the Rules: Balancing the Needs of the Student and the Client*

The student practice rules, Rules of Professional Conduct, and the Guidelines for Clinical Legal Education can generally be interpreted as defining a minimum standard for teacher intervention. This standard requires intervention only in cases where a student is in a position to irreparably damage the client. Although intervention to assure more than minimal compliance with professional responsibility rules is surely contemplated, these authorities do not go so far as to impose a standard which would assure the client the quality of representation which the clinical teacher could personally provide.

This "irreparable damage" approach to intervention appears to be the practice of at least some clinical teachers. Based on my discussions with other clinical teachers, including my colleagues at Gonzaga, the standard for intervention actually employed varies from teacher to teacher. Roughly speaking, there are two camps. Some teachers will intervene only when they believe it necessary to avoid irreparable harm. Others tend to intervene when they believe student work or performance, while minimally competent, seriously departs from the level of skill and judgment the teacher would bring to bear on the particular case.

The "irreparable harm" group views learning from mistakes and self-discovery as crucial to the student's clinical education. Some proponents of this view question the presumption that the teacher's judgment of how to handle a case is always better or more accurate than the student's. They are willing to sacrifice efficiency and control for the perceived educational benefits derived from student autonomy so long as malpractice is avoided and the Rules of Professional Conduct are not violated. Individuals in this group implicitly see themselves more as teachers than lawyers.

The other group represents the view that the client's interests are generally superior to the student's educational needs and desires. The proponents of this view are concerned that clients not be used as guinea pigs in the effort to train law students. They believe that it is not sufficient simply to avoid malpractice. The client also has an interest in reasonably efficient representation and in avoiding anxiety and demands caused by student mistakes and delays. An additional concern is that it is not appropriate to inflict on the legal system and other participants in the adjudicative process inordinate strain on resources and time which may result from repeated, albeit remediable, student mistakes. Intervention for teachers of this persuasion is therefore more likely to occur because the teacher implicitly places the interests of the client (and perhaps the system) over those of the student. Put another way, intervention is more likely when the teacher identifies more with his or her role as lawyer than teacher.

The difference in views on intervention is not surprising. The purpose of clinical student practice, in addition to technical skills training, is to provide students an opportunity to develop sound and independent legal judgment, including good moral judgment. The naked assumption of professional responsibility for a real client will not guarantee ethical or competent behavior on the part of the student any more than it does for the practicing lawyer. However, the failure to allow a student to, in fact, be responsible for a client increases the likelihood the student will not fully explore or reflect on what it means to be a lawyer and will treat professional responsibility as simply another set of rules to be learned on the path to the bar. Intervention, therefore, may be regarded as an obstruction to the student's professional growth, or may be viewed as appropriate in order to protect the client and avoid the student's perception that it is acceptable to subordinate the client's interest to that of the student.

For the clinical teacher, somewhere between the roles of teacher and lawyer lies the obligation to assess the dangers that can result from allowing a student to "practice" professional responsibility on a real human being. Criteria must be identified and articulated for determining when client-centered experiential learning presents an unacceptable risk of harm to the client or others.

C. *Using Core Values as Criteria for Intervention Decisions*

Clinical teaching, like the practice of law, is an endeavor complicated by many variables. Students, like clients, will differ in their strengths, weaknesses, and goals. The personality, experience, intelligence and moral vision a student brings to the clinic will affect how that student relates to clients, perceives problems, formulates solutions, makes decisions, and evaluates results. The same variables will affect how a teacher relates to and interacts with students.

Because of the dynamic and variable nature of the process, the task of the clinical teacher is both routinized and endlessly creative. The unique combination presented in every new mix of student, teacher, client, and legal problem makes it difficult to define or prescribe with any precision a uniform standard for teacher intervention. Nonetheless, there are discrete professional responsibility values common to all intervention decisions. These values emanate from codified ethical rules and can be identified by asking the following questions:

1. Is the client's relationship primarily with the student or with the clinical teacher?
2. Has the client consented to primary representation by the law student and been adequately informed of the advantages and disadvantages of student representation?
3. Is the clinical teacher familiar with the personality type, technical skill, and overall competency of the law student?
4. Is the clinical teacher as fully apprised of the facts, law and legal strategy as the student?
5. Will intervention by the clinical teacher, even if not required to prevent irreparable harm, significantly avoid the imposition of additional burdens on the client, court and other interested parties?

1. The Student-Client Relationship

The first question focuses the teacher's attention on the reality of who is representing the client. If the student is assigned primary responsibility for the case or a particular task but in reality that responsibility has been assumed by the clinical teacher, then considerations about disturbing the student-client relationship will be less important. Communication and decision-making take on a markedly personal and confidential quality in the lawyer-client relationship. A client's confidence in one individual is not automatically transferable to another. The client is likely to expect that the person with whom the client has an established primary working relationship will be the person who performs a given task. If that person is the clinical teacher and not the student, it would be appropriate for the teacher to carry out the required lawyering task both from the standpoint of honoring the client's legitimate expectations and because the teacher may be better informed and prepared. On the other hand, if the primary lawyer-client relation is with the student, intervention by the teacher could be disruptive.

2. The Client's Informed Consent

The second question, dealing with the client's "informed consent," is related to the first but goes further by requiring the clinical teacher to ascertain the degree to which the client comprehends and voluntarily assumes any risks associated with representation by a student rather than a more experienced lawyer. Some states and the ABA model student practice rule require the written consent of the client before a student can appear in court or an administrative tribunal on the client's behalf. Washington's APR 9 requires only that the client be informed of the "legal intern's status."[51] No jurisdiction appears to formally require a detailed explanation of risks which might inhere in the client's acceptance of student representation.

Both common sense and ethical standards suggest the importance of selecting a lawyer on an informed and intelligent basis. While it is true that many low income persons come to law school clinics as the last resort for legal representation, this is certainly not always the case, and should not in any event justify a failure to fully apprise a prospective client that primary responsibility for his or her case will rest with a relatively inexperienced student. To the extent a client lacks information or receives ambiguous information concerning the nature of the representation, the client arguably has a claim to a level of services which can be personally delivered or performed by the licensed lawyer charged with professional responsibility for the case—the clinical teacher. In such circumstances intervention may be appropriate to avoid exposing the client to risks which he or she did not knowingly and voluntarily assume.

3. The Teacher's Familiarity with the Student

The third question relates to the clinical teacher's ability to diagnose and evaluate the student's aptitude and competency for accomplishing a particular lawyering activity. If the teacher is not in a position adequately to judge and anticipate how the student will respond to unexpected events, the question whether to intervene will call for speculation and should be resolved in favor of the more reliable representation by the clinical teacher.

There is no such thing as competency *per se*. There are, however, certain generic competencies which would apply to most, if not all, lawyering tasks. If the teacher observes that necessary underlying skills appear to be manifested adequately or inadequately by the student over a number of occasions, the teacher will be more able to generalize about what is likely to occur in the future. The student may be regarded as more or less competent in relation to the observation processes that lead to the teacher's conclusion. Hence, even if a student has never actually conducted jury *voir dire* before a live jury, the clinical teacher might confidently predict how the student will perform if the teacher knows something of the student's proficiency in the relevant underlying competencies (*e.g.*, oral, problemsolving, and professional responsibility competencies).

---

51 WASH. SUP. CT. ADMISSIONS TO PRACTICE Rule 9(c)(2) . * * *

The clinical teacher will also want to be familiar with the personality type of the student in order to predict future behavior and judgment. Character traits are important dimensions of lawyering competency and should be evaluated as such. The clinical teacher should take special care to protect the client from the immature or emotionally unstable student. This may be especially difficult for the busy teacher who is otherwise blinded by the student's intellectual brilliance or technical skill.

Ideally the clinical teacher should not be in the position of supervising the performance stage of lawyering activity without having adequately evaluated the student regarding relevant competencies and emotional maturity. The need to intervene will largely correspond to the teacher's confidence in predicting how the student will handle the unexpected. Where the teacher, for whatever reason, lacks the diagnostic data necessary to predict student competence, intervention should be liberally employed to ensure reliable representation.

4. The Teacher's Familiarity with the Case

The fourth question dovetails with the concerns raised in the third question but with a focus on the clinical teacher's competency to perform the lawyering activity in question. Intervention implies that the teacher can personally perform the task more competently than the student, or in a manner more likely to comply with relevant ethical demands. The clinical teacher will presumably be more proficient in both the generic and specific competencies expected of a lawyer. But if the teacher is not personally well prepared and apprised of the facts, law and legal strategy necessary for competent representation in the specific case, it is less likely intervention would accomplish its intended purpose of remedying unsatisfactory student performance. This is, of course, the worst of all possible situations for the clinical teacher and a dilemma which, in itself, arguably constitutes unprofessional conduct. While the chances of a conscientious clinical teacher being totally unprepared to take over for a student are remote, the teacher's level of preparation and knowledge will not be constant from case to case. A teacher's ability to improve on the performance of a student will be limited by the degree to which the teacher lacks relevant and specific information. To that same extent, the clinical teacher should exercise caution in assuming direct responsibility for representation. A conservative approach to intervention in such circumstances will also minimize any danger that the uninformed teacher will merely substitute his or her style of advocacy or preferred choices for the disparate and possibly more thoughtful conduct of the student.

5. Burdens on the Client and the System

Issues raised by the fifth question relate to the need for intervention in those situations where student representation is not inimical to an ultimate outcome favorable to the client but significantly impacts the client or legal system in collateral ways. Even if intervention is not necessary to assure the desired result, the clinical teacher should consider the consequences of student performance in terms of delay, financial and emotional costs to the client, and impact on the resources of the court and interested parties.

A lawyer has a duty to "act with reasonable diligence and promptness in representing a client"[63] and to make "reasonable efforts to expedite litigation consistent with the interests of the client."[64] Unnecessary or excessive delay in handling a client's case can adversely affect the client's interests. Even if the delay does not affect substantive or procedural rights, it may cause the client needless anxiety. It may also frustrate the prompt and efficient work of courts or administrative tribunals.

Lawyers also have a duty of fairness to the opposing party and counsel and an obligation to respect the rights of third persons. A lawyer's responsibility to the client does not imply that it is acceptable to unnecessarily embarrass, delay or burden others. Substantial legal reasons may, of course, dictate a course of conduct which does have these effects. But responsible professional conduct should take into account the larger context in which the lawyer operates and the power he or she has over lives of others.

Where the clinical teacher believes intervention will expedite resolution of the legal problem and save time, money and anxiety for the client and others, there should be less reluctance to take over primary responsibility for the relevant task. For example, in supervision of a student-conducted deposition, intervention may not be necessary to prevent irreparable harm to the client's cause. But it may be desirable and appropriate to avoid the necessity of having to reconvene the deposition at a later time to ferret out information which the student missed.

It may be argued that the clinical teacher will always be in a superior position to expedite litigation and minimize emotional and financial costs to the client and others. The discussion concerning other intervention considerations indicates this is not the case. In any event, this criterion for intervention will necessarily have to be weighed and balanced against those other considerations.

The five listed considerations are by no means exclusive. They do, however, encompass values at the core of the clinical teacher's professional responsibility to clients. These can be summarized as follows:

1) Respect for the client's professional relationship with the student and expectations flowing from that relationship;
2) Respect for the client's right to make an informed decision about student representation and its advantages or disadvantages;
3) Concern for the client reflected by the clinical teacher's ability to adequately diagnose and predict student competencies;
4) Concern for the client reflected by the clinical teacher's personal readiness and competence to assume client representation responsibilities; and
5) Concern for adverse collateral consequences to the client and others which might be avoided through intervention.

* * *

---

63   MODEL RULES OF PROFESSIONAL CONDUCT Rule 1.3 (1990).
64   *Id.* at Rule 3.2.

A unitary code of ethics might be counterproductive to a diverse bar. In the next excerpt Eleanor W. Myers considers whether different rules of conduct ought to be adopted for different types of law practice.

Eleanor W. Myers, *"Simple Truths" About Moral Education*, 45 AM. U. L. REV. 823 (1996)*

* * *

* * * Lawyers do different kinds of work, ranging from high stakes business litigation to counseling individuals. Lawyers work in different organizational settings, ranging from private law firms of varying sizes to in-house legal departments to government and public interest practices. Lawyers work in different geographic settings, ranging from urban to rural. Lawyers represent different kinds of clients, ranging from wealthy corporations to poor individuals. Authors of a 1982 study of the Chicago Bar, documenting these differences, characterized the notion of a single unified profession as one that "no longer fit[s] the facts."[83]

We are told that the tumultuous process that led to the ABA's adoption of the Model Rules of Professional Conduct included arguments from all sectors of the profession over the proper definition of professional conduct. Controversy regarding issues such as confidentiality and entity representation highlighted how lawyers in different practices expressed their professional concerns in different ways.

> Taking trial lawyers, corporate counsel, legal services lawyers, code enforcers, judges, private practitioners in large and small firms, law professors, and others properly into account . . . one is struck by the heterogeneity of ethical views in today's profession. . . . Legal services lawyers want rules that guarantee their zealous commitment to clients and special attention to the problem of advancing litigation expenses for the indigent and the problem of maintaining professional independence from lay employers. Securities lawyers want ethics rules that buffer them from an aggressive SEC. Small-town lawyers do not want to formalize their ongoing client relationships by putting fee agreements in writing. Bar counsel want the easiest rules to enforce. Trial lawyers want to minimize the perception that they might have to betray their clients' trust, even at the risk of having to blink at perjury. And so on.[85]

---

*   Reprinted with permission.

[83]   JOHN P. HEINZ & EDWARD O. LAUMANN, CHICAGO LAWYERS: THE SOCIAL STRUCTURE OF THE BAR 3 (1982). * * *

[85]   [Theodore Schneyer, *Professionalism as Politics: The Making of a Modern Legal Ethics Code*, *in* LAWYERS' IDEALS/LAWYERS' PRACTICES: TRANSFORMATIONS IN THE AMERICAN LEGAL PROFESSION] at 140-41 [(1992)].

Professional diversity stems from at least three important sources: the nature of the professional work itself, the diversity of the people engaged in practice, and the contextualized nature of ethical decisionmaking. This means that each ethical question is, in important ways, distinct from every other one because of its unique context. * * *

* * *

The diversity of practice and the discretion afforded by the professional mores to construct alternative conceptions of lawyering to accommodate those differences have led scholars to a more comprehensive theory of professionalism. They reject the notion of a unitary vision and substitute the idea that different workplaces and practice situations produce differing professional visions; that there are multiple "arenas of professionalism."[89] "[L]awyers possess widely varying conceptions of professional ideals that correspond to the historical and practical circumstances of their work."

Indeed within those arenas, lawyers have constructed multiple, even conflicting, ideas of what constitutes professional lawyering. The struggles over, and debates about those competing visions are themselves as important as arenas in which notions of professionalism are forged.

Conflicting articulations of professional values of loyalty and confidentiality in different practice settings provide good examples of the various professional visions that result from the diversity of professional work.

The conflict of interest provisions of the Model Rules of Professional Conduct provide that, absent consent, a lawyer should not represent a client whose interests are directly adverse to another client, or in circumstances where the lawyer's representation may be materially limited by the lawyer's responsibilities to another client or to a third person. The comments to that Rule advise that a lawyer should not seek consent "when a disinterested lawyer would conclude that the client should not agree to the representation under the circumstances."

The conflict of interest rule is often invoked in a litigation or adversarial context to preclude a lawyer from simultaneously representing clients whose interests actually or potentially diverge. Lawyers who represent clients in non-adversarial settings, however, face distinct issues in multiple client representation. For example, lawyers who do estate planning for married couples face a situation in which clients share many goals, but also may have potential conflicts with one another regarding such matters as distributive schemes or the disposition of separate assets. The ethical dilemmas of estate lawyers were so distinct from those arising in the litigation context that the ABA Section of Real Property, Probate, and Trust Law (Section) wrote a separate set of recommendations and commentaries setting forth its "pre-

---

89   Nelson & Trubek, *Arenas of Professionalism[: The Professional Ideologies of Lawyers in Context, in* Lawyers' Ideals/Lawyers' Practices: Transformations in the American Legal Profession] at 177 [(Robert L. Nelson et al., eds. 1992)].

scriptive guide" on those ethical questions.[97] In those recommendations, the Section characterized the ABA's Model Rules "as a code of conduct for lawyers, written primarily to govern the conduct of advocates," describing the limitations of the Rules as they apply to lawyers representing married couples as follows:

> From an ethical standpoint, the risk is that, in counseling the couple as a unit for tax and planning purposes, neither individual will receive the representation a single individual might receive under the same circumstances. Yet family needs, tax incentives and the very nature of marriage often make separate counseling unnecessary, and indeed, inappropriate. Lawyers may look to the Model Rules to guide them in the representation, but will find only a set of rules that assumes the existence of well-defined conflicts between well-defined clients.

The Section's recommendations as to modes of representation under the Model Rules, guidelines for observing confidentiality, and standards for obtaining consent, all departed from the litigator's conception of a lawyer single-mindedly representing an individual client.

The Real Property, Probate and Trust Section's report attempted to harmonize the reality of a distinct kind of practice with the adversarial ethic that the Section perceived to dominate the ABA Model Rules. It is an uneasy alliance. It highlights a distinct notion of professionalism that animates that arena of practice.

The American Academy of Matrimonial Lawyers provides another example of a distinct ethic developed to meet the special attributes of a particular field of practice. In its Preliminary Statement to Bounds of Advocacy, a guide to ethical conduct for family lawyers, the Academy stated: "Existing codes do not provide adequate guidance to the matrimonial lawyer. . . . [T]heir emphasis on zealous representation of individual clients in criminal and some civil cases is not always appropriate in family law matters . . . . Many [family law practitioners] have encountered instances where the [Rules of Professional Conduct] provided insufficient, or even undesirable, guidance."[105] The Matrimonial Lawyers' guide set forth standards of conduct that departed from the traditional conception of lawyering responsibilities, particularly with respect to children. Those recommendations included considering the welfare of the children in any marital dispute, prohibiting the use of child custody demands for financial leverage or vindictiveness, and requiring disclosure of a substantial risk of child abuse, even if the information was otherwise confidential under the ethics rules or the attorney-client privilege. The special regard for children in the Matrimonial Lawyers' guide is a departure from the traditional conception of a lawyer single-mindedly pursuing client goals with minimal regard for the interests of third parties.

---

97   Reports of the Special Study Committee on Professional Responsibility of the Section of Real Property, Probate and Trust Law of the American Bar Association, *Editor's Introduction*, 28 REAL PROP., PROB. & TR. J. 763, 763 (1994). * * *

105   AMERICAN ACADEMY OF MATRIMONIAL LAWYERS, STANDARDS OF CONDUCT 3-4 (1991).

* * *

Questions of appropriate professional behavior are not answered simply, nor are they susceptible of answers *a priori*. Such questions require assessments of context, competing values, and one's own responsibilities. That someone has faced and resolved a similar question before does not mean that the same answer is appropriate in a different context, with a different client or for a different lawyer. Often such questions raise profound issues at the core of our profession. Two examples will illustrate this point.

Lawyers in practice make mistakes. A relatively common example is the misdelivery of a privileged document to an opposing party. The professional responsibility questions are: (i) what the receiving lawyer should do upon discovering the mistake, i.e., read the document, return it unread, or turn it over to a judge (if the matter is in litigation); and (ii) whether the lawyer may make that decision without consulting the client. These relatively straightforward and recurring questions have generated ethics opinions, contradictory court decisions, and scholarly commentary. To resolve the questions, the ABA and the courts have balanced the confidentiality concerns of the client against the duty of diligent representation. The opinions are conflicting, sometimes resulting in the return of the document and other times not. The ultimate resolution of the question implicates our deepest notions of what it means to behave professionally. Are we bound to capitalize on our opponent's mistakes? Must we defer to our client's wishes on this point? Does merely raising the question contradict fundamental notions of trust and shared humanity which ought to characterize our dealings with others?

As another example, a lawyer counsels a client about whether or not to accept a proffered settlement of a case. The client, strapped for funds and nervous about testifying, is inclined to accept. The lawyer thinks the offer is inadequate and that the client's chances of obtaining substantially more money at trial are excellent. The professional responsibility question is how much pressure the lawyer should exert to influence the client to follow the lawyer's recommendation. This relatively straightforward question raises profound issues about the allocation of power in the lawyer-client relationship. It is a subject that has attracted legal scholarship, moral philosophy, and writing about practical skills. Although practitioners face this question every day, it is complex and deserves sustained attention.

The message that professional responsibility questions are profound and difficult, and that it is professional to raise such questions is one that every teacher in law school can impart, even if that teacher does not "know the answer." It is important for our students to be encouraged to raise and ponder these issues, and to "rehearse" their conversations about them.

* * *

Cases often pose the potential for conflicts of interest. In the following excerpt, Debra Bassett Perschbacher and Rex R. Perschbacher look at conflicts of interest inherent in a lawyer's representation of a city in a civil rights action. The lawyer's initial consultation with a codefendant of the city can raise tremendous ethical dilemmas for the lawyer. The authors use this scenario as a vehicle for exploring the parameters of the rules regarding conflicts.

Debra Bassett Perschbacher and Rex R. Perschbacher, *Enter at Your Own Risk: The Initial Consultation and Conflicts of Interest*, 3 GEO. J. OF LEGAL ETHICS 689 (1990)*

INTRODUCTION

Despite a regular and increasing volume of commentary addressing lawyers' conflicts of interest, the preventing, detecting, and resolving of conflicts remains a difficult and elusive problem for lawyers in every area of practice. In lofty and direct terms, lawyers are directed to exercise their professional judgment "solely for the benefit of [the] client and free of compromising influences and loyalties." Unfortunately, in practice, it is never this easy. It may be difficult or impossible to decide who the client is; to determine whether there is one client or several; to inform the client about possible conflicts and still retain the client's confidence; and to investigate conflicts and effectively represent the client. Representation begun entirely above-board may result in conflicts requiring the lawyer to cease representing the client. The court may disqualify a lawyer from representing a client over their joint and vigorous objection. And preventative steps taken to cure or avoid a conflict, even when affected parties consent, may fail or even backfire.

Consider this possible situation. One morning, Lawyer receives a telephone call from the Town of Reddirt, California, a regular client. The Town has just received notice of a section 1983 action filed against it by Traveler. Traveler alleges that he was stopped by a Reddirt police officer for a traffic violation, and that in the course of that stop, the officer used unnecessary force and called him racial epithets. Traveler has also named the police officer as a defendant in the lawsuit. The Town asks Lawyer to represent it in this action, and asks if Lawyer could also represent the police officer. After discussing the matter at some length over the telephone, Lawyer agrees to meet with the police officer in her office that afternoon, intending to do some preliminary investigation into the charges.

When the officer arrives, Lawyer introduces herself as the Town's counsel and asks the officer to tell her what happened. During the course of her afternoon discussion with the officer, the officer reveals that indeed he did throw Traveler against the side of a wall and use racial slurs, because he didn't like the way Traveler looked. Lawyer informs the officer that she will contact him again soon.

---

    *   Reprinted with permission of the publisher, © 1990 Georgetown Journal of Legal Ethics & Georgetown University.

At this point, Lawyer might wish, for various reasons, to elect one of the following options: (1) decline any role in the case; (2) attempt to represent both the Town and the police officer; or (3) attempt to represent only the Town. Assume for the moment that Lawyer sees no problems and proceeds as lawyer for the Town.

Not too much later, Lawyer realizes there could be a potential conflict of interest if she represents both the Town and the officer. She then telephones the police officer and informs him that she is unable to represent him because it is likely that a conflict of interest would develop between the officer's legal position and that of the Town, who is Lawyer's regular client. Discovery begins, and the officer obtains independent counsel. Approximately two months later, Lawyer receives a call from the officer's attorney. The attorney states that when the officer met with Lawyer that afternoon two months ago, he believed Lawyer was representing both himself and the Town, and that due to that belief he revealed confidential information to Lawyer. The attorney demands that Lawyer withdraw from the case, and threatens to file a motion for disqualification if necessary. The Town does not want to substitute lawyers. What can Lawyer do? What could Lawyer have done to avoid this problem?

This not-too-hypothetical example illustrates that the label "conflict of interest" may oversimplify a series of difficult issues in legal regulation and professional responsibility. These include the fundamental issue of who is a client; whether some kind of "Miranda warning" must be given by a lawyer-investigator to persons she deals with at the request of the nominal client; and how a lawyer can possibly fulfill her duties of loyalty and zealous advocacy and at the same time retain the chance to continue with a valuable representation undertaken for a long-standing client.

Although lawyers' conflicts of interest are nothing new, adversaries and judges are only now giving them increased attention. Not only are lawyers subject to closer scrutiny for potential conflicts, but the changing nature of law practice, particularly the growth in average law firm size, and increased procedural complexity in litigation, create an increased likelihood for conflicts where none existed before.

* * *

I. THE GENERAL RULES CONCERNING CONFLICTS OF INTEREST

A. INTRODUCTION

Generally, an attorney may represent more than one client in a matter involving a potential conflict of interest only if the attorney reasonably believes that he or she can adequately represent both clients' interests and both clients consent after full disclosure of the implications of joint representation.[12] Even with client consent, an attorney may not represent multiple parties to the same transaction whose interests or positions are fundamentally antagonistic. But it is ethically permissible for a lawyer to represent

> multiple parties whose interests are generally aligned, such as the parties
> to the formation of a corporation. However, should it become evident dur-

---

[12]   MODEL RULES OF PROFESSIONAL CONDUCT Rule 1.7 (1983) * * *.

ing the multiple representation that the lawyer cannot adequately represent the interests of each party, or should any party revoke consent, the lawyer must withdraw and may not thereafter represent one party against another on the same matter.

Among co-parties in litigation, conflicts of interest may arise explicitly and unquestionably if they assert cross-claims against each other. With regard to cross-claims, co-parties are indistinguishable from traditional litigation adversaries, a situation in which joint representation is universally proscribed. However, conflicts are just as real when co-parties ought to make cross-claims although they have not formally done so. Thus, an attorney for co-parties is under a continuing obligation to consider possible claims among her clients and inform them if there are grounds to make such claims.

Potential co-parties' cross-claims include claims for affirmative relief among co-plaintiffs (in effect re-aligning one or more co-plaintiffs as defendants on such claims); and claims for contribution or indemnity among co-defendants. Although this kind of co-defendant conflict may be limited or avoided by an indemnification agreement, it is no panacea. The agreement must be comprehensive enough to encompass the foreseeable indemnity claims that have been or may be made. If unforeseen situations arise, the conflict will reemerge. Such agreements may limit the lawyer's ability to assert claims that fall within the indemnity agreement, thus compromising the lawyer's duty of loyalty and zealous advocacy on behalf of one or more of the co-parties. Obviously, before allowing her clients to enter into an indemnification agreement, full and informed consent is necessary, including full disclosure of potential conflicts and how the lawyer's effective advocacy may be limited. But this is not surprising. Indemnification agreements are merely a subspecies of the initial client consent necessary before a lawyer may undertake any joint representation.

"An impermissible conflict may exist by reason of substantial discrepancy in the parties' testimony, incompatibility in positions in relation to an opposing party or the fact that there are substantially different possibilities of settlement of the claims or liabilities in question."[18] Whether multiple representation is proper is determined on a case-by-case basis after considering the interests involved.

An attorney has an affirmative duty to disclose to clients any potential conflicts of interest. If a lawyer, for example, represents multiple defendants, such multiple representation is permissible if each client is fully apprised of the potential for a conflict of interest, is given the opportunity to consult independent counsel, and waives any claims against the other clients. However, should conflicts later develop, the lawyer must withdraw.[22]

An attorney has a duty to withdraw if the representation will violate the attorney's professional responsibility. If the attorney does not withdraw, opposing counsel may bring a motion to disqualify or recuse the attorney.

---

18   MODEL RULES Rule 1.7 comment (1983) * * *.

22   MODEL RULES Rule 1.16(a)(1) (requiring attorney to withdraw if "the representation will result in violation of the rules of professional conduct or other law") * * *.

Conflict of interest rules also limit lawyers' ability to represent clients because of previous representations. The rules here are not as strict as for simultaneous representations. Generally, a lawyer cannot represent a client in an ongoing matter when that representation is substantially related to a prior representation in which the lawyer represented an adversary of the current client.[25] The two disqualifying elements must each be satisfied. The former and current representations must be adverse, and the two representations must be substantially related. In this way the twin objectives of protecting client confidences and preserving the lawyer's preeminent duty of loyalty guide any inquiry into a possibly disqualifying conflict of interest.

By demonstrating a "substantial relationship" between the former representation and current litigation, opposing counsel establishes a prima facie case that the attorney received confidential information. There is a split of authority as to whether disqualification is mandatory or discretionary once a "substantial relationship" is shown, with the majority finding disqualification mandatory. Any doubts as to the existence of a conflict of interest should be resolved in favor of disqualification.

B. RULES OF PROFESSIONAL CONDUCT

The American Bar Association *Model Code of Professional Responsibility* provides that an attorney may not represent a client "if it would be likely to involve him in representing differing interests."[29] No distinction is made between concurrent and successive conflicts.

The conflict analysis is more complex, but more precise, under the *Model Rules*.[30] Concurrent conflicts are treated under Rule 1.7; successive client conflicts under Rule 1.9. Rule 1.7 prohibits directly adverse representation and representation that may be limited materially by the lawyer's responsibilities to another client unless the lawyer reasonably believes the clients will not be adversely affected and each affected client consents after consultation. Potentially disqualifying successive client conflicts also require consent of the former client but are limited to representations in "the same or a substantially related matter" in which the present client's interests are "materially adverse" to the former client's interests. Waiver by client consent is clearly favored in the successive conflicts situation.

---

25   MODEL RULES Rule 1.9(b) * * *.

29   MODEL CODE DR 5-105(A) (1982). DR 5-105(B) provides:
A lawyer shall not continue multiple employment if the exercise of his independent professional judgment in behalf of a client will be or is likely to be adversely affected by his representation of another client, or if it would be likely to involve him in representing differing interests, except to the extent permitted under DR 5-105(C). [footnote omitted].

30   MODEL RULES Rule 1.7(b). Rule 1.7(b) provides:
[a] lawyer shall not represent a client if the representation of that client may be materially limited by the lawyer's responsibilities to another client . . . unless . . . the client consents after consultation. When representation of multiple clients in a single matter is undertaken, the consultation shall include explanation of the implications of the common representation and the advantages and risks involved. * * *

There are several considerations underlying the various rules concerning professional conduct. Perhaps the most important of these considerations is the preservation of any confidences communicated by the client to the attorney.[33] Another consideration is the client's expectation of receiving the attorney's loyalty.[34] Finally, these provisions are meant to protect "[b]oth the fact and the appearance of total professional commitment."[35]

"Regardless of the particular language used by the courts and the rules of professional conduct to define the standards, a common principle underlies all of them: the interests of the clients are primary, and the interests of the lawyers are secondary."[36] "Doubts as to the existence of an asserted conflict of interest should be resolved in favor of disqualification."[37]

A lawyer caught in a conflict of interest representation is subject to discipline. If a client is harmed by the conflict, the lawyer may be subject to a malpractice action and possible damages. In litigation, however, the most frequent consequence is a motion brought to disqualify the lawyer from representing one or more of her clients. When conflicts arise after the initial engagement, ethical rules require the lawyer to withdraw from the representation.[41] In addition to the individual lawyer or lawyers directly involved in the conflict of interests, imputed disqualification will usually disqualify other members of the individual lawyer's firm.[42] The imputed disqualification rule is not absolute. It may be waived by consent of the affected clients,[43] and it is limited when applied to lawyers joining and leaving affected firms. Some courts have further limited the imputed disqualification rule by treating it as a rebuttable presumption, not an absolute bar.

II. WHEN DOES (AND WHEN SHOULD) AN ATTORNEY-CLIENT RELATIONSHIP ARISE?

A. WHEN DOES THE ATTORNEY-CLIENT RELATIONSHIP ARISE?

The basic ethical rules regulating conflicts of interest between clients assume that the lawyer already knows who the client is. However, at times one of the

---

33   MODEL CODE Canon 4; *id.* DR 4-101(B)(2); MODEL RULES Rule 1.6 (1983) * * *.

34   MODEL CODE EC 5-1 ("The professional judgment of a lawyer should be exercised, within the bounds of the law, solely for the benefit of his client and free of compromising influences and loyalties. Neither his personal interests, the interests of other clients, nor the desires of third persons should be permitted to dilute his loyalty to his client. [footnote omitted]"); MODEL RULES Rule 1.7 comment ("[l]oyalty is an essential element in the lawyer's relationship to a client.") * * *.

35   *Trone* [v. Smith], 621 F.2d [994], at 998 [(9th Cir. 1980)] * * *.

36   Haagen-Dazs Co. v. Perche No! Gelato, Inc., 639 F. Supp. 282, 286 (N.D. Cal. 1986).

37   Westinghouse Elec. Corp. v. Gulf Oil Corp., 588 F.2d 221, 225 (7th Cir. 1978) * * *.

41   MODEL RULES Rule 1.16(a)(1) (attorney shall withdraw if representation will violate the rules of professional conduct); MODEL CODE DR 2-110(B)(2) (attorney will withdraw if continued representation will violate the disciplinary rules) * * *.

42   MODEL RULES Rule 1.10(a), provides: "While lawyers are associated in a firm, none of them shall knowingly represent a client when any one of them practicing alone would be prohibited from doing so by [the concurrent and successive conflict of interest rules]" * * *.

43   MODEL RULES Rule 1.10(d) * * *.

lawyer's most difficult and critical issues is to determine who the client is. Although the proposition that an attorney would have difficulty determining the identity of his or her client sounds absurd at first blush, this problem arises with some regularity. Oddly, an inexperienced or incautious lawyer may also discover that he or she has involuntarily acquired an unintended client. This, too, arises fairly often in some areas of practice. Returning to this Article's beginning hypothetical, Lawyer believed she was conducting a "preliminary investigation" by meeting with the police officer. Yet she subsequently was threatened with disqualification because she inadvertently had acquired an additional client. How could this happen?

Two approaches exist to the attorney-client relationship issue. The first is that the meeting between Lawyer and the police officer constituted an initial consultation; the second is that the officer reasonably believed Lawyer represented him as well as the Town. It is important to note that no specific formalities are required to create an attorney-client relationship. For example, the lack of a fee agreement is of no consequence in this determination. "When a party seeking legal advice consults an attorney at law and secures that advice, the relation of attorney and client is established prima facie."[49]

Lawyer's meeting with the police officer closely resembles an initial consultation. Clearly the protection of the attorney-client relationship extends to those individuals who meet with an attorney with the intent to retain him or her. "The fiduciary relationship existing between lawyer and client extends to preliminary consultation by a prospective client with a view to retention of the lawyer, although actual employment does not result."[51]

Second, even in the absence of a formal attorney-client relationship, attorney-client protections have been extended to individuals who conveyed confidential information to an attorney with a reasonable belief the attorney was acting on their behalf.

Thus, two possible approaches exist to the attorney-client relationship issue. The first is that the meeting between Lawyer and the police officer constituted an initial consultation, which seems likely. The fact that Lawyer and the officer did not formally enter into an independent private relationship is of no consequence in determining whether attorney-client protections apply. The second approach is that the officer reasonably believed Lawyer represented him as well as the Town. Under the facts of this situation, whether the police officer "reasonably" believed Lawyer represented him is a question of fact. One could argue that because Lawyer stated that she was the Town's attorney and that she had to assess the situation, the officer should be precluded from any reasonable belief that Lawyer was representing him.

On the other hand, a court would likely take a sympathetic view toward a layperson who was instructed to meet with counsel, and who was not specifically

49   [Perkins v. West Coast Lumber Co., 129 Cal. 427], at 429, 62 P. [57] at 58 [(1900)] * * *.

51   Westinghouse [Electric Corp. v. Kerr-McGee Corp.,] 580 F.2d [1311], at 1319 [(7th Cir.), *cert. denied*, 439 U.S. 955 (1978)] * * *.

admonished that counsel was not acting on his behalf. The police officer might convince the court that he believed Lawyer intended to represent both himself and the Town, and a court might consider the officer's communication of confidential information to Lawyer additional evidence of the officer's belief that Lawyer was representing both parties.

Thus, a court likely would conclude that an attorney-client relationship was formed between Lawyer and the police officer on the theory that their meeting constituted an "initial consultation." It is also possible that a court would invoke attorney-client protections on the basis of the officer's reasonable belief that Lawyer was providing joint representation.

* * *

B. THE RESULTS OF DISQUALIFICATION

1. Disqualification of Lawyer's Firm

If an individual lawyer is disqualified, then other members of his or her firm will also be disqualified under imputed disqualification rules. The American Bar Association *Model Code of Professional Responsibility* provides that "[i]f a lawyer is required to decline employment or to withdraw from employment under a Disciplinary Rule, no partner, or associate, or any other lawyer affiliated with him or his firm, may accept or continue such employment." Similarly, the courts have ruled that when an attorney is counsel for an adverse party in a substantially related matter, the attorney's entire law firm is disqualified.

Some courts have found certain screening procedures, such as "ethical walls," acceptable under certain circumstances. However, absent an "ethical wall," if Lawyer is disqualified, no other attorney in her firm could act as substitute counsel.

* * *

IV. AN OBJECTIVE STANDARD FOR EVALUATING DISQUALIFICATION MOTIONS: A PROPOSAL

One of the difficulties in evaluating a situation for potential conflicts of interest is in defining what constitutes a "conflict." Conflicts are not limited merely to situations in which clients fall on different sides of a lawsuit. Conflicts of interest encompass both "objective" conflicts and "subjective" conflicts.

"Objective" conflicts involve adverse client interests in the litigation or the subject matter, such as when clients take inconsistent legal positions. "Subjective" conflicts look beyond the clients' interests to whether the representation would violate the attorney's duty of undivided loyalty owed to each client. Any standard for evaluating disqualification motions must take both types of conflicts into account.

The greatest difficulties lie within the "subjective" conflicts area. Originally, the lawyer's duty of loyalty was contained in Canon 9 of the *Model Code*, which provided that a "lawyer should avoid even the appearance of impropriety." The purpose of this rule was to "promote public confidence in our system and in the legal profession."[91] Despite its good intentions, Canon 9's language could be construed as sweeping very broadly and providing no guidelines for its application. When the American Bar Association's House of Delegates adopted the *Model Rules of Professional Conduct* in 1983, they excluded the prohibition against "even the appearance of impropriety" and instead attempted to provide more detailed standards. Rules 1.7 and 1.9 deal with conflicts of interest: Rule 1.7 addresses the basic approach to conflicts and discusses simultaneous representation, and Rule 1.9 addresses conflicts involving former clients. The ethical focus, however, did not change: loyalty to the client remains an essential concern.

Although "appearances of impropriety" may have been all-inclusive, the *Model Rules'* language does not include enough. The *Model Rules* have relegated the discussion of loyalty to the comments, and even then conflicting loyalties are not well-defined. Of particular concern is the *Model Rules'* seeming emphasis upon "objective" conflicts, because such an emphasis detracts from the more difficult loyalty issues. Most attorneys likely would recognize the potential for a conflict of interest when co-defendants take incompatible positions. However, when a lawyer is faced with a request to represent, for example, a town and one of its police officers before any factual investigation into the matter has begun, the *Model Rules* provide little help.

Thus, in our hypothetical, Lawyer would have found no guidance by reading the *Model Rules* before meeting with the police officer. Further, if a disqualification motion is made against Lawyer, the *Model Rules* do not provide the court with sufficient guidelines to issue a ruling. Rule 1.9 adopts the "substantial relationship" test, but provides no definition of this test nor any method for determining when two representations are substantially related. If the appropriate resolution to the hypothetical situation nonetheless seems apparent, consider the following modification: during Lawyer's meeting with the police officer, no confidential information is revealed. However, concerned that a conflict might later develop, Lawyer directs the police officer to obtain independent counsel. Several months later, the officer moves to disqualify Lawyer from the case.

Nondisclosure of confidential information, interestingly, makes absolutely no difference to the vast majority of courts. This approach protects client confidences and appears to preserve client loyalty, but it comes at a very high cost. Disqualification is a harsh result, causing the disqualified attorney injury to his or her reputation as well as financial loss. In addition, the client may suffer embarrassment, additional expense, and delay in the preparation of its case. As a result, some courts permit evidence that the lawyer had no access to confidential information.

What is needed are guidelines that encompass both objective and subjective conflicts adequately without being overinclusive. To attain this goal, this Article recommends modifications in two areas: the *Model Rules of Professional Conduct* and the "substantial relationship" test as developed by the courts. The "substantial relationship" test reaches too far; the *Model Rules* do not reach far enough.

---

91   MODEL CODE EC 9-1 * * *.

To reach both areas, this Article recommends revisions to Rules 1.7 and 1.9. These revisions would make explicit that client loyalty is the first concern in evaluating conflicts of interest; that client loyalty can cause disqualification after merely an initial consultation; and that client loyalty encompasses "appearances of impropriety" as well as differing legal positions. In applying these standards, courts should adopt an objective standard in disqualification motions: Should a reasonable lawyer, concerned with the appearance of impropriety, continue to represent Client X? In answering this question, courts should consider five factors: (1) Should the attorney have foreseen the potential for a conflict of interest? (2) Was deception involved, either by the attorney or by the client? (3) Is there a "'substantial relationship" between the two representations? (4) Would continued representation create an appearance of impropriety? (5) Were client confidences revealed in fact?

* * *

In the next excerpt Michelle Jacobs explores the Model Code's requirement of zealous representation as it affects poor clients. She suggests that lawyers often afford less zealous representation to poor clients than to other clients. By defining client problems as "routine," lawyers can do a disservice to clients.

Michelle Jacobs, *Legal Professionalism: Do Ethical Rules Require Zealous Representation for Poor People?*, 8 St. Thomas L. Rev. 97 (1995)*

Do ethical rules permit zealous representation for the poor? Every lawyer reading that question will immediately think, "Yes, of course the rules permit zealous representation. In fact, they require it." However, consider the following:

> QUESTION: The canons and rules of ethics require lawyers to represent their clients zealously. What does zealous representation mean to you?

> ANSWER: Zealously representing a client means doing everything within the borders of the ethical rules and the confines of law that you can do to best represent your client. If it means going to the edge of your ethical obligations, then so be it. However, it does not mean crossing over that edge. In some cases, it may require you to step on that edge, but in no case should you step over it. In the Public Defender context, it will be much

---

more difficult to do due to the volume of cases and the nature of some of the clients. However, even Public Defenders should keep in mind who they are representing and their duty to zealously represent them.

The standard of client representation has always been one of zealous advocacy. Moreover, the Model Code of Professional Responsibility (Model Code) includes the expectation that lawyers will represent their clients zealously.[3] These rules make no distinction based on economic classifications, so that lawyers representing indigent clients are held to the same standard of "zealous representation" as those representing non-indigent clients. We certainly teach students that we expect them to provide zealous representation to their clinical clients and to exhibit professionalism in everything they do, not only on behalf of the clients and the clinic, but for their own benefit as well. Life is not a classroom and in reality, for those attorneys representing indigent clients through legal aid/legal services, the zealous representation and professionalism typically demanded by the affluent client may not be the standard expected of lawyers by the legal community. The Model Code does not define "zealousness"; no examples of zealousness are provided, and the interpretative language is far from being mandatory. Indeed, the majority of the comments to Canon 7 are concerned with the issue of actions that may not be within the bounds of the law. The examples we cite when teaching exemplify lawyers who assist clients with the fabrication of evidence or lawyers who materially mislead the court. Alternatively, professors scrutinize lawyers who fail to inform their clients of case progress, or usurp their clients' decision-making authority. In other words, the teaching methods we employ focus on the failure of the aspiration for zealous representation, as opposed to exploring the lofts of the aspirations. Has that been a problem for our students? On the surface, it would appear that it has not.

* * *

In the initial question and answer stated above, the student's response seemed appropriate, and the mention of the difficulty in providing zealous representation in the public defender context was duly noted. However, when this student's answer is combined with the answer to the next question, one begins to suspect that things may not be going well under the surface.

> QUESTION: Your client is an elderly black man who has been arrested for a second DUI offense within a year of a previous DUI offense. He cancels several appointments. You send an investigator to his home and it turns out the client is caring for his elderly wife who is ill. Health costs are stretching their meager resources to the breaking point. You want to talk to the client face to face. Should you go to the client's house and meet with him?

> ANSWER: You really shouldn't be required to meet with such a client at the client's home, but if there is no other way then perhaps you should go

---

3   MODEL CODE OF PROFESSIONAL RESPONSIBILITY Canon 7 (1981) (stating that a lawyer should represent a client zealously within the bounds of the law).

to the client's home. I think this decision is up to the individual lawyer. If time permits, meaning the lawyer has the time to do so, then I think it would be alright to go to the client's home. However, making a habit of this could be detrimental to that lawyer's practice.

What the Model Code requires is ambiguous in this type of situation. In the above scenario, does the Model Code require the lawyer to send an investigator out to the client's home, or would a telephone conference do? More likely than not, our reaction in the poverty law context would be to send an investigator to the indigent client. After all, lawyers working in the poverty arena are burdened with very heavy caseloads and, as the response of this student seems to suggest, a personal visit with the client could be disruptive to the attorney's law practice.

Nevertheless, what would the notion of zealous advocacy require? I suggest it would require going to the client's house. I reach that conclusion by analyzing what a lawyer would do for a private, fee-paying client. Suppose, for a moment, that a fee-paying client has retained us to draft a will. If the client is unable to travel to the lawyer's office because of advanced age or illness, the lawyer goes to the client. This is not a matter of lawyer discretion—the lawyer is doing what he or she has to do to accomplish a satisfactory resolution of the client's objectives. Similarly, if the client is a corporate executive with a busy schedule, none of us would find it unusual or extraordinary for the lawyer to go to the client's office to accommodate the corporate client's schedule. Yet, with an indigent client, the initial reaction would be to dismiss the notion of a visit to the client as being impractical and inappropriate.

Standing alone, the notion that the lawyer representing indigent clients has time pressures that prevent her from providing the client with full and zealous representation is damaging enough. However, in the poverty context, the issue of allocation of time resources is complicated by notions of client worth. Zealous representation is further diminished when the lawyer makes a value judgment as to which client matter is important enough for the lawyer to give it more than minimum attention. For the lawyer pressed for time and with too many clients to serve, there will be a tendency to give routine treatment to those matters that appear similar. However important as a political or moral issue, poverty is presented to legal assistance offices in a stream of individual problems, each of which already has been defined as insignificant in its social ramification. Our students, who do not even experience the true pressures of a poverty caseload, learn how to categorize their cases as routine before they are even half way through their clinical experience.

* * *

From the client's perspective however, the matter is hardly routine. Certainly in the context of a criminal prosecution, even at the misdemeanor level, matters should not be treated as routine. Does the fact that a lawyer has handled twenty worthless check misdemeanor cases in one day mean that the twenty-first case is entitled to only a perfunctory handling? As noted by Paul Tremblay, if clients are presented with the choice of having only minimally adequate service or full service, clients will presumably choose full service.[12] However, full service is not the service we provide. As the student suggests, an unspoken process of deeming which case is worthy of full attention takes place. All those deemed unworthy are handled as routine, uninteresting matters.

> I am enjoying PD clinic a lot because I like interacting with people and helping them. It's enjoyable to finally get two clients who I feel I can really help and who I believe are really being victimized. All my other clients this semester have flat out admitted they committed the crime and just want to plea to it. . . .

As this student's language suggests, a value judgment has been made as to whether the clients are truly deserving of zealous representation. The two clients this student speaks of are deemed to be deserving because the student feels they have been victimized. The student assumes, for example, that the other clients who admitted their guilt have not been victimized, or that they can not be helped. Similarly, a tenancy action or a divorce proceeding where there are no major assets exemplifies matters that affect lives in significant ways, even though these actions may not seem "deserving" of zealous representation. As the face of each client changes, as advocates for the poor, we must understand that the nature of the case changes. To the lawyer, a case may simply appear to be just another visitation schedule in a divorce proceeding; to the client, the divorce is likely to be one of the most traumatic events in his or her lifetime. Categorizing the case as "routine" trivializes the importance of the client's crisis.

* * * For the poverty lawyer this is further complicated because both the Model Rules of Professional Conduct and the Model Code of Professional Responsibility endorse the fiction that poverty lawyers can fulfill their functions in the same way that private lawyers do. Yet, it is clear that both the lawyer and the client in a legal services context are different from the lawyer and client in the private arena. The poverty lawyer can neither adjust the provisions of services based on the amount of money the client can pay, nor effectively control the number of clients he or she will serve to adequately ensure that enough time is devoted to each of the cases. The non-paying client has no resources to employ to demand fuller attention from the lawyer or to press for prioritization of her/his case. In combination, these factors leave the indigent client virtually powerless when compared to the paying client. Thus, ironically, in a legal system that recognizes only one standard of representation—zealousness—the indigent client has no power to demand that he or she be represented in accordance with this standard. Even more frightening is the fact that lawyers who practice in the poverty law arena seem to have accepted the notion that, it will in fact, be impossible to provide their clients with the level of "zealous representation" reflected by the standards and demanded by the paying client.

In examining some of the suggestions for dealing with the issue of representation of indigent clients, proposals have been made to redefine the acceptable standard

---

12   Tremblay, [*Toward a Community-Based Ethic for Legal Services Practice*, 37 UCLA L. Rev. 1101] at 1136 [(1990)].

of service to the poor as that of "minimally adequate services." As enticing as redefining the standards of representation for poor people to better reflect the reality of the poverty law practice might be, the actual effect of such a redefinition would be to further reduce the level of service that is presently only minimal at best. Indeed, removing the standard of zealous advocacy would only align the poor client against an adversary, whether it be a state agency or an individual such as a landlord represented by private counsel, in a system that will expect zealous representation on behalf of the adversary while allowing less for the economically disadvantaged client. The disempowerment of the indigent client will be compounded as she already enters the legal arena with less real power than her adversary. Such a redefinition only heightens the disadvantage to the indigent client. The first student's answers indicate that even under the zealous representation standard, we are all too willing to accept a lesser performance on behalf of indigent clients. Human nature, combined with the dynamics of the poverty caseload, would still place pressure on the poverty lawyer to provide less service, even under a minimally adequate standard.

* * *

What lawyer behavior will the traditional detached lawyering generate with our elderly black client? Consider the following:

QUESTION: You come to the conclusion that the client is an alcoholic. Do you have any obligation to deal with the issue of your client's alcoholism?

ANSWER ONE: No. I believe that zealous advocacy only applies to protecting the client's legal interests. I don't have any obligation to deal with his alcoholism and I probably would not.

ANSWER TWO: No. In the scope of representing him, the court will treat him more favorably if it appears that he is taking steps to deal with the problem.

ANSWER THREE: You don't have a legal obligation to deal with it but you may have a moral obligation.

These students, who have had the benefit of exposure to a lawyering style opposite that of the traditional norm, at least for a semester in my clinic, are still shaped by the normative professional framework. They believe, as the answers suggest, that they can separate "legal" duties from other obligations that may or may not be owed to the client. * * *

Returning to our hypothetical alcoholic client, the general conception of this client is that he is not worthy of full attention or zealous representation. Our students are comfortable making this assessment as the client is seen as not having a "legal" problem. Yet, in contrast, let us return once again to our roles as private attorneys. Through the use of zealous representation and professionalism, how would this client's case have been handled if he had had the economic resources to retain a private attorney? In the role as advocate, the lawyer attempts to explore as many options for the client as his money will support. A zealous advocate will want to position the client as a primary care-giver who is under pressure because of his wife's condition. In that way, the advocate can argue for the most lenient treatment of the client. To encourage the court to be lenient, the advocate will want to demonstrate that the client has taken steps to resolve the alcoholism. In so doing, the private attorney puts the client in the most favorable position for resolution of his legal problem.

* * *

How then can we, as lawyers, participate in establishing a higher expectation of the quality of legal services rendered to indigent clients? One possible approach that could provide some guidance may be found with a different definition of "professionalism." An alternative definition of the professional ideal is outlined by Sammons.[47] He redefines professionalism as "a way for people to participate in a meaningful fashion in the resolution of their social disputes or in prevention of social disputes or both." Moreover, he states:

> Service to the ideal of meaningful participation defines our profession and the moral value of meaningful participation justifies it. . . . Meaningful participation means that the client's participation will reflect, and reflect upon, the person of the client in dispute. In other words, only through meaningful participation can the client be an author of his own life in the dispute. . . . When we are functioning as we should, that is, when we are trying to reflect the person of the client, we assist the client in exploring many alternative definitions of the problems. . . . These processes keep the client and the lawyer tentative about the dispute and tentative about the ends of the representation, which is essential if the client is to continue to participate. The client and the lawyer are constantly reflecting on the ends of the representation and, in doing so, they are constantly redefining what it means to be a lawyer for this client in this dispute.

In this process the lawyer and the client stay open about what the client wants. Both recognize that the ends of representation are complex and ambiguous. For example, some have said that winning is the end of all legal representation. But what does winning mean? Winning is a complex and ambiguous end. In the example of our elderly client, winning is not just obtaining a reasonable resolution of the current DUI charge. Winning might be helping him obtain a home attendant to help with his wife so that he can participate in a rehabilitation program. Or, it might mean helping him to obtain food stamps or some kind of supplemental assistance. Can those options be incorporated in our notion of providing "legal advice"? The private lawyer analysis shows that they certainly can be.

Rather than adjusting our expectations downward to the notion that we can only provide minimally adequate services to the indigent client, why not adjust the expectation upward, to strive to provide zealous representation? Why shouldn't we advocate acceptance of the reality that indigent clients are not identical to clients who can demand high quality services? Why shouldn't we advocate that in the poverty area,

---

47   [JACK] SAMMONS, [LAWYER PROFESSIONALISM] at 5-6 [(1988)].

zealous representation means providing holistic assistance to the client? Thus, if alcoholism has been identified as a non-legal problem that is affecting the client's legal status, as in our example where the criminal charge is DUI, then the lawyer has an affirmative obligation to seek out means of helping the client resolve the underlying problem.

Under this interpretation of zealous representation, if the lawyer has made no effort to direct the client to treatment for the alcoholism or no effort to direct him to resources that could help with his wife, then that lawyer has not met the standard of zealous representation. Such a standard requires neither that the lawyer be held responsible for the client actually going to counseling nor that the lawyer become an expert in Supplemental Security Income benefits or home nursing; nor should the lawyer take action to which the client has not consented. However, the lawyer would not be able to end his or her representation of that client without assisting the client in exploring options that would help resolve the issues that created the legal problem.

* * *

Chapter 3

LAWYER-CLIENT COMMUNICATION

A. The Lawyer-Client Relationship

The practice of law requires communication not only about facts and law but about the interests and values of both lawyer and client. The first excerpt presents the story of a case as seen by a law student and by her client. It illustrates the challenge of resolving the tension between the interests and desires of the client and the interests and desires of the law student.

Nancy Cook, *Legal Fictions: Clinical Experiences, Lace Collars and Boundless Stories*, 1 CLIN. L. REV. 41 (1994)*

* * *

The Story of the Case

Last summer, the summer of 1992, a woman was arrested in Albuquerque for disorderly conduct. The statute she was alleged to have violated prohibits "... engaging in violent, abusive, indecent, profane, boisterous, unreasonably loud or otherwise disorderly conduct which tends to disturb the peace." Through connections with the local Public Defender's office, our law school clinic, which provides supervised student representation to a limited number of individuals, acquired the case. I read through the police report, which was virtually all there was to the file we received from the Public Defender, and assigned the case to one of my eight students, Rachel Kolman.[3]

In the beginning, this is all we knew about the case: The police responded to a call "in reference to a male and female fighting" in a motel room on Central Avenue. Central Avenue is the old Route 66, and this particular section is known for having

---

*   Reprinted with permission.

3   I am using Rachel's real name here with her permission. She has been not only gracious enough to let me tell her part of this story, but has volunteered her time and assistance in pulling it together. Rachel's client, "Debra" in this essay, could not be located and so has not given her permission to be identified. For that reason, her name and some details of her life have been changed.

more than its fair share of drug related activities and prostitution. On arrival, the two responding Anglo male police officers encountered several people in the parking lot, one of whom advised them that "a crazy woman" had come to his room and wouldn't leave.

As the men were conversing, this woman came around the corner. When she saw the police and the man they were interviewing—the man from the motel room— she began screaming at them. The officers attempted to calm her, but she "just got louder and more uncooperative." First the officers merely asked the woman to leave, but when she continued to yell, they advised her that she was under arrest for disorderly conduct. She then went to her car and locked herself in. At this point, under the threat of being forcibly removed from her vehicle, the woman got out and was handcuffed and transported to the detention center.

This information was contained in the police report that served as the basis for the criminal information filed against the woman. Buried in the middle of the report was this sentence: "We couldn't find anyone or find any reason to support her claim of rape."

Subsequent conversations with the police revealed that the man who spoke to them about the "crazy woman" was calm and articulate. The woman had asked him for money which he would not give her. Asked if they had seen any animals around, a fact that was significant to the defendant's version of events, the officers said that they had not. The defendant appeared to be intoxicated, but the officers' main concern was that she had been creating such a disturbance that many of the motel residents were coming outside and shouting back at her.

Rachel arranged to meet with the defendant, Debra, who was out on bond. Briefly, what Rachel learned in the interview was that Debra, a twenty-six year old, single, black woman, had recently arrived in New Mexico from the east coast. She and her boyfriend, with whom she was living, had moved to Albuquerque because they had heard that it was a tolerant place. At the time of the interview, Debra was unemployed, having lost her job because of her several days absence while she sat in the Bernalillo County Detention Center trying to make bail on this charge.

On the day of her arrest, Debra had gone to a bar with a female friend and there flirted with a man whom she thought was very good looking. She had three or four drinks, after which she left, voluntarily accompanying the man to his nearby motel room.

When she left the bar, Debra wasn't sure whether she was "interested" in the man. It was after they were in his room for a while and he started getting "aggressive" that she decided to cut the evening short. She tried to leave, but was stopped by a pit bull that was positioned in front of the door. The man tore off her clothes and raped her. She was yelling, which brought the motel manager to the room. Her assailant opened the door to speak to the manager and when he did, Debra screamed out that she was being raped. The manager left, but after that, the man backed off. She was able to grab her clothes and run from the room.

Debra called the police from a pay phone around the corner, unaware of the fact that the motel manager had already done so. When she returned to the motel, she was surprised to see that a patrol car was already there. She immediately went up to the officers, who were standing with the man who had raped her, to tell them what happened. They wouldn't listen to her, which made her very angry. In the end, they arrested her and let the rapist go. She spent the weekend in jail, during which time she received no medical attention.

This was the point in the semester when we were dealing in the classroom with case planning and investigation. I thought this case provided an excellent opportunity for working through case theory and investigative plans. In class, Rachel presented the "facts" as we knew them and I then divided students into two groups, four representing the prosecution and four representing the defense. As anticipated, the two teams came up with widely different perspectives on the case, both of which were potentially credible to a fact finder, factually supportable, and predictable. The prosecution theory was, she's a prostitute on the run, possibly a drug addict, she didn't get paid for her services, so she cried rape to get back at the john who stiffed her; she had been "violent, abusive . . . , unreasonably loud" and "otherwise disorderly" in the motel parking lot, drawing a crowd and disturbing the other residents at the motel. The defense theory was, two racist, sexist, white cops saw a poor black woman and immediately thought junkie whore and couldn't be bothered to listen to her; under the circumstances (she had just been raped), any disturbance she caused was more than justifiable.

By all outward appearances, this was a successful class. The students went away feeling that they had been smart and creative and that they had properly analyzed the facts and come up with rational explanations from both perspectives. Rachel had a theory to work with, another to prepare to defend against, and a long list of investigative tasks that could help her evaluate the competing theories and hone her defense.

But.

Debra's Story

Here is the but: When Rachel spoke to Debra, client, defendant, victim, with our "theory" of the case in mind, Debra, unique, whole, independent individual, balked. She didn't see racism. She didn't see sexism. She didn't see a great social structure built to disadvantage the poor, women, people of color, poor women of color. What did she see? Her own innocence. A rapist's guilt. Simple injustice. She expected simple justice to prevail in the courtroom. She expected vindication. If we tell the truth, she maintained, motives, class, and race differences won't matter. All that feminist cow dung doesn't mean anything when the truth is so simple.

Was that all she saw? We don't know. After their first several conversations, in which Debra expressed to Rachel her heartfelt thanks that Rachel had been assigned to the case because finally, *finally* someone was listening to her, Debra changed her mind about having student representation. She had described Rachel as "a godsend," but as the investigation proceeded, she grew distant, she avoided Rachel, and spoke of her boyfriend wanting her to hire private counsel. Privately, Rachel sought to understand why. Had she alienated her with her whiteJewishmiddleclassfeminist "theories"? Was Debra's boyfriend exerting pressure because *he* didn't trust a woman, a white woman, a student? Had Rachel been naive? Was the boyfriend Debra's pimp and the whole rape story a scam?

These questions remain unanswered for us. Most of Debra's story is now, and probably forever, outside our reach. The reason for this is that Debra fired us about a week before the case was set to come up for trial.

Rachel's Story

Rachel was not chosen lightly for this assignment. The single line in the police report making reference to rape had sent up warning flares and I wanted to assign the case to someone who would proceed with open ears and an open mind. Rachel had come to law school after five or six years of post-graduate community service work. She had extensive experience in working with unprivileged people and had earned a local reputation for her unfailing willingness to lend a hand to important social causes. I had—and have—complete confidence in Rachel's ability to be sensitive to issues involving race, gender, poverty, and lifestyle. In addition, I had personally observed her to be a good listener, reflective and insightful, and conscious of how her own needs might affect her personal interactions.

Rachel identified potentially troubling aspects of the case from the police report alone; she was disturbed by the reference to a rape and the apparent lack of response to that. When she spoke to Debra, who recounted the rape incident without any prodding from Rachel, her concerns about the police officers' disregard of the rape complaint were confirmed. Her analysis of the situation was that "If the same thing had been happening at the Sheraton, and a white woman had called [the police], they would not have arrested her."

Following her interview with Debra, Rachel conducted a thorough investigation and found considerable support for Debra's version of events, including statements from a number of witnesses who were not identified in the police reports and the record of a phone call made by the motel manager to the police reporting the "fight" as a possible rape. According to some witnesses at the scene, at least one of the officers was condescending to women and disrespectful to blacks. There was sufficient evidence to make the police look bad, if we chose to pursue the racist-sexist theory that had been developed in class.

There was, in addition, a fair amount of available evidence to make Debra look bad, more than enough to make the outcome at trial far from certain, if the prosecutor on the case cared to investigate. Some witnesses stated that the door to the motel room had been open all the while that Debra was there and that the male resident of the room had tried to make her leave. According to the police, Debra had been assaultive and verbally abusive in the squad car, and the Detention Center personnel reported that she was similarly combative on arrival there. In addition, Debra had subsequently picked up a domestic violence charge. We were not representing her on that charge, but because of its potential importance to plea negotiations and any sentencing, it was part of the background to our trial preparation.

Rachel's dilemma was, what to do in light of the client's unwillingness to make race, class, or gender an issue? She was uncomfortable about pursuing a theory of discrimination in the courtroom if Debra opposed it. From Rachel's perspective, "part of being an advocate" was allowing Debra's voice to come through, since, as Rachel put it, "it's *her* story." At the same time, she did not share Debra's faith that simple truth would win out. Having come to law school believing, as Debra apparently did, in "the myth that courts give fairness," and having quickly been disabused of that notion as a first year law student,[5] Rachel searched in vain for a satisfactory way to explain to Debra what she might reasonably expect in a courtroom. "How was I going to tell her story," Rachel asked, "in a way a judge would understand, a jury would believe?"

We considered alternatives other than trial that might result in reforms of police procedures as well as in dismissal of the charges against Debra. The Police Department was already under scrutiny for its handling of several investigatory stops that had resulted in the deaths of two young men the previous spring, and this increased the likelihood that, if approached, the press would take an interest in the department's handling of rape complaints. Media pressure might have some desirable effects. There was also the option of filing a civil suit against the police department in either state or federal court. One thing that was appealing about these alternatives was that they focused attention on a problem that was much larger than the charge pending against Debra; they gave Rachel (and Debra) the opportunity to make a difference on a grander scale.

Debra, however, was not interested in discussing these options. She wanted the charges to go away, yes, and she wanted the police to conduct themselves differently, but she did not want to be involved in a major law reform effort. As far as she was concerned, the sooner this mess got cleaned up, the better; she had been inconvenienced enough.

The offense with which Debra was charged was not a serious one, of course, and the fact that she had already spent three days in jail opened up the possibility of working out a deal with the prosecutor. Debra was adamant about not entering any kind of a plea, however, so any negotiating would have to result in dismissal of the charges. How much to reveal in a discussion with the prosecutor was a big question since, if she did not see matters our way, she would then be better prepared to counter our trial strategies.

In the end, Rachel opted for a straightforward but subtle approach. Ten days before trial, she called the district attorney and said simply, "I think you ought to take a serious look at this case." She disclosed nothing about what our defense was going to be or who our witnesses were. The prosecutor agreed to take a look at the case (not a normal pre-trial occurrence in Albuquerque's Metropolitan Court) and said she would get back to Rachel in a day or two.

The D.A. never called Rachel back. A few days later, however—on the same day that the phone call came in saying Debra was firing us—Rachel received in the mail a notice of dismissal from the State.

Although she was pleased that, for whatever reason, the State had seen fit to dismiss the charges and that Debra would not have to face the risk of a conviction, Rachel was disheartened. She was distressed by her own sense of powerlessness, partly in regard to her client, and partly with respect to the unresolved problem of

---

5   With respect to her first few weeks in law school, Rachel said, "I can't believe how many times I heard in the first weeks, 'If you want justice, go to Divinity School.'"

how the Albuquerque police handled complaints of rape. In her self evaluation, she wrote:

> I was a bit discouraged that I became very involved with this case from my heart, that I saw the problem in the larger context of a social issue regarding how poor women of color are treated by the APD [Albuquerque Police Department] and the client did not. I suspect that I will either become jaded and learn not to care or will re-live this scenario. I was also a bit discouraged that this case will not turn into a civil suit against the police department. However, I understand that not every client wants to be tied to litigation for years and that that was my hidden agenda of being a public watch on the APD.

At this point, of course, the "case" had been concluded. Rachel wrote to Debra to let her know what the State had done and enclosed a copy of the dismissal. She encouraged Debra to contact her if she had any questions, but not surprisingly, there was never any response to this letter. We closed out the file, and that might have been the end of matters had Rachel not been so concerned that the next non-titled woman to allege rape, and the one after that, and the one after that, would be summarily dismissed as "uncooperative" in much the same way Debra had been. Regardless of how Debra might be feeling about matters, *Rachel* did not want Debra's experience to be a permanent state of affairs. As she expressed it,

> My feeling was whyever she was there [at the motel] shouldn't matter. To me it didn't even really matter if she was raped or not. It was the fact that she was *yelling* rape. It should not be for the cops on the street to decide then and there whether this woman was raped or not and to judge that.

It is difficult to recreate the conversations between Rachel and me which led to the next steps each of us chose to take. As a graduate of the client-centered school of decision making, and a believer that those same interactive techniques can be profitably applied to student supervision, I am certain that I peppered our discussions with such questions as, What do you want to accomplish? What options do you see? What effect do you think that would have? How would you go about doing that? How might that ease your frustration? But I can't honestly say that I have a distinct memory of those conversations.

What I do have a clear memory of are the moments when we relaxed our student/teacher roles and just talked story, eye to eye, voice to voice, person to person. This was the year (if you begin counting the months, as I do, with the start of the new academic calendar) of the William Kennedy Smith and Mike Tyson trials. It was the year of the Clarence Thomas confirmation hearings and of the first criminal trial of the police officers who beat up Rodney King. Those stories frequently diverted Rachel and me from our assigned educational tasks; we discussed the hows and whys of unequal justice, we asked each other what if?, and we exchanged other tales of rapes and lynchings, silencing and denial. Out of the exchange of stories came new insights, new perspectives, new possibilities for action. Debra's case acquired meaning and context far beyond what showed up between the covers of her case file.

Rachel's response to these talks was to use her skills in networking to find a useful role for herself. During her investigation of Debra's case, she had discovered that the Albuquerque Police Department manual provided no real instructions on what an officer was to do when faced with the situation of a person claiming rape. No policy existed with respect to obtaining medical attention or providing psychological support. Rachel's first act after closing Debra's case file was to look into this situation; she spoke first to the police department's liaison, who acknowledged the problem and expressed a willingness to remedy it. Rachel then spoke to a local rape crisis center and found that staff workers were in the process of writing a policy that could fill in the gap in the police manual. Rachel offered her services in this effort.

* * *

In the next excerpt Robert D. Dinerstein contrasts the "client-centered" approach to lawyering with the traditional approach and summarizes the philosophical and political arguments for client-centered lawyering. The model for legal interviewing and counseling associated with client-centered lawyering stresses communication techniques that encourage client decision making.

Robert D. Dinerstein, *Client-Centered Counseling: Reappraisal and Refinement*, 32 ARIZ. L. REV. 501 (1990)*

* * *

The traditional view of legal counseling (and the lawyer-client relationship generally) maintains that the client should make the critical decisions concerning the overall goals of the representation, with the lawyer exercising a great deal of influence over how such decisions are made and what the actual decisions are. This view holds that the client should stand by passively while the lawyer lays out all relevant legal considerations for the decision and indicates what decision he believes, as a matter of his professional judgment, the client ought to make. The lawyer then urges the client to make the recommended decision. The client-centered or participatory model of counseling, with the client empowered to make decisions for him- or herself, is a response to this traditional model.

Advocates for the client-centered model have made a number of arguments, based variously on philosophical, political, psychological, ethical and utilitarian grounds, for their model's superiority over the traditional approach. Some of the

---

model's most committed advocates are clinical law teachers, who have adopted it for use in both live-client clinical law programs and simulation courses. David Binder and Susan Price's 1977 text, *Legal Interviewing and Counseling: A Client-Centered Approach*, has been the primary influence on these teachers. In their book, Binder and Price propose a counseling model that concretizes their particular version of client-centeredness. Both the number of educators who have adopted the book and the relative paucity of academic criticism that it has received suggest the extraordinary influence of the model within clinical education circles.

But if the Binder and Price model has not been subjected to substantial academic criticism, the concept of client-centered counseling has, at least implicitly. Some writers have criticized its emphasis on client autonomy to the exclusion of other values, especially in circumstances in which the client is not the powerless, disadvantaged client that most clinical programs represent. Others have suggested that client-centered counseling is too time-consuming and economically infeasible for practicing attorneys. They see the strict client-centered lawyer's reticence towards his client—his unwillingness even to suggest what the client ought to do for fear that he will unduly influence the client's choice—as denying guidance to the clients that need it most. And if, as some argue, one goal of the counseling process is to foster an often contentious dialogue between lawyer and client, the client-centered lawyer's excessive deference to her client denies important dialogic opportunities and results in an unnecessarily impoverished decisionmaking process.

* * *

II. CLIENT-CENTERED COUNSELING DEFINED

A. *The Traditional Model*

Traditional legal counseling reflects an absence of meaningful interchange between lawyer and client. The client comes to the lawyer with some idea about his problem. The lawyer asks questions designed to adduce the information necessary to place the client's problem within the appropriate conceptual box. At the proper time, he counsels the client by essentially conducting a monologue: the lawyer tells the client something of the nature of his actions on the client's behalf and then advises the client about the course of action he recommends. The lawyer may go into great detail about the rationale for his advice. Alternatively, she may provide a relatively terse recitation of technical advice and let the client decide how to proceed. The lawyer is concerned with the client's reaction to his advice but tends not to value client input, for he believes that the client has little of value to contribute to the resolution of his legal problem. Lawyer and client are likely to talk at, rather than with, each other. Any assurance that the lawyer provides to the client—and it could be substantial—is likely to be based on the client's perception that the lawyer is "taking care of matters" rather than on a belief that the lawyer truly tried to understand the client as a whole, complex person.

In general, the traditional legal counseling model assumes that clients should be passive and delegate decisionmaking responsibility to their lawyers; that ineffective professional service is relatively rare; that professionals give disinterested service and maintain high professional standards; that effective professional services are available to all who can pay; and that professional problems tend to call for technical solutions beyond the ken of laypersons.

B. The Binder and Price Counseling Model

Client-centered counseling is a critical component of client-centered lawyering. Client-centered counseling may be defined as a legal counseling process designed to foster client-decisionmaking. Its goal is not only to provide opportunities for clients to make decisions themselves but also to enhance the likelihood that the decisions are truly the client's and not the lawyer's. To accomplish these goals, client-centered counselors must attend to the means they employ in the counseling process, as well as the end of client decisionmaking they attempt to achieve.

Binder and Price describe a relatively straightforward, but highly structured, legal counseling model to be used in litigation contexts. With respect to the basic go/no-go decision about whether to litigate, the lawyer first sets out the legal alternatives for the client. Next, she solicits the client's input on generating additional alternatives. Then, the lawyer engages the client in a discussion of the positive and negative consequences of the options. These consequences include not only the legal consequences, as to which the lawyer is enjoined to make predictions of the most likely outcome of each alternative, but the social, psychological and economic consequences as well. Finally, the lawyer assists the client in weighing these consequences with an eye towards having the client make the final decision.

Binder and Price set out their philosophy of client decisionmaking and its rationale as follows:

> The ultimate decision regarding which alternative should be chosen should be based upon an evaluation of which alternative is most likely to bring the *greatest client satisfaction*. If a decision is to be made on the basis of maximum client satisfaction, there first must be knowledge of the importance or value which the client attaches to each of the consequences involved. Only when the client's values are known can there be a determination of which alternative, on balance, will provide maximum client benefit. However, it is our belief that, by and large, lawyers cannot know what value clients really place on the various consequences. We therefore conclude that lawyers usually cannot determine which alternative will provide maximum client satisfaction and that decisions should be left to the client.[29]

The authors argue further that the ABA Code of Professional Responsibility supports client decisionmaking and that the client will be more likely to accept a decision if she has made it herself.

The most controversial aspect of Binder and Price's client-centered counseling model is their great resistance to the lawyer giving the client her opinion as to what action the client should take. The authors are concerned that if the lawyer commu-

---

29   D. Binder & S. Price, [Legal Interviewing and Counseling: A Client-Centered Approach], at 148-49 [1977] (emphasis in original).

nicates her opinion to the client the latter will end up making the decision that he believes the lawyer wants him to make rather than the decision that is best for him. Because clients frequently "are remarkably sensitive to, and easily swayed by, what they guess their lawyer thinks is best for them," it is crucial that the lawyer consciously communicate her neutrality to the client. Although Binder and Price allow for the possibility that a client who is an independent decisionmaker could receive the lawyer's opinion without being overwhelmed by it, they are concerned about clients who are passive decisionmakers or clients whom the lawyer is unable to categorize as independent. They argue that, in cases where the client asks for the lawyer's opinion about what to do, the lawyer should "parry the initial request with an explanation about why the decision should be made by the client." Moreover, as Stephen Ellmann observes,[36] Binder and Price apparently would not recommend that the lawyer tell the client at the beginning of the counseling session that the client could choose to have the lawyer give him her advice. While Binder and Price describe a number of situations in which client decisionmaking may be inapplicable, their emphasis on a client decisionmaking model that eschews the lawyer's explicit presentation of advice establishes them as perhaps the strongest advocates of unmediated client-centeredness.

The Binder and Price model is an important contribution to our understanding of legal counseling in general and client-centeredness or client decisionmaking in particular. The model's emphasis on the client's role in the counseling process provides a needed response to the worst excesses of the traditional lawyer-dominated model of counseling. Its view of the professional's role is also refreshing. Implicit in the model is a view of professionalism that does not depend upon mystification of laypeople or obfuscation of those areas in which the professional's expertise is of questionable value to the client. The assumptions of the model are fully consonant with developing notions of informed consent in law and other disciplines. The model's emphasis on psychological aspects of the lawyer-client relationship, while not without controversy, serves a useful purpose in challenging the lawyer's traditional view of facts as objective and given.

* * *

1. The Philosophical Argument: Enhancing Client Autonomy

The core argument supporting client decisionmaking is that it enhances the client's individual autonomy. Autonomy, or self-determination, means that a person can choose and act freely, according to her own life plan. There are many possible definitions of autonomy, but the capacity to make choices is a key component of the concept. Recognizing a person's autonomy is essential to according respect to that person; respect for autonomy is a cornerstone of liberal legal theory and of the

---

36   Ellmann, [*Lawyers and Clients*, 34 UCLA L. REV. 717] at 745 [(1987)] (commenting that in the Binder and Price lawyer's "Preparatory Explanation" at the beginning of the counseling session the lawyer makes no mention of the possibility of giving advice to the client regarding his decision).

American political system. It can be justified for its intrinsic value and on utilitarian grounds.

A person's autonomy can be compromised in a number of ways. One such way is through paternalism, which operates in counterpoint to autonomy. Pure paternalistic actions, which by definition are taken to benefit the person(s) whose will is being overborne, are problematic precisely because they deny people their fundamental right to make their own decisions in their own ways, even if those decisions could somehow objectively be shown to be wrong.

At least in American society, law plays an important function in facilitating an individual's ability to function autonomously. As mediators and interpreters of the law, lawyers are the conduits through which people can express their autonomy. By creating mechanisms that empower their clients to make their own decisions in their own way, client-centered lawyers contribute to their clients' autonomy.

The importance of autonomy led at least two commentators to argue that client decisionmaking with respect to all aspects of a lawsuit is presumptively required. Few scholars dispute the importance of autonomy as a value. The dispute is over: (1) the extent to which other values, such as the moral autonomy of the lawyer or third parties, may limit the exercise of autonomy, and (2) whether a client-centered model of lawyering is the best route to maximizing autonomy. * * * [T]wo preliminary observations are in order. First, in examining models of client counseling the question is less whether client-centeredness fosters client immorality than whether it is any more likely to do so than other client-counseling models. Second, it is not a necessary part of the autonomy argument for client-centeredness that a client's autonomy can never be overridden. Rather, if autonomy is an important value, client-centered counseling is desirable if it furthers autonomy and is especially desirable if it tends to further it more than other client-counseling models, so long as it does not unduly trench upon other important values.

That leaves the second issue respecting autonomy and client-centered counseling: does the model in fact maximize client autonomy? The principal autonomy objection to the client-centered counseling model is that if the lawyer acts paternalistically and exercises more power over her client's choices (and over the manner in which the client considers those choices) the client's autonomy will actually be enhanced. The traditional lawyer's decisionmaking superiority over the client is deemed to be based in part on the lawyer's professional and technical training and in part on the lawyer's status as a dispassionate decisionmaker.

This argument fails on several levels. First, even if lawyer paternalism increased client autonomy in the long-run it would violate the notion of autonomy as a side-constraint. Second, the danger is great that a paternalistic lawyer would construe a client's disagreement with her views as indicative of the client's lack of sophistication and need for the lawyer's expertise rather than a different (though rational) calculation about what choice to make. Third, clients must make many decisions that do not primarily implicate the technical expertise of the lawyer but instead implicate the client's personal values, wants and desires; the client, not the lawyer, is the expert on these issues. Finally, the traditional model's assumption that the lawyer will have the best interest of the client at heart is overbroad and insufficiently sensitive both to conflicts of interest between lawyer and client and questionable lawyer competence.

When compared to the traditional counseling model, then, the client-centered counseling model provides more assurance of client autonomy. Yet in one important sense, client-centered lawyering, at least as defined by Binder and Price, may be inconsistent with maximizing client autonomy. As noted previously, Binder and Price in general require lawyers to refrain from giving clients their opinions on what alternatives the clients should choose. They apparently allow no room for lawyers to attempt consciously to persuade their clients to make particular decisions. But some informed consent theorists have asserted that persuasion is not only an acceptable but a necessary part of an autonomous relationship. If so, the Binder and Price lawyer denies her client autonomy by eschewing the use of persuasion.

This is a serious argument, but one that, in my judgment, proves too much. Although I will postpone, for now, the full consideration of persuasion's role in enhancing client autonomy, several preliminary considerations are in order. Whether persuasion enhances or detracts from client autonomy will depend on a number of circumstances, including the nature of the relationship between lawyer and client, the power difference between them, their values, and the nature of the legal problem. Where, in particular and carefully limited cases, persuasion may enhance autonomy, the client-centered lawyer is, or ought to be, permitted to use the technique. But given the propensity of lawyers, and perhaps law students, to act paternalistically toward their clients, a client-centered model that establishes a presumption against the lawyer's use of persuasion is preferable to one that presumes persuasion is acceptable behavior.

2. Client-Centeredness: The Political Argument

Like all social relationships, the lawyer-client relationship does not exist in a vacuum. It is subject to political, social and economic trends in society. Client-centered lawyering must be placed in the particular political and historical context in which it arose. Moreover, political situations change. Even if client-centered lawyering and counseling served certain political values when it was introduced, there is no assurance that it continues to serve those same values, or that those values have the same significance today. In this sub-section, I will attempt to analyze briefly two aspects of the politics underlying client centeredness: the political influences upon the development of client centeredness and political values that continuing fealty to the concept might serve. My goal here is to place client-centeredness in context and thereby suggest both the possibilities and some potential limitations on its broad applicability.

The origins of client-centered lawyering are inextricably bound up with the development of "modern" clinical legal education itself. Full exploration of this development would present a fascinating story but one that unfortunately is beyond the scope of this article. Nevertheless, modern clinical legal education developed in the crucible of the political activism of the 1960's and early 1970's. Many of the proponents of the client-centered approach were former legal services or public interest lawyers who entered academia as clinical law teachers.[82] The experience of these lawyer-teachers with poor clients had a profound effect on their assessment of problems in the lawyer-client relationship and their proposed solutions. In particular, these teachers' goals of empowering politically disadvantaged clients provided a rationale for client-centered practice on behalf of poor people.

Any discussion of clinical teachers must start with Gary Bellow, one of the founders of modern clinical education, as well as one of its most prominent influences. Consequently, Bellow's background and views about lawyering assume particular importance in charting the origins of client-centered counseling and lawyering. Bellow's short but influential 1977 article, *Turning Solutions Into Problems: The Legal Aid Experience*,[86] described a number of practices in which legal services lawyers engaged that raised troubling questions about how those lawyers dealt with their clients. Among other things, Bellow asserted that, in the main, legal services lawyers tended to process their clients' cases routinely; to define client problems narrowly; to impose solutions upon clients without meaningful discussion; and to push their clients into accepting settlements. He urged that legal services lawyers recognize the political dimension of their practice and discuss with clients the immanent political choices their cases presented. He also stressed the need for legal services lawyers to educate their clients and provide for greater client participation in their cases.

Bellow's advocacy for politically-conscious lawyering, empowerment of poor clients, and increased client participation did not, of course, spring forth suddenly in the 1977 article but was consistent with views he expressed considerably earlier.[89] His approach suggests a pressing concern with clients' experience of powerlessness and their need for greater participation in both societal institutions and the lawyer-client relationship. That focus on increased client participation and empowerment was consistent with much of the citizen participation and community control rhetoric of the 1960's and 1970's. As Stephen Wexler wrote in a 1970 article:

> The hallmark of an effective poor people's practice is that the lawyer does not do anything for his clients that they can do or be taught to do for themselves. The standards of success for a poor people's lawyer are how well he can recognize all the things his clients can do with a little of his help, and how well he can teach them to do more.[92]

---

82   Barnhizer, [*The University Ideal and Clinical Legal Education*, 35 N.Y.L. Sch. L. Rev.] at 1, 18 & n.3, 70-71 [(forthcoming 1990)] * * * .

86   34 NLADA Briefcase 106 (Aug. 1977).

89   * * *

Interestingly, Bellow's views do not necessarily support a Binder and Price version of client-centeredness. In particular, his criticism of the professional pose of neutrality and his advocacy for active engagement with the client's cause seem to distance him from the Binder and Price technique. * * * In Chapter 2 ("Being a Lawyer: The Problem of Values"), Bellow and Moulton attempt to convey the complexity of current conceptions of legal practice and the lawyer-client relationship. While noting their view that the legal profession "does not offer an adequate conception of justice" and pays insufficient attention to issues of class, race, and power, they note also the problems with the alternative visions of lawyer-as-client's tool and lawyer-as-imposer-of-values. [G. Bellow & B. Moulton, The Lawyering Process: Materials for Clinical Instruction in Advocacy] at 116 [(1978)]. * * *

92   Wexler, *Practicing Law for Poor People*, 79 Yale L.J. 1049, 1055 (1970).

While Wexler's observation was made in the context of advocating that poverty lawyers focus more on community organizing than on solely legal solutions, it is consistent with an enhanced role for the client within the lawyer-client relationship.

The political pedigree of client-centered lawyering is of more than historical interest. The realization that it arose out of a law practice that dealt primarily with poor people is essential to understanding the concept as it has developed. Yet when clinical teachers write about clinical education issues today, few stress the political underpinnings of client-centered approaches. Rather, it is Critical Legal Studies adherents and others concerned with developing more explicitly political law practices who have stressed the need for greater client participation in the lawyer-client relationship. Indeed, some of these writers, far from embracing developing notions of client-centeredness, forcefully criticize the concept. But if poor and disadvantaged clients needed empowerment in the 1960's and 1970's, it can hardly be contended that they need it less so in the 1990's.

* * *

The next excerpt focuses on how lawyers and clients can work together on a basis of equality to formulate joint goals and strategies. Alex J. Hurder contends that the need to reconcile the interests and values of the client with the interests and values of the lawyer requires negotiation between the lawyer and client about their joint goals and the means of pursuing them.

Alex J. Hurder, *Negotiating the Lawyer-Client Relationship: A Search for Equality and Collaboration*, 44 BUFFALO L. REV. 71 (1996)*

I. INTRODUCTION

Two law students under the supervision of a law professor represented M. Dujon Johnson by court appointment on a misdemeanor charge in a Midwestern state's trial court.[1] The lawyers[2] investigated the case thoroughly, interviewed their client, developed a theory of the case, and represented Mr. Johnson aggressively. When the case came to trial the prosecutor asked the judge to dismiss the case, a victory for the defense. The client was furious. He was angry at the court and angry at his lawyers. Taking advantage of their unexpected free time, the law professor, the

---

*   Copyright © 1996 by the Buffalo Law Review.

1   The story of M. Dujon Johnson is taken from an insightful article by Clark D. Cunningham, the law professor who represented Johnson. See Clark D. Cunningham, *The Lawyer As Translator, Representation As Text: Towards An Ethnography of Legal Discourse*, 77 CORNELL L. REV. 1298 (1992). Johnson insisted that Cunningham use Johnson's real name in telling his story. *Id.* at 1383.

2   The term lawyer is used to include law students practicing under the auspices of a law school legal clinic.

two law students and their client began a discussion of their relationship. It was a discussion that should have begun when they first met.

The story of M. Dujon Johnson's case is told by Clark Cunningham as a vehicle for examining the lawyer's role as a translator. Reading Cunnningham's careful account of the development of the relationship between the lawyers and their client suggests that the cause of Johnson's dissatisfaction was not solely in translation, but also in prevailing conceptions of what the relationship between a lawyer and client should be.

Johnson's correspondence with Cunningham after the case was closed afforded a unique opportunity to hear the voice of the client and to view the lawyer-client relationship from a client's perspective. In his comments on how his case was handled, Johnson explained that he wanted to participate as an equal in a process of collaboration with his lawyers.

At the initial interview with Johnson, the lawyers learned that he had been arrested by two state troopers when he pulled into a service station at night near Ann Arbor, Michigan. The troopers called out, "Hey, yo," to Johnson, an African American undergraduate at the University of Michigan. They ordered him out of his car and asked him to submit to a pat-down search. When Johnson refused, claiming that a search would violate his constitutional rights, the troopers arrested him for disorderly conduct, searched him, pressed his face on the hood of the car while handcuffing him, and took him to jail. At his arraignment, the judge appointed the lawyers to represent him.

What the lawyers did not ask at the initial interview was as significant as what they did ask. They did not ask Johnson what his goals were. If they had, they would have learned that he wanted more than simply to be cleared of a misdemeanor charge. As he said later, "I would like to have my reputation restored, and my dignity."

The lawyers did not ask Johnson what means should be used to pursue his goals. If they had, they would have learned that he wanted a public trial. They would have learned that, at Johnson's arraignment, the prosecutor had offered to dismiss his case if he would pay court costs of fifty dollars, and he had refused. The trial itself was the relief Johnson sought. Without discussing it with their client, the lawyers filed a motion to suppress evidence that, if successful, would have drastically shortened the trial.

The lawyers did not ask Johnson how to divide the responsibility for conducting his defense. If they had, they would have learned that he was eager to play a significant role in the defense of his case. When his lawyer proposed, shortly before the trial, that Johnson cross examine the trooper who arrested him, Johnson agreed. He was willing to take a heightened risk of conviction in order to have an active role in the case. By then it was too late. Both sides had already testified at the hearing on the suppression motion, and the trial never took place.

Johnson's lawyers did not ask him about the rules of the relationship they were forming. If they had, they would have discovered that he was not content. In a conversation after his case had been dismissed, Johnson said the lawyers had been "patronizing." He said he was always the "secondary person." He felt that they had treated him like a child. Johnson's perception of factors defining his relationship with his lawyers were more detailed than the lawyers expected. He pointed out that on several trips in the car he rode in the back seat while the two law students rode in front. At his final appearance in court, Johnson sat behind the bar with the spectators rather than at the counsel table with his lawyers. Johnson interpreted these physical arrangements as signs that he was in the backseat, not only literally, but in the control of his case as well.

Johnson's case poses the question for clinical legal education of how relationships of equality and collaboration between lawyers and clients can be created and sustained. The texts on legal interviewing and counseling that have been most influential in clinical legal education have not provided a satisfactory answer to the question. Leading texts on professional responsibility also fail to answer the question.

The demand for equality and collaboration expressed by M. Dujon Johnson is being raised in every field of law. Changes in the nature of the work lawyers do are forcing changes in the way lawyers relate to clients. The rigid roles of lawyer and client developed in response to the formalities of courtroom litigation do not serve well in the less formal setting of negotiating sessions, mediation conferences or administrative hearings. For instance, representing clients in negotiations requires continuous communication between lawyer and client about goals, strategies and the roles to be played by lawyer and client. The use of mediation to resolve disputes requires similar intensity of communication between lawyer and client. This communication takes place primarily in the process of legal interviewing and counseling.

The issues that were not raised in the initial interview with Johnson—his goals, the means he would choose to pursue the goals, the division of responsibility between Johnson and his lawyers, and the rules governing the interaction between Johnson and the lawyers—were all critical terms of the lawyer-client relationship. They are issues that must be decided jointly by the lawyer and client because they determine the actions to be taken by both. The process for making joint decisions is negotiation.

* * *

II. Negotiating the Lawyer-Client Relationship as an Aspect of Interviewing and Counseling

Negotiation of the terms of the lawyer-client relationship is an essential function of legal interviewing and counseling. Negotiation is the process for making joint decisions. The importance of lawyer-client negotiation as a part of the legal interviewing and counseling process has been overlooked in approaches to lawyering that emphasize the autonomy of either the lawyer or the client in the decision making process.

In the traditional approach to lawyering, the client identifies a problem, and virtually all other decisions remain the professional domain of the lawyer. The client-centered approach developed in reaction to the dominance of the lawyer in traditional models of lawyering. The client-centered approach requires the lawyer to let her client make autonomous decisions about a case to the maximum extent possible. To protect the client's autonomy, the lawyer identifies all decisions that have a significant impact, legal or nonlegal, on the client and helps the client make them through the process of counseling. Decisions about the skill and craft of lawyering remain the domain of the lawyer.

Both the traditional approach and the client-centered approach assume that the lawyer and client operate autonomously, with some decisions belonging to the domain of the lawyer and some to the domain of the client. Tensions develop when the interests of either side, lawyer or client, make it necessary to influence a decision in the domain of the other.

Both approaches divide decisions into those in which only the client has a legitimate interest and those in which only the lawyer has a legitimate interest. Reflection on actual practice demonstrates that such a division is impossible. Clients often have an intense interest in aspects of a case that are typically considered the domain of the lawyer. For example, the decision to file a motion to suppress evidence, typically considered a matter of professional judgment, conflicted with the client's interest in going to trial in M. Dujon Johnson's case. Lawyers frequently have such strong interest in substantive goals, normally considered the domain of the client, that they will not continue a relationship if mutually acceptable goals cannot be found. For example, in Johnson's case a policy that prevented the lawyers from filing civil cases deterred them from agreeing to goals that could not be accomplished in criminal court.

An approach favoring equality and collaboration would require that all decisions about the terms of the lawyer-client relationship be made jointly by the lawyer and client. Such decisions include selecting mutual goals, choosing the means of pursuing mutual goals, dividing responsibility between lawyer and client, and establishing rules governing the relationship between lawyer and client. Such an approach assumes that both lawyer and client might have legitimate interests in any decision about the terms of the relationship. Therefore, neither lawyer nor client has a special domain. It also assumes that the client is capable of making decisions in her own interest if given full access to the relevant information available. Such information includes knowledge of the law, knowledge of facts about the case, and knowledge of interests that could potentially affect the lawyer's participation in the case. The client's interests are protected, not by carving out domains of autonomous decision making, but by providing space within the lawyer-client relationship for open negotiation of every decision that has an impact on the interests of the client or the lawyer.

A. *Lawyer-Client Negotiation*

Negotiation is a necessary process for joint decision making. A study by William Felstiner and Austin Sarat of lawyer-client interaction in 40 divorce cases suggests that negotiation is an aspect of the lawyer-client relationship whether it is planned or not.[53] The negotiating process was often complex. The negotiations concerned the goals that would be joint objectives of the lawyer and client as well as the division of responsibility within the relationship for accomplishing different tasks.

---

[53] Felstiner & Sarat, [*Enactments of Power: Negotiating Reality and Responsibility In Lawyer-Client Interactions*, 77 CORNELL L. REV. 1447] at 1450 [(1992)]. * * *

The negotiating tactics employed by clients included withholding information and excluding the lawyer from entire fields of inquiry. Felstiner and Sarat found that both lawyers and clients exercise "various levels of procrastination, vacillation, disapproval, withdrawal, repression, and [manipulation of information] that delayed, distorted and jeopardized what [the lawyer or client] was trying to accomplish."[57] They interpreted these actions as "covert enactments of power" used to gain advantage in ongoing negotiations within the lawyer-client relationship.

Negotiation produces better results for both sides if not done covertly. In their influential book, *Getting To Yes*, Roger Fisher and William Ury introduced a strategy for negotiating decisions by focusing on the interests of each side, searching for options that permit mutual gain and resolving conflicting interests by looking for objective criteria independent of either side.[59] If incorporated into the process of legal interviewing and counseling, the Fisher and Ury strategy of principled negotiation would enable lawyers and clients to make joint decisions about mutual goals and the scope of their relationship in a way that would preserve and strengthen, rather than weaken, the lawyer-client relationship. Negotiating the lawyer-client relationship is typical of many transactional negotiations in which maintaining the ongoing relationship ranks among the highest interests of both parties to the negotiation.

The possibility of lawyer dominance of negotiated decision making is a valid concern. Generally, the lawyer has more experience negotiating and more knowledge of the law. However, clients also have power in lawyer-client negotiations. Being a voluntary relationship, the client has the power to withdraw from the relationship if her interests are not satisfied. The client's ability to withdraw from the relationship is the client's most fundamental power, but withdrawal is an ultimate act and may lead to unwanted consequences for the client as well as the lawyer. The client has other sources of bargaining power. They include control over the payment of fees, the use of grievance procedures, the disciplinary procedures of bar associations, the client's ability to influence other clients or potential clients of the lawyer, and the client's ability to withhold information or action needed for the case.

Negotiating does not imply acquiescence by the lawyer to the impossible or the unlawful. At times the lawyer may have to meet the client's proposals by explaining that rules of civil procedure or rules of professional responsibility prevent the lawyer from agreeing to the client's proposed course of action. For instance, rules of civil procedure limit the number of interrogatories a party may use. If a client wants to use extensive written interrogatories without good cause the lawyer must explain that the procedure is unavailable. Rules of professional responsibility prohibit the lawyer's complicity in giving false information to the court. A client who proposes giving false testimony to a court must be told that the proposal is unacceptable. If a client insists on an unlawful course of action, the lawyer might have to end the relationship. However, just as a lawyer would not reject a potential cause of action without research-

---

57   *Id.* at 1467. * * *

59   *See* ROGER FISHER & WILLIAM URY, GETTING TO YES: NEGOTIATING AGREEMENT WITHOUT GIVING IN at xii (Bruce Patton ed., 1981). * * *

ing possible arguments, a lawyer should not reject proposed goals, procedures or divisions of responsibility without exploring their legal and practical feasibility.

At times a client might express an interest in taking a non-traditional but lawful role (e.g., conducting the cross-examination of a witness) or following an ill-advised but permissible procedure (e.g., refusing to negotiate with an adversary before the trial of a case). The client's interest might be equaled by the lawyer's interest in following a different course of action, such as an interest in pleasing the court by following local customs. The process of negotiation allows the lawyer to disclose significant interests to the client and to search for options that satisfy the interests of both lawyer and client. An attempt by the lawyer to appear neutral would possibly foreclose opportunities to discover a mutually acceptable course of action.

Recognition of the role of negotiation in lawyer-client interaction also does not mean that every decision would require detailed negotiations. Ordinarily, lawyers and clients can agree to follow standard procedures and customary divisions of responsibility without discussing every possible option. Differing interests are not likely to manifest themselves in every aspect of the relationship. However, when differing interests do arise, resolution of the differences through negotiation should not be hindered by restrictions arising out of unjustifiable assumptions about the role of the lawyer or the client. If the client's interests require extensive negotiation to arrive at joint decisions, the possibility of developing a relationship unique to the needs of the case should not be foreclosed by preconceptions of the lawyer's or the client's role.

An approach to lawyering that emphasizes the importance of negotiating the terms of the lawyer-client relationship could move lawyer-client negotiating from the covert, self-defeating activity documented by Felstiner and Sarat, to planned and organized discussion. To insure that issues are addressed openly and honestly, negotiation of the terms of the lawyer-client relationship should be an integral element of the legal interviewing and counseling process.

* * *

III. Organization of the Interviewing and Counseling Process

An approach that integrates the negotiation and renegotiation of joint decisions with the other essential functions of legal interviewing and counseling can provide lawyers with objective criteria for planning and organizing interactions with clients, for making judgments about how to communicate with clients, and for evaluating the lawyer's role in lawyer-client communication.

Like the other functions of legal interviewing and counseling (information gathering, informing and advising the client, and building rapport), negotiating and renegotiating joint decisions occurs at every stage of the lawyer-client relationship, from the initial interview to the final lawyer-client conference. Many decisions cannot be made in the early stages of the relationship, and many joint decisions must be renegotiated as new information is learned and new options develop. The legal interviewing and counseling process must allow the lawyer to move back and forth freely from the negotiation and renegotiation of joint decisions to the communication of information and advice necessary to implement joint decisions. The process is cyclical.

The legal interviewing and counseling process enables lawyers and clients to work in harmony to solve legal problems. It also creates the lawyer-client relationship. Before examining the progression of activities and decisions that create and define the lawyer-client relationship, it is helpful to consider the forms that the joint decisions of lawyers and clients can take. Joint decisions can take a variety of forms ranging from formal written contracts to informal mutual expectations.

A. *Forms of Joint Decisions*

The lawyer-client relationship is the product of a series of joint decisions made by the lawyer and her client. A joint decision might take the form of a formal written contract (e.g., a retainer agreement). It might take the form of an oral understanding (e.g., a promise to appear in court). It might also take the form of informal mutual expectations (e.g., both sides will be courteous, or both sides will be straightforward). The lawyer-client relationship is both contractual and social. It is contractual in that the lawyer and client exchange express or implied promises to behave and perform in certain ways. The lawyer-client relationship is a social relationship in that the lawyer and client also develop patterns of behavior and expectations in the course of their relationship that are not based on an exchange of promises.

The express contractual agreement between lawyer and client might be extremely detailed or very brief. It might include the legal problem to be addressed, how fees will be calculated, and actions to be taken by the lawyer or client. Implied agreements between the lawyer and client are also a part of the contractual relationship. They might include the lawyer's implied promise to file a pleading before the statute of limitations expires or the client's implied promise to pay the expenses of an expert witness. Both the express and implied contractual agreements between the lawyer and client are negotiated and renegotiated throughout the lawyer-client relationship.

Issues such as the frequency and nature of communication between the lawyer and client can be made the subjects of contractual agreement, but ordinarily they remain a part of the social relationship that the lawyer and client develop. The patterns of behavior that make up the fabric of the social relationship between the lawyer and client are no less important to the accomplishment of their joint objectives than the contractual agreements. The behaviors might include such expectations as how much authority is delegated to the lawyer to make decisions, what types of information the lawyer will share with the client, and, also, what information the client will share with the lawyer.

Many aspects of the social relationship between the lawyer and client acquire significance because of the age, race, class, gender, sexual orientation, ethnicity, disability or social background of the lawyer or client. For instance, the lawyer's decision to call a client by first name instead of by a courtesy title might communicate a sense of equality in some relationships but might communicate a lack of respect in others.

The terminology used by a lawyer might be an issue in the lawyer-client relationship. For example, widespread objection by persons with disabilities to use of the term "handicapped" led to amendment of the Individuals with Disabilities Education Act in 1990 to eliminate use of the term handicapped throughout the statute. A lawyer can adapt to changes in terminology by listening to how clients describe themselves or matters in which they have an interest and by initiating discussion, if necessary, of what terminology should be used.

A lawyer or client who desires a change in the character of a lawyer-client relationship must renegotiate the social as well as the contractual terms of the relationship in order to bring about the change.

B. *Four Essential Functions*

Recognition of the importance of incorporating lawyer-client negotiation into the legal interviewing and counseling process influences the way that a lawyer plans and organizes interaction with a client. The organization of communication between a lawyer and client must provide for four essential functions of legal interviewing and counseling: (1) gathering information; (2) informing and advising the client; (3) building rapport; and (4) negotiating and renegotiating the terms of the lawyer-client relationship. The organization of lawyer-client conferences should take into account the progression of decision making from more general threshold issues to more specialized decisions that must be made in the course of negotiations or litigation. Furthermore, at each stage of the relationship the organization of the legal interviewing and counseling process should balance the four essential functions so that they complement and reinforce each other as much as possible.

1. *A Progression of Joint Decisions.* An approach that incorporates the negotiation of joint decisions requires that information-sharing and decision-making proceed cyclically. The Binder, Bergman and Price model for information gathering can be an effective method of organizing the lawyer's search for information. The progression from broad inquiry with open-ended questions to theory verification through more focused questioning advocated by Binder, Bergman and Price[112] gives the lawyer an opportunity to identify the facts and concerns of greatest interest to the client. However, the path from information gathering to decision making is not always a straight line. Information gathering might have to be interrupted to permit negotiation of issues that affect the scope of the lawyer's questioning, or even to negotiate the types of information that the client will make available.

The agenda of the lawyer-client conference might itself be a subject of negotiation as the client might have interests in how the conference is conducted. The lawyer should be prepared to modify a proposed process for information gathering, especially if cultural or experiential differences give a client an interest in pursuing a different process. Research by John M. Conley and William M. O'Barr suggests that telling a story in chronological narrative form is difficult for some people and could lead to the omission of important information.[114] Some clients might prefer to organize the story around individuals and their relationship to the critical event rather than

---

112   [DAVID A. BINDER ET AL., LAWYERS AS COUNSELORS: A CLIENT-CENTERED APPROACH] at 112-114 [(1991)].

114   *See* CONLEY & O'BARR, [RULES VERSUS RELATIONSHIPS: THE ETHNOGRAPHY OF LEGAL DISCOURSE], at 58-81 [(1990)].

chronologically. The lawyer should be prepared to negotiate a suitable format for information gathering if the interests of the client require it.

Preliminary issues that might need to be negotiated or renegotiated should be raised early in each lawyer-client conference. The lawyer should begin a conference with a client by proposing an agenda for the meeting. The proposal can be informal, such as, "I would like to ask you some questions, and then we can talk about what needs to be done. Is that all right?" The lawyer's initial inquiry should be not only, "What kind of problem are you having?" but, "How would you like to approach it?" or "What do you want to do?"

Threshold issues in the development of the lawyer-client relationship must be decided before information gathering, informing and advising can be narrowed. Such threshold issues might include the degree of confidentiality of lawyer-client communication, whether or not the client wants a role in planning the organization of the conference, and whether the client's problem, broadly defined (e.g., whether it is a criminal matter, a civil matter, or a regulatory matter) is a matter the lawyer can undertake.

As the exchange of information and advice progresses, the negotiation of the terms of the lawyer-client relationship requires decisions about the boundaries of the relationship, such as the scope of the lawyer's authority to act for the client, limitations on the lawyer's responsibility, and the division of responsibility between the lawyer and client. At later conferences between the lawyer and client the issues that must be negotiated and decided become more specific and might deal with how the client's case should be presented, how to frame the story of the case, what forum should be selected, and what specific roles the lawyer and client will have.

The roles of the lawyer and client in the investigation of a case or in negotiations with an adversary cannot be fully negotiated until both lawyer and client have substantial information about facts and alternatives available to them. As the lawyer and client learn more about a case, and eachother, negotiations between lawyer and client will encompass a growing range of issues. For instance, the lawyer might believe that taking a deposition would increase the chance of prevailing and the client might not want to bear the expense. Issues agreed upon at the beginning of a case might have to be renegotiated as the client becomes more sophisticated and the lawyer learns more about the client and the case. A decision made early in the case to rely on alternative dispute resolution procedures might have to be renegotiated if it appears that the adversary is not participating in good faith.

Although it is important to plan the organization of legal interviewing and counseling, the organization must be flexible. If difficulty arises in gathering information it might signal that the organization of an interviewing and counseling conference needs to be renegotiated. The lawyer must exercise judgment in deciding whether it is possible to take action in union with the client or whether it is necessary to resume the negotiation or renegotiation of mutual goals or strategies.

2. *Balancing the Essential Functions of Legal Interviewing and Counseling.* The organization of lawyer-client interaction should balance the essential functions of legal interviewing and counseling so that they complement and reinforce each other as much as possible. The functions of information gathering, informing and

advising the client, building rapport, and negotiating and renegotiating joint decisions might reinforce each other, but often they are in conflict, and the pursuit of one might jeopardize accomplishment of the others. When the functions are in conflict, it is particularly important for the lawyer to be sensitive to the organization of the lawyer-client interaction.

For example, at the initial conference between lawyer and client it might be a mistake for the lawyer to begin gathering information without first negotiating guidelines for the lawyer-client relationship. A common problem at an initial interview is the failure to negotiate a mutual understanding about the protection of client confidences. The client's reluctance to divulge information does not stem from a failure to understand rules of professional responsibility. The client is justified in wanting to negotiate an explicit understanding of how the lawyer will use information revealed by the client. In the absence of an understanding that the client's confidences will be protected, the client might be unwilling to reveal important data to the lawyer. The degree of confidentiality of the lawyer-client relationship is a matter for negotiation. Although professional ethics require a lawyer to preserve the confidences of clients, the client makes an express or implied waiver of confidentiality in many cases. If the client asks the lawyer to initiate negotiations with an adversary, the request implies authorization to reveal some information that would otherwise be confidential. If the facts of the case are sensitive, the client might be willing to reveal some facts but not others to the adversary and might withhold facts from the lawyer in the absence of an explicit understanding that the lawyer will reveal only what the client authorizes. The lawyer should make it clear that information will be used in the negotiations only with the specific agreement of the client. Thus, negotiating guidelines for the confidentiality of the relationship early in the lawyer-client interaction reinforces the other function of gathering information. The client is likely to provide more information after a full discussion with the lawyer of how it will be used.

The use of confidential information is only one of many issues that might require negotiation before the other functions of interviewing and counseling can unfold. Negotiations about the structure of the lawyer-client relationship can also facilitate the functions of gathering information and building rapport. For example, if the client needs an order for protection from domestic violence, local statutes might require the petitioner to supply detailed information to the court. Some of it might be embarrassing to the client, and both lawyer and client might prefer to have a more developed relationship and better rapport before discussing sensitive topics. If the lawyer and client discuss the problem and agree to postpone usual steps in developing the relationship between them in order to respond to the emergency, loss of rapport can be avoided and the client might be more willing to communicate sensitive information. At a later encounter, the lawyer can ask about the client's ultimate goals and gather detailed information about the case.

Negotiating some issues in the lawyer-client relationship might conflict with the other functions of legal interviewing and counseling. For instance, it is important for the lawyer to negotiate a fee arrangement at an early stage. Disclosing the lawyer's conditions of employment and seeking the consent of the client is essential to the integrity of the relationship. However, presenting the client with a retainer agreement specifying the steps the lawyer will take to collect unpaid fees risks a loss of rapport. The organization of lawyer-client conferences could provide for such potential conflicts by deciding on joint objectives and means of pursuing them before discussing the proposed agreement on fees.

Often building rapport and gathering information are in conflict. For some clients building rapport might require that the lawyer take time to tell about herself and her experience (or lack of experience) before any other communication takes place. The time the lawyer spends telling about herself might delay the collection of important facts. However, the confidence and trust that results from full rapport between lawyer and client can justify the time spent.

Recognition that legal interviewing and counseling is a cyclical process of sharing information and negotiating joint decisions enables a lawyer to plan and propose agendas for lawyer-client conferences that meet the needs of both lawyer and client.

* * *

B. Communicating Interests and Values

Because the communication between a lawyer and client is usually confidential, very little is known about how practicing lawyers interpret the law and the legal system to their clients. In the unique study described in the following excerpt, Austin Sarat and William L.F. Felstiner observed and recorded the lawyer-client conferences in forty divorce cases. They found striking similarities throughout the United States in how lawyers talk to clients.

Austin Sarat and William L.F. Felstiner, *Lawyers and Legal Consciousness: Law Talk in the Divorce Lawyer's Office*, 98 YALE L.J. 1663 (1989)*

Two very different pictures of mass legal consciousness have wide currency in contemporary legal scholarship. The first is one of public cynicism, of instrumentalism without conviction, of citizens both litigious and, at the same time, alienated from the legal system. This image of mass legal consciousness informs many accounts of the so-called "litigation explosion" and suggests that legal institutions are no longer accorded sufficient legitimacy and respect. It is deployed to identify and respond to the alleged erosion of public confidence in legal institutions.

---

    *   Reprinted by permission of The Yale Law Journal Company and Fred B. Rothman & Company from The Yale Law Journal, Vol. 98, pages 1663-1688.

The second view of mass legal consciousness presents a picture of a loyal and trusting public, deeply attached to law and legal institutions, taken in by law's manners, myths, and legitimating narratives. This portrait is rooted in the Tocquevillian assertion that Americans understand their social relationships and their social problems through the lenses of law: To resolve "their daily controversies," they "borrow . . . the ideas and even the language peculiar to judicial proceedings."[4] Tocqueville believed that the pervasiveness of the language of law in the activities of everyday life reflected and reinforced widespread allegiance to legal institutions. Today, a similar portrait of unquestioning public respect for the rules and institutions of law underlies most critical scholarship.

Specifically, critical scholarship has identified three characteristics of mass legal consciousness which help explain the hegemony of law. First, Americans are said to regard their legal institutions as legitimate and, therefore, to acquiesce in the social order which those institutions help maintain. Second, the legitimacy of law is said to be a product of "mystification," an illusory picture which law constructs of itself. Americans are alleged to subscribe to myths about law produced and disseminated by legal officials, the foremost being that law is neutral, objective, and governed by rules. The third characteristic of mass legal consciousness is said to be the pervasive belief in the inevitability and immutability of existing legal arrangements. By unearthing these three elements, critics hope to undermine what they see as excessive public respect for, and belief in, the existing legal order.

In both pictures of mass legal consciousness lawyers are recognized as important intermediaries between clients and the legal system; many more people see lawyers than have direct contact with formal legal institutions. Much of the conversation between lawyers and their clients is educational: lawyers provide knowledge of how particular legal processes work and introduce their clients to ways the law might be used in their favor. Practicing lawyers thus play an important role in shaping mass legal consciousness and in promoting or undermining the sense of legitimacy that the public attaches to legal institutions.

* * *

I. LEGITIMATION AND PROFESSIONALISM:
A DEBATE ABOUT THE LAWYER'S ROLE

* * *

Critical scholars want lawyers to demystify and delegitimate law by exposing the inconsistency and arbitrariness of legal doctrine to their clients. They want lawyers to teach clients that rules are used by legal officials as instruments to achieve personal and political purposes or as post hoc rationalizations. Rights and responsibilities cannot be deduced from pre-existing rules because rules are so

---

4   A. DE TOCQUEVILLE, DEMOCRACY IN AMERICA 357 (F. Bowen ed. 1876).

numerous, complicated, and ambiguous that they can accommodate almost any result. In short, critics want lawyers to help politicize mass legal consciousness.

The replacement of legal formalism with a less rule-centered portrait of law is part of the effort of critical scholars to reform lawyer/client relations and to provide an alternative to traditional understandings of professionalism and professional power. Critical scholars assume that undermining formalism will contribute to the reorganization and reorientation of the legal profession. Stripped of the illusion of rule determinacy, clients will demand a more active role in the management of their own legal problems; lawyers will be free to come to terms with the constitutive effects of their activities, and, finally, lawyers and clients working together can break down the artificial boundaries separating law and politics. As Gabel and Harris put it, lawyers should demystify the law and help their clients to "reconceptualize the way the legal system itself is organized."[38]

II. The Empirical Project

A. *Methods*

Whether the assumptions of the organized bar or of the critics bear any relationship to actual legal practice is currently unknown. To develop a clear understanding of lawyers' contributions to the maintenance or critique of legal legitimacy, and to assess the implications of what lawyers actually tell their clients about the legal process for a theory of mass legal consciousness and professional authority, we conducted an observational study of lawyer/client conferences. Over a period of 33 months, we observed and tape-recorded 115 lawyer/client conferences in California and in Massachusetts. This effort consisted of following one side of 40 divorce cases, involving 20 different lawyers, ideally from the first lawyer/client interview until the divorce was final.

We chose to examine divorce, in part, for tactical reasons. Divorce, however, is by no means typical of all areas of practice. Thus the generalizations that can be drawn from this data may be limited. Nonetheless, our findings are highly consequential, given the prevalence of divorce and the fact that it is one of the areas of most frequent contact between citizens and the legal system.

B. *The Data*

Conversations between lawyers and clients are frequently about the nature, operation, and efficacy of legal institutions and the characteristics, motivation, and competence of legal actors. They range from perfunctory recitation of rules governing the divorce process to complicated explanations of particular results. While discussions of the legal system—what we call law talk—are spread throughout our sample of lawyer/client conferences, they are not spread evenly. Law talk tends to occur when prompted by significant events in the course of litigation. It is, in addition, more likely to be initiated by a client inquiry than volunteered by a lawyer. Finally, what is perhaps most striking is the relative uniformity in law talk among the many

---

38   Gabel & Harris, [*Building Power and Breaking Images: Critical Legal Theory and the Practice of Law*, 11 N.Y.U. Rev. L. & Soc. Change 369] at 376 [((1982-83)].

different kinds of lawyers in our sample. Differences in experience, type of practice, and degree of specialization are not associated with differences in the picture of law presented in the divorce lawyer's office. Moreover, despite important differences in legal culture and the rules governing divorce, there are no significant differences in the frequency, range, or pattern of law talk in Massachusetts and California.

1. *The Significance of Rules*

How do lawyers describe the law, particular laws, or legal processes to their clients? What characteristics are attributed to law and the legal system? Before addressing these questions it is important to note that there is a rather regular progression in law talk—a constant narrative structure. Almost all divorce cases start with the lawyer's brief explanation of divorce procedures as they are laid out in statutes. This law talk is full of explicit references to rules. Lawyers begin, if you will, with formalism. They describe the *rules* that frame the process, establish its limits and provide alternative routes. However, the written law is only a starting point. Formalism fades rather quickly as the interaction progresses. Descriptions and characterizations of the legal system now occur mainly when clients ask why a particular result occurred or what results might be predicted. In response to these unsolicited inquiries, lawyers rarely make explicit reference to rules. Rules and their relevance are taken for granted by lawyers who generally act as if clients already shared their empirical understanding of the legal process. As a consequence, at this point in the interaction, lawyers do not take the time to introduce their clients to the subtle manner in which rules penetrate and permeate the legal process.

Lawyers often talk about what can or cannot be done or what is or is not likely to happen without explicitly noting that their views are shaped by statutes or court decisions, although the trained ear would recognize that their formulations are clearly rooted in an understanding of rules. Typical of such implicit rule references is the response of a lawyer to a client's inquiry about what would happen to child support if his income were reduced:

> You should keep in the back of your mind . . . that if your financial situation changes in the future the judgment can be modified. That's not a problem. It is not etched in stone. . . . Anything to do with a child is always modifiable by the court.

How and why judgments in court "can be modified" is not explained. The client is not told whether that possibility is a result of the ease with which lawyers escape from earlier agreements, or of the sympathy that judges display toward children, or of the rules governing support, custody, and visitation. This failure to identify rules and highlight their relevance prevents clients from having access to law's public discourse and the resources for argument provided by an understanding of rules. In addition, it helps lawyers maintain a monopoly of those resources and focuses client concerns on the professional skills and capacities of their particular lawyer.

Lawyers, in fact, talk to clients in much the same way that they talk to each other. There is no acknowledgment that clients may not already understand the salience of rules. The normal conventions of lawyer-to-lawyer discourse are not translated for divorce clients, who most often bring an incomplete and unsophisticated understanding to their encounters with the legal process. There is no concerted effort to bridge the gap between professional and popular culture.

Even when rules are explicitly noted, there are few references to or discussions of their determinate power. Lawyers do not describe the legal process of divorce as rule driven or rule governed. Nor do they usually provide an explicit evaluation of the rules themselves. However, when rules do at times emerge as part of the explicit conversational foreground, they are generally disparaged; contrary to the assumptions of both the organized bar and critical scholars, lawyers rarely defend the rationality, importance, or efficacy of legal rules.

For instance, it is common for lawyers to mock rules as irrelevant or useless in governing the behavior of legal officials involved in the divorce process. Rules, according to one California lawyer, do not give "clear-cut answers. If they did we wouldn't even have to be talking." A Massachusetts lawyer spoke more generally about the irrelevance of rules in describing the way the local court system operated: "There really are no rules here, just people, the judge, the lawyers, the litigants." Another maintained that the scheduling of cases reflected the virtually unchecked power of the bailiff:

> When you get heard is up to the court officer . . . he's the one who controls the docket. They don't have a list prepared and they don't start at the top and work down. They go according to his idea of when people should be heard.

Other lawyers extended the argument about the ambiguity or irrelevance of rules to more important aspects of the legal process of divorce. Several suggested that judges refuse to be guided by rules of evidence and that such rules therefore have no bearing on the way hearings are conducted. One Massachusetts lawyer explained that he would not be able to prevent the opposing spouse from talking about his client's alleged adultery even though such testimony would be technically inadmissible according to the literal rules:

> I think we just have to realize that it is going to come out. We just have to take that as a given. You know, they teach you in law school about how to object to that kind of testimony: 'I object, irrelevant,' 'I object hearsay.' But then when you start to practice you realize that judges, especially in divorce cases, don't pay any attention. They act as if there were no rules of evidence.

Other lawyers expressed frustration about the ineffectiveness of rules governing filing periods, establishing times in which responsive pleadings are to be submitted or governing the conduct of discovery.

Moreover, statutes concerning property division are, as lawyers tell it, often irrelevant to actual outcomes. Lawyers in both Massachusetts and California regularly criticized judges for failing to pay attention to those statutes or to the case law interpreting them. As one Massachusetts lawyer told her client in a case involving substantial marital property,

[i]n this state the statute requires judges to consider fifteen separate things, things like how long you were married, what contributions you and Tom made, whether you have good prospects. It is a pretty comprehensive list, but I've never seen a judge make findings on all of those things. They just hear a few and then divide things up. Things generally come out roughly even, but not because the rules require it.

Thus, what lawyers do make visible as they respond to their clients' questions are the personalities and dispositions of actors within the legal process and the salience of local norms rather than legal rules. Emphasizing people over rules, law talk acquaints clients with a process in which judges exercise immense discretionary power. The message to the client is that it is the judge, not the rules, that really counts. What the judge will accept, what the judge will do is the crucial issue in the divorce process. With respect to property settlements, Massachusetts clients are reminded that since all agreements require judicial approval there is, in effect, "nothing binding about them. The judge will do what he wants with it." Another lawyer explained that in dividing the marital property, "the judge can do with it as he chooses to do." Still another lawyer informed his client of what he called the "immense amount of power and authority" which judges exercise and suggested that the particular judge who would be hearing his case would use that power "pretty much as he deems fit."

A second way in which lawyers denigrate rules is by characterizing them as unnecessarily technical. They claim that, as a result, even judges and lawyers frequently do not know what they mean. For example:

> Client: Tell me the mechanics of this.
> Lawyer: You should know. It's your right to know. But whether or not I'm going to be able to explain this is questionable. . . . It's sort of simple in practice, but it's very confusing to explain. I've an lawful lot of really smart people who've . . . who've asked me after the divorce is over, now what the hell was the interlocutory judgment?

A third criticism of rules focuses on their weakness in guiding or determining behavior outside the legal process. Lawyers identify the limits of law. They acquaint their clients with the limited efficacy of legal rules and caution them not to rely too heavily on rules or court orders. This is particularly the case when a lawyer is trying to discourage his client from pursuing a certain course of action. Thus, in one California case, where the client was very disturbed by her husband's continuing refusal to obey a restraining order [restricting contact with the spouse], the lawyer's response was to stress the futility of going to court to obtain a contempt order:

> Lawyer: Okay. So what you would like is what? You'd like phone calls if he needs to . . .
> Client: Limited to the concern of the children or medical bills, and, you know, never mind giving me all his heartache trouble.
> Lawyer: You know, he's in violation of the court order [restricting contact with the spouse], but to take him to court, it can be done, I'm not saying that we won't do it or anything, it's a matter of proving contempt. We can prove it, but then what do you get out of that. You don't get anything. . . .

"You don't get anything" suggests that since rules and orders are not self-executing, they do not necessarily govern behavior or resolve problems. This lawyer is schooling his client in what has been called the "gap" problem, the extremely loose coupling between legal rules and social behavior.

The same emphasis on the limited efficacy of rules is conveyed in the following discussion of joint legal custody, where a Massachusetts lawyer talks to his client about the irrelevance of joint legal custody. The client brings substantial preconceptions about the meaning of joint custody to this exchange. The lawyer's effort is to disabuse him of those preconceptions, to emphasize that what matters is the ongoing relationship between spouses rather than the posture of official arrangements:

> Client: The custody order I would like to be requested is joint custody. That means, and correct me if I'm wrong, that I shall be aware and informed and be able to have input in my daughter's life as well as she would have the right to be aware, informed and have input in my daughter's life whether my daughter is there with her or here with me.
> Lawyer: There's no such thing as court ordered joint custody. In a realistic sense, real sense of joint custody. You are thinking of it as if there is. Just like it's a court ordered step. You get custody and she has visitation rights. That means definite things. You have the custody and you control the child's life: She becomes a visitor. On joint custody that's something that is worked out between the two individuals who right from the start are able to deal with the child with at least no major problems. They would deal with the child in a normal manner. . . .

This lawyer's comparison of court orders and what really happens suggests a parallel between the ineffectiveness of rules governing the behavior of those who are part of the legal apparatus—lawyers, court officers, judges—and the limited power of rules to control the behavior of people outside the legal process.

2. *The Critique of Legal Officials*

When attention is turned from assessment of rules to evaluation of the behavior of actors in the legal process, lawyers continue their law talk in a critical, realistic mode. In their characterizations of judges, lawyers tend to think in comparative terms, often noting that different judges react differently to similar combinations of facts and rules. Thus law talk turns discretion into difference. The legal process is said to individualize results, not on the basis of the idiosyncratic fact patterns or the litigants' particular needs, but as a reflection of the propensities of the individual judge. In one case, for example, the lawyer suggested that he might have difficulty getting the judge to accept a particularly favorable division of property. As he explained,

> [s]ome judges wouldn't care. I could do it by representation. Just present the papers to the judge, tell him what we've done, and he'd shake his head and go okay, and sign an order and we'd be all done. Okay. Judge Max doesn't let that happen. . . . Other judges, excuse me, most other judges,

would not even ask questions other than saying something like 'Are you satisfied?' But this judge . . . will very likely want to ask her if she indeed understood the agreement before she signed it and he'll want to run through the thing.

As another lawyer put it, "[t]here are no 'for sures,' you are dealing with the antithesis of science . . . at the other end, with opinion, viewpoint."

While some judges are considered better than others, and better judges are deemed "smart" or "experienced" or "savvy" or "reasonable," the clear tendency of lawyers' talk about judges is to call into question their skill, dedication, and concern. In the lawyers' vocabulary, no word is more prominent in describing judges than "arbitrary." Judges are portrayed in ways that suggest that they are capable of making decisions on grounds that have nothing to do with facts or rules. As one Massachusetts lawyer said in explaining to his client what to expect in a hearing, "[y]ou have to be careful in terms of how you do certain things because you can really prejudice the judge against you by bringing up certain issues in a certain way."

In another conversation, a lawyer encouraged his client to adopt a particular demeanor in the courtroom:

Lawyer: But you sit there somewhat respectful. Do the same thing in this courtroom, okay? Hands in front of you are just fine, or on the table just fine. I don't care, but don't cross your legs.

Client: (Crosses legs)

Lawyer: Okay. I asked you not to do that. If you do it I'll probably nudge you in the shoulder and ask you to stop crossing your legs. Okay? No arms over the back of the chair. Okay?

Client: (Sits up very straight)

Lawyer: That's alright. You look nice and neat and scared that way, that's okay. But sit up with your arms and hands in front of you; I don't care where they go, but in front of you, and without the crossed legs. Okay? And then one other thing I ask of you. Don't go like this (puts head on his desk), or anything, but don't go like this. Okay? No matter how tired you are tomorrow morning I want you to look pretty alert. It's best if you can just remember to keep your hands on the table or in your lap, and you'll be all set. Okay? Why? Why am I asking you to do this? Only because the judge will be looking at you. Okay? And he's going to make a decision, a fairly important one, and I don't want that decision to be influenced just by the way you sit.

Client: Like, he don't care.

Lawyer: Well, he might, if he doesn't like you. Okay? And even if he doesn't like you but you look concerned and you're interested, he'll probably go your way anyway. Okay. Judges are people, and well, I'll tell you, we might as well play the odds rather than have some surprises develop just because the judge doesn't like the way you're sitting. Okay?

Client: Some would do that?

Lawyer: Yup, some do.

In explaining why he must talk about such things as posture and appearance, this lawyer is guarding against the possibility that the judge's decision may be "influenced just by the way you sit." While this is an extreme case, law talk is peppered with references to extra-legal factors that influence judges, including their backgrounds and experiences. Thus one lawyer cautioned a female client that her chances of arranging joint custody for her child were not great because

> [j]udges don't have a real good sense of what to do about this. . . . It is a very male dominated view, because most of the judges are in the 40s and 50s or over and the concept anybody would . . . They find it hard in their own experience to digest the notion . . . In their day, when they were practicing lawyers, you either get custody or you don't. So they don't quite know what to do with joint custody.

While judges are influenced by minute details of client dress and behavior in the courtroom, they are also alleged to be incapable of grasping the nuances and subtleties of legal arguments, uninterested in the details of particular cases, and to act in ways that make their decisions difficult to understand. As one Massachusetts lawyer said in explaining a judge's ruling:

> I don't think he's totally oblivious to some of the more obvious things. The more subtle things I'm not sure he's catching on to. And he's not exercising his authority to allow us to delve into a lot of the more subtle things. Perhaps the judge doesn't want to rule on the motion for sanctions because he wants you to get your evidence in . . . okay . . . and because he wants to hear enough so that he can grant you your divorce . . . there is the possibility . . . that he can see at least the obvious things down below him and those are enough for him. And that he doesn't care about the subtleties and that those things that are so obvious to him are all he needs and he wants to give you . . . what we want to obtain. Now that's a possibility, and we shouldn't discount it yet. . . . However . . . as much as I hope and pray that that's just what he's doing I'm not all that optimistic on it either. And I wouldn't guess that he was doing that based on the reputations developed among other . . . attorneys. Based on that reputation I have my doubts that he is that bright . . . he's that aware of what's going on. But if he is we should be aware that he might be.

This lawyer's critique is doubled in the rhetorical play of the words obvious and oblivious. At the same time, the general criticism is softened by the suggestion that the judge's limitations may work, in this case, to the client's advantage.

In other cases, judges are said to lack the requisite qualifications or knowledge to make the decisions that the law requires them to make. As one California lawyer put it, in explaining why he was not optimistic about a favorable ruling on a complicated property issue, "[y]ou've got a judge with a 110 IQ who is sitting there, and he says, 'Hey, I don't want to hear all the god damned complications . . . Let's do it the simplest way.'" Or as another lawyer suggested:

[h]ere's the problem. . . . What they really ought to do in domestic law is every judge who hears domestic law ought to have, literally a CPA, or somebody familiar with financial data, prepare for him or her something before the case to say somehow there is magic going on here. . . . [Judges] don't think even logically to say where's the money going to come from.

Criticism of judges does not end with issues of competence and qualification; it also includes issues of motivation, sensitivity, and concern. Many judges are said to be lazy, insensitive, concerned more with their own convenience than with the issues, and generally uninterested in "justice." As one lawyer put it, they "don't want to make tough decisions." Another suggested that

[j]udges are not tolerant of subtleties. . . . All they want you to do is, they want you out the door and the rulings are usually gross. They're gross rulings. They don't consider and factor in the subtleties of what the people are trying to do.

The talk of this and other lawyers indicates that the ease of making decisions is a major influence on the judiciary. It suggests that the inattentiveness, insensitivity, and incompetence of judges must be taken into account in deciding how to process cases. As one lawyer says, "whatever arbitration system you choose is better than the judge."

These explanations describe the legal system as idiosyncratic and personalistic, and, in so doing, they endow lawyers with a mystique of insider knowledge and experience that is unavailable to even well-educated, well-read clients. They suggest that the skilled lawyer is more than a good legal technician; he is someone who knows the back corridors of legal institutions, the personalities of judges and how to present client desires in such a way as to appeal to the judges' proclivities. They highlight a "private knowledge" the full details of which cannot be shared with clients, and, at the same time, serve to shift responsibility for bad results from lawyers to powerful and unapproachable legal authorities. The critique of judges thus works to empower lawyers at the expense of their clients.

* * *

IV. CONCLUSION

In a legal order whose legitimacy rests on the claims of formalism and, to a lesser extent, on those of equity, the law talk of the divorce lawyer's office may be partially responsible for the common finding that people who use legal processes tend, no matter how favorable the results of their encounter, to have a less positive view of the law than those with no direct experience. Law talk in the divorce lawyer's office, as it interprets the internal workings of the legal system, exposes law as failing to live up to the expectations which people have about it. The law talk of the divorce lawyer's office is replete with "rule skepticism." Moreover, while it acknowledges the importance of discretion, and of the particular proclivities of the actors who exercise it, it is highly critical of their motivations, capacities, commitments, and concerns. If the presentation of a formalist front, or of a legal system whose officials are fully committed to doing substantive justice, is necessary to legit-imate the legal order, then the presentation of the legal process at the street level may work to unwind the bases of legitimation that other levels work to create.

* * *

_____

Lawyers not only interpret the legal system to clients, they also convert clients' experiences into stories with legal significance. In the next excerpt Clark D. Cunningham uses two case studies to illustrate the challenge of trans-lating clients' experiences into the language of law and translating the lan-guage of law for clients.

Clark D. Cunningham, *A Tale of Two Clients: Thinking About Law As Language*, 87 MICH. L. REV. 2459 (1989)*

* * *

* * * The central activity of lawyering is generally described as representing clients. * * *

* * *

The very familiarity of the phrase "representing a client" prevents us from rec-ognizing the profound ambiguities created by describing lawyering as representation. * * * [In this article] I tell two true stories from my experience of representing clients. As I suggest in the titles of these stories, in one case the lawyer's work was reduced to mere "re-presentation," while in the other "the representation" of the client that "appeared" in court seemed to be an autonomous creation unconnected to the client's own words. Although both stories are therefore about "representation," in neither tale does the lawyer achieve the kind of identity with his client that seems to me to be at the core of what it means to be a lawyer: the achievement of two persons somehow speaking with one voice. Instead, in one story the client is struck mute while in the other the lawyer is silenced.

* * *

In the "Case of the Silenced Client," our client was charged with the misde-meanor of Operating a Vehicle While Under the Influence of Liquor ("OUIL") and a companion per se violation of operating a vehicle with a blood-alcohol level in excess of 0.10%. When the students presented the case to me after the intake inter-view, they reported that the client admitted that he was guilty. They therefore assumed that the representation would involve routine plea bargaining with most of our energy focused on sentencing and obtaining a restricted driver's license.

_____

*   Reprinted with permission.

The representation had an unusual complicating factor: the client's native language was Spanish and his ability to speak English was limited. Accordingly, we had arranged for a law student fluent in Spanish to attend the intake interview as a translator. As we reviewed the video tape, I noted that when the students asked the client, "What happened?" his first response was *Yo soy culpable.* The translator paused for a moment and then said, for the client, "I'm guilty." The students confirmed that this exchange was the basis for their report that the client "admitted" he was guilty.

I was curious to find out why the client's words were translated as "I'm guilty," and so I sought out the translating law student. The translator confirmed my suspicion that the Spanish word used by our client, "culpable," was a close cognate of the English word bearing the same form. As a result, the client's statement could have also been translated: "I am culpable" or "I am blameworthy." Thus the client could have been saying something more like, "I feel bad about what I did," or "I accept personal responsibility for the consequences of my action." If the client's words had been given these latter possible translations, the students might well have reached a different conclusion about his admission of "guilt."

I first met our client myself a few days later when we went to court for his arraignment. The court file did not contain the police report or the results of the breathalyzer test our client told us he was given at the police station. The test results were important because different levels of blood alcohol bring into play both different statutory presumptions and different plea bargaining positions under the operating policies of the local prosecutor's office. We were also eager to see whether the police report corroborated our client's story that the test was administered despite his indicating to the police that he did not speak English. Because administration of the breathalyzer test requires consent, the police must read a *Miranda*-type statement of "chemical test rights" before giving the test. We thought there might be a good argument for suppressing the test results on the theory that our client did not give an informed consent.

We decided that our lack of necessary information made plea negotiations at the arraignment unwise. We therefore told our client, through the law student interpreter, that we recommended a plea of "not guilty." Our client said he did not understand and insisted that he was "guilty." At that point our case was called and we advised our client to "stand mute," which he did. When we told the judge that our client was "standing mute," he entered a plea of not guilty "on behalf of" the defendant, as is customary. It is because our client was thus "struck mute" in court that I call this the "Case of the Silenced Client."

Even though the client was silent, the judge, in effect, put words into his mouth: according to the record, he "pled" not guilty. The court (with our tacit connivance) "made up" a defendant who took the proper adversarial position so that the case could proceed. In this sense, the defendant who "appeared" in court was indeed only a "representation," an image projected by the institutional needs of the judge and lawyers.

I was intrigued and troubled by the gap between ourselves and our client over the word "guilty." On what authority, with what justifications, could we proceed to "represent" him if we did not understand what he meant by "culpable" and he did not understand what we meant by "not guilty"? It was while this experience was fresh in my mind that the next story took place.

* * *

One day a local federal magistrate called our clinic to ask whether we would represent a prisoner who had a civil rights case ready to go to trial. The prisoner had litigated this federal lawsuit himself for several years, surviving two summary judgment motions brought by the defending prison officials. Early in the litigation he had filed a motion for appointment of counsel, but later fired the appointed counsel for reasons not entirely clear from the record. On the day of trial, the judge had concluded the prisoner needed the assistance of counsel, adjourned the case, and asked the magistrate to contact us.

We accepted the appointment only after receiving and reviewing the extensive record, which included the transcript of an evidentiary hearing and several opinions on the summary judgment motions. Upon acceptance, we filed an appearance before meeting with our prospective client, contrary to our usual practice. Communication with the prisoner was difficult because he had been placed in solitary confinement in a high-security prison.

By the time we filed our appearance, a deadline was fast approaching for a hearing on the defendants' third motion for summary judgment. I discussed with the team of students whether we should try to meet with our client before filing a supplemental brief on the motion. The students understandably felt that filing the brief was the more urgent task and plausibly suggested that our first meeting with the client might go better if we had the finished brief to show him.

Our plan of action seemed for a time to work well. When the students met with the client for the first time, they gave him a copy of the brief and he seemed pleased with them and their work. However, at the next meeting, in court for the summary judgment hearing, the client showed the students a page in the brief where he had written "Wrong!" in the margin next to a sentence that stated: "Plaintiff's claim is that he was placed in segregation and deprived of good-time credits based on false misconduct reports and hearings of which he received no notice and was not permitted to attend." Several days after the hearing, our client mailed to the court a handwritten motion invoking the right of self-representation and asking the court to terminate our appointment to represent him. The stated ground for the motion was that "false/wrong claim and/or statement of fact has been advanced/made" by the appointed counsel, specifically citing the one sentence in the brief.

Because of the timing of our entry into the case, in preparing the brief and our trial strategy we had relied largely on the court's previous opinions as defining the factual and legal issues. "The case" as we thus understood it centered on our client's claim that several prison disciplinary hearings had been conducted in his absence. The key factual dispute was whether he had received notice of these hearings and refused to attend, as the prison officials claimed, or whether, as he contended, he learned of the hearings only afterwards when discipline was imposed. The sentence our client had marked as "wrong" in the brief reflected this understanding of "the case." I have placed "the case" in quotation marks because, as we soon learned, "the case" that our client had in mind was different from "the case" we learned about by reading the court's opinions.

Of course, when we received the motion, the students and I went back out to the prison. Because another faculty member had supervised the summary judgment hearing, it was my first face-to-face encounter with our client.

We met in a kind of cage between the prison control center and the solitary confinement wing. The only chairs were welded together in a straight line, so I ended up squatting against the wall in order to look at my client while we spoke. Without the security of a desk and armchair, I felt somewhat naked and no doubt looked a bit foolish. It was, in retrospect, perhaps an appropriate posture for an unusual interview.

I found myself looking slightly upwards into the eyes of a very intense and determined man. He began by insisting that there was no need for a trial because there were "no factual issues." He kept saying that the defendant officials had "violated the eighth and fourteenth amendments" by disciplining him without legal authority. As we talked it became increasingly clear to me that he viewed "his case" not as a complaint about lack of notice but as an assertion that the entire prison disciplinary system was illegal. His central point seemed to be that the disciplinary system was not authorized by specific state statutes and regulations but was only based on administratively adopted policy statements and operating procedures. Although he agreed that he had said in his complaint (and still insisted) that he had received no notice of the hearings, he saw no need for a trial on that disputed fact issue in light of his more systemic attack on the legitimacy of the prison's entire disciplinary system.

We tried to accommodate his vision of the case with our trial strategy by suggesting that ours was simply an alternate theory of liability: even if the court would not accept his sweeping attack on the system, he might still prevail by showing that the defendants had failed to follow due process in his particular case by not notifying him of the hearings and by conducting them in his absence. He would have none of it. He did not want us to assert *our* theory of "the case" precisely because that theory was not *his* case, even though the events described in his *pro se* complaint gave rise to the claim both we and the court had assumed he was making.

My interview ended on a somber note. I asked the prisoner what he wanted us to do at this point. His terse reply: "Don't show up in court."

We did show up in court because the judge asked us to withdraw formally on the record, on the morning of trial. Our client reaffirmed in open court his desire to represent himself, but before the judge granted his request the judge attempted to review with our client what the issues would be for trial. He was surprised to hear our client assert that there was no need for trial but, despite admirable patience, the judge was unable to get our client to explain clearly the position disclosed in our interview with him.

At that point I felt placed in a very peculiar position. My client had told me in no uncertain terms that he did not want me to represent him, yet I felt a desire to help him make himself clear to the judge. But without a client to "speak for," it was I who "stood mute" in the courtroom. I realized that without a client I had no identity in that court, in that case. Nonetheless, I decided to speak.

I rose to my feet, but first addressed not the court but my erstwhile client. Turning to him, I explained how I felt, that I knew he did not want me to "speak for him" yet I thought it would help if I shared with the judge my understanding of what he had said in our interview. I told him to feel free to stop me at any point and asked him to listen carefully so that he could correct anything I said when I was done. I then faced the judge and stated my understanding of how my client's idea of his claim differed from the claim described in the court's earlier opinions and our brief, carefully choosing my words in an effort to make sure that my client could understand everything I said. It was a challenging experience, this effort to speak to the court in my client's voice rather than my own. At the conclusion, I turned to my client and asked him if what I had said was a fair statement of his claim. He looked slightly surprised but pleased and said, "yes, that's about right."

The judge then granted the request for self-representation and the student attorneys and I left.

By silencing his lawyers, our former client gained the right to speak for himself in court but, ultimately, he still did not feel he was heard. I am told that after we left the judge continued the dialogue with the plaintiff and eventually allowed him to proceed on his claim that the disciplinary policies were without legal authority. Although the trial resulted in a judgment for the defendants, the judge did not treat the claim of systemic illegality as frivolous. In fact, the court noted that the challenged prison disciplinary policy had been invalidated by the state supreme court three years earlier because it had not been promulgated through formal rulemaking in accordance with the state's Administrative Procedures Act. Unfortunately for the plaintiff, the state supreme court's declaration of invalidity was not given retroactive effect and plaintiff's claim related to discipline imposed before the state supreme court decision.

* * *

The titles and epilogues to these two tales represent my retrospective interpretation of the events in the two cases. At the time, * * * I was primarily aware simply of the gap between lawyer and client and, as a result, between court and client. The traveler on the London subway, the "Tube" or "Underground," hears a warning whenever a train pulls into a stop: "MIND THE GAP," intones a forbidding, mechanical voice. The warning causes the traveler to notice that the platform and threshold of the train car are not a continuous surface, that a narrow but potentially perilous gap separates the two. The tales of the mute client and the silenced lawyer served for me as such a warning; like the busy and preoccupied Tube traveler, I needed to be reminded that a deep gap can sever client from lawyer.

This kind of gap seems a common feature of lawyer-client relationships. Austin Sarat and William Felstiner are in the process of publishing the results of a monumental study of lawyer-client conversations. Their data consist of 115 tape-recorded conversations taken from forty divorce cases observed over thirty-three months, in two sites from different states. Their detailed study of these conversations shows a consistent pattern:

Clients focus their interpretive energy in efforts to construct an explanation of the past and of their marriage's failure. Lawyers avoid responding to these interpretations because they do not consider that who did what to whom in the marriage is relevant to the legal task of dissolving it. In this domain clients largely talk past their lawyers, and interpretive activity proceeds without the generation and ratification of a shared understanding of reality.[26]

Indeed Sarat and Felstiner go so far as to suggest that the lawyers and clients seem to be dealing with two different divorces.

Although I was not familiar with Sarat and Felstiner's study at the time of the two cases, almost the same point had come to mind when a sentence surfaced in my mind from the depths of my memory: "We don't care about what happened; we only care about what is going to happen." This sentence seemed to describe the arraignment in the Case of the Silenced Client: although the plea appeared to be a statement about what had happened (whether our client had committed a crime), as lawyers we only seemed to care about what was going to happen as a result of the plea. "Not guilty" was not a faithful description of our client's culpability, but rather only a rhetorical move in a verbal game in which the client was silent and largely powerless.

I recalled the sentence as the title of an article I had assigned for reading several years earlier to a class in legal ethics.[28] I then reread the article, which was based on a nine-month study by social scientist Carl Hosticka of lawyer-client interactions in two different law offices. The title was a direct quote from a conversation between Hosticka and one of the attorneys studied. Hosticka concluded that the lawyers studied often redefined "what happened" to their clients in order to change "what is going to happen":

> "[W]hat happened" is not immutably fixed in an objective reality, but is a social construction based on experience and interaction. . . . [T]he primary issue may not be what happened to the client, nor what kind of trouble the client is in, but who has the power to say what happened and to define the kind of trouble. Indeed the power to define the client's problem is one tool professionals may use to induce client cooperation with their prescription of appropriate behavior. . . .
>
> This control over the interaction is reflected in the official definition of reality that results from the interaction. . . . [P]ower is exercised *through* the definition of reality. . . .

I found myself uncomfortable with Hosticka's assumption that lawyers are autonomous creators of meaning, not bound in any way to the client's account of "what happened." Nonetheless, both of my cases seemed to authenticate Hosticka's view: in the Case of the Silenced Client, by instructing our client to stand mute know-

---

26   Sarat & Felstiner, *Law and Social Relations: Vocabularies of Motive in Lawyer/Client Interaction*, 22 LAW & SOC'Y. REV. 737, 742 (1988) (footnote omitted).

28   Hosticka, *We Don't Care About What Happened, We Only Care About What Is Going to Happen: Lawyer-Client Negotiations of Reality*, 26 SOCIAL PROBS. 599 (1979).

ing that a not guilty plea would be entered, we "re-defined" our client's reality, to control what was going to happen; in the Case of the Silenced Lawyer, the client realized that the only way he could regain control over "his case" was to deprive his lawyers of the power to define "what happened."

I found myself focusing on Hosticka's initial premise: that "what happened" is not "fixed in an objective reality" but is rather "a social construction." The subtitle of his article, "Lawyer-Client Negotiations of Reality," is based upon this premise. The assertion that "reality" is socially constructed, negotiable, although familiar in the academic world, would be startling to many of our clients. Indeed, the gap in both tales seems related to this point. The silenced client stood mute because in his view he was "really" guilty and it would be a lie to plead not guilty. My other client silenced me, claiming I had literally misrepresented his case. By constructing a different legal claim than his out of the same facts, I made a "false" statement. Neither client seemed to think that "reality" was something that could be "negotiated" between him and his lawyer or with the court. "Something" *really* did happen and when their lawyer's story, told on their behalf to the court, failed to correspond to that reality, the lawyer ceased to "represent" them.

Yet the lawyer's work for a client cannot be limited to mere representation. New meaning *is* given to the "reality" the client brings to the lawyer and in some way that "reality" is altered. But how can the lawyer explain to the client, and to himself or herself, this process of creation and alteration without losing a sense that something really happened? How can the lawyer continue to care about what happened while creating what is going to happen? How can the lawyer tell a story that is nonetheless *true*?

In trying to answer these questions I turned to thinking about the relationship between experience and knowledge and the relationship of language to both.

* * * In trying to communicate her experience to her lawyer, the client typically is struggling herself to organize, structure, and relate that experience to other experiences she has *known* and thereby to understand herself what happened. Her inability to *speak* the language of the law prevents her from *knowing* her experience as a legal event. This desire for knowledge is often expressed in the question, "Do I have a case?" As the lawyer attempts to "make a case" out of the client's lay narrative, there is indeed a transformation of "reality," but only at one level, the level of knowledge. The lawyer cannot change the client's raw memories of the experience but can and indeed must alter the client's knowledge of "what happened" by reconstituting that experience into a different symbolic form.

If law is seen as a language, then the lawyer becomes a translator. Unlike "representation" and "creating a representation," the idea of translation captures that elusive sense of two persons speaking with one voice. If language is intimately bound up with the way we think about experience, then talking about experience in a different language necessarily entails knowing that experience in a somewhat different way. Thus the translator must give new meaning in the process of translation, yet at the same time the translator strives to speak, not as herself, but as another.

* * *

Good translation is a hard job. It is easier either to just re-present or to create your own representation. If the lawyer merely re-presents, then the client's experience may not gain legal significance. But if the lawyer "creates a representation," the legal significance may not be rooted in the client's own experience. Either way, both client and judge are poorly served because the failure of communication is a loss of potential new knowledge. * * *

As illustrated by the Case of the Silenced Lawyer, it can be a mistake to assume that a client is interested only in "winning" the case rather than in understanding both "what happened" and what is happening. In that case, the student lawyers and I had made the common assumption that our client was interested only in an outcome measured by dollars and that he did not particularly care what route was used to reach that outcome. In fact, he cared very much what route was used, what story was told on his behalf. Words mattered very much to our client; one sentence in a brief submitted in his name made all the difference in our representation of him.

More than anything else, this client wanted to project his inner mental certainty onto the world in which he lived by asserting that the system that very literally constrained him was fundamentally unfair. He wanted to give his own meaning to the events that led to his solitary confinement and thereby control a world that had as its definitive quality the prisoner's utter lack of control. The case we planned to try would instead have reaffirmed the rules of the constraining system while giving him in return, at best, only money.

* * *

Failure to translate for the client not only risks a dissatisfied client; it also impoverishes the law. Like all forms of knowledge, law arises out of experience. Clients are the source of that experience. Their understanding of that experience is likely to retain elements lost in the legal understanding, elements that might enrich our legal knowledge. * * *

* * *

* * * Thinking about law as language and lawyering as translation will not bring me to a full understanding of my experience of being a lawyer nor fully communicate that experience to you. But it is a beginning. Tell tales to yourself and others about your own lawyering experiences and compare them to my own two tales. Then * * * apply the metaphor of translation; see if it "fits"; think about what meaning is added and left out. And then, consider writing to me so that this story may continue. * * *

In the next excerpt James B. White elaborates on the role of the lawyer as a translator by examining what a good translator does.

James B. White, *Translation as a Mode of Thought*, 77 CORNELL L. REV. 1388 (1992)*

* * *

[I]f the lawyer is a translator, should we not teach our students how to do what translators do? This would include giving prominence to the process of interviewing clients and witnesses, seen not simply as bureaucratic "intake" or as the occasion for emotionally supportive (or destructive) behavior but as an essential part of all lawyering. More than that, this kind of teaching would insist, across the curriculum, on bringing to the surface of attention some sense of the different ways in which the stories of cases we read could be told in different languages and voices. It would lead us to call upon our students' sense of ordinary language, ordinary life, not just as a matter of intellectual curiosity or political ideology, but with the sense that to do this is an important part of training in the activity of lawyering.

* * *

It is one thing to criticize someone else for failing to hear your voice, for failing to accord you respect, and so forth, but is quite another to criticize *oneself* for failing to hear another or accord that person respect. In the first case the objects of complaint are salient and visible—the speaker feels injured by them—while in the second the occlusions and erasures and insensitivities are one's own and, however visible they may be to others, they tend in the nature of things to be invisible to oneself. Take racism as an example: as Professor Delgado and his co-author argue in their paper in this symposium,[5] a great deal of racism is simply invisible to most white people, partly because it takes place out of their sight or because they miss, or misunderstand, what they actually see; but more profoundly and disturbingly, often because it is unwittingly their own. This is a feature not only of racism and sexism, I think, but of cultural power more generally: it tends to be invisible to the person who exercises it.

To try to learn what your conduct looks like from another's point of view, then, is not so easy. The natural first step is to read or try to listen to what others say, but when I, at least, read accounts of the experience of African Americans, today or under slavery or Jim Crow—say in the autobiographies of Frederick Douglass, Malcolm X, Dick Gregory, or Maya Angelou, or in the novels of Alice Walker or Toni Morrison, or in *Black Ice*, Lorene Cary's recent story of her early life—I find that it is easier for me to identify with the person suffering injustice and talking about it than it is to see myself on the other side of things, in the slavemaster or bigot or patronizing white liberal.

This is not surprising, I think, for it arises not only from the desire to avoid painful truths, but from our common understanding of the relation between narrator

---

5   Richard Delgado & Jean Stefancic, *Images of the Outsider in American Law and Culture: Can Free Expression Remedy Systemic Social Ills?*, 77 CORNELL L. REV. 1258 (1992).

and audience in such a text, which invites the sharing of the speaker's point of view.[6] In reading *David Copperfield*, for example, one feels with the narrator how horrible the Murdstones are, how lovable Peggotty, without asking how lovable or brutal one is oneself. As readers we are always on the right side, except in the greatest works of art: The *Iliad*, which teaches its audience both the equal reality of all human experience and our irresistible need to forget that knowledge; the novels of Jane Austen, which implicate the reader in misreadings that parallel the misreadings the reader makes in life; or *Huckleberry Finn*, which involves the white reader in the impossibility of his language of race. * * *

It is related to another point, suggested above, namely that to think of conversation as a kind of translation entails an ethic of fundamental equality. If it is recognized that translation always involves significant gains and losses in meaning, there can be no universal language in which universal truths are uttered. This means that every act of interpretation, every conversation in the world, takes place across differences in language, for none of us speaks exactly the same dialect as anyone else, and these differences cannot be resolved by the imposition of a super-language. We are each entitled to our own meanings and these can never be the same. This point is eloquently made, in somewhat different form, by Mari Matsuda in her recent article on accent discrimination,[8] which maintains, and in a literary way demonstrates, that every American speaks English with an accent. There is no "normal" or "standard" pronunciation, and we should not talk as if there were. The same thing is true of our languages as well: each of us speaks a dialect, or a set of dialects; to see this is to recognize that lines of communication must be established among us, and among our languages, from positions of mutual equality, across whatever lines of power may deny this truth. * * *

* * *

* * * The language of the law, with all of its distortions—in fact by means of these distortions—enables us as a society, and as citizens and litigants, to achieve something we could not do through our own unmediated voices. Consider here as one example the finding of Sarat and Felstiner * * * that lawyers in divorce cases seem to disregard much of what their clients are really saying to them.[9] In particular, we are told, they do not seem interested in "who did what to whom."

---

6   How can a writer avoid this blunting of her story? If she attacks her audience directly, she risks alienating it entirely. And in some sense the deepest point of much of this writing is to demonstrate the human reality of one's experience, which depends upon the very sympathetic identification I describe. I have no ready answer, but can simply report that James Baldwin's THE FIRE NEXT TIME (1963) did seem to persuade many white people of their own implication in the system of race, in part by describing it persuasively as a white invention. Something of the same thing is true of Catharine MacKinnon's work, especially FEMINISM UNMODIFIED (1987), I think for the same reason.

8   Mari J. Matsuda, *Voices of America: Accent, Antidiscrimination Law, and a Jurisprudence for the Last Reconstruction*, 100 YALE L.J. 1329 (1991). * * *

9   Austin Sarat & William L.F. Felstiner, *Law and Social Relations: Vocabularies of Motive in Lawyer/Client Interaction*, 22 LAW & SOC'Y REV. 737 (1988).

What might an experienced divorce lawyer say on her own behalf? Perhaps something like this:

Of course it is wrong if we fail to hear and respond to what our clients are telling us, and I am sure I do that all too often. We should listen with special care when they talk about their children, for example, and try to provide a conversational context in which they can discover more fully their own wishes as they come to recognize more fully the reality of their own situation.

But this very phrase suggests that we have a role that cannot be reduced to meeting their wishes, or translating their stories without distortion, even if that were possible, namely to help them to come to see the reality of their situation and to form wishes appropriate to that. It is so common as to be nearly universal that divorcing people think unrealistically about their futures, both in economic terms and in terms of their children's lives. In fact they often deny that they are really getting divorced—they see the future as a continuation of their marriage, which has often by then dissolved into a fight. And an essential part of the fight is blame and retaliation: wanting to retell the story of what the other spouse did wrong and they did right, over and over, as a way of justifying themselves to themselves and others, and indeed as a way of justifying their own present hostility, their refusal to cooperate, their insensitivity to their children's needs, their denial of changes in their economic and social circumstances, and the like. If all goes well, someday they will in fact give up the fight, and the claims of right and wrong by which they carry it on. The question, who did what to whom, will then have meaning only diagnostically, as they try to figure out their own contribution to what was bad about the marriage so that they will not repeat it.

One of our objects as lawyers is to help them move in that direction earlier than they otherwise might: to help them to accept their circumstances and to form appropriate wishes based upon them. As an essential part of doing that, we divert their attention repeatedly from what they wish to tell us to what they are denying. Part of our task, that is, and a good part, is the education of our clients. Two good lawyers, working with such an attitude on opposite sides of a bad divorce, can greatly reduce the amount of misery the divorcing partners inflict on themselves and others, and do so in ways for which they will later often be grateful.

And think of this too: bad as the language of divorce law is, and the institutions through which it works, suppose that we tried to deal with the breakdown of relations solely in the language of the parties themselves. We would have nothing but negotiation, and ill-focused negotiation at that—no way to learn from the past, and no way to reach a collective judgment about important matters, such as the value of work in the home or the way to think about custody and visitation.

The legal process works a translation that entails a loss, but it also entails, or can entail, a gain. The proper duty of the translator is not solely to the language and text out of which she works, but runs as well to the language in which she speaks, and to the demands of the social and cultural context in which she functions.

This explanation has considerable appeal to me, and not only in connection with divorce. Think of the relation between police officer and suspect: here the law of the Fourth Amendment and unlawful arrest provides a language for thought and speech about this relation, and for its regulation as well. It will never reflect without distortion whatever an officer or suspect might say. But it may nonetheless be a good language—one that can make possible thought and argument about the transaction that they share in a way that does more to include the legitimate concerns of both, and of the rest of society too, than either of their own ways of talking, standing alone, would do. I think, then, that we need to give attention not only to the erasures and occlusions and misrepresentations that take place in legal discourse but also to what we think to be the merits and values of this language, or the opposite of these things, and hence of translation into it.[11] A part of our subject, in fact, is the analysis and comparison of different languages, or different versions of the same language, of which we can ask what they enable us—as lawyers, as people, and as a society—to achieve, as well as what they inhibit or prevent.

A great deal of attention has recently been focused on the way the law disadvantages the powerless. Law is indeed sometimes conceived of simply as a disguise or legitimization for the exercise of power, a huge fraud. Of course there is the element of disguised power, but that should not blind us to what else is present, namely that the law also can and does provide protection to the powerless. The cynical and power-hungry Callicles in the *Gorgias* showed that he knew this when he said that all talk about justice should be discarded as pointless sentimentalism; it is only a convention, he said, imposed on the powerful by the weak, and those who are powerful, like him, should deny its force. But for this very reason it is right for those of us who live with the law as its caretakers to assert its possibilities, knowing that it is partly on behalf of the powerless that we do so.

* * * But there is another side: the law is not only a source of violence, it reduces violence; it not only oppresses the weak, it defends them. The conversion of the language of the people into the law, while always an effacement, may also be right, both from their own point of view and from the point of view of the larger world the law is trying to create. There is thus in the law an ineluctably tragic element that the image of translation captures: translation is always imperfect; but it is nec-

---

[11]   It is important to recognize that the client or witness often has not one single story, which will be translated well or badly, but a variety of possible ways to tell his story, among which choices must be made. The very process of translation may draw attention to this circumstance and help the speaker work out the version of his experience which is most satisfactory to him in this context.

essary that it be done if we are to listen to each other at all, and certainly if we are to maintain a generally shared language of justice. * * *

C. Transcending Differences

Lawyers and clients must always transcend differences between them to work together. When the differences relate to class, race, ethnicity, gender, sexual orientation, disability or age, a lawyer must pay special attention to the need for effective communication. As the next excerpt points out, learning from each other's experiences can make differences a source of strength.

Gerald P. Lopez, Rebellious Lawyering, One Chicano's Vision of Progressive Law Practice (1992)*

* * *

Growing Together While Remaining Divided. When a client asks a lawyer to intervene in his life, he seeks help at the risk of further subordination. In agreeing to intervene, the lawyer extends uncertain help at the risk of further estrangement and reprobation. Each must receive the other and collaborate on these terms, however tentative and fragile the bond. Each must learn not only to accept but to embrace this tension in their relationship. Just as tension can forestall and undermine their collaboration, so too can it inform their understanding of just how they must both grow together and remain divided in their work.

In seeking a lawyer's intervention, a client necessarily invites scrutiny of his life. "Understand my situation," he urges, "and help me to understand what I might do, if at all and perhaps through law, to change it." To help the lawyer make sense of and optimally empathize with his situation, a client must expose how and with whom he lives life, and how he would have himself understood. He must make available, insofar as he can, his ways of acting, talking, perceiving, and coping with the world. At the same time, a client must grow in his understanding of how others view his situation. He must be willing to help the lawyer represent him to himself: "This is how you look to the world, this is how you look to the law." In requesting a lawyer's help, a client not only jeopardizes his sense that he can manage on his own but exposes his way of life to an outsider—worse still, to a professional member of a subordinating culture, a representative licensed by the state.

In making his life available in his own terms and in understanding his life in other (including law's) terms, a client always teaches and always learns. Obviously, he instructs the lawyer about his own practices; but he learns, too, most immediately about what the lawyer needs to understand. Obviously, he learns about how others, particularly those in the legal culture, perceive his situation. But he teaches as well, perhaps about what those in the law take for granted or never venture to learn—how it feels to experience the problem he faces, how he thinks it could be solved most effectively, how exactly certain legal practices modify his life. As teacher and as student, a client must both appreciate and critique, at once operating together with and in opposition to his collaborator, the lawyer. In engaging in this collaboration, the client agrees to play an active role in the resolution of what is often a crisis situation in his life. And both the lawyer and the client must understand and accept the responsibilities that this effort demands.

On her part, a lawyer necessarily undertakes a delicate and presumptuous project in agreeing to intervene to help a client help himself. She holds herself out as sufficiently curious and skilled to learn about and eventually understand the client's situation *in* the client's terms. "I think I can understand your situation; at least with your help I'll try," she proclaims through her intervention. "And I think I can help you understand what, if anything, you can do (perhaps through me, perhaps through the law) to change it." At the same time, she recognizes the practical and moral limits on her project. She asks a client to expose his life to someone whom she too thinks *should* be perceived as possibly endangering his capacity to help himself in other ways and further entrenching his already subordinated status.

Moreover, she at least secretly aspires to an understanding of her client and his situation perhaps beyond her reach. With a client's help, she can know a great deal about her client's life, but not all. Much of what she knows may tell more about her than about her client since, at some level, she likely "monopolizes" the conversations through which her client must make himself understood in his terms. After all, countering the force of privilege, power, and special knowledge of the legal culture is no easy task and no permanent achievement. * * *

Together with the client, the lawyer must combat monopolized conversations without abandoning her obligation to challenge her client—to critique as well as appreciate his understanding of his situation, the legal culture, and the strategies he pursues. Yet at the same time, the lawyer must guard against that element of critique which squelches the client's resourcefulness and imagination: "You don't fully understand the complexity of the situation, the rules by which this game is played, or you wouldn't be so outraged by that particular aspect of it." It is all too easy for the lawyer to cut off approaches to or insights into a problem by writing off the client's fury as naiveté.

Like the client, the lawyer always teaches and always learns. In trying to understand the client's situation, she learns about the client's practices and about the relationships in which she intervenes. Even here she teaches when she lets the client see what she needs to learn, and, less obviously, when, as an outsider, she challenges thoroughly accepted ways of thinking and acting. Obviously she teaches about the legal culture, about its story/argument strategies, about its ways of understanding and responding to problems. But thankfully she learns here too, sometimes about law's limited imagination, sometimes about its irrelevance on the street, its failure to penetrate the lives of subordinated people. In mutual appreciation and critique, she learns to collaborate with another problem-solver. Together they bring what they are doing with one another under scrutiny and devise strategies for putting their ideas into action.

Continuous practical knowledges, distinct and converging, collaborate best when they confront one another. As part of a larger collective effort within the rebellious idea of lawyering against subordination, a client and a lawyer do not want simply to add to each other's knowledge, a bit of this and a bit of that coexisting easily. Instead, they desire to challenge what each knows—how each gained it, what each believes about it, and how each shares and uses it. In so doing, they work constantly (if often in unglamorous and fragmented ways) to change the very understanding most people cling to both about what clients and lawyers share and about how they use what each knows about living and lawyering.

* * *

Although clients might have personal identification related to class, race, ethnicity, gender, sexual orientation, disability or age, each client is unique. A lawyer must be prepared to learn about a client's background and experience, and must not make assumptions about the client's personal identification or perspective. The next excerpt discusses the importance of learning about personal identification issues.

Bill Ong Hing, *Raising Personal Identification Issues of Class, Race, Ethnicity, Gender, Sexual Orientation, Physical Disability, and Age in Lawyering Courses*, 45 STAN. L. REV. 1807 (1993)*

* * *

* * * [A]n effective community lawyer must be aware of the personal identification differences of the various players involved in a case. Imagine the following situation: I am a twenty-seven-year-old male, Chinese American lawyer who is hired as the housing attorney for the East Palo Alto Community Law Project, located in East Palo Alto, California. East Palo Alto is a poor, small, incorporated community located adjacent to several affluent communities. In 1950 East Palo Alto had fewer than 2,000 residents and almost no African Americans. The population grew to 15,000 by 1960, with about 3,300 African Americans. By 1980, the city of 18,850 was about 64 percent African American and 13 percent Latino. Today, almost a third of the population is Latino. The Law Project is a community poverty law office which handles housing, public benefits, and education related cases. Suppose that one of my first clients is Ms. Pierce, a 30 year old, single, African American

woman who has two children. She has sought my help because her apartment is in terrible shape. There are plumbing problems and roach infestation, not all the burners on the stove work, and plaster is falling away in certain parts of the unit, and she cannot get the manager of the building to fumigate and make necessary repairs. In addition to the manager, there are an array of possible players in this case. Other tenants, the building owner, the health inspector, tenant rights advocates, rent board officials, Ms. Pierce's children, and media reporters come to mind.

* * *

This attorney-client hypothetical illustrates why training in dealing with personal identification differences is important to the success of the community lawyer. Every client is unique, and the effect of identification differences will vary from client to client. However, I am convinced of the need to be conscious of and sensitive to these differences in the development of all attorney-client relationships.

An attorney who differs from a client in personal identification terms can be effective, but must be conscious of these differences and work towards developing the necessary rapport. This rapport can be critical to the success of the relationship and the outcome of the case. An attorney who is out of touch on these issues may be able to get by and even achieve good results for clients. However, learning about identification differences and understanding their potential significance can only enhance the attorney-client relationship and the attorney's effectiveness. Even if one is skeptical of their significance, most people will recognize the value of being tactful when confronting at least one of the following issues: class, race, ethnicity/culture, gender, sexual orientation, disability, or age difference. For example, most attorneys realize that sensitivity to gender difference with the client can help the relationship. Practicing and learning how to deal with that difference is the honing of a skill helpful to the practice of law. Similarly, developing an approach in the case of racial or cultural differences is also useful, especially when the client may have strong separatist feelings and the attorney would benefit from understanding the source of that sentiment.

Some individuals may view all this as a matter of common sense. But the truth is that most young community lawyers need training on how to respond to personal identification issues. We all have opinions on these matters, but we have had little opportunity to review these issues in the critical format of the classroom. Common sense, without training, is dangerously fashioned by our own class, race, ethnicity/culture, gender, and sexual background. What we think of as common sense may make little sense or even be offensive to someone of a different identification background. Thus, the opportunity to learn and discuss different approaches with the help of different perspectives from readings, the opinions of others, and self-critique is unique.

Continuing the hypothetical example of the Chinese American attorney and the African American client, one can imagine that personal identification differences with other players will impact the case as well. In the interaction of lawyer and/or client with the manager, the apartment owner, the health inspector, other tenants, tenants' rights advocates, and rent board officials, these differences will affect the cooperation, ability to communicate, and receptivity to unique perspectives. For example, if one strategy which Ms. Pierce and I conclude is worth pursuing involves contacting other tenants in the building in order to form a tenants group, the fact that some tenants are Spanish speaking, undocumented immigrants will be quite important to the success of such organizing. Communication problems have to be solved if those tenants don't speak English and neither Ms. Pierce nor I speak Spanish. Ms. Pierce and I will have to deal with the fact that some tenants may be biased against undocumented workers or non-English speakers. All tenants who are asked to organize may fear retaliatory eviction by the owner, but undocumented tenants might also fear being reported to immigration officials. In addition, suppose that two tenants supportive of a tenants' organization are a lesbian couple who has been ostracized by many other tenants in the building. Ms. Pierce and I would need to sensitize other tenants to accept homosexual lifestyles.

In short, understanding personal identification differences and how to manage them is integral to my vision of good community lawyering. * * * Similar to training in alternative approaches to legal problems, training on identification issues, working in partnership with the client, working with community allies, and respecting the client's own talents contributes to establishing an attorney-client relationship that is not simply another subordinating experience for the client, but is productive.

* * *

––––––––––––––

In the next excerpt Naomi R. Cahn warns against letting beliefs about social categories become stereotypes about individuals. She examines styles of lawyering that have been labeled male and female, but observes that no single style of lawyering can be attributed to men or women.

Naomi R. Cahn, *Theoretics of Practice: The Integration of Progressive Thought and Action: Styles of Lawyering*, 43 HASTINGS L.J. 1039 (1992)*

* * *

I. Thinking About a Female Style of Lawyering

A. Women in the Law

* * *

What has caused a contemporary rethinking of the existence of male or female styles of lawyering? The answer is complex and includes stereotypes about men and women, studies of differences between male and female lawyers, theories about the

––––––––––––––

construction by males of the current legal system, perceptions about male and female lawyers, and the celebration of women's differences from men in some feminist writing. Sometimes, perhaps, the cause is a longing for an alternative style to the hardball, aggressive tactics of many lawyers. Or, it simply may be that because women have been excluded for so long, we imagine, and hope, they will act differently. The idea has pervasive, even seductive, appeal. Indeed, studies do show differences in how some men and women react to law school, how they respond to the legal system and decide moral issues, and how their styles are perceived by others, lending even more credibility to the supposed existence of different styles.

* * *

Studies of women's responses to the legal system also show some gender-based distinctions. * * * [A Stanford study] found that women responded somewhat differently than men to two hypotheticals—one on media law and one on legal standing—designed to test whether moral reasoning was dissimilar. The media law hypothetical asked respondents to balance the right to a free press against an individual's right to privacy where a reporter snapped a picture of a naked woman being dragged from her house by police.[23] In the standing hypothetical respondents were asked whether a mother could appeal her son's murder conviction and imminent execution. The study found some limited support for the conclusion that male and female lawyers would find different factors relevant in reaching their decisions.

In another study of lawyers' attitudes, Stacy Caplow and Shira Scheindlin surveyed 1975 and 1976 female graduates from fourteen law schools (there was no male comparison group).[25] Approximately one half of the respondents believed that their sex had hampered their success. Caplow and Scheindlin concluded that, underlying many of the problems for the women attorneys they surveyed, "perhaps too amorphous to touch, is the very nature of the practice of law. . . . Many of our respondents said they would prefer that the law was constructive, proactive, and that the bottom line was less important than the person the lawyer seeks to help." The authors believe that if these seemingly female qualities affect how law is practiced, the relationship between lawyers and their clients, and the lawyers' decisionmaking process, then women will have a "profound" effect on the law.

In one extensive study of the different moralities, the authors found that female lawyers were more likely to be care-oriented than male lawyers.[29] * * * Women seem more likely to prefer less adversarial methods of resolving disputes that do not harm the other side—relying on methods of problem solving and reconciliation rather than aggressive posturing—and women are more likely to be the primary, and expected, caretakers of children.

---

23   [Janet Taber et al., *Gender, Legal Education, and the Legal Profession: An Empirical Study of Stanford Law Students and Graduates*, 40 STAN. L. REV. 1209] at 1277 [(1988)].

25   Stacy Caplow & Shira A. Scheindlin, *"Portrait of a Lady": The Woman Lawyer in the 1980s*, 35 N.Y.L. SCH. L. REV. 391 (1990).

29   RAND JACK & DANA CROWLEY JACK, MORAL VISION AND PROFESSIONAL DECISIONS: THE CHANGING VALUES OF WOMEN AND MEN LAWYERS (1989).

Studies also have supported the belief that women suffer discrimination in their legal employment and in the courts. Various studies of gender bias in the courts have found that judges treat women differently, and that male lawyers are even worse than judges in their discriminatory treatment. Women also are the subject of differing perceptions by courts, other lawyers, and clients. The profession has been, and is still, primarily composed of white male lawyers. There are real differences in how seriously women are taken as attorneys. Even if women do not act differently from men, they look different. One comparatively recent article pointed out (in all earnestness) that women face "[t]he initial 'minus' of being recognizably non-male," but counseled that this could be "immediately superseded" if the women were knowledgeable and well-prepared.

Judges, attorneys, and court personnel do not give as much credibility to women as to men, and perceive women as acting differently from men. The ABA Commission noted:

> Not all male lawyers resort to the stereotypical aggressive, hard-ball, 'male' style of lawyering. Many are soft-spoken and conciliatory in nego-tiations. They may be more skilled at listening than at arguing. But when men display these varieties in lawyering styles, it is regarded as just that—a difference in style. When women depart from the stereotypical style of aggressive lawyering, it is more likely to be regarded as a gender difference and a basis for questioning competence.[38]

Women and men, then, both use different styles at different times. Women, however, are perceived as using a female style when they depart from traditional patterns of lawyering; men are not. Men's differences are accepted, while women's differences are ascribed to gender and, correspondingly, devalued.

There is evidence that men and women experience substantial differences in treatment within the legal profession. Given these differences, in conjunction with stereotypes about the appropriate roles of men and women and theories about dif-ference, it is understandable why the question of whether men and women use dif-ferent styles is relevant. The existing system reflects male experiences and viewpoints. I thus focus on examining the existence of a female style. An image of a female style suggests that it is different from what currently exists, and, implicitly, that what currently exists is male.

B. A Female Lawyering Process

This section suggests what a female style of lawyering might look like. By drawing on the work of feminists who have suggested that men and women speak in a different voice, it is possible to outline some of the dimensions of this alternative style.

Let us start by imagining a female style of lawyering based on these studied dif-ferences, together with observations from the work of relational and affiliational fem-

---

38   ABA [COMM. ON WOMEN IN THE PROFESSION, REPORT TO THE HOUSE OF DELEGATES 13] at 4 [(1988)]. * * *

inists such as Carol Gilligan and Nel Noddings.[41] Simply summarized, these feminists assert that women use an ethic of care in their moral reasoning, while men are more oriented to an ethic of rights. Women are more caring and more oriented towards relationships than are men. Women tend to perceive morally troubling problems as situations in which people might be hurt, and then try to resolve conflicts by strategies that maintain connection and relationship. Correspondingly, women are contextual, looking at surrounding circumstances. Men, by contrast, are oriented towards individual autonomy and impartial rules. They tend to see problems in terms of violations of rights, rather than relationships between people. Men are more likely to resolve conflicts by examining competing rights, and applying neutral and abstract standards.

The implicit critique of the legal system is that it has been constructed by (white) men to accord with male values, overlooking or devaluing female values. The legal system values claims of individual rights, and overlooks claims that are based on connection. A legal system based on connection, rather than on competing rights, would result in valuing different aspects of each case. For example, in pregnant substance abuser cases the issues are currently framed as a conflict between the rights of the fetus and those of the mother, rather than a valuing of the connection between mother and fetus. When such a problem is viewed as a conflict between competing rights, it leads to state prosecution of mothers for substance abuse; when viewed in terms of connection, it suggests that a more appropriate outcome would be better information about birth control and improved prenatal care for pregnant substance abusers.

Using ethic of care principles, what would lawyering look like? Others have begun to answer this question by imagining lawyering in the following terms:

1. More negotiation, mediation, and other alternatives to traditional adversarial dispute resolution;
2. more appreciation of the other party's perspective—more understanding and recognition of that party's interests;
3. more appreciation for the relational context in which the client's problem arises, more understanding of the totality of our client's experience and more listening to her;
4. less aggressive, confrontational trial and pretrial tactics—more disagreement on real issues than creation of disputes solely to disagree; and
5. more altruistic reasons for choosing to become lawyers—more public interest work.

* * *

---

41   *See* CAROL GILLIGAN, IN A DIFFERENT VOICE: PSYCHOLOGICAL THEORY AND WOMEN'S DEVELOPMENT (1982); MAPPING THE MORAL DOMAIN (Carol Gilligan et al. eds., 1990); NEL NODDINGS, CARING: A FEMININE APPROACH TO ETHICS & MORAL EDUCATION (1984).

II. Critiques of a "Female Style of Lawyering"

Notwithstanding its articulation of improvements to the existing system, the preceding discussion does not describe accurately a female style of lawyering. Instead, it models a style of lawyering based on an ethic of care, and then ascribes this model to women. While I appreciate the insights from the ethic of care, it seems dangerously inaccurate to correlate a women's style with this ethic of care. The following sections explain why. I discuss three major problems with this analysis: first, there is a theoretical problem in using unmodified terms such as male or female to describe any lawyering style; second, psychological and sociological research does not support such broad definitions of styles; and third, an ethic of care is, at best, an incomplete description of a female style that limits alternative perceptions of lawyering.

A. The Problem of Essentialism

As theoretical and analytic categories, the unmodified terms "male" and "female" are problematic. By identifying characteristics as male or female, we ignore differences based on race, class, sexual orientation, or other significant social and cultural experiences which shape how we view the world and act in it. In this essentialist position we simplify without acknowledging the diversity within groups. For example, to talk about male or female assumes that generalizations about white and black women, and white and black men are accurate. But, we know this is not true. The recent study of Boalt law students illustrates the fallacies in these generalizations. The differences in response varied by both gender and race. Questions often elicited very different responses from members of different racial groups. For example, fifty-one percent of all women questioned felt pressured to set aside their own values in order to think like a lawyer; but white women and women of color differed by thirteen percentage points: sixty-one percent of women of color said they felt pressured, compared to forty-eight percent of white women. Additionally, thirty percent of women of color but only sixteen percent of white women—constituting twenty percent of all women questioned—felt negatively about their lives since entering law school. While the differentials may not be dramatic, they do show the difficulties of generalizing about a particular group.

Even if, notwithstanding difficulties inherent in essentialism, we recognize styles as male or female, we risk perpetuating the very subordination of "the female voice" that many of us, as feminists, are trying to overcome. When something is characterized as female, it is generally devalued or deliberately and self-consciously overvalued. At one extreme, this results in exclusion of women from the legal profession because they are so different from the correct, male style. At another extreme, this results in celebration of a female style, presumably supplanting the currently dominant style, and thus privileging one style as the correct way to practice law. Neither of these extremes is desirable. While we should not be frightened to characterize something as female lest it be devalued, we should be careful in deciding what is female and what we wish to defend as so. Similarly, we should not construct a new, although female, style to be emulated. Characterizing lawyering methods with the labels of male and female is limiting; it excludes alternative styles, and pretends that there are no overlapping attributes. As shown by the research briefly discussed below, people exhibit a mixture of "male" and "female" traits.

B. The Problem of Research

As a practical matter, the research does not support essentialist categories of male and female that correlate with moral orientations. * * *

Moreover, we must remember that what researchers find depends, at least to some extent, on what they look for and how they look for it. Research on boys and girls has been characterized by a focus on analyzing the duality of gender. Instead, and more productively, it could focus on cross-gender groupings, examining boys and girls playing together, and analyzing differences among boys and among girls that show the variations within gender.

Like the researchers, we, as observers, are influenced by our own gendered expectations. Babies who are born of indeterminate sex can be socialized to become either boys or girls. External stimuli have an enormous impact on young children. One of my favorite stories about gender socialization concerns the three year-old daughter of friends. My friends refused to put a dress on Randy until she asked for it; consequently, Randy always wore pants or overalls. People who did not know what sex she was frequently commented, "What an active boy you have." When my friends responded by saying they thought their daughter was pretty special, the commenters began to coo, and exclaimed, "She is so adorable." This child was experiencing, in a visible manner, how children learn gender-appropriate behavior; the commenters were displaying their expectations of how little girls and boys act. Clearly, there are powerful, and presently uncontrollable, influences that reinforce stereotypes of men and women.

C. The Problem of Incompleteness

Finally, the list of characteristics ascribed to women by relational feminists is incomplete. Only the strongest of those attributes traditionally ascribed to women emerge in the depiction of an ethic of care. These positive aspects of womanhood include caring and nurturing, as well as a focus on relationships. The definition of an ethic of care does not include other conventional attributes of femininity, such as passivity and dependence, in its canon. A female style of lawyering would not be a completely positive model, and should account for negative attributes of femininity. An ethic of care does not do this. While an ethic of care presumes to describe women, it is inaccurate for several reasons. First, just as women have been socialized to be caring, they have also been socialized to be passive and dependent on others; second, as discussed earlier, many women have escaped this socialization.

A wonderful example of how the theory of care does not always account for the reality of women's lives is the story of the little girl in Margaret Atwood's *Cat's Eye*.[72] Elaine is "friendly" with three other girls. Among other things, the girls force her to walk three steps in front of them; they bury her in a deep pit, covering it with planks and then with dirt; and they abandon her after she falls into ice, where she almost

---

72 MARGARET ATWOOD, CAT'S EYE (1988).

freezes to death. In short, they demean her, and almost kill her. These little girls do not conform to our image of children who play together cooperatively and stop a game when it appears that they will hurt someone. These are cruel girls who delight in torturing their "friend."

This story resounds with many women, who recognize themselves as either Elaine or her "friends," and also remember how unpleasant little girls can be to each other. An ethic of care does not explain this cruelty. For that matter, neither does an ethic of rights, showing the limits of both paradigms.

Instead, we need to put alleged differences into a context so that we can describe the actualities of law practice, see the limits of using the paradigms of ethics of care and rights to describe behavior, and only then determine the meanings of differences.

III. A Contextual Approach

Given the difficulties of correlating an ethic of care with women's style, I now explore a second position from which to analyze methods of lawyering: a contextual approach. This approach does not deny that some male and female lawyers are different, but rather examines how lawyers actually practice; it then evaluates the impact of these differences in practice; and then questions whether they can form the basis for new methods of lawyering. As such, it goes beyond the descriptive. By looking at the social context, we first shift "analysis away from fixing abstract and binary differences to examining the social relations and contexts in which multiple differences are constructed, undermined, and given meaning." At that point, we can challenge the meanings ascribed to what have been observed as differences.

To show how context helps to interpret allegedly gendered styles, I will reinterpret one of the hypotheticals used in the Stanford University Law School survey of 1500 graduates, which was designed to test women's supposedly different reasoning process. I then discuss the societal attitudes that help form the expected responses to this hypothetical.

A. Reinterpreting Hypotheticals

The hypothetical was designed to test whether there was a distinct women's perspective on moral problems presented by legal issues. The hypothetical concerned the issue of standing: A mother wanted to appeal her son's conviction for murder, and respondents were asked to decide whether she should be able to do so, notwithstanding her son's objections. The respondents then were asked to rank the importance of seven factors to their answer: (1) whether the son's desire not to appeal was more important than the mother's desire to appeal; (2) what the mother's motive for appealing was—was it because she loved her son or was she seeking publicity; (3) whether the son realized the effect on his family of his decision not to appeal; (4) whether the mother loved her son; (5) whether the son liked his mother; (6) the fact that the woman was the defendant's mother, rather than his second cousin; and (7) whether allowing the mother to appeal would mean that more distant relatives would be able to appeal. The study categorized the first five factors as "contextual" factors—regarding concerns for relationships, care, and communication—and the last two factors as "abstract"—determinations based on rights, logic, and abstract justice.

Men and women responded similarly to five factors, including whether the son realized the effect on his family of his decision not to appeal and the basis of the mother's motive for appealing. Male and female graduates rated differently only two factors: whether the mother loved her son, and whether the son liked his mother. The study's authors concluded that, when men and women differed, women rated contextual factors higher than did the men, although they did not know why men and women differed on only some of the contextual factors. The authors reasoned that women appeared to focus more readily on the quality of the mother-son relationship, which might explain the varying importance placed on factors regarding the mother's and son's feelings towards each other. Ultimately, the authors believed that the responses provided "some, although limited, support to Gilligan's theory" about different moral approaches.

I have a slightly different theory. The responses to this hypothetical do not show a distinctively feminine voice that considers connection and context to be more relevant. Men and women both considered equally relevant the mother's motive and whether the son had considered the effect on his family of his decision. These are both connection and contextual factors that go beyond rules of law; neither of these factors was legally relevant to the Supreme Court decision that inspired the hypothetical. Instead, the responses show that, for purposes of only two of the five contextual factors, women may have identified with the mother and respected the mother-son bond. This is not because the women were necessarily more caring; rather, it is because women are socialized into motherhood, into stereotypes that the mother-child bond is theirs to establish and hold sacred. Based on this socialization process, women should rate as more important to their decision the factors that relate to the mother-son bond. The responses do not necessarily show that women have a universal voice that is more focused on relationships and connection; they show, instead, that many (though not all) women identified more with the (female) mother than with the (male) son. While the authors suggest that the relatively few differences between male and female respondents might result from the socialization process into a legal mindset, I believe that they show more about the socialization into motherhood than about the process of becoming a lawyer.

B. Context

Feminist jurisprudence, and feminism in other areas, has become preoccupied with the existence and meaning of gender differences. How does a feminist analysis of gender differences affect legal practice?

First, a feminist analysis (or other outsider-based analysis) can begin to identify what the dominant style has left out of the conventional view by questioning the inevitability and neutrality of that dominance. The "female" style discussed earlier may not correlate with women, but it does point to alternatives (some of which already exist within practice). Second, the feminist analysis shows us how society constructs gender, how gender constructs society, and how dangerous these constructions are because they ignore variations within and among men and women. Third, by challenging what has been left out, feminist theory adds in some of the missing context.

This analysis of social construction leads to a questioning of existing methods of practice. Thinking about who has developed existing models gives us an appreciation of the social context that fosters these practices. Thus, gender, when defined as a socially constructed term, is useful analytically as part of a feminist analysis that seeks change. I agree with Deborah Rhode when she states:

> The sameness/difference dilemma cannot be resolved; it can only be reformulated. . . . To make significant progress, our strategies must rest on feminist principles, not feminine stereotypes. The issues of greatest concern to women are not simply "women's issues." Although the feminist platform incorporates values traditionally associated with women, the stakes in its realization are ones that both sexes share.[94]

Instead, given that gender is a social construct, and that society constructs different meanings for gender, it is clear that there are no universal descriptions within each gender. For example, it means something different to me than to Phyllis Schlafly to be a white woman. People can make some choices as to what being a woman means to them. Being male or female does not invariably determine behavior. The meaning and organization of gender varies widely. The sociologist Barrie Thorne notes that, when girls and boys are organized on opposing sides, children on each side may ally themselves within that gender, with some antagonism to the other side, but, when situations are based on lines other than gender, then boys and girls interact without "gender-marked ways," often, for example, playing some games in mixed groups.

The stories and studies recounted in this Article show differences in socialization and perception, and they show that some women learn to behave in certain ways that result in, and conform to, feminine stereotypes. However, these differences do not show an identifiably female style of being a lawyer. There are many women who do not exhibit the attributes I have ascribed to a female style of lawyering, and some men who do.

What is most important is the recognition that there is no one way to practice law effectively, and that monolithic male models do not describe how the profession practices law, nor how best to serve clients. Indeed, as Nina Tarr shows in her examination of two rural female lawyers, an ethic of care already exists in the reality constructed by rural society of a lawyer's role.[99] We need to look at how lawyers actually practice, what techniques individual lawyers use, as well as how legal profession norms create an ideal worker and penalize others. What studying male and female styles can do is open us up to appreciate the diversity in practice. There is a hierarchy of gender differences that values men over women, that makes male style

---

94   Rhode, *The "No-Problem" Problem* [: *Feminist Challenges and Cultural Change,* 100 YALE L.J. 1731], at 1790-91 [(1991)] * * * .

99   Nina W. Tarr, *Two Women Attorneys and Country Practice,* 2 COLUM. J. GENDER & L. (forthcoming 1992) (manuscript at 36, on file with the *Hastings Law Journal*).

the norm, and nonmale styles aberrational. In practice, however, both styles are used, and men and women need to understand each style's strengths and weaknesses.

Through this recognition, we should strive to value the differences, to learn what alternative styles teach us about our own practice. As a feminist, I must take seriously those values that have traditionally been identified as feminine. Rather than identifying a monolithic female style, however, I want to use these values to examine and to challenge existing structures, to change our ways of understanding what lawyers do well, and to recognize the importance of methods that have been overlooked, or excluded. Because of the power of existing methods of practice, it often is difficult to see behind them or beyond them. Beginning to talk about what has been excluded is the first step in the process of change. While this is not sufficient, it serves to broaden the agenda—to begin the process, called for by Ann Shalleck, of "creat[ing] a framework for challenging what is dangerous or harmful within dominant forms of lawyering activity" and to inform a process of creating something new.[107]

The legal system may be unable to accommodate new styles, or even to acknowledge the existence of a multiplicity of styles. Indeed, some of these innovations, such as the need to restructure the workplace, might permanently change lawyering. The need to address how gender structures attorney-client relationships may result in other changes. Nonetheless, the legal profession is changing and accepting new styles. Many of these changes result from different people entering the legal system—people who have different backgrounds and who have been socialized to be mothers, rather than fathers—that, for example, value family as well as work. The changes result, in part, from a different way of thinking—not only by women, but also, and perhaps more importantly, about women.

* * *

In the following excerpt Abbe Smith uses the personal accounts of students in a legal clinic to show that dealing with difference can be difficult and uncomfortable. She encourages law students and faculty to tell their stories of dealing with difference and to talk about their implications.

Abbe Smith, *Rosie O'Neill Goes to Law School: The Clinical Education of the Sensitive New Age Public Defender*, 28 HARV. C.R.-C.L. L. REV. 1 (1993)*

Introduction

Lawyers are all right, I guess—but it doesn't appeal to me. . . . I mean they're all right if they go around saving innocent guys' lives all the time,

---

[107] Shalleck, [*The Feminist Transformation of Lawyering: A Response to Naomi Cahn*, 43 HASTINGS L.J. 1071] at 1073-74 [(1992)].

* Reprinted with permission.

and like that, but you don't *do* that kind of stuff if you're a lawyer. All you do is make a lot of dough and play golf and play bridge and buy cars and drink Martinis and look like a hot-shot. And besides. Even if you *did* go around saving guys' lives and all, how would you know if you did it because you really *wanted* to save guys' lives, or because you did it because what you *really* wanted to do was be a terrific lawyer, with everybody slapping you on the back and congratulating you in court when the goddam trial was over, the reporters and everybody, the way it is in the dirty movies? How would you know you weren't being a phony? The trouble is, you *wouldn't*.

—Holden Caulfield, *The Catcher in the Rye*[1]

I know that I make a difference.

—Rosie O'Neill, *The Trials of Rosie O'Neill*[2]

Holden Caulfield's lament is not unfamiliar, whether one is grappling with an adolescent identity crisis or is engaged in clinical legal education. Why do we do the work we do? How do we come to choose it, and once we choose it, how do we sustain meaning in it? Can lawyers—especially criminal defense lawyers—be genuine, decent and caring, instead of back-slapping, egocentric and phony? Can criminal lawyers and would-be criminal lawyers ever hope to feel "whole" given the nature of the work?

Then along comes Rosie O'Neill. Instead of being played by Vanessa Redgrave in some one-shot PBS production, she is played by Sharon Gless in prime time, once a week, on CBS. Rosie O'Neill is a product of the 1960s, a feminist and a public defender. She has a sense of humor, a sense of perspective, a sense of the absurd, and sense enough to see a shrink to help her make sense of what doesn't seem to make any. She wears pants to court. She is committed to her work, but she raises questions about it. She struggles to keep a handle on the big picture as she gets deeply involved in smaller ones. In short, she is a role model for clinical students and public defenders everywhere.

How did Rosie O'Neill, this feminist public defender, come to light? Maybe because there are more and more women lawyers, many of whom came of age during the second wave of the women's movement in this country. Maybe because of the obvious gender hierarchy in criminal law, in criminal courtrooms, even within a criminal case. Maybe because there is a politics to being a public defender—a challenge to institutionalized inequality within the criminal justice system—that is consistent with being a feminist.

Suddenly when you go to the movies or you turn on the T.V. you find hip, feisty, women criminal lawyers: Cher in *Suspect*, Debra Winger in *Legal Eagles*, Glenn Close in *Jagged Edge*, Ellen Barkin in *The Big Easy*, Kelly McGillis in *The Accused*,

---

1   J.D. SALINGER, THE CATCHER IN THE RYE 172 (Bantam Books, 1964) (1951).

2   *The Trials of Rosie O'Neill* (CBS television broadcast, Nov. 7, 1991).

Susan Dey in *L.A. Law*, Marlee Matlin in *Reasonable Doubts*, and, of course, Sharon Gless in *The Trials of Rosie O'Neill*.[7] Does art imitate life or life art?

Rosie O'Neill and her crowd offer a new public defender sensibility which is not for women only. They offer a reflective, critical, concerned sensibility that stands in marked contrast to the "staggering indifference" with which traditional criminal defense lawyers approach their role and their work.[9] Defense lawyers traditionally express little concern about the guilt or innocence of their clients, little concern about larger questions of "truth" or "justice," and little concern about what happens to victims in court.[10] Defense lawyers traditionally detach themselves from difficult moral questions, focusing instead on legal questions, the adversary system, and a "litany of constitutional ideals."[11]

It may not be possible for a public defender in the heat of battle, under the weight of a staggering caseload, to reflect on personal conflicts, moral questions and ideological dilemmas. But it is important that the clinical law student (and clinical law teacher) do so. The clinical student ought to grapple with the hardest and deepest questions while learning the meaning of professional role and professional responsibility. Clinical legal education provides the best opportunity for this kind of reflection, and the best pedagogical method for guiding that reflection. * * *

* * *

The first thing clinical students encounter is difference. They then try to grapple with it. Everything and everybody is different from what they have ever encountered, at least in law school: the clients, the neighborhoods, the courthouse, the jail. Even the teachers are different. Students have many different reactions to all this difference:

> I . . . feel so *different* from [them]. I grew up in white middle class Long Island. I attended Catholic grammar school and high school. I went to a private college. . . . I wonder how my clients will perceive me. Will they see this white guy in a suit telling them he understands their situation when they feel he has nothing in common with them?

> Everyone seems to know everyone. Prosecutors, defense attorneys, clerks, probation officers, judges. Everyone but me at least. Pretty intimidating.

---

7   SUSPECT (Tri-Star Pictures, Inc. 1987); LEGAL EAGLES (Universal Studios, Inc. 1986); JAGGED EDGE (Columbia Pictures Industries, Inc. 1985); THE BIG EASY (Kings Road Entertainment, Inc. 1987); THE ACCUSED (Paramount Pictures Corporation 1988); *L.A. Law* (NBC Television); *Reasonable Doubts* (NBC Television); *The Trials of Rosie O'Neill* (CBS Television).

Three of these criminal lawyers are actually prosecutors. Just checking to see whether you were paying attention.

9   Barbara Babcock, *Defending the Guilty*, 32 CLEV. ST. L. REV. 175, 180 (1983).

10   *Id.* * * *

11   LISA MCINTYRE, THE PUBLIC DEFENDER: THE PRACTICE OF LAW IN THE SHADOWS OF REPUTE 139-70 (1987).

Probably even more intimidating for the defendants—although it appears many have been here before.

> The apartment was neat, but it still had that grim look of a project. Mrs. Jones was very talkative and helpful . . . and very nice. She is young, probably thirty-five or so, and she has a seventeen year old daughter who has a six month old child (by my client). There were also two other little boys running around who were very curious about the two white men sitting in the living room.

In the first excerpt, the student is concerned about his own difference from his clients. He's worried about being disingenuous and inauthentic in his clients' eyes. Though the student is reflective in his self-consciousness, consistent with the clinical method, he is not reflective *about* his self-consciousness. He fails to raise the epistemological questions that feminist method demands. What does it mean to have "something in common" with clients? What would happen if he had "something in common" with clients that wouldn't happen if he had "nothing in common" with clients? While there's no apparent prejudgment in the excerpt about clients' difference—about what it means to be an indigent criminal defendant (except that they are not white, middle-class, Catholic school educated, and from Long Island)—there is a Chinese fable-like presumption about how the clients might feel about the student's "difference."

The student in the second excerpt feels excluded from a ritual. Rightly so, in many respects. There is self-consciousness again, though not piercing. What does it mean that "everyone knows each other?" How do they know each other? What does knowing each other get them? How is this experience like or unlike the experience of walking into a crowded room of strangers, all drinking Chardonnay, and assuming everyone else has known each other since kindergarten? What does "having been here before" get the accused client? The student perceives himself to be the newcomer, the outsider. But won't he soon transcend that role entirely? Aren't the criminal defendants who are the student's clients also outsiders, notwithstanding their apparent familiarity with the system? How does the one outsider role compare with the other? Clinical methods of reflection and critique focus on how to break down the mystery of the courthouse scene in order to be a player in it. Feminist epistemological questions would inquire more deeply into the nature of the mystery.

The third student remarks both on his difference and the difference of the witnesses with whom he is meeting. He does so more descriptively than reflectively, though what he chooses to describe reveals a great deal. He starts by noting that "the apartment was neat." It's an interesting place to start. Why is the tidiness of the apartment noteworthy? The student seems surprised. What did he expect? "Neat" apparently has definition for him, it has value, it meets a standard. But where do the definition, the value, the standard come from?

There is more: the place is "neat but . . . grim." One wonders and wonders about "grim." It's a good word. But grim to whom? Unlike "neat," which apparently needs no further description, "grim" is elaborated upon: the apartment has "that grim look of a project." "That" connotes a familiarity with projects. Is there a "look" to a project that's familiar enough to refer to as "that grim look?" What makes the student say so? Stereotypes lurk just beneath the surface. Only their absence is noted. Nothing is affirmed.

The student is a white man. Mrs. Jones is black, which is made clear only by the reference to the student's own whiteness. While this may seem self-referential at first, it can also be seen as a refreshing reference to another perspective not his (the two little boys'). The student observes that Mrs. Jones is young, this time not in relation to himself (he is twenty-five or so) but in relation to Mrs. Jones' daughter and more, her granddaughter. The student acknowledges that Mrs. Jones is a thirty-five-year-old grandmother, something apparently different from his experience. The description is noticeably flat. The reader gets no picture of the person the student meets, and no picture of the life the student has entered. Mrs. Jones was "talkative," "helpful," and "nice." The apartment is "neat." Mrs. Jones could almost be played by Doris Day. The clinical method would focus on getting past the race, class, and cultural differences in order to effectively interview the witnesses. Feminist method would ask why the student has selected the particular traits he selects to focus on.

Dealing with difference can be difficult. In fact, students frequently complain about "difficult clients." The nature of the difficulty runs the gamut:

> I waited two hours for Linda F. to show up today, and became highly disappointed when she didn't. . . . My clients don't seem to care about their cases.

> I was brought upstairs to the holding cells. This was a shock to me. I didn't know that the Roxbury court had actual prison cells in it! I also got my first dose of abuse by some of the other prisoners as I looked for my client's cell. "Hey punk!" one called out. "Come here and help me," one yelled as he and his fellow inmates laughed. I wasn't sure how to react to these other people. They were potential clients also . . . yet they were annoying me. Do I treat them as I do the beggars in Harvard Square and just walk by not acknowledging their presence? Or do I look at whoever spoke to me and express my sympathy with a certain look? Or do I get right up next to them and tell them to shut up. I chose the first option and walked to my client's cell. It smelled so bad in there, though. How can anyone stand to be in there regularly meeting clients? Does representing your client zealously mean that you must lose your olfactory capability?

In the first excerpt, the student has an experience shared by many engaged in poverty law practice. Sometimes clients don't show up for appointments, sometimes they're late, sometimes they're hard to track down because of changed addresses and disconnected telephones, and sometimes they fail to appear in court. It's hard not to get "disappointed," though I wonder whether "frustrated" or "pissed off" might not be more accurate. Both clinicians and feminists would ask why Linda F. didn't show up. (The clinician might ask why the student waited for *two hours* and whether the student at least did other work during that time.) There may be a particular reason. If not, the clinical method of learning from synthesis combined with the feminist method of contextual reasoning would lead a student to ask a series of questions about what might underlie the client's conduct: What is the institutional context in which the client and lawyer first encountered each other? Under what circumstances was the lawyer-client relationship established?

What differences might there be between indigent criminal clients and court-appointed counsel and middle-class criminal clients and privately retained counsel? What is the interpersonal context? Who made the appointment with whom? Why was the appointment made? Was the client given a choice about whether she wanted to meet? More specifically, what are the details of Linda F.'s life? Does she have children? If so, was there anyone available to take care of them while she went off to see her lawyer? Does she live far away from the clinic office? If so, can she easily get transportation? Does she have the money to pay for the transportation? How might the client rank this appointment with her lawyer as compared to other life demands?

The second excerpt is so full it threatens to spill over. The student confronts several layers of difference exacerbated by a clear demarcation: the bars of a jail cell. A student confronting a client in a holding cell might well be "shocked" by the conditions there: holding cells are often filthy, cold, overcrowded and in serious disrepair. The conditions are made worse by urgency. Those being held are focused only on getting out. Even without the inmates' taunts, there is no question who is on one side of the bars and who is on the other. But the student's "shock" still should be probed. What does it mean for a third-year law student, a few months away from being a practicing lawyer, to be shocked by the very existence of jail cells within courthouses? What do they teach in those law schools anyway?

The student's word choice leads to a list of questions. Why does the student use the word "abuse?" Are the people behind the bars the student's abusers? How is he abused? The student, who apparently is new at all this, remarks that this is his "first dose of abuse." Why the "first" when the experience is actually his *only*? And why "dose of abuse," as if it's some kind of bad medicine to be parcelled out like castor oil? What preconceptions are revealed by this phrase? What about the actual words called out by the people behind the bars? Is "punk" a devastating epithet? Is it made worse by the laughter that follows? How? What about these "other people" about whom the student feels uncertain. What about these "potential clients?" It sounds like there is a difference between the student's client, whom he hasn't met yet, and these "other" people—these "potential" clients. Does it help to humanize these "others" by thinking of them as "potential clients" when in fact they are already clients, though somebody else's clients, not his?

Then there are the "beggars." Why do we reduce people to a piece of their existence, the means of their existence, the narrowest computation of the sum of their parts? The word "beggar" is almost Dickensian: it conjures up images of Fagan and his protégés, wrapped in thread-bare coats, jostling and begging for a dime. It's a pretty hostile word. Unlike "homeless," "destitute" or "needy," the word "beggar" connotes a bothersome relationship. The student feels put upon both by beggars and by his prison "abusers." It's a curious comparison: those whose freedom has been taken and those with only the flimsiest freedom left. The student is probably searching for a frame of reference, a normative range of behavior, but he rather blithely tells of walking by the "beggars in Harvard Square" without acknowledging their existence. What power "acknowledgment" possesses.

That the student may have made an appropriate "choice" of conduct does not end the discussion, though clinicians would rightly credit the student's common sense and practical judgment. The paths not followed are as interesting as the one taken. Where does the "expression of sympathy" option come from? Has the student expressed any up to this point? What does it mean to "get up right next to them and tell them to shut up?" Why get up close to make a connection that severs connection? Why engage in posturing of this sort at all; how tough is it to tell a bunch of guys behind bars to shut up? Why would confrontation of this sort come to mind? Does the student widen the gulf when he declines connection and acts as if "the others" don't exist, or does he actually respect territoriality?

Now wait a minute, let's not get too carried away with this epistemological stuff. There has to be a reality out there somewhere. The student has a few seconds and needs to pick a course of conduct. The student shouldn't have to feel lousy no matter what he chooses. Is there some sort of clinical/feminist analysis that will help the student reconcile himself to being the butt of a joke he doesn't find terribly funny? Probably not. Is the student wrong to feel uncomfortable? I don't think so. I don't think the student needs to reconcile himself to an unpleasant role. I don't think the student needs to disavow his "annoyance" at the hazing he received. It seems to me that both feminist and clinical methods would take seriously the student's experience and then talk about what it means. The student ought to be encouraged to tell the story, to tell how he felt. Women law students and lawyers who go to men's jails and prisons must regularly endure a steady stream of sexual taunts, come-ons and insults as part of the job. We too should be encouraged to tell the story, to tell how it felt.

There is much that remains untold in this excerpt, and one thing in particular: the student seems terrified. But he doesn't talk about the terror, he focuses on the bad smell instead. The smell is real and unpleasant, though surely more acutely experienced by the people in the cells than by those who "regularly" meet them. That people are caged with that smell and cannot get away from it is deeply disturbing. It makes you feel sick. It gives you a headache. It distracts you from everything else.

Why does the student suddenly mention the smell just as he is finally about to make a connection with his client? The smell becomes a powerful distancing device. The people trapped with the smell have got to be different, different in some blameworthy way. The smell becomes as much a symbol as a reality. The "olfactory capability" line is witty, but why end on a joke? Why doesn't the student talk about how horrible it must be to be locked up with no fresh air to breath? Why doesn't he talk about the utter indignity of the conditions? Why doesn't he talk about how frightening it all is?

Sometimes the stories students tell about difference are stark and seem to speak for themselves. Yet these stories are deceptively complex and rich:

> "I'm a woman, I'm black, and I'm a lesbian. That's why I'm in all of this trouble right now." Sharon Wilson, my latest client, looked me right in the eye as she spoke these words. I felt very uncomfortable as she said this—

at one point during my conversation with her I said, "Listen, as you can tell I am white and male. I'm also heterosexual. If any of this makes you very uncomfortable, I'll get you another lawyer." I wonder if she would feel better with a black woman lesbian lawyer. I told her at the outset of our conversation that I was going to do my best to make sure that any of her *characteristics* would not force her to accept any more punishment than someone without her characteristics; only the events leading up to her arrest as well as her prior criminal record would be relevant. To my surprise, she kept telling me how much she trusted me—how enthusiastic I looked—how I had "honest eyes."

This case was a prosecution for trespass and assault and battery on a police officer. The student's client, Sharon Wilson, had recently moved to Boston and was living in a shelter for women. She was asked to leave the shelter when she "made the mistake of telling one of the homophobic woman residents that she was attractive." Ms. Wilson agreed to leave, but wished to do so with dignity, so she asked the director of the shelter to call a taxi. The director called the police instead.

The student begins his account in the same powerful way that the client began the interaction. "I'm a woman, I'm black, and I'm a lesbian. And that's why I'm in all of this trouble right now." The client doesn't wait for the student lawyer to introduce himself, to set the ground rules, to establish roles; she takes charge, she frames her own legal problem, then she presents it to him. There is a directness, a sharpness, an immediacy to the client's engagement. She looks the student in the eye and tells him what's what. The student immediately undercuts that intimacy in his account. He refers to Sharon Wilson as his "latest client," like "did you hear the latest?" and "the latest movie" and "the latest fashion."

The student confesses his discomfort. But he fails to explore why he is uncomfortable. Is it that she is the powerful one when he is supposed to have the power? Is it that she is open about who she is without hedging or shrinking, thereby "violating the 'norm,' . . . the conventions of gender identity, the boundaries of gendered sexuality, and heterosexuality itself"? Is it being looked in the eye? Is it because his vulnerability is suddenly more central than hers?

The student responds to his client's self-revelation by offering his own: "As you can tell, I am white and male." He then adds, "I'm also heterosexual." Interestingly, the student separates his self-description into two sentences, whereas the client puts it into one: woman, black, lesbian. The student sees those words as parts, mere "characteristics." The client experiences them as a whole, inseparable for her. The student's language is the language of privilege: he is the norm, needing only adjectives as modifiers—white, male, heterosexual. He moves comfortably through the world as white, male, heterosexual. The words seem to mean the same thing. While, in a way, the student has responded to the client on her terms, the truth is that her terms are markedly different from his rendition of her terms. Each of the client's words standing alone presents a risk and a challenge: Woman. Black. Lesbian. The student has barely begun to share.

Somewhat transparently, the student says to the client, "If any of that makes you uncomfortable I'll get you another lawyer." Now, who's the uncomfortable one here? In the name of respectful acknowledgment of difference, the student offers the solution of getting the client another lawyer. But what does that say about his desire to bridge the difference? His proposal is not to engage with the client, to talk about what there is to talk about, but to end it right there. The student doesn't reflect on this. Will the client be more comfortable with a "black woman lesbian lawyer?" (The student's phrasing is tellingly redundant here. There is a nervous desire not to leave anything out.) What about the role of class here? Would the lawyer need to be a poor, black lesbian? What about the role of personality? What if the lawyer was an obnoxious, arrogant, poor, black lesbian? What if the student lawyer is an excellent advocate? What if that's all the client wants? In fact, the student's "enthusiasm" and "honesty" and "trustworthiness" seem most important to the client. What does it say about indigence and the criminal justice system that enthusiasm and trust are striking enough to comment upon? Isn't the student actually doing some back-pedaling by suggesting other counsel? What has the client said or done to cause this? By the student's own account, the client seems to like him.

Out of discomfort, the student, otherwise clear-headed and well-spoken, babbles on about doing his "best" and the "event" and the "arrest" and the client's "prior criminal record" and "punishment" and "relevance" and "characteristics." Just let me please play the lawyer for one moment, he seems to say. But who is right about what is most relevant in this case? The client's first words have the makings of a closing argument.

* * *

Chapter 4

GOAL SETTING, DECISION MAKING, AND PLANNING

A. Framing the Story of the Case

A lawyer and client begin to frame the story of a case at their first meeting. In the next excerpt Lucie White tells about a case in which the story as framed by the client turns out to be more effective than the lawyer's strategy.

Lucie White, *Subordination, Rhetorical Survival Skills, and Sunday Shoes: Notes on the Hearing of Mrs. G.*, 38 BUFF. L. REV. 1 (1990)*

* * *

A. *The Story*

Mrs. G. is thirty-five years old, Black, and on her own. She has five girls, ranging in age from four to fourteen. She has never told me anything about their fathers; all I know is that she isn't getting formal child support payments from anyone. She lives on an AFDC[79] grant of just over three hundred dollars a month and a small monthly allotment of Food Stamps. She probably gets a little extra money from occasional jobs as a field hand or a maid, but she doesn't share this information with me and I don't ask. She has a very coveted unit of public housing, so she doesn't have to pay rent. She is taking an adult basic education class at the local community action center, which is in the same building as my own office. I often notice her in the classroom as I pass by.

* * *

---

[79]   Aid to Families with Dependent Children, 42 U.S.C. §§ 601, 615 (1982).

Mrs. G. and two daughters first appeared at our office one Friday morning at about ten, without an appointment. I was booked for the whole day; the chairs in the tiny waiting room were already filled. But I called her in between two scheduled clients. Mrs. G. looked frightened. She showed me a letter from the welfare office that said she had received an "overpayment" of AFDC benefits. Though she couldn't read very well, she knew that the word "overpayment" meant fraud. Reagan's newly appointed United States attorney, with the enthusiastic backing of Senator Jesse Helms, had just announced plans to prosecute "welfare cheats" to the full extent of the law. Following this lead, a grand jury had indicted several local women on federal charges of welfare fraud. Therefore, Mrs. G. had some reason to believe that "fraud" carried the threat of jail.

The "letter" was actually a standardized notice that I had seen many times before. Whenever the welfare department's computer showed that a client had received an overpayment, it would kick out this form, which stated the amount at issue and advised the client to pay it back. The notice did not say why the agency had concluded that a payment error had been made. Nor did it inform the client that she might contest the county's determination. Rather, the notice assigned the client a time to meet with the county's fraud investigator to sign a repayment contract and warned that if the client chose not to show up at this meeting further action would be taken. Mrs. G.'s meeting with the fraud investigator was set for the following Monday.

At the time, I was negotiating with the county over the routine at these meetings and the wording on the overpayment form. Therefore, I knew what Mrs. G. could expect at the meeting. The fraud worker would scold her and then ask her to sign a statement conceding the overpayment, consenting to a 10 percent reduction of her AFDC benefits until the full amount was paid back, and advising that the government could still press criminal charges against her.

I explained to Mrs. G. that she did not have to go to the meeting on Monday, or to sign any forms. She seemed relieved and asked if I could help her get the overpayment straightened out. I signed her on as a client and, aware of the other people waiting to see me, sped through my canned explanation of how I could help her. Then I called the fraud investigator, canceled Monday's meeting, and told him I was representing her. Thinking that the emergency had been dealt with, I scheduled an appointment for Mrs. G. for the following Tuesday and told her not to sign anything or talk to anyone at the welfare office until I saw her again.

The following Tuesday Mrs. G. arrived at my office looking upset. She said she had gone to her fraud appointment because she had been "afraid not to." She had signed a paper admitting she owed the county about six hundred dollars, and agreeing to have her benefits reduced by thirty dollars a month for the year and a half it would take to repay the amount. She remembered I had told her not to sign anything; she looked like she was waiting for me to yell at her or tell her to leave. I suddenly saw a woman caught between two bullies, both of us ordering her what to do.

I hadn't spent enough time with Mrs. G. the previous Friday. For me, it had been one more emergency—a quick fix, an appointment, out the door. It suddenly seemed pointless to process so many clients, in such haste, without any time to listen, to challenge, to think together. But what to do, with so many people waiting at the door? I mused on these thoughts for a moment, but what I finally said was simpler. I was furious. Why had she gone to the fraud appointment and signed the repayment contract? Why hadn't she done as *we* had agreed? Now it would be so much harder to contest the county's claim: we would have to attack *both* the repayment contract *and* the underlying overpayment claim. Why hadn't she listened to me?

Mrs. G. just looked at me in silence. She finally stammered that she knew she had been "wrong" to go to the meeting when I had told her not to and she was "sorry."

After we both calmed down I mumbled my own apology and turned to the business at hand. She told me that a few months before she had received a cash settlement for injuries she and her oldest daughter had suffered in a minor car accident. After medical bills had been paid and her lawyer had taken his fees, her award came to $592. Before Mrs. G. cashed the insurance check, she took it to her AFDC worker to report it and ask if it was all right for her to spend it. The system had trained her to tell her worker about every change in her life. With a few exceptions, any "income" she reported would be subtracted, dollar for dollar, from her AFDC stipend.

The worker was not sure how to classify the insurance award. After talking to a supervisor, however, she told Mrs. G. that the check would not affect her AFDC budget and she could spend it however she wanted.

Mrs. G. cashed her check that same afternoon and took her five girls on what she described to me as a "shopping trip." They bought Kotex, which they were always running short on at the end of the month. They also bought shoes, dresses for school, and some frozen food. Then she made two payments on her furniture bill. After a couple of wonderful days, the money was gone.

Two months passed. Mrs. G. received and spent two AFDC checks. Then she got the overpayment notice, asking her to repay to the county an amount equal to her insurance award.

When she got to this point, I could see Mrs. G. getting upset again. She had told her worker everything, but nobody had explained to her what she was supposed to do. She hadn't meant to do anything wrong. I said I thought the welfare office had done something wrong in this case, not Mrs. G. I thought we could get the mess straightened out, but we'd need more information. I asked if she could put together a list of all the things she had bought with the insurance money. If she still had any of the receipts, she should bring them to me. I would look at her case file at the welfare office and see her again in a couple of days.

The file had a note from the caseworker confirming that Mrs. G. had reported the insurance payment when she received it. The note also showed that the worker did not include the amount in calculating her stipend. The "overpayment" got flagged two months later when a supervisor, doing a random "quality control" check on her file, discovered the worker's note. Under AFDC law, the insurance award was considered a "lump sum payment." Aware that the law regarding such payments had recently changed, the supervisor decided to check out the case with the state quality control office.

He learned that the insurance award did count as income for AFDC purposes under the state's regulations; indeed, the county should have cut Mrs. G. off of welfare entirely for almost two months on the theory that her family could live for that time off of the insurance award. The lump sum rule was a Reagan Administration innovation designed to teach poor people the virtues of saving money and planning for the future. Nothing in the new provision required that clients be warned in advance about the rule change, however. Only in limited circumstances was a state free to waive the rule. Without a waiver, Mrs. G. would have to pay back $592 to the welfare office. If the county didn't try to collect the sum from Mrs. G., it would be sanctioned for an administrative error.

I met again with Mrs. G. the following Friday. When I told her what I had pieced together from her file, she insisted that she had asked her worker's permission before spending the insurance money. Then she seemed to get flustered and repeated what had become a familiar refrain. She didn't want to make any trouble. She hadn't meant to do anything wrong. I told her that it looked to me like it was the welfare office—and not her—who had done something wrong. I said I would try to get the county to drop the matter, but I thought we might have to go to a hearing, finally, to win.

* * *

Mrs. G. brought all five of her girls to my office to prepare for the hearing. Our first task was to decide on a strategy for the argument. I told her that I saw two stories we could tell. The first was the story she had told me. It was the "estoppel" story, the story of the wrong advice she got from her worker about spending the insurance check. The second story was one that I had come up with from reading the law. The state had laid the groundwork for this story when it opted for the "life necessities" waiver permitted by federal regulations. If a client could show that she had spent the sum to avert a crisis situation, then it would be considered "unavailable" as income, and her AFDC benefits would not be suspended. I didn't like this second story very much, and I wasn't sure that Mrs. G. would want to go along with it. How could I ask her to distinguish "life necessities" from mere luxuries, when she was keeping five children alive on three hundred dollars a month, and when she had been given no voice in the calculus that had determined her "needs."

Yet I felt that the necessities story might work at the hearing, while "estoppel" would unite the county and state against us. According to legal aid's welfare specialist in the state capital, state officials didn't like the lump sum rule. It made more paper work for the counties. And, by knocking families off the federally financed AFDC program, the rule increased the pressure on state- and county-funded relief programs. But the only way the state could get around the rule without being subject to federal sanctions was through the necessities exception. Behind the scenes, state officials were saying to our welfare specialist that they intended to interpret the exception broadly. In addition to this inside information that the state officials would prefer the necessities tale, I knew from experience that they would feel comfortable with the role that story gave to Mrs. G. It would place her on her knees, asking for pity as she described how hard she was struggling to make ends meet.

The estoppel story would be entirely different. In it, Mrs. G. would be pointing a finger, turning the county itself into the object of scrutiny. She would accuse welfare officials of wrong, and claim that they had caused her injury. She would demand that the county bend its own rules, absorb the overpayment out of its own funds, and run the risk of sanction from the state for its error.

As I thought about the choices, I felt myself in a bind. The estoppel story would feel good in the telling, but at the likely cost of losing the hearing, and provoking the county's ire. The hearing officer—though charged to be neutral—would surely identify with the county in this challenge to the government's power to evade the costs of its own mistakes. The necessities story would force Mrs. G. to grovel, but it would give both county and state what they wanted to hear—another "yes sir" welfare recipient.

This bind was familiar to me as a poverty lawyer. I felt it most strongly in disability hearings, when I would counsel clients to describe themselves as totally helpless in order to convince the court that they met the statutory definition of disability. But I had faced it in AFDC work as well, when I taught women to present themselves as abandoned, depleted of resources, and encumbered by children to qualify for relief. I taught them to say yes to the degrading terms of "income security," as it was called—invasions of sexual privacy, disruptions of kin-ties, the forced choice of one sibling's welfare over another's. Lawyers had tried to challenge these conditions, but for the most part the courts had confirmed that the system could take such license with its women. After all, poor women were free to say no to welfare if they weren't pleased with its terms.

As I contemplated my role as an advocate, I felt again the familiar sense that I had been taken. Here I was, asking Mrs. G. to trust me, talking with her about our conspiring together to beat the system and strate-gizing together to change it. Here I was, thinking that what I was doing was educative and empowering or at least supportive of those agendas, when all my efforts worked, in the end, only to teach her to submit to the system in all of the complex ways that it demanded.

In the moment it took for these old thoughts to flit through my mind, Mrs. G. and her children sat patiently in front of me, fidgeting, waiting for me to speak. My focus returned to them and the immediate crisis they faced if their AFDC benefits were cut. What story should we tell at the hearing, I wondered out loud. How should we decide? Mechanically at first, I began to describe to her our "options."

When I explained the necessities story, Mrs. G. said she might get confused trying to remember what all she had bought with the money. Why did they need to know those things anyway? I could tell she was get-ting angry. I wondered if two months of benefits—six hundred dollars—was worth it. Maybe paying it back made more sense. I reminded her that we didn't have to tell this story at the hearing, and in fact, we didn't have to go to the hearing at all. Although I was trying to choose my words care-fully, I felt myself saying too much. Why had I even raised the question of which story to tell? It was a tactical decision—not the kind of issue that clients were supposed to decide. Why hadn't I just told her to answer the questions that I chose to ask?

Mrs. G. asked me what to do. I said I wanted to see the welfare office admit their mistake, but I was concerned that if we tried to make them, we would lose. Mrs. G. said she still felt like she'd been treated unfairly but—in the next breath—"I didn't mean to do anything wrong." Why couldn't we tell both stories? With this simple question, I lost all pretense of strate-gic subtlety or control. I said sure.

I asked for the list she had promised to make of all the things she bought with the insurance money. Kotex, I thought, would speak for itself, but why, I asked, had she needed to get the girls new shoes? She explained that the girls' old shoes were pretty much torn up, so bad that the other kids would make fun of them at school. Could she bring in the old shoes. She said she could.

We rehearsed her testimony, first about her conversation with her worker regarding the insurance award and then about the Kotex and the shoes. Maybe the hearing wouldn't be too bad for Mrs. G., especially if I could help her see it all as strategy, rather than the kind of talking she could do with people she could trust. She had to distance herself at the hearing. She shouldn't expect them to go away from it understanding why she was angry, or what she needed, or what her life was like. The hearing was their territory. The most she could hope for was to take it over for a moment, leading them to act out her agenda. Conspiracy was the theme she must keep repeating as she dutifully played her role.

We spent the next half hour rehearsing the hearing. By the end, she seemed reasonably comfortable with her part. Then we practiced the cross-examination, the ugly questions that—even though everyone conceded to be irrelevant—still always seemed to get asked . . . questions about her children, their fathers, how long she had been on welfare, why she wasn't working instead. This was the part of these sessions that I disliked the most. We practiced me objecting and her staying quiet and trying to stay composed. By the end of our meeting, the whole thing was holding together, more or less.

The hearing itself was in a small conference room at the welfare office. Mrs. G. arrived with her two oldest daughters and five boxes of shoes. When we got there the state hearing officer and the county AFDC director were already seated at the hearing table in lively conversation. The AFDC director was a youngish man with sandy hair and a beard. He didn't seem like a bureaucrat until he started talking. I knew most of the hearing officers who came to the county, but this one, a pale, greying man who slouched in his chair, was new to me. I started feeling uneasy as I rehearsed how I would plead this troubling case to a stranger.

We took our seats across the table from the AFDC director. The hearing officer set up a portable tape recorder and got out his bible. Mrs. G.'s AFDC worker, an African American woman about her age, entered through a side door and took a seat next to her boss. The hearing officer turned on the recorder, read his obligatory opening remarks, and asked all the witnesses to rise and repeat before God that they intended to tell the truth. Mrs. G. and her worker complied.

The officer then turned the matter over to me. I gave a brief account of the background events and then began to question Mrs. G. First I asked her about the insurance proceeds. She explained how she had received an insurance check of about six hundred dollars following a car accident in which she and her oldest daughter had been slightly injured. She said that the insurance company had already paid the medical bills and the lawyer; the last six hundred dollars was for her and her daughter to spend however they wanted. I asked her if she had shown the check to her AFDC worker before she cashed it. She stammered. I repeated the question. She said she may have taken the check to the welfare office before she cashed it, but she couldn't remember for sure. She didn't know if she had gotten a chance to talk to anyone about it. Her worker was always real busy.

Armed with the worker's own sketchy notation of the conversation in the case file, I began to cross-examine my client, coaxing her memory about the event we had discussed so many times before. I asked if she remembered her worker telling her anything about how she could spend the money. Mrs. G. seemed to be getting more uncomfortable. It was quite a predicament for her, after all. If she "remembered" what her worker had told her, would her story expose mismanagement in the welfare office, or merely scapegoat another Black woman, who was not too much better off than herself?

When she repeated that she couldn't remember, I decided to leave the estoppel story for the moment. Maybe I could think of a way to return to it later. I moved on to the life necessities issue. I asked Mrs. G. to recount, as best she could, exactly how she had spent the insurance money. She showed me the receipts she had kept for the furniture payments and I put them into evidence. She explained that she was buying a couple of big mattresses for the kids and a new kitchen table. She said she had also bought some food—some frozen meat and several boxes of Kotex for all the girls. The others in the room shifted uneasily in their chairs. Then she said she had also bought her daughters some clothes and some shoes. She had the cash register receipt for the purchase.

Choosing my words carefully, I asked why she had needed to buy the new shoes. She looked at me for a moment with an expression that I couldn't read. Then she stated, quite emphatically, that they were Sunday shoes that she had bought with the money. The girls already had everyday shoes to wear to school, but she had wanted them to have nice shoes for church too. She said no more than two or three sentences, but her voice sounded different—stronger, more composed—than I had known from her before. When she finished speaking the room was silent, except for the incessant hum of the tape machine on the table and the fluorescent lights overhead. In that moment, I felt the boundaries of our "conspiracy" shift. Suddenly I was on the outside, with the folks on the other side of the table, the welfare director and the hearing officer. The only person I could not locate in this new alignment was Mrs. G.'s welfare worker.

I didn't ask Mrs. G. to pull out the children's old shoes, as we'd rehearsed. Nor did I make my "life necessities" argument. My lawyer's language couldn't add anything to what she had said. They would have to figure out for themselves why buying Sunday shoes for her children—and saying it—was indeed a "life necessity" for this woman. After the hearing, Mrs. G. seemed elated. She asked me how she had done at the hearing and I told her that I thought she was great. I warned her, though, that we could never be sure, in this game, who was winning, or even what side anyone was on.

We lost the hearing and immediately petitioned for review by the chief hearing officer. I wasn't sure of the theory we'd argue, but I wanted to keep the case open until I figured out what we could do.

Three days after the appeal was filed, the county welfare director called me unexpectedly, to tell me that the county had decided to withdraw its overpayment claim against Mrs. G. He explained that on a careful review of its own records, the county had decided that it wouldn't be "fair" to make Mrs. G. pay the money back. I said I was relieved to hear that they had decided, finally, to come to a sensible result in the case. I was sorry they hadn't done so earlier. I then said something about how confusing the lump sum rule was and how Mrs. G.'s worker had checked with her supervisor before telling Mrs. G. it was all right to spend the insurance money. I said I was sure that the screw up was not anyone's fault. He mumbled a bureaucratic pleasantry and we hung up.

When I told Mrs. G. that she had won, she said she had just wanted to "do the right thing," and that she hoped they understood that she'd never meant to do anything wrong. I repeated that they were the ones who had made the mistake. Though I wasn't sure exactly what was going on inside the welfare office, at least this crisis was over.

* * *

1. *Why Did Mrs. G. Return to the Lawyer?* The lawyer thought she understood the answer to this question. In her view, Mrs. G.'s life had taught her that to be safe, she must submit to her superiors. Mrs. G. was faced with conflicting commands from the welfare agency and the legal aid office. So, like the archetypical woman, shaped to mold herself to male desire, Mrs. G. said "yes" to everything the Man asked. She said yes when the lawyer asked her to go through with a hearing, yes again when the fraud investigator asked her to drop it, and yes once more when the lawyer demanded her apology. In the lawyer's view, this excess of acquiescence had a sad, but straight-forward meaning. It marked Mrs. G.'s lack of social power: this woman could not risk having a point of view of her own.

Yet the lawyer was not situated to see the whole story. Though she aspired to stand beside Mrs. G. as an equal, she also sought to guard her own status—and the modicum of social power that it gave her. She *saw* Mrs. G. as a victim because that was the role she needed her client to occupy to support her own social status. For if Mrs. G. was indeed silenced by the violence around her, she would then be dependent on the lawyer's expertise and protection, and therefore compliant to the lawyer's will. With such clients, the lawyer could feel quite secure of her power, and complacent about the value of her work.

But Mrs. G.'s survival skills were more complex, more subtle, than the lawyer dared to recognize. There might be another meaning to Mrs. G.'s ambivalence about what she wanted to do. Perhaps she was *playing* with the compliance that all of her superiors demanded. By acquiescing to both of the system's opposed orders, she was surely protecting herself from the risks of defiance. But she was also undermining the value—to them—of her own submission. By refusing to claim any ground as her own, she made it impossible for others to subdue her will.

Self-negation may not have been the *only* meaning that Mrs. G. felt positioned to claim. She finally *came back* to the lawyer, repudiated the settlement, determined to pursue her case. Was this merely one more deft move between two bureaucrats, searching them both for strategic advantage while secretly mocking the rhetoric of both spheres? Or did Mrs. G. finally get fed up at the unfairness of the welfare, and at her own endless submission? When she returned to the lawyer, she was offered a bargain. She might get money, and some limited protection from the welfare, if she went along with the hearing plan. But she might have also heard the lawyer to promise something different from this *quid pro quo*. In her talk of rights and justice, the lawyer offered Mrs. G. not just money, but also vindication. In going forward with the hearing, was Mrs. G. simply making a street-wise calculation to play the game the lawyer offered? Or was she also giving voice to a faint hope—a hope that one day she might really have the legal protections she needed to take part in the shaping of justice?

2. *Why Did Mrs. G. Depart from her Script?* The lawyer had scripted Mrs. G. as a victim. That was the only strategy for the hearing that the lawyer, within the constraints of her own social position, could imagine for Mrs. G. She had warned her client to play the victim if she wanted to win. Mrs. G. learned her lines. She came to the hearing well-rehearsed in the lawyer's strategy. But in the hearing, she did not play. When she was cued to perform, without any signal to her lawyer she abandoned their script.

The lawyer shared with Mrs. G. the oppression of gender, but was placed above Mrs. G. in the social hierarchies of race and class. The lawyer was paid by the same people who paid for welfare, the federal government. Both programs were part of a social agenda of assisting, but also controlling, the poor. Though the lawyer had worked hard to identify with Mrs. G., she was also sworn, and paid, to defend the basic constitution of the *status quo*. When Mrs. G. "misbehaved" at the hearing, when she failed to talk on cue and then refused to keep quiet, Mrs. G. pointed to the ambiguity of the legal aid lawyer's social role. Through her defiant actions, Mrs. G. told the lawyer that a conspiracy with a double agent is inevitably going to prove an unstable alliance.

The lawyer had tried to "collaborate" with Mrs. G. in devising an advocacy plan. Yet the terms of that "dialogue" excluded Mrs. G.'s voice. Mrs. G. was a better strategist than the lawyer—more daring, more subtle, more fluent—in her own home terrain. She knew the psychology, the culture, and the politics of the white people who controlled her community. She knew how to read, and sometimes control, her masters' motivations; she had to command this knowledge—the intuition—to survive. The lawyer had learned intuition as a woman, but in a much more private sphere. She was an outsider to the county, and to Mrs. G.'s social world. Mrs. G.'s superior sense of the landscape posed a subtle threat to the lawyer's expertise. Sensing this threat, the lawyer steered their strategic "discussion" into the sphere of her own expert knowledge. By limiting the very definition of "strategy" to the manipulation of legal doctrine, she invited Mrs. G. to respond to her questions with silence. And, indeed, Mrs. G. did not talk freely when the lawyer was devising their game-plan. Rather, Mrs. G. waited until the hearing to act our her own intuitions. Although she surely had not plotted those actions in advance, she came up with moves at the hearing which threw everyone else off their guard, and may have proved her the better *legal* strategist of the lawyer-client pair.

The disarming "strategy" that Mrs. G. improvised at the hearing was to appear to *abandon* strategy entirely. For a moment she stepped out of the role of the supplicant. She ignored the doctrinal pigeonholes that would fragment her voice. She put aside all that the lawyer told her the audience wanted to hear. Instead, when asked to point a finger at her caseworker, she was silent. When asked about "life necessities," she explained that she had used her money to meet *her own* needs. She had bought her children Sunday shoes.

* * *

The next excerpt describes how the stories created by "outgroups" can change the perceptions of a dominant group. The experiences of outgroups who have challenged the status quo by creating new stories contain valuable lessons for every lawyer and client.

Richard Delgado, *Storytelling for Oppositionists and Others: A Plea for Narrative*, 87 MICH. L. REV. 2411 (1989)*

INTRODUCTION

Everyone has been writing stories these days. And I don't just mean writing *about* stories or narrative theory, important as those are. I mean actual stories, as in "once-upon-a-time" type stories. Derrick Bell has been writing "Chronicles," and in the *Harvard Law Review* at that.[2] Others have been writing dialogues, stories, and metastories. Many others have been daring to become more personal in their writing, to inject narrative, perspective, and feeling—how it was for me—into their otherwise scholarly, footnoted articles and, in the case of the truly brave, into their teaching.

Many, but by no means all, who have been telling legal stories are members of what could be loosely described as outgroups,[8] groups whose marginality defines the boundaries of the mainstream, whose voice and perspective—whose conscious-ness—has been suppressed, devalued, and abnormalized. The attraction of stories for these groups should come as no surprise. For stories create their own bonds, repre-sent cohesion, shared understandings, and meanings. The cohesiveness that stories bring is part of the strength of the outgroup. An outgroup creates its own stories, which circulate within the group as a kind of counter-reality.

The dominant group creates its own stories, as well. The stories or narratives told by the ingroup remind it of its identity in relation to outgroups, and provide it with a form of shared reality in which its own superior position is seen as natural.

The stories of outgroups aim to subvert that ingroup reality. In civil rights, for example, many in the majority hold that any inequality between blacks and whites is due either to cultural lag, or inadequate enforcement of currently existing beneficial laws—both of which are easily correctable. For many minority persons, the princi-pal instrument of their subordination is neither of these. Rather, it is the prevailing *mindset* by means of which members of the dominant group justify the world as it is, that is, with whites on top and browns and blacks at the bottom.

---

*   Reprinted with permission.

2   D. BELL, AND WE ARE NOT SAVED (1987) [hereinafter AND WE ARE NOT SAVED]; Bell, *The Supreme Court, 1984 Term—Foreword: The Civil Rights Chronicles*, 99 HARV. L. REV. 4 (1985) [here-inafter *The Civil Rights Chronicles*].

8   By "outgroup" I mean any group whose consciousness is other than that of the dominant one.
* * *

Stories, parables, chronicles, and narratives are powerful means for destroying mindset—the bundle of presuppositions, received wisdoms, and shared understandings against a background of which legal and political discourse takes place. These matters are rarely focused on. They are like eyeglasses we have worn a long time. They are nearly invisible; we use them to scan and interpret the world and only rarely examine them for themselves. Ideology—the received wisdom—makes current social arrangements seem fair and natural. Those in power sleep well at night—their conduct does not seem to them like oppression.

The cure is storytelling (or as I shall sometimes call it, counterstorytelling). As Derrick Bell, Bruno Bettelheim, and others show, stories can shatter complacency and challenge the status quo. Stories told by underdogs are frequently ironic or satiric; a root word for "humor" is humus—bringing low, down to earth. Along with the tradition of storytelling in black culture there exists the Spanish tradition of the picaresque novel or story, which tells of humble folk piquing the pompous or powerful and bringing them down to more human levels.

Most who write about storytelling focus on its community-building functions: stories build consensus, a common culture of shared understandings, and deeper, more vital ethics. Counterstories, which challenge the received wisdom, do that as well. They can open new windows into reality, showing us that there are possibilities for life other than the ones we live. They enrich imagination and teach that by combining elements from the story and current reality, we may construct a new world richer than either alone. Counterstories can quicken and engage conscience. Their graphic quality can stir imagination in ways in which more conventional discourse cannot.

But stories and counterstories can serve an equally important destructive function. They can show that what we believe is ridiculous, self-serving, or cruel. They can show us the way out of the trap of unjustified exclusion. They can help us understand when it is time to reallocate power. They are the other half—the destructive half—of the creative dialectic.

Stories and counterstories, to be effective, must be or must appear to be non-coercive. They invite the reader to suspend judgment, listen for their point or message, and then decide what measure of truth they contain. They are insinuative, not frontal; they offer a respite from the linear, coercive discourse that characterizes much legal writing.

* * *

Often, the challenge of practicing law is finding a way to look at facts and reality from a new perspective in order to construct a story that protects the interests of a client. The next excerpt summarizes methods that have been used by feminists and others to interpret and express experiences as members of an excluded group.

Phyllis Goldfarb, *A Theory-Practice Spiral: The Ethics of Feminism and Clinical Education*, 75 MINN. L. REV. 1599 (1991)*

* * *

A. FEMINIST METHODS, FEMINIST THEORY

* * *

None of the methods described in this section are uniquely used by women or by feminists. Nor would every feminist subscribe to them or to the artificial but heuristically useful categorization of methods presented here. Neither have feminist thinkers alone constructed these methods. Although once again mindful of the potentially misleading nature of labels, I believe that this set of methods is properly designated "feminist" because its contents have been collected, developed and endorsed by a considerable number of feminists engaged in an effort to understand and undermine gender hierarchy.

No feminist method is grounded explicitly in the established methodology of a particular discipline. Although feminists have chosen to avoid the confines of a single disciplinary approach, they have often borrowed helpful approaches from other disciplines. Feminist methodology is deliberately eclectic, discouraging artificial separations of related ideas and promoting cross-disciplinary thinking that furthers its animating values. I urge readers, regardless of any preconceptions about the substantive goals of various activities identified as feminist, to evaluate each method that feminists have adopted on its own merits. I have attempted to make the descriptions that follow vivid enough to permit such evaluation.

1. Consciousness-Raising

Any description of contemporary feminist practice must begin with reference to consciousness-raising, the preeminent method of the movement. As a method, consciousness-raising developed organically from women's coming together, drawn by a shared sense of need, to describe their lives' experiences to one another. Through the collaborative telling of and listening to individual women's experiences, many participants noticed similarities and repetitions. As story-patterns began to form, the collective nature of their various situations emerged. Once having glimpsed "the social dimension of individual experience and the individual dimension of social experience," their reactions to their experiences took the shape of structural critique.

Consciousness-raising is a collective, interpersonal, reflective method aimed at articulating and advancing authentic ways of understanding and interpreting lived experiences. The cooperative nature of the exploration discourages hierarchical arrangements within the group that would reproduce, in part, the problem generating the need for gathering. Stated differently, feminist method incorporates an understanding of interpersonal relationships as revealing and expressing political content.

---

*   Reprinted with permission.

One should not misread the summary nature of this description as underplaying the difficulty and the power of consciousness-raising as a form of emancipatory struggle enacted in language. Participating in consciousness-raising is not a simple matter of speaking one's thoughts, but of discovering one's thoughts with the support and assistance of the other participants' tentative reports and statements. To know one's pain and one's experience, and to trust what one knows sufficiently to name it, in a culture that has never recognized the existence of such pain or the validity of such experience, is an extraordinary feat, involving a long process of grappling to find language that can facilitate and express that understanding. The method depends on "train[ing] ourselves to respect our feelings and to transpose them into a language so they can be shared."

* * *

2. Storytelling

Storytelling, a concept much in vogue in academic circles generally, is a specific form of consciousness-raising that serves as corrective. Speaking one's experiences can disrupt theory through the power of personal stories for which the theory cannot account. Many have challenged theories of law and other dominant social theories through this process of "narrative critique." It is also a process through which women of color, lesbians, poor women, and disabled women have confronted feminist theories of women's situation that did not account for them. Not surprisingly, feminists advocate storytelling as, among other things, an antidote to the application of preconceived rules to ritualized stories consisting of spare, refined facts—a practice privileged by some sectors of academic law.

The narratives offered as consciousness-raising, especially when articulated by the excluded, hold possibilities for changing the listeners' consciousness through empathetic understanding. Stories, whether real or potentially real, provide listeners with the vivid historical detail necessary for a vicarious experience that may awaken empathy. They also allow the storyteller to explore and develop a sense of identity and subjectivity, elusive capacities under social conditions which widely objectify her. Drawing on the storyteller's experiences and feelings, narratives can move listeners emotionally and intellectually. This emotional and intellectual engagement can contribute to careful interpretation and analysis of the story's data, promoting a fuller human understanding than analytic reasoning alone can sometimes provide. Under conditions of openness, theory can be built through the consciousness-raising practice of storytelling, disrupted by the same practice, then reconstructed.

* * *

3. Exclusion Questions

In a recent article, Katharine Bartlett has named and described methods related to consciousness-raising and storytelling that feminists have added to the standard array of approaches to legal reasoning.[136] One of these methods she calls "asking the woman question" (or "asking the exclusion question"). Exclusion questions help feminists develop structural theory from the narratives of experience explored in consciousness-raising. Asking such questions entails asking about the exclusion of various women's needs, perspectives, and experiences from law itself or from other social and political institutions. Storytelling and consciousness-raising provide participants with the basis for knowing how different women understand and report their needs, perspectives, and experiences, such that participants can identify institutional forms excluding various women. Understanding the commonalities and differences of many women is a necessary aspect of discovering the mismatch between them, or particular groups of them, and cultural institutions. And understanding how various women experience institutions precedes discovery of how institutions respond to or ignore various women's interests. Critical theory develops from analyzing the perceived reasons for, and implications of, women's exclusion, and the consequences of their imagined inclusion.

Nothing can limit these methods to use in women's exploration of the workings of a gender system. Indeed, one cannot understand the gender system in isolation from other social structures, because women come in a full complement of races, classes, cultures, sexual orientations, and physical abilities, all of which affect the meaning, the quality, and the security of their lives in a multitude of daily ways. To speak of one's experience as a woman is to speak of one's experience in a society which makes gender, and all of these other categories as well, such powerful socializing forces that they simultaneously influence one's identity, treatment, and opportunity. Any structural critique that emerges from viewing women as a diverse class must reflect their multiple identities and their multiple and varied experiences in the social world. As pure method, asking a genuine and inclusive woman question always means asking a broader question about exclusion across all of the strata in which women, and many men, are found.

* * *

4. Contextual Reasoning

* * *

The value of all the feminist methods described here is their capacity to expand context. Faithfulness to these methods requires vigilance in searching for and carefully attending to perspectives and interests often overlooked because they are unfamiliar to the reasoner. The following example illustrates how these features of feminist practical reasoning, as described by Bartlett, can affect the legal decision-making process.

Consider the prosecution of a battered woman who uses a weapon against her batterer during a period of quiescence in the abuse cycle. She claims self-defense, but the prosecution insists that the charged acts constitute excessive force in violation of

---

136 Bartlett, [*Feminist Legal Methods*, 103 HARV. L. REV. 829, 835 (1990)].

the duty to retreat. A court applying self-defense doctrine to these circumstances will likely consider the state's policy interests in excluding excessive force and including a duty to retreat in the construction of self-defense. The court also may consider the common law interpretations of what constitutes excessive force and the duty to retreat. As in any prosecution, the court also would likely consider the interests of the person harmed, the man who has been assaulted in this instance, and others like him, as well as the reasons for, and interests of, the defendant in claiming self-defense.

A feminist decisionmaker employing contextual reasoning would consider all of the information above, but also would stretch the scope of the context by including the "stories" and perspectives of these litigants, and others who are involved in battering relationships. The decisionmaker might consider women's typical size and strength disadvantages; their absence of training, such as in the military and on football teams, in physical protection; the extent to which their physical efforts to defend themselves are met with increased violence immediately or later; and data about battered women whose batterers seriously injured or killed them without using weapons, for purposes of evaluating whether a woman's use of a weapon is truly excessive. Sensitized by this context, the reasoner would listen to the story of *this* battered woman and try to take her perspective, evaluating her story by paying special attention to its similarities to, and its differences from, important features of the collected stories. The reasoner also would inquire about the defendant's perceptions of the imminence of her danger in light of the past patterns of her abuse and her understanding of these patterns. Additionally, the decisionmaker would seek to understand the perspective of the man who has been assaulted in these circumstances. Contextual reasoning dictates that the decisionmaker weigh this welter of complex information before making the legal and moral choice about how to apply notions of self-defense in this case.

Opening up the actual circumstances of the battering experience and the social and psychological conditions under which it occurs may generate insights that aid in the resolution of cases involving battering, insights that would remain submerged in a purely logical analysis of the meaning of self-defense. Moreover, the decisionmakers in such cases may find themselves moved by the process of plumbing human misery so directly. Feminists would urge them to reflect on these feelings, and not suppress any influence these feelings have on their understanding of the real human consequences of legal judgments.

* * *

5. Epistemological and Ethical Questions

The narrative and consciousness-raising methods that uncover a range of perspectives, when combined with exclusion questions and contextual reasoning, have helped feminists to develop a powerful epistemological critique of law and other disciplines. By using their experiences in general and their experiences of legal institutions in particular, feminists have shown that doctrinal categories presented as neutral and objective often exclude the perspectives of many while enshrining a particular point of view. For example, when courts faced with the issue of self-defense ruled that a repeatedly battered woman's use of a weapon against her batterer during a lull in the abuse cycle constituted excessive force in violation of a duty to retreat, many women realized that the law of self-defense captured the imagery of two men of comparable size, strength, and physical training engaged in a single confrontation.

Not surprisingly, those whose experiences are reflected in the law of self-defense are likely to view the law as neutral, objective, and sound. Those whose experiences are at odds with the dominant position embedded in the doctrine can see more easily the particularity and partiality of the law and its implicit assumptions about how the world works and about whose perspectives count. Accordingly, if those whose perspectives are reflected in the structures and institutions of dominant legal culture hold exclusive official authority to judge others, and if they exercise that judgment without self-reflection or criticism, then those who differ from the dominant norms will look not only deficient but deviant. To render fairer judgments, decisionmakers must seriously consider the multiplicity of perspectives.

* * *

B. Making Decisions

Clients come to lawyers for help with making decisions. Because the decisions a client makes can have substantial impact on the interests of the lawyer, in the form of economic consequences, commitment of time, or satisfaction with the goals of their joint endeavor, a lawyer has to decide how much to intervene in a client's decision making. Consider the guidelines offered in the next excerpt for the lawyer's role in decision making.

David A. Binder, Paul Bergman and Susan C. Price, LAWYERS AS COUNSELORS: A CLIENT-CENTERED APPROACH (1991)*

* * *

Chapter 15
THE NATURE OF THE COUNSELING PROCESS

* * *

1. INTRODUCTION

Numerous decisions are made as clients' matters move toward resolution. Some of these decisions involve resolution of the principal problems themselves: Should a settlement offer be accepted? Should a contract be signed, despite its failure to include an exclusive dealing provision? Often, however, decisions involve subsidiary strategies: Should discovery be undertaken immediately? Should the draft of

---

*   Reprinted from Lawyers as Counselors: A Client-Centered Approach, David A. Binder, Paul Bergman and Susan C. Price, 1991, with permission of the West Publishing Corporation.

a proposed agreement omit an arbitration clause? Who should prepare the draft—you or the other party?

This chapter explores issues that arise when you counsel and advise clients with respect to either type of decision. Those issues include:

a. Who, as between you and a client, should have the final say?
b. What decisions regarding the handling of a matter should you explore with a client?
c. With respect to decisions which require client consultation,

    1. What information should you elicit from a client before a decision is made?
    2. What information should you insure is available to a client before a decision is made?
    3. When should you provide an opinion as to what decision should be made?
    4. What criteria should you use in arriving at an opinion as to what decision should be made?
    5. How fully must you counsel a client?
    6. When, if ever, may you suggest that a client's decision is wrong?

Understanding these issues, and having some approach to resolving them whenever a decision looms, is critical. Answers to these questions define the counseling role and thus are at the heart of what it means to practice law.

2. COUNSELING AND ADVICE-GIVING DEFINED

Begin by considering the terms "counseling" and "advice-giving." They reflect related but quite different tasks. Usually you must both counsel and advise clients to help them make decisions.

Counseling

Counseling is the process by which lawyers help clients decide what course of action to adopt in order to resolve a problem. The process begins with identifying a problem and clarifying a client's objectives. Thereafter, the process entails identifying and evaluating the probable positive and negative consequences of potential solutions in order to decide which alternative is most likely to achieve a client's aims.

Advice-Giving

Advice consists of your opinion. You may advise a client both about what consequences (legal and/or nonlegal) are likely to flow from alternative courses of action or about which alternative a client should adopt.

An example clarifies the distinction between these two forms of advice. Assume that you represent Snider, who is negotiating to lease space in a shopping center. The owner has indicated that she does not want to give Snider an option to renew the lease. Snider has to decide whether or not to insist on the option. Your opinion about whether or not Snider should insist on the option is an opinion about what course of action Snider should follow. Your opinion about how insisting on the option may affect upcoming negotiations constitutes an opinion about the likely consequences of selecting a particular course of action.

Generally, when counseling you provide advice about consequences far more often than you do about which alternative a client should adopt.

3. AFFORD CLIENTS AN OPPORTUNITY TO MAKE DECISIONS

Inherent in the above definitions of advice-giving and counseling is the idea that clients should generally have the opportunity to make decisions. This is not to say that you never venture your opinion about what course of action a client should adopt, that you never make a decision without consulting a client, or that you must always carry out a client's decision. Our point is a more limited one. With respect to the many decisions that typically must be made as a matter progresses, usually you must give a client the opportunity to decide.

As a starting point, a client should have primary decision-making power because of the simple truth that *a problem is a client's problem, not yours.* For the most part a client, not you, will have to accept the immediate as well as the long term consequences of any decision. For example, deciding to take depositions may result in a client, not you, expending thousands of dollars. Similarly, a client will receive the benefits or suffer the losses attendant to decisions to hire an expert, leave an arbitration clause out of an agreement, or accept a settlement offer.

Given that clients bear the brunt of decisions' consequences, clients presumptively should have the opportunity to determine what course of action to take. Our society highly values each individual's right of self-determination, and you ought to abandon that value only in the face of strong reason for doing so. Because client autonomy is of paramount importance, decisions should be made on the basis of what choice is most likely to *provide a client with maximum satisfaction.*

Clients almost invariably are better able than you to assess which potential decision is most likely to be satisfactory. For one thing, as you recall from Chapter 1, resolving problems typically requires consideration of nonlegal consequences. And clients are likely to be able to predict nonlegal consequences far better than you can. Moreover, even if both you and a client agreed precisely on the likely consequences of a decision, you would not necessarily weigh those consequences equally in making the decision. The process of weighing consequences heavily depends on each person's unique values, and autonomy notions assign primary importance to a client's values.

* * *

You might respond, "I realize that what is best for any client typically rests on subjective personal values which are unknown to me. But that doesn't mean I shouldn't make decisions for a client. It just means that in addition to eliciting the 'facts,' I should also find out about each client's predictions and values." Such a response is not entirely without basis. As you will see, counseling does consist in part of asking clients about predicted consequences and personal values. However, in most instances such an inquiry will not give you a full understanding of a client's personal values. As noted elsewhere,

> "[I]t is often very difficult, if not impossible, for clients to precisely quantify the value they place on specific consequences. Thus, clients cannot usually say, even to themselves, such things as, 'On a scale from one to ten, getting $2500 now has a value of plus 5; avoiding the strain of trial has a value of plus 2; however, giving up the opportunity to obtain an additional $5500 has a value of minus 5;' etc. All that clients can usually do is give general statements of the value they place on the various consequences. Thus, clients can sometimes quantify consequences to the extent of labeling them as 'very important,' 'important,' 'not so important,' etc. However, this quantifying process does not usually allow clients to distinguish between consequences which they see as fitting into the same general category of importance. Thus, typically, clients cannot distinguish between two or three consequences, each of which they see as 'important,' 'not so important,' etc. This inability to distinguish between consequences is particularly pronounced when the consequences are of different types. For instance, a client typically cannot distinguish between an 'important' economic consequence and an 'important' psychological consequence. When asked to rank or weigh the relative importance of such consequences, clients will typically say such things as 'I can't say which is more important. Getting an additional $1500 is important, but it's also important that I not be under a lot of stress. My friends say go for the additional money, but they don't have to face testifying in court. I can't say which is more important; they're both important.'"[15]

Moreover, what is true about conveying values and preferences is also true with respect to conveying risk averseness. Most clients have a difficult time articulating precisely the degree to which they are willing to risk possible losses to achieve possible gains. * * * Clients' typical inability to express accurately their subjective thoughts about their willingness to take risks is another reason that you must give clients the opportunity to decide what course of action to follow.

Finally, even if you could become fully conversant with a client's value and preference structure, you perhaps ought not be trusted to make important decisions because of your potential conflicts of interest. When it comes time to make decisions, your interests and those of a client frequently are adverse. For instance, in making decisions about what provisions to include in a deal, lawyers often want to include a great many more contingency provisions than do clients. Lawyers often want clients to insert such provisions in agreements not only to protect the client but also to make sure that if the contingency ultimately does arise, the lawyer cannot be sued for malpractice. Clients, on the other hand, are often more interested in making a deal than

---

15   See Binder & Price, [LEGAL INTERVIEWING AND COUNSELING: A CLIENT-CENTERED APPROACH], at 149 [(1977)].

in being fully protected if an agreement should ultimately break down. Clients often predict that insistence on a contingency provision may kill the deal and they are therefore willing to drop the provision and take the risk that the contingency will not arise.

Other common examples of potential lawyer-client decision-making conflicts include whether to accept an offer, whether to take depositions, and whether to call a witness to testify. In each of these instances, what may be financially beneficial or convenient for a lawyer may conflict with what is financially best for a client.

That lawyers and clients often have conflicting interests suggests once again that decisions ought to remain in a client's hands. Even if you could determine a client's values and preferences, the temptation to decide the matter in a way which advances your personal interests is reason to allow a client to make the ultimate choice.

4. WHAT DECISIONS CAN YOU MAKE WITHOUT CONSULTING A CLIENT?

An emphasis on clients as primary decision-makers may suggest that clients should have the opportunity to make each and every decision. Some commentators, in fact, have urged such a position.

However, the "client makes all the decisions" position is unworkable and, in fact, inconsistent with client-centeredness. If a client were to make every decision, you would have to inform a client each time a decision were necessary and engage a client in a discussion of potential options and consequences. Yet, as you recall, even a simple matter typically requires scores of decisions. Accordingly, you and your clients would have to be in nearly continuous communication. Undoubtedly, most clients would not have the time, the desire or the financial resources to hire you under these conditions. Moreover, you would undoubtedly soon regard practicing law under such conditions as a sentence to a career of virtually continuous communication with a small number of clients.

If consultation about every decision is unacceptable, how might you decide what decisions to call to a client's attention? There is no easy answer to this question. In the past, some authorities attempted to draw a distinction between matters' "substantive" and "procedural" aspects. They suggested that lawyers should review with clients decisions affecting the objectives of representation, but need not do so with respect to decisions which only affect the means by which the objectives were secured. Many courts continue to echo this ends-means distinction.

However, a moment's reflection suggests that drawing a meaningful line based on "ends" and "means" is often impossible. For example, clients are often concerned both about what is achieved and how it is achieved. Assume that you represent a client charged with burglary, and a decision arises about whether or not to call the client's sister as an alibi witness. You believe the sister will make an excellent witness, but the client insists that she not be called because in the client's view testifying will cause the sister undue stress. Is the decision of whether to call the sister one of ends or means? If the client's objective is seen simply as avoiding conviction—winning the trial—the decision about calling the sister is arguably merely a question of tactics or means. However, if the client's objectives are seen as avoiding a conviction and also avoiding stress to the sister, both decisions involve objectives.

Asking a client early on to indicate what kinds of decisions he or she wishes to be consulted about has sometimes been suggested as an approach to the issue of when you need to consult a client. However, this "waiver" approach too is typically inadequate. A client who is legally experienced may have a basis for making an informed choice about which decisions he or she wishes to be consulted on. You may therefore be justified in relying on that choice, at least when the client asks for frequent consultation. When consultation occurs frequently, a client has repeated opportunities to reassess the decision about the kinds of issues on which he or she wishes to be consulted.

However, legally inexperienced clients usually cannot foresee the twists and turns that even relatively simple matters may take, and hence cannot know what decision points are likely to arise. Accordingly you should probably not rely on an inexperienced client's waiver of decision-making responsibility.

Moreover, whether or not a client is experienced, the kinds of decisions a client wishes to be consulted about at one point in time are not necessarily the kinds of decisions the client will wish to be consulted about at some later time. As a client's life situation changes, and as a matter ages, the kinds of decisions which a client views as important and on which the client hence wants to be consulted may well also change. Thus, any initial guideline delineating when consultation is desired is a very soft decision which needs periodic review.

Hence, neither "ends-means" nor "prior waiver" adequately determine which decisions require client consultation. In our view, a different standard should apply. You ought to provide a client with an opportunity to make a decision whenever a lawyer using "such skill, prudence, and diligence as other members of the profession commonly possess and exercise," would or should know that a pending decision is likely to have a *substantial legal or nonlegal impact on a client.*

This standard instructs you to consult a client if, measured by the presumed awareness of the legal community, a decision is likely to have a substantial legal or nonlegal impact on a client. Admittedly, the standard is not without its difficulties. For example, the standard may differ from one community to another. Also, it may burden a novice attorney with finding out whether experienced attorneys are likely to view a decision as one likely to have a substantial impact. However, the standard is one to which professionals are commonly held. Moreover, it is client centered. It focuses on the likely impact on an individual client, rather than fuzzy distinctions between "ends" and "means."

Since helping clients resolve problems is a lawyer's major role, it is legitimate to require lawyers to be aware of clients' objectives and concerns throughout the attorney-client relationship. Moreover, many lawyers undoubtedly now gather information about clients' objectives and concerns. Finally, using a client-centered approach invariably elicits such information. For example, preliminary problem identification seeks to unearth objectives and concerns at the outset of a relationship. Hence, the standard is both fair and realistic.

Indeed, many lawyers undoubtedly comply with the standard in their everyday practices. When a decision may cause a substantial impact, many lawyers regularly consult clients about a wide variety of decisions that many would define as involving "means." For example, when decisions are likely to have a substantial legal or nonlegal impact, litigators often consult with their clients about matters such as continuances, filing of motions, taking of depositions, and negotiation strategy. Indeed, a lawyer might even consult a client as to the wisdom of asking a question on cross examination in circumstances where the impact of a critical admission might be undercut by an explanation, and the lawyer believes that the client may know whether the witness will give that explanation. Likewise, when substantial impact decisions arise in transactional matters, lawyers discuss with their clients such issues as how to word provisions, which side will draft the agreement, and what negotiation strategy to pursue.

* * *

5. EFFECT OF THE "SUBSTANTIAL IMPACT" STANDARD ON "LAWYERING SKILLS" CONCERNS

You may worry about whether a standard obligating you to consult a client whenever a decision is likely to have a substantial impact unduly interferes with your exercise of professional skills. For example, if a decision to pursue a certain line of questioning on cross is likely to have a substantial impact, are you therefore obligated to consult the client regarding cross examination questioning strategy?

Clients, recognizing their own lack of expertise, undoubtedly assume you will make such decisions, and do not expect to be consulted about them. By analogy, consider that a plumber does not consult a customer as to what type of wrench to use on a stopped drain. The customer's act of hiring the plumber indicates the customer's desire for the plumber to make those decisions which are in the plumber's traditional domain. Similarly, a client's decision to hire you is tacit willingness for you to make lawyering skills decisions free from consultation. Thus, such matters as how you cross examine, write briefs, or phrase contingency clauses are generally for you alone to decide, even though they may have a substantial impact. They involve primarily the exercise of the skills and crafts that are the special domain of lawyers.

However, "lawyering skills" are often not a sufficient excuse for failure to consult a client. When a decision is likely to have an impact beyond that normally associated with the exercise of lawyering skills and crafts, the "substantial impact" standard obligates consultation. For example, consider these situations:

a. A witness you are considering calling on behalf of your client is the client's boss.
b. You are considering phrasing a contingency clause in a purposely vague manner because you do not think the other party will agree to the precise language your client desires, and the vague wording may at a future date be interpreted in your client's favor.
c. You are considering whether to remove an action from state to federal court.
d. You are considering whether to defend an action vigorously, as opposed to simply countering the plaintiff's moves.

You probably should consult a client in each of these situations. The decisions carry impacts beyond those normally associated with the use of professional skills and crafts.

Thus, in "a," developing the case-in-chief may usually lie entirely within your professional judgment. But calling a client's boss raises sensitive issues beyond those normally associated with direct examination. Hence, the need for client consultation.

Similarly, in "b," the question of how to phrase the contingency clause is not simply one of professional craft, but of risk averseness, of a client's willingness to live with uncertainty. That decision too does not involve primarily the craft of legal writing, but may have a substantial impact on the client's position in the event the contingency arises. Hence, the need for consultation.

In "c," whether an action is tried in state or federal court is likely to have many effects, such as what evidentiary rules apply and when the action may come to trial. Again, even though the decision rests in part on the exercise of professional judgment, the potential impacts suggest the need for client consultation.

Finally, in "d," costs to a client may be very different depending on how vigorously a suit is defended. Costs, of course, are the type of impact which very much suggest the need for client consultation.

Admittedly, knowing when an impact is beyond that normally associated with the exercise of professional skills and crafts will often be difficult. We make no pretense that our line is a bright and unwavering one. However, we do think that the "ends"-"means" test leaves far too many decisions in an attorney's hands alone. The four examples above may help you understand why many "lawyering skills" decisions require client consultation.

* * *

In the next excerpt Binny Miller focuses on the client's role in making decisions and urges lawyers to collaborate with clients on the essential task of developing a theory of the case.

Binny Miller, *Give Them Back Their Lives: Recognizing Client Narrative in Case Theory*, 93 MICH. L. REV. 485 (1994)*

* * *

In recent years the concepts of lawyering as storytelling and client voice as narrative have come into vogue. As a practical matter, lawyers have always seen their work as in part "storytelling," but only recently has legal scholarship framed lawyering in these terms. By and large, legal scholars have approached storytelling and narrative from the standpoint of theory—critical race theory, critical literary and legal theory, feminist theory, lesbian and gay theory, and ethnographic theory. In contrast, clinical theory has long grounded narrative in the actual practice of lawyering. The emerging theoretics of practice literature draws on all of these vantage points in looking at the intersection of theory and practice in legal advocacy.

Although these approaches differ in some respects, they share enough in common that they can be grouped under the rubric of "critical lawyering." These critical theorists posit that client voices have been muted by the narratives that lawyers tell on their behalf, and urge lawyers to set aside their own stories in favor of client stories. They follow in the footsteps of the client-centered movement, which has argued that clients should play a greater role in their own cases.

The critical and client-centered movements add to our understanding of the role that client voices can and should play in legal representation. But in the rush to embrace client voice, these scholars have virtually ignored the critical role that case theory can play in linking client stories to the narratives that lawyers tell on behalf of clients.

Case theory—or theory of the case—can be seen as an explanatory statement linking the "case" to the client's experience of the world. It serves as a lens for shaping reality, in light of the law, to explain the facts, relationships, and circumstances of the client and other parties in the way that can best achieve the client's goals. The relevant reality combines the perspectives of the lawyer and the client with an eye toward the ultimate audience—the trier of fact.

Despite the view of many lawyers that case theory is central to the task of lawyering, and despite its prominence in highly publicized trials, most accounts of lawyering do not explore the richness of case theory. For writers of trial advocacy texts, case theory is an important lawyering "skill," yet their works contain at best only skeletal analyses of the concept. For client-centered theorists, case theory plays little role in client decisionmaking; at best, it is one of a number of decisions that permit some client participation, and at worst, it is a task for lawyers alone. For critical theorists, both the concept of case theory and the role of clients in decisionmaking about case theory remain partially obscured.

This article is about case theory and its implications for incorporating client narratives in litigation. In seeking to understand the connections between voice, narra-

---

*   Reprinted with permission.

tive, and case theory, I look not only to theory but to my experience as a clinical teacher and criminal defense attorney. I explore how the practice of lawyering can be reconstructed to embrace a greater role for clients in constructing case theories, both through the images of the client the lawyer presents in the case theory and through active client participation in developing and choosing the case theory. Although one aim of case theory is to persuade the trier of fact, my focus is not on the sorts of inferences and arguments that might persuade a jury but rather on the role of the client in shaping case theory.

* * *

I. THE ROLE OF CASE THEORY IN LAWYERING

* * *

A. *Traditional Model: Where Is the Client?*

1. *Concept of Case Theory*

Case theory provides a framework for trial preparation and ultimately for trial. It has been defined as "the basic underlying idea that explains not only the legal theory and factual background, but also ties as much of the evidence as possible into a coherent and credible whole."[38] Case theory is not simply a statement of the applicable law or of the facts that support this legal interpretation, but rather it is the "basic concept around which everything else revolves."[39]

Case theory is often described as comprising two separate theories, a legal theory and a factual theory. The legal theory is "a legal framework developed by a lawyer from interpretation, analysis, and expansion of legal rules and standards,"[41] while the factual theory is "the party's 'story' justifying relief under the legal theory."[42] The case theory should be supported by the facts, meaning that it should explain the party's version of the facts, the unfavorable facts, and any undisputed facts. The theory must also be measured against its legal sufficiency and in terms of how well it responds to the likely theory of the opponent.

* * *

Once a case theory is selected, it serves as the centerpiece for all strategic and tactical decisions in the case. The case theory is incorporated in the pleadings and serves as a guide for conducting the pretrial investigation and discovery, including client and witness interviews, formal discovery, and motions. Later, case theory "dictate[s] virtually every word the attorney utters at trial."[57] The theory of the case is not only stated explicitly in the opening statement and reiterated in closing argument, but it also shapes every aspect of the trial, including trial tactics, witness examinations, and evidentiary issues. Thus, a trial becomes a contest between competing theories of the case.

---

38   JAMES W. MCELHANEY, TRIAL NOTEBOOK 78 (3d ed. 1994). * * *

39   MCELHANEY, TRIAL NOTEBOOK, *supra* note 38, at 78. * * *

41   BERGER ET AL., PRETRIAL [ADVOCACY: PLANNING, ANALYSIS AND STRATEGY], at 18 [(1988)].

42   *Id.* * * *

57   CARLSON & IMWINKELRIED, [DYNAMICS OF TRIAL PRACTICE: PROBLEMS AND MATERIALS], at 35 [(1989)].

Case theory remains an elusive concept, beyond the seemingly simple statement that case theory is the legal and factual framework for organizing and presenting a case. Lawyers often mistake case theory for narrow tactical decisions, and this confusion is compounded by the use of other terms that loosely approximate the idea of case theory but are not identical. While the terms *theory of the case* and *theme* are sometimes used interchangeably, they seem to mean different things. *Theory* implies a linear, rational concept that drives the fact finder inexorably to a favorable result; *theme*, while geared to the same end, instead suggests a potent mixture of facts and emotion. Other efforts to define *case theory* are colorful and quaint at best; at worst, they are cliches. The often-cited admonitions that case theory should be straightforward and consistent with common sense, human experience, and the values of the judge or jury add little to these barebones explanations.

* * *

2. *Critique—Visible Doctrine and Invisible Clients*

The heart of traditional case theory is what I call "element-crunching": case theory is the law with facts playing a supporting role. Under this view, case theory is derived from the close study of court decisions, statutes, rules, regulations, and treatises. The attorney simply turns to these sources of information, determines which elements she needs to prove, and then gathers those facts that establish each and every element of her theory.

* * *

Although the best of the traditionalists recognize a back-and-forth interplay between legal theory and "what happened," facts nonetheless serve a purpose secondary to legal doctrine. Even when "factual theory" is identified as a piece of case-theory structure, this bipartite structure severs factual theory from legal theory. Stories are subsumed in legal theory, which serves as both the starting point and ending point for case theory. Facts exist simply to be plugged into legal theory, and facts that cannot find a home in some legal element are deemed virtually irrelevant. The process of theory development is quantifiable, neat, and quite sterile.

For the traditionalists, there are a finite number of possible case theories in any case. If the lawyer is a good detective, she will ferret out all potential case theories, discard those theories that do not fit the facts, and from the remaining available theories select the one that is most persuasive. Yet even the novel theories she derives from creatively reading existing law or discovering new law lack the boundless possibilities that any one set of facts presents.

But traditionalists do not see these possibilities because they picture a world of objective facts in which the lawyer can really *know* "what happened" if only she pushes the right buttons. In their view, the worst kind of lawyer is one who "desperately grop[es] for anything in order to win, without any regard to what really happened."[98] In their rush to reject different factual scenarios, traditionalists provide no

---

98   Berger *et al.*, Pretrial, *supra* note [41], at 23 * * * .

sense that objective facts are often few, that perspective is everything, and that what happened may be a meaningless concept apart from the lens of the particular viewer.

Contrast the traditionalist view with the videotape shown in the trial of the Los Angeles police officers charged with beating Rodney King. Although at first glance the videotape seemed susceptible to only one interpretation—a black man being brutally beaten by four white officers—the defense relied on the videotape to show King as a madman raging out of control. Even those jurors who were not persuaded that King was a madman experienced a "deadening" of facts through the constant replaying of the video, which at first seemed horrific.

Finally, clients are almost invisible in the traditional concept of case theory. Indeed, for some traditionalists, the process of defining the world of available theories begins even before the lawyer interviews the client. Although others recognize that clients can serve as a source of factual "stories" in developing case theory and may be counseled about the impact of a decision on the success of a particular case theory, this recognition does not translate into an active role for the client. The active role belongs to the lawyer and her view shapes the case theory. The real challenge for the lawyer lies in developing a viable case theory, not in understanding the client and her world. Lawyers are given the task of matching the theory to client goals, and clients are nearly always assumed to want to win, whatever the trade-offs. Even those traditionalists who recognize that an effective case theory should achieve the client's objectives give clients only a limited role in identifying objectives and assign them no role at all in selecting or shaping a theory to meet these objectives.

The defense lawyer's "lecture" to his client about the law in *Anatomy of a Murder*[107] stands as the classic example admonishing lawyers not to discuss case theory with their clients. In that book—and in the movie version as well—the lawyer raises a potential insanity theory with his client and, through thinly veiled suggestion, deliberately encourages the client to adopt the story. The message is that a lawyer should obtain all the "facts" from clients without revealing potential theories; otherwise, clients will shape their stories to fit the theory. Although in this example the attorney may have overstepped ethical boundaries by putting words in the client's mouth to fit the attorney's theory, the more unfortunate legacy of the story is that clients and case theory do not mix.

B. *Client-Centered Theory: Who Decides?*

While the traditional model lays out the contours of case theory, the client-centered model calls attention to the issue that the identity of the person who makes the decision about case theory—the lawyer or the client—should be critical. In the context of a particular legal procedure—whether trial, negotiation, or settlement—what role can clients play in conceiving the strategy to carry out the procedure? Or more broadly, even outside the context of a particular decision, what role can clients play in simply conceiving of the *case*? What is the case and what does it mean to the client?

---

107 ROBERT TRAVER, ANATOMY OF A MURDER 35-49 (1958). * * *

* * *

With few exceptions, client-centered writers analyze the decisions facing the client in generic terms, without distinguishing the type of decision at stake. When they discuss the context of a decision specifically, the most active arena of client decisionmaking appears to be in the area of legal process, either in initiating legal procedures—by filing a lawsuit or an appeal or invoking an informal mechanism, for example—or in disposing of a case through settlement or trial. This focus in process implies that other kinds of decisions are relegated to lawyers and thus are excluded from the lawyer-client dialogue.

* * *

Perhaps the reluctance to embrace client decisionmaking about case theory stems from a failure to understand the real differences in the degree to which strategy decisions can be the subject of collaboration between lawyers and clients. Indeed, many trial decisions must be made quickly and on the spot. But an understanding of the process of case theory development debunks the notion that *all* trial strategy must be left to lawyers because decisions must be made quickly without time for consultation. It is the nature of the decision, rather than the legal forum, that should determine the appropriateness of shared decisionmaking. Case theory is the quintessential question that can, and indeed should, be decided in advance of trial. It is precisely the kind of decision suited to brainstorming and collaboration with clients.

Client-centered theorists need to take the insight that the choices lawyers make create the official conception of what the case is about in the legal system one step further by truly integrating the client's perspective. Rather than seeing each case as a series of discrete choices, each segregable from the other—should I settle, go to trial, make this objection, or call this witness?—lawyers and theorists should instead view a case as a unified whole, bound together. This is the mistake that the traditionalists make in creating the ends-means dichotomy, a mistake that client-centered theorists quickly call them on. Ironically, client-centered theorists miss the opportunity that case theory offers—the opportunity to play out the futility of the distinction between ends and means. For some clients, case theory is a means to an end; for others, it may be an end in itself.

* * *

C. *Critical Lawyering Theory: Whose Story Is It?*

The critical lawyers make a major contribution to the traditional understanding of case theory by involving clients in the choice of which story to tell and thus recognizing the importance of client life experience and strategic skills in this endeavor. Because many of these theorists do not talk in terms of case theory, I consider how their insights about the related concept of storytelling can be translated to case theory development.

1. *Theory of Critical Lawyering*

Critical theorists view lawyers as tellers of stories or narratives. In considering narrative, critical theorists differentiate between the stories that clients tell about their lives and those that lawyers tell about clients' lives in the courtroom. The content of client narratives is the fabric of the client's life, not just the client's version of "what happened." The traditionalists also see storytelling possibilities in different versions of "what happened," but in the eyes of critical theorists, the gap between legal narratives and client narratives in traditional lawyering practices is too wide.

Critical theorists see legal narrative through the lens of power. In this picture of power, legal narrative is a battleground of competing lawyer and client narratives in which lawyer narratives always emerge victorious. Lawyers reject client stories as implausible unless they fit into lawyer-endorsed strategies in which legal doctrine predominates. They construct fixed, predictable, and unimaginative stories that exclude client experience. Lawyer narratives drown out the voices of client narratives, marginalizing and subordinating them.

In seeking to bridge the gap between lawyer and client stories, critical theorists offer two competing visions of lawyering. In one vision, client stories should be victorious in the narrative contest. In these contests, critical lawyers see the client's story as the only story worth telling—as they worship pure, unadulterated client narratives over any form of lawyer narrative. Only by "speaking out" can clients reclaim their narratives, deviating from prepared testimony in depositions and hearings.

In the other vision, client narratives inform, but do not overthrow, legal narrative. The lawyer translates the client's story so it can be heard and understood in the legal system. In both visions, the legal stories ultimately told present vivid images of clients and are enriched by client life experience.

Yet even when lawyers incorporate client stories in their storytelling, critical theorists see legal forums as ultimately inadequate to capture the full range of client stories. Thus, client stories must also be related both in lawyer-client interactions—when clients can be seen as teachers, not as students—and in interactions between clients. The informality of these settings makes it possible to tell the whole range of client stories, unhampered by the constraints legal rules and procedures impose on conveying the life experiences of clients in legal forums.

* * *

3. *Critique—Metaphors of the Narrative Contest and the Lawyer as Translator*

When translated into case theory, however, the critical lawyers' approach to legal narrative has both theoretical and methodological shortcomings. Despite their focus on client storytelling, critical lawyers are ultimately pessimistic about the opportunities for clients to tell their stories. But a broader concept of case theory provides many opportunities for client stories, because case theory is only "law-talk" to the extent that it is law-driven. Ultimately, there is more room for storytelling about clients in legal forums than critical lawyers contemplate.

Indeed, if client voices are to be heard and clients are to be empowered, the process of developing case theory is central to this task. Rather than seeing case theory as a bridge between client and lawyer stories, however, many critical theorists envision an inevitable narrative contest between lawyers and clients. Lawyer and client stories are always at war, even for those lawyers who are conscious of the power dynamics in the lawyer-client relationship, and so a choice must be made between two opposing stories. This contest metaphor misses the mark in several important respects.

Although the stories lawyers and clients tell often diverge, not all stories lawyers tell differ from their clients' stories. A single story may be told *not* because the lawyer story has displaced the client story but because the stories are the same.

Even when lawyer and client stories diverge and lawyer stories predominate, this cannot always be explained by the exercise of power. Not all clients want to tell their stories. A client might *choose* silence or a lawyer narrative over her own narrative to improve her chances of winning or to achieve some other goal. * * *

* * *

III. RECONCEIVING CASE THEORY: IMPLICATIONS FOR THE
LAWYER-CLIENT RELATIONSHIP

A. *Creating a Theory of Case Theory*

* * *

My aim is to articulate a theory of case theory that is truer *both* to the client's life experience *and* to what it is that lawyers actually do. By defining case theory as an explanatory statement linking the case to the client's experience of the world, we create a context for seeing what we might not otherwise see. Case theory creates a perspective for the facts, relationships, and circumstances of the client and other parties that is grounded in the client's goals. Case theory makes actions seem quite reasonable that at first seemed unreasonable, and it allows us to accept the client's story and at the same time have a plausible explanation for other stories.

* * *

B. *Enhancing Client Participation and Control*

* * *

Although the traditional concept of case theory as a pivotal piece of legal strategy could also provide some role for clients, its legal and instrumental focus narrows the possibilities for client involvement. In contrast, the new vision creates a broader role for client expertise in both instrumental and noninstrumental terms, while still acknowledging that case theory matters a great deal to the ultimate result. Once case theory becomes more than just legal doctrine, clients have more to contribute than the facts about what happened.

For example, a client may know as much as his lawyer does about whether a case theory based on race would persuade the jury. Whatever else lawyers may be expert at, there is little reason to think that a lawyer knows more about racism than does the average person. While a lawyer, through experience, may learn a great deal about how local juries react to different kinds of theories, this knowledge is not technical, nor is it exclusive. Awareness of racism is knowledge acquired in day-to-day life; it is hardly the exclusive province of lawyers.

Client expertise extends not only to developing a more winning case theory but also to assessing whether the theory satisfies other client objectives. Strategy, rather than being any action making it more likely that the client will win, becomes richer and more complex. At the same time, it becomes something clients are capable of weighing—perhaps even more capable than lawyers. Even if lawyers are better than clients at assessing the likelihood that judges and juries will accept a particular argument, they are less expert than clients in knowing whether a case theory portrays the client in the way he wants to be portrayed, advances an argument that matters to him on a personal or political level, or makes room for his voice.

Finally, this model also values client choice for its own sake even if it does not lead to "better" results in either of the above senses. Rather than being relegated to the netherworld of "mere" strategy, case theory is the piece of the case that goes most to the heart of who the client is by determining how his story is told. Because the client is inside the story, the client has the right to decide how to tell it.

This vision of case theory also leads to a much different lawyer-client counseling dialogue from the one envisioned by client-centered theorists. Rather than focusing on the choice of procedural mechanism—trial, negotiation, or plea—as the key decision, the counseling dialogue would focus on case theory. Lawyers and clients would discuss the advantages and disadvantages of different case theories from many vantage points, including standard considerations such as which theory is most likely to prevail and whose testimony is necessary to support each theory.

The conversation would also turn to other, less instrumental concerns, such as how the client would be presented in each theory and whether he likes the story that the theory tells. In choosing one case theory over another, a client might seek vindication by asserting a particular right; he might even demonstrate that he cares more about vindication than he does about acquittal. Or a client might forgo an alibi defense because the alibi witness is his secret lover and also the spouse of his closest friend. A client might veto an insanity defense for reasons of personal integrity or choose a novel legal defense with little likelihood of success on the chance that it might establish an important legal principle.

Lawyers and clients might also discuss procedural mechanisms, but not in the conventional sense. While for a lawyer the choice of forum is driven by the goal of achieving the best legal result, each forum may also provide different opportunities for storytelling. A client who cares about how she is portrayed by case theory, or who has some other goal for case theory, would want to know how case theory would play out in a given forum. The answer to what the case is about also informs the choice of a particular legal procedure. For example, if a client seeks vindication, then a trial is typically a better alternative than a plea.

Once the collaborative energy of lawyer and client is focused on case theory, the question of who decides other issues assumes less importance because the choice of case theory makes many tactical decisions fall neatly into place. * * *

Not only might theories change in this discussion, but also facts. Although some clients may make up facts to fit the case theory, this risk is outweighed by the contributions of truthful clients who know what facts matter. Case theory discussions are likely to reveal new factual dimensions because clients tell lawyers what they think is important and case theory reveals which facts matter. Once the lawyer broadens the frame of what is relevant, then the lawyer, assisted by the client, will see new facts and emphasize those facts consistent with case theory.

In this dialogue, the client is truly a teacher and a contributor, not simply a recipient of the lawyer's noblesse oblige, as in the prototypical client-centered discussion about nonlegal consequences. The client engages deeply in the process of developing case theory because of what he knows and what the lawyer does not. The client might educate us in ways we cannot even imagine. Once we cede control over case theory to our clients, we must remember that as lawyers we may not be in the best position to understand their choices. We want desperately to ascribe a "why" to their words, yet our understanding is limited by our own frame of reference. We perceive legal strategy as the reason for their actions and only reluctantly consider other possible strategic goals. We forget that the legal consequences of their actions may be entirely accidental. They may have intended something entirely different.

* * *

C. *Recognizing Lawyer Life Experience*

Finally, in this process, we might also learn that much of how we as lawyers shape case theory has to do with who we are. It is not that we dominate our clients, as critical theorists argue, but rather that we are either more or less creative than our colleagues, more or less risk averse, more or less fearful of taking on the system, or have more or less life experience with the theory in question. By engaging with the client in these discussions, we might come to know more about ourselves, become better lawyers in the process.

* * *

_____

The lawyer's role in making decisions becomes more complex when the lawyer represents multiple clients, such as a group of individuals, a corporation, an unincorporated association, or a class in a class action. The next excerpt examines the role of the lawyer representing multiple clients with potentially different interests and values.

Stephen Ellmann, *Client-Centeredness Multiplied: Individual Autonomy and Collective Mobilization in Public Interest Lawyers' Representation of Groups*, 78 VA. L. REV. 1103 (1992)*

* * *

* * * [A] tremendous amount of what lawyers do they do for groups of people. The vast bulk of corporate representation is in a sense the representation of the many individual owners of the corporation's stock. Union representation is, probably a good deal more directly, representation of the union's members. Class action litigation expressly deals with the interests of groups of individuals who share common concerns but are too numerous to be individually represented, and the members of many smaller groups are individually named in the cases that concern them. There remain, to be sure, many cases or matters in which the only formal client is an individual, but few of these will implicate only that individual's interests. A single child may demand the desegregation of a school system; one homeless family's vindication of a right to emergency housing may help others win the same benefit in the future; and the gains and losses from any transaction or litigation are likely to be reaped not only by the "client" but by the client's family.

For lawyers whose work is aimed at achieving social reform on behalf of people who would otherwise lack adequate representation—those lawyers whom I will call "public interest lawyers"—the role of groups is particularly significant. Faced with needs far greater than they can hope to meet, these lawyers must make decisions about what cases and causes to undertake. The problems their clients encounter are not the product of some series of unique individual accidents; rather, they result at least in part from social conditions that affect many people at once. Meaningful assistance to these clients depends, to some extent, on finding legal strategies that target broad situations rather than just individual circumstance, and public interest lawyers can properly make case selection decisions that take into account whether potential cases will have this broad impact. The success of these strategies, in turn, may depend on the extent to which they empower clients outside as well as inside the courts, and so may hinge on the degree to which they transform this multiplicity of people into a group.

The upshot is that a great deal of what public interest lawyers do will be done on behalf of groups, either explicitly or implicitly. But the various groups of disadvantaged or underrepresented people in our society are not monolithic. They consist of individuals, whose needs may in fact be unique and whose relations to the groups to which they may be said to belong may range from hostile to harmonious. Poor people, like rich people, are formed in and are part of communities. However, they equally may seek to change or even to shed some of the ties that bind them to these communities. Thus there is an inevitable danger that the lawyer who sets out to help disadvantaged people as members of groups may inadvertently succeed in oppress-

---

*   Reprinted with permission.

ing them (or some of them) as individuals. So long as we acknowledge and value the capacity of individuals to make choices that are not entirely dictated by their preexisting group affiliations—in other words, so long as we value individual autonomy—we must be troubled by the danger to this autonomy inherent in a focus on group interests. My purpose in this Article is to examine the extent of this danger in certain forms of public interest lawyers' representation of client groups. I will argue that proper representation of groups demands radical alterations in our usual methods of protecting individual client autonomy in the lawyer-client relationship, but that it is possible for lawyers both to limit the intrusions on individual autonomy that group interactions generate and to protect a crucial element of individual autonomy—our choices to make connections—that would be jeopardized by a resistance to group representation.

* * *

I. THE DEFINITION OF THE CLIENT

A. *Four Frameworks for Representation*

Defining the client is often difficult, even when only one person is being represented. In individual representation, the lawyer's task, and the client's, is to ensure that the lawyer comes to understand this particular client as he or she is, and not as the lawyer finds it natural, or convenient, or attractive to imagine the client to be. This is no easy matter, particularly for lawyers who are overburdened by caseload and look to routinized systems of legal triage for relief. Even lawyers who want to provide individualized service are in danger of misreading their clients, for the ways that clients describe themselves are inevitably influenced by the questions they are asked, and the desire clients articulate are affected by the sense of the possible that lawyers provide. These effects, moreover, are not merely a matter of self-presentation, because clients, like the rest of us, change in response to what they experience, so that what the lawyer says to the client may affect who a client *is*.

Whatever the intricacies of defining the individual client, matters are vastly more complex when the lawyer is dealing with more than one individual. Consider the following situation:

> Eight tenants from a particular apartment building meet with a lawyer at the local legal services office. The tenants explain that they, and the forty other families in the building, have struggled for years to make their landlord provide them with a minimally safe and habitable building. Many of them have, as individuals, protested to the landlord; some have temporarily withheld their rent; and some have moved out when they could. Now, however, these eight men and women have decided that conditions in their building are intolerable, and that they want to take action together to seek redress. In the course of the meeting, it becomes clear to the lawyer that although most of these eight people are quite determined to continue living in the building, two or three might be tempted to take a cash settlement that would enable them to find better housing elsewhere—

even though their doing so might jeopardize the chance of the other tenants' obtaining needed repairs. The lawyer agrees to help them formulate and carry out a plan of attack that will put the maximum legal pressure on the landlord to accede to the tenants' demands.

This lawyer might characterize her relationship to the tenants in any of four quite different ways. These different characterizations, as we shall see, span a continuum from an insistence on the status of each individual as a client to a vision of these individuals, and their many other co-tenants, as a class. The consequences of these characterizations, not surprisingly, can powerfully affect the work the lawyer does for the tenants, and the relations the tenants will have with each other. Where individual representation is the model, the lawyer must assiduously work for each individual client, but may well have to withdraw altogether if the clients develop conflicts of interest. In group representation, on the other hand, the lawyer's fidelity to each individual is considerably curtailed, but her ability to help the individuals to achieve their collective ends is enhanced. These points will become more clear as we examine each of the four possible characterizations.

1. Individual Representation, Multiplied

First, a lawyer might see herself as representing eight separate individuals. This, of course, would be ethically unproblematic if the eight had identical interests, but they do not. Instead, after the first meeting it is already apparent that the tenants may eventually have quite different preferences as to the remedies they seek, and that these different preferences might result in sharp disagreements within the group. Under the Model Rules, however, "a possible conflict" does not necessarily bar the lawyer from representing all eight.[23] If the lawyer reasonably believes, in light of her experience with such cases, that the tenants will ultimately agree on the issue of relief, or that each will be able to get his or her preferred relief without undercutting the others' positions vis-a-vis the landlord—and if the clients consent to her representing them all despite the possibility of future conflict—then she is free to do so. Each tenant will then be her client, and she will owe a duty of loyalty and confidentiality to each one as an individual. If a true conflict of interest does emerge, then she may well have to withdraw from the representation of all eight, whatever the difficulties they may face in finding alternative counsel.

2. Intermediation

Not every disagreement ripens into a conflict of interest, however, and if disagreement among the tenants on the issue of relief does develop, the lawyer can continue to represent all eight if she can characterize her relationship to the tenants in a second way—as a mediator or, in the language of the Model Rules, an "intermediary."[27] Under this rubric, the lawyer is free to help the clients to reach a compromise

---

23   Model Rules [of Professional Conduct], Rule 1.7 cmt. [(1983) (as amended through February, 1990)].

27   Model Rules, supra note [23], Rule 2.2. * * *

that is in their collective best interest, rather than vigorously defending each individual's preexisting preferences. However, the lawyer can play the role of intermediary only in rather narrow circumstances. Each client must consent, after consultation, to the lawyer's playing of this part—and if any of the clients revoke their consent she must withdraw. In addition, she herself must

> reasonably believe[] that the matter can be resolved on terms compatible with the clients' best interests, that each client will be able to make adequately informed decisions in the matter and that there is little risk of material prejudice to the interests of any of the clients if the contemplated resolution is unsuccessful . . . .[29]

These conditions are not easily met. The lawyer is obliged to protect each client's confidentiality *and* to keep each client adequately informed, and these duties can be directly at odds: the more any client insists on confidentiality, the harder it will be for the lawyer to keep her other clients adequately informed. And because a failure of the mediation will likely preclude her from representing any of the clients and probably subject all of what any one of them has said to her to discovery by the others, she can hardly believe that there is little risk of material prejudice unless she can say that the matter not only *can* but *probably will* be resolved on terms compatible with the clients' best interests.

3.   *Organizational Representation*

Given the vigilance on behalf of individual clients reflected in these first two formulations of the lawyer's role, it is startling—even stunning—to encounter the radically different regime envisaged by Model Rule 1.13. The first subsection of this rule declares that "[a] lawyer employed or retained by an organization represents the organization acting through its duly authorized constituents."[36] This simple sentence adopts the "entity theory" of organizational representation, under which the lawyer for the organization does *not* represent its shareholders, or officers, or employees, but instead represents an artificial entity, the organization. No doubt the most frequent application of this proposition is in the field of corporate representation, but it may apply in a variety of other contexts, including our housing lawyer's relationship to this group of tenants.

Its bearing on this situation stems from the fact that Rule 1.13 applies to unincorporated associations as well as to organizations having corporate form. Neither the Rule itself nor the accompanying Comment defines "organization," but two influential commentators have urged a very expansive treatment of the term in this context. Geoffrey C. Hazard, Jr. and W. William Hodes suggest that the rule would also apply to seventeen homeowners who "form a group that hires lawyer L to prosecute a nuisance action" and agree that they will all abide by any settlement that twelve of

---

29   Id. Rule 2.2(a)(2).

36   Model Rules, supra note [23], Rule 1.13(a). * * *

their number approve.[39] These facts, Hazard and Hodes indicate, give this set of people "an identity apart from the individuals who comprise it,"[40] and thus transform them into an organization.

On this logic, the eight tenants, too, can readily be seen as such an organization. It is true that these tenants have not, so far as the stated facts reveal, agreed among themselves on any such decisionmaking process. Perhaps they need not do so; perhaps they become an organization if they simply think of themselves as a group. But if they do need to adopt some structure, then their lawyer can help them do so. After all, lawyers help clients establish organizations all the time. The lawyer could suggest that the tenants agree on a procedure for resolving disagreements among themselves, and if, after proper counseling about the potential consequences, they did reach an appropriate agreement, the lawyer could represent them as an organization rather than as eight separate clients.

The consequences of this recharacterization are striking. Because the lawyer now represents the entity, she no longer owes unqualified loyalty or confidentiality to any of the eight tenants as individuals. Hence if one tenant provides her with information, she need not convey this information to each of the others unless doing so is required by her duty of loyalty to the organization. Conversely, if providing the information to the group is necessary in order to keep it adequately informed, the lawyer has no duty to protect the individual tenant's secrets. So, too, if the eight constituents of the organization develop disagreements, her obligation is *not* to remain neutral as between them. Rather, her obligation is to provide the best counsel she can to the organization (though adopting a neutral stance might still be appropriate, if neutrality best served the organization).

Even if the tenants' disagreements ripen into actual conflicts of interest, their lawyer will not automatically have to withdraw, for she does not represent the tenants as individuals. Her client is the group itself, and the fact that some constituents of the group now dissent from its collective decision does not automatically bar her from continuing to do the bidding of the group as an entity. So, for example, if the tenants have agreed to abide by any settlement that two-thirds of them approve, the lawyer can settle the case on behalf of the group despite the wishes of the minority. The shift from the norms of individual representation is particularly vivid here, for if the eight tenants constituted eight individual clients, each of them might have an *unwaivable* right to approve or reject any settlement. In short, the modest steps by which a set of people can transform themselves into a group sharply alter the role the lawyer can play, and in ways that facilitate group action at the expense of individual prerogatives.

4. Class Representation

The fourth characterization of the lawyer's relationship to this set of eight people is scarcely mentioned in either the Model Code or the Model Rules. This char-

---

39   Hazard & Hodes, [The Law of Lawyering: A Handbook on The Model Rules of Professional Conduct] § 1.13:203 [2d ed. 1990]. * * *

40   Id. §1.13:103. * * *

acterization treats the eight individuals as the named representatives of a class of all the tenants in the building (a group of perhaps 150 people or more). The lawyer cannot turn the tenants into class representatives without their consent, but once this consent has been granted the lawyer acquires a freedom from the wishes of the individual clients that in some ways exceeds even that conferred by Model Rule 1.13.

Indeed, whereas Rule 1.13 facilitates a group's collective *action*, the class action device is primarily concerned only with the group's collective *representation*. The result of class action status may well be to empower groups of people by facilitating their access to court, but the people so empowered are not empowered as against their lawyer. Certainly this is true as to the named class representatives, for according to the standard interpretation of Rule 23 of the Federal Rules of Civil Procedure, the lawyer owes her most fundamental duty of loyalty not to them but to the class itself. With judicial approval, she may settle the case despite the objections of a majority of the named representatives. Moreover, the existence of disagreements within the class by no means automatically precludes class certification, although if these disagreements are profound enough they may lead to the designation of subclasses with separate representation. Finally, even—or especially—the class as a whole lacks the power to direct the lawyer's actions, because the class typically has no decisionmaking structure through which it can act. As a result, the lawyer's responsibility for gauging what is in the class's best interests is profound, and a court may approve a settlement endorsed by the class lawyer even if most class members—and, it would seem, most named class representatives—object.

B. The Lawyer's Role in Selecting a Framework

It may be surprising to learn how far existing ethical and legal principles permit lawyers to depart from the stringent safeguards of individual client autonomy that play so important a part in the profession's norms. But because this discretion does exist, lawyers must decide how to use it. It might be objected that this potential departure from the protection of individual autonomy is unproblematic, because it is the clients themselves who decide whether to be characterized as individuals, an organization, or representatives of a class. In that sense, organizational or class representation can be seen as resting on a valid waiver of some amount of individual autonomy. But as a practical and a legal matter, this choice of characterization does not rest exclusively with the clients. One source of the lawyer's influence on this decision is that it is plainly her responsibility to counsel these individuals on their choice. Perhaps the eight tenants who arrived in the lawyer's office did not conceive of themselves as an "organization" or as the representatives of a class; it is up to the lawyer to explain the significance of these characterizations and to counsel these individuals on what characterization they and the lawyer should adopt. In addition, the lawyer may well have the authority to condition her representation of the clients on their agreement to one status or another. Although clients may object to these conditions, clients who have few options for obtaining counsel are not in a good position to insist on their objections, because the lawyer is likely to have the authority to decline to represent them if she considers the form of representation they seek to be repugnant or imprudent. Having rejected these clients, she may then solicit others, through advertising, personal letters, or even if the lawyer is a public interest lawyer—through in-person contacts.

Indeed, the lawyer's discretion to enter into individual or group representation would have come into play even if only a single tenant had originally consulted her. Had she learned that her first client was one of many facing similar problems, she might have concluded that collective efforts were needed. At that point, she might have assisted this tenant to begin organizing a tenants' group. Alternatively, she might have developed a court case naming this individual as a representative of a class, or she might even have declined to represent this tenant, if the tenant was uninterested in collective action, and launched her own effort to find a group to represent.

Because lawyers can wield so profound an influence on the characterization of their clients, they must be sensitive to the values at stake in its exercise. The rules of ethics suggest that the bond between an individual client and his lawyer, a bond in which the client's secrets are jealously guarded and his interests zealously advocated, is an essential protection of individual autonomy. Principles of client-centered practice suggest that even within this attorney-client dyad, the client's autonomy is still in danger from lawyers who wittingly or unwittingly override the client's own wishes in favor of outcomes that the lawyers prefer. Group representation cannot protect individual autonomy in the same ways, or perhaps to the same extent, as individual representation does. * * * [H]owever, group representation is by no means always opposed to individual autonomy; instead, group representation is essential to protect those aspects of autonomy that people express through their membership in groups—as well as those values beyond autonomy's purview that republicans, feminists and others suggest collective engagement may serve. * * *

* * *

C. Planning the Investigation of Facts

The framing of the story of the case and the choice of a case theory provide a roadmap for the search for evidence. In the next excerpt David A. Binder and Paul Bergman describe a strategy for investigating facts.

David A. Binder and Paul Bergman, FACT INVESTIGATION, FROM HYPOTHESIS TO PROOF (1984)*

* * *

2. OVERALL PLANNING STRATEGIES

a. General Decision-Making Strategy

The complexity of investigatory planning is similar to the complexities faced by planners in other fields. All planners try to identify and select options in the face of an uncertain future. Hence, awareness of general decision-making strategy, which probably applies whether one is investigating a legal dispute or deciding where to dine, may be useful.

Organized decision-making is typically thought of as a four step process, in which one asks and attempts to answer the following questions:

(a) What are my objectives?
(b) What are the alternatives?
(c) What are the pros and cons of each alternative?
(d) On balance, which alternative seems best?

The answers generally do not point toward a single, radiant truth. However, the questions produce an approach that allows one to make considered choices.

As for objectives, one may have a number of goals in mind. For instance, one may seek to uncover "all the documents," learn all evidence pertaining to a certain theory of relief, or learn sufficient evidence to support a motion for summary judgment. Moreover, one may have tactical, non-informational objectives in mind. For example, with an eye to negotiation, one may want to learn an adversary's underlying needs and interests, or to demonstrate that one is prepared to expend considerable resources on a case.

After identifying one or more objectives, one then considers alternative ways of accomplishing them. There exist a host of formal and informal avenues for pursuing potential evidence. At the very least, one must be aware of available alternatives. For example, unless one is aware that in civil cases depositions can be taken upon written interrogatories, or that in criminal cases motions to suppress may be used as discovery vehicles, one's awareness of discovery alternatives is incomplete. Research, both in a law library and in the offices of more experienced litigators, may be necessary to ensure that no reasonable alternative is overlooked.

---

*   Reprinted from FACT INVESTIGATION, FROM HYPOTHESIS TO PROOF, David A. Binder and Paul Bergman, 1984, with permission of the West Publishing Corporation.

Next, one evaluates the alternatives. From both a legal and a practical standpoint, what are the likely advantages and disadvantages of each? For example, for reasons that will be discussed in Chapter 17, interrogatories are useful for learning the identities of witnesses and the existence and location of documents. But they are not well suited to the task of learning the events and details in a party's story. Moreover, sending out interrogatories may alert an adversary to one's theories and areas of factual concern. If nothing else, that knowledge may enable opposing counsel to do a more thorough job of preparing witnesses for later depositions and trial.

Depositions are not without their drawbacks. Though one may compel testimony, opposing counsel has a right to be present, to listen to the evidence, and to ask questions. Moreover, depositions are not an effective way of learning an adversary's legal theories. During depositions, even a party may not be asked for the legal theories on which he or she relies.

Moreover, the timing of discovery is also important. If one conducts discovery of one's adversary before the adversary has had a sufficient opportunity to conduct its own investigation, one may learn little. On the other hand, one needs to find out about an adversary's legal theories and factual contentions, lest one waste time on irrelevancies.

Apart from such standard advantages and disadvantages, considerations of alternatives in a particular case usually involve examining a plethora of assumptions about the future. For example, as a general rule one advantage of interrogatories is that they are cheaper and less time consuming than depositions. But how well does one know the adversaries, both lawyer and client? Are they likely to respond in thirty days or to seek an extension? Will a series of follow-up telephone calls and letters be necessary? How about motions to compel answers and impose sanctions? Only by forcing oneself to examine predicted behavior in specific contexts can one fully evaluate likely consequences.

Usually, one lacks the data to make exact predictions. If a decision appears vitally important, one may seek additional predictive data. Otherwise, one makes do with judgments based on experience with the typical consequences of various alternatives, together with the limited specific data available. In many instances, that judgment will be aided by actually writing down the alternatives and their perceived pros and cons. The process of writing down and then staring at choices often leads to more considered judgments.

Finally, perhaps together with a client, one makes a decision. That decision may vary from a clear choice to adopt one alternative to a realization of the need to identify and consider additional alternatives. In the mushy world of investigatory planning, one usually has the comfort of knowing that often there is no single "right" alternative. A variety of tacks may produce good results. Use of the general decision-making approach often enables one to find at least one of those tacks.

b.   Preliminary Investigatory Considerations

The task of considering alternative methods of accomplishing objectives is aided by one's undertaking a few preliminary investigatory considerations. These considerations typically give one a sense of the "lay of the land," and thus may facilitate one's choice of an effective alternative to accomplish a particular objective. This section describes some of these more specific considerations. While we discuss the considerations separately for purposes of clarity, in practice they may well be combined.

(i) Connect Potential Evidence with Witnesses and/or Documents

Presumably one has already identified potential affirmative and rebuttal evidence which appears to be favorable to one's client. Before embarking on investigation, one considers sources through which one can convert potential evidence into evidence on hand. Who is likely to have the information? Or, stepping back, who might be able to identify someone else who might have the information? Is the information likely to be included in a document? If so, who might have prepared the document, and in whose possession might it be?

Connecting evidence to witnesses may serve a number of valuable functions. It may indicate that at least for certain potential evidence, one has more than one possible source. Or, if one source keeps popping up, that may help one decide where to begin questioning. And, if one must embark on investigation without possible sources for certain evidence, one is reminded to update the listing as new information is unearthed and additional sources uncovered.

(ii) Consider Whether Potential Witnesses Are Likely to be "Friendly" or "Adverse"

Witnesses are rarely totally helpful or totally harmful. Nevertheless, for one reason or another witnesses are often aligned with one of the parties. Perhaps a witness is employed by one of the parties or is a close friend. Or, perhaps a witness has a socio-political or emotional bias which favors one of the parties.

A number of consequences typically flow from a witness' alignment with a party. If one represents the party adverse to the witness, the witness may not agree to an informal interview. Even if an informal interview is arranged, the witness may be less willing to disclose information than he or she would be under oath, at a deposition. If one imparts information, a "friendly" witness may consider it to fairly reassess an initial story, whereas an "adverse" witness may only report the information to one's adversary (though one may in fact want this to happen). A "friendly" witness may be more flexible in changing the time of an interview, agreeing to a follow-up interview, or accompanying one to scenes of events. Hence, one should generally make at least a preliminary assessment of a witness' possible alignment.

* * *

4.   AM I READY TO TALK TO THE WITNESS?

a.   How Important Is It To Talk To The Witness?

Frequently, certain aspects of cases are more important, or at least more urgent, than other aspects. Therefore, though a given witness might provide information which satisfies one objective, one might compare that objective to others. The comparison may lead to the conclusion that even though one is in other respects "ready" to speak with a witness, one should first pursue more important urgent objectives.

For example, of two legal theories, does one lead to speedier, perhaps injunctive relief? Does one offer the opportunity for greater damages? Are some theories already amply supported by evidence, while as to other theories the factual cupboard is bare? Such questions lead to an assessment of a witness' importance and may suggest that one pursue a goal involving different witnesses.

b.   Do I Need More Familiarity With Scenes of Events and Tangible Evidence?

One is routinely advised to be as familiar as possible with physical locations where important events took place and with important pieces of real evidence. However, the ease with which this advice is given should not obscure its purpose. For, in the long run, it is usually a witness' knowledge, not an attorney's, which is critical. One does not view a scene or physical evidence simply to enhance one's own knowledge. Rather, one often does so in order to question witnesses more effectively. For example, a witness may describe something as having happened "sort of off to the right of where I was standing." If one is unfamiliar with the scene, it may be difficult to probe for more exacting detail. But if one has been to the scene personally, one may force the witness to be precise: "You say it was off to the right. Where was it with respect to the bus bench with the tasteful advertisement for Louis the Lawyer?"

If it seems important to see a scene or an item of tangible evidence before talking to a witness, one then decides how to go about doing so. A public location usually presents no difficulty. A "Motion to Produce Mount Diablo" is rarely in order.

But if a physical location or an item of real evidence is under the control of an adversary or a non-party, some awareness of potential alternatives is required. Do not overlook informal discovery. Perhaps whoever has the evidence will share it. A deal is often possible: "I'll let you see mine if you let me see yours." If this does not work, then resort to more expensive formal discovery may be needed. For example, if real evidence is in the adversary's control, a "Request to Produce" is usually in order. If a non-party has it, a "Subpoena duces tecum re Deposition" or its equivalent is typically used. When a physical location is involved, a "Request to Permit Entry Upon Land" can be considered.

c.   Do I Need To Gather Any Documents First?

Ever more frequently, the road to litigation is littered with letters, reports, memoranda, written messages, and other indicia of a highly bureaucratized society. Many disputes concern events that happened over a period of months or even years, and without access to relevant documents a witness may not be able to recall all that occurred. Imagine a witness on the receiving end of this question: "They say that your company's use of various sales forms is an unfair business practice. How did you go about developing those forms?" Most likely that development involved a series of meetings with accompanying memoranda and proposed forms. The witness probably could not meaningfully respond to such a question in the absence of a personal calendar indicating his or her presence at those meetings, the memoranda or reports detailing the development of the forms and the various forms themselves and their predecessors. Hence, one often needs to gather pertinent documents which a witness can review before or during the interview.

Again, if certain documents are under the control of someone other than one's client, one needs to consider formal or informal methods of gaining access to them.

If one knows the documents one seeks, and if they are in the hands of the adversary, the appropriate formal discovery device is typically a "Request to Produce." If a known document is in the hands of a non-party, one may need to serve a "Subpoena Duces Tecum re Deposition." Lastly, if one suspects that documents exist but does not know their whereabouts, one may have to take depositions or send out interrogatories before talking to a witness.

d. Are There Other Witnesses I Should Talk to First?

Aficionados of the "renvoi" doctrine of choice-of-law particularly enjoy this consideration, as the seamless web truly turns in upon itself. One may desire to speak with a witness—say, an expert who may suggest areas of inquiry with other witnesses. But before one speaks to that witness, one may first have to view a physical location or obtain documents from other witnesses. But to do that one may have to talk to other witnesses, take depositions or send out interrogatories. But first . . . .

If any "master plan" adherents still exist, these possibilities may convince them of the futility of planning beyond a few tasks. Like a drawing by M.C. Escher, everything seems to be preliminary to everything else. Escher had the luxury of stopping at the portrayal of the dilemma—it was enough for him to "spot the issue." Lawyers have to resolve dilemmas by making choices that are less than perfect. All one can do is carefully consider which witness to talk to next, and go from there. Alternatively, become an artist.

* * *

The results of fact investigation contribute to development of the story of the case. The next excerpt uses a memorandum to the law firm's investigator in a hypothetical case to explore the interplay of facts, storylines and potential audiences in the development of a case.

Gerald P. López, *Reconceiving Civil Rights Practice: Seven Weeks in the Life of a Rebellious Collaboration*, 77 GEO. L.J. 1603 (1989)*

* * *

THE INITIAL LAWYER-CLIENT MEETING

An initial meeting held in the lawyer's office often signals the beginning of the relationship between a client and a lawyer. As a favor to one of its better small business clients, Martha's firm has agreed to talk with Jesse Cruz. All the firm knows about Cruz is that he lives and works in 'Zalaipa,' California—a small city near Riverside, about one hour southeast of Los Angeles and within the jurisdiction of the federal court in Los Angeles—and that he claims to have been discriminated against because he is Chicano. * * *

* * *

---

*   Reprinted with permission.

The Early Brainstorming Stage

From the time of the initial interview of Jesse Cruz forward, Martha Fisher finds herself in what may be described as "The Early Brainstorming Stage." She doesn't know whether or not she can be of any help to Jesse and, nonetheless, on the basis of the available information, must critically assess his situation as she now understands it. Two aspects of this brainstorming stage now concern her. First, what is a court likely to do if forced to respond to this situation translated and transformed into a § 1983 lawsuit? Second, what audiences other than a court are available potentially to respond to Jesse's needs and concerns?

These two questions are intimately related and interact as a lawyer like Martha thinks about Jesse's or any client's situation. While both lawyer and client will typically want to and should try to solve the client's problem without resort to litigation, problems and their possible solutions are typically analyzed, negotiated, and bargained over and otherwise handled in the shadow of a single question: "What is a court likely to do if this situation is litigated?" The answer to that question depends, of course, on the stories and arguments one can anticipate from each side and the likely response of a court in light of its way of establishing meaning in the midst of a dispute. However much a court's interpretation of the situation shadows all that is done in shaping the relationships in question, a lawyer must take seriously the need to identify other audiences with the potential to satisfy more or less a client's needs or desires. This aspect of lawyering is underappreciated and is too often pursued uncritically and haphazardly. Failing to appreciate that a court is not the only audience with a defined remedial culture (constituted in large part by an "approved" repertoire of stories and arguments and storytelling and argument-making practices), lawyers often blow a chance to help a client by overlooking or crudely responding to the practices of an available audience.

Martha's next move, a familiar one for her, will be to draft a Fact Investigation Memo. In her effort to learn all that she can about Jesse and Sylvia's situation in Zalaipa, she will brainstorm about local audiences, other than a court, potentially relevant in trying to help Jesse and Sylvia change their situation. What stories and storytelling practices govern the remedial ceremonies of each such audience? The Mayor or the Chief of Police? Or the state ABC or the City Council? Or the white business community? Or potentially sympathetic Zalaipa citizenry? She will try to be imaginative in identifying audiences and be specific in hypothesizing about the nature of the respective remedial ceremonies (again, the stories and the storytelling practices). At the same time that she brainstorms about local audiences as potential sources of relief, Martha will brainstorm about Jesse and Sylvia's possible § 1983 storylines, about the information she needs to confirm and to fill in gaps and details. Though her knowledge of § 1983 law may be modest by expert standards, she feels the need to begin exploring its promise as well as its limits.

This brainstorming demands that Martha speculate about Zalaipa, its people, and its constitutive practices. Imagining what Zalaipa is like is a way of prompting curiosity about local knowledge. She must think hard about precisely what she would like to learn about each of the audiences she thinks relevant to Jesse's situation, about whether the information is likely to be anecdotal or empirical, and about how she might gather this information either through others or on her own.

A lawyer and her client inevitably shape, indeed help make over time, the very situation in which they find themselves acting and as to which they seek some response. Martha has to consider how fact investigation itself shapes a client's situation. Suggesting that certain information be gathered in Jesse and Sylvia's circumstance might raise concerns, requiring Martha to think about what precautions she can and should take.

Martha will address her memo to Samantha Rivers. Samantha is a savvy investigator who lives in the Redlands area and who occasionally works for Martha's firm on personal injury, criminal, and domestic cases. Samantha acquired her research and investigative skills working with community organizations in Southern California. She's been involved with a number of low-income organizations and issues over the past eight years.

Most recently, Samantha worked with community leaders in Compton, a predominantly black and Latino city in metropolitan Los Angeles, to prevent displacement of low-income blacks by developers wishing to upgrade housing for higher income groups. Samantha provided technical assistance: she researched the relevant land use regulations, found out what anti-displacement legal measures other communities had tried and how successful they'd been, and investigated nonlegal alternatives. Using Samantha's information, the community leaders decided to confront the county planning commission with the situation directly. One hundred Compton residents, accompanied by members of the local and L.A. press, went to the planning commission office and demanded that action be taken to permit them to continue living in their homes. While the strategy certainly slowed the gentrification process, its long term impact remains to be seen.

Samantha likes knowing why she's being asked to nose around about things; knowing what the lawyer is thinking in serving a client helps her, she claims, to do a better job. The purpose of the memo is to help both Martha and Samantha try to figure out what's going on and what, if anything, they might help Jesse and Sylvia do in response. The fact that Samantha may not be able to gather certain information will not dissuade Martha from asking for it—Martha will try to be as thorough as possible. She knows that her work at this early stage of the case will help immeasurably in understanding the options available in trying to help a client like Jesse.

FACT INVESTIGATION MEMO

TO: Samantha Rivers
FROM: Martha Fisher
RE: Fact Investigation—Jesse Cruz
DATE: July 13, 1988

I. REVIEW OF FACTS AND PURPOSES

A. FACTS

Clients Jesse Cruz and his wife Sylvia live in Zalaipa and for years have wanted to run their own Mexican restaurant. In April 1986, they bought out a restaurant from the daughter of the deceased owner, Jack Nat, on the assurance that a beer and wine license would be easy to acquire from the Dept. of Alcoholic Beverage Control (ABC). At a hearing, however, Mr. Cruz was denied his license on the grounds that too many licenses had already been granted and that the Mexican community had been causing problems in Zalaipa. The Chief of Police, City Attorney, police officers, and community members all testified to this effect at the hearing. Nearly a year later, the Cruzes were granted their license by the appeals board after it found insufficient evidence to justify the denial.

Once the license was granted, however, clients began to have trouble with police harassment. Police regularly wait down the block from the restaurant, checking customers for drunkenness, drugs, and undocumented alien status as they depart. In addition, cars parked by restaurant patrons are towed almost as soon as the meters expire.

The Cruzes believe their restaurant has been singled out for such treatment, noting that other restaurants in the area seem to have acquired licenses with no trouble and do not have their customers harassed. One exception is Maggie O'Connor, who runs a nearby pool hall and caters to the same black and Chicano clientele as clients' restaurant. O'Connor has encountered similar difficulties.

B. PURPOSES

The Cruzes suspect there is a conspiracy in Zalaipa, which comprises at the least top city officials, to discriminate against minorities, especially Chicanos, in both affirmative freedoms, such as running their own businesses, and negative freedoms—being left alone, for example. Clients think this unequal treatment is getting worse as minorities become more established in downtown Zalaipa.

I want to find out as much as possible about how much Jesse's suspicion (I have spoken only to him as yet) is warranted. If there is a citywide conspiracy at work, I don't expect it will be easy to uncover. I am interested, nonetheless, in any significant evidence—empirical or anecdotal—you can assemble that would seem to corroborate ill will, a simple misunderstanding, or anything in between. By no means do I doubt Jesse's perceptions, but I want to assume as little wrongdoing as possible at the start to avoid injecting hostility into a situation which at the moment may only be suffering from overzealous licensing and police work.

Specifically, we must avoid jeopardizing one of the Cruzes' employees, who is undocumented. I would also prefer to avoid ruffling any feathers until we are certain something is amiss. The dynamic of power in a small town like Zalaipa is such that needlessly antagonizing people, especially in the power structure, can only breed even more trouble for clients in the future.

For these reasons, as well as my usual preference for solving matters through accommodation and understanding, litigation is not my first choice of strategies. Depending how deep the corruption, if any, runs, this matter could be settled with a few simple phone calls. Moreover, although the lack of a license inconvenienced clients for nearly a year and may well have led to a loss of profits, Jesse stressed that he considers the harassment the larger problem and primarily wants the police to leave him and his customers alone. If the problem turns out to be a simple one, my sense is that Jesse, not a very contentious person, would prefer a straightforward and informal resolution to the expense and routinization of a lawsuit.

On the other hand, if indeed Zalaipa is under the thumb of a conspiracy or even if only a few top officials are involved in discrimination, I am entirely willing to prepare and pursue litigation or, for that matter, any other mobilized action that seems to be a good idea. I expect that a section 1983 action (for deprivation of constitutional and perhaps statutory federal rights) is our most likely avenue from what I know now. Even if we never tried such a suit, we must be prepared to gather the relevant evidence and present to those implicated a credible threat of legal action if we are to seem a worthy adversary. We needn't threaten them; neither, however, need we shrink from exercising fully our legal options.

Hence, I would ask that you perform a dual function in your fact investigation. First, gather as much information as you can to illuminate Jesse's story. In doing so, pay special attention to what you are able to discover easily and what people seem less than interested in revealing. A good deal of what I ask here should be a matter of public record. Encountering more than the usual red tape should be a sign to you either that Zalaipa is overly bureaucratized or that someone may not want you to get the information. Second, once you've established a core of data and we have consulted again (but even in your initial investigation), I'll want you to be presenting our case in the form of a "story" that the audience will appreciate and, for lack of a better term, relate to. What I mean by that will be spelled out in the body of this memo; just realize that even as a mere information-gatherer, you will have inserted yourself into the tight Zalaipa community and become a player in whatever drama is being acted out. We might as well present ourselves with maximum flexibility and a minimum of confrontation at first.

This memo is organized to walk you through the general strategy I've developed. Since we know very little at this point, I want to keep the flow of information as wide as possible, while keeping a vigilant lookout for chances to resolve the Cruzes' circumstances. I should note here that even if Jesse's rather grand suspicions are not borne out, that by no means tells me that he and Sylvia do not have a problem. So long as they even perceive unfairness in the community, there is a problem, and one I want to do something about.

The next section outlines the general groupings of questions I would like answered. Section III briefly details the groups of audiences with whom we will have to deal sooner or later and discusses how relevant information can best be gotten from those audiences without either compromising Jesse and Sylvia's wishes or (unduly) misleading those with whom we interact. The final section sets out what we would need to establish to have a chance at bringing a successful section 1983 lawsuit. As our ultimate approach to the problem will depend largely on what you discover, please perform the impossible, and keep in mind that we may eventually want to do anything from offering the Police Chief a friendly meal at the Cruzes' restaurant to cross-examining every official in the city in a federal court.

II. GENERAL FACT FAMILIES

Facts I want range from the detailed and specific to the broad and unquantifiable. As discussed above, facts will play at least two roles: setting a foundation for filling out your investigation and breathing life into the stories and arguments we'll present. How facts are presented to you means as much to me as what, on their face, they tell us.

First, let's find out about towing practices. Get as much as you can: who tows, when, on whose orders, in what neighborhoods, who sets the policy, and so on. Evidence that every car in Zalaipa is towed the minute its meter runs out will take a lot out of the Cruzes' harassment fears.

I also want to know what I can about Jesse and Sylvia. I don't want to be digging around behind their backs—in fact, I may elicit most of this information myself from talking to them—but I think it's important to know to whom Jesse has complained about this, whether they've owned a business before, and any other connections they may have to the people whom they perceive as mistreating them.

As important as anything is learning about Zalaipa. While the business climate is certainly relevant, getting a handle on the general tenor of race relations and social attitudes is equally useful. I suspect (as I'm sure you've gathered) that whatever the factual basis of the Cruzes' concerns, perceptions play heavily in this situation. And perceptions rest on attitudes and surroundings more than on towing practices or the election procedures of the City Council. If Zalaipa is just an old, formerly all-white California town then the worst sin of the citizenry may be mere outdated social attitudes. At any rate, anything we do will be based on guesswork alone until we get a better idea of what makes Zalaipa tick.

Fourth, minority relations: the police will ably combine the less statistical "attitude" evidence I just asked for with hard numbers about what percentage of the population is minorities and how relations are perceived both by minority groups and the police. Like information about towing practices, finding no evidence of wrongdoing at this stage will require us to shift focus dramatically so don't assume answers to the questions you'll be asking.

Minority relations with the community in general will give you related information, but focused less on their interactions with the power structure and more on what happens to Zalaipa minorities on the whole. Empirical evidence will be worthwhile to establish, say, the usual procedure for liquor licenses and minority businesses. Anecdotal evidence, especially from the community, may bear out or belie the Cruzes' situation.

Finally, Maggie O'Connor and her story are vital. In fact, if I were you I'd start with her, paying particular attention to similarities with Jesse's story. And be sure to ask if she's done anything about it and, if so, what success she's had.

III. AUDIENCES AND STORYLINES

"Audiences" in this context is a term of broad usage. It will include anyone who has (or may have) had an effect on the Cruzes in the past, who could be of help in the future, and third parties who can offer information useful for learning more about

Zalaipa and the general treatment of minorities. That should remain your primary focus at the start and a corollary purpose throughout your investigation: learning everything possible about Zalaipa. Realities and hard facts are, of course, of interest and will be of compelling interest if we have to resort to litigation. But perceptions are often more important even than what is objectively "real"; don't slight what people think just because there's no "confirmation" of it. And no less important than the perceptions of the minority community is what the power brokers and disinterested third parties think, for actions are motivated more by perception than anything else.

Each audience will have something different to offer you, yet many will offer the same sort of information. I have therefore taken the somewhat artificial but more easily understood step of grouping the relevant audiences into three broad categories. It scarcely needs repeating that as with any categorization, this method is merely an aid to better grasping the approach desired. Many, if not all, of the audiences will fit into more than one of the groups. Please bear in mind, then, that flexibility is the bedrock of the story/argument approach. The groupings are organized primarily around the relationship of each of their constituencies to the Cruzes and their situation.

A. THE POWER BROKERS

This group comprises those unseen forces that clients suspect may be in league and that are the furthest removed from the public eye. They determine the fate not only of the Cruzes' restaurant but also how minorities are treated overall, especially in their interactions with authority.

The Audiences

The Mayor. If Zalaipa resembles the small towns I know, the Mayor is the law. That doesn't necessarily mean the law is an ass in Zalaipa or even that the Mayor doesn't consider all points of view. It may well mean, however, that along with the City Council, the police, and the City Attorney, the Mayor is the driving force (or, alternately, the unwilling hostage) of the system of justice and the popular reception of changing social norms. I don't mean to prejudice your fact finding. But whether for good or ill, it's important to find out the role of the Mayor.

The Chief of Police. The Chief testified against granting the Cruzes a license at the initial hearing. Given clients' perception of police misconduct, the Chief is among the most important players. Knowledge or encouragement of discrimination would, of course, lead to serious consequences for the Chief. On the other hand, if what the Cruzes are suffering is mere overzealous police work by a young cop, the Chief may well be grateful to know about it and eager to correct misunderstandings. He is in perhaps the most powerful position either to help or hinder our efforts.

The Police. Especially the cop sitting outside the Cruzes' restaurant. He is likely personally responsible not only for any harassment of patrons but also for the rigid rules for towing customers' cars. If he's just following orders, he'll be useful for finding out who has been giving such orders. If he's acting on his own volition, it may or may not be indicative of a more widespread practice in the department. And don't lose sight of the possibility that all restaurants and cars are treated like this in the town.

The City Council. On largely the same rationale as the Mayor, the Council weighs heavily in our balance for holding most of Zalaipa's power and, probably, setting much of its public policy. Whether its actions are malicious, omissions, or merely misunderstood, the Council will be vital either for winning relief or for negotiating change.

ABC. Although Jesse considers the delay of the license the lesser of the offenses against him, it may be a good deal easier to prove unequal treatment there than isolated discrimination on the street. Depending on whether the ABC functions more as a state or a local agency, it may have important and telling ties to the rest of the power elite in Zalaipa. I consider this a less promising lead than other sources, but as it was the beginning of the Cruzes' troubles, it's important.

The City Attorney. Also testified at the initial hearing. Clearly, as the official in charge of law enforcement in Zalaipa, s/he has a good deal to say about the policy of the police and, perhaps, the liquor board. Finding out how close the City Attorney is to the Mayor and the City Council will be especially instructive in determining whether policy in Zalaipa is a unitary guideline or a more open and pluralistic process.

The Towing Company. It hardly seems among the powers that be, but for the Cruzes, its power is among the most important of all those listed here. Whether it takes it upon itself to tow so quickly or is merely following a set program will be an instructive place to start your inquiry.

The Storylines

To begin with yet another broad generalization, I'd like at the outset to talk with the power brokers on the assumption that one of four storylines is developing. Hence your investigation should uncover information that will be of use in exploring any of these stories, while avoiding locking us into one approach. Specifically, I suspect one of the following is an accurate portrayal of what's happening, at least at a general level:

There is no intentional discrimination in Zalaipa. What the ruling white elite thinks is fair often (usually) diverges wildly from what those under their control believe is fair, but that doesn't make those in charge racists (except in the sense that we all are). Frankly, if we can resolve this whole situation simply by establishing better understanding, that would make me—and, I think, the Cruzes—happiest. I most definitely do not want to accuse anyone, even indirectly, of unfair treatment until we know more. We can catch more flies with honey than vinegar; let's not assume guilt without proof.

The low level functionaries of Zalaipa have it in for minorities, unbeknownst to their superiors. Again, offending those at the top will not help us remedy the situation. Rather, presenting our clients' concerns reasonably and inviting alternative interpretations will tell the power brokers that we intend to be fair and open-minded. They may well want an honest police force as much as the Cruzes. We should give them a chance to show it.

Isolated people at the top are compelling their underlings' unequal treatment of minorities, but the problem is not citywide. In this situation, although the officials worthy of blame are unlikely to help us, those who appoint them, work with them, and trust them will, if we are reasonable, welcome what we have to tell them. Even talking with those responsible for the discrimination will be valuable; inconsistency between what they tell you and what others do will help us begin to make a case to others who aren't aware of their activities.

The system is rotten to the core. This, of course, is always a possibility. That everyone from the Chief of Police to the rookie cop on the street might want nonwhites out of Zalaipa is something you should be prepared to find. If you do, our options may well narrow quickly to a section 1983 suit (or some other forceful mobilization). At that point, you'd have to recast your fact finding strategy toward getting information that will prove much more difficult to garner.

In approaching your task, please approach each situation as though the first scenario applies until you get substantial evidence to the contrary. My goal is to solve the Cruzes' problem at its root. That could mean anything from a monthly community meeting of leaders and minority groups to appointing some sort of special committee to oversee minority concerns. It might also mean litigation, but even were we to win a suit, I wouldn't consider that a very lasting solution. So long as animosity continues in the community, incentives to treat minorities fairly will be stifled.

To talk with those in control, then, we should begin by speaking their language. Although I might profitably meet with the city potentates myself, I think the presence of a lawyer has an immediate tendency to polarize the situation and set up barriers. I'd prefer, therefore, that you make the initial communication with the power brokers. You'll also seem more objective to them if you're merely working for someone who's representing a client, rather than representing someone yourself.

You needn't mislead them. If someone asks what you're doing, tell them you're working for a lawyer who's looking into minority business opportunities, but stress that you're basically after facts and are not out to hang anyone. You may be asked if you're threatening or planning to sue. The truth probably serves best here. Just say something to the effect that we certainly don't want to litigate if we don't have to, and at any rate we're not even certain there's any problem worth suing over at the moment. You're talking to them precisely to see how possible non-litigation change is.

With all this in mind, I'd recommend an approach that emphasizes the following elements. Put them in your own words; the quoted passages are mere suggestions.

"Some of the minority residents of Zalaipa feel that they aren't being treated equally. I know how much perceptions can differ and we're interested in hearing your side of it. Have you had particular troubles in minority areas that have convinced you to patrol more regularly there?" Ask in a non-confrontational way and show you really are interested in how the mayor or the Council or the police see the situation.

"Our clients want to run a nice family restaurant. Most of their customers are young families with children who come to relax and spend some time together. They think perhaps there has been trouble downtown with raucous younger bars; they really aren't interested in running that kind of establishment. Has there been trouble downtown? What's your understanding of the situation?" This will show that you understand that the treatment of the Cruzes may just be overzealous police work and gives whomever you're talking to plenty of latitude to offer reasonable counter-explanations.

"We're mainly interested here in increasing understanding between the people we represent and those in charge in the city. Do you have any conduits for communication with the minority community? Have you had many complaints? Would you be interested in setting up either a panel or perhaps a periodic open forum to hear citizens' comments? How do you feel about relations in Zalaipa?" Be sure here to admit your slight knowledge of the situation; there's nothing worse than an out-of-towner who thinks she knows it all.

I think conversations within these sorts of stories will show the police, the mayor, and the city that you understand their legitimate concerns and how misperceptions can arise on both sides. Stressing what Jesse and Sylvia perceive ("Our clients feel discriminated against") rather than the evil qualities of others in Zalaipa ("You're a racist") will allow whomever you're talking with not to take the defensive. In fact, if you state the Cruzes' case without too much emphasis on accusation, the other person could, in theory, even agree: "Yes, we've heard many complaints about unequal treatment. Why do you think your clients feel that way?" This orients you toward solving the problem together right from the start, rather than both having to defend your views in a tit-for-tat exchange.

Of course, you may find that a widespread conspiracy does exist. In that case, we'll need substantial evidence both to prepare any lawsuit and to show the other side we mean business. For this reason, it seems best for you to gather what you can in empirical and anecdotal evidence before going "to the top." That way you'll be prepared either to give a cooperative member of the City Council figures to show why Zalaipa Chicanos feel locked out or to show an intransigent city attorney that you at least have a prima facie case of civil rights violations and would like to talk seriously.

Necessary Facts and Ways to Gather Them

Who decides what the towing company tows and when? Is there a written contract with the City detailing towing procedures? Is it at the company's discretion? Are certain parts of town targeted for more frequent tows? Is there a great difference between what the company is supposed to do and what it does? For all this, I'd urge you to rely on a broad range of sources, including the company itself, any public record of its contract with the City, police information, other businesses, and anecdotal evidence from the streets.

Compare whatever is available in the file of the Cruzes' initial hearing and their appeal with records of other hearings and appeals. Do the figures bear out the City's contention that licenses have been limited in number? Is it true that downtown minority liquor licenses have led to more than the usual amount of trouble? How long do license applications usually take? Is there a pattern to how many are granted and denied and to whom? How many hearings does it usually take? Do such high officials as the Police Chief and City Attorney usually testify at such hearings? Who runs the ABC in Zalaipa? What's the minority participation on the ABC? How are members chosen? Are there published criteria for granting licenses? Does Maggie O'Connor know anyone else who suffered similar delay? Is there a record of complaints against the ABC anywhere?

What is the current mood and ethnic makeup of downtown Zalaipa? Are there many restaurants? Many owned by minorities? Are any major changes planned for downtown in coming years? Has a center City renovation been planned? Are any eminent domain projects in the works (such that the City would have an incentive to drive down the value of the Cruzes' land by making their restaurant fail)? Is parking seen as a problem; is it tight or readily available? Is there even a minority business community or organization? Are minorities concentrated into pockets? Is their income level commensurate with the citizenry at large, or are they predominantly poor? Much of this should be clear in the public records or in California abstracts and census charts; old newspaper articles, especially from "Metro"-type sections, are useful for finding out what's planned for downtown. Is it possible Jesse and Sylvia are simply out of step with what Zalaipa wants for itself in coming years? Is what Zalaipa wants discriminatory or just different?

Are the police and minorities (especially Chicanos) generally thought of as being at odds? How often are minorities arrested in relation to: the Zalaipa population as a whole, others of the same socio-economic class, whites? How serious is the undocumented worker "problem," if any? What anecdotal evidence exists either to verify or refute the Cruzes' perceptions? Is the same cop always outside Jesse and Sylvia's restaurant? Has he been the subject of any investigation? (You'll probably have to rely on people's memories or the newspapers for this—internal affairs departments are, understandably, tight-lipped.) Are there many Chicano cops; are they perceived among other Chicanos as "genuine" or Uncle Tom types (Tio Taco types)? How real is the problem posed by minority restaurants in the downtown area? Much of this information, at least from the police perspective, might be in records of proceedings of the City Council with regard to police funding or specific police policies from year to year, where the department draws up proposals and defends the focus of its approach.

What is the minority sentiment in general toward Zalaipa, the rest of the City, and the power brokers? Who has the wealth and power in town? How are the power brokers chosen? Are minorities a significant voice in that process? Are minorities proportionally represented in the power structure? Have they shown any interest in being properly represented? How open is the process, especially to the poor? Are minorities at all united? Who runs the media? How large a segment of Zalaipa is on government assistance? What percentage of such people are minorities? How strong are minority organizations? How prevalent are complaints of the sort the Cruzes have made here?

This seems an overwhelming amount of information and hardly the types of questions with which to take up a high city official's time. That's why I want you to get what you can from public records, clerks, low-ranking personnel, and anecdotal evidence before approaching top people. Then you can select striking information (should you turn up any) to ask them about; how well their perceptions comport with reality may help underscore your argument to them that others perceive things differently, or it may be the first bit of proof that someone is lying. In either case, it will pay to be informed and prepared to respond to anything you may hear.

Summary and Concerns

To summarize, the value of the power brokers is twofold. First, they are in the best position immediately to solve the Cruzes' problem and, in the longer term, to help remedy what may be a widespread perception of unfairness in Zalaipa. Second, their information is invaluable to us not only for its own sake, but as evidence of on what grounds official City policy is being made, and to what ends.

Should any of the first three story lines prove true, the potential for overall improvement is tremendous. Especially in a small town unhampered by miles of red tape or dozens of offices performing the same functions, most of the town probably knows most of the rest of the town and things can get done. My aim is to discover as many of the problems as possible from the outset so any solution we create can be comprehensive. Unless the problem is strictly isolated (to one person, for example), it bespeaks a breakdown in the process somewhere, which may be best addressed on a community-wide level.

And, should the worst turn out to be true, we will have confronted the power brokers from the start and gotten a first look at their justifications and likely defenses. I realize the tone of much of this seems overly optimistic about what we will discover. I am neither optimistic nor expecting the worst. But approaching the situation willing to talk reasonably will avoid putting everyone on highest alert while still letting us gather information. A section 1983 suit is a real possibility. Dealing with the potentates right off the bat will inform us as to the balances and uses of power in Zalaipa and help us immeasurably when the heavy flak begins after we file suit.

In closing this section, I would like to stress that at any crucial juncture, the Cruzes' needs and desires will, of course, take prominence. Should they decide they would rather not pursue a citywide communication improvement program, that is perfectly their prerogative. I want only to understand the full range of the problem and possible solutions before expecting them to make a choice. If they choose to limit their choice to their own immediate situation, that won't necessarily prevent our handing over what we've found to Zalaipa community groups. It merely means any decision we reach should weigh their wishes heavily.

* * *

Chapter 5

ADVOCACY IN
THE LEGAL SYSTEM

A. Telling the Story of the Case

Effective advocacy requires persuasive storytelling, whether it occurs in the context of traditional litigation or alternative dispute resolution. The next excerpt illustrates how advocacy might be approached as storytelling using the example of the oral arguments in the landmark case of *Brown v. Board of Education*.

Anthony G. Amsterdam, *Telling Stories and Stories About Them*, 1 CLIN. L. REV. 9 (1994)*

* * *

5.

Suppose (the oldster said), we were to look at the arguments of Thurgood Marshall and John W. Davis before the Supreme Court of the United States in the 1952 public school desegregation cases—the cases that became *Brown v. Board of Education*—not only as legal argumentation but as story telling. Now, I don't mean (he said) only those parts of the argument that were couched in overtly narrative form—the description of the events that brought about the litigation, the statement of proceedings in the lower courts. I mean the entire arguments, including the parts that invoke legal doctrine, that explicate and apply legal reasoning.

You needn't scrunch up all your eyebrows (he said). You look like a convention of caterpillars with the stomachache. Stories can take varied forms. A story doesn't have to begin "Once there was a princess" and then tell what she did, in historical fashion and in chronological sequence. Ordinarily, the events that are told about will unfold in time in an order that makes sense to human beings for whom "time . . . is the primary category of experience."[7] But the *telling* of those events—what is sometimes called "utterance" as distinguished from "statement"—can assume a wholly different temporal structure and stylistic form. There is no reason why the sequence and

---

* Reprinted with permission.

7 NORTHROP FRYE, *The Rhythms of Time*, in MYTH AND METAPHOR 157 (1991). * * *

the language which an appellate lawyer uses to describe the issues before the court and to formulate legal-sounding arguments addressed to those issues cannot tell a story. The only test of a story is whether it functions as a story: whether it creates a world of characters and actions and experiences and necessities entangled in "situations which change or to the changes of which . . . [the characters] react[,] . . . giving rise to a new predicament which calls for thought or action or both."[11] So let us see whether Marshall's and Davis' arguments in *Brown* do something of that sort— begging your leave (he added apologetically) for whatever else they also do.

6.

Thurgood Marshall began his argument by reciting succinctly the procedural history of the litigation. Next he read to the Court "the two provisions of the law of South Carolina under attack in this particular case."[13] One said that "'It shall be unlawful for pupils of one race to attend the schools provided by boards of trustees for persons of another race.'" The second said that "'Separate schools shall be provided for children of the white races [sic] . . . and no child of either race shall ever be permitted to attend a school provided for children of the other race.'"

Marshall then stated that his position in the lower court had been "that these statutes were unconstitutional in their enforcement because . . . evidence would be produced by expert witnesses to show that governmentally imposed racial segregation in and of itself was . . . a denial of equality." He adverted to expert testimony in the record that "there were no recognizable differences between children" in educational capacity. He summarized his legal theory: that when an "attack [is made] on a classification statute," the State must show that "there is a difference" between the "persons being classified" and that "the difference has a significance with the subject matter being legislated." He detailed the testimony of witnesses that segregation "deterred the personality development of . . . [African-American] children," "destroys their self-respect," "denies them full opportunity for democratic social development," and stamps them "with a badge of inferiority." He noted that the State had presented no countervailing evidence and that the record showed "no effort whatsoever . . . to support the legislative determinations of the State of South Carolina." Rather, the "Court is being asked to uphold those statutes . . . because of two reasons. One is that these matters are legislative matters, as to whether or not we are going to have segregation." The other is that "Negroes as Negroes—all Negroes—are different from everybody else." As Marshall framed the case:

> "the only issue is to consider whether . . . [an African-American] individual or small group, as we have here, of appellants, . . . [are entitled to have] their constitutionally protected rights . . . weighed over against

---

    11   PAUL RICOEUR, *The Narrative Function*, in HERMENEUTICS & THE HUMAN SCIENCES 274, 277 (John Thompson trans. 1981).

    13   ARGUMENT: THE ORAL ARGUMENT BEFORE THE SUPREME COURT IN BROWN V. BOARD OF EDUCATION OF TOPEKA, 1952-55, at 37 (Leon Friedman ed. 1969). * * *

what is considered to be the public policy of the State of South Carolina
. . . and . . . affirmed"

because

"if what is considered to be the public policy of the State of South Carolina
runs contrary to the rights of that individual, then . . . this Court, reluctantly or otherwise is obliged to say that this policy has run up against the
Fourteenth Amendment . . . ."

In closing, Marshall addressed the concern that if the Court struck down segregation, there would be public resistance to its decree. "[All] of these predictions of
things that were going to happen, they have never happened." "I for one do not
believe that the people in South Carolina or those southern states are lawless people."
"Even if the concession [to fears of racial friction] was necessary in 1895, it is not
necessary now because people have grown up and understand each other."

"They are fighting together[28] and living together. For example, today
they are working together in other places. As a result of the ruling of this
Court, they are going together on the higher level.[29] . . . I know in the
South where I spent most of my time, you will see white and colored kids
going down the road together to school. They separate and go to different
schools, and they come out and they play together. I do not see why there
would necessarily be any trouble if they went to school together."

Arguing for the State of South Carolina, John W. Davis began by reciting in
detail everything that South Carolina had already done "to furnish not merely physical facilities . . . but educational facilities, equipment, curricula, and opportunities
equal on the part of the state for the Negro as for the white pupil." He summarized
and then quoted the findings of the court below "that the defendants had made
every possible effort to comply with the decree of the court, [and] that they had done
all that was humanly possible . . . [to achieve] equality between the races in this area.
. . . ." This, he added, had involved enormous effort and expenditure. "[I]n South Carolina, under the leadership of its present Governor, there was a surge for educational
reform and improvement, which I suspect has not been exceeded in any state in this
Union." The Legislature "adopted . . . [an] act providing for the issuance of a maximum of $75,000,000 in bonds for school purposes," serviced by a state sales tax
which, "[s]peaking from some slight personal experience, I can assert . . . escapes
very few transactions in that state." "That being done, the legislature set up an educational finance commission" with broad powers. "Thereupon, the commission goes
to Clarendon County, which is the seat of the present drama . . . [and] finds that in
Clarendon County there are thirty-four educational districts, so-called, each with its

---

28   The reference is to African-American and white soldiers in the Korean War. * * *

29   The reference is to *Sweatt v. Painter*, 339 U.S. 629 (1950), and *McLaurin v. Oklahoma State
Regents*, 339 U.S. 637 (1950), invalidating the consignment of African-American students to separate
facilities in University graduate schools. * * *

separate body of officers and administrators, and all of them bogged down, I take it, by similar poverty." Things are promptly, thoroughly, and expensively reorganized; new schools are constructed for African-Americans; and the "State of South Carolina appropriated money to furnish school buses for black and white." "Of course, in these days, the schoolboy no longer walks. The figure of the schoolboy trudging four miles in the morning and back four in the afternoon swinging his books as he went is as much a figure of myth as the presidential candidate born in a log cabin. Both of these characters have disappeared."

After summarizing again "the progress that had been made in the public school system in South Carolina . . . with particular reference to the improvement of the facilities, equipment[,] curricular [sic], and opportunities accorded to the colored students," Davis came to "what is really the crux of this case. That is the meaning and interpretation of the Fourteenth Amendment to the Constitution . . . ." Davis argued that the Congress that "proffered" the Fourteenth Amendment and the States that "ratified" it all demonstrated through their "conduct by way of interpretation" that they did not conceive it to "touch . . . [the States'] power over their public schools." He cited judicial decisions to this effect. It would be, he said,

> "an interesting, though perhaps entirely useless, undertaking to enumerate the numbers of men charged with official duty in the legislative and judicial branches of the Government who have declared that segregation is not per se unlawful. The members of Congress, year after year, and session after session, the members of the state constitutional conventions, the members of state legislatures, year after year and session after session, the members of the higher courts of the states, the members of the inferior federal judiciary, and the members of this tribunal—what their numbers may be, I do not know, but I think it reasonably certain that it must mount well into the thousands, and to this I stress for Your Honors that every one of that vast group was bound by oath to support the Constitution of the United States and any of its amendments—is it conceivable that all that body of concurrent opinion was recreant to its duty or misunderstood the constitutional mandate, or was ignorant of the history which gave to the mandate its scope and meaning? I submit not."

Finally, Davis summarized, criticized, and disparaged the expert testimony regarding harm to African-American children on which Marshall had relied; he recited South Carolina's assertedly disastrous experience with integrated schools from 1865 through 1877; and he quoted W.E.B. Du Bois to the effect that African-American children would develop better balanced spirits and personalities "'by putting . . . [them] in [separate] schools where they are wanted, and where they are happy and inspired, than in [sic] thrusting them into hells [in integrated schools] where they are ridiculed and hated.'" He closed by asking: "Is it not a fact that the very strength and fiber of our federal system is local self-government . . .?" "Is it not of all the activities of government the one which most nearly approaches the hearts and minds of the people, the . . . education of their young?" "Is it not the height of wisdom that the manner in which that should be conducted should be left to those most immediately affected by it, and that the wishes of the parents, both white and colored, should be ascertained before their children are forced into what may be an unwelcome contact?"

Marshall's and Davis' arguments diverge in their analysis of the legal issue that the Court must decide, in their interpretation of the relevant precedents, and in their ordering of the relevant values. But they diverge still more in the basic stories they configure, the worlds of narrative action they create.

Marshall's story has three major characters: the segregating Legislatures as enforcers of the will of the white majorities of their respective States; children, who learn and think and live and feel and hurt and play and grow; and federal judges as the guardians of the Constitution. The story begins when the children come to court, asserting that the Legislatures have afflicted them. And indeed it is shown that the Legislatures have directed laws against the children, making it unlawful for them to go here rather than there, separating them from one another despite their natural instincts to be together. The separation brands and cripples and scars the African-American children, for no earthly reason. So the children appear as supplicants before the federal judges. The Legislatures tell the federal judges to butt out, first because the matter is none of federal judges' business, second because the federal judges should take the Legislatures' factually unsupported word that African-Americans are inherently inferior. Now, how are the federal judges to respond to this contention?

Davis' story, in sharp contrast, is full of governmental actors—a cast of thousands, polled. They are as numerous as gods in the Greek Pantheon and they act much like those divinities. They bestow munificent benefits on humankind and they tithe it. The order of the universe depends upon the maintenance of their respective realms of authority; they use humans, in large measure, to mark out and reinforce the boundaries of those realms. Humans make trouble when they ask the gods to meddle in the wrong realms.

Children are conspicuously absent from the main plot of Davis' tale. Things are done *for* them but not *to* them; and they act not at all. They are bodiless—the "schoolboy," a "figure of myth." Children appear only in a Davis subplot. This is the subplot spun by African-American advocates for and against school desegregation. Those of Marshall's ilk bring unprecedented claims and irresponsible witnesses before the federal judiciary to malign responsible officials. (The homonymic counterpoint is Davis' own: "Not a one of . . . [these witnesses] is under any official duty in the premises whatever; not a one of them has had to consider the welfare of the people for whom they are legislating or whose rights they were called on to adjudicate.") Others, like W.E.B. Du Bois, "perhaps the most constant and vocal opponent of Negro oppression of any of his race in the country," share Marshall's concern about the mysteries of children's minds but disagree with Marshall's witnesses regarding the nature of those mysteries. The debate between them has been blown up into a case to lay before federal judges so as to induce those judges to depart from their own realm of dignity, gainsay the wisdom and authority of tradition, and invade the realm of the States, their Legislatures, their Constitutional Conventions, and all their cognizant officialdom. Now, how are the federal judges to respond to this concoction?

7.

So I ask you (the oldster said), are these not stories? Are they not powerful narratives that have a narrative beginning and a narrative middle and that dictate different narrative endings, different judgments of the Court? Do they not point to those different judgments, to some extent, *narratively*—quite apart from the *legal* arguments in which they are embedded?

Oh, I grant you that the legal arguments are quite important, too. In fact, I once wrote a small piece—for a volume in Thurgood Marshall's honor—examining the structure of his legal arguments in *Brown*. The damnedest thing was, I came to the conclusion that his choice of legal theory might itself be best explained in narrative rather than in doctrinal terms. I suppose each one of us sees pretty much what his or her own head is screwed on to see—or heads (he said), begging your pardon—but that's beside the point just now. The point is, if you agree with me that Marshall and Davis are telling stories in their *Brown* arguments, it might be instructive to examine some of the ways in which they go about it.

8.

Macrostructure

The macrostructure of Marshall's argument constitutes a half-finished tale that requires judicial action to conclude it. His opening words put the action in the Court's arena[61] and his closing words leave the action there.[62] Despite heavy questioning by the Justices, Marshall's movement from beginning to end is relentlessly direct, its dramatic urgency unremitting:

> We are rightly in this Court. We claim
> that South Carolina has declared a ban
> coercing children to be put apart
> whom Nature made the same.
> Ever has the lore of this Court run:
> No law can stand
> unbased on reason. Yet unreasoningly are
> our children ravished of their birthright and undone.
> We indict these acts. The segregating States retort
> that they are higher than the law of the land,
> cocksure the Court will share their scorn of Blacks.
> So. We await an answer from the Court.

The macrostructure of Davis' argument consists of three movements:

> "The first thing I want to contend . . . is that the mandate of the court
> below [requiring equalization of educational resources] . . . has been
> fully complied with. The question is no longer in the case."

---

61   "May it please the Court, this case is here on direct appeal from the United States District Court for the Eastern District of South Carolina. The issue raised in this case was clearly raised in the pleadings, and was clearly raised throughout the first hearing." * * *

62   "As to whether or not I, as an individual, am being deprived of my right is not legislative, but judicial." * * *

"The second question . . . I wish to address . . . is that [the segregation laws] of South Carolina do not offend the Fourteenth Amendment . . . ."

"Third, I want to say something about the evidence offered by the plaintiffs upon which counsel so confidently relied."

As legal reasoning alone, this suite is plausible but hardly compelling. The first point is avowedly aimed at documenting the mootness of a claim for equal, separate facilities that Marshall is not making and, indeed, has just expressly disavowed. The second point is the whole case. The third point—the trashing of Marshall's expert witnesses—is logically anterior to the conclusion of the second.

The force of the suite lies in its story structure. For the tale that Davis has spun is an easily recognized narrative: the narrative of the insatiate beneficiary. First, a beneficiary is endowed with a generous but measured gift. Second, the fitness of the state of affairs produced by that gift is shown or feted. Third, the same or a similarly situated beneficiary ungratefully or greedily seeks to extort a bigger gift. The outcome follows inescapably. The grasper comes to grief.

But Davis' macrostructure serves another function, too. By discussing the ultimate Fourteenth Amendment issue before discussing the testimony that Marshall has presented as bearing on that issue, Davis uses an inversion of the play-within-a-play device to divide the scene into two separate stages. The big stage is the real world, a world of governmental authority and action, of history and experience: the world in which Congress proposes and the States ratify the Fourteenth Amendment, courts construe it, state constitutional conventions and legislatures deal with vital issues of public policy, state and local officials struggle with the difficult practical problems of raising moneys, building schools, and educating masses of children. The small stage is the federal courtroom to which Marshall has enticed a bare handful of poor actors—professorial types and impractical visionaries all—who, having each observed a few children playing with a few dolls, are willing to hazard vasty mentalistic conclusions contrary to those of equally committed and hypersensitive African-American advocates like W.E.B. Du Bois. It is through this fantastical farce on the little stage that Marshall proposes to inveigle the Justices of the Supreme Court of the United States to take momentous action on the big stage. Who's he trying to kid?

* * *

10.

Microstructure

Marshall's and Davis' 1952 arguments show marked differences in the incidence of particular linguistic components.

Consider first their use of verbs. What do they portray African-American people **doing**, white people **doing**, governments and government officials **doing**? What do they depict as being **done to** and **done for** each of these groups? It will be useful to distinguish the portions of their arguments in which they discuss the evidence presented in the trial court (along with the writings of W.E.B. Du Bois and a book of

Kenneth Clark's, both of which Davis juxtaposes to that evidence) from the remainder of the arguments. Let's call these the "evidentiary passages" and the "general passages," respectively.

* * *

The numbers in themselves are interesting. Notice the asymmetry between the levels of action predicated of the various actors in Davis' evidentiary passages on the one hand and in Davis' general passages on the other. This asymmetry reflects—and contributes to creating—Davis' play-within-a-play motif. It implies an incongruity between the real world and the make-believe world fabricated by academics obsessed with the emotional ills of African-American children, including academics who disagree about the proper cure for those ills. Evidently, the academics' hangups are unworldly. In Marshall's argument, by contrast, there is a fair consistency between the world depicted by the evidence and the world at large.

Davis' world—i.e., Davis' real world—is dominated by government activity. Government actors appear more often and do much more than in Marshall's argument. In Davis' real world, more is done for African-Americans than to African-Americans, and most of what is done to or for African-Americans is also done to or for whites. In Marshall's argument and in Davis' evidentiary passages, considerably more is done to African-Americans than is done for them, and most of what is done to them is not done to whites. Although Davis' version of the evidence portrays African-Americans as quite active, they do little—and nothing distinctive—in Davis' real world. As agents, they do not exist there.

Marshall's verbs portray African-American children as *going through* humiliation, *putting up with* humiliation, *having* rights, and *asserting* rights. He uses more motor verbs than copulas to situate them: [85] they *go* to school; and "[e]ven if you *get stuck* in one [school] district," "[t]hey could *move over* into . . . [a different] district, if necessary." In the general passages of Davis' argument, the motor verbs ordinarily associated with human agents are instead attributed to governments and their instrumentalities: "South Carolina does not *come* to this policy as a stranger." "South Carolina *moved* from mixed to segregated schools [in 1877]." "[T]he commission *goes* to Clarendon County . . . [and] finds that in Clarendon County there are thirty-four educational districts, . . . each with its separate body of officers and administrators, and all of them *bogged down* . . . by similar poverty." Having been "'[r]equired . . . *to proceed* at once to furnish'" African-Americans equal educational resources and to "report what progress *they were making*," state officials "*brought* these districts *into* unity and strength," and so forth. The comings, goings and journeyings that make governmental actors the protagonists in Davis' story are denied to human beings except in passages connoting unreality.

In both Marshall's and Davis' arguments, of course, governments enact statutes, provide schools, administer them, and assign students to them. Marshall makes con-

---

85   A *motor* verb is one that conveys motion, activity or drive; a *copula* (or *linking verb*) is a verb that connects its subject to a predicate complement without expressing any action (*i.e.*, "be," "seem," "appear"). * * *

siderably less of this activity than Davis does, 23 verbs (out of 8600 words) to Davis' 45 (out of 5500). Marshall portrays the State of South Carolina as *imposing* racial segregation and as *violating* the Fourteenth Amendment; its legislators "have never . . . recognize[d] . . . [the] pleas" of African-Americans. Davis portrays the State of South Carolina as having "obeyed the . . . injunction" of the district court requiring equal educational opportunities for African-Americans, as having proceeded "'promptly and in good faith to comply with the [c]ourt's decree,'" as having "made every possible effort to comply," and as having "done all that was humanly possible." Thus do Davis' governments not only journey but *strive*: they "think"; they "*conceive* it their power and right to maintain separate schools if it suits their policy"; they "*conceiv[e]* . . . that . . . [the Fourteenth Amendment] did not touch their power over their public schools"; they "had *solemnly accepted*" the Fourteenth Amendment, and "[c]ertainly it cannot be said that a legislature conducting its public schools in accordance with the wishes of its people . . . [is] acting merely *by* caprice or *by* racial prejudice."

As for what is **done to** whom, in Marshall's argument "Negroes are taken out of the main stream of American life in these states"; they are "excluded"; they are "harmed"; they are "denied equality," "den[ied] their rights," and "deprive[d] . . . of their constitutional rights." Their children are "injured," "deprive[d] . . . of equal status," and "denie[d] full opportunity for democratic social development." They "have road blocks put up in their minds as a result of . . . segregation"; this "deter[s] . . . the development of . . . [their] personalities," "destroys their self-respect," and "stamps . . . [them] with a badge of inferiority." In the general passages of Davis' argument, the only thing that is done to African-Americans that is not done to whites is that African-Americans are *caught* in the grasp of Marshall's argument. In Davis' evidentiary passages, he quotes (and denigrates) Kenneth Clark's testimony that African-American children "'have been definitely *harmed*,'" and he recites the views of W.E.B. Du Bois that African-American children in integrated schools are "'despised,'" "'resented,'" "'mock[ed],'" "'neglected or bullied,'" and "'thrust[] . . . into hells where they are ridiculed and hated.'" Notice that even in these passages, which, Davis implies, recount the opinions of African-American psychologizers, the nature of the harm done to African-Americans is different than in Marshall's argument. In Davis' passages, African-Americans are psychologically *injured*; in Marshall's, they are injured and *denied their rights*.

The notion that African-Americans **have** rights is alien to Davis' argument. Indeed, he accords them few attributes of any sort.

* * *

The things that African-Americans possess in Marshall's evidentiary passages also include *personalities* and *minds* and *development* and *self-respect*. But here African-Americans have other and more rights-based attributes as well: they are given "humiliation" and "a badge of inferiority," and they are subjected to the deprivation of "*equal status* in the school community." Parallel language appears in Marshall's general passages, where African-Americans additionally possess *rights, individual rights, constitutional rights and privileges* and *personal and present rights*. Davis nowhere uses the term *rights* or anything like it in connection with African-Americans; he does use *rights* once in connection with "the people" at large; he speaks often of the *right* and *power* of governments. His nouns of possession, like his verbs, endow governments and their officials with the vital powers of living beings: they have *minds*; they act *in good faith*; they are moved by a "*surge* for educational reform and improvement"; they have "strength and fiber." Davis' adjectives describing governmental entities are in the same vein: these entities are neither *ignorant* nor *recreant*. They have the cognitive and moral faculties that Davis' argument, in its general passages, almost never grants people.

The compositional elements of the lawyers' arguments show both their basic narrative strategies and the way in which each advocate deals with the plausibility problem inherent in his chosen strategy. Marshall's primary plausibility problem is to tell a story of oppression that escapes becoming maudlin. To present segregated African-American children as judicial supplicants with a claim of right rather than an appeal for pity requires a fine balance: their plight as victims must be portrayed in language that preserves their agentivity, their authenticity, and their integrity as human beings. Davis' plausibility problem stems from the need to say as *little* as he says about African-American children in a case that inescapably is all about them. They must be talked about enough to avoid the appearance of belittling them, but they can neither do nor have done to them so much that they become live or important actors.

Marshall's depiction of African-American children as "going through" the kind of "humiliation" that "nobody should put up with" and his use of agentive and rights-based language in describing their situation and their injuries respond in part to his particular narrational problem. So do Davis' play-within-a-play tactic and his use of terminology that deprives African-American children of the agentivity that Davis ascribes to governmental actors. The lawyers' word choice and grammatical structure reinforce their respective themes.

* * *

Marshall's verb usage in his evidentiary and general passages is reasonably consistent. It tells a story in which governments and their African-American citizens are both active agents. Governments are the more active, as befits an oppressor in a tale of oppression. But they are far from all-powerful; African-Americans are down but not out; judicial action to redress the balance is possible and necessary.

Davis' verb usage in his evidentiary passages contrasts starkly with that in his general passages. In the evidentiary passages, which depict the beguiling fabrication that the advocates of desegregation are attempting to foist on the judiciary, African-Americans are frenetically active and governments are left almost wholly out of account. In Davis' general passages, depicting reality outside the courtroom, governments are all-powerful and all-important—although not wholly unrestrained—and African-Americans are nonentities.

* * *

Pleadings are potentially powerful vehicles for telling the client's story in a persuasive manner. The next excerpt suggests that lawyers can tell more compelling stories in pleadings by incorporating the language of their clients and styles of writing used by journalists and historians.

Herbert Eastman, *Speaking Truth to Power: The Language of Civil Rights Litigators*, 104 YALE L.J. 763 (1995)*

* * *

A. *Hattie's Story*

I once had a client named Hattie Kendrick. She was a woman and an African-American, a school teacher and a civil rights warrior, spit upon, arrested, and tossed out of restaurants and clothing stores that did not "cater to the colored trade." She marched and spoke out for integration and against oppression. Her school fired her, but not before she had taught generations of black children in Cairo, Illinois, that participation in American democracy was their right and their duty. In the 1940's, she sued to win equal pay for black teachers, with Thurgood Marshall as her lawyer. And in the 1970's, she was a named plaintiff in a class action asserting the voting rights of black citizens in Cairo against a city electoral system rigged to reduce the value of their votes to nothingness. All she wanted was to cast a meaningful vote in a democratic election before she died—she was in her nineties, growing blind and weak. Such a woman. Such a story. And such a voice. Listen to how she discerns the problems of her town: "'Too long have the two races stood grinning in each other's faces, while they carry the fires of resentment and hate in their hearts, and with their hands hid behind their backs they carry the unsheathed sword.'" Yet here is how the complaint filed in federal court identifies the named plaintiffs, including Hattie Kendrick: "All plaintiffs are Blacks, citizens of the United States and of the State of Illinois, and residents of Cairo, Illinois registered to vote in Municipal Elections conducted in Cairo."[5]

This Article springs from the recurring disappointment and frustration I have felt after consultation with clients in cases presenting outrages that, in a phrase loved by my mother, cried out to heaven. I have represented and continue to represent these clients in civil rights cases, broadly defined. These are my clients: a young woman, sexually abused as a child, forced to undergo unjustified strip searches that aroused the nightmares of her childhood. A black laborer finding his lunch in the toilet and racist threats in his locker. A gay man staring death from AIDS in the face and denied the only available treatment because of bureaucratic indifference and homophobia. A recovering drug addict holding his addiction at bay with the support of a group

---

*   Reprinted by permission of The Yale Law Journal Company and Fred B. Rothman & Company from The Yale Law Journal, Vol. 104, pages 765-777, 789.

5   First Amended Complaint at 3, Kendrick v. Mass (S.D. Ill. filed July 3, 1979) (No. 73-19C) [hereinafter *Kendrick*].

home, yet in jeopardy of losing that home when fearful neighbors complained to a cowardly city government.

My frustration and disappointment began when I reviewed the pleadings I drafted for them. I could barely see over the chasm separating what those clients told me about their lives and what I wrote to the court as factual allegations in the complaint—sterile recitations of dates and events that lost so much in the translation. What is lost in a description that identifies a woman like Hattie only as a registered voter? Details, of course. Passion, certainly, but more than that. We lose the identity of the person harmed, the story of her life. But even more is lost. This was a class action aimed at remedying a systemic problem harming thousands, over generations. The complaint omits the social chemistry underneath the events normally invisible to the law—events that create the injury or compound it. In this complaint, we lose the fullness of the harm done, the scale of the deprivations, the humiliation of the plaintiff class members, the damage to greater society, the significance of it all.

The complaint omits the frustration of the democratic process and the powerful metaphors that claim an exception to the rules restricting the court's involvement. The complaint leaves intact the walls between the clients and the court, the clients and the lawyer. In a strange way, it even effaces the lawyer by denying her the dynamic and creative role of responding to the tragedy witnessed.

I wondered how we, as lawyers, could plead the horror of wrong done on a mass scale. In reviewing the pleadings in other famous civil rights class actions, I found similar failings. This Article explores why we fail and wonders whether we can do better.

To begin with, this Article demonstrates our failure by comparing lawyers' pleadings with the reality of clients' situations as described by journalists and historians. Much is lost by words alone, by the words of journalists and historians no less than those of lawyers. But with their losses and omissions, these contrasting descriptions will prove useful in my analysis. As Stanley Fish argues, all we have of "what really happened" is a collection of competing descriptions.[7] The descriptions make visible the extent to which law as a language omits something significant from the reality it purports to portray.

These contrasts are not merely academic. In this Article, we do not observe the legal interpretations of distant or dead judges' precedent. Rather, we read the work of a lawyer speaking through a complaint to a judge who will then, as part of the interpretive process, engage the lawyer in an ongoing conversation that is begun and framed by the complaint. The conversation ends with a decision, favorable or adverse.

The very high social stakes and moral imperative of civil rights cases invite literary treatment, in order to present worlds in conflict. In a systemic civil rights lawsuit brought by a class against a governmental or corporate system, the surface of everydayness is ripped open and we inspect the layers underneath. We then find the routine that grinds along, churning out the little injustices, the grinning faces that con-

---

7   STANLEY FISH, DOING WHAT COMES NATURALLY: CHANGE, RHETORIC, AND THE PRACTICE OF THEORY IN LITERARY AND LEGAL STUDIES 158 (1989).

ceal resentment. The civil rights plaintiff may stand in the courtroom as an equal to her adversary, but she did not enter the courtroom in that condition and may leave with that inequality deepened. An adverse verdict can mean continued oppression, even death.

But this dramatic quality transcends the civil rights context. Every client has a story that deserves to be told—from the corporate client trying to survive in a harshly competitive climate, to a spouse embroiled in a bitter divorce. While the need to tell a story is present in many different kinds of litigation, the civil rights field is a good place to begin. * * *

B. *Speaking Is What We Do: The Importance of Complaints*

> Liberty, lives, fortunes often are at stake, and appeals for assistance and mercy rend the air for those who care to hear * * *. In all questions men are frequently influenced by some statement which, spoken at the eventful time, determines fate.[14]

Clarence Darrow

What does it matter? What is wrong with a pleading that simply offers a short and concise statement of the claim, as the rules expect? Why are pleadings so important?

At one time in our history, these questions would have sounded odd to most lawyers. Justice Story wrote that pleading "contains the quintessence of the law, and no man ever mastered it, who was not by that means made a profound lawyer."[15] Littleton called pleading "one of the most honourable, laudable, and profitable things in our law."[16] Of course, Story and Littleton were speaking of common law pleading, long since worn down by waves of reform to simplicity and plainness. Still, the reforms do not lessen the importance of the pleading.

Certainly, the persuasiveness of the stories lawyers tell for their clients matters. "People, including judges and jurors," Michael Tigar writes, "understand and restate events in terms of stories."[18] Nevertheless, many lawyers view the complaint simply as the mechanism by which they get the case into a court and in front of a jury—irrelevant once defense motions attacking the pleading have been overcome. Viewed from their angle, the complaint only needs to meet legal sufficiencies; it need not tell a story. These lawyers might think that the trial, specifically the closing arguments, serves as a more appropriate vehicle for telling the tragic stories they seek to remedy.

Even so, civil rights pleadings in particular should tell stories, for these reasons: First, in civil rights cases seeking injunctions, there is no jury. The judge is the per-

---

14   CLARENCE DARROW, VERDICTS OUT OF COURT 321-22 (Arthur Weinberg & Lila Weinberg eds., 1963).

15   *Quoted in* JONATHAN LANDERS ET AL., CIVIL PROCEDURE 347 (2d ed. 1988).

16   LITTLETON, TENURES, bk. 3, ch. 9, § 534 (London, Henry Butterworth 1825) (1481).

18   MICHAEL E. TIGAR, EXAMINING WITNESSES 5 (1993). * * *

son who must be persuaded. She is the trier of fact who will then decide to issue an injunction or not. The complaint, while certainly not the only opportunity for persuasion, is the first in time and the one that frames the remaining discussion of the case. Second, not only will there be no jury, it is likely that there will be no trial. Years will be spent managing a complex discovery process, punctuated by scrimmages over various motions. Often the parties bypass trial by negotiating a consent decree, often with guidance from the court. While the parties may negotiate the relief, the court must approve of the terms and maintain a "continuing involvement in administration and implementation." Abram Chayes has noted that "[a]ll these factors thrust the trial judge into an active role in shaping, organizing and facilitating the litigation."[25] When the decision maker shapes the development of the case and grants the relief without a trial, the complaint grows in significance. It is the first and perhaps the only means of communicating the client's story.

Third, even where a trial results, it will take years to get there. Erving Goffman has observed that in most personal encounters, one or the other of the participants in an interaction will shape that interaction, at the outset.[27] In litigation, one participant—the judge—exercises much more power than the others in deciding who speaks, at what length, and at what time. The complaint—read by the judge, one would hope, before her first face-to-face interaction with plaintiffs' counsel—may present the lawyer with the sole means of shaping the continuing interaction "at the outset." The complaint may color the judge's perception throughout the trial and beyond—from motions, discovery disputes, and settlement conferences, through postdecree enforcement proceedings.

Fourth, the court's construction of the "real" problem dictates how the problem will be considered and addressed. For example, if a prison case is defined as a problem of resources rather than as a dispute over particular rights, the court may rule that it has no power to act. On the other hand, if the case is defined as a dispute over rights, then the lack of resources provides no defense.

> If the right is to an integrated classroom, then the transportation of pupils to achieve that end is appropriate. Suppose, on the other hand, a court asks why a school has become segregated. It may conclude that residential patterns are responsible. If it does, then its order may deal as much with housing as with the school. The definition of the issue dictates the direction of the response and the scope of the resulting remedy.

Since we criticize judges who reach adverse decisions by using labels that misrepresent our client's reality, we should pause to consider how our complaints can educate the judge about that reality.

Fifth, federal judges who sit in isolation, economically and socially, from the problems of poor blacks in Cairo or of felons in maximum security prisons, need

---

25   Chayes, [*The Role of The Judge in Public Law Litigation*, 89 HARV. L. REV. 1281] at 1298 [(1976)]. * * *

27   GOFFMAN, [THE PRESENTATION OF SELF IN EVERYDAY LIFE] at 10-12 [(1973)].

more vivid and complete pictures painted for them if they are to understand the problems sufficiently, to care about them enough to guide the litigation, and, ultimately, to remedy those problems. Beyond the personal life experiences of the judge, other obstacles restrict the view of the judge, e.g., the restraints of the role, limited resources, and even more limited access to the facts of a case.

Civil rights lawyers have an opportunity and an obligation to expand that view, starting with the complaint. Unavoidably, they will be reduced to speaking of the case in shorthand—metaphors or cliches—that is cramped by the claims made in the complaint. "Good morning, Judge. This is a Section 1983 prisoner case." They can advance their persuasion, or fail to: "Counsel, is this that case where the prisoners were herded like cattle?"

One federal judge has candidly written that

> [R]egardless of who appointed them, judges react negatively to the "gotcha" lawsuit. By that I mean the lawsuit based on some technical nonobservance of a law or regulation whose consequences are undocumented, or at best vague. We judges want to know the facts, the real-life conditions, the actual practices underlying a legal challenge * * *. Judges search for meaning in what we do. You need to convince us that the law or the regulation is important in poor people's lives.[33]

Other judges—and their law clerks—have emphasized, in prisoner cases, that it is the "compelling" story that moves them to act.

Sixth, the complaint is even more important to lawyers who perceive themselves as representatives of a cause or constituency beyond the immediate client. Civil rights "litigation is itself an excellent constituency-building device." A lawyer can further her larger cause by drafting a pleading that serves as a "dramatic and decisive gesture, stating a claim in its most extreme and visible form—as a legal right." Impact litigation can give poor clients a chance to mobilize for change. Robert Jerome Glennon even argues that litigation contributed more to the success of the mid-1950's civil rights movement in Montgomery, Alabama, than did the bus boycott.[38] The complaint, filed with the court and disseminated to clients or "constituents" and the media, communicates what the problem is all about.

Seventh, through the media, the complaint speaks to the greater community. That community includes the defendants, the defendants' superiors, and possibly their friends and colleagues. That community may come to see hidden problems in a new light, consider change, and press for settlement.

Eighth, the complaint offers the litigator the only chance to tell the client's story—a dramatic, compelling story—in a literary way. It is a rare chance for creativity. Civil rights lawyers should not resist this opportunity. Civil rights complaints, because they are of more recent vintage and so deeply fact sensitive, are

---

33   Patricia M. Wald, *Ten Admonitions for Legal Services Advocates Contemplating Federal Litigation*, CLEARINGHOUSE REV., May 1993, at 11, 13. * * *

38   Robert J. Glennon, *The Role of Law in the Civil Rights Movement: The Montgomery Bus Boycott, 1955-1957*, 9 LAW & HIST. REV. 59 (1991).

rooted less often in common law pleading rules and techniques and written less frequently from formbooks. Civil rights lawyers find themselves compelled to go beyond the boilerplates, which do not lend themselves to portraying the unique position of their clients, who are socially marginalized underdogs.

All this is summarized in an aphorism, which echoes from Story's time as well as from Littleton's: Pleading matters because it is what we do.

* * *

1. *Cairo:* Kendrick v. Moss

In 1973, Hattie Kendrick and other African-American leaders in Cairo, Illinois, filed a federal class action lawsuit under the Fourteenth and Fifteenth Amendments to the U.S. Constitution. In their lawsuit, they challenged the structure of municipal elections by arguing, in essence, that the at-large system diluted the votes of black citizens. Although Cairo was forty percent black, city officers were elected by citywide vote and racially polarized voting patterns prevailed whenever a black candidate faced a white opponent. As a result, a black citizen's vote for a black candidate would be rendered meaningless. In order to prevail under existing law, the Cairo plaintiffs had to plead and prove a history of segregation in the community, a lack of responsiveness to minority constituents, and unequal access to the electoral process.

A few years after the Lawyers' Committee for Civil Rights Under Law filed the Cairo lawsuit, I arrived in Cairo fresh out of law school and found myself assigned to Hattie's case. Hattie became a grandmother to the little outpost of civil rights lawyers in Cairo and her case came to matter to us as the duty not only of lawyers but of grandchildren. We added a claim under the Voting Rights Act, named another community activist, Preston Ewing, as a plaintiff, and began to push the case toward trial. In other respects, I did not alter the original complaint.

The factual allegations in the complaint can be compared to a 1972 account written by journalist Paul Good and published by the U.S. Commission on Civil Rights after it held hearings in Cairo. The complaint pleads "systematic" discrimination in employment, citing statistics of higher unemployment and lower median income for blacks. The journalist's account contains similar statistics but it also includes additional information.

> When jobless blacks went on welfare, they were forced to pick cotton in season at substandard wages or lose their welfare rights. Since local plants—including governmental contractors—would not hire black seamstresses, one welfare mother with five children had to travel 50 miles a day to work, arising at 3 a.m. to feed and dress the children before carrying them to a sitter. When eventually she could find no one to mind them, she lost her welfare allotments.
>
> . . . .
>
> Mrs. Rosie Bryant, an 84-year-old welfare recipient so poor that she and her husband had to mortgage their mule, has a more down-to-earth summation of things. [She discussed] at the 1966 meeting [of the Illinois Advisory Commission to the U.S. Civil Rights Commission] what civil

rights laws had done for her. "Listen," she says, "I don't see a bit of difference now than I did way back in '51 or '52 in the civil rights. It hasn't reached us. I reckon it's on its way, but it ain't got here yet."[48]

The complaint plainly lacks colorful prose; but more than that, it misses the poignant personal stories of the two women. Additionally, it loses the context of their problems, which involve far more than the Voting Rights Act. "The problem" encompasses even more than a poor economy in which the few employers hire fewer blacks than they might. Employers, cotton growers, and the local welfare office combined their power to control Cairo's black citizens. Finally, the complaint fails to note that the purported racial progress of recent decades had yet to reach Cairo. As lawyers, we failed to argue that racial justice would only reach the town if the court brought it.

The complaint alleges the maintenance of segregation throughout the history of Cairo, and cites examples:

> Public facilities owned by private individuals have been historically operated on a racially segregated basis . . . . Entertainment facilities in Cairo often have been closed to avoid court ordered integration. The only public swimming pool was closed in the mid-1960's.

Contrast this with the journalist's version:

> [Anthony Patterson] was eight when Cairo's only swimming pool closed rather than integrate; through quiet hot summers he watched weeds grow until they choked the pool. * * * He says: "This town is so far behind and backwards, it's really a shame. You don't think about staying and looking for a job. You can't even work as a bagboy in a supermarket. You just think about going away all the time."
>
>   . . . .
>
> There were small, sporadic boycotts by blacks trying to force desegregation of public accommodations, and answering violence from whites. In 1962, the city's only swimming pool, which had been operated by the Rotary Club, integrated for two weeks after blacks complained to state officials, then closed for good. From that day until now, the young people of Cairo during the scorching southern Illinois summers have had to drive 30 miles to swim in a pool or risk the Mississippi currents where some have died.

On this issue, the complaint loses the personal perspective, here a story of hopelessness. This hopelessness can only be contagious when those who would otherwise be hopeful are confronted by a resistance to integration so fierce as to deny all children the benefit of a pool in the near-tropical temperatures of Cairo.

The complaint misses something else: the role blacks played in the racial history of their town. They were more than numbers, more than passive observers

---

48   GOOD, [CAIRO, ILLINOIS: RACISM AT FLOODTIDE] at 13-14 [(U.S. Comm'n on Civil Rights, 1973)].

awaiting the intervention of the federal government. They demanded equality and fought for it. Elsewhere in his account, the journalist turns to another example of segregated public facilities:

> At the roller skating rink, there was no bargaining. When blacks in 1964 picketed to gain admission, vigilantes were waiting with clubs. Among those beaten was a 16-year-old named Charles Koen who was destined to become a minister and leader among the blacks, and a living symbol to whites of criminal anarchy seeking to destroy the old order.

This symbol is important to a court that will hear the defendants' worries about black militants and criminal anarchists as an excuse for not involving blacks in their own government.

The journalist reports his interview with John Holland, the City Attorney, and Tom Madra, a leader of the White Hats, a white vigilante group:

> "Listen," Holland says, "I told Preston Ewing [leader of the local NAACP chapter] a dozen times I'm looking for a good colored leader who can control his people. Everybody looks for a good black man nowadays. You find one and you've got liquid gold."
>
> "They put one on the Fire Department," Madra says, "Even though he couldn't pass the test. He quit. Said he didn't like to sit around."
>
> Holland relaxes in a smile and adds, "He must have been a pretty good kind of Negro," he says, "If he didn't like to sit around."
>
> Madra . . . sits on the edge of his chair, feet drumming and says: "There's no good black leadership in this community. There are some good Negro undertakers and doctors. But that's all."
>
>   . . . .
>
> Do blacks have any legitimate complaints? Housing, for example?
>
> "There's no doubt," Madra replies, "That blacks from other states did gravitate here into Illinois because of the welfare programs and did inherit bad housing. They came here for the largesse. They were unemployed and unemployable. They live by preference in a shanty."
>
> Attorney Holland explains that there are no blacks in government because "there are very few to choose from. There's nothing better than having a good black man on your city council. But the black militants drive them out. We're thinking now of putting two on the council."

The complaint pleads only the result of this matrix of attitudes:

> Black residents of Cairo have been systematically excluded from elective politics in the community. The political processes leading to the nomination and election of partisan candidates for elective office have not been open to Black residents of Cairo . . . . Only one Black, Jacob Amos, has ever been elected to office in the Cairo city government . . . in 1894.

. . . Black residents of Cairo have been systematically denied appointment to and membership on various boards, departments and agencies . . . . [54]

Compare the following passages. Which justifies more compellingly a court's intervention in the electoral politics of a city?

Option One:

The abolition of a ward system of election, and the adoption and perpetuation of the present at-large system for electing City Council members have resulted and will continue to result in immediate and irreparable injury to plaintiffs herein, who have no adequate remedy at law.

Or, Option Two:

It is said by some veteran observers, white and black, that the Cairo power structure . . . discerned in this century that the city was never going to make it big. Many of the vast warehouses along the Ohio levee, once burgeoning with goods in transit among river, road or rail lay empty, padlocked. The bulk of industry coming in was runaway, lured by the promise of cheap, tractable, non-union labor that included unskilled and impoverished men off broken-down farms on the far side of both rivers. A desperate competition among whites for jobs guaranteed their continuing solidarity against blacks who, in turn, could be had for next-to-nothing to do whatever dirty or menial work whites disdained. . . . All these elements, according to observers like former Cairo newspaper publisher Martin Brown, persuaded white men of authority to run the city as a limited fief, resisting change that might challenge their entrenched position, reaping the fruits of stagnation.

　　Robert Lansden, a 62-year-old white attorney and banker whose grandfather wrote Cairo's official history and has a park named in his honor, says: "There are a lot of white people who would sooner see Cairo float down the Mississippi than give a black man a break."

Given my lack of experience in law and life at that time, we might conclude that I omitted these stories from the amended complaint because of my inability to reconcile my two halves (lawyer and person) in a whole life. Another young lawyer, cautious and unskilled. But even the most seasoned attorneys have made similar omissions.

* * *

At this point, we need only acknowledge three propositions. First, there is something in the language journalists and historians use to describe events and people that is missing from the language lawyers use to describe and analyze that same reality. Second, the missing element may have some significance. Third, given the

---

54   *Kendrick, supra* note 5, at 8.

persuasive importance of complaints, it is unlikely that lawyers omit that missing element through mere accident.

In *Kendrick*, we had no other chance to present the lost elements to the court because the case settled. During the years of pretrial discovery and motions, the court acted without the benefit of the stories that make judicial intervention a moral imperative. After the entry of the consent decree, the court enforced the decree. But even then, the court did not act because it truly had been persuaded by force of the story. As one of the lawyers, I grasped some of the elements omitted from our pleading that were present in Good's account of Cairo's history. Hattie told me these stories. I had read Good's book, but I never placed these stories in the complaint. Instead, the complaint thinly pleads the Cairo story, with omissions that are glaring only when we squint past them to the story as told by others. Why do we write complaints so that we must squint to see the stories behind them?

* * *

In the next excerpt Anthony Alfieri urges lawyers and clients to collaborate as equals in telling the client's story. Focusing on the client's narrative can enhance the power of clients and make lawyers more effective.

Anthony V. Alfieri, *Reconstructive Poverty Law Practice: Learning Lessons of Client Narrative*, 100 YALE L.J. 2107 (1991)*

* * *

I. CLIENT STORY

They shut off my lights in November, when my kids' food stamps were first reduced. It was around Thanksgiving. I was twenty-four hours without gas and electric. They shut it off because I couldn't pay the gas and electric bill. I had taken the money from my public assistance check to buy food for that month for me and my kids. I used some of the money for food because I have no food for myself and my kids. I figured I had to buy food for me and my kids or pay the gas and electric bill. It was $121 which I didn't have. I went and took the welfare money and put it together with mine. I even paid the rent. Sometimes I take the money to pay the rent. The rent is too high. Except I couldn't pay my gas and electric.

I went right up to the Department of Social Services and I told them. I had to pay the rent and to buy food. I was there all day long, and finally my case worker gave me the check for Con Edison. To put it back on. And I took it to Con Edison.

---

    *   Reprinted by permission of The Yale Law Journal Company and Fred B. Rothman & Company from The Yale Law Journal, Vol. 100, pages at 2109-2111, 2114-2118, 2131-2136, 2138-2141.

The other shut off I know was my son's graduation, Victor's graduation. I didn't have the money to buy him a suit. So I took the money from the gas and electricity and buy him a decent suit for the graduation. Of course he had a cap and gown over it, but still he needed something to wear. I can't be positive about it, but I remember these two times because my services were shut off. It's a very bad experience when they shut off the electricity.

I remember two times I had to go to them. I go to the Department of Social Services and I show them the disconnection notice. And they tell me they give me the money, to sign some papers. And I sign the papers. Every time they send me a notice is when I go there and I sign the papers, and they send me a notice that they are going to reduce my check so much because they had to take it out. I never know what the papers say. To my knowledge, if I don't sign them I don't get the money for the gas and electricity. So I sign them. That's why I have the money taken out of public assistance every month.

I received a notice when my food stamps were first reduced. I don't know why the food stamps go down. I don't know why they go up either. They sent me my public assistance check. But my food stamps were discontinued. I was without food stamps in November and then December. I made sacrifices. It's very hard. Public assistance money is not enough, let's put it that way.

II. LAWYER STANCE

The above story was told to me by a woman named Mrs. Celeste. I met Mrs. Celeste in the neighborhood legal aid office where I used to work. She told me this story over the five years I helped represent her in a food stamp case. In the years since, I often have revisited the story to gather lessons of lawyering for my teaching and to settle doubts which arose later when those lessons were tested by clients, colleagues, students, and my own research. What I have discovered is that the story Mrs. Celeste told is not the story I originally heard nor the one I told in advocacy.

Mrs. Celeste, a divorced Hispanic foster parent, was a long time food stamp recipient dependent on public assistance for survival. As a consequence of a state food stamp reduction and economic need, she was forced to reallocate her public assistance income to pay rent and purchase food and clothing. The reallocation caused her twice to forego payment of gas and electricity until the local utility discontinued her service, at which time she sought emergency assistance. In short, Mrs. Celeste's story is about state-sanctioned impoverishment.

The reduction of a client's public welfare benefits and the resulting shortage or loss of basic necessities is a common crisis in impoverished communities. For poverty lawyers devoted to serving those communities, the crisis character of a client's situation dictates specific legal tactics and strategies.

This Essay will not review the wisdom of poverty lawyer tactics and strategies in Mrs. Celeste's case. For my purpose, it is sufficient to observe that the tactics and strategies applied satisfied the twin objectives of safeguarding Mrs. Celeste's entitlement to food stamps and invalidating federal regulations abrogating that entitlement. The Essay focuses instead on the discursive and interpretive methods of lawyering, specifically the notion of poverty law advocacy as a medium of storytelling.

I began the Essay with Mrs. Celeste's telling of her story because of my abiding suspicion towards the poverty lawyer's, and therefore my own, method of storytelling. My suspicion is that a lawyer's telling of his client's story in advocacy falsifies the normative content of that story. The normative content of a client's story consists of substantive narratives which construct the meanings and images of the client's social world. Both the lawyer and the client speak in narratives. Lawyer storytelling falsifies client story when lawyer narratives silence and displace client narratives.

* * *

III. Client Narratives

I have been a public assistance recipient since 1970. Be seventeen years. I was employed way back in 1970 before Daniel was born, in Rochester, New York. I was working 1965, 1966, 1967, when my children all were small. Their names are Rosa, Victor, and Daniel. Rosa is twenty-two, Victor is eighteen, and Daniel is seventeen. I also have a granddaughter, Azalia. She is just two years old.

I receive a public assistance grant, food stamps, and Medicaid for Daniel and myself and Rosa. Not the foster children. Victor does not receive public assistance. I don't know how they work it, but I took him out, because he's away at school. So I don't know about that. Azalia does not receive any public assistance either. The public assistance is in a check. Everything is included in that, public assistance and electricity come together. I don't understand how it's computed. The food stamps are in coupons.

A. *Dignity*

My food stamps were decreased from November to approximately February. Five months. Of course it caused me hardship. First of all, there were a lot of things that my kids, I couldn't afford to buy them. I couldn't buy them fresh vegetables, fresh fruits. Everything had to come from cans. Sometimes I run out of rice for my kids and they don't eat no rice. They eat anything; maybe they eat Cheerios or something like that. No-frills food, you know, things that had no frills. I paid less money for them.

But not all the time I have the money. When I don't have the money they have to go without it. There were a lot of things that I had to make cut-downs. I remember what they were. The foods was there, and both my boys always go into the baseball league. They couldn't go because I couldn't afford it. Christmas, they didn't have nothing. You know, there are a lot of things that they didn't do. They couldn't go to the movies, they couldn't go to the Skate Key, where they skate. Sometimes I had to buy in the thrift shop, you know, Salvation Army to buy some things that wasn't even fit to use, so I could use the money for food.

B. *Caring*

I first became a foster parent way back about 1983 some time, March 25, 1983. In that same day I got four kids, that night. When the lady came to my house, she put me down for two; I got four. Right now I have six foster children. You can never say. It could change tomorrow. I received the prior four. All of a sudden I had two, then three, then four. That's the way it goes. Now it's six. They age from eleven years to seven months. Starting with the oldest one, Nilsa, she is eleven years old; she's been with me since June of 1986. Salas is eight, Vilma is six, and Sarmiento is five; they have been with me three and a half years. Pablo is two, he has been with me since he was fifteen days old. Tyrice is seven months; she has been with me on and off, six months.

I didn't know about the foster care money. I found out when I went to the interview. It wasn't much, but you'd get something to provide for the kids. I would take them in because I love kids. I always loved kids. And to have six kids in your house you have to love kids, because money is not everything, you know. The money they give you is not even enough to go around. If you think you are going to get rich on that money, forget it. Don't take care of no kids, then, because it's not going to work out. You really have to have some love, consideration, and know what these kids need.

When they first came to recertify me, they explained everything. They told me the monies you get for the kids you're supposed to use it for the kids, and when, if a child gets sick, or falls down, you know, you have to have money ready to take him to the hospital. If something happens to that child, and you say I haven't got the money, they're going to ask you what you did with the money.

I don't mingle their money, the foster payment of the kids, with my money. I keep it in a separate place in the top drawer in an envelope. When the check comes I just go and cash it. Then I go out and buy all their food. And, whatever is left, then you're going to have to go out and buy clothes and Pampers. Maybe at the end of the month I will have like, twenty or thirty dollars left, and still that's, you know, that's their money. You have to have that money with you at all times to keep the kids. I mean, I want to keep them.

I don't use the money for rent or utilities. I buy sheets for the children's beds. For their towels. You have to get everything separate for those children. You have to have separations in the rooms for everything, dressers, clothes, bedclothes, pillows, everything. They don't give you no bedclothes or anything like that. Sometimes I have to put from my own pocket because the money for the foster kids is not enough. I got reimbursed for some of it, not for everything.

They come to the house and they check the way I keep the kids, how they, you know, the progress. They come visiting from one to three months. It all depends on the time you have the child. They come to find out how much food, the clothing, the sleeping area, how I keep the kids, you know, what are the privacy, what are the things they do. I mean if they are skinny or heavy or they look good, healthy. Many times they asked me how the kids eat, what do they eat, do they like what I make for them, how many times a day do I feed them, do I give them snacks, things like that.

They go with me to the school to visit with the teachers of every child. They do that like in the school year, they do that three times. And court visit. When I go to court for one of the kids or any of the kids. This is about extension of placement, to ask for more time to be left in foster care, or if the child should be returned with the natural parents or with somebody that could take care of them, like related to them. And the natural parents will be there and the foster parents will be there.

The girls have gone back to their home and they have come back even worse than when I first had them. From their mother's house. They came back dirty and everything. I even had to buy special shampoo for lice because these children, when they came back to me, they came back with lice, bugs. I had to buy special shampoo, and I had to buy Tylenol. They were sick with a cold. They come out worse, they got bad habits, swearing and everything. They come to my house and they stop all this. The judge orders the child to go back to the mother and nine months later the child has to be ordered to my house again.

C. *Community*

You have to go once a month for a meeting and they tell you the rule what you can do and what you cannot do with a child. How to discipline the children. What you could do with them, what you can't do with them. When the child is taken out of your house, how to prepare you to be disattached from that child. And when a child comes into the house, how you should behave with them, what to expect. If you get a child that is in need, like a special-need child, maybe he has muscular dystrophy, how to deal with him. If he has a mental or physical problem, how to deal with that. And we have to go to these meetings every month.

There is a psychologist in the agency. And there are other people that come from the outside, talk to you about it. People that go there, you know, the experts, whatever they call them. It's a lot of people that go there. The psychologist talks to us about how to behave with the kids, how to discipline the kids. This meeting has been going on for three and a half years that you have every month, starting in October and ending in June.

D. *Rights*

In order for me to become a foster mother, I have to have earned income for me and my kids. And, the welfare and the food stamps, and the Medicaid, that's my only income. And, that's what makes me, you know, a foster mother. If I had no kind of income, I couldn't be a foster mother. They will take them out of the home, you know, they would figure that I wouldn't have enough income to really take care of them. To become a foster parent you have to have some kind of income. And the only income that I had was public assistance. To be certified as a foster parent, I needed to be either working or on public assistance, food stamps, and Medicaid. That was the certification for me. I was approved by that.

I don't care if they don't pay me. I consider Sarmiento and Pablo my kids even though I have no authority over them. I consider them my kids, and unless the judge orders them to go back to the mother, it is going to be hard on me, but I want to adopt. If they take Pablo and Sarmiento out of my house, I lose the priority of adopting them, and that is my main concern.

I don't want to lose Pablo because supposing you are a mother, how would you feel if they take a child away from you two and a half years old when he comes to you fifteen days old? What trauma is that baby going to feel? It is like putting a child through so many things. The child needs a head start and Pablo has it. He has a head start with me, and if they put him out, I lose the priority of adopting the child. That is the one I want.

I have a baby in the hospital, Tyrice. I don't care if you pay me the money, I want Tyrice. I went to the hospital every day and I don't get paid for that, but I am there every day, not the mother. She will be put in the hospital, and nobody is going to adopt a child who has problems, problems with her nerves, muscular problems. I look at Tyrice and how sick she is. I say she is a baby and she needs love, and that is what I am here for, to give her love. A lot of people don't want this work because it is too much trouble, but if you love kids like I do, it is not too much trouble.

At the time Rosa was with me, I didn't have Azalia. Rosa kept on living with me for a while and then she broke out. I don't know where she went. She used to hang out. Then when she came back to the household, she told me that she was pregnant. She is my daughter; I was not going to tell her, "You can't come into my house." I am her mother. So I left her in the house, I put her back on the budget.

Then I tried to get the baby's father. I spoke to him and told him he was the child's father, he had to come and provide for the child, I couldn't afford to do it, and he said, "Okay." He wanted to give Azalia only ten dollars. I said, "No, that is not going to be the way. You have to go by the court." The court made it thirty-five dollars.

* * *

V. RECONSTRUCTIVE PRACTICES

The task of reconstruction is to find room to maneuver within the traditional practices governing the poverty lawyer's pre-understanding and interpretation of client story. It is not an attempt to overturn interpretive practices. In my view, the traditions of poverty law are too settled to be completely dislodged. I aim instead to pose an alternative set of interpretive practices to counter the interpretive violence of tradition.

* * *

Client voices and narratives exist in both the public and the private spheres of the client's life. Spoken by Mrs. Celeste in welfare and utility company offices, foster parent meetings, and administrative hearings, the narratives emanate from the complex social relations of individuals and families subjugated by economic impoverishment and the miscarriages of the welfare state. The struggle to accommodate and overthrow subjugation is the story told by client narratives.

* * *

This alternative vision affirms the client's ability to muster and assert power both in the lawyer-client relation and in associated legal settings, such as welfare offices, administrative hearings, and courts. Because each client is different, the assertion of power is distinctive in each case. For Mrs. Celeste, the twice-asserted demand for an emergency assistance grant is one form of power. Her insistence on the court-ordered increase of her granddaughter's child support payments is a second form. Her request for an administrative hearing to halt the reduction of her family's food stamps is a third form, and her sharing information with other foster parents about her effort to challenge the reduction in a lawsuit is a fourth.

Specific to each form is a substantive assertion of power tailored expressly to the context in which Mrs. Celeste found herself. When the context switched (for example, from welfare office to foster parent meeting), the substance of her assertion changed. Mrs. Celeste's ability to adjust her assertion to combat the fluctuating aggressions of impoverishment in public and private life is a mark of an empowering subject. That mark is available to the poverty lawyer in client voices and narratives. But as Mrs. Celeste's demands for emergency assistance grants demonstrate, the incidents of power recounted by the client may seem mundane and even redundant to the lawyer.

The client's daily struggle to assert power enables her to resist depictions of dependence and inferiority. In the case of Mrs. Celeste, her struggle materialized in commonplace acts of dignity, caring, community, and rights. Unnoticed in the routine spaces of her public and private life, these acts symbolized alternative forms of knowledge, practices of discourse, and models of individual and collective social action. The experience of daily struggle is the bond connecting client knowledge, discourse, and action.

The ongoing project to expose the ideological underpinnings of poverty law practice does not require absolute renunciation of its traditions; reconstruction rather than disavowal is needed. Reconstruction of the lawyer's narrative meanings and images of the client's world conjoins four practices: suspicion, metaphor, collaboration, and redescription. Suspicion investigates the competing images of the client's world sketched in lawyer and client narratives. Metaphor connects those images to the meanings of withheld narratives. Collaboration integrates the revealed narratives into client story. Redescription announces the client story in advocacy.

A. *Suspicion*

Suspicion is the practice of investigating the primary contradiction of the poverty lawyer's interpretive tradition: the image of client dependency. This image and its attendant meaning are contradicted by the client's public and private assertions of power. These assertions interlace Mrs. Celeste's client narratives which emerge in her continuing struggle to procure emergency assistance grants, feed, clothe, and house her natural children, care for her foster children, assist other foster parents threatened by food stamp reductions, and obtain adequate child support payments for her granddaughter.

The falsification of Mrs. Celeste's struggle to assert power occurred in lawyer narratives. The narratives failed to assign normative meaning to Mrs. Celeste's talk of emergency assistance applications and delays, food stamp budgets and reductions, and child support payments. Similarly, the narratives failed to grant normative significance to Mrs. Celeste's talk of troubled foster children, uncertain agency placements, unpredictable family court decisions, and monthly foster parent meetings. Bound by a traditional narrative stance, I presumed that talk of these experiences was immaterial, except as it might pertain to my legal aid-endorsed strategy of litigation.

In the absence of suspicion, the poverty lawyer pursues an advocacy strategy which overlooks his narrative falsification of the client's story. Yet at the same time, the lawyer is keenly aware of the falsifications inflicted by the courts and welfare bureaucracies constraining his advocacy. He daily witnesses such falsifications in the inconsistency of executive, legislative, and judicial decisionmaking, and in the contradictions of the welfare state. Examples of state falsifications are illustrated by Mrs. Celeste's narratives of erratic family court placements, emergency assistance delays, and food stamp reductions.

Because he bears witness to the events of falsification, the poverty lawyer is able to cast suspicion on the formal procedures, substantive rules, and institutional structures of the "juridical field" within which he practices. In a moment of suspicion, the lawyer can transcend juridical falsification; that moment of transcendence, though ephemeral and fragmentary, is the key to reconstructive practice. Reconstruction compels the lawyer to connect his experience of juridical contradiction with the client's experience of narrative contradiction. The connection may be discovered and vocalized in the lawyer-client contexts of interviewing, counseling, and investigation.

* * *

B. *Metaphor*

Metaphor deciphers the "doubleness" of client events described in lawyer narratives to reveal the meanings and images of client narratives. The promise of metaphor does not lie in the total unfastening of the poverty lawyer's interpretive stance. Metaphor supplies a practical means of revealing a translatable glimpse of an alternative client normative world, a different reality.

Through the practice of metaphor, the lawyer imagines that events composing client story may signify a double meaning or constitute a double referent. The first meaning is prosaic, referring to the concreteness of specific events. This is the meaning inscribed by traditional lawyer practice. In describing these events, the poverty lawyer believes that he brackets his perspective, treating the events as objective phenomena. A prosaic description of the events surrounding Mrs. Celeste's emergency assistance applications concentrates on her utility "shut offs," visits to the welfare center and utility company, case worker negotiations, benefit issuance delay, and recoupment procedures. While accurate, this description refers to only a portion of the meanings and images of Mrs. Celeste's story. A more complete account requires the lawyer to search for a deeper, normative meaning within client events. A metaphorical search of Mrs. Celeste's story reveals underlying narratives describing her struggle to survive while providing for nine natural and foster children. Mrs. Celeste tells of this struggle in powerful narratives in which the metaphors of dignity, caring, community, and rights signify normative references to an alternative meaning of the events in her story.

Metaphorical description and revelation seek to incorporate the empowering meaning of client narratives into the poverty lawyer's hearing and telling of client story. The incorporation need not, indeed cannot, be total. Even if the result is incomplete, the practice of metaphor may enable the lawyer to tell a fuller story of the client than otherwise would be possible. This possibility hinges on the lawyer's willingness to experiment with the practice of metaphor throughout the lawyer-client relation, especially in interviewing—the stage of interpretive practice where the violence of silencing is most destructive to client narrative.

To establish the connection between client metaphor and narrative, the lawyer must look beyond prosaic descriptions of events to discern the metaphorical references within client narratives. Even when obliquely stated, the references speak of alternative client meanings and images. In the case of Mrs. Celeste, the metaphor of dignity represents the narrative of her family struggle to survive a state levied food stamp reduction. The metaphor of caring signifies her narrative of foster parenting, particularly her desire to adopt Pablo and Tyrice. The metaphor of community symbolizes her narrative of foster parent association, while the metaphor of rights represents her narrative of food stamp entitlement and parent-child connection. Each metaphor refers to narratives vital to Mrs. Celeste's story and therefore is essential to reconstructive practice.

Client narratives otherwise silenced by interpretive violence at the interviewing stage may emerge through dialogue in counseling. Counseling dialogue can sharpen the contradiction between prosaic description of events and metaphorical reference. By focusing dialogue on client metaphorical referents the lawyer can increase the likelihood of revealing that contradiction. Had I recognized the multilayered dimensions of Mrs. Celeste's narratives, our counseling dialogue may have been greatly enriched. For example, we might have discussed whether federal litigation best served her needs as a food stamp recipient and her aspirations as a foster parent. Based on that discussion, we might have established a more collaborative advocacy strategy in which we decided together what narratives to present in my telling of her story.

Of course, lawyer-client interpretive boundaries tend to conceal the connections between metaphor and narrative. Narrative revelation is made possible only by the lawyer's ability to recontextualize his investigation outside of traditional boundaries. This recontextualization may involve a series of collaborative acts calculated to remove the hierarchical imprint of lawyer narrative in order to reconstitute the meaning of client story. The goal of lawyer-client collaboration is to permit the lawyer to eclipse momentarily his dominant-dependent relational vision in order to experience an alternative social arrangement. For the lawyer, recognition of this possibility is the threshold to integrating empowering client narratives into storytelling.

C. Collaboration

The practice of collaboration commands lawyer-client co-equal participation in the telling of client story. As a means of guiding all aspects of lawyer-client advocacy, collaboration overrides lawyer claims of neutral and universal narratives. Because client narratives may be unspoken at the outset of the advocacy relation, the lawyer must employ an interpretive paradigm which immediately affirms client voice and narrative. That affirmation must occur at the initial client interview.

The poverty lawyer's affirmation of the client's right to speak her narratives collides with the lawyer's pre-understanding of the client's incapacity to speak. Collaboration challenges the image of the unspeaking client, affirming the client's inherent capacity to speak out in her story, just as in everyday life. By way of collaboration, the lawyer may realize that the banishment of client speech from the public discourse of legal advocacy is due to interpretive practices, not the client's incompetence.

The integration of client-spoken narratives into the public storytelling of advocacy will not come easily. Lawyers are neither sorcerers nor wizards. Client voice and narrative cannot be magically summoned; silence cannot be exorcised. But speech can be nourished when it is prized as the touchstone of client integrity.

The materialization of client speech rests on the inclusion of client voice and narrative not only in interviewing, counseling, investigating, and negotiating, but also in litigation. Making room for client voice in the public telling of client story is a crucial element of collaboration. Because that room must be carved out of lawyer-dominated space, the loss may render him vulnerable as he loses his power to silence. With the fading of lawyer interpretive privilege, the client may experience a change in *public* status, relinquish her strategy of capitulation, and take up the role of collaborator.

The role of collaborator entitles the client to speak her narratives as a full participant in the storytelling of advocacy. Conversely, collaboration obliges the lawyer to center the voices of the client's narratives in the telling of the client's story. Although defined by reciprocity, the paradigm of collaboration does not offer lawyer-client unity; lawyer-client difference usually militates against such union. What collaboration does offer is the commitment to the negotiation of shared responsibilities: the responsibility of the lawyer to discern and integrate client narratives into the storytelling of advocacy, and the responsibility of the client to speak her narratives in public when she believes speech will not endanger her well-being. This last proviso is important due to possible retribution from case workers, landlords, or public officials angered by the client's public act of speaking out.

The mutuality of collaboration permits the lawyer to appreciate the diversity of client narratives, forestalling reliance on a generalized lawyer narrative that is incomplete. To give practical effect to those narratives, the lawyer and client must redescribe the story told in advocacy. There should be no expectation that the advocacy story will comprise the fullness of the client's narratives. Likewise, there can be no guarantee that the narratives will be entirely reliable or reconcilable. Holding the client to a standard of wholly consistent narratives denies the contradictions of the client's world, one defined by the tension between dependent treatment and independent struggle.

* * *

B. Negotiation

The ability to use non-adversarial methods for resolving disputes is an important dimension of advocacy. This excerpt from the now classic text on negotiation presents the "problem-solving" approach to negotiation. The approach focuses on discerning clients' interests, rather than their positions, as a means of finding mutually satisfying solutions.

Roger Fisher, William Ury and Bruce Patton, GETTING TO YES, NEGOTIATING AGREEMENT WITHOUT GIVING IN, (2d. ed. 1991)*

3 Focus on Interests,
Not Positions

Consider the story of two men quarreling in a library. One wants the window open and the other wants it closed. They bicker back and forth about how much to leave it open: a crack, halfway, three quarters of the way. No solution satisfies them both.

Enter the librarian. She asks one why he wants the window open: "To get some fresh air." She asks the other why he wants it closed: "To avoid the draft." After thinking a minute, she opens wide a window in the next room, bringing in fresh air without a draft.

For a wise solution reconcile interests, not positions.

This story is typical of many negotiations. Since the parties' problem appears to be a conflict of positions, and since their goal is to agree on a position, they naturally tend to think and talk about positions—and in the process often reach an impasse.

The librarian could not have invented the solution she did if she had focused only on the two men's stated positions of wanting the window open or closed. Instead she looked to their underlying interests of fresh air and no draft. This difference between positions and interests is crucial.

Interests define the problem. The basic problem in a negotiation lies not in conflicting positions, but in the conflict between each side's needs, desires, concerns, and fears. The parties may say:

"I am trying to get him to stop that real estate development next door."

Or "We disagree. He wants $100,000 for the house. I won't pay a penny more than $95,000."

But on a more basic level the problem is:

"He needs the cash; I want peace and quiet."

Or "He needs at least $100,000 to settle with his ex-wife. I told my family that I wouldn't pay more than $95,000 for a house."

Such desires and concerns are *interests*. Interests motivate people; they are the silent movers behind the hubbub of positions. Your position is something you have decided upon. Your interests are what caused you to so decide.

The Egyptian-Israeli peace treaty blocked out at Camp David in 1978 demonstrates the usefulness of looking behind positions. Israel had occupied the Egyptian Sinai Peninsula since the Six Day War of 1967. When Egypt and Israel sat down together in 1978 to negotiate a peace, their positions were incompatible. Israel insisted on keeping some of the Sinai. Egypt, on the other hand, insisted that every inch of the Sinai be returned to Egyptian sovereignty. Time and again, people drew maps showing possible boundary lines that would divide the Sinai between Egypt and Israel. Compromising in this way was wholly unacceptable to Egypt. To go back to the situation as it was in 1967 was equally unacceptable to Israel.

Looking to their interests instead of their positions made it possible to develop a solution. Israel's interest lay in security; they did not want Egyptian tanks poised on their border ready to roll across at any time. Egypt's interest lay in sovereignty; the Sinai had been part of Egypt since the time of the Pharaohs. After centuries of domination by Greeks, Romans, Turks, French, and British, Egypt had only recently regained full sovereignty and was not about to cede territory to another foreign conqueror.

At Camp David, President Sadat of Egypt and Prime Minister Begin of Israel agreed to a plan that would return the Sinai to complete Egyptian sovereignty and, by demilitarizing large areas, would still assure Israeli security. The Egyptian flag would fly everywhere, but Egyptian tanks would be nowhere near Israel.

Reconciling interests rather than positions works for two reasons. First, for every interest there usually exist several possible positions that could satisfy it. All too often people simply adopt the most obvious position, as Israel did, for example, in announcing that they intended to keep part of the Sinai. When you do look behind opposed positions for the motivating interests, you can often find an alternative position which meets not only your interests but theirs as well. In the Sinai, demilitarization was one such alternative.

Reconciling interests rather than compromising between positions also works because behind opposed positions lie many more interests than conflicting ones.

Behind opposed positions lie shared and compatible interests, as well as conflicting ones. We tend to assume that because the other side's positions are opposed to ours, their interests must also be opposed. If we have an interest in defending ourselves, then they must want to attack us. If we have an interest in minimizing the rent, then their interest must be to maximize it. In many negotiations, however, a close examination of the underlying interests will reveal the existence of many more interests that are shared or compatible than ones that are opposed.

For example, look at the interests a tenant shares with a prospective landlord:

1. Both want stability. The landlord wants a stable tenant; the tenant wants a permanent address.
2. Both would like to see the apartment well maintained. The tenant is going to live there; the landlord wants to increase the value of the apartment as well as the reputation of the building.
3. Both are interested in a good relationship with each other. The landlord wants a tenant who pays the rent regularly; the tenant wants a responsive landlord who will carry out the necessary repairs.

They may have interests that do not conflict but simply differ. For example:

1. The tenant may not want to deal with fresh paint, to which he is allergic. The landlord will not want to pay the costs of repainting all the other apartments.
2. The landlord would like the security of a down payment of the first month's rent, and he may want it by tomorrow. The tenant, knowing that this is a good apartment, may be indifferent on the question of paying tomorrow or later.

When weighed against these shared and divergent interests, the opposed interests in minimizing the rent and maximizing the return seem more manageable. The shared interests will likely result in a long lease, an agreement to share the cost of improving the apartment, and efforts by both parties to accommodate each other in the interest of a good relationship. The divergent interests may perhaps be reconciled by a down payment tomorrow and an agreement by the landlord to paint the apartment provided the tenant buys the paint. The precise amount of the rent is all that remains to be settled, and the market for rental apartments may define that fairly well.

Agreement is often made possible precisely because interests differ. You and a shoe-seller may both like money and shoes. Relatively, his interest in the fifty dollars exceeds his interest in the shoes. For you, the situation is reversed: you like the shoes better than the fifty dollars. Hence the deal. Shared interests and differing but complementary interests can both serve as the building blocks for a wise agreement.

* * *

In the following excerpt, Carrie Menkel-Meadow highlights how the problem-solving approach to negotiation enables parties to express their underlying needs and objectives more successfully than adversarial approaches. She also suggests that the problem-solving approach leads to more just and satisfying results.

Carrie Menkel-Meadow, *Toward Another View of Legal Negotiation: The Structure of Problem Solving*, 31 UCLA L. Rev. 754 (1984)*

"To sue is human, to settle divine"
    – Sign in U.S. Magistrate's Office

* * *

INTRODUCTION

When people negotiate they engage in a particular kind of social behavior; they seek to do together what they cannot do alone. Those who negotiate are sometimes principals attempting to solve their own problems, or, more likely in legal negotiation, they are agents acting for clients, within the bounds of the law.

When lawyers write about this frequent social activity they join commentators from other disciplines in emphasizing an adversarial or zero-sum game approach to negotiation. In their view, what one party gains the other must lose. Resources are limited and must be divided. Information about one's real preferences must be jealously guarded. If the negotiation fails, the court will declare one party a winner, awarding money or an injunction. Successful negotiations represent a compromise of each party's position on an ordinal scale of numerical (usually monetary) values. This Article suggests that writers and negotiators who take such an adversarial approach limit themselves unnecessarily because they have not fully examined their assumptions.

Recently, several analysts have suggested that another approach to negotiation, an approach I will call problem-solving, might better accomplish the purposes of negotiation. This problem-solving model seeks to demonstrate how negotiators, on behalf of litigators or planners, can more effectively accomplish their goals by focusing on the parties' actual objectives and creatively attempting to satisfy the needs of both parties, rather than by focusing exclusively on the assumed objectives of maximizing individual gain. Unfortunately, some of this new literature tends to confuse collaborative negotiation styles or strategies with what must be antecedent to any negotiation behavior—a conception of negotiation goals.[8] These recent analysts have also failed to fully explore their own assumptions concerning the objectives in negotiation. This Article explores those assumptions and elaborates on a framework for problem-solving negotiation that responds to the limitations of the adversarial model.

In order to contrast the adversarial model with the problem-solving model several key concepts must be defined and criteria for evaluation of the models made explicit. The negotiation models described here may seem unduly polarized, yet they represent the polarities of approach exemplified both by the conceptions of negoti-

---

    *   Originally published in 31 UCLA L. Rev. 754. Copyright 1984, The Regents of the University of California. All rights reserved.

    8   Negotiation goals, in general, encompass that which the client seeks to accomplish. It could mean "maximizing gain" but in many negotiations the client will have particular substantive goals that may not include maximizing individual gain. Thus, the particular goals should be considered before any given set of strategies or behaviors are utilized.

ation we construct as well as by the strategies and behaviors we choose. The models described here are based on orientations to negotiation, that is, how we approach our purpose in negotiation, rather than on the particular strategies or tactics we choose. It must be noted, however, that the tactics and strategies we choose may well be affected by our conception of negotiation. A general model demonstrates the relationship of negotiation orientations to negotiation results:

$$\text{Orientation} \rightarrow \text{Mind-Set} \rightarrow \text{Behavior} \rightarrow \text{Results.}$$

The orientation (adversarial or problem solving) leads to a mind-set about what can be achieved (maximizing individual gain or solving the parties' problem by satisfying their underlying needs) which in turn affects the behavior chosen (competitive or solution searching) which in turn affects the solutions arrived at (narrow compromises or creative solutions).

* * *

II. Toward a Model of Problem Solving Negotiation: A Theory of Needs

Problem solving is an orientation to negotiation which focuses on finding solutions to the parties' sets of underlying needs and objectives. The problem-solving conception subordinates strategies and tactics to the process of identifying possible solutions and therefore allows a broader range of outcomes to negotiation problems.

A. *The Underlying Principles of Problem Solving: Meeting Varied and Complementary Needs*

Parties to a negotiation typically have underlying needs or objectives—what they hope to achieve, accomplish, and/or be compensated for as a result of the dispute or transaction. Although litigants typically ask for relief in the form of damages, this relief is actually a proxy for more basic needs or objectives. By attempting to uncover those underlying needs, the problem-solving model presents opportunities for discovering greater numbers of and better quality solutions. It offers the possibility of meeting a greater variety of needs both directly and by trading off different needs, rather than forcing a zero-sum battle over a single item.

The principle underlying such an approach is that unearthing a greater number of the actual needs of the parties will create more possible solutions because not all needs will be mutually exclusive. As a corollary, because not all individuals value the same things in the same way, the exploitation of differential or complementary needs will produce a wider variety of solutions which more closely meet the parties' needs.

A few examples may illustrate these points. In personal injury actions courts usually award monetary damages. Plaintiffs, however, commonly want this money for specific purposes. For instance, an individual who has been injured in a car accident may desire compensation for any or all of the following items: past and future medical expenses, rehabilitation and compensation for the cost of rehabilitation, replacement of damaged property such as a car and the costs of such replacement, lost income, compensation for lost time, pain and suffering, the loss of companionship with one's family, friends and fellow employees and employer, lost opportunities to engage in activities which may no longer be possible, such as backpacking or playing basketball with one's children, vindication or acknowledgment of fault by the responsible party, and retribution or punishment of the person who was at fault. In short, the injured person seeks to be returned to the same physical, psychological, social and economic state she was in before the accident occurred. Because this may be impossible, the plaintiff needs money in order to buy back as many of these things as possible.

In the commercial context, a breach of contract for failure to supply goods might involve compensation for the following: the cost of obtaining substitute goods, psychological damage resulting from loss of a steady source of supply, lost sales, loss of goodwill, any disruption in business which may have occurred, having to lay off employees as a result of decreased business, restoration of good business relationships, and retribution or punishment of the defaulting party. In the * * * case described above, the litigation model structured the parties' goals in terms of the payment of money, when in fact one party sought to purchase and own a reliable form of transportation and the other sought a profit. It may be more useful in any contract case to think of the parties' needs in terms of what originally brought them together—the purpose of their relationship. Can the parties still realize their original goals? Charles Fried describes the classic function of contracts as attempts by the parties to mutually meet each other's needs:

> You want to accomplish purpose A and I want to accomplish purpose B. Neither of us can succeed without the cooperation of the other. Thus, I want to be able to commit myself to help you achieve A so that you will commit yourself to help me achieve B.

Some of the parties' needs may not be compensable, directly or indirectly. For example, some injuries may be impossible to fully rehabilitate. A physical disability, a scar, or damage to a personal or business reputation may never be fully eradicated. Thus, the underlying needs produced by these injuries may not be susceptible to full and/or monetary satisfaction. The need to be regarded as totally normal or completely honorable can probably never be met, but the party in a negotiation will be motivated by the desire to satisfy as fully as possible these underlying human needs. Some parties may have a need to get "as much X as possible," such as in demands for money for pain and suffering. This demand simply may represent the best proxy available for satisfying the unsatisfiable desire to be made truly whole—that is to be put back in the position of no accident at all. It also may represent a desire to save for a rainy day or to maximize power, fame or love.

It is also important to recognize that *both* parties have such needs. For example, in the personal injury case above, the defendant may have the same need for vindication or retribution if he believes he was not responsible for the accident. In addition, the defendant may need to be compensated for his damaged car and injured body. He will also have needs with respect to how much, when and how he may be able to pay the monetary damages because of other uses for the money. A contract breaching defendant may have specific financial needs such as payroll, advertising, purchases of supplies, etc.; defendants are not always simply trying to avoid paying a certain sum of money to plaintiffs. In the commercial case, the defendant may have needs similar to those of the plaintiff: lost income due to the plaintiff's failure to pay on the contract, and, to the extent the plaintiff may seek to terminate the relationship with the defendant, a steady source of future business.

As Carol Gilligan noted in her study of gender differences in moral reasoning, there may be more solutions when one takes account of both parties' needs than when one tries to evaluate the moral hierarchy of whose needs are more deserving.[162] When asked, as part of a larger study on rights and responsibilities, whether a man should steal a drug to save his wife's life when a pharmacist demands a price the man cannot afford, a boy sees the problem as one of property versus life and argues that the drug should be stolen. A girl, in seeking to meet the needs of the man, his wife, and the pharmacist, tries to find other solutions such as borrowing money (either from the pharmacist or a third party) or trying to persuade the druggist to give the man the drug because he comes to see the importance of the woman's life. Amy, the girl in the study, is confident that "if Heinz (the man) and the druggist had talked it out long enough, they could reach something besides stealing."

Whether a focus on the needs of both parties is a particularly female mode of problem solving is still unknown. To the extent that it focuses on a broader way to solve problems it obviously should be of use to all legal negotiators—male or female.

To the extent that negotiators focus exclusively on "winning" the greatest amount of money, they focus on only one form of need. The only flexibility in tailoring an agreement may lie in the choice of ways to structure monetary solutions, including one shot payments, installments, and structured settlements. By looking, however, at what the parties desire money for, there may be a variety of solutions that will satisfy the parties more fully and directly. For example, when an injured plaintiff needs physical rehabilitation, if the defendant can provide the plaintiff directly with rehabilitation services, the defendant may save money and the plaintiff may gain the needed rehabilitation at lower cost. In addition, if the defendant can provide the plaintiff with a job that provides physical rehabilitation, the plaintiff may not only receive income which could be used to purchase more rehabilitation, but be further rehabilitated in the form of the psychological self-worth which accompanies such employment. Admittedly, none of these solutions may fully satisfy the injured plaintiff, but some or all may be equally beneficial to the plaintiff, and the latter two may be preferable to the defendant because they are less costly.

Understanding that the other party's needs are not necessarily as assumed may present an opportunity for arriving at creative solutions. Traditionally, lawyers

---

162 In her discussion of how a boy and girl attempt to decide what is morally correct in Heinz's dilemma (a moral problem developed by Kohlberg to establish the stages of moral development) the boy reasons hierarchically and must come up with "a" solution. The girl attempts to figure out if there are other possibilities that would permit the man to obtain the drug and would also provide payment for the pharmacist. C. GILLIGAN, [IN A DIFFERENT VOICE: PSYCHOLOGICAL THEORY AND WOMEN'S DEVELOPMENT,] 24-32 [(1982)].

approaching negotiations from the adversarial model view the other side as an enemy to be defeated. By examining the underlying needs of the other side, the lawyer may instead see opportunities for solutions that would not have existed before based upon the recognition of different, but not conflicting, preferences.

An example from the psychological literature illustrates this point. Suppose that a husband and wife have two weeks in which to take their vacation. The husband prefers the mountains and the wife prefers the seaside. If vacation time is limited and thus a scarce resource, the couple may engage in adversarial negotiation about where they should go. The simple compromise situation, if they engage in distributive bargaining, would be to split the two weeks of vacation time spending one week in the mountains and one week at the ocean. This solution is not likely to be satisfying, however, because of the lost time and money in moving from place to place and in getting used to a new hotel room and locale. In addition to being happy only half of the time, each party to the negotiation has incurred transaction costs associated with this solution. Other "compromise" solutions might include alternating preferences on a year to year basis, taking separate vacations, or taking a longer vacation at a loss of pay. Assuming that husband and wife want to vacation together, all of these solutions may leave something to be desired by at least one of the parties.

By examining their underlying preferences, however, the parties might find additional solutions that could make both happy at less cost. Perhaps the husband prefers the mountains because he likes to hike and engage in stream fishing. Perhaps the wife enjoys swimming, sunbathing and seafood. By exploring these underlying preferences the couple might find vacation spots that permit all of these activities: a mountain resort on a large lake, or a seaside resort at the foot of mountains. By examining their underlying needs the parties can see solutions that satisfy many more of their preferences, and the "sum of the utilities" to the couple as a whole is greater than what they would have achieved by compromising.

In addition, by exploring whether they attach different values to their preferences they may be able to arrive at other solutions by trading items. The wife in our example might be willing to give up ocean fresh seafood if she can have fresh stream or lake trout, and so, with very little cost to her, the couple can choose another waterspot where the hikes might be better for the husband. By examining the weight or value given to certain preferences the parties may realize that some desires are easily attainable because they are not of equal importance to the other side. Thus, one party can increase its utilities without reducing the other's. This differs from a zero-sum conception of negotiation because of the recognition that preferences may be totally different and are, therefore, neither scarce nor in competition with each other. In addition, if a preference is not used to "force" a concession from the other party (which as the example shows is not necessary), there are none of the forced reciprocal concessions of adversarial negotiation.

The exploitation of complementary interests occurs frequently in the legal context. For example, in a child custody case the lawyers may learn that both parties desire to have the children some of the time and neither of the parties wishes to have the children all of the time. It will be easy, therefore, to arrange for a joint custody agreement that satisfies the needs of both parties. Similarly, in a commercial matter, the defendant may want to make payment over time and the plaintiff, for tax purposes or to increase interest income, may desire deferred income.

B. *The Structure of Problem Solving*

1. Identifying the Parties' Underlying Needs and Objectives

Unlike the adversarial model which makes assumptions about the parties' desires to maximize individual gain, problem solving begins by attempting to determine the actual needs of particular clients. The problem-solving model seeks to avoid a lawyer who acts for a hypothetical, rather than a real, client by creating a "standardized person to whom he attributes standardized ends."[175]

Ascertaining the client's needs will, of course, begin with the initial interview. This is not the place to review the extensive interview literature, but in thinking ahead to the negotiation which might occur, a lawyer might begin by asking the client such general questions as "how would you like to see this all turn out?" or "what would you like to accomplish here?" before channelling the client's objectives in directions the lawyer knows are legally possible. The client may be the best source of ideas that go beyond what the court or the legal system might commonly permit. Once the client's ideas are brought to the surface, the lawyer can explore the needs they are meant to satisfy, and the legal and nonlegal consequences of these and other solutions.

Since so many legal problems are reduced to monetary solutions, consideration of the economic needs and objectives of the client faced with a dispute or transaction is a good place to begin. What are the monetary requirements now—compensation, return on investment, liquidity for payment? What might be the future monetary needs? What is the money needed for? Are any cheaper means available? Are there cash substitutes that are available and acceptable? What are the tax consequences of payment/receipt now? Later? What payment structure is desirable—lump sum, installments? Why? What are the transaction costs or solution costs of negotiation as opposed to litigation?

Next the lawyer might consider that with which she is most familiar—the legal issues. What legal regulations govern the parties' situation? Must there be an admission of liability? Is a legal judgment necessary? Why? Is a formal document evidencing agreement desirable or required? What are the likely future legal consequences of actions taken? What are the parties likely to do if one of them breaches an agreement? What assets will be available in the future for legal action, if necessary?

The negotiator might consider how any solution affects the client's relationship to others. What are the social needs of the parties? How do others feel about this dispute or transaction? Will family members, friends, business associates, employers, employees be affected by actions taken by the parties? If not affected now, how will any of these people feel if things change in the future?

---

[175] Lehman, [*The Pursuit of a Client's Interest*, 77 MICH. L. REV. 1078,] 1087 [(1979)] (paraphrasing Simon, *The Ideology of Advocacy: Procedural Justice and Professional Ethics*, 1978 WIS. L. REV. 29).

The negotiator might also ask the client to consider the personal feelings generated by the dispute or transaction. What are the psychological needs of the parties? Does one desire vindication, retribution, power? Why? What will be the long-term psychological consequences of satisfying or not satisfying these needs? How risk averse are the parties? What are their motivations for pursuing their aims in the negotiation? How might some of these feelings change if they forego litigation now or if they insist on obtaining some advantage?

Finally, the negotiator might also consider the ethical concerns of the parties. How fair do they desire to be with each other? What are the consequences of acting altruistically or dishonestly now? In the future? Will there be feelings of guilt later for "taking advantage" of the other side?

For each of these basic categories of needs the negotiator should also consider how the needs may change over the long run. There may be additional needs which the client has not articulated and which have as yet unrealized consequences. Frequently, some of the latent needs or concerns can be ascertained by simply following up a client's statement of need with an inquiry as to why that item or thing is desired. For each stated need, the lawyer should engage in a systematic inquiry into long and short run consequences and the latent concerns behind those which are manifest.

Ideally, this framework for determining the parties' needs must be considered from both parties' perspectives. At the very least, it should encourage lawyers and clients to consider whether all the potential needs presented by a negotiation have been canvassed. The following chart summarizes this identification or inventory of needs:

	Now (Short Run)	Later (Long Run)	Manifest (Articulated)	Latent (Unstated)
Economic (Including Transaction Costs)				
Legal				
Social (Relationships)				
Psychological (Feelings) (Risk Aversion)				
Ethical/Moral (Fairness)				

As important as ascertaining the parties' needs is the consideration given to the weight or value of clients' needs and preferences. Professor Lehman illustrates the sad consequences of lawyers' assumptions that legal or economic needs are always pre-eminent in importance to clients. In one case he tells us of a couple whose desire to make a gift was thwarted. Listening to their lawyer's advice about deferring the gift for tax reasons, they decided not to make the gift and died before the tax year was over. In another case, a grieving widow headed toward alcoholism in her marital home, refused to consult a lawyer about selling the house. She feared the lawyer would urge her to stay until she reached age 55, an additional year, in order to avoid capital gains taxation. The lesson of such unfortunate tales is that, as Lehman tells us: "the lawyer needs to be careful to discover what it is the client is really about, to give [the] fullest possible opportunity for her interests to be explored, and to avoid the over-bearing assertion of simple money saving." [185]

In negotiation, as in counseling, the lawyer should be certain that she acts with full knowledge of the client's desires. Within the suggested framework, the lawyer ranks the client's preferences in terms of what is important to the client rather than what the lawyer assumes about the "typical" client.

In order to engage in problem-solving negotiation the lawyer must first ascertain her clients' underlying needs or objectives. In addition, the lawyer may want to explore whether there are unstated objectives, pursue those which she thinks appropriate to the situation, or probe the legitimacy and propriety of particular goals. It should be noted, however, that the lawyer's role in exploring latent concerns or discussing the propriety of objectives can come dangerously close to the role of the lawyer in the adversarial model who imposes his own values or makes assumptions about what the client wants to accomplish. Finally, in order to pursue solutions that will be advantageous for both parties, the lawyer must ascertain the likely underlying needs and objectives of the other party. The client is a primary source for this information, but the lawyer should pursue other sources throughout the negotiation process.

* * *

c.   *Just or Fair Solutions* For those who seek the most effective or efficient solutions from a utilitarian perspective, it is enough to settle at a point where no party can gain without hurting the other party. This is the best solution that can be reached when all preferences and needs are taken into account. But legal negotiations leave us with two special non-Pareto optimal problems. First, should the zealous advocate pursue a gain for his client that would cause a loss to the other side? Second, when might the negotiator choose to pursue less gain for his client or actually cause his client to suffer some loss so as to benefit or not hurt the other side? In some sense these questions are on opposite sides of the same coin. Without solving either definitively, the problem-solving model of negotiation may provide some avenues of inquiry.

In the first case the lawyer and client together can consider whether the pursuit of an additional gain at an equivalent or higher cost to the other side is likely to effect the result in an adverse way. The second party may be so hurt, angry or defeated that the solution will be difficult or more expensive to implement. Having answered the utilitarian question, the legal negotiator must then take into account the rules of her profession. If she abides by the rules which require her to be a zealous advocate for her client, she may pursue the "harsh" result. As Bellow, Moulton & Kettleson have noted,[232] there appears to be nothing in the Code of Professional Responsibility which

---

185   [Lehman, *supra* note 175], at 1089-90.
232   G. BELLOW & B. MOULTON, [THE LAWYERING PROCESS: NEGOTIATION] 263-73 [(1981)].

prohibits a lawyer from achieving a result which even she may regard as unfair. Murray Schwartz has suggested that, at least in nonlitigation matters, a slightly different standard of conduct ought to be applied; that the lawyer not necessarily extract that last gain if to do so would be unconscionable as measured by the law in other areas.[234] Still, as a matter of current rules a tough negotiator could (indeed some would say she must) pursue with impunity that additional gain unless, of course, her client instructs otherwise.

Regarding the second case, and as part of the first, the following formulation is offered to those who wish to take the evaluation of a problem-solving solution beyond a utilitarian analysis. In considering the acceptability of a particular solution, both lawyer and client might engage in a dialogue about the fairness or justness of their proposals. Putting aside for the moment philosophical debates about the appropriate measures of justness or fairness, lawyer and client might simply ask each other what, if any, detrimental effect their solution has on themselves, the other party, third parties, or the larger society. No current rule requires the lawyer or her client to act on such a dialogue. However, in considering whether the negotiation problem has been solved in a way which meets the underlying objectives of the parties, asking such questions might prevent clients and lawyers from seeking objectives that they ought not or do not want. Under the present Code, the withdrawal rules will govern those lawyers and clients who may have a differing sense of justice or fairness and who choose to part company over their differences.

In one sense this moral dialogue is simply part of ascertaining the client's needs and thus falls squarely within the problem-solving model. By not discussing these issues with her client, the lawyer may be assuming the standardized, self-interested profit maximizer that dominates the adversarial model. Thus, to the extent that the client does have a need to act fairly, morally, or justly, the lawyer must determine such needs as carefully as she determines how much money the client needs.

Consideration of the justness or fairness of a solution, however, may go beyond a simple needs analysis of the problem. Or, as Fisher & Ury suggest, meeting needs may be secondary to achieving just and objective results. To the extent that the Fisher & Ury model of "principled negotiation" depends on reaching a fair agreement measured by objective standards as a way of avoiding the costs of positional negotiation, it places a greater emphasis on an "objective" agreement than on meeting the parties' needs.[243]

In a sense, consideration of the justness of the solution may be a "need" of the lawyer who seeks to participate in a process that accomplishes just results, or at least is conducted in a manner which gives full expression to the autonomy and dignity of the participants. Some commentators would go further and suggest that consideration of the justness or fairness of a solution is not a need, but an obligation derived either from the special duties and obligations of our profession, or from the ordinary duties and obligations of our humanity.

---

    234 Schwartz, [*The Professionalism and Accountability of Lawyers*, 66 CALIF. L. REV. 669,] 678-90 [(1978)].

    243 R. FISHER & W. URY, [GETTING TO YES: NEGOTIATING AGREEMENT WITHOUT GIVING IN] 84-98 [(1981)].

For the lawyer who engages in problem-solving negotiation, assessment of the fairness of the solution may be made easier by all that has gone before. Professor Gilligan points out that moral judgments may be more deeply embedded in the contexts and relationships of the moral dilemmas than in any abstract principles. To the extent that this is true, the problem-solving negotiator who has canvassed a richer set of needs will know more about the context and relationships affected by the problem than the negotiator who simply tries to maximize financial gain.

Negotiations result in agreements which affect the lives of the parties. Parties and their lawyers must finally decide what they want to do. They may consider the rightness of what they do or they may avoid such issues. There is nothing in the problem-solving model which necessarily compels parties to consider the justice of their solutions, unless that is a need, expressed or unstated, of one of the parties. But, if the purpose of the problem-solving model is to accomplish a result which most satisfies the parties, there is no reason why satisfaction shouldn't include knowing that one has done right.

The justness or rightness of a negotiation can be considered not only from the ends produced, but also from the process—the acts of which it consists. This aspect of negotiation is beginning to be explored with some seriousness. Aside from whether one is justified in lying or in overstating preferences in negotiation, the question of how one feels about the process used to accomplish negotiated solutions is not unrelated to the justness of the solution. A problem-solving orientation toward negotiation may lead not only to better solutions, but to a process which could be more creative and enjoyable than destructive and antagonistic.

* * *

Lawyers often make decisions for clients in the course of negotiations. In the next excerpt Robert F. Cochran, Jr., explores the lawyer's duty to let clients make decisions that arise in negotiation.

Robert F. Cochran, Jr., *Legal Representation and the Next Steps Toward Client Control: Attorney Malpractice and the Failure to Allow the Client to Control Negotiation and Pursue Alternatives to Litigation*, 47 WASH. & LEE L. REV. 819 (1990)*

I. INTRODUCTION

There is a broad consensus within Western ethical systems in support of the principle of autonomy; to the extent reasonably possible, individuals should control decisions that affect them. Based on this principle of autonomy, doctors are subject to malpractice liability if they fail to obtain the informed consent of patients prior to medical treatment; they must inform the patients of the risks of and alternatives to

---

*   Reprinted with permission.

medical treatment, and allow the patient to choose whether to undergo the treatment. However, the legal system has been slow to apply a similar duty to lawyers. While lawyers have a professional duty to allow clients to make some choices during legal representation, they are not required to allow clients to make many other significant decisions. It is ironic that the lawyer, who under our system of legal representation is intended to protect the client's autonomy from unjustifiable interference by the state or other individuals, can become an additional source of interference with the client's autonomy. This article addresses the question of what decisions the client should control during legal representation, and the steps that courts are likely to take in the development of a right of client control.

* * *

V. Next Steps Toward Client Control: The Client's Right to Control Negotiation and to Pursue Alternatives to Litigation

* * *

A. The Client's Right to Control Negotiation

1. The Interests of the Client in Negotiation Decisions

The outcome of negotiations is generally of great importance to clients in legal representation, whether the lawyer is negotiating a transaction or the resolution of a dispute. In negotiation of a transaction, if a favorable agreement is lost because the lawyer does not involve the client in decisionmaking, then the client has lost the benefit of the favorable agreement. In negotiation of a dispute, avoiding litigation can have several potential advantages to the client. It can limit uncertainty, speed resolution, and enable the parties to tailor a settlement to meet their special needs. If an attorney fails to negotiate a settlement that could have been obtained had the client controlled the negotiation, the case is tried, and the client loses, the client has lost the benefit that the client would have had if the parties had settled.

Many decisions that are made during negotiation are likely to affect the outcome. Some choices enhance the likelihood that a settlement, if obtained, will be favorable to a client, but also create a greater risk of deadlock. It is the client that will suffer the most significant loss if there is a bad settlement or if there is a deadlock, and the client should control the significant decisions during negotiation.

2. Negotiation and the Lawyer's Conflict of Interest

Courts require a lawyer that is representing both a defendant in a civil case and the defendant's liability insurance company to provide the defendant with a substantial amount of information that will affect the decision whether or not to settle. The attorney must:

> advise and counsel a client as to all facts, circumstances and consequences which are necessary to enable the client to make an informed decision on matters such as the likelihood of an excess verdict and the desirability of attempting settlement within the policy limits.[156]

---

156 Garris v. Severson, Merson, Berke & Melchior, 252 Cal. Rptr. 204, 206 (Cal. Ct. App. 1988) (Order not published). * * *

This duty is based on the conflict of interest between the insurance company and the defendant, both of whom are clients of the attorney. However, this is not the only situation in which a conflict of interest is likely to interfere with an attorney's decisionmaking during negotiation. Often, there is a conflict of interest between the lawyer and the client in negotiation decisions, and the lawyer should always have the responsibility to allow the client to make significant negotiation decisions. Conflicts of interest between the lawyer and the client during negotiation are both likely to arise and likely to affect the lawyer's actions.

Several types of conflicts of interest are likely during negotiation of a dispute because lawyers have a great interest in whether or not a case is litigated, and the lawyer's interest often differs from that of the client. First, the financial arrangements between the attorney and the client may create a conflict of interest. If lawyers are handling a case on a contingency fee basis, it is generally in their interest to get a quick settlement, even if substantial negotiation or litigation might generate a larger recovery for the client. Second, the workload of the attorney may create a conflict of interest. If lawyers are overworked, it will be in their interest to settle cases quickly, whereas if they are underworked and they are employed on an hourly basis, it will be in their interest to negotiate for a longer period of time or litigate. Third, potential publicity from the trial of a case may create a conflict of interest. In some cases, it may be in a lawyer's interest to litigate a case and get some publicity, rather than negotiate a settlement. In cases that lawyers are likely to lose, they may be tempted to settle rather than risk negative publicity. Finally, the interest of the lawyer in developing a reputation for handling cases in a certain manner may run counter to the interest of the client. For example, a lawyer may want to develop a reputation for hardball negotiation, and may not want to undercut that reputation by taking a conciliatory approach, even when a conciliatory approach would be in the interest of the client.

In addition to the likelihood that the lawyer and client will have a conflict of interest in negotiation, a conflict of interest is more likely to influence the attorney's actions in negotiation than in litigation. Whereas litigation takes place in public, in front of the client, the judge, and, in some cases, the press, negotiation generally takes place in private between the attorneys. During negotiation, the client is not present to oversee the behavior of the attorney, and attorneys do not risk bad publicity from a performance that is influenced by their own interests. An attorney for the opposing side is likely to be more than happy to quietly take advantage of an attorney that is ineffective because of a conflict of interest. The effects of these conflicts of interest can be diminished if the client has the right to make the significant negotiation decisions.

3. The Ability of the Client to Make Negotiation Decisions

It may be that there is justification for leaving much of the decisionmaking authority with the lawyer in litigation, where many of the decisions are technical or urgent, but negotiation decisions, generally, are not so technical or urgent as litigation decisions. Negotiation choices may be difficult, but, generally, the client can understand the risks and benefits of the alternatives. The lawyer should play an important role in explaining the likelihood of various results under the alternatives, but lawyers should allow clients to make the choices in light of their own values and risk preferences.

In many situations, the client may have advantages over the attorney in making negotiation decisions. The client may know the opposing party and have a better understanding than the attorney of how that party is likely to react to various strategic behavior. The client also may have a better knowledge of some aspects of the subject over which the parties are negotiating. This knowledge may enable the client to think of creative means of arranging a deal or settling a case that will benefit both sides.[164] These abilities justify client control of negotiation decisions.

4. Beyond the Settlement Offer Precedent

Courts have established that lawyers must have client authority before they make settlement offers and that they must present settlement offers to clients. This right is justified by the importance of the decision to the client and the likely conflict of interest between the lawyer and the client. The settlement offer rules, however, do not sufficiently protect the interest of clients in controlling settlement choices. There are many other choices that are made during negotiation that are important to the client.

A decision by the Pennsylvania Supreme Court in 1989 suggests a willingness on the part of courts to broaden the choices attorneys must give to clients during negotiation. In *Rizzo v. Haines*,[167] the plaintiff had been injured when a Philadelphia police car struck the plaintiff's car in the rear.[168] The plaintiff was paralyzed. Plaintiff, represented by an attorney, brought suit against the city of Philadelphia. During the course of a settlement conference, the trial judge suggested a settlement figure of $550,000. Plaintiff's attorney immediately rejected this figure. Later, during the course of the trial, the attorney for the city told plaintiff's attorney, "Look, I've got more than 550, what do you really want," to which plaintiff's attorney's only reply was "$2 million," the amount of the plaintiff's previously rejected offer. The plaintiff's attorney never discussed the judge's suggested settlement figure or the city attorney's statement of authority with the plaintiff. "[T]here was also evidence that [plaintiff's attorney] considered the opportunity to try the case to be a cornerstone in building his reputation as a successful plaintiff's attorney." The case was tried and the jury awarded the plaintiff a verdict of $450,000.

The plaintiff brought a malpractice suit against his attorney. In the trial against the attorney, the city attorney revealed that he had had authority to settle the initial suit for $750,000. For the malpractice cause of action, the trial court awarded the plaintiff $300,000, which represented the difference between the verdict obtained in

---

164 An initial decision that attorneys often do not even consider is the question of who does the negotiating. In recent years, there has been a growing interest in having direct negotiation between the parties to a business dispute. Such negotiations can yield superior results to those conducted by the lawyers because the parties to the dispute are more familiar than their attorneys with their business and can respond more quickly and creatively to proposals. They can look at the complete business picture, unconstrained by the parameters imposed by legal doctrine. * * *

167 520 Pa. 484, 555 A.2d 58 (1989).

168 Rizzo v. Haines, 520 Pa. 484, 488, 555 A.2d at 60 (1989).

the original trial and the city attorney's settlement authority. The Pennsylvania Supreme Court affirmed the trial court's order, which stated that:

> [Plaintiff's attorney] did not properly discuss [the City's] inquiry/offer with the plaintiff. He did not properly disclose [the trial judge's] recommendation or [the city attorney's inquiry]. He did not comply with a duty to properly inform plaintiff and to assure that plaintiff heard and understood.

The Pennsylvania Supreme Court also pointed to a policy justification of encouraging settlement as one of the grounds for its decision.

Though the court cited the rule that the lawyer should convey settlement offers to a client, that rule, by itself, does not explain the decision. The city's attorney never gave the plaintiff's lawyer an offer of $550,000, much less $750,000. The city's attorney merely stated that he had authority to settle for $550,000 and requested a counter-offer. The court expanded the right of clients to be informed of settlement offers to include the right to be informed of the judge's settlement recommendation, statements by the other side of their settlement authority, and requests of the other side for a counter-offer.

Rizzo, however, suggests far more than that the attorney merely must report to the client the judge's recommendations and the opposing attorney's statements of authority and requests for counter-offers. If the plaintiff's attorney had merely told the plaintiff, "The judge suggested settlement at $550,000, the city attorney said he has authority to offer that much, but that is not enough money and I said that wasn't enough," it is unlikely that the parties would have reached settlement. However, if plaintiff's attorney had informed plaintiff of the judge's and city attorney's statements and had allowed plaintiff to control the settlement negotiations, it is reasonable to assume that the parties would have settled. Implicit in the court's judgment may be a requirement that clients control significant negotiation decisions.

* * *

B. The Client's Right to Pursue Alternative Methods of Dispute Resolution

In recent years, there has been a substantial growth in interest in alternative means of dispute resolution. The major alternatives to litigation and negotiation are mediation and arbitration.[202] In mediation, the parties meet with a neutral third party, generally chosen by the parties, who attempts to facilitate the parties' negotiation of a settlement. The mediator helps to facilitate negotiation by helping to define the problem and suggesting options for its resolution. Mediation is like nego-

---

202 Other forms of alternative dispute resolution include the mini-trial (lawyers present their cases to the principals of institutional clients, who then, with the help of an advisor, seek to reach agreement) and mediation/arbitration (begins as mediation, proceeds to arbitration if the parties do not agree). * * * Each of these has proven to be helpful in resolving some disputes, but they have not yet become so common or so widely known that the failure of an attorney to alert clients to their use should subject the attorney to liability for malpractice.

tiation, in that the parties must reach agreement for there to be a resolution of the dispute. In many cases, agreements worked out by the parties through mediation are subject to the review of counsel before final approval by the parties.

In arbitration, an arbitrator, generally chosen by the parties, conducts a hearing and resolves the dispute. The parties generally are represented by counsel. Arbitration is like litigation in that a third party, the arbitrator, decides how to resolve the dispute. The ground rules of the arbitration generally are created by the agreement of the parties. They determine how many arbitrators there will be, how the arbitrators will be chosen, what rules of evidence will apply, and whether or not the decision may be appealed. Courts have generally upheld agreements to binding arbitration.

There are risks and potential benefits to both mediation and arbitration. An attorney should inform the client of these risks and potential benefits and allow the client to choose whether to pursue these means of dispute resolution.

1. The Potential Benefits and Risks to the Client of Mediation and Arbitration

Mediation and arbitration may differ from litigation in time required before resolution of the dispute, cost, effect on the future relationship of the parties, likely result, and procedural protections.

a. Time and Attorneys' Fees

Mediation and arbitration may save the client both time and money. They can save the client time in two respects. First, the parties generally can arrange to have the dispute mediated or arbitrated at a much earlier date than they could have a trial. In litigation, the delay between the filing of a complaint and the trial of a case can be substantial. For example, in 1985, in Los Angeles County Superior Court it took an average of thirty-six months for civil cases to get to trial. Parties can begin to mediate or arbitrate a dispute as soon as they agree on a mediator or arbitrator and arrange for a meeting.

Mediation and arbitration can save the client time in a second respect. Once one of these methods of dispute resolution begins, it may require a shorter amount of attorney and client time than litigation or attorney negotiation. In some cases, mediation will resolve a dispute faster than attorney negotiation, in some cases it will not. Some characteristics of mediation may expedite resolution of a dispute. When the parties meet directly with each other during mediation, they can answer each other's questions and make offers and counter-offers without delay. On the other hand, during mediation, the parties may spend time dealing with underlying emotional conflicts that are not related to the specific problem in dispute.

Arbitration generally will require a shorter amount of time than litigation. The arbitrator is typically an expert in the subject matter of the dispute, and may understand the facts of the case more quickly than a judge or jury. Arbitration results also may not be subject to appeal, and thus arbitration may prevent the long delay that can accompany appellate review.

In addition to the potential time savings, the parties may save attorneys' fees through mediation or arbitration. In mediation, generally, the parties meet with the mediator, without their attorneys. Negotiations between the parties during mediation will require less expense than negotiation for a similar amount of time by attorneys. Mediation requires only one professional fee, the fee of the mediator, during the time of the mediation. However, this savings may be offset, to some extent, by the expense of having an attorney review the agreement. If the mediation is successful, the parties will probably save money. If the mediation is unsuccessful, however, the parties will pay the mediator's fees, as well as their future attorneys' fees.

Mediation creates the largest savings of time and money in cases in which the parties reach agreement and attorney negotiation would not have been successful. Of course, it is difficult to tell whether or not any one case that has been settled through mediation would have been settled through attorney negotiation, but it appears that mediation is somewhat more successful at resolving disputes than attorney negotiation. Therefore, if the parties mediate, the client is likely to save time and money if the mediation is successful. When the client knows the other party, the client may be best able to determine whether mediation is likely to lead to an agreement.

The attorneys' fees in arbitration are likely to be somewhat less than the attorneys' fees in litigation. In arbitration, attorneys represent the parties in hearings that are like trials in many respects. The arbitrator is typically an expert in the subject matter of the dispute, and so the hearing may be shorter, requiring less attorneys' fees than a trial. However, the parties will generally have to pay the expense of the arbitrator, and this may reduce the savings of attorneys' fees created by the shorter hearing. The parties are likely to have a big savings in time and attorneys' fees if they agree that the decision of the arbitrator will be final and thereby avoid the expense of an appeal.

b. The Future Relationship Between the Parties

Litigation discourages communication and trust between the parties. They are adversaries: one party wins, the other party loses, and victory is reduced to a money judgment. Litigation is likely to increase friction and animosity between the parties. The friction that litigation creates can be especially troublesome in commercial cases in which the parties want to maintain a future business relationship, and in child custody cases in which the parties must maintain a future family relationship.

Possibly the greatest value of mediation is that the parties are likely to have a better future relationship after mediation than after litigation. Whereas litigation and attorney negotiation are likely to inhibit communication between the parties, one of the central goals of mediation is to create trust and communication between the parties. Maintaining a good relationship with the other party may be important to the client.

c. Results

The likely result if a case is mediated or arbitrated may be better or worse for the client than the likely result if the case is litigated. Whether, for an individual client, mediation is likely to lead to a more favorable resolution than litigation or attorney negotiation will depend on the client, the other party, the case, and the mediator. Clients with good negotiation skills, i.e., clients that are intelligent, articulate, forceful, and meticulous, are likely to do well in mediation. Clients that have poor negotiation skills are likely to do poorly. If the parties have had a relationship in which one party has dominated the other party, often the case in a domestic dispute, the dominant party may have a great advantage. Additionally, the party with the greater knowledge of the subject of the litigation is likely to do better in mediation. Some mediators will attempt to equalize the bargaining strengths of the parties, others will not.

In some cases, the results of mediation are likely to be better for both parties than would a result reached through litigation or attorney negotiation. The parties may develop a creative compromise through mediation that differs from any remedy a court has power to provide. Attorneys, of course, may reach a creative compromise through negotiation, but the parties will often be more familiar than their attorneys with the subject matter of the dispute and may be more likely to develop a creative compromise. For example, assume that there is a contract dispute between two commercial parties. A court may have only the option of determining which party breached and awarding damages to the innocent party. Attorneys may be concerned primarily with the dispute at issue and may attempt to compromise and settle for an amount somewhere between the likely result if plaintiff had won and the likely result if the plaintiff had lost. However, in mediation, the parties may be able to structure a new agreement in a way that will be beneficial to both parties.

Studies comparing the attitudes of parties toward litigation and mediation show that the parties are more satisfied with the results that they achieve in mediation. They are more likely to comply with and less likely to litigate over agreements that they have reached through mediation.

An advantage of arbitration is that an arbitrator may be more likely to give a correct decision than a judge or jury. The parties can choose the arbitrator based on experience, expertise in the subject of the dispute, and reputation for good judgment. The arbitrator's expertise may be especially beneficial if the resolution of the dispute depends on trade custom and usage. In a dispute concerning a complex area of business, it may be in the interest of a client who wants a correct decision to have an arbitrator with a background in the subject area resolve it.

d. Privacy

A final advantage to the parties of alternative methods of dispute resolution is privacy. Mediation sessions and arbitration hearings of private disputes are not open to the public. The information that the parties convey in the meetings will not be a matter of public record unless the result later becomes the subject of a court proceeding. Privacy can be especially important to parties in a domestic dispute, who consider the matters discussed to be personal, or to parties in a business dispute, who want to avoid releasing information that might place them at a competitive disadvantage.

2. Mediation, Arbitration, and the Lawyer's Conflict of Interest

The decision whether to adopt mediation or arbitration as a means of dispute resolution should be made by clients, rather than by attorneys, not only because of the risks and potential benefits to the client of each of these methods, but because lawyers are likely to have a conflict of interest over whether to pursue alternative methods of dispute resolution.

As to the decision whether to pursue mediation, an attorney's conflict of interest is likely to be great. Mediation generally is conducted by the parties, without the presence of their attorneys. The attorneys lose work because mediation generally does not require as much attorney time as negotiation or litigation. Attorneys will also have a conflict of interest as to whether to pursue mediation or arbitration if they are not familiar with these processes. If a client wishes to pursue mediation or arbitration and the lawyer is not experienced with these methods of dispute resolution, the lawyer may have to refer the case to another attorney. In light of this risk, lawyers that are not familiar with alternative means of dispute resolution will be tempted to avoid presenting clients with these options.

3. Policy Considerations

Courts may be inclined to recognize a cause of action for the failure to allow the client to choose mediation or arbitration, not only because this is an important decision for the client, but also because such a cause of action will encourage mediation and arbitration of disputes. Courts may want to encourage mediation and arbitration because these methods of dispute resolution may help to relieve overloaded courts and encourage reconciliation. On the other hand, alternative means of dispute resolution may limit the quality of justice. This section discusses each of these arguments.

a. Overloaded Courts

As noted in a prior section, the delay before a case can be tried may be substantial. This delay occurs, in part, because of the great increase that has occurred in the number of cases that are filed. For example, between 1960 and 1980, the number of cases filed per capita in the Federal District Courts nearly doubled. This creates problems, not only for individual litigants, but also for the legal system. Numerous commentators and judges have advocated alternative dispute resolution as a means of relieving the backlog of cases in the court system.

An example of the effectiveness of mediation at resolving cases quickly and promptly is the New York "Neighborhood Justice Center" program, in which volunteers from the community mediate interpersonal, neighborhood, domestic, consumer, landlord-tenant, and minor criminal disputes. The neighborhood justice centers have been able to resolve a substantial number of disputes quickly, at a very small cost to the state. It may be that many of the disputes that such programs resolve would otherwise have been litigated.

This article advocates the extension of malpractice liability to attorneys who fail to allow clients the choice of whether to pursue mediation or arbitration. Adoption of this proposal may initially create some new attorney malpractice suits. Eventually, however, the number of suits that are avoided because clients choose to pursue alternative means of dispute resolution are likely to greatly outnumber the attorney malpractice causes of action that the cause of action would initially generate. Once courts clearly establish the right of the client to choose alternative means of dispute resolution, the number of situations in which attorneys fail to present these options to the client should greatly diminish.

b. The Value to Society of Reconciliation

The ultimate goal of many advocates of alternative methods of dispute resolution is not merely dispute resolution, but reconciliation of the parties. This can benefit, not only the individuals involved, but society as a whole. Reconciliation of the parties can reduce the likelihood of future disputes and prevent conflict from escalating into serious, violent, criminal confrontation. As noted previously, the New York neighborhood justice mediation program resolved many disputes that might have otherwise been litigated. It also may be that without mediation, some of the disputes would have led to violence.

c. Will Informal Justice Inhibit the Development of Justice?

There is a concern among some legal scholars that alternative means of dispute resolution will dispense inferior justice in three respects. First, it is argued that alternative methods of dispute resolution create a risk of injustice in individual cases; the more powerful party might take advantage of the less powerful party. Since mediation often does not rely on substantive or procedural rules of law or procedure or on other protections of the adversarial process, less powerful individuals and groups may be treated unfairly. They may be forced into an inferior settlement because they need funds immediately or because they cannot afford the expense of litigation. In litigation, however, judges lessen the impact of inequalities, for example, by asking questions at trial or inviting *amici* to participate.

Second, beyond the risk that alternative means of dispute resolution will yield unjust results in individual cases, is the risk that removing cases from the judicial system will reduce the ability of the system to develop just rules of law. Courts will not be confronted with the opportunity to develop precedents that benefit the disadvantaged. This is an especially great risk if alternative means of dispute resolution become the primary methods of dispute resolution that are available to the poor. As to many issues, there is a genuine social need for an authoritative interpretation of law. If the problems of the poor are increasingly handled through alternative means of dispute resolution, the judicial development of legal rights for the poor may diminish.

A third argument against alternative methods of dispute resolution is that through their use, those not responsible to the public may resolve issues of great significance to the public. One of the values of adjudication is that it vests the power of the state in highly visible officials who act as trustees for the public, and are therefore answerable for their actions. Owen Fiss argues on behalf of litigation that the job of the courts "is not to maximize the ends of private parties, nor simply to secure the peace, but to explicate and give force to the values embodied in" the law.[250] Federal Circuit Court Judge Harry T. Edwards is troubled, for example, by settlement of environmental disputes through negotiation and mediation. Negotiation over environ-

---

[250] Fiss, [*Against Settlement*, 93 YALE L.J. 1073,] 1085 [(1984)].

mental protection standards that Congress or a governmental agency has enacted may yield results that are inconsistent with the rule of law.[251] There is a danger that private groups will set environmental standards, without the democratic checks of governmental institutions.

Based on these problems with alternative means of dispute resolution, some have argued that we should not adopt rules that push parties toward alternative dispute resolution. The proposals advanced herein would not impose on anyone the duty to engage in alternative methods of dispute resolution, but it would probably lead to greater use of alternative methods of dispute resolution and may therefore take some disputes out of the judicial system.

Nevertheless, clients should have the right to choose how their cases are handled. If a client wants a case to be handled in a way that will establish a rule that will be beneficial to society, that should be the client's choice. But, if a client wants to pursue a method of dispute resolution that may require less expense, less time, and less conflict, the client should be able to do so.[254] It may be helpful to consider a medical analogy. In some medical cases, it might be better for society if a patient underwent a new, experimental treatment, but, based on the principle of autonomy, we allow medical patients to control their destiny. The client should control the way that a case is handled, just as the patient controls the choice of medical treatment.

* * *

VI. CONCLUSION

The right of the client to control the important decisions during legal representation should be a part of the client's right to autonomy. Client control will generally yield better results for the client, will limit the effect of conflicts of interest that accompany the attorney/client relationship, and will build on the precedent of medical informed consent. Courts should extend the right of client control, both by giving the client the right to control those decisions which a reasonable client, in what the lawyer knows or should know to be the position of the client, would want to control, and by continuing to identify specific choices that, as a matter of law, are for the client.

Whether or not courts adopt a general standard of client control, they should identify the significant choices in negotiation, and the choice whether to pursue mediation or arbitration, as decisions that are for the client. These choices are of great significance to clients and are within the competence of clients. Client control over the decision to use alternative dispute resolution is likely to lead to greater use of mediation and arbitration, a reduction in the load on courts, and more reconciliation among litigants. If clients can show that the failure of the attorney to allow them to control negotiation decisions and to choose mediation or arbitration caused them to suffer loss, courts should allow them a malpractice recovery.

---

251 Edwards, [*Alternative Dispute Resolution: Panacea or Anathema?*, 99 HARV. L. REV. 668,] 677 [(1986)].

254 Owen Fiss has stated that he would "not urge that parties be 'forced' to litigate, since that would interfere with their autonomy." * * *

C. Mediation

Mediation has become an important alternative avenue for relief. In the mediation process clients have a chance to tell their own stories and express their own needs and interests. In the next excerpt James H. Stark discusses the basic skills and competencies required in mediation.

James H. Stark, *Preliminary Reflections on the Establishment of a Mediation Clinic*, 2 Clin. L. Rev. 457 (1996)*

* * *

A. What Are the Skills of Mediation?

Here is my list of mediator skills or competencies, culled from four diverse but representative sources. Presenting any list of competencies is daunting. Mediation is pluralistic and highly contextual and commentators therefore tend to disagree about the specific skills that comprise mediator competence. Some even doubt that mediation can be reduced to a definable set of behavioral activities. For the time being, I postpone discussion of several mediation skills and strategies that are especially controversial, and present a list that I believe would command substantial (though by no means universal) agreement among mediation practitioners and scholars. (Note also that I focus here only on the skills that mediators utilize once the parties are at the bargaining table.)

1. Communication

An effective mediator must have well-developed communication skills, including the ability to explain, listen, question and, in many settings, to facilitate the communication of others.

Explanatory skills include the ability to introduce the mediation process in terms the parties can understand, answer questions, convey information as appropriate during the process, and to speak tactfully but directly.

Listening skills include the ability to attend to verbal and nonverbal nuance and to convey that attentiveness, to read and understand underlying emotions, to clarify responses empathically and nonjudgmentally, and to summarize content.

Questioning skills comprise the full variety of familiar questioning techniques necessary to develop facts, inferences, feelings and motivations of parties in the middle of conflict.

Facilitation skills refer to the mediator's ability to assist the parties in communicating effectively with each other by promoting honesty in communication, restraining destructive or abusive behavior, uncovering distortions in communication, translating or reframing party statements into positive language that can produce mediation progress, and by regulating, as appropriate, the tension between the par-

---

*   Reprinted with permission.

ties as the mediation proceeds. Effective facilitation requires an understanding of interpersonal dynamics and the ability to deal with strong emotions.

2. *Impartiality*

An effective mediator must convey impartiality, by treating both parties even-handedly and each party with empathy and respect. An effective mediator must recognize and monitor her own biases regarding the parties and struggle not to let them affect the mediation.[30] An effective mediator recuses herself from the mediation if some personal interest, or a prior relationship with, or strong negative reaction to, one of the parties makes it impossible to act evenhandedly.

3. *Agenda Development*

An effective mediator helps the parties develop the issues necessary to resolve their dispute, which may include issues that are suppressed or unacknowledged. An effective mediator assists the parties in determining what issues are amenable or not amenable to mediation and helps them frame the issues in a way that can lead to constructive discussion. An effective mediator helps the parties decide in what order the issues can most productively be addressed.

4. *Problem-solving*

An effective mediator must establish a climate in which effective problem-solving can occur. This includes a number of separate skills: assessing the readiness of the parties to resolve their dispute; helping the parties determine their underlying interests; building, to the extent possible, an atmosphere of cooperation; assisting the parties in developing realistic alternative solutions to their dispute; and assessing these potential solutions in light of the parties' shared and differing interests.

Dissecting these skills in greater detail, an effective mediator must be able to determine whether each party is psychologically prepared to work toward resolution of her dispute, asking questions to determine whether mediation is justified and deferring or terminating mediation where appropriate. This skill requires some understanding of the psychology of conflict.

A skilled mediator must be able to recognize the difference between positions and interests and work with both parties to identify their needs and priorities as well as their rights.

To build a cooperative climate, an effective mediator must recognize when information is being withheld, work to assist open and honest communication, emphasize common values and shared concerns, squelch inappropriate threats and coercion and help each party, to the maximum extent possible, recognize the legitimacy of the other's needs. This skill requires not only empathy, but some understanding of the dynamics of competitive bargaining.

---

30   Although the terms "impartiality" and "neutrality" are often not defined or used interchangeably in the mediation literature, I find Josh Stulberg's distinction useful. According to Stulberg, "neutrality" means that the mediator has no personal preference that the dispute be resolved one way or the other, and that she will help the parties develop settlement terms that *they* find acceptable, even if the mediator finds them objectionable. STULBERG, [TAKING CHARGE, MANAGING CONFLICT (1987)] at 8, 37. * * *

A skilled mediator must create an atmosphere in which creativity and innovation are valued, and in which the full resources of the parties are used to find constructive solutions to their dispute. Included here are the abilities to encourage the free exchange of ideas and to help the parties be patient and keep an open mind in the face of inevitable frustration and impasse.

An effective mediator must be able to help the parties choose effectively from the options they have generated. This skill includes working with the parties to ensure that the solutions they choose are realistic and durable.

5. Drafting

Where appropriate, an effective mediator helps the parties draft a mediation agreement that clearly, fully and accurately reflects their agreement.

B. Specialist or Generalist Training?

Even a cursory examination of this list makes plain that while many mediation skills are generally useful in the practice of law, some are not, or at least not obviously so. All effective lawyers must be skillful listeners, questioners and explainers, but the relevance of "communication facilitation" to many legal practitioners is less clear. Understanding how to draft executory agreements is undoubtedly an important skill for lawyers to acquire; learning to master the skill of evenhandedness—so fundamental to the mediator's role—seems not only irrelevant to, but wholly at odds with, what most practitioners do.

What about agenda development? Josh Stulberg describes the mediator as a "chairperson" who "establishes the format of each meeting" and "is responsible for focusing the discussion and maintaining the control over the parties' behavior." Are these peculiarly lawyering skills? It's hard to say so. And yet lawyers are frequently called upon to preside over meetings and to exercise the self-discipline necessary to keep others on task. Surely these are useful generic skills for law students to learn.

Similarly, the skills listed in "problem-solving" seem to a greater or lesser degree, fundamental to the practice of law. Certainly, effective negotiators must help their clients determine their interests and establish their priorities. Effective legal counselors must be able to help their clients brainstorm and assess potential solutions to their problems. And if assessing the psychological state of one's clients and "building cooperation" are not part of the standard job description of most lawyers, perhaps they ought to be; these are skills that all lawyers can utilize in appropriate circumstances.

Readers will draw their own conclusions, but I agree with Carol Liebman and Barbara Schatz that the skills of mediation are, to a substantial degree, generically important skills for the practice of law. The deeper and more interesting question is how teaching, learning and practicing these familiar skills change—and become more challenging—in the specialized context of mediation.

C. Aspects of Mediation that Complicate Skills Training

1. The Problem of Two

The single characteristic that most distinguishes the mediator-disputant relationship from the lawyer-client relationship is this: Unlike a lawyer representing a single client, or multiple clients with shared interests, a mediator must assist and navigate between two or more disputants with differing, if not hostile, interests. Mediation is often conducted in an atmosphere of high tension and emotion. Within this atmosphere, the mediator's job is to help each disputant state her case, develop an understanding of her interests and priorities and engage in problem-solving—all the while maintaining, as best as possible, balance and equilibrium between the parties.

The need to maintain balance between two people experiencing strong emotions makes the mediator's role uniquely precarious. Mediators must constantly monitor how their interventions affect not one, but both parties. As one of my students wrote, mediation is like "piloting a small plane on an important mission through an uncharted area and a storm"; if any of the mediator's techniques "backfire . . . it might take a very long time to make up ground." Consider how this dynamic may affect the teaching and practice of three representative mediator tasks:

Initial Questioning. It is a commonly stated axiom in the literature that, after preliminary introductions and explanations are completed, a mediator should permit each party to make an opening statement. During this initial "story telling" stage, interruptions by the other party are discouraged, and the mediator assists the party who is speaking to vent feelings, describe facts and broadly develop his or her understanding of the issues at stake. Then it is the other party's turn.[35] Christopher Moore lists a variety of techniques that can be used at this stage to facilitate each party's communication: including restatement, paraphrasing, active listening, summarization, expansion, grouping and generalization.

For any clinician familiar with the lawyer-client interviewing literature, this is of course well-trod ground: The initial "story-telling" phase of mediation is much like the "problem-identification" phase of an initial client-lawyer interview—not an accident, inasmuch as these techniques are premised on common psychological assumptions about communication and information exchange.[37]

But the mediation skills texts are vague when it comes to describing how these initial questioning interventions should be timed and balanced by the mediator. At the beginning of a mediation session, both parties generally are anxious to speak, and any perceived unfairnesses are likely to be strongly felt. How much time can a mediator spend with one party before the other begins to feel aggrieved? If one party is less well organized or articulate than the other, can the mediator take the extra time necessary to help that party develop her story and still appear evenhanded? I do not mean to suggest that there are clear-cut "rules" for dealing with such problems, only that

---

35   *See, e.g.,* CHRISTOPHER MOORE, THE MEDIATION PROCESS 168-69 (1986). * * *

37   The leading skills texts in both mediation and client interviewing and counseling tend to draw heavily on the work of Carl Rogers and other humanistic psychologists. Rogers' "person centered" psychology emphasizes the importance of demonstrating empathic understanding and sincere positive regard for the client. * * *

the tasks of fact development and problem development are more complex and challenging in the context of mediation than in an initial client interview, because the mediator must serve two masters.

Active Listening. Ever since I began teaching mediation, I have had the inchoate sense that active listening is an especially critical skill for mediators to master, and I have therefore spent substantial class time teaching it. As Christopher Moore has written, active listening is a communication technique that allows the speaker and listener to verify the precise content of a statement, ensuring that a speaker has been heard, permits the venting and exploration of emotions and "demonstrates the acceptability of expressing emotions."[38] Learning this skill is obviously important in the lawyer-client relationship, but it seems especially significant in the heightened emotional atmosphere of most mediations.

But as important as active listening may be in mediation, there are also distinctive challenges in utilizing the technique in this context. Again, the need to monitor the effect of one's statements on both parties may complicate the mediator's task of demonstrating empathy to each party.

Consider the following example, taken from Folberg and Taylor:[39] In response to an opening narrative statement by one of the parties, the mediator says: "You are angry and ashamed that you have been accused of not paying your debts." The authors hold this statement out as a type of reflective comment that permits the direct acknowledgment of feelings, that "contribute(s) to rapport and * * * reduce(s) tension for the participants."

Folberg and Taylor's illustrative statement is the kind that a psychologically-oriented legal interviewer possibly might use if she wanted to capture the full emotional content of a client's narrative. Perhaps it is the case that a mediator serves the parties best by making similar kinds of statements, without regard to the presence of the two parties, thereby modeling a willingness to address all the psychological ramifications of the parties' dispute. More likely, however, empathy in mediation must be practiced with some concern for diplomacy, given the presence of two parties. To continue with Folberg and Taylor's example, arguably a skillful mediator should not identify one party's "shame" in front of the other party, or at least should defer naming it until later in the mediation, when a safer atmosphere has been established for the candid expression of feelings.

I have seen no discussion of this issue in the mediation literature and I recognize that its resolution will depend a good deal on context. But it does complicate the task of teaching students active listening—a skill which, as most clinicians know, many law students find awkward enough to master in the lawyer-client relationship.

Issue Framing and Agenda Development. I have previously alluded to the mediator's role in *helping* the parties frame and order the issues for discussion. In fact, scholars disagree about the role a mediator should play in issue framing and agenda development. Some contend that the mediator should take a directive role in

---

38   MOORE, *supra* note 35, at 128.

39   FOLBERG & TAYLOR, [MEDIATION: A COMPREHENSIVE GUIDE TO RESOLVING CONFLICTS WITHOUT LITIGATION] at 112-115 [(1984)].

framing and ordering the issues for discussion. Others argue that the mediator should work with the parties to perform these tasks themselves if possible, taking control only as a last resort and with the parties' consent. Whatever one's view on this issue, issue framing and agenda development are challenging skills to teach students in the context of mediation, again because of the presence of two parties.

The task of "issue framing" in mediation is analogous to the task of problem diagnosis in legal interviewing: In both cases, the professional's job is to define, organize and develop the issues facing clients in a manner that will be most helpful to them. The legal interviewing literature describes some of the challenges lawyers encounter in fully and accurately diagnosing their clients' problems: clients are reluctant to share sensitive information, especially at the beginning of the interview, or misperceive the nature of their own problems, or see their case in unduly narrow terms. For their part, lawyers—who, like physicians, are taught to think in diagnostic categories—often prematurely "classify the flow of reality" into the wrong categories, because of insufficient training or insufficient sensitivity to the unique aspects of each client's situation. This tendency to pigeonhole prematurely, an occupational hazard for all lawyers, is especially a risk for beginning lawyers; how many times have each of us had to send a student back for a second or third client interview, because the student reached a hasty and incomplete diagnosis of the client's case?

Such difficulties are compounded in mediation, and the risks are greater. If the mediation student wishes to assist parties frame the issues themselves, she must frequently negotiate between contesting "images of reality"—conflicts between the parties in their agendas, their views of the relevant historical facts, and/or their fundamental values. Sometimes such conflicts in perception and belief can help elucidate the issues for the mediator. Often, however, they complicate the mediator's task, which is not only to diagnose the issues at stake, but to try to help the parties articulate the issues in a neutral manner which does not favor either side. Articulating the issues fairly requires the mediator to have developed all the relevant underlying facts, including sensitive facts, a task that is also generally more challenging in the highly charged atmosphere of a mediation than in a typical lawyer-client interview.

The mediator who takes it upon herself to frame and order the issues faces an additional danger: the risk of what Greatbatch and Dingwell call "selective facilitation."[48] This is a phenomenon similar to the problem of pigeonholing in interviewing: The mediator leads the discussion in certain directions but not others, facilitates the examination of particular subjects but not others—a consequence of poor listening or deficient imagination or some bias, perhaps unconscious, on the mediator's part. In an ongoing lawyer-client relationship, such oversights will generally be discovered and remedied. Many mediations, however, are one-shot affairs. In such cases, the mediator's selective facilitation creates a risk not just of inefficient service, but of biased, weak and deficient agreements.

The preceding examples are intended to be illustrative, not exhaustive. In ways that I must leave to the reader's imagination, I believe that it is harder to listen, harder

---

48   David Greatbatch & Robert Dingwell, *Selective Facilitation: Some Preliminary Observations on a Strategy Used by Divorce Mediators*, 23 LAW & SOC. REV. 613 (1989).

to question, and harder to assist in brainstorming, assessing and choosing among potential solutions to a dispute when dealing with two disputants in a mediation rather than a single client * * *.

2. *Disputed Visions, Disputed Norms*

As Leonard Riskin has written, "almost every conversation about 'mediation' suffers from ambiguity. People have different visions of what mediation is or should be."[50] Small wonder. Mediation is practiced by persons with widely divergent backgrounds in such varied settings as community storefronts, courthouse corridors, diplomatic anterooms and high school principals' offices, as well as in judges' chambers, if one considers judicial settlement conferences a form of "mediation." Some practitioners and commentators view mediation primarily as a method of case management and docket control. Others speak of its potential for individual empowerment or community self-government. Some writers are attracted by the problem-solving potential of mediation, focusing on its capacity to produce integrative, "win-win" agreements. Others emphasize the relational or spiritual side of mediation, pointing to its capacity to foster communication, ameliorate conflict, "transform" relationships and engender peace. These different and sometimes conflicting visions of the goals of mediation often give rise to different or conflicting norms of practice * * *.

The mediator's proper role is less well developed and more controverted than the advocate's; and as a result some really fundamental questions are up for grabs. This substantially complicates the task of skills training in a mediation program. Consider just two examples:

a. *Should A Mediator Try To Persuade the Parties to Reach A Settlement?*

Conscientious readers may recall one of Carol Liebman and Barbara Schatz's listed goals, thus far not addressed: to teach "in the context of mediation, generic . . . *persuasion* . . . skills that are fundamental to the practice of law." Persuasion and argumentation certainly are the lawyer's stock in trade. Are they also part of an effective mediator's repertoire?

The dominant view in the literature is that mediation's purpose is to solve problems and promote settlement, and many of the skills texts provide mediators with persuasion and argumentation strategies to accomplish these goals. Josh Stulberg tells his readers, for example, to "highlight needs" and "point to common interests,"[58] as well as "to capitalize on inconsistencies as well as vulnerabilities," "try role reversal," and "stroke 'em." He argues that, once a mediator has resolved for herself that mediation is an appropriate procedure for the parties and their dispute, "any agreement [is] better than no agreement at all."

---

50   Leonard L. Riskin, *Mediation Orientations, Strategies and Techniques*, 12 ALTERNATIVES TO HIGH COST OF LITIGATION 111 (1994).

58   STULBERG, *supra* note [30], at 102.

Robert Baruch Bush and Joseph Folger, in a provocative and important new book,[63] take precisely the contrary position. Bush and Folger argue that the "settlement uber alles" orientation of many mediation practitioners often produces agreements that are "either illusory or unjust because of mediator directiveness." Mediation is successful, in Bush and Folger's terms, first "if the parties have been helped to clarify goals, options and resources and then make informed, deliberate and free choices regarding how to proceed at every decision point"; and second, if the parties have experienced a "greater actualization of their capacity for relating to others." Theirs is a transformative vision of mediation, in which progress and success are judged not by the number of settlements reached, but by the fairness of those settlements and by the opportunity afforded to the parties "to handle their conflicts for themselves with dignity, self-respect, and consideration for the other side." Notably, the word "persuasion" is not part of Bush and Folger's lexicon. Indeed, they view any form of shaping or steering by the mediator as inappropriate, because it cannot be done neutrally and risks "displac[ing] or obscur[ing]" "the parties' problems and needs."

What is a mediation skills trainer to do if she believes that both visions of mediation have validity? Perhaps what I intend to do this semester: have her students read both books. Bush and Folger quite clearly assert, however, that a problem-solving, settlement-oriented approach to mediation cannot be integrated with a transformative approach, because "taking one approach means doing the opposite of what is called for in the other." Because I do not know whether they are right or wrong, I do not know whether introducing students to these contrasting visions of mediation will empower students to make their own choices or simply confuse them.

b. Should a Lawyer-Mediator Provide Legal Information to the Disputants and Evaluate their Positions?

This may seem like a no-brainer to litigators whose principal exposure to mediation consists of judicial settlement conferences, special master proceedings, or private mediations in such fields as construction or personal injury law. Court-annexed and lawyer-controlled mediations tend to be highly evaluative: the participants, usually lawyers themselves, want and expect the mediator to "provide some direction as to the appropriate grounds for settlement—based on law, industry practice or technology." They also assume "that the mediator is qualified to give such direction by virtue of her experience, training and objectivity."

In fact, however, the question of whether a mediator should provide such information and evaluation is vigorously contested. The principal tension here is between providing advice and information on the one hand, and retaining the appearance of impartiality on the other. The mediator wants disputants to make fully informed decisions. However, if the mediator gives her opinions, "such opinions might impair the appearance of impartiality and thereby interfere with the mediator's ability to function." Bush and Folger argue that the mediator should never "tak[e] sides, express[ ] judgments or be[ ] directive, all of which are central aspects of advice-giving and

---

63   See generally BUSH & FOLGER, [THE PROMISE OF MEDIATION (1994)].

advocacy," and which add to the strength of one party at the expense of the other. Lela Love has stated categorically that "evaluative mediation is a contradiction." Nancy Rogers, who was one of the first law school mediation clinicians in the country and whose book, *A Student's Guide to Mediation and the Law*, was the first aimed specifically at a law student audience, spends no less than 28 pages addressing unauthorized practice of law considerations facing law student mediators if they provide legal information or advice. She and her co-author conclude: "The widely varying interpretations reached in past advisory opinions make it difficult to predict whether the lawyer-mediator will be deemed to have acted unethically in giving legal information or advice . . . . With their licenses at stake, lawyer-mediators may be hesitant to provide any legal assistance in jurisdictions where the ethical situation has not been clarified . . . ."

I have tried to steer a middle course here. I have no doubt that directive, evaluative law-based mediations can be conducted in an extremely narrow and coercive manner, disempowering parties from settling on the basis of "community norms or values that are broader than those the court can consider." On the other hand, I think that it is misguided to argue that a mediator with knowledge of the law should not share her knowledge with the parties in a law-based mediation—especially if the parties are *pro se*. As Jackie Nolan-Haley has argued, for "parties who choose to bring their conflicts into the public domain of the court . . . law may be an important, if not predominant, value."[80] When settling their disputes, disputants must be permitted to invoke legal norms if they choose to, and the mediator must take steps to ensure that the parties' choices are knowing and informed. In my view, any threat to the appearance of neutrality and impartiality is a necessary price that mediators must pay for party empowerment and informed consent.

* * * Again, these examples are meant to be illustrative, not exhaustive, of the problem of disputed norms. I have already alluded to a dispute in the literature regarding how directive a mediator should be in developing and organizing a mediation agenda. I have mentioned in passing that the relative importance of "communication facilitation" may vary on the setting in which the mediation occurs. Mediation practitioners and scholars differ on other important questions as well, such as, for example, the role of caucusing in mediation, i.e., whether the parties should be separated and what kinds of conversations may properly take place between the mediator and an individual party. The main reason why such disputes occur is because mediation is pluralistic and contextual: parties and program providers will have different goals and objectives in different mediation settings and these varying goals will often help define what is meant by "competent" practice in that setting. Thus, while there no doubt exists a core of generic mediation skills necessary for competent practice in all settings, it is also true, as the Society of Professionals in Dispute Resolution (SPIDR) has recently concluded, that "[a] practice appropriate in one context may be inappropriate in another."

* * *

---

80   Jacqueline Nolan-Haley, *Court Mediation and the Search for Justice Through Law*, 74 Wash. U. L.Q. 501, 518 (1996). * * *

3. The Contingent Nature of Mediation and the Problem of Planning

What kinds of mediation strategies and interventions work in what kinds of disputes? Recent empirical research suggests that mediator behaviors that are effective in improving relationships or producing settlement in one dispute may be ineffective or even counterproductive in another, and that successful mediators are, above all, adaptive: they utilize different substantive and contextual tactics depending on the contingencies that arise in a particular case. Thus, for example, making suggestions for settlement may be positively and strongly associated with settlement when resistance to mediation is low, but negatively associated with settlement when resistance to mediation is high or there are other "dispute problems," such as poor leadership or poor preparation by the negotiators. Substantive pressure by the mediator will impair party relations in most types of disputes, but will less clearly do so when the "dispute level" is already high. Successful mediators utilize a variety of emotive tactics, such as controlling expressions of hostility or, conversely, letting everyone blow off steam, depending on the circumstances of the particular dispute.

Because the contingencies that can arise in a mediation are virtually limitless, the range of potential mediator interventions is also virtually limitless, and some commentators despair that mediation can be taught at all. Beryl Blaustone, who strongly argues that mediation can and should be taught in law school, acknowledges that "[m]ediation is a process which involves complex human behavior,"[96] and which "requires a scientific understanding of conflict and dispute behavior." While many mediation theorists have described identifiable "stages" of the mediation process, it seems widely recognized that because mediation is flexible, informal and reactive, these stages do not necessarily follow a set or linear pattern.

* * *

As Bush and Folger have written, the skilled mediator never knows how the mediation will unfold or what her next steps will be. She must remain always in a psychologically *responsive* posture, reacting to the unique interactions of the parties in each case. * * *

4. The Psychological Dimensions of Mediation Practice

An effective mediator is a skilled conflict manager, able to analyze the parties' relationship, help them negotiate their disagreements and resolve their conflicts. As Bush and Folger have written, mediators "enter" the parties' conflict; they "become participants in the unfolding interaction and have an influence on the way it develops."[105]

In order to be effective conflict managers, mediators must first have some understanding of the psychology of conflict: how strong conflict generally affects people's perceptions and behaviors, the various stages or cycles of feelings that are

---

96   Beryl Blaustone, *Training the Modern Lawyer: Incorporating the Study of Mediation into Required Law School Courses*, 21 Sw. U. L. Rev. 1317, 1326 (1992).

105   [BUSH & FOLGER, *supra* note 63,] at 70.

associated with conflict, and their own individual styles of handling conflict. I believe that effective conflict management also requires a high degree of what Daniel Goleman calls "interpersonal intelligence"[107]: the capacity to understand and empathize with other people, to "discern and respond appropriately to [their] moods, temperaments, motivations and desires," to handle relationships well and "interact[ ] smoothly with others."

* * *

* * * In order to be truly effective in mediation, students must be able to work comfortably at the intersection of thought and feeling. In addition to analyzing and predicting and assessing options (skills ordinarily associated with academic intelligence and I.Q.), students need to be attuned to the often hidden and suppressed emotions that underlie conflict * * *.

* * *

These are no doubt critical life skills, and the notion of improving the emotional literacy of law students is an attractive ideal. But the jury is still out on the question of whether and to what degree these skills can be taught, at least to adults. The difficulty is that these interpersonal skills—empathy and the ability to manage other people's relationships, for example—are believed to be advanced competencies, resting on more fundamental *intra*personal skills, such as self-awareness, self-confidence and the ability to manage and harness one's own emotions productively in the service of one's goals. The roots of all these skills lie very deep within each of us, tracing their origins to early childhood and, perhaps, to the neurology of the brain.

One therefore wonders how much these skills can be improved in a law school mediation program. * * *

In the following excerpt Isabelle R. Gunning expresses concern that, without the mediator's injection of fundamental values, negative cultural myths might reinforce the powerlessness of disadvantaged groups. She recommends that the mediator take an "activist" role to ensure fairness and equality.

---

107 GOLEMAN, [INTELLIGENCE] at 38 [(1995)]. * * *

Isabelle R. Gunning, *Diversity Issues in Mediation: Controlling Negative Cultural Myths*, 1995 J. DISP. RESOL. 55*

* * *

B. Shared Values

Mediation, as a method of resolving disputes, has a long tradition, that is not exclusively American. The American emphasis on non-intervention as the mark of neutrality is a product of the culture. Other cultures have made different choices on the "activism" of mediators. For example in both the Navajo Peacemaker Court and the Filipino Katarungang Pambarangay system, traditional methods of non-adversarial dispute resolution are kept alive which involve "mediators," called peacemakers or barangay captains, who intervene much more actively than their American counterparts even though they too are not decision-makers for the parties. In both these kinds of mediation, the mediators have confidence in their own knowledge of the community values which all participants are assumed to share. Two aspects of these mediations mark them especially: 1) the mediators openly inject concerns larger than the participants themselves; for example, community harmony and even spiritual guidance which they understand the parties share; and 2) the mediators are rarely ever strangers or unknown volunteers or professionals even though they are not to be biased towards one side or the other.

The Navajo peacemaker does not make American style claims of neutrality. He will often be a relative of the disputing parties and his role will involve teaching and even "lecturing" the parties on Navajo values and "how their behavior comports with shared values." The ground rules for a peace making session are steeped in ceremony and tradition, beginning and ending with prayers. Filipino mediators, somewhat like Navajo peacemakers, are comfortable making strong recommendations to the participants on how they should resolve their disputes. Like Navajo peacemakers, Filipino mediators often know the parties. The mediator is not likely to be a relative, but as the local barangay captain (or precinct captain) they will often be familiar with the parties or their situation. Also similar to the Navajo peacemaker, the Filipino mediator, with his familiarity with the community, will have an interest in maintaining the peace within the larger community. The attitude is reflected in the practice of the mediator getting personally involved with helping the disputants achieving agreement. The session does include a spiritual component, like the Navajo Peacemaker Court, and often begins with prayer.

American mediation, in contrast, is more individualistically oriented since American culture is more individualistic than the cultures described (or indeed most cultures). But Americans cannot be said to be without concerns for the larger community and connections amongst its varied members. The non-interventionist model leaves to the parties the decision whether to discuss openly any conflicting feelings between one's individual concerns and one's communal concerns. The parties' ability to make individual, isolated decisions is augmented by the fact that in American

---

    *   Reprinted by permission from the Journal of Dispute Resolution, the Curators of the University of Missouri, and the author.

mediation the mediator and the parties are generally unfamiliar with each other and so all are unaware of anyone's personal values or community status. However, the notion that the mediator should be a stranger to the parties is not one that is necessarily universally shared. It is an interesting comment on the amount of distance and distrust among Americans that we think that we will be more fairly treated by strangers of unknown quantities than by people we know. One can imagine that there are people who find it difficult and unnatural to discuss painful and personal matters in front of strangers; who might well prefer a mediator about whom they have some knowledge or respect or with whom they have had some contact. These aspects of American culture suggest that, as in Navajo or Filipino culture, a more interventionist style of mediation which responds more directly to needs for connectedness and community may be appropriate. On the other hand, the comparatively heavy influence of religion in these other societies' mediation forms underscores the problem of intervention. While many Americans practice some form of religion or nurture a spiritual life and increasingly feel that a religious belief system is important, not all Americans will practice their spiritual beliefs in the same way. Indeed conflicting spiritual beliefs have been and continue to be the source of much conflict between different segments of American society.

The value of respect for the individual reflected in the structure of American mediation is appropriate for our culture and its shared values on individual rights. But it is important to keep sight of the fact that connectedness and community are also values shared in American culture and that the mediation process, in other ways, very consciously nurtures and encourages those values. In a typical, even non-interventionist mediation, certain values of community are assumed to be shared; for example, connection, the ability to agree, mutual respect and peaceful resolution of conflict. Opening statements typically include remarks encouraging the parties to think in terms of their ability to agree and flagging for the parties that treating each other with respect (no name calling or interrupting) constitutes one of the few "rules" of mediation.

Shared values around community are already a part of American non-interventionist style mediation. The issue activist mediation raises involves accepting that the American Creed values of equality are in fact a shared value that consequently is as appropriately injected into a mediation as mutual respect is. Equality as a core American Creed value dates back to the birth of the United States as a separate nation. We really can all agree that equality is a shared American value. But the concern the mediator will just impose her values upon the parties still arises as we struggle with the questions of what "equality" means under any particular set of circumstances. The history of the notion of equality in American culture shows that it is a concept that has expanded over time. For example, "All men are created equal" moved from meaning only propertied white men to adult human beings, both male and female and of all races. But while the fluidity of the definition of equality historically can show how difficult it is to define, it also reveals that defining and redefining core values is an essential aspect of American political and legal life. Constitutional law, in particular, reveals through appellate cases the history of the adversarial legal system in defining the redefining core concepts like equality of various "out" groups—racial minorities, religious minorities, women and gays and lesbians—raising challenges to old definitions and becoming the catalyst for the entire society to craft new definitions.

While the identification of shared values in a homogeneous society can be daunting enough, it perhaps seems impossible to do so in a heterogeneous society like the United States. While the political and legal history of the United States reveals that it is difficult to define and redefine shared values, it also shows that it can and must be done. Some array of articulated or unarticulated shared values will be applied in social life. Without the conflict of definition and redefinition one is only assured that the status quo, the value of the most economically powerful minority will be imposed, not that shared values will result.

In order to structure mediation so that it can work most of the time in favor of everybody, the value of equality must be introduced, injected when necessary. Mediation, then, becomes another locus in American political, social and legal life where ideas about equality are defined and redefined. When parties' conflicts are stymied by the presence of negative cultural myths and interpretive frameworks about disadvantaged identity groups, then the injection of equality values is appropriate so that the parties can try to either identify shared positive cultural myths and interpretive frameworks or to create them.

* * *

The practice of mediation is still in its infancy when compared with the long tradition of litigation. The final excerpt in this chapter contrasts mediation with traditional adversarial approaches and describes the mediation process not simply as a means of resolving a dispute, but as an opportunity for learning and healing on the part of the parties.

Donald T. Saposnek, *The Art of Family Mediation*, 11 MEDIATION Q. 5, (1993)*

* * *

Science and Art

In virtually every area of expertise, some combination of science and art exists. Science describes the structure, methodology, logic, and predictability of a phenomenon, the lineality of an approach, discriminations of the content, and elucidation of the steps for teaching and learning and evaluating particular skills. The word *science* is derived from the Latin for "to know" and characterizes the systematized knowledge, facts, and principles derived from observation, study, and experimenta-

---

*   Reprinted with permission.

tion on what is being studied. The factual knowledge basis of "science" is suggested by its antonyms, *intuition* and *belief*. *Art*, on the other hand, captures the intangible, spontaneous, flowing, unpredictable, intuitive aspects of the expertise. In contrast to science, art does not follow the rules of logic but operates more on intuition, feeling, and style. The Latin source of the word *art* means "to join, or fit together." As such, art is not about systematically breaking down the problem into finer and finer discriminations, but rather it attempts to view the problem holistically, creatively, systematically, from different angles, seeing the parts in their relationship to one another. It does not easily break itself into teachable steps but instead is organically developed. Art demands of the student an intuitive grasp, a conceptual integration, and emotion-based impressions.

Mediation is both a science and an art. The science of meditation has been well documented in the host of books and articles published over the past decade. However, little attention has been directed to the art of mediation.* * *

* * *

Attitude of the Mediator as Artist

In moving from a scientist's perspective to an artist's perspective, the intervenor's outlook shifts in fundamental ways across a number of dimensions. The basic shift in emphasis is from what might be termed linear, logical, analytical, rational, task-oriented thinking to nonlinear, intuitive, holistic, emotional, metaphorical thinking. This might also be viewed as a shift in emphasis from left-brain thinking to right-brain thinking, or as Weil (1972) wrote, a shift from what he termed "straight" thinking to "stoned" thinking. By these terms, he designated not people (as was commonly misunderstood in the 1970s), but thought processes. He noted that everyone has the capacity to think both in a "straight" way (as we do in logical problem solving) and in a "stoned" way (as we do in our most creative moments and in our dreams). Some people use one of these modes predominantly, and most people use each of these modes at different times for different purposes.

The various dimensions across which the evolving artful mediator shifts includes the following (it should be kept in mind that these shifts are always ones of *emphasis*, not of absolute categories):

1. *Shifts from an individual perspective to a systems perspective.* With this shift, the practitioner moves from seeing two disputants who each have opposing points of view that compel the mediator (at least internally) to sort out who is truthful and lying, who is right and wrong, and who should prevail and yield, to seeing the participants as engaged in a systemic dispute that has no single right, truthful, or necessarily correct outcome. From the latter standpoint, the dispute requires resolution via higher principles, through a paradigm shift to a win-win model. Such a perspective gives the practitioner more leverage for moving the couple to focus on a common purpose, since focusing on the details of their disputes is less important than developing a more integrated overview of the bigger picture for their mutual gain. Moreover, in this bigger frame, their needs as well as those of their children can be met simultaneously.

2. *Shifts from a problem-solving perspective to a healing perspective.* This involves viewing the mediation task as more than just reaching agreement; it also involves exploring a host of feelings that may include pain, anger, sadness, grief, anxiety, guilt and regret. This perspective requires that the mediator "connect" with the parties on a deep, empathic level. When the mediator incorporates exploration of feelings (especially those underlying impasses) as a central goal in the mediation process and is able to carry out this process of exploration, a powerful psychological atmosphere is created for helping to heal the wounds of divorce—an atmosphere beyond the basic techniques of mediation.

3. *Shifts from a mechanistic perspective to a perspective of compassion.* Compassion is a mode of relating that involves a deep understanding and acceptance of the pain and personal struggles of each client; through such acceptance, it allows a more natural and healing interactional process to take place between the couple. When operating as a technician, a mediator can help a couple reach agreement in spite of their pain and suffering. However, it is reasonable to assume that a mechanistic approach will produce a qualitatively different outcome than an approach based on compassion. Without compassion, the job may get done but the degree of mutual understanding of the couple, spontaneity of communications, and sensitivity to each other will be of a different quality than what could be possible if the mediator operated out of a mode of compassion for the clients.

4. *Shifts from viewing mediation as just one of many equally valued options for resolving family conflicts to a perspective that proactively affirms that the mediation process is better than the adversarial process (for cases in which there are no contraindications for mediation, such as, perhaps, a significant history of abuse within the family).* This view includes a conviction that mediation is better for minimizing conflict within the ongoing coparenting relationships, is better for the child by optimizing cooperation between the parents, and operates toward a higher goal than simply winning, with its negative by-products of revenge and resistance. In the larger sphere, mediation also models for all the participants and their children an attitude of harmonious resolution of conflict, and thus it is within a spirit of reconciling the world * * * so urgently needed in our global community.

Levels of Analysis

When one considers the practice of mediation in terms of levels of analysis, it becomes easier to appreciate how, as the frame of view enlarges, one moves in emphasis from the mechanics to the art of mediation. A mediator's view of the purview of mediation can be considered on four levels, with each one including and expanding beyond the ones preceding it:

Level I: Solving a Problem. At this level, the goal and frame of mediation remain fixed simply on the presenting content. Solving the immediate problem at hand is the singular goal of the mediation process. This level may operate when a quid pro quo approach is used to divide the assets of a couple or to design some regular schedule of time sharing with their child simply based on the work schedules of each parent. The degree of creativity needed on the part of the practitioner is minimal, since the solution is logic based and involves trading one concession for another. This step of solving a problem, albeit limited in the scope of what may be possible, is certainly one large step up from the adversarial goal of "winning a battle."

Level II: Developing a Dispute Resolution System. This perspective moves the mediator's task beyond the mere resolution of the particular presenting problem to dealing with the couple's communication patterns and rules (Ury, Brett, and Goldberg, 1988). It is based on the adage that it is better to teach starving villagers methods to grow their own crops than to just repeatedly feed them. Developing with the participants preventive measures to quell potential conflicts and establishing systematic rules and principles for resolving and managing conflicts that arise is, in the long run, a farther-reaching and more helpful level of intervention. In addition to resolving the matter at hand, it provides tools for the self-management of future conflicts. This approach demands more creativity on the practitioner's part and requires seeing beyond the particular problem to the future of the couple's problem-solving approach.

Level III: Integrating Conflicting Forces. From this perspective, presented as early as 1924 in the works of Mary Parker Follett, the mediator attempts to continually integrate conflicting forces so that no compromise need take place and neither side must sacrifice anything. Thus, in the now-classic example of two parties desiring a single orange, an integrated solution results when creative inquiry reveals that one party wants the fruit of the orange to eat, while the other party wants the rind with which to make an orange cake. * * *

Such integrated resolutions of conflict demand that the mediator continually blend conflicting forces into a common focus to find a new, integrated solution different from the ones the parties propose. The integrated solution is a growth-engendering perspective and represents a model of creative cooperation in the truest sense of the term.

Level IV: Practical Spirituality: Viewing Conflict as Opportunity. From this perspective, conflict is not seen as a battle to be won, or as a problem to be solved, or even as forces to be integrated. Rather, conflict is seen as an opportunity for creating, learning, and spreading harmony in the world (Crum, 1987). Defining *spirituality* as "connectedness" (see Zumeta, this issue), the goal of practical spirituality is to connect with the parties at such a deep level of empathy and understanding that they are encouraged to redefine their conflicts as common "challenges." Thus, they are empowered to learn about and meet those challenges as partners in a common enterprise, not as antagonists fighting over limited resources.

The mediator's task is to interact intuitively and sensitively with the couple's emotional energies to guide them to a common focus of connectedness across the content of their discussions. Thus, from this perspective, the mediation process is best viewed as an artful learning and harmonizing process for all involved. Through observing, listening, understanding, empathizing, and truly accepting the parties regardless of how they present themselves or their positions, mediators establish a sense of connectedness with each party and between the parties. When it pervades the entire process, this sense of connectedness can greatly contribute to the healing of the relationship as well as to the resolution of the conflicts (challenges) the parties present.

* * *

Success Reconceptualized

The traditional concept of successful mediation is simply the reaching of a written agreement on all matters before the mediator. However, the research on mediation suggests that interventions on levels beyond the mechanics of simple negotiation may be crucial for effective and lasting outcomes. We must move beyond the mere techniques for reaching agreement and reach toward higher levels of awareness and understanding. An effective mediator must demonstrate interpersonal sensitivity to the emotional aspects of the dispute, to the unique thoughts, interests, values, meaning, and goals of each individual participant. Moreover, the mediator must artfully utilize this sensitivity to respond to the deeper needs of each person in a way that reduces defensiveness and hostility through mutual understanding and empathy.

On a broader social level, we must begin to see conflict as opportunity to create change that will benefit more people than just disputants. As our artful interventions for harmonious resolution of their conflicts touch the couple at higher levels of awareness, understanding, empathy, and connectedness, a ripple effect may set in, as they begin to spread these new learnings to their family, friends, divorce professionals, and even strangers with whom they interact. With true global consciousness, we must begin to think beyond the immediate dispute to larger systemic perspectives. As such, each act of mediation not only gives us the opportunity to effect a more fundamental change in our client's ways of seeing and thinking about conflict, but also allows us to increasingly become artists of harmonious interactions for social healing in the world. This, then, could serve as our new expanded vision of success in mediation—blending the science with the art of mediation to effect positive change in the world.

References

* * *

Crum, T. *The Magic of Conflict.* New York: Simon & Schuster, 1987.

* * *

Ury, W. L., Brett, J.M., and Goldberg, S.B., *Getting Disputes Resolved: Designing Systems to Cut the Costs of Conflict.* San Francisco: Jossey-Bass, 1988.

* * *

Chapter 6

THE PUBLIC ROLE
OF THE LAWYER

A. The Justice Mission of Lawyers

In the following excerpt Peter Margulies explores the ways in which clinical education fosters civic republicanism. Shared risk and narrative, two essential features of civic republicanism, also pervade clinical legal education.

Peter Margulies, *The Mother with Poor Judgment and Other Tales of the Unexpected: A Civic Republican View of Difference and Clinical Legal Education*, 88 Nw. U. L. Rev. 695 (1994)*

* * *

I. CIVIC REPUBLICAN THEORY AND THE LAW SCHOOL CLINIC

Civic republicanism addresses how societies can govern themselves. Central to self-government are shared risk and narrative. Such sharing brings community, knowledge, and an openness to the unexpected which is precluded by obedience to any universal, reductive system of rules.

Sharing risk with others affirms that governance is a public concern—a *res publica*. One risk is that things will turn out not to be as one expects, that one will have to relinquish one's assumptions. Sharing the unexpected gives people a stake in each other's lives.

Narratives capture the unpredictability of experience, the possibility of connection, and the proximity of new beginnings. Only the concrete experience conveyed in narrative can persuade others; an exegesis of doctrine without narrative is an engine of alienation. Small encounters, such as moments of self-disclosure which embrace difference, can subvert an entire oppressive regime.

This narrative approach rejects any form of political orthodoxy, either of the left or right. Reductive models which seek to isolate a single factor, such as class, to

---

* Reprinted by special permission of Northwestern University School of Law, Volume 88, Issue 2, *Northwestern University Law Review*, pp. 701-704, 706-720 (1994).

explain change, wilt in the face of narrative's unpredictability. Shared narratives also counter the use of stereotypes—stock stories, told by oppressors without the input of the oppressed. In addition, the concept of shared narratives counsels against overreliance on professionals, who screen out stories which fall outside of professional roles. Immersion in professional roles makes openness to the unexpected impossible.

Shared risk lends special insights to the narratives of subordinated people. Although dominant cultures often seek to suppress these narratives, the stories of subordinated people can teach transformative lessons. Hannah Arendt cites the civil rights and labor movements as central examples. She also focuses on pre-Holocaust Jewish writers and critics, including Kafka and Walter Benjamin, as people who shared risks. These risks included genocide at the hands of the dominant culture, and opprobrium from an assimilation-minded Jewish community which wished before World War II to deny the existence of anti-Semitism. The risks which these writers confronted—Benjamin, for example, took his life at the Franco-Spanish border, rather than be captured by the Vichy forces—granted them a special vision. As Arendt quotes Benjamin, "by climbing to the top of a mast that is already crumbling"[40] in a shipwreck, "tempestuous times could be surveyed better than from a safe harbor."

One ubiquitous risk of narrative is that the listener will get it wrong. Civic republicanism transforms this risk into a strength. Mistakes under a civic republican vision are opportunities for awareness. Stories such as Isak Dinesen's, for example, reveal life's resistance to plans. In Dinesen's own life, Arendt sees a story of hubris—Dinesen's determination to build a new world for herself in Africa. Dinesen's acknowledgment of this hubris fuels great stories about the folly of imposing one's vision of the world on others. Narratives of the revolutionary experience capture this same sense of spontaneity. Arendt discusses mistakes which galvanized the American Revolution, particularly the colonists' belief that by protesting the overreaching of King George III they were merely invoking the authority of a British constitution. The British system has no written constitution. This "mistake" of the framers about the fundamental rightness of self-government subsequently empowered movements for social change in this country. For example, the movement to empower African-Americans, whom the framers had declined to include in their vision of self-government, used the framers' rhetoric to help make its case. Similarly, for Arendt, the martyred activist Rosa Luxembourg's overconfidence in the commitment of the German Social Democratic Party to genuine democracy—crushed when she realized that the party cared more about internal party politics than about effecting change—paved the way for her assertion that revolution comes "from below."

Sharing narratives with other groups can multiply the risk of mistakes. Yet, this sharing also has immense transformative capacity. It can lead to seeing a problem in a whole new way, which suddenly makes the experience of others compelling. Arendt notes that movement toward racial justice in the United States requires dialogue between whites and blacks.[47] She takes as a special indication of the common

---

40   [HANNAH] ARENDT, MEN IN DARK TIMES [Harvest ed. 1968] at 172.

47   *See* HANNAH ARENDT & KARL JASPERS, CORRESPONDENCE 1926-69, at 558 (Lotte Kohler & Hans Saner eds. & Rita Kimber trans., 1st ed. 1992) (critiquing racial polarization in United States).

ground between different subordinated groups the story of a New York City high school contest during World War II which asked students to choose the most appropriate punishment for Hitler. The winner was an African-American female student who argued that Hitler "should have a black skin put on him and be forced to live in the United States." Subordinated groups' determination to make their experience accessible to others permits public action in the larger society.

Sharing narratives is as important within a group as between groups. Shutting off new stories because some group members "insist on talking about facts or events that do not fit [a group's] image,"[50] ultimately shuts off learning for the group, which itself becomes not a force for change, but a crucible of routine. Here, as well, Arendt's examples of Rosa Luxembourg, who struggled against the bureaucratization of the left in Europe, and of Jewish intellectuals between the wars, who dared to openly discuss the anti-Semitism which their parents wished to deny, demonstrate the importance of intragroup dissent.

At its best, clinical education represents the same form of shared risk and narrative. Civic conceptions of education have stressed the importance of risk. For example, Rousseau urged that children be allowed to make mistakes, even those that put them at risk of being hurt, in order to learn.[52] If one makes one's own mistakes, one will "own" the learning one derives from those mistakes. Imposing knowledge from the top down is never as effective. Sharing the risk of making mistakes allows each learner to learn from others. Similarly, people learn best when they listen to narratives which resonate with their own experience. Openness to the questions of students is vital to this process, just as the questions of citizens are vital in civic republican governance.

Clinical education embodies this civic view of learning. In a clinic, new stories happen daily. Clinic stories emerge from modestly scaled encounters; that is what makes them important. Hearing these stories should shake up even the most devoted acolyte of any orthodoxy. No orthodoxy captures the richness of the stories which walk into a law school clinic.

* * *

II. Two Stories Of The Clinic

A. The Case of the Dubious Disability Benefits

Along with students in a seminar that I ran at the City University of New York Law School at Queens College, I represented a citizen who had been terminated from the federal Supplemental Security Income (SSI) program, which provides benefits to people whose long-term disabilities prevent them from working. Our client had a learning disability, diabetes, hip braces, and no fingers on his right hand. He originally went on SSI as a child, based on the presence of mental illness, apparently pre-

---

50   [HANNAH] ARENDT, BETWEEN PAST AND FUTURE [(1954),] at 255.

52   *See* JEAN JACQUES ROUSSEAU, EMILE 111 (Everyman ed. 1911).

cipitated by seeing his father murder his mother. He is also a graduate of a well-respected law school.

It was this last fact that got our client, whom I will call Mr. Gaines, into trouble with the Social Security Administration (SSA), which runs the SSI program. The idea of a law graduate receiving SSI was too counterintuitive for the SSA. Although Mr. Gaines required substantial accommodations from his law school, including tutoring and additional time, to complete the program, this cut no ice with the bureaucracy; weeks after Mr. Gaines's graduation, he was terminated. At this time, SSI benefits were Mr. Gaines's sole source of support. Pending appeals, however, he continued to receive benefits for several months, until he found a job at a government agency. Mr. Gaines had always taken care to notify SSA of his educational and employment plans.

Mr. Gaines had aspirations which, admittedly, were difficult to reconcile with the images of dependency associated with disability benefits. He had gone to law school precisely so he could work at a job he found fulfilling. He did not want to stay home and collect benefits; nor did he want a job which SSA said he could do, such as a ticket taker, gate tender, or minder of automatic machines. Mr. Gaines wanted to be a lawyer because he found the law stimulating. He also believed that, as an African-American, it was important to achieve professional status. He was concerned about biased Caucasians who would label him as indolent; he wanted to be a role model.

However, in the short term, termination of benefits created practical problems, even after Mr. Gaines secured employment. Given the challenges Mr. Gaines faced in law school, he was not sure that he could "hack it" at his new position. He also felt that SSA was sending him and other people like him a message: don't even think about getting an education or a job.

My students over two separate semesters raised provocative questions about this case. One student, one of the most diligent and insightful I have ever worked with, felt that taking this case was an unwise allocation of scarce resources. She felt that we should focus on people who were unable to do work of any kind. Those people had no alternatives; moreover, unlike Mr. Gaines, who as a law graduate arguably was competent to represent himself, other citizens might be unable to do so. In addition, this student, whom I call Mary, felt that the whole notion of using SSI as a transition to employment buttressed the expectation that all recipients could or should work. She felt that this expectation was unfair and oppressive—people should be free not to work, she said, whether or not they had the ability.

Another student also raised resource allocation questions. He noted as well, that he felt Mr. Gaines *could* work, and that saying that someone could not work when in fact he could presented ethical issues. He wondered if we could win this case, and, if it seemed likely we could not, whether we should be working on it.

B. The Case of the Mother with Poor Judgment

In another case, involving obtaining a legal lease for a woman with two children, one with moderate to severe mental retardation, somewhat different issues arose. When the students went to interview the client, whom I will call Ms. Esperon, they returned shaken. Ms. Esperon, who at the time was residing illegally in a city-owned apartment, had overwhelming problems, they reported; she was living from day to day. Ms. Esperon's daughter with mental retardation, an adolescent, had never been to school; her mother ministered to all of her needs. The kicker for the students, who were male—one Jewish, one Latino—was that, with all these challenges, Ms. Esperon was pregnant.

Both students were greatly concerned about Ms. Esperon's situation. They felt that another child would simply multiply her challenges. Of what use was their representation, they wondered, if their client would be stuck on a treadmill of poverty and uncertainty? Both students also expressed the view that it was simply "bad judgment" for Ms. Esperon to have gotten pregnant.

I responded to the students with an attempt to speak for the absent client. What the students viewed as simply poor judgment, I told them, might in fact be one of the few positive things Ms. Esperon could do to affect her life. Having a baby might give her a sense of fulfillment that she found otherwise difficult to achieve. Besides, Ms. Esperon's community might value having children, which would also enhance her sense of self-worth.

I was somewhat directive throughout this process, perhaps because the subject made me nervous. The students seemed to have an attitude that could be construed in one of two ways. On one view, they were questioning the nature of lawyers' roles—what were they really contributing to this client's life through their representation? On another view, they were serving up a vintage middle class stereotype—inveighing against the poor judgment of the "undeserving poor."

The semester ended with Mr. Gaines's benefits case unresolved. It took Mr. Gaines to tell us, some time later, that termination of benefits was in a way a source of empowerment for him—a "graduation" from incapacity, he called it, to match his graduation from law school. On one level, pursuing the benefits case meant to Mr. Gaines that, despite having graduated, he was now to be held back.

I also had some very interesting conversations with Ms. Esperon. Ms. Esperon's daughter with mental retardation was summarily removed from the apartment by the city. The summary action was most likely illegal, and Ms. Esperon's daughter was subsequently returned to her. One reason given for the daughter's removal was that she had never been to school. Ms. Esperon told me she had tried to find a school for her daughter, whom the city placed in a regular boardinghouse with no provision for the daughter's special needs, but no school was good enough. While discussing this difficult subject, Ms. Esperon mentioned that she was pregnant. She told me, without any questions from me—much of my time in conversation with Ms. Esperon was spent listening—that she was concerned about having the baby, because of the difficulties which she confronted already. Although, she said, she was also excited about having the baby—a feeling that grew as the summer wore on and her due date approached—she sometimes wished she could have seriously considered having an abortion. However, she said, her religious beliefs precluded this. I said I realized that her situation presented her with many difficult choices. We ended our talk.

Upon hanging up the telephone, I realized that my students' concern about Ms. Esperon's judgment found an echo in Ms. Esperon's own assessment. My own cozy platitudes about the role of children in fostering self-esteem were also part of Ms. Esperon's perspective. The religious dimension, however, had been a blank for both me and my students. Nor was this the only instance in which Ms. Esperon confounded my expectations. At one point Ms. Esperon told me she had a breakdown, as well as asthma, and could barely leave her apartment. Ever ready with lawyerly advice, I suggested that if she truly found it difficult to keep to her routine, she might wish to consider applying for SSI benefits. Ms. Esperon replied that although her children received SSI, AFDC, and Medicaid, she did not feel that she was disabled enough to seek SSI.

Ms. Esperon ultimately received a lease, more because of her own resourcefulness than because of our advocacy on her behalf.

* * *

III. A CIVIC REPUBLICAN CRITIQUE OF STORIES FROM THE CLINIC

* * *

A. Stereotypes

My students and I let stock stories obstruct a genuine sharing of narratives with both Ms. Esperon and Mr. Gaines. We made two complementary mistakes here. Either we gave the people we represented no credit for possessing agency—the capacity to control their own lives—or we submerged them in images of group behavior, without considering society's role in constructing those images.

Our blind spots were numerous. Most seriously, we did not acknowledge that Ms. Esperon's situation as a single Latina receiving AFDC emerged from the intersectionality of ethnicity, class, and gender. The combination of these three factors marginalized Ms. Esperon not only within the larger society, but also within groups who share one or two marginalizing factors with Ms. Esperon. For example, Anglo society has never viewed Latinas as participants in the polity, but instead has typically relegated them to the caricatured role of the "hot-blooded" female. Feminists have objected forcefully to women being portrayed as exclusively sexual beings. However, these objections have not necessarily aided Latinas, who, as people of color, remain marginalized even within women's groups. As women in poverty, Latina single mothers on AFDC are not merely marginalized, but as a practical matter virtually shut out from the mobilized resources which professional women can generate. Finally, as women, Latina women are marginalized both within the Spanish-speaking and the larger community.

One striking aspect of this intersectionality in Ms. Esperon's case was that we applied male standards to assess her behavior, yet never considered whether men had anything to do with her situation. None of us considered that Ms. Esperon might have gotten pregnant because a *man* failed to use birth control. We also ignored the appalling history of eugenics which for years sanctioned involuntary sterilizations of women in poverty. Moreover, we implicitly held Ms. Esperon to be at fault somehow because she was a single mother. Yet we did not consider the welfare system that still frequently penalizes women for having a "man in the house." We may not have been alone in these marginalizing moves. Indeed, even Ms. Esperon's own community marginalized her by assuming that child care was "women's work," which men need not do.

Mention of work raises another issue: why do we assume that the market is correct when it does not deign to pay mothers for the work they do? In focusing on Ms. Esperon's judgment, we did not consider the role society plays in making larger judgments about what work is worth reimbursing. These social judgments cry out for the exercise of some critical judgment.

A final indicator of our failure to hear Ms. Esperon's story arises in the area of abortion. Our failure even to consider that Ms. Esperon might have religious beliefs which affected her views about abortion stemmed not only from lawyers' tendency to discount phenomena which rational self-interest cannot explain, but also from the habit of viewing reproductive issues as abstractions. For many men, the issue is whether abortion is permissible or not. Since abortion concerns women's bodies, women do not have the luxury of taking an abstract view. For Ms. Esperon, the choice was far more concrete than whether or not abortion is permissible. Ms. Esperon may indeed have been pro-choice in her politics; but the choice she happened to make was to carry her pregnancy to term.

Our interactions with Mr. Gaines were also characterized by stereotypes which ignored the intersectionality of subordination. In Mr. Gaines's case, the intersection of race and disability was salient. The cross Mr. Gaines had to bear was the suspicion that he was trying to "get over" on the world. Because his learning disability was "invisible," he had to contend with society's fear of malingering. Mr. Gaines also had to contend with the dominant culture's stereotype of African-Americans as malingerers. This perception flourishes despite the insights of Jesse Jackson, who notes that African-Americans "work every day" and "take the early bus" to jobs which white Americans do not want. Such inconvenient facts are often lost on white America. Moreover, even the disability community, which has grown steadily over the past twenty years, often tacitly excludes African-Americans, perhaps not deliberately, but simply because no attention is paid to how to include them. Indeed, in its domination by white, middle class persons, the disability rights movement bears a disconcerting resemblance to feminism. Finally, it seems that the African-American community is not necessarily any more effective than the white community at integrating people with disabilities into the mainstream. One group of people protected by federal legislation which bars discrimination based on disability, people with AIDS, has been the target of fear within communities of color, as within virtually all communities in the nation.

Mr. Gaines experienced the ignorance of white, temporarily able-bodied America much more acutely than we expected. His assurance and determination were in constant conflict with a nagging loss of self-esteem which afflicts both people with disabilities and African-Americans coping with a racist society. For Mr. Gaines, the Kafkaesque process of proving eligibility for disability benefits, in which the claimant must demonstrate as completely as possible her incapacity for productive work, ensured a constant drag on self-esteem.

My students and I never appreciated the depth of Mr. Gaines's dilemma. We invested too much in a *homo economicus* view of the world in which getting some sum of money for someone, at whatever price to self-worth, could not be bad. We were thus unprepared for the vigor of Mr. Gaines's conviction that his termination from benefits represented a graduation from dependency.

B. Religion

My students' and my failure to listen to the narratives of citizens we represented led to other unexpected developments. Ms. Esperon's invocation of religion is a good example. We had not considered the possibility that Ms. Esperon might hold religious views which made abortion unacceptable to her. A couple of different strands may account for this failure of perception. First, I am a largely secularized Jew whose religious observance is mainly confined to the annual gathering of family at the Passover seder, celebrating the Jews' release from slavery in ancient Egypt. I identify myself culturally as a Jew, yet I suspect that I am a free rider on that cultural heritage, absorbing it but engaging in little of the religious practice which provides the context for Jewish cultural life. Because we tend to assume that our values are "natural" and widely shared, I probably assumed that Ms. Esperon maintained the same distance from religious practice that I did.

Another, more invidious perspective may have shaped our attitudes toward Ms. Esperon's religion. We may have assumed that because secular liberals and progressives assert their allegiance with Latinas and other people of color, Latinas uncritically endorse a secular discourse of rights which leaves little room for religion in public life. This notion is only slightly more benign than the more visible stereotype of the "hot-blooded" Latina.

Our failure points up problems in contemporary political orthodoxies' treatment of religion. For liberalism, shaped in Enlightenment rationality, religious faith is a suspect incursion of the irrational. Yet Ms. Esperon, like most of us, lives in a world where rationality is often conspicuous by its absence. Lawyers treat the discourse of rights and constitutionalism as a secular religion. Yet this secular religion of rights lacks the compelling narratives needed to move masses of people toward political action. Radicals have a different problem. They dismiss religion on the same grounds that they dismiss rights talk: as another specimen of false consciousness, following Marx's famous assertion that religion is the opium of the people.

In contrast, civic republicanism offers a much more satisfying account of religious experience. Republicanism views religion as a *religare*—a tying back or recollection—of beginnings. Through these ties to origins, people can judge if their society has fallen away from first principles, and take action to reinvent themselves. This kind of recollection and renewal through religion has been a vital source of political action for oppressed people. Viewed in such a light, Ms. Esperon's religious faith is a commitment to renewed beginnings amidst oppression. However, both liberalism and much of what passes for progressive theory ignore this phenomenon. Narratives can help shake up such complacency.

Ms. Esperon's view of abortion illustrates how taking religious narratives seriously can enrich public life. For conservatives, the religious disfavoring of abortion by some poor people is a challenge to extend the concern for life which putatively animates "pro-life" forces beyond the fetus to children already born. At the same time, Ms. Esperon's distaste for abortion poses a challenge to putatively progressive forces. Stressing abortion rights may have less immediate relevance to some poor women, as they define their own needs, than decent housing, freedom from violence, and good schools. Listening to the narratives of women like Ms. Esperon will help create a popular movement more fully responsive to their concerns.

C. Class

Sharing narratives also challenges political orthodoxies about class. Both citizens discussed here had extensive experience with poverty. However, each client had aspirations which both conservatives and conventional critical thinkers associate with middle class values. Mr. Gaines wanted to practice law, a high status occupation, rather than take tickets or mind machines. Ms. Esperon did not want to obtain government benefits to which *she* did not feel she was entitled. She believed that receiving government benefits without meeting the relevant criteria was not a windfall worthy of celebration but an encumbrance to be avoided.

Ms. Esperon's selectivity in applying for benefits did not stem from contentment with the status quo. Ms. Esperon acknowledged to me in our conversations that she was subordinated, because of her class, as well as her ethnicity and gender. She knew government thought it could ignore her, or injure her, without worrying about her doing anything to stop it. This made her angry. Her rage, coupled with her resourcefulness, gave her a small but real quotient of power.

The reality of this situation does not jibe with any orthodox political view of class. The traditional liberal view of class is that it does not exist. In a liberal domain of rights, the same rights are given to all; what people do with them—where they start out and where they finish—is their own affair, and not the province of politics. Anatole France's classic aphorism, "The rich and the poor have the same right to sleep under bridges," expresses this view.

Conservatives, on the other hand, readily acknowledge the importance of class—but only as an index of pathology. "Lower class" people are at the bottom of an entirely legitimate hierarchy in which "merit" rises to the top, and socially deviant behavior defines the bottom. Poor people are poor precisely because they deserve to be. Middle class people are "above" the poor because their values and behavior are superior.

It would be welcome relief to look to the Left for a more nuanced perspective. Unfortunately, conventional critical views mirror conservative doctrine. The conventional critical dictum is that class explains society and history. This perspective tends to essentialize poor people as a univocal mass, opposed categorically to middle or upper class consciousness. The difference between conventional critical and conservative approaches is simply that while conservatives deplore the perceived immorality of poor people, conventional critical theorists celebrate it as resistance to hierarchy.

Our clinical interactions with Mr. Gaines and Ms. Esperon demonstrate that none of these political orthodoxies does justice to the diversity of poor people's experience. Both Mr. Gaines and Ms. Esperon had a consciousness of class which the liberal view discounts. At the same time, their stubborn efforts at self-help subvert conservative arguments that "poverty equals pathology." Poor people historically have practiced mutual aid to secure a semblance of the safe space which the middle and upper classes enjoy. In many ways, it is easier for those on the Right to ignore this history and focus on images of poor people's lawlessness. These images pose no threat whatever to Rightist stereotypes; indeed, they confirm them. Effective mutual aid by subordinated groups is much more difficult to accommodate within the Rightist poverty as pathology model.

Ms. Esperon and Mr. Gaines also reveal the essentialist core of conventional critical views of class. For my student Mary, for example, Mr. Gaines's view of disability benefits as a bridge to employment was simply a legitimation of bourgeois ideology—false consciousness that demonstrates the extent of poor people's subordination.

Classifying Mr. Gaines's views as false consciousness illustrates two problems with conventional critical theory. First, it elevates theory over experience. Second, it amplifies the views of middle class professional theorists over the voices of poor people. Unlike theorists conveniently spared from living the consequences of their theories, Mr. Gaines appreciated that a job, good shoes, and a decent apartment blunt the necessity which rules poor people's lives. Similarly, Ms. Esperon's disdain for benefits whose eligibility criteria she did not meet was not the conceit of a bourgeois *manque*. Instead it was the product of the hardheaded realization that the pittance provided by needs-based government benefit programs permits welfare bureaucracies to exert more control over poor people's lives. For poor people, as for the middle class, paying for something is a sign of voice, worth, and belonging. As a result, poor people's organizations have frequently charged dues.

A civic republican view takes this context into account. Under this view, class is a concept which shifts in its normative and descriptive implications. Poor people can be beaten down—rendered incapable of action by the assumptions of the dominant culture. Yet, at other times, as the example of the labor movement reveals, they can muster forces of innovation which transform politics. Class exists, but its consequences are often unexpected. Normatively, civic republicanism envisions a mutuality between classes, which surpasses the one-dimensional images of class in conservative, liberal, and conventional critical thought. Viewing class in this way is risky; it leaves one without recourse to the pat assumptions of orthodoxy. Compared with the nuances revealed by a civic republican attentiveness to the unexpected lessons of experience, political orthodoxies display a bureaucratic rigidity.

D. Bureaucracy

Bureaucracy clashes with the civic republican themes of shared risk and narrative in two areas addressed in this Article: the lawyer's role and legal education. In each case, high volume and the urge to maintain a quiet life discourage the sharing of risk and narrative.

The bureaucratic nature of some conceptions of lawyers' roles is apparent from my thoughts when students expressed concern about what would happen to Ms.

Esperon even if our legal representation achieved the results desired. In essence, my reflexive response to this concern was, "It's not your problem—you're a lawyer." The "it's not your problem" theme is a prime example of how modernity has compartmentalized responsibility through rigid roles. Narrow role conceptions have alienated people from the shared risk and narrative at the heart of civic republicanism. Hannah Arendt, perhaps the foremost modern exponent of civic republicanism, has gone so far, in her most controversial work, as to lay much of the blame for the Holocaust on bureaucrats who were "just following orders."[106]

Similarly, the Anglo-American conception of lawyering in an adversary system carves out a narrow niche for lawyer-client interaction. Under this liberal legalist regime, the client becomes a deracinated rights bearer, her *res* or defense abstracted from a web of relationships in which legality may play only a small role.

This model of liberal legalism requires an impossible detachment of role from self. Making judgments about the actions of people with whom we interact is at the heart of what we do *as* people. If we require that lawyers detach themselves from this faculty in order to exude the requisite warm zeal on a client's behalf, we extract some essential humanity from the bar and also perversely encourage attitudes which undermine lawyer-client relations. Rather than disappear from the lawyer's character, judgments about clients instead reassert themselves *sub rosa* as corrosive cynicism about clients generally. This is consistent with bureaucrats' tendency to value the appearance of order while declining to confront fundamental differences which desperately require robust debate.

In contrast, a civic republican conception situates lawyers in a larger landscape of culture, politics, and narrative. Changes in those areas will change the legal terrain, and vice versa. Neither law nor any other profession is exclusively "private"—instead, law always possesses the potential to transcend the private and enter the public realm. Lawyers and other professionals must be prepared to make this leap.

My students' approach, although it is fraught with problems, points up the artificiality of a bureaucratic approach to law and the virtues of an expanded lawyer's role. The students' peculiar position in purgatory—no longer laypersons, not yet lawyers—opened them to experience banished by ideals of professional detachment. A clear link with civic republican principles is found in my students' concern about allocation of resources in the case of Mr. Gaines. Here, the students looked beyond the atomistic level of individual representation and considered the public interest. They recognized that the distribution of legal services is a political decision, which affects whose voice and narrative is heard. Moreover, they wanted to make decisions based on some conception of context and circumstance—whether we would be better employed helping other people perhaps less able than Mr. Gaines to raise their own voices above the din of the marketplace. The students eschewed the bureaucratic modes of determining access to services, which typically involve developing cumbersome procedures to discourage access whenever possible.

---

106   *See* HANNAH ARENDT, EICHMANN IN JERUSALEM (1963).

The students' concern about Ms. Esperon's pregnancy is a more ambiguous instance of the extension of lawyers' roles. We have already discussed the role of stereotypes in their perception of Ms. Esperon's judgment. Yet, their concerns about Ms. Esperon also illustrate a refusal to divide up the world neatly into "public" and "private." Legal protection of reproductive freedom has typically centered on the right to privacy. However, divorcing issues of reproduction from debate because those issues are somehow "private" only makes reproductive choices more vulnerable to political interference. The movement for reproductive rights has been strongest when it argues that such rights are important precisely because they have public implications for women's ability to participate as equals in society.

Here, having another baby could have conflicting effects on Ms. Esperon's ability to participate. It might enhance her participation by giving her a greater stake in her community, a possibility which the students did not consider. Or it might reduce that ability by so multiplying her family's needs that advocacy for any one need would seem hopeless. To neglect those effects in the interest of a "lawyerly" concern solely with receipt of AFDC benefits would have sliced up Ms. Esperon into neat bureaucratic compartments. That the students saw Ms. Esperon as a person, rather than a walking intake file, reveals affinity with a civic humanist approach. To my students, Ms. Esperon was not a mere passive recipient of benefits so beloved by the liberal bureaucratic state. In ascribing poor judgment to Ms. Esperon, at least my students gave her the capacity for judgment, an essential element of participation in society.

Addressing these issues with citizens also provides a valuable "witness" who can prompt public action. Ms. Esperon, for example, talked about these issues with me. However, she may not have felt as comfortable in discussing her apprehension about her pregnancy with family or friends. Sometimes professionals' independence from a citizen's usual circle can be an invitation to dialogue. Such dialogue can in turn fortify the individual for more meaningful involvement within the group.

* * *

Ultimately, every lawyer must undertake the long and arduous struggle to define his or her own conception of justice, and every lawyer must infuse his or her legal practice with that individual conception of justice. As the next excerpt suggests, law faculty are not, nor should they be, immune from this struggle.

David R. Barnhizer, *The Justice Mission of American Law Schools*, 40 CLEV. ST. L. REV. 285 (1992)*

* * *

Most faculty in American law schools would deny the appropriateness of any mission that requires them to either understand or advance justice. Their hesitance is understandable. Practical people, and law faculty generally fit into this category, tend to suspect what they perceive as particularly loose concepts and terms capable of being abused and manipulated to serve any end. Justice is admittedly such a term. Justice reeks of oft maligned metaphysics, and sounds far too much like natural law, an idea fraught with the vagaries and polemics of religion and propaganda. For the past two centuries the ideas of methods of metaphysics and its subset, natural law, concepts intimately linked with justice, have been condemned as unscientific pap— the refuge of superstitious fools and demagogues who lacked either the discipline or the willingness to pursue the mysteries of the universe through the rigorous and demanding methods of science. "Justice," as the claim might go, is as ignorant and sisyphean a quest as were the medieval searchers for the Philosopher's Stone, through which base metals were thought to be transmuted into gold, or the Holy Grail.

* * *

Justice in application operates on a different level of intensity and detail than does justice in theory. The difficulty of understanding the volumes of existing material developed through millennia on questions of the nature and functions of justice is increased because justice is a fundamentally political phenomenon, even in its theoretical dimensions. As the debate concerning the nature of justice moves from more abstract considerations of the various and competing theories of justice to increasingly concrete areas of concern, the interactions become steadily more intense and bitter. This is because the conclusions reached or implied are not only created with awareness of their implications but are inevitably used in decisions that dictate and justify the allocation and reallocation of social goods, rights, responsibilities, opportunities and privileges. They become the deep grounding principles we take for granted and rarely even seek to understand because truth is not an essential condition for the success of functioning political systems, a fact which exacerbates the intrinsic dilemma in which legal scholars find themselves.

The scholar's dilemma, particularly those scholars in disciplines such as law that are irreversibly linked to the operation of power and implicit willingness to do violence if necessary, is that societies require shared consensus far more than truth. Negative truths about the scientifically unsupportable premises of our fundamental beliefs might interfere with the quality of the operating consensus, at least for those satisfied with their lot. The stark truth about opportunity, fairness, racial and gender bias, about who received economic benefits and so forth would not be knowledge that

_____

*   Reprinted with permission.

"sets us free" but "set us at each other's throats." If this sounds familiar, welcome to the final decade of the Twentieth Century, a period in which we have facilely "deconstructed" our fundamental principles, sought to reveal the underlying truths of an unfair social system, and created a political context filled with hollow slogans based on intense propaganda campaigns both defensive and offensive in character, designed to mask the emptiness into which our "intellectuals" have cast us and designed to either retain or obtain power for their advocates. For many, even if gaining power is not a realistic probability, there is at least some satisfaction in wounding the source of one's perceived injustice or, like Samson, suicidally bringing the temple down on their heads.

This is the dilemma from which we must struggle to extract ourselves and our political community. Understanding justice and developing the richer dimensions of law in an effort to incorporate its principles are essential aspects of our justice mission which is of course at least as important as an on-going and fluid process as any assumptions concerning singular truths, goals, or visions of right. As I suggest at the conclusion of this article, the answer to the dilemma must begin from within us, not with institutional and intellectual externalities. Our problems go to the core of the humanity, our very conception of our selves, and will not be resolved short of that source of energy, values, creativity and destructiveness.

* * *

III. THE ELUSIVE MEANING OF JUSTICE

* * *

One of the main difficulties with pursuing justice only at theoretical levels is that it means and can be made to mean many different things in a wide variety of contexts. Is justice, for example, a mystical, magical grail that has touched the lips of God, or is it a kind of intangible life-giving substance equivalent to water, air, food, etc., without which we humans cannot survive? On one level, for example, justice is cosmic, the very mind or motive force of the universe or God, or emanations from the pattern of deep principles embedded by our Creator in the structure of existence. On another level, justice can be seen in the choice to cut a two-thousand year old Sequoia, converting it from a living, stately giant to an inanimate board feet of lumber, or the willingness to extinguish a species of owls due to our own failure to plan sustainable economic activity.

How is justice realized on the level of specific acts or omissions between individual entities or groups, and, as the example of the Sequoia impliedly asks, is sentience a necessary condition of the existence and definition of justice? Are humans part of a natural order in which justice is a wide and richly textured value and force integral to all elements of our universal reality, or is justice only a matter of the specific affairs of the human species relevant in relation to human concerns and interactions? I ask these particular questions because Aristotle described justice as "the highest virtue," arguing that the special essence of justice is that it exists not only for ourselves but in relation to how we behave toward others.

IV. Justice As Choice

Whether we ask such questions about the meaning and nature of justice, how we ask them, and how we choose to answer them are critical considerations. How we demonstrate the validity of the answer is equally critical. This is because the particular answers we choose about the origin, nature and content of justice help define the conditions and terms of society that we are likely to consider legitimate. What the Langdellian legal scientists and most law faculty since then have failed to understand or sought to ignore is that we still make covert choices about the answers to these questions, consciously or unconsciously, choately or inchoately.

We *must* make these choices. To refuse to choose is inevitably itself a choice. We cannot escape them in our reasoning and decisions as judges, lawyers, legislators, law professors and citizens because they are the grounding principles of our decisions and doctrines. We can pretend that the choices were part of the historical social contract, derived from a non-existent state of nature or hypothetical original position, dependent on scientific principles, human nature, or God. We invent such legitimating constructs because we need something larger than ourselves on which to ground our political systems. This is because we are afraid to face the reality of our rather violent and nasty selves and the responsibility the freedom of choice imposes. Our fictions are less an indication of our lack of knowledge or of our ability to understand than they are an indication of our fear of the implications and consequences of the truth. We fear telling the emperor he is naked.

The truth is far simpler than we pretend. The truths of justice are within us. The only certainty is that we are the responsible center of our political, legal and moral universe. It is a troubling and existentialist truth, but we can demonstrate the validity of nothing else. At a minimum, therefore, we must accept that it is our responsibility to understand that we are the architects of justice. Therefore, the quality and intensity of justice emerges from within us. We choose, we accept, we generate the principles of justice not only as atomistic individuals, but as a community of humans committed to a positive vision of a just society. We choose the fundamental terms.

Private property, for example, is nothing more nor less than a proposition containing an implicit assertion about the just, fair, and necessary conditions of society. It is, of course, also a justification for keeping what one has seized. The minimalist state, such as forms the basis of Robert Nozick's philosophy, is also a major statement about what is just and a way of keeping what one has seized. So is the Marxist principle of "from each according to his ability, to each according to his need." This principle not only allowed a complete restructuring of ownership and property rights, legitimating an enormous abuse of power, it simultaneously served as a justification for seizing more. Each principle is an implicit claim about such fundamental matters as human nature, the appropriate functions of government, and the validity of distributions of rights, privileges and resources. Each is also a principle of empowerment and of human nature. Private property, the "free market," the minimal state, and Marxism are potent metaphysical preconditions that, once chosen, lead inevitably to distinct positions concerning what is just. They are devices of power and legitimation and, as such, ones of justice and injustice. Regardless of our attempts to reject such first principles, whether we label them metaphysics or natural law, they are inescapable. Our responsibility as active scholars is to penetrate to their fundamental assumptions, their truth conditions and their real consequences.

Like the rancorous arguments over original intent and the appropriate methods of judicial interpretation of the Constitution, not one of these metaphysical propositions can be proved as opposed to believed in or chosen. I can argue, assert premises and attempt to muster supporting evidence, give my belief or opinion, speak more or less eloquently about my positions, collect examples that seem to make the best sense, and find the statements of others that strike me as compelling. I cannot, however, *prove* the nature, content and functions of justice, as opposed to *choosing* and *justifying* those which make the most sense to me.

Even Aristotle's descriptions of justice, which I often use, or Rawls's closely related idea of justice as fairness, do not provide answers as opposed to ammunition in support of our particular choices. They are only more or less well-reasoned rhetorical arguments about which I can make choices. Stripped down to basics, therefore, our views about justice and injustice are *belief systems*, some of which compete with each other, particularly at applied levels of action, each representing a set of values that has been inculcated within us at some point by parents, teachers, peers, experiences, churches, readings, television, etc. We learn the values and internalize them to be brought out when we need them.

This does not mean that the impulse to justice, or God, or food, sex, territoriality and dominance do not emerge from genetically imprinted characteristics of the human species as a reasonably sophisticated animal. It seems obvious that our basic biological nature does have much to do with our behavior. But admitting that to be a valid point by itself establishes almost nothing other than that we should seek to understand these characteristics better and should take them into account in setting our limits. We may be able to ground arguments for justice in such things as genetic urges and species preservation, in animalistic tendencies toward aggression, territoriality and social clustering. Such characteristics are not entirely irrelevant. But if we are being honest with ourselves, these characteristics do not tell us very much about what is just but tell us more about the traps and limits that our innate biological factors create and impose. These ideas may explain something about why we tend to behave in ways we consider unjust and vicious, or why we fear or punish those not of our "herd" or tribe. They will not establish, however, the conditions of a system that most of us would want to describe as just.

Arguments about justice that derive from biological factors and innate drives and characteristics are necessarily incomplete. Each represents only a small part of what we would have to know in order to understand the workings of a potential construct of justice. Even then they would be inadequate, and to some extent dangerous, because they would not be able to take into account the special architecture of a just society that we would choose to create rather than the consequences of an unjust society appropriate to the nature of our species in its natural, savage or bestial state. The related quests to first understand and then to realize justice are in fact part of the human attempt to transcend the limits and barbarism of our biological natures and to behave toward each other in ways that, at a minimum, neutralize our innate savagery and even go beyond that minimum to emphasize and nurture the best of our characteristics. The very premises of the Rule of Law are in large part such a governing system, one designed not only to protect the interests of those in power but to inhibit the worst in us while allowing us to explore some of our best potentialities. Justice, and the willingness to challenge injustice, is the defining and evolutionary principle of humans.

V. JUSTICE AS PREFERENCE AND BELIEF

Our most cherished principles of justice are grounded in preference and belief. The particular preferences and beliefs are deeply rooted and powerful. They often have, as part of their tradition, centuries of religious, cultural, constitutional and philosophical tradition. They may be deeply set, core beliefs, untouchable by evidence or argument. However, they are beliefs and preferences about which we have made choices, usually subtle and unknowing.

The fact that justice is a preference does not trivialize it. The opposite is true. Because the principles of justice are part of powerful belief systems which, once set, are virtually unalterable, they help determine the basic fabric of a particular society. They provide, for example, the value systems drawn upon by American presidents and legislators in determining the limits of government. They guide and limit the decisions of lower court and Supreme Court justices. The fit is neither neat nor explicit but people rely upon their belief systems when making decisions about conflicts between fundamental matters.

This suggests several considerations about any undertaking that insists on having justice as a primary focus. One is that I (and anyone else) can speculate about, but never prove the ultimate nature of justice. I can assert, but never establish beyond the fact of my assertion, that God created a universe within which justice not only exists but possesses a definable character. I would like this to be so, and may believe it to be so, but honesty requires that I admit complete ignorance about the truth of the proposition. The best I can say is that it is true that many people believe the proposition to be valid and that therefore it is not politically irrelevant to society and to decisions made pursuant to the belief. I can argue that humans possess a quality or faculty, either natural or God-given or both, that links them to the natural justice of the universe. About these and similar propositions voluminous *summas* have been written. For all their massive elegance, however, the main content of everything we actually *know* about justice rather than what we *believe* could have been said in a few pages. That is all we can know and are likely to ever know about the ultimate truth of those propositions. On the other hand, this does not make the beliefs irrelevant because humans use them to implicitly ground their systems and guide their decisions.

VI. PRACTICAL JUSTICE

A system of governance and political order dependent upon widespread acceptance of shared fundamental values such as opportunity, tolerance, fairness and rationality begins to disintegrate when those shared beliefs lose their force. In our system they have, over the past twenty years, become victims of a combination of both truth and ignorance. We have become overwhelmingly selfish, a nation of opportunists and hustlers, racists of every skin color abound, and we refuse to tolerate any position but our own. Of course, such attitudes have always been with us but we have struggled to overcome them or at least to keep them under control. Now they have been somehow glorified as desirable, undoing painful centuries of progress. If we do not commit ourselves to strengthening the quality of personal awareness and commitment, the institutions and the positive shared beliefs of our society as a community committed to taking others' well-being into account, we will experience a period of decline into a political and economic dark age from which it is unlikely we will be able to climb back out within our lifetimes or our children's lifetimes. * * *

* * *

There is a continuing tension among legal scholars about whether lawyers should be absolved from responsibility for the consequences of their actions because their role is to serve as advocates for their clients, regardless of the moral rectitude of the clients' positions. In the next excerpt Paul R. Tremblay asks whether lawyers have an obligation to serve justice at the same time they are serving their clients.

Paul R. Tremblay, *Practiced Moral Activism*, 8 St. Thomas L. Rev. 9 (1995)*

* * *

II. CONSTRUCTING A WORKING IMAGE OF MORALLY ACTIVIST LAWYERING

We encounter certain difficulties when we endeavor to articulate a reasonably coherent vision of this moral activism. Such a vision should be congruent with the philosophers' teachings and should differ in some observable way from the traditional view that lawyers have possessed of their roles in the past. The problem, though, is that the activists do not speak with anything close to one voice. Disagreements exist at quite fundamental levels, reflecting in many cases controversies within moral philosophy that are decades, or even centuries, in the making. To describe one activist vision, then, I would need either to resolve those controversies, or ignore them in some way. Neither choice seems quite principled. This difficulty represents a central element of my argument in this Article, which is that lawyers who choose to be activist cannot avoid precisely this quandary. In order to justify her chosen brand of activism, that lawyer must overlook or resolve arbitrarily some of the metaethical questions with which the philosophers struggle.

* * *

* * * [M]oral activism in its broadest sense demands accountability from lawyers for their actions, and tends not to permit the mere fact of occupational role expectations to justify lawyer conduct. The morally activist view appeared first, it seems, with Richard Wasserstrom's 1975 polemic questioning whether it ought to be right for lawyers to do free from censure things that those who are not lawyers could not do in similar shameless fashion.[13] Wasserstrom's article was descriptive and questioning, but not particularly prescriptive. Other writers developed his critique, however, and began to structure an alternative view of lawyer role which would try to accommodate his concerns. The following year Charles Fried published his famous (or infamous) contrasting article *Lawyer as Friend*, which defended the standard conception of lawyer role by stressing its value in enhancing client and lawyer autonomy.[14] Together the Wasserstrom and Fried articles set the contours of the ensuing conversation. In the late 1970s, Murray Schwartz[16] and Gerald Postema crafted sophisticated objections to Fried's (and the traditional) nonaccountability arguments, William Simon produced a profound deconstruction of the adversary system, challenging traditional role views in a more critical way,[18] and Alan Goldman offered a philosopher's sophisticated view of an activist lawyer's world.[19] It was David Luban, though, who established the issue of role morality in the central position it possesses in legal ethics today. In 1983, Luban edited *The Good Lawyer*,[20] a rich collection of philosophical and legal essays written by prominent philosophers and law scholars about the "good lawyer versus good person" question. He followed that effort in 1988 with *Lawyers and Justice*,[21] an articulate and advanced defense of the activist conception. *Lawyers and Justice* provoked two sophisticated responses, with rejoinders from Luban. That same year saw the publication of William Simon's pioneering article, *Ethical Discretion in Lawyering*.[23] In this significant work, Simon presented an activist model that departs from the customary "role morality" language by arguing that legal merit and justice, and not morality, ought to serve as the governing criterion for an activist stance. While neither Simon nor any other scholar has yet refined Simon's critique beyond his 1988 formulation, his attractive argument for ethical discretion has garnered great attention within the academy. As noted earlier,

---

13   Richard Wasserstrom, *Lawyers as Professionals: Some Moral Issues*, 5 HUM. RTS. 1, 1-2 (1975-1976) [hereinafter Wasserstrom, *Lawyers as Professionals*]. * * *

14   [Charles] Fried, [*Lawyer As Friend: The Moral Foundations of the Lawyer-Client Relation*], 85 YALE L.J. 1060 [(1976)].

16   Murray L. Schwartz, *The Professionalism and Accountability of Lawyers*, 66 CAL. L. REV. 669, 673-74 (1978). * * *

18   [William H.] Simon, *Ideology of Advocacy*[: *Procedural Justice and Professional Ethics*, 1978 WISC. L. REV. 29.]

19   ALAN H. GOLDMAN, THE MORAL FOUNDATIONS OF PROFESSIONAL ETHICS 90-155 (1980).

20   [DAVID] LUBAN, THE GOOD LAWYER[: LAWYERS' ROLES AND LAWYERS' ETHICS (1983)].

21   [DAVID] LUBAN, LAWYERS & JUSTICE[: AN ETHICAL STUDY (1988)].

23   William H. Simon, *Ethical Discretion in Lawyering*, 101 HARV. L. REV. 1083 (1988) [hereinafter Simon, *Ethical Discretion*].

Luban and Simon remain the two most prominent spokespersons for activism, appearing regularly in modern ethics scholarship. Few scholarly efforts, though, have sought to contrast the two from the standpoint of legal practice.

My brief history of activist development cannot be compete [sic] without a mention of two other contributors, Thomas Shaffer and Gerald López. Shaffer's avowedly religious and theological perspective on lawyering contrasts with the more secular philosophical arguments of most of the activist debate, as does his attention to virtue and character, instead of the more common attention to conduct and actions. * * * If Shaffer's influence is a religious one, that of Gerald López is a political one. López * * * deserves considerable credit for rethinking the moral relationship and interactions between lawyers and poor clients.[30] * * *

* * *

B. Two Activist Models: Luban and Smith

* * * [T]wo contrasting visions of activism remain prominent in both teaching and scholarship. David Luban's "common morality" based conception[62] and William Simon's "legal merit," or "justice" based, conception are the two versions of non-traditional lawyering which have received the most intense attention. Together the two offer lawyers a plausible choice between competing arguments about the underpinnings of an activist stance. An activist-sympathizing lawyer feeling perplexed or overwhelmed by the philosophy debates just described might comfortably choose between a Luban and a Simon approach to her work, if only because the two are the most visible choices and differ in understandable ways.

1. David Luban's Commitment to Common Morality

It is not my purpose here to describe in great detail the Luban thesis, but I do need to highlight two aspects of his work if we are to understand the message to a lawyer in practice. First, there is Luban's underlying skepticism about the adversary system excuse. Luban employs what he terms the "Fourfold Root of Sufficient Reasoning" to demonstrate that lawyers ought not be morally exempt from criticism because they are performing an important role within the adversary system. Whenever a person in a role intends to act in a way which, but for that role, would be morally troublesome, and wishes to employ the role as a justification for acting in that way, she must rely upon the Fourfold Root, which Luban describes as follows:

> [T]he institutional excuse, fully spelled out, will take the [following] form . . . : the agent (1) justifies the institution by demonstrating its moral goodness; (2) justifies the role by appealing to the structure of the institution; (3) justifies the role obligations by showing that they are essential

---

30   *See* Gerald P. López, Rebellious Lawyering: One Chicano's Vision of Progressive Law Practice (1992).

62   *See* Luban, Lawyers & Justice, *supra* note [21], at 105.

to the role; and (4) justifies the role act by showing that the obligations require it.

Luban's argument is that mere reliance on a role is insufficient to justify questionable actions, but using ordinary morality as a trump is equally inappropriate. The Fourfold Root suggests a method of separating those acts that have justification because of their institutional role flavor from those that do not. Luban contends that this justificatory process and analysis may be applied by practicing lawyers in the "hurley-burley" of their practice.

The standard by which he expects assessment of (but not trumping of) role acts is that of ordinary morality, which Luban argues is susceptible to coherent understanding. In his Fourfold Root analysis Luban affords a weak justification to the adversary system, the "pragmatic" realization that the system, despite its flaws, seems to be as effective as any other system. Thus, a lawyer's deliberations cannot rely heavily on that system to license acts that otherwise would be significantly troublesome from a standard of common morality. When the justification for the role-acts are insufficient to trump moral considerations, several things follow: at a minimum, the lawyer must accept moral responsibility for her actions; she also ought not continue to assist that client and, in some instances, she may be justified in betraying her client.

2. William Simon's Commitment to a Conception of Legal Merits

William Simon's article *Ethical Discretion in Lawyering* has had a significant impact upon the world of legal ethics. Like Luban, Simon opposes the "neutral partisanship" stance of the traditional defense of advocacy and lawyering, captured by the "zealous advocacy" conception so often repeated in conventional ethics discourse. Unlike Luban, though, Simon rejects the common opposition of "private" moral decision-making to legal decision-making. Instead, Simon proposes a realm of "ethical discretion," which he describes as a mandate to lawyers to "seek justice," but which, on further reflection, appears to be largely purposivist in intent and in implementation. I use the term "purposivist" to capture a sense of obligation to respect the obvious and apparent purposes of the substantive law to "vindicate our legal ideals."

Simon's conception is more easily cognizable than Luban's, in that it relies upon a set of criteria (substantive law standards) for which, he argues, we possess more of a common shared language. Yet, Simon's suggestion is also more inscrutable and complex in application, in that his definition of "legal merits" encompasses more than a straightforward purposivist perspective on substantive law. This point needs brief development here if we are to understand how a working lawyer might apply Simon's reasoning.

Simon argues that lawyers ought to possess ethical discretion to "take those actions that, considering the relevant circumstances of the particular case, seem most likely to promote justice." He divides that task into two realms, "relative merit" and "internal merit." The questions of internal merit are of the greater interest for present purposes. They are the insights for which Simon has attracted the most attention. The internal merit obligation "requires that the lawyer make her best effort to achieve the most appropriate resolution in each case." Simon takes pains to emphasize that the "most appropriate resolution" means the most appropriate *legal* resolution, not the most appropriate *moral* resolution. As he writes,

> [The discretionary approach] differs from many critiques of prevalent legal ethics doctrine that would appeal to moral concerns outside the legal system against values associated with the legal role. The argument here is that ethical discretion would best vindicate *our legal ideals* and contribute to a more effective functioning of the lawyer role.

* * *

III. A LAW STUDENT, AN EVICTION, AND MORAL CONFLICT

* * *

B. ONE EVICTION STORY (AMONG MANY)

Christopher was a second year student who enrolled in the law school's civil clinic for the Spring semester. His third case of the term was the Hunter matter. It was, in the parlance of the office, an "eviction case." The intake form told Christopher that Cathy Hunter was thirty-three years old, married to Patrick, age thirty-four, and with two children, one age three and the other ten months. Cathy had called the clinic after receiving a Summary Process complaint, which is the Massachusetts device for commencing an eviction proceeding in court. The short write-up noted that the Hunters' landlord claimed that they owed $3,750 (or five months) in rent, but that the tenants were complaining about unsafe and unsanitary conditions at their home.

Christopher interviewed Cathy, who came in with her two children but without Patrick. He found her story compelling. When Cathy moved into the apartment about a year ago the building was in the process of being taken over by her current landlord, Carl LeBlanc, from a bank that had foreclosed on the previous owner's interests. Cathy and Patrick dealt with a bank official, not with Carl, in arranging their rental. The bank representative offered them an incentive when they moved in; if they could find a tenant for one of the other vacant units, they would get a month's rent free. The Hunters were able to do this. They knew of a friend's friend who needed an apartment, so they did not have to pay for the second month they lived in the unit.

Cathy described Carl LeBlanc as a nasty, frugal, judgmental, absentee landlord—in short, not a very nice man. The Hunters had a number of serious problems with the apartment from the time they moved in, including drafty windows in the winter, mice scurrying across the floor, plumbing that did not work right, and an occasional lack of hot water. Cathy admitted that they had fallen behind on the rent, but not nearly as much as LeBlanc was claiming. She pointed out that LeBlanc was not giving them credit for the bank's free month, and furthermore had never credited them with some rent they had paid. She believed that the family was behind in rent only by about a month and a half or two months at most. Cathy had heard from the local tenants' organization that, given the problems with the unit, a court should forgive that amount. She told Christopher that when the family moved in, Patrick was working for a food distributor in town, but he was laid off soon after. He had been looking for work off and on, but he also applied for disability benefits because of back pain of long duration that was getting worse. Cathy asked whether the clinic could help out with that issue. In the meantime, the family lived off of Aid to Families with Dependent Children (AFDC), which provided a monthly cash grant of $668 for a family of four (which was less than the monthly $750 rent), plus $195 in food stamps and Medicaid coverage.

Cathy was very angry at the landlord. She felt he had been harassing them ever since they began having trouble paying the rent. On three separate occasions, LeBlanc came into the apartment without their permission, once surprising them at 11:00 a.m. on a Saturday while the couple slept on a fold-out couch in the living room. Christopher's interview also turned up the following facts: The landlord had taken a $750 security deposit from the Hunters, but had never sent them a receipt telling them that the funds were deposited into a separate, interest-bearing account free from the claims of LeBlanc's creditors. Christopher also learned that, while the tenants had received a properly drafted Notice to Quit, the Constable had left the notice under the door of the apartment across the hall, where their friend lived. Cathy had received the notice on the same day it was delivered, but she had received it from her friend, not from the Constable.

Cathy's goal was to avoid eviction for as long as possible. It was March and still cold in New England. Her youngest child was ten months old and was often sick. It would take the Hunters several months to find a new apartment, especially with the need for the first month's rent, last month's rent, and security deposit (which together could easily total $2,250) most new landlords would demand. She was desperately fearful of being homeless. Her family was in Ireland, so she had no chance of staying with them if she was evicted. Her husband had some relatives living nearby, but he was not on very good terms with them, so living with his side of the family was also out of the question.

Christopher was quite moved by his interaction with Cathy, who seemed to be the victim of so much bad luck. Her landlord sounded like a mercenary who ran roughshod over his tenants' rights. Christopher liked Cathy a lot, and her children were well-behaved and gentle, not what he was expecting in a family in such apparent distress. After the interview, he met with his faculty supervisor, Linda, to plan his strategy. After completing the research to which Linda directed him, Christopher developed an impressive strategy. He learned that the entire action against the Hunters could be dismissed because the Notice to Quit had not been served in the manner required by statute. If LeBlanc started over again after the dismissal, or if the dismissal motion was denied, Christopher discovered that he could win Cathy's case on the merits, for LeBlanc had not complied with several of his obligations. Christopher easily and reasonably could assert the following counterclaims: (1) violation of the security deposit statute, with a treble damages penalty ($2,250) and attorney's fees, (2) interference with quiet enjoyment (the unauthorized entries), which allows a statutory three months' rent penalty and attorney's fees, (3) breach of the implied warranty of habitability by maintaining an unsafe and unsanitary dwelling, (4) violation of the state's Consumer Protection Act by renting a dwelling that was not in compliance with state law, with possible treble damages and attorney's fees, and (5) retaliatory eviction, if one saw LeBlanc's action as evicting the Hunters for their lawful refusal to pay rent for a less than habitable dwelling, with three months' rent as a statutory penalty along with attorney's fees.

Christopher learned that Massachusetts has a statute which declares that if a tenant prevails on any counterclaim, she can retain possession of the rental unit. While nervous about his ability to pull it off, Christopher was delighted that he could find a way to help this family so much. Indeed, he could demand as much as $20,250 in damages, if all of the treble damages and statutory penalties of the counterclaims were aggregated. Linda warned Christopher about the conservative nature of all district court judges, in an effort to reality-test his judgments about what this case might be worth, but Christopher also knew that tenants in Massachusetts had an absolute right to appeal any judgment of the trial court, and have an entire trial *de novo* in superior court, where he understood that the judges were likely to be less jaded and more comfortable with figures like $20,500.

This appeal, in fact, was Christopher's ace in the hole. If Linda was right that local district court judges were not favorably inclined toward tenants, all that meant was that Cathy would have a legitimate right to appeal the case. While the appeal was of right, and could take up to a year to complete, Cathy would still be required to pay the fair market rent during that period, which could be a real problem if what she was looking for was free time (recall that as of now she could not pay the rent of $750 while on AFDC, and her income was not likely to increase in the reasonable future).

However, Christopher was not without ideas about how to get around this serious problem. How much rent Cathy and her family would be required to pay during the appeal was a function of the condition of the apartment, and likely to be in dispute. The district court judges tended to use the contract rent as the chosen figure. But *that decision* was itself appealable to the Superior Court, and perhaps even beyond that. Until there was a definitive ruling on the question of appropriate rent, Christopher might be able to get Cathy the ability to stay in the apartment rent free. While there were certainly limits on Christopher's ability to manipulate these procedural devices, he was comfortable in his prediction that Cathy could live in her apartment at least for the next few months without paying any rent and without any fear of eviction.

There was, finally, one last real-world advantage to the Hunters that Christopher's research unearthed. Whenever LeBlanc obtained his eviction order from a court, whether sooner from the District Court, later from the Superior Court, or through some negotiated agreement, LeBlanc would have to finance the dispossession of the tenants from his unit. The cost of moving, and perhaps even packing, the tenants' belongings, and storing them for several months must be borne by the landlord, although the landlord does have a right, in theory, to seek recompense from the tenants through a separate civil action. While this fact had some relevance to the plans of the Hunters, who knew that if they must move they would not forfeit their property, its greatest strength was in the negotiating leverage it offered Christopher with the landlord, whose costs even after a successful eviction could approach $2,000.

Emboldened by his research results, Christopher called Cathy to tell her his belief that she had a pretty compelling case, and that the clinic would accept the matter for representation. Christopher wished to discuss the various options with Cathy and with Patrick before filing either his Motion to Dismiss or his Answer and Counterclaims. Christopher arranged to visit the Hunters at their apartment the next evening.

That visit to the apartment was one of two back-to-back events that caused Christopher to begin to have serious personal discomfort with his role in what otherwise was a model piece of clinic litigation. The meeting was quite disenchanting to Christopher. The apartment that he had imagined as a tribute to slumlordism turned out to be quite nice. It was nicer, in fact, than the place he shared with his law school roommates. This did not mean that Cathy's claims were not true, for nice apartments could have mice and infrequent hot water, etc., but Christopher began to have doubts about Cathy's perspective on things. These doubts were more than encouraged by his reaction to Patrick, whom Christopher perceived as angry, manipulative, and less than honest. In talking to Patrick that evening Christopher just could not get Patrick's story to feel right, even though Patrick never altered the tale Cathy had first recounted. Proof of their story was weak or implausible or, at times, nonexistent. The Hunters had no receipts for the rent they claimed LeBlanc had failed to credit them. They had called the local Health Department on three separate occasions over the past year complaining about substandard conditions, but on each occasion the Health Department had found no violations at all, or only minor ones like chipped tiles in the bathroom. Patrick told Christopher that LeBlanc had the health inspectors "in his pocket," so the Hunters could never get a fair visit from them.

Patrick was very excited by what Christopher had told Cathy on the telephone about the case being strong. He had been in touch with the city's tenants' union, and he pressed Christopher about the counterclaims and the various treble damages awards that the Hunters might get. He knew about the appeal process and wanted to think through with Christopher just how long they could stay in the apartment without paying any rent. He hoped that they could play out the process long enough for Patrick's disability claim to be heard. If they had to leave earlier, they might be able to move in with Patrick's parents in their house in the next town. While there was room there, Patrick saw that as an absolute last alternative because his parents disapproved of some of Patrick's friends and would, as he described it, "always be on my case."

Christopher, with Linda assisting from time to time, explained to the Hunters his various theories, although neither mentioned the $20,500 figure. He agreed to think through with Linda the various ways to proceed, although Patrick expressed a preference for holding back the Motion to Dismiss to try for the greatest delay.

Soon after this meeting, a second sobering event occurred. With Linda's blessing, Christopher called LeBlanc's lawyer, Jeannette Sinclair, ostensibly to begin negotiations and perhaps to learn something about LeBlanc's theory that might aid in Christopher's strategy. The conversation with Jeannette was extraordinarily depressing for Christopher. Jeannette was nice to Christopher, and seemed a principled, smart, and collaborative lawyer (to the extent that one can discern this from a single call). She also painted a picture of LeBlanc, and of the Hunters, that was very different from what Christopher had created for himself. LeBlanc was a married man with three children, working at a nearby computer company, who had purchased this three unit building as an investment. His mortgage payments on the building were a bit less than the income from the three units, and the Hunters' refusal to pay him was causing him not only severe financial distress, but serious personal health concerns as well. Jeannette painted the Hunters as unfortunate victims (neither party had planned on Patrick losing his job) who had turned on LeBlanc with a vengeance. They called his home repeatedly and harassed both LeBlanc and his wife, they called the Health Department again and again hoping to find a way to avoid liability for the back rent, and they kept threatening to bring claims against LeBlanc if he tried to evict them.

Christopher was at a loss about how to proceed in this telephone conversation. He did not (and felt he could not) disparage LeBlanc in return, but he did opt to lay out his legal claims in an effort to show Jeannette that the Hunters had grounds on which to stand. She responded to each. On the security deposit claim she possessed records showing that the deposit had been placed in the correct kind of bank account and that a receipt had been mailed to the Hunters; however, she now noticed, that receipt, like the notice to quit, seemed to have been sent to Apartment B, not the Hunters' Apartment A. Because the resident of Apartment B was the Hunters' friend, she did not view that misstep as of any substantive concern. She denied all of the other claims. She did not wish to be unreasonable, though, and wanted to talk about a possible compromise. She offered to allow the Hunters three weeks to move. If they moved without LeBlanc's resort to the expensive constable, mover, and storage arrangement, LeBlanc would forgive all of the back rent. Christopher agreed only to discuss the offer with his clients.

With Linda present, Christopher met with Patrick and Cathy at the clinic office. The meeting did not go well. Patrick sensed Christopher's sympathies for LeBlanc and accused him of not siding with his own clients. Patrick said that Jeannette Sinclair was a liar and a slumlord lawyer who should not be believed. The documents to which she had referred in the telephone call, and which she had now faxed to Christopher for his review, were, Patrick pointed out, either irrelevant (the Health Department papers did not expressly rule out mice) or supported their claim (the security deposit papers were sent to the wrong address). Patrick did not see anything different between the last meeting and now; all of the counterclaims could still be filed, and all of the delays and procedural steps were still available. He wished to proceed as before. He could not afford to move in three weeks, so he needed to use the court for as much time as he could get. Cathy quietly agreed.

After the meeting, even though it was late, Christopher and Linda moved into her office to think all this through. . . .

I wish to end my story at this point. We leave Christopher and Linda in a state of some moral ambiguity. The conversation they are about to begin may be informed by the notions of morally activist lawyering Linda might have tried to teach in the clinic, or that Christopher might have encountered in his professional responsibility course. Let us assume that each has read the central Simon and Luban works, Linda perhaps more closely than Christopher. Their conversation, and its various possibilities, is explored in the following Part.

IV. WORKING WITHIN AN ACTIVIST CONCEPTION

* * *

My argument in the last section has been that a traditionalist, a neutral partisan, will perceive his obligation to be to defend the Hunters with all "arguably legal" means. I have constructed the case in such a way that all of Christopher's original tactics remain "arguably legal," but are morally troublesome. The standard conception has little place, though, for Christopher's moral concerns. The emerging morally activist lawyering conception, however, purports to offer just such a place. As it is no longer the 1970s, Christopher and Linda have available to them a melange of ideas from the productive philosophers, all suggesting that the tension between Christopher's professional role demands and his personal integrity ought to be addressed in a way in which the integrity element is not so easily sacrificed.

* * *

I think it should become clear that "choosing" in fact is *not* the most apt description of Christopher's experience as he reacts to the Hunter tension. For the moment, though, I want to maintain that metaphor. If we could break down his moral thought process at this juncture, there appear to be two parts to this moral calculus. First, does he opt for a traditional stance, or an activist one? If I am correct that there are differences between these two universes, then it is not illogical to think of lawyers as falling into one "camp" or the other. If Christopher is a traditionalist, and if my assessment of the standard conception is reliable, then he proceeds as I described above, which means essentially litigating this "arguably legal" defense. If he is not a traditionalist, but instead is an activist, then his second decision point arises: which of the activist arguments does he accept, and which does he reject? If I am correct that there are cognizable differences among the activists, then it is not illogical to expect that those differences will affect the practice experience (or, equally relevantly, the moral assessment) of the resulting lawyering.

Two things seem to be true at this point in the argument. One is that Christopher most likely will not perform (and will not have done so in the recent past) a philosophical investigation and analysis of the competing theories, judging then one to be superior, before acting. The second is that Christopher *will act* in some way on this case, a way which in hindsight will be describable as consonant with one or another of the philosophical theories. That is to say, he cannot (unless he is a rare law student) resolve the philosophers' debates, but he will have to act as though he has done so, at least provisionally and at least for his conception of his career at this moment. These observations are apt to apply to *both* of the two hypothesized decision points that I have described: whether to be an activist, and (if chosen) what kind of activist to be. But, as I alluded to above, it is unfair to refer to these as *choices*, for that may accord an overstated sense of deliberative judgment to this process. It is more likely that Christopher will search in some imperfect, "satisficing" way to reconcile his moral beliefs, his legal obligations, and his personal reactions to his clients and their case. What looks like a series of decision points might instead be a complex blend of tactical and ethical sentiments.

If my description is accurate, then the philosophers' richly textured arguments are nearly beside the point for Christopher's proceeding on this case, except as follows. The arguments, whether richly textured or not, are critically important in affording an intellectually pedigreed justification for the *initial orientation* that Christopher will already hope to follow. It ought to be easier to be morally activist in 1995 than in 1974, thanks to Luban, Simon, Wasserstrom, etc. In addition, the arguments, and here preferably richly textured ones, will aid Christopher in his post hoc defense for what he opts to do within his morally ambiguous professional experience. Differing activist conceptions can justify different lawyering postures, and my best guess is that, once the abandonment of the standard conception is accomplished, the differences among the activist experts are more valuable after the fact than as principled direction ex ante for one posture among several choices.

* * *

There is not sufficient space to explore Christopher's range of choices in any great detail, but I do want to consider a couple of questions regarding the *lawfulness* of Christopher's options. Christopher does not live in some future morally superior world. He practices in Massachusetts in 1995, with whatever limits and mandates the professional responsibility laws of that state might impose upon him. Do those mandates *permit* him to be as morally activist as he might believe he ought to be? *Can he* act in the way that his teachers and the philosophers are suggesting he act?

There are, it seems, two ways to approach these questions, a simple way and a complicated way. The simple response offers two suggestions for Christopher, neither of which causes him any risk of professional censure. He may of course *talk* to his clients about his moral or legal concerns, and hope to come to an accommodation between what he perceives as their less-than-principled instructions and his moral or legal limitations. As many have pointed out, we too often assume that our clients would be unwilling to consider the moral implications of their choices. I do not want at all to belittle the importance of this process, but it is not an "activist" one; it is fully permitted, perhaps encouraged, by the traditional rules. I therefore need not address it fully here. The second "simple" choice is to withdraw, if the moral dialogue does not accomplish a satisfactory accommodation of Christopher's concerns. Withdrawal is "activist." Depending on one's jurisdiction and the prevailing interpretation of norms, it is probably allowed. I call it "simple" because one can readily find out whether it is permitted within the jurisdiction, even though it is never easily chosen by a lawyer.

Christopher might try, though, to practice morally activist lawyering in a more subtle way. For instance he might: (1) not file the motion to dismiss based upon the faulty notice to quit, (2) not plead a security deposit counterclaim, or (3) not serve discovery if he thinks that, while not frivolous, doing so is purely instrumental and not justified under the standards he has chosen to follow. This, to me, is activism in an affirmative sense. It limits the scope of the representation without withdrawing, and without informing the clients about the availability of the unchosen tactics. Christopher could simply diminish the range of available options that an ethical lawyer might consider, excluding those which he deems not fitting that definition.

Just as Christopher would not include perjury as a choice he would discuss with his clients, as a moral activist he might leave the instrumental ploys off the table.

This latter strategy is what I refer to as the complicated one, for reasons that should be apparent. The complicated practice is more consistent with an activist orientation, and truer to its mission than is a practice in which withdrawal is the only remedy available for clients who choose the instrumental route. It is probably not lawful, however, as I read existing standards, and it may well constitute malpractice. While one might predict that a malpractice liability judgment would be very unlikely in a case such as the one I have chosen to observe, an activist lawyer in the private market who costs a client substantial sums of money by failing to employ instrumental procedural devices cannot feel so confident.

If I am correct about this supposition, that activism is only lawful in the simpler but not in the more complicated fashions, that realization is a bit sobering for proponents of the activist position. It does not diminish the force of the activist message that lawyers cannot avoid responsibility for their actions, a message which (as it becomes more widespread) will consequently call for increased dialogue and more trepidation about instrumental, loophole lawyering. But one senses that the tremendous intricacy of the scholarly debate about the scope and the limits of various kinds of activism has presupposed that activists would be able to accomplish more, in actual practice alongside clients, than what they have always had permission, if perhaps considerably less incentive, to do.

* * *

Earlier excerpts have emphasized the importance of lawyer-client deliberation for the development of an effective relationship. Amy Gutmann posits that attorney-client deliberation is also essential to the lawyer's goal of serving justice. Zealous advocacy on the client's behalf does not necessarily lead to just results. By discussing the implications of action with the client, the lawyer and client may together choose a path which better comports with the ideal of justice.

Amy Gutmann, *Can Virtue Be Taught to Lawyers?*, 45 STAN. L. REV. 1759 (1993)*

"Can virtue be taught?" Plato rightly thought this a most challenging question. But our question—Can virtue be taught to lawyers?—presents a still greater challenge. We can begin to meet the challenge, as Socrates might suggest, by addressing the prior question: What is virtue for lawyers? For without figuring out what legal virtue is, we can only pretend to know whether lawyers can be taught virtue, or learn it.

---

* * *

Consider the view of legal virtue offered by the standard conception of lawyering. "When acting as an advocate, a lawyer must, within the established constraints upon professional behavior, maximize the likelihood that the client will prevail."[1] To maximize the likelihood that your client prevails, you must be not just an advocate of your client's preferences or interests, but a zealous advocate.

The obligation of zealous advocacy has been amply criticized by David Luban, among others, for losing sight of the larger aim of the law in furthering social justice.[2] The standard conception makes most sense in the context of the adversary process of criminal law, which does not of course comprehend most of what lawyers do. Even zealous advocates of their clients' preferences or interests may be held responsible— legally, professionally, and morally—for their actions. Authorization by clients does not immunize lawyers from responsibility for doing wrong any more than authorization by military officers exonerates soldiers from wrongdoing. What constitutes legal wrongdoing is often a tricky question, but the principle of responsibility does not stand or fall on hard cases.

A partial truth of the standard conception remains, and I want to pursue its implications here. Far worse than being a zealous lawyer is being a lazy or incompetent one, unwilling or unable to take on someone else's cause as your own. Lawyers who represent their clients simply for the sake of making a living, and therefore do not represent them well as long as they can get away with it, use their clients merely as means to their own self-interested ends. In criticizing the standard conception, we should not lose sight of the virtue of ardent (and perhaps at times zealous) advocacy. This is a virtue entailed in the legal obligation to argue other people's causes, not one's own. The advocacy virtues are necessary to safeguarding the basic interests of citizens in the face of threats to their civil and political rights.

But they are not sufficient, and for a reason that even proponents of the standard conception should acknowledge. The standard critique of zealous advocacy focuses on the need for lawyers to temper their defense of clients' causes with an appreciation of the larger purpose of their legal actions: social justice. Before we consider tempering advocacy for the sake of social justice, we should look carefully at the requirements of advocacy itself. What constitutes adequate representation? Ardent legal advocates, like good doctors, need to know not just the preferences of their clients, but their informed preferences. Like good friends, good lawyers do not take every and any preference of their clients as dispositive of what they should do in their clients' defense. Unlike good friends, good lawyers know, or should know, a lot more than their clients about the probable consequences for their clients' lives of various legal strategies. Proponents of the standard conception and critics alike can grant that ardent advocacy is sometimes a great virtue of lawyers. But we also should recognize that lawyers are not in a position to know what their obligation of ardent advocacy

---

1   Murray L. Schwartz, *The Professionalism and Accountability of Lawyers*, 66 CAL. L. REV. 673 (1978).

2   DAVID LUBAN, LAWYERS AND JUSTICE: AN ETHICAL STUDY 3-147, 393-403 (1988).

entails unless they understand their clients' informed preferences. Such an understanding cannot be taken for granted, or assumed to be apparent from simply asking clients about their preferences for legal services.

An internal critique of the standard conception follows from its central premise. The case of an ardent advocate should reflect her clients' informed preferences. In general, if lawyers do not make special efforts to understand the informed preferences of their clients, then the standard conception becomes indistinguishable from the indefensible claim that lawyers cannot be held accountable for anything to which their clients consent, whether or not they are well informed.

Clients are typically not experts in the law, or at least not in the part of the law for which they seek legal counsel. We need to rely upon legal counsel to develop informed preferences regarding legal services. Whether we know it or not, we are dependent on lawyers for becoming informed about the nature of legal processes and outcomes, and their likely impact on our lives. But the process of legal understanding is not one-way. Lawyers also depend, or should depend, upon their clients for understanding whether and what legal strategies would best serve their clients' interests. And clients depend on lawyers for advising us on whether and how to proceed with our cases. The decision in the end is ours, not theirs. But lawyers have a responsibility for helping us make an informed decision by engaging with us in a deliberative process which entails the give-and-take of information, understanding, and even argument about our alternatives. Whenever ardent advocacy is a legal virtue, so is the willingness and ability of lawyers to deliberate with clients, explaining the aims and likely consequences of alternate strategies, listening to the clients' concerns, reacting to them, and arriving at an understanding of their clients' informed preferences after mutual evaluation of the possibilities. The deliberative virtues include the disposition to discuss various legal strategies with clients, and to understand clients' goals and their informed reaction to relevant legal strategies to the extent feasible. These deliberative virtues are a precondition of good advocacy.

A mundane example illustrates this internal criticism of the standard conception. Suppose a group of divorce lawyers are excellent at arguing court cases for their clients but spend little or no time trying to understand their clients' informed preferences with regard to marriage and divorce. The vast majority of their clients do not start out with anything close to an expert knowledge of legal possibilities, let alone of the probable consequences and experiences attached to arguing their cases in court or settling them out of court. The lawyers take their clients' preferences at face value. When a client comes into their office saying that he does not want to pay his spouse a penny if he can get away with it, they tell him they will do whatever they can within the limits of the law to help him. They can threaten his spouse with litigation over custody and scare her into settling for a minimum amount of child support. And the lawyers often succeed in this strategy or in others that are also well-designed to satisfy their clients' expressed preferences. Their clients, on the other hand, typically fail miserably. They are never encouraged to consider the bad consequences of their desire to punish their spouses, and by extension, their children, who may never forgive them for the excessive misery wrought on their family for the sake of selfishness or revenge.

This group of successful divorce lawyers could practice their profession differently and still be successful as zealous advocates, far more successful in one important sense. They could help their clients examine the broader implications of their initial preferences, and explore with them the pros and cons of alternative strategies. The initial preferences of clients are sometimes, perhaps often, contrary to what their informed preferences would be. It is not reasonable to expect clients to inform themselves, even to know the questions they need to ask, independently of the guidance of legal counsel. These divorce lawyers, therefore, may seem like ardent advocates but in one critical sense they fail to fulfill the responsibilities of ardent advocates. They have not tried to understand, and to help their clients understand, their informed preferences. These lawyers bear some responsibility (not necessarily "full" responsibility) for their clients' uninformed preferences, because clients typically have no reasonable alternative but to depend on lawyers for informing them about the pitfalls and possibilities of the legal strategies available to them. (These lawyers do not bear full responsibility because clients also have some responsibility for informing themselves, and public officials are also responsible for instituting legal reforms that make it easier for ordinary people to inform themselves about the law.) On its own terms, the standard conception is incomplete if it does not ally the virtues of deliberation with clients with those of ardent advocacy.

But this defense of deliberative virtues is incomplete, and we can expose its incompleteness by considering a more compelling conception of law: the justice conception. Ardent advocacy may be a necessary virtue for lawyers in their roles as advocates, but lawyers cannot know if and when they should be advocates without thinking about the larger social purposes of law, in particular about the central place of law in serving social justice in a constitutional democracy. (Of course, this is not to say that legal practices as we know them consistently serve the cause of social justice, but rather that the social justification of some legal services rests critically on their doing so.) The core of the justice conception is captured by the Model Rule's characterization of a lawyer as a "public citizen having special responsibility for the quality of justice."[5]

The justice conception, as one might infer from its label, shifts the primary virtue of lawyering from advocacy to justice. Advocacy, even zealous advocacy, may still be an important virtue for (some) lawyers, but only insofar as justice demands. It would be surprising, moreover, especially in a society where some people are economically disadvantaged and socially stigmatized, to find that justice always, or even generally, demands zealous advocacy of lawyers, regardless of the nature of their clients' cause. The justice conception does not demand that lawyers aim directly at what they deem just, even if that means arguing against their clients' cause. Where the adversary system is justified, so are lawyers justified in ardently arguing their clients' cases. But the adversary system is not justified in all legal contexts, and even where it is, it may not justify zealous advocacy, meaning maximizing the likelihood that one's client cause will prevail (which is what the standard conception requires).

---

5   Model Rules Of Professional Conduct Preamble (1989).

The virtue of justice, to follow David Luban's "fourfold root of sufficient reasoning," requires that lawyers be able to justify (1) the legal institution within which they act (e.g., the adversary system of criminal justice), (2) their legal role (e.g., advocate for clients) as necessary to that institution, (3) their role obligation (e.g., zealousness in advocacy) as necessary to the role, and (4) their role acts (e.g., cross-examining an alleged victim of rape about her irrelevant sexual history) as necessary to the role obligation. If the justification fails at any stage, as it does in stages three and four of the parenthetical example, then lawyers are not justified in acting as zealous advocates.

Whereas the standard conception defends zealous advocacy as the primary legal virtue, the justice conception views as virtuous only those dispositions and acts required by the legal pursuit of social justice. The justice conception highlights an important legal virtue that the standard conception neglects, or even denies: the willingness and capacity of lawyers to act according to the demands of justice, rather than the preferences (even the informed preferences) of their clients when the two conflict. Partisan advocacy is not justified for all legal roles. Even when advocacy is justified, zealous advocacy may not be. And zealous advocacy does not justify certain tactics on behalf of one's clients (such as discrediting a plaintiff by raising irrelevant facts about her sexual history).

* * *

Proponents of the justice conception conflate the idea that lawyers have a greater responsibility to pursue justice (by virtue of their role and/or their having more power to do so) with the idea that they are more likely to subscribe to the correct conception of justice (by virtue of their practical judgment). The practical judgment of lawyers, their capacity for "logical thinking, a nose for facts, good judgment of people, toleration"[8] does not translate into a comparative advantage over other thoughtful people in discerning what constitutes just social policy or the most justifiable of competing principles of social justice. Deception of clients in the service of social justice is therefore suspect for both deontological and consequentialist reasons. Justice is not well-served by authorizing lawyers to pursue just ends independently of their clients' authorization, because the unauthorized means are morally suspect, and the ends lawyers choose to pursue may be worse than those that would be chosen by well-informed clients.

* * *

If their cause is just, why be so concerned with the means that lawyers use to pursue justice? Why recommend deliberation between lawyers and clients, a sharing of information and understanding on relevant matters, rather than that lawyers use their legal expertise and authority simply to convince clients to do what they, the expert lawyers, believe is just? * * * Deliberation demands far more. It requires an active engagement with clients that aims at a better understanding of the value of legal action and its alternatives than either party to the deliberation probably had at

---

8   David Luban, *The* Noblesse Oblige *Tradition in the Practice of Law*, 41 Vand. L. Rev. 717, 725 (1988).

the outset. The value of the best legal action on behalf of a client may often be its contribution to the pursuit of social justice, but social justice cannot routinely be pursued by a legal counsel independently of the client's informed consent.

The demand for deliberative virtues has two distinct sources internal to the justice conception of law, and one external to it (to which I will return in discussing the character conception of legal virtue). The first internal source has to do with the distribution of the virtue of justice, the second with its content. Regarding the distribution of justice as a virtue, it is not in practice reasonable to rely upon lawyers as a group for a firmer commitment to social justice (beyond the rule of law) or just social policies than their clients. Lawyers are more expert in navigating the law than their clients, but they are also, by virtue of their expertise and professional autonomy, politically more powerful and therefore potentially more likely to subvert social justice in pursuit of their own professional or personal interests. Legal expertise does not make lawyers more committed to the cause of social justice than their clients, and it is hard to see why it would. The justice conception therefore cannot credibly claim that the disposition to pursue just ends is a virtue more distinctive to lawyers than their clients. Nor can it authorize lawyers to act upon their substantive conception of justice independently of deliberating with their clients about its content. Were the justice conception to recommend such independent action beyond upholding the rule of law, it would be justifying a form of tyranny.

It does not follow that lawyers must defer to their clients' preferences as required by the standard conception, but rather that deliberation with clients places an important internal constraint on (and opportunity for) the legal pursuit of justice. This constraint is important both because it respects the principle of informed consent, and because it increases the chances that justice will actually be pursued and the virtue of justice will be as widely distributed among citizens as constitutional democracies require. An analogous (although relevantly different) set of internal constraints applies to judges, where judicial deliberation issues in one or more opinions that are informed by, and addressed to, competing legal and moral perspectives on the case.

The recommendation that lawyers deliberate with their clients follows also from an understanding of the content of social justice in a constitutional democracy. Constitutional democracies are created to cope with reasonable disagreements, including disagreements over the content of social justice and just social policy. At the same time, constitutional democracies must be constituted by, and authorize public officials to act upon, a public conception of social justice which itself is not universally accepted. Ongoing deliberation over its contents is one requirement of a conception of social justice suitable to constitutional democracy. Saying that lawyers should deliberate with their clients about justice is another way of saying that they should act justly, where the conception of justice now includes consideration of the social process of reasoning, not just its content. Reasoning by lawyers themselves is not enough, however logical, cognizant of the facts, tolerant and understanding of human nature legal reasoning is. Neither is deliberation a sufficient condition of legal justice, although it is both necessary and neglected.

I have outlined two reasons internal to the justice conception for lawyers to deliberate with their clients. There is a third reason that becomes apparent only after considering the limited scope of the justice conception in motivating what many lawyers do for a living. The justice conception would of course claim too much were it to require lawyers always to manifest the virtue of justice in their actions. In some situations of adversary justice, we rely upon legal institutions rather than lawyers for pursuing justice. This is the insight the standard conception carries too far. But there is yet another limit of the justice conception that rests on the distinction between furthering social justice and helping people live good lives according to their best lights, where social justice does not demand such help but simply permits it. Social justice need not be the primary aim of legal counsel and action on behalf of clients. Helping people live good lives is an aim of legal counsel consistent with social justice, but not dictated by it or directly aimed at it. Some legal services simply help people live good lives according to their best lights.

* * *

We often need help in thinking about our own well-being, and lawyers can help us in situations where legal services are a potential means of furthering individual well-being. Many nonadversarial legal services are only indirectly relevant to social justice, but directly relevant to a client's well being. Lawyers who further the well-being of their clients without injuring others do good in the world, even if they do not contribute to the cause of justice. The differential ability of citizens to afford legal counsel is of course a matter of social justice, but income maldistribution does not obliterate the good of this common form of legal counsel. Wherever legal services have the potential for enhancing human well-being, they also have the potential for harm, which is yet another reason why the disposition of lawyers to deliberate with their clients is a legal virtue. Deliberation is a necessary condition for informed consent, and informed consent is a safeguard against the potential tyranny of legal counsel.

* * *

As Richard A. Boswell explains in the next excerpt, clinicians are in a unique position to animate legal theory with the stories of lawyers and clients. A clinical faculty member's aspiration to justice should necessarily encompass the infusion of real life into theoretical legal constructs.

Richard A. Boswell, *Keeping the Practice in Clinical Education and Scholarship*, 43 Hastings L.J. 1187 (1992)*

* * *

A general survey of writing by clinicians leads me to the preliminary conclusion that much of the recent writing emulates more traditional scholarship. * * * This clinical scholarship has not taken advantage of the clinic's great strengths. It does not speak in the language of clients, lawyers, or even judges. In short, it does not serve as a bridge between these important participants in our sociolegal system. Whereas traditional doctrinal scholarship was more accessible to lawyers and judges, much of the new clinical scholarship is becoming less accessible to all groups, with the exception, perhaps, of some segments of the academy.

The question that we should be asking is whether we are going to be a bridge between the academy and the larger world of lawyers and clients, or whether we will merely inform others in the academy of our own perspectives on law. The roles are quite different. In the former we are communicating amongst all of the groups that shape the law; in the latter we communicate only within the academy. While this need not be an either/or proposition, I believe the choice must include providing a bridge between the academy and the larger world. This is the proper choice because we stand in two positions: within the academy, and in the midst of the larger world of the law in practice. As active practitioners within the academy, we are uniquely able to contribute to legal education's understanding of the outside world. Each of our constituencies has an important contribution to offer the academy, and we are in an excellent position to talk with and among those constituencies.

Much has been written about the gap between that which we teach in law school and that which actually goes on in the practice of law. The extent of the division between the theorists and the practitioners does not appear to be narrowing. I believe that bridging this widening gap will become even more difficult. * * *

The modern clinical movement presently stands at a crossroad. The path it takes will either marginalize its capacity to contribute meaningfully to social justice and legal education or make it the catalyst of a morally revitalized practice. This brings to mind Professor Gary Palm, of the University of Chicago's Mandel Legal Aid Clinic, who called on us to return to our roots.[20] He warned of the demise of in-house clinical programs, and he called on clinicians not to forsake the origins of the clinical movement. Professor Palm was referring to the modern clinical movement's roots in direct client representation during the late 1960s.

If we delve into the original *raison d'etre* of the clinical movement, we see that it sought to fill a moral vacuum plaguing legal practice and education. This moral vacuum, which was "discovered" during the Vietnam War era, still exists and needs

---

20 Gary Palm, Remarks at the Association of American Law Schools Annual Conference (Jan. 1989).

to be filled. Moral questions and hard choices are the heart of the law school clinic and the work of clinicians. Therefore, we must not be afraid to raise such questions in our scholarship, for the failure to raise these questions itself represents an implicit moral choice.

A more morally emphatic, living scholarship is needed to fill the gap between theory and practice. The legal theoretical movements of the last twenty years have provided excellent critiques of the dominant legal order. At their core, these movements cry out for a greater sensitivity to justice. But justice is a hollow word unless it has moral content and appeal. New clinical scholarship need not supplant the critical theories of the past two decades, but could inform each constituency about the other: scholarship that focuses on what clinicians talk about and experience on a daily basis in our interactions with clients, students, lawyers, judges, social workers, legislators, and countless others; scholarship that willingly addresses and grapples with moral and ethical questions. This kind of scholarship might help to draw links between each of these important constituencies of our work. Indeed, it might well lead us to a deeper mutual understanding.

B. Access to Justice

Tigran W. Eldred and Thomas Schoenherr describe how cutbacks in funding to the Legal Services Corporation have resulted in a "crisis of unmet legal needs" of poor people. Since the time when the article was written in 1993, there have been further cuts in funding for the program. Even more significantly, recent legislation has limited the types of cases which legal services lawyers can handle. Thus, the imperatives undergirding the obligation of each lawyer to represent poor people have become even more urgent.

Tigran W. Eldred and Thomas Schoenherr, *The Lawyer's Duty of Public Service: More Than Charity?*, 96 W. VA. L. REV. 367 (1993/1994)*

* * *

II. THE CRISIS IN LEGAL SERVICES FOR THE POOR

At the end of the nineteenth century, the first legal aid organizations were established to meet the legal needs of narrowly defined social groups, such as newly freed blacks, immigrants, children, and women. These benevolent associations, organized through charitable contributions of money and service, expanded in the early part of the twentieth century—by 1919, in fact, forty-one cities had legal aid

---

*   Reprinted with permission.

societies, with a staff of approximately two hundred full- and part-time attorneys, and an aggregate budget of nearly $190,000. Of these, however, only one—the Kansas City Bureau—was organized as a municipal office and received public funding. The remainder depended exclusively upon the charitable contributions of professional talent and financial support. This trend continued through the 1950s, when the prevailing political climate heightened fear against socialization of legal services for the poor. By 1960, two hundred legal aid offices operated with a total staff of 132 full-time attorneys. Unfortunately, these charitable contributions were insufficient to meet the legal needs of the poor, as less than 1 percent of the nation's 39 million poor people in 1960 received legal assistance from legal aid societies.

In 1965, legal aid became a national priority through the federal government's creation of the Legal Services Program (LSP), which funded initiatives in hundreds of communities throughout the country to help meet the vast array of the poor's legal needs. By 1967, for example, LSP issued $40 million in grants to more than three hundred agencies in over 210 communities, demonstrating for the first time that the federal government recognized that an important method in fighting poverty was to provide the nation's poor with access to essential legal services. By 1971, the aggregate amount of funding had increased to $61 million, which allowed 2,500 full-time staff attorneys in 934 legal services offices to handle over 1 million cases annually. The expansion in services continued through the 1970s, and by 1981, the Legal Services Corporation (LSC)—which had been created in 1974 to replace LSP—was budgeted at $321 million. By the 19s [sic], however, LSC had fallen out of favor with the Reagan administration, which drastically slashed the corporation's budget to $241 million in 1982, and appointed directors who were hostile to LSC's very existence. The effect of these financial cutbacks has been devastating: as reported by one research group in 1983, sixty-one LSC-funded programs reported a loss of *thirty* percent of their staff attorneys, many of whom were the most experienced attorneys. Moreover, LSC reported a *twenty-five* percent decline in the number of legal services offices operating nationwide. Although support for legal services has been restored in recent years, funding still lags well behind the pre-1982 levels.

Unfortunately, despite the federal government's efforts to meet the legal needs of the poor, today there exists what often has been described as a "crisis of unmet legal needs." Although quantifying the extent of the crisis is difficult, there is almost universal acceptance that the poor have been denied needed legal services. One survey by the ABA, for example, has concluded that no more than twenty percent of poor people's legal needs are being addressed. Given that most people living in poverty encounter legal difficulties on a regular basis, it is not surprising that, on a national scale, the aggregate unmet legal needs of poor Americans are staggering. Extrapolating existing data, a leading commentator has concluded that, "very conservatively," the amount of unmet legal needs of the poor nationwide is *twenty million* hours per year. The legal problems for which the poor can find no representation fall into various categories; for example, in New York State, the most frequently reported legal troubles include housing issues, public benefits problems, health care concerns, consumer and utility problems, discrimination and employment matters, and family issues. Given current poverty trends, the legal needs of the poor can only be expected to escalate.

To describe the problem simply as a quantitative matter, however, is to understate the true gravity of the legal services crisis. To those living in poverty, the margin of survival is precariously narrow. Often, one significant adverse legal result, such as the termination of public benefits, can be the difference between survival and disaster. In New York City, for example, over a quarter of the families entering the city's shelter system cited eviction by their landlords as the cause of their homelessness.[22] It is not surprising that in New York City Housing Court, 80-90% of landlords have counsel, whereas tenants are represented by an attorney no more than 15% of the time. Significantly, when tenants are represented by counsel, eviction rarely occurs. The conclusion is inescapable: legal counsel is an essential resource to prevent homelessness, a calamity not only for the [sic] those who no longer have homes, but also for society as a whole, which must finance public shelters. This example of the devastating personal and societal consequences of inadequate access to legal services is representative of the results of the crisis in legal services in general. Viewed in this light, the failure of the poor to receive needed legal services can only be considered catastrophic.

III. THE LAWYER'S AMBIGUOUS "DUTY" OF PUBLIC SERVICE

Despite the desperate need by the poor for legal services, the legal profession has displayed consistent confusion over whether lawyers have an ethical duty to render free legal services to those who cannot afford to pay for legal counsel. Throughout American legal history, the dominant view has been that lawyers are not obliged, as a matter of professional responsibility, to provide legal services free of charge to those in need. Rather, the legal culture in this country has understood *pro bono* work to be an act of personal charity, to be performed at the discretion of the individual attorney. According to this view, the imposition of a *pro bono* duty would violate the discretionary ideal of public service, the virtue of which depends upon the fact that such service is propelled by the lawyer's individual conscience, rather than forced compulsion. Of course, there have been exceptions to this rule, the most notable being the long history of courts appointing counsel to represent indigent clients in pending civil matters. Notwithstanding the judiciary's unique perspective on the lawyer's professional responsibilities, however, the profession as a whole has been unwilling to accept the notion of a professional duty to serve, and instead has viewed legal counsel similar [to] any other scarce resource—to be purchased in the marketplace by those who are able to pay. * * *

* * *

---

22   *See* [COMMITTEE TO IMPROVE THE AVAILABILITY OF LEGAL SERVICES, FINAL REPORT TO THE CHIEF JUDGE OF THE STATE OF NEW YORK (April 1990)] at 16-17 (citing the ASSOCIATION OF THE BAR OF THE CITY OF NEW YORK, COMMITTEE ON LEGAL ASSISTANCE, HOUSING COURT PRO BONO PROJECT: REPORT ON THE PROJECT, PARTS I AND II (June and Nov. 1988)).

V. The Lawyer's Duty of Public Service

A. *The Lawyer's Unique Role in Distributing Legal Services*

The traditional notion that lawyers do not have an affirmative duty to serve fails to account for the special and unique role that lawyers play in the system of justice. As a leading proponent of a lawyer's duty of service, David Luban points out in his seminal study *Lawyers and Justice: An Ethical Study*[102] that there are compelling reasons why lawyers must accept, as a matter of professional duty, an obligation to help serve those in need. This duty, Luban explains, derives not merely from the poor's needs for legal services, but instead from categorical arguments grounded in the very ideals that legitimize the American polity.

The argument in favor of a duty of public service is based on two postulates, the first being that it is imperative that the poor have access to the legal system. As Luban notes, the essential legitimatizing principle of the American legal system is that all people are afforded "equal justice under the law." This ideal implies not only an equality of political right, such as the right to vote, but also "equality of legal right," meaning that each person must have the opportunity to redress legal grievances through the adjudicative process. Because legal rights are meaningless unless they can be enforced, "the principle of equal access to the legal system is part of our framework of political legitimacy . . . [and] to deny a person legal assistance is to deny her equality before the law, and that to deny someone equality before the law delegitimizes our form of government."

The second premise Luban puts forth is that meaningful access to the legal system requires the assistance of a lawyer. Model Rule 6.1 acknowledges the essential truth of this conclusion. In describing what he calls the "necessity claim," Luban notes:

> It is an obvious fact . . . that all of our legal institutions (except small claims court) are designed to be operated by lawyers and not by laypersons. Laws are written in such a way that they can be interpreted only by lawyers; judicial decisions are crafted so as to be fully intelligible only to the legally trained. Court regulations, court schedules, even courthouse architecture are designed around the needs of the legal profession.

There can be little dispute on this matter, as an illustration makes clear. In federal courts throughout the country, indigent *pro se* prisoners pursue legal claims under the federal civil rights statute for a variety of constitutional deprivations, including the denial of due process in disciplinary hearings and the unauthorized use of excessive force by prison personnel. Invariably, these lawsuits languish on what are known as "pro se lists" until a lawyer either volunteers or otherwise accepts an appointment. Once appointed, the lawyer can achieve what the client cannot—including: conducting pre-trial discovery (drafting meaningful document requests and taking depositions); appearing in court for motion practice; and ussing [sic] the available technology necessary to advance a legal claim (including the use of word

---

102 David Luban, Lawyers and Justice: An Ethical Study (1988). * * *

processors, secretarial assistance, and paralegal support). Even assuming that an incarcerated litigant could proceed through discovery and pre-trial proceedings, very few (if any) will have the legal acumen to comprehend the perplexing legal issues of law, and, if trial is warranted, to master the basics of federal civil procedure. In the end, meaningful access to the legal system for a *pro se* prisoner can only occur after counsel has been appointed. Litigating in federal court may entail some of the more complicated aspects of our legal structure; nevertheless, it goes without saying that virtually all of our legal institutions are designed to be operated by lawyers, and not laypersons. As a result, meaningful access to the legal system unavoidably requires the services of competent counsel.

Given that the legitimacy of the legal system requires that every member of society, including the poor, have access to a lawyer, the remaining question is who must assure that access? Due to the unique and privileged role granted to members of the bar, lawyers have an affirmative obligation to provide the poor with needed legal resources. Lawyers are not artisans; instead, they are professionals who retail in an extremely valuable commodity—"the law"—which must be available to all for the system to retain its legitimacy. And yet, because the state has created a monopoly over legal services, which restricts the practice of law exclusively to licensed attorneys, lawyers alone are in a unique position to meet the legal needs of the poor. In fact, any layperson who attempts to assist the poor with their legal needs would be punished under unauthorized practice of law statutes. Given this restriction on the availability of legal resources, lawyers are the only members of society who can help meet the legal needs of the poor. As a result, to maintain the legitimacy of the legal system, each lawyer must help ensure that legal services are available to all, including those who are too poor to pay for them.

Despite the force of this argument, some have claimed that it is unfair to single lawyers out and burden them with solving the legal needs of the poor. According to this view, the burden of distributing legal services to the poor should be borne by society as a whole, rather than by lawyers alone. The problem with this claim, however, is that it ignores the fact that the monopoly that lawyers retain over legal services confers substantial benefits on lawyers, including granting lawyers the privilege of retailing lucrative legal services at prices that are higher than could be commanded in a deregulated market. As such, requesting lawyers to expend a percentage of time to assist those in need is nothing more than a fair surcharge for the windfall that accrues from the legal monopoly. Moreover, because access by the poor to legal services is a necessary precondition to the legitimacy of the legal process, lawyers must accept a duty of service, notwithstanding that society has shunned the legal needs of the poor. Any other conclusion would allow lawyers to retail their trade—providing legal services to paying clients—in a legal system that has lost its legitimacy. Although some lawyers would undoubtedly be willing to continue to practice law [in] such an unjust system, fundamental notions of legal ethics require that every lawyer work to maintain the integrity of the legal profession. As a result, lawyers cannot ignore the legal services crisis, even if society chooses to do so.

In conclusion, for the legal system to be legitimate, society must afford legal services—access to a lawyer—to the poor. Because the monopoly that benefits lawyers limits the poor's access to the legal system, lawyers have a unique obligation to help legitimize the very system in which they practice. Consequently, all attorneys have a fundamental duty to assist in meeting the legal needs of the poor. This is not an argument borne of necessity; rather, the duty of public service arises from the very nature of a system that seeks Equal Justice Under Law.

B. *Implications of a Duty of Public Service*

Several implications result from the notion that lawyers owe an affirmative duty of public service. First and foremost, the rules governing the professional responsibilities of lawyers must be amended to reflect the fact that every lawyer, as a condition of membership, has a professional responsibility to help assure that legal services are available to those in need. The revised rule should unambiguously articulate the notion that every lawyer has the responsibility to engage in *pro bono* legal activities on behalf of those who cannot afford legal services. This does not necessarily mean that the amended rule should mandate that each lawyer spend a certain number of hours per year providing direct legal services to those in need. Rather, a flexible approach should be adopted to allow each attorney to determine how best to comply with the professional obligation of public service. Undoubtedly, some will choose direct legal services; others will make a financial contribution to appropriate legal services organizations; still others may decide to become active in a bar association subcommittee that is devoted to maximizing the poor's access to legal services. Ultimately, the point is not to dictate how the professional service obligation is performed, but rather to articulate a clear rule that will inform each member of the profession that a basic professional responsibility exists to help assure that legal services are available to all.

Second, the bar should make a special effort to help educate lawyers about their public service responsibilities and to help facilitate lawyer *pro bono* activities. For states that mandate Continuing Legal Education for lawyers, training about public service should become an integral part of the educational process. For states that do not require CLE, special programs should be created to discuss the professional duty of public service. Topics to be covered in such seminars should include the nature and extent of the duty of service, an overview of the crisis in legal services for the poor, and training sessions to help practitioners learn the substantive areas of poverty law, such as housing law, government benefits law, and the like. Bar associations should also distribute training materials to all practitioners to help explain the nature and extent of the professional duty of public service and to suggest methods on how to perform the duty.

In addition, law schools must begin teaching students about their duty of public service as part of the required professional responsibility curriculum. As the ABA Commission on Professionalism has stated, "law schools . . . constitute the greatest opportunity" to instill an ethic of public service in young lawyers. To communicate to students the importance of the duty of public service, several concrete modifications to the curriculum should be implemented. First, law schools should make a concerted effort to expose students to the legal needs of the poor, so as to sensitize students to the nature and scope of the legal services problem. One method to achieve this result may be to establish a curricular requirement that each student, as a condition of graduation, is expected to perform a designated amount of *pro bono* work. Second, the ethic of public service should not be confined to professional responsibility classes alone, but instead should be taught and discussed pervasively throughout the law school curriculum. Third, each law school should offer a variety of different substantive courses and clinical programs related to various aspects of poverty law to increase student exposure to the legal needs of the poor. Courses devoted to the ethical considerations of public interest law would also be very useful in helping law students appreciate their public service responsibilities. Finally, law schools should focus attention on whether there is merit to the charge that the law school experience tends to devalue the importance of public interest law by sending messages to law students that work for the poor is less worthy than work for corporate and business interests. To counteract these negative signals, law schools must work to create a more positive atmosphere towards public interest law, so that student desires to engage in *pro bono* activities are nurtured, and not inhibited.

Finally, establishing a clear duty of public service should relieve some of the pressure surrounding mandatory *pro bono* initiatives. Hopefully, rates of attorney *pro bono* activity will significantly improve once lawyers begin to understand that their professional responsibilities include the fundamental duty to perform public service on behalf of the poor. However, if after an appropriate period of time, lawyers continue to ignore their public service responsibilities, then mandatory *pro bono* programs should be instituted. Although active resistance to such programs is sure to continue, such opposition will be easier to overcome after the profession has clearly articulated a vision of legal ethics that includes a basic duty of public service. Moreover, irrespective of the resistance, however, the bar will be justified in imposing mandatory *pro bono* requirements to ensure that lawyers fulfill the basic responsibility of public service.

VI. CONCLUSION

Given the crisis in legal services for the poor, the legal profession needs to acknowledge that the basic tenets of the system of justice require that each lawyer accept, as a matter of professional responsibility, the duty to help assure that the poor have access to needed legal services. As such, lawyers can no longer conceive of public service as a matter of mere charity, to be performed at the discretion of each individual lawyer. Once the bar articulates a clear basis for the duty of service and implements appropriate initiatives to encourage *pro bono* efforts, lawyers must begin to take their public responsibilities seriously. If they do not, alternative methods to secure legal services for the poor, including mandatory *pro bono* programs, should be explored and implemented.

Barlow Christianson identifies two philosophical bases for the lawyer's pro bono obligation. First is the lawyer's personal conscience and perceived duty to assist the public. Second, as discussed more fully in the preceding excerpt, is the fact that lawyers are given a monopoly on access to one branch of government. The price for holding that monopoly is the obligation to provide pro bono service.

Barlow F. Christensen, *The Lawyer's Pro Bono Publico Responsibility*, 1981 AM. B. FOUND. RES. J. 1*

* * *

One of the most controversial sections of the American Bar Association's proposed new Model Rules of Professional Conduct[2] has been the so-called "mandatory pro bono service" provision:

> A lawyer shall render unpaid public interest legal service. A lawyer may discharge this responsibility by service in activities for improving the law, the legal system, or the legal profession, or by providing professional services to persons of limited means or to public service groups or organizations. A lawyer shall make an annual report concerning such service to appropriate regulatory authority.

This seemingly modest step toward a real mandatory system has generated heated debate within the legal profession, and opposition to it apparently poses a threat to the acceptance of the whole of the Model Rules. Accordingly, the ABA commission has deleted the reporting provision of the rule, at least for the present. The mandatory pro bono service notion is probably not dead, however: its proponents are insistent, and the legal profession will almost surely have to deal with the issue again.

SOME DEFINITIONAL PROBLEMS

Before further examination of the lawyer's pro bono publico obligation, perhaps a few comments on the matter of definition would be useful. The subject is often discussed without any attempt at definition, and some differences of opinion may result from the fact that different people are using the same terms to talk about different concepts.

Views of what constitutes pro bono publico service range from the extremely broad to the very narrow. On the one hand, there are those who appear to regard as pro bono service anything that a lawyer may do of a public nature, including, for example, membership on school boards, participation in the activities of service clubs such as the Lions or Kiwanis, and even political activity. On the other hand, some would limit the term to actual no-fee or low-fee representation of needy clients. The

---

2   American Bar Association, Commission on Evaluation of Professional Standards, Model Rules of Professional Conduct (Discussion Draft, Jan. 30, 1980) (hereinafter referred to as Draft Model Rules).

definition used in the proposed new Model Rules—"service in activities for improving the law, the legal system, or the legal profession, or . . . professional services to persons of limited means or to public service groups or organizations"—occupies a middle ground.

The broadest definition would seem to go too far. A distinction should probably be drawn between those public service obligations arising directly out of the lawyer's membership in the legal profession and those that flow from his status as a citizen and member of the community. Political activity, participation in the work of service organizations, and membership on the governing boards of educational or beneficent organizations would seem generally to be expressions of civic rather than professional duty. But even this distinction leads to some close questions. For example, an invitation to serve on the board of a charitable institution is intended in most cases to draw upon the lawyer's analytical and decision-making skills, which are clearly professional. And, indeed, it may be intended in most cases to draw upon his knowledge of the law, or even upon other lawyering skills. Still, a genuine difference would seem to exist between the gratuitous performance of what are clearly legal services on behalf of a public service group or organization and the performance of deliberative, supervisory, or administrative services in which the employment of lawyering skills may be only incidental. The line may be difficult to draw, but pro bono obligations would seem best limited to those that arise primarily because a person is a lawyer and not extended to those that derive primarily from citizenship or membership in the community.

The narrowest definition—actual representation of needy clients—would appear to be too restrictive. Involvement in the work of law reform or in developing and supervising legal service delivery programs, for example, is unquestionably public service effort arising directly from the lawyer's status as a professional. In some instances, such service may be of greater overall value to the public than the same amount of time spent in actual service to needy clients. Of course, there is something to be said for the position that the public, the profession, and the individual lawyer would all benefit significantly if all lawyers were to devote at least some of their public service time to the performance of their quintessential role—the actual representation of clients—in the cause of the defenseless and oppressed. But perhaps this would best be left as an ideal rather than as a definition of the pro bono obligation.

The above quoted definition from the proposed Model Rules, or something like it, would seem, then, to be appropriate as a frame of reference for thinking about the lawyer's pro bono obligation, and this is the definition used in the discussion that follows. But even with this working definition, questions remain. For example, should all bar association work be regarded as public interest activity, so that simply attending bar meetings or serving on internal committees discharges a pro bono obligation? Even these activities may contribute, at least indirectly, to the improvement of the law, the legal system, or the legal profession. Or should the effort be clearly and directly related to those ends before it can be regarded as pro bono publico? And what kind of improvement of the legal profession qualifies as a public service? That question no one seems yet to have addressed in any definitive way. The conclusion is inescapable that decisions about mandatory pro bono publico service will require far greater attention to definition than seems thus far to have been given.

* * *

The proponents of mandatory public interest service have not always been entirely clear about the philosophical bases for their conclusion that lawyers must be compelled to pro bono service. They do sometimes talk about the profession's tradition of service above gain, of course. And some see pro bono service as required in self-defense; if lawyers do not accept a mandatory obligation to provide public service, they say, others may impose it upon them or even take away their exclusive privilege to practice law. But the most consistent rationale seems to be the notion that the lawyer's obligation to render unpaid public interest legal service arises out of his essential position in the justice system and his monopoly of the business of performing legal services.

* * *

TRADITIONAL VOLUNTARY PUBLIC SERVICE

Historically and traditionally, the lawyer's public interest obligation has been regarded as a matter of personal conscience and aspiration to a professional ideal, exemplified so nobly by such public interest service pioneers as the late Reginald Heber Smith. Roscoe Pound's definition of a profession is well known: "[A] group of men pursuing a learned art as a common calling in the spirit of a public service—no less a public service because it may incidentally be a means of livelihood."[21] Similarly, in his classic work on legal ethics, Henry Drinker declared, under the heading "Noblesse Oblige," that the first of the "[p]rimary characteristics which distinguish the legal profession from business" is "a duty of public service, of which the emolument is a by-product."[22] This characteristic he traced back to what he called "our legal ancestors, the barristers, in their Inns of Court." And, the recommended oath of admission for lawyers, adopted by the American Bar Association in 1908 and now a statutory requirement in many states, contains an avowal that the lawyer "will never reject, from any consideration personal to [himself], the cause of the defenseless or oppressed."

The "spirit of public service" about which Pound spoke is broader than the mere obligation to render legal service to those in need, of course. The same spirit prompts many of the lawyer's other ethical obligations, particularly those relating to the duty of fidelity to clients. Some have used this fact to justify the position that the lawyer discharges his public service obligation when he does nothing more than serve paying clients faithfully and competently. But clearly, the traditional obligation, as articulated by Pound and Drinker and as honored by many dedicated lawyers throughout the history of the profession, goes beyond mere service to paying clients. It goes, as well, to "the cause of the defenseless or oppressed."

---

21   Roscoe Pound, The Lawyer from Antiquity to Modern Times: With Particular Reference to the Development of Bar Associations in the United States 5 (St. Paul, Minn.: West Publishing Co., 1953).

22   Henry S. Drinker, Legal Ethics 5 (New York: Columbia University Press, 1953).

A significant characteristic of the traditional pro bono publico obligation is its essentially passive—even negative—nature. Traditionally, the individual lawyer has had no affirmative duty to seek out and serve the defenseless or oppressed, or even to see that they are served; rather, his duty has been to "not reject" them when they come to him. Thus, the extent of the obligation is defined, to begin with, by the happenstance of needy clients coming to lawyers and ultimately by the individual lawyer's personal sense of professional obligation, without reference to externals such as aggregate unmet legal need. Indeed, from the traditional point of view, public needs are largely irrelevant to professional obligation except as they may affect the individual lawyer's sense of duty.

Some of the consequences of the passive character of the traditional pro bono obligation are central to the issue here being considered. These are those consequences relating to the amount of public interest legal work done voluntarily by reason of the traditional pro bono obligation and the locus of its performance—that is, which lawyers do the pro bono work.

* * *

Although no hard data support the observation, it would seem that a substantial number of lawyers do an appreciable amount of pro bono work out of genuine commitment to the traditional professional ideal. No one can say how many or how much, of course. But these dedicated lawyers are those who would be most directly affected and would have the most to lose from the adoption of a mandatory pro bono program. While imposition of a mandatory duty would be unlikely to lessen the commitment of these lawyers to the traditional ideal—they would no doubt continue to render public interest service, and for noble reasons—it would to some extent rob them of the personal satisfaction that they now find in such service. This threatened loss is at least a part of the reason for opposition to mandatory pro bono. As one noted bar leader has said, many lawyers "resent the whole business of mandatory pro bono!"[32] One might also speculate whether mandatory public interest service might not inhibit the development among succeeding generations of lawyers of a comparable group with such deep commitment to the traditional ideal. If so, the loss to the profession and to the public would be serious and substantial.

One commentator has suggested that much work that might be regarded as pro bono service is done at least partly out of self-interest:

> The solo and small firm general practitioner inevitably provides a lot of legal service on a no fee or low fee basis. That is, such a practitioner needs a steady flow of clients, has to take some chances that new clients will not or cannot pay, and suffers loss on some of the chances taken. The gratuitous services are simply the by-product of a strategy of business-getting.[33]

---

32   Robert W. Meserve, as quoted in [Scott] Slonim, [Commission Votes Down Pro Bono Reporting, 66 A.B.A.J.] at 951 [(1980)]. * * *

33   Geoffrey C. Hazard, Jr., The Lawyer's Pro Bono Obligation 2, Discussion paper for the American Bar Association Second National Conference on Legal Services and the Public, Dec. 7-8, 1979.

It is suggested that while these lawyers may be motivated partly by the traditional ideal of service before gain, the incentive of personal economic interest provides a more solid foundation for good works than does "a mere sense of duty" or than would any formal or legal obligation. Perhaps this is so, but the notion that the profession's collective pro bono obligation is to be discharged largely through no-fee or low-fee work done as a business-getting strategy by solo practitioners and small-firm lawyers motivated primarily by economic self-interest carries with it some disquieting implications.

To begin with, this economic incentive shares one of the limiting characteristics of the traditional professional ideal, its essentially passive nature. Those lawyers who do such no-fee and low-fee work do it for those clients who happen to come to them. And this may have something to do both with the quantity of pro bono work done and with the nature of the work or the clients for whom the work is done. While the gratuitous work done in this manner is without doubt substantial in quantity—probably the largest amount done by the bar—it almost surely represents but a fraction of the pro bono work that needs to be done and that would be done if affirmative action were taken to serve those who need service and if the entire bar, and not just a segment, were doing it.

* * *

The nature of the gratuitous work done in this way is also likely to be quite different from that which would be done if the mechanism were not passive. The client who, on his own initiative, comes to a lawyer for service and then ends up not paying for it may very well be significantly different from the potential client who never comes to a lawyer because he knows that he cannot pay the fee. And the kinds of cases brought by each may well be different. The possibility exists, then, that the pro bono work done as a business-getting strategy does not reach those clients and those cases where the need is greatest. Put the other way, pro bono work as a business-getting strategy may be devoted disproportionately to those clients and cases that need it least.

* * *

Finally, what of those lawyers who do little or no pro bono work for any reason? Again, we have no way of knowing for sure how many there may be, but there would appear to be far too many of them—perhaps more than the profession would care to acknowledge openly. * * *

These lawyers may be divided into two groups. The first comprises those who do little or no pro bono work because of lack of opportunity. Because of the passive nature of the traditional pro bono obligation, they are under no compulsion to seek out public interest work. And, because of their practice situations—usually in the larger urban firms—clients in need of no-fee or low-fee work do not often seek them out. Perhaps an interview response obtained in another study would serve to illustrate. A senior partner in one large and prestigious urban firm, when asked about limitations on his firm's ability to do work for the poor or people of moderate means, replied: "Very frankly, I find that the work for either the poor or the first and middle income [groups] does not gravitate to an office of this sort. We do it if it comes, but it does-n't get here very often for one reason or another." It is submitted that this statement probably describes the pro bono activity of a large number of lawyers. They might render some public interest legal service if the opportunity arises, but the opportunity doesn't often arise.

* * *

The other group of lawyers who render little or no public interest legal service is composed of those who have no personal commitment to the traditional professional ideal of service above gain and who have no economic need for pro bono cases as a business-getting strategy. These are they who refuse to accept certain kinds of cases without a full cash fee in advance and who take only that work for which they are virtually certain of being paid. These are also they who take small fees from clients unable to pay more and then neglect those clients' matters in favor of more lucrative work or give no service at all. Indeed, much of the unprofessional behavior with which the bar is regularly charged is probably attributable to lawyers who also refuse to do pro bono work. Once more, it is impossible even to speculate about their number, but the persistence and extent of public criticism of the bar for such unprofessional conduct would seem to suggest that disregard of the professional ideal is far too common.

The failure of many lawyers to do any significant amount of pro bono work is surely one of the most distressing consequences of the traditional voluntary approach to pro bono service. All too willing to bask in the light of reflected honor, claiming the benefits of professional status while refusing to accept the burdens of professional obligation, these lawyers make a mockery of the profession's noble aspirations. And it is here that mandatory pro bono would be likely to have its greatest impact. Without in any way diminishing professional self-image, professional satisfaction, or adherence to the professional ideal—these lawyers have no commitment to the professional ideal to start with—mandatory pro bono would compel a substantial number of lawyers to assume their fair share of the burden of professional responsibility, ensuring at least the substance of public service if not the "spirit of public service."

Looked at solely from the perspective of the traditional professional ideal, the issue of mandatory public interest service would seem to be a fairly close one. Some benefits would probably be obtainable through a mandatory system, but some serious losses would also occur. On balance, the traditional voluntary approach would seem to be preferable, at least from this perspective. The issue would appear ultimately to turn, then, on the validity and force of the obligation claimed to arise by reason of the lawyer's so-called monopoly. Is there such an obligation? If so, is it of sufficient consequence to tip the balance in favor of mandatory pro bono?

* * *

Rights and privileges, by definition, carry with them duties and responsibilities. So with the exclusive privilege of law practice. It carries with it the responsibilities of competence and honesty, for example. And, unlike the same responsibilities that arise out of the traditional professional ethic, those that stem from the lawyer's exclusive status are imperative duties. The duty of competence is enforced by academic qualifications for admission to law practice, by bar examinations, and by civil liability for negligence. The duty of honesty is enforced by disciplinary action for malfeasance and in some instances by criminal sanctions.

I submit that the exclusive privilege of law practice also carries with it a similarly imperative duty to see to it that any injury to the public caused by the monopoly is eliminated. This duty does not depend upon the happenstance of people with needs coming to lawyers. Nor does it depend upon the vagaries of individual conscience. It has nothing to do with charity or largesse or benevolence. It is an imperative duty that flows from the exclusive privilege of law practice to every lawyer who claims the privilege. It comes with the territory. But the question remains. Just what is the obligation arising from the lawyer's monopoly?

* * *

* * * [T]he obligation stemming from the lawyer's monopoly is an imperative duty of *all* lawyers who share in the privileges of the monopoly. The extent of the obligation is defined not in terms of the extent of public legal needs to be met but in terms of the bar's reasonable capacity. The essence of the concept of "reasonable capacity" must be the involvement of *all* lawyers—not just the public spirited and not just those impelled by economic considerations to provide no-fee and low-fee service—in whatever measures are developed to alleviate the injury to the public by reason of the lawyer's monopoly. Nothing that has thus far been done or proposed, short of mandatory pro bono service, offers even slight promise of involving all lawyers. It would appear that a large number of lawyers will not shoulder their part of the professional burden unless they are compelled to it.

So, we are led, reluctantly and sadly, to the conclusion that mandatory pro bono must be accepted. Even though one consequence may be the loss, by some lawyers, of professional self-image and professional satisfaction, only a mandatory system of public interest service offers any reasonable prospect of meeting adequately the professional obligation arising out of both the lawyer's monopoly and the legal profession's tradition of public service.

* * *

In the following excerpt Barbara Bezdek describes the Legal Theory and Practice course at the University of Maryland Law School. One purpose of the course is to provide students with experience representing poor persons.

Barbara Bezdek, *Reconstructing a Pedagogy of Responsibility*, 43 HASTINGS L.J. 1159 (1992)*

Candidly speaking, the Legal Theory and Practice (LTP) courses' essential purpose is to inculcate values leading our graduates to represent poor and underrepresented people and communities.[1] * * *

* * *

A principal lesson of the traditional first year curriculum is that lawyers' responsibility is limited. Even with today's expanded use of problems and role-plays in classroom courses, the standard conception of lawyers' functions and social roles sells to each class of incoming lawyers an excused status. If harms were inflicted, disputing parties are responsible; if decisions have objectionable results or effects, they were made by judges; robbers are entitled to counsel at public expense, so surely robber barons are if they can pay the freight. Lawyers merely facilitate transactions, solve problems, make the legal system go. Lawyers' work is to provide the technical know-how by which clients pursue each other, and lawyers are explicitly absolved from the taint of their clients' evil ends so long as the means are "clean."

Law schools' explicit instruction about responsibility delivers a similarly limiting message. Three overt curricular expressions coexist. The most common, and most vigorously criticized, is the application of legalism to "responsibility." The teaching of what purport to be ethical rules for the legal profession lapses into an imitation of the legalistic methodology of the bulk of the curriculum. It is deadening, taught as ahistorical, apolitical, and removed from social contexts. It teaches students to regard legal relationships as separate from the world in which they exist, having no history and no ramifications for others or for social institutions. The effect, and it is fair to say the effort, is to separate the lawyer and her own ethical sensibilities from the broader social world in which she will function.

A second approach is professionalism. It proceeds from a broader notion of lawyers' role, making reference to sociohistorical context, and extolling the positive role of lawyers in shaping society. From this vantage point, it makes a call on lawyers to act in the public interest and enact American liberal-democratic political ideals of inclusion. Some purveyors of professionalism have the aggravating tendency to speak in noble abstractions. They speak of the responsibility of "the legal profession" to represent "the poor," a plea that is made personal for most of the bar only when the prospect of mandatory pro bono looms. One further note in the chorus urging a return to halcyon days of a public-regarding legal profession, is the concern that the practice of law has become overly commercialized, a business rather than a "profession."

---

1 This was a charge directed to the Law School by the Advisory Council of the Maryland Legal Services Corporation (also known as the Cardin Commission, for its Chair, Congressman Benjamin Cardin). * * *

A third avenue for addressing lawyers' responsibility that has ventured into law schools is a kind of pragmatics. Its focus is to render ethical dilemmas of law practice more relevant, interesting, or compelling by grounding them in actual practice. It may take the form of classroom-based problems, or, as in recent years, it may serve as an argument for the recognition of clinical courses in the core curriculum. While incarnations of this spirit may be concretely helpful to some poor people in that some real legal services may be offered through law school clinics or required pro bono programs, the larger effect of the approach is to contribute to the marginalization of poor people in the curriculum. Exhorting students to the pragmatic quick-fix approach to isolated legal problems of poor people does not promote, and actually discourages, lawyers' attention to the systemic hostility of law's operation to poor people.

None of these three visions of professional responsibility renders a picture of the world, or of lawyers' work in it, that reaches the nub of "responsibility" to which the LTP [Legal Theory and Practice] courses are directed. What each lacks is concern with the deepest question lawyers' work poses: Who should I be?, or who should I become? This is, of course, a lifelong inquiry. In LTP courses, which occur early, but briefly in our students' legal careers, the question takes a more specific form: Who am I in relation to poor people?

* * *

The premise undergirding the Cardin Report directive is that each lawyer is implicated in the structures of law and their consequences, which privilege certain interests at the dullingly regular expense of impoverished others. This premise of responsible connectedness is a moral position, a core question-and-answer for living one's life. By lodging the question perpetually in the life of each "responsible" lawyer, it responds to the question posed earlier: Who am I in relation to poor people?

The perception of obligated and responsive connectedness is not a stance that has immediate widespread appeal. It is discouraged by the individualist tradition dominant in legal culture and in the larger culture as well. Furthermore, we all have much more experience of ourselves as innocent, than we have impulses to see ourselves so connected as to be implicated in others' oppression and vulnerability. It is others who jail people, evict people, set the benefits levels, and create the cultural disdain for "the undeserving poor." Isn't it? Unlike most of law schooling, LTP courses invite students to reexamine this comforting conclusion.

Students' reported experiences in Socratic classrooms suggest that one of the first lessons learned in law school is to witness others made to suffer and be forced to stand silent in the face of that suffering. The instruction to hold one's tongue in the law school classroom "prepares one to [tolerate] the suffering that one sees out in the world."[31] If law school delivers the lesson that compassion must give way to process, little wonder that many students acknowledge so little about the functions and effects of legal arrangements in the society.

---

31   *Id.* [James R. Elkins, *Pedagogy of Ethics*, 10 J. LEGAL PROF. 37, 58 (1985).]

The classroom example illustrates a fundamental aspect of social conditioning about responses to wrongs. It presents the sort of moment when, squirming under the discomforting weight of whether to object or accede to an exercise of dispropor- tionate power, one perceives the individual who is suffering, or the social system that enables the harm. Some may respond through empathy with identifiable other per- sons—the victim or victor. Others may, instead, perceive the net of socially allocated resources—such as power, authority, self-possession, and confidence in the classroom example—in which the suffering one is now ensnared.

Law students' work with poor clients offers parallel problems of perceptual focus. Numerous clinical students in any given year develop empathic, caring, iden- tifying relationships with their clients, across culturally significant boundaries of race, class, gender, and related life circumstances. However, too seldom does this priva- tized relational experience work its way into students' awareness of the ideological and sociocultural constructs of the legal world in which they move.

Venturing into a poor people's law practice in Baltimore makes vivid for LTP students that ours is a world marked by wide disparities in the distribution of money, of political power, and of personal opportunity for making significant life choices. Many LTP students observe first-hand that the social system that accomplishes these distributive outcomes is supported by legal rules and institutions that take little or no account of their clients' justifiable claims. This discovery opens students to consider the challenges thus posed to social and legal arrangements they now see as problematic.

The LTP/Property students discovered in Rent Court, not the neutral body adjudicating conflicting factual or legal claims rendered by their other first-year courses, but instead a forum operated for the speedy and convenient collection of rent by landlords, at taxpayers' expense. To the surprise of several students, few tenants they met were scofflaws. Many struggled each month to pay some sixty percent of their meager household incomes to rent hovels, and the effort to scrape it together each month left little time, energy, or expectation that telling the judge about the trou- ble with the heat and the leaky pipes was likely to make much difference.

Students' reactions to the poverty, the people, and the legal responses they encountered, created numerous openings for conversation between teacher and stu- dent about the possible meanings for their responsibilities as lawyers. Most students departed the course with a sharper awareness that to be poor in Rent Court meant as little, and as much, as the utter inability to raise another fifty dollars from family or friends. This led to some introspection far removed from the ordinary discourse of the classroom. Some students shared moments of surprising candor. "I never would have believed one could work so hard, and still make so little." "He needed that sum to avoid an eviction; I spent that much on the weekend, and I can't even think what it was for." "It occurred to me to wonder, can I stand outside the courtroom and talk with one more tenant, wearing a ninety-eight dollar 'barn jacket'?"

The day that tenants waited in line for advice from the white law students, believing the black law students must be tenants too, provoked pained and halting efforts later to express aloud the differing perceptions within the group about the links between race and the maldistribution of resources about which we shared some data: access to habitable housing, to lawyers, to law school. Others wrestled with the ways they saw themselves as like, and not like, the tenants with whom they worked. Each of these is, I contend, a form of inquiry into the moral dimensions of one's lawyering.

* * *

The adversary system is predicated on the concept that each lawyer zealously represents his or her clients. In order for this model to work, however, poor persons must also be represented, especially when their adversary is represented. Thus each lawyer has an obligation—as one who engages in and benefits from the adversary system—to provide pro bono representation to indigent persons.

Steven Lubet, *Professionalism Revisited*, 42 EMORY L.J. 197 (1993)*

Why are lawyers (on a good day) so roundly vilified and execrated?

One reason for the widespread popular dislike of lawyers was identified in a recent essay by Timothy Terrell and James Wildman.[1] Lawyering is misunderstood and mistrusted because it, unlike medicine, "exists largely because of moral ambiguity, not to resolve it." Moral ambiguity is uncomfortable but necessary to a democratic life. Like other necessary discomforts, it is resented.

Life would be so much easier if everyone did things the same way, if someone would simply *impose* order. The imposition of order, however, negates freedom; the price of constant order is too high. The rule of law, by striking the balance between order and freedom, imposes costs at both ends of the equation: it deprives us of order by stressing ambiguity, and at the same time it limits our freedom by creating constraints. Viewed in this light, it might even be said that a good legal system ought to be unpopular since a system could only satisfy everyone if there existed a generally diminished expectation of either freedom or order. People who do not care for freedom would be happy with a legal system that only provided order, and vice versa, but there will be frequent dissatisfaction with a system that values both.

Lawyers, at least in the contexts with which most people are familiar, are almost invariably the bearers of bad news. From the perspective of any (and therefore every) individual, the end result of lawyering is likely to be too much limitation on one's own freedom, but not enough imposition of order on anyone else.

---

*   Reprinted with permission.
[1]   Timothy Terrell & James Wildman, *Rethinking "Professionalism,"* 41 EMORY L.J. 403 (1992).

* * *

WHAT CAN LAWYERS DO?

* * *

Terrell and Wildman identify two areas in which the legal profession has been criticized for failing to live up to professional standards. The first issue is the "civility" crisis, which Terrell and Wildman appropriately dismiss as the lawyers' equivalent of bedside manner. Civility, of course, needs no academic justification; it is important in and of itself. But lawyers' rudeness to one another, however undesirable, is unlikely to be the root cause of public unhappiness with the profession. Most discourtesy, after all, is employed on behalf of clients. As economists would be quick to point out, hardball tactics would atrophy if they did not result in some measure of success. While the bar must address the problem of outrageous conduct, this is ultimately an internal predicament. Terrell and Wildman similarly discount the ideal of pro bono service, at least as a mandatory attribute of professionalism. Here they are wrong. Public service is a quality to be required of all professions, and an apparent lack of dedication to public service is, at least in part, responsible for the diminished stature of lawyers today.

SERVICE AS A PROFESSIONAL IDEAL

Terrell and Wildman argue that a moral claim for pro bono representation reduces the concept of professionalism to "a single, politically biased value—helping the poor." "Helping the poor" is a reasonably useful shorthand phrase, but it can be misleading. The concept of pro bono service concerns unremunerated representation, but it is not limited to indigent legal services. Lawyers can find it possible to donate their professional time to all manner of nonindigent clients, ranging from the American Civil Liberties Union to the Right to Life Legal Defense Fund to Lawyers for the Creative Arts. Such work can cut across the entire political and nonpolitical spectrum.

Nonetheless, it is reasonable for Terrell and Wildman to limit their discussion to indigent representation, since that is where the greatest needs are found, and that is also where the legal profession has been the most neglectful. Even still, it is hard to see why they consider representation of the poor to be so overtly politicized. As Terrell and Wildman put it, "what had been a discussion of means (how best to supply legal services) is now one about ends (how best to supply those services for a specific purpose)." But pro bono representation, even for "the poor," does not imply representation for a specific purpose. Quite the contrary, it suggests only the distribution of legal services with no particular goal in mind.

To be sure, many "poverty lawyers" have their own ideological agendas, and as laudable as their aims might be, it is not the burden of the profession to advance them. On the other hand, most of the legal needs of the poor are decidedly nonpolitical. Not all indigent representation involves a lawsuit against the welfare bureaucracy or class actions against consumer finance companies. Helping the poor need not be the equivalent of engaging in class warfare.

* * *

The depoliticization of indigent representation removes Terrell's and Wild-man's principal differentiation between pro bono work and professionalism, but does not provide a justification for the necessity of the work itself. Terrell and Wild-man believe that the legal profession bears a special "responsibility for adequate distribution of legal services" as a consequence of "the importance of law to our culture." This duty does not, in their view, extend to individual practitioners. Rather, they adopt the position that the profession need only "enable" those who wish to do pro bono work; they argue that no individual ought be required to do so. Terrell and Wildman reject the "monopoly" theory that lawyers are obligated to provide free services in exchange for their exclusive right to practice law, positing that lawyers are no longer able to extract "monopoly rents."

Terrell's & Wildman's argument works on its own terms. The service obligation is generalized; it exists because of the importance of law, not because of any specific benefits to lawyers. In consequence, no specific lawyer must take any particular action. The bar should "enable" pro bono activity, or at most self-assess a legal services tax, but no lawyer would ever have to handle a matter without charging a fee. Of course, if lawyers did benefit individually, then a quid pro quo in the form of personal service would be appropriate.

* * *

Clients are willing to hire lawyers because they know that their confidences will be kept, that their options will be evaluated, that their goals will be sought, and that their causes will be championed. Without the guarantee of individual, independent representation, and particularly without the guarantee of confidentiality, fewer lawyers would be retained, and at lower fees. Our system, by allowing the single-minded pursuit of a client's needs, in turn allows lawyers to charge a premium for their services. Thus, monopoly or not, legal counsel is made more valuable by the adversary system.

That system, however, is only justified by an ethic of universal, or near-universal, access to counsel. If everyone has a lawyer looking out for his or her own good, then it is all well and fine to keep confidences and to pursue zealously a client's cause. The farther we stray, though, from this ideal, the less warrant there is for adversary justice. Accordingly, if counsel were only available to the wealthy few, there would be less social basis for the attorney-client privilege and all of the accompanying entitlements that make lawyers' services so valuable.

But we do have an adversary, independent system, and every attorney's fee therefore includes some amount that is a direct reflection of the latitude that lawyers are given to serve their individual clients' needs. Moreover, this premium would exist irrespective of licensure, and it does not at all depend upon the existence of a monopoly.

Thus, lawyers benefit directly and personally from the institution of a legal system that prizes individual representation. Since that system is predicated on a broad distribution of legal services, it is reasonable to expect lawyers to repay some of that benefit in the form of free legal services.

In other words, client confidentiality and related attributes of advocacy can be seen as a sort of public concession, granted to lawyers for resale to their clients. Part of the profit from the use of this publicly-created good can, in turn, be reappropriated for public use. In that sense, mandatory pro bono obligations can be viewed as comparable to severance taxes or user fees.

Terrell and Wildman, however, have a second objection to pro bono representation, at least if it is to be required of individual attorneys. They argue that the work is too complicated:

> Many kinds of indigent services today involve areas of law that are quite detailed in their own right, meaning that competent service to that client will require levels of investment by a lawyer that cannot be justified by occasional involvement in pro bono service.

Thus, the argument runs, lawyers required to engage in pro bono activities will be put to an impossible test. They must either develop a superfluous expertise at the expense of their regular clients, or they must resign themselves to halfhearted, and therefore unprofessional, pro bono efforts.

There is, however, a third choice that Terrell and Wildman do not recognize. While it is true that many kinds of indigent services are achingly complex, many others are not. Mandatory pro bono representation need not be concentrated at the sophisticated end of the lawyering spectrum. Poor people have use for will drafting, probate administration, real estate closings, domestic relations representation, social security appeals, contract negotiation, and all sorts of simple litigation. True, death penalty defense, federal civil rights litigation, and consumer class actions are more high-profile, but they are not the sole, or even the principal, components of poverty law.

The potential complexity of indigent representation provides a solid reason to adopt only a measured program, one that matches the skills of the lawyer to the needs of the client, but it provides no reason to absolve all lawyers of individual responsibility for pro bono work. There should not be a lawyer in practice who is incapable of drafting a basic will, or who could not learn overnight how to defend a simple collection case. Pro bono work will, by definition, take some time away from ordinary law practice, but there is no reason to think that it will compromise the "ethic of excellence" with regard either to free or paying clients.

Moreover, there is an additional reason to view pro bono obligations as personal. I call it the Eleventh Floor Principle, and it is best explained through a vignette from my own early days in practice.

For two years after I graduated from law school, I worked in a legal services office on Chicago's west side. From my first day on the job I became our office's "consumer law expert," which required me to spend considerable time in the courtrooms on the eleventh floor of the civic center. While the words "eleventh floor" are unlikely to evoke a phobic reaction from lawyers outside of Chicago, anyone who ever practiced there will recognize immediately the terrible scene that I am about to describe.

In the early 1970s the eleventh floor was a no-man's land for poor people. It housed the landlord-tenant and collection courts, and therefore saw an endless stream of hapless individuals come before the bench to be processed. The all but inevitable outcome of every case was either an eviction or a wage garnishment. The plaintiffs' bar ran the courtrooms, to the point that these lawyers virtually organized the judges' calendars. The defendants were almost always unrepresented. If they had defenses, they had no way of recognizing or raising them. The best result that a defendant could hope for, whether liable or not, was usually a few extra days in his or her apartment or a few extra months to pay a debt.

The worst feature of the eleventh floor, however, was not the judgments that were entered. The worst feature of the eleventh floor was the way that the defendants were treated. The judges were nasty and peremptory. They rushed through the cases without allowing the defendants to talk, and they ridiculed defendants who attempted to say a few words in their own behalves. The clerks and bailiffs were worse, refusing to answer questions or to give explanations. The only advice they would give was "sit down and wait until your case is called." A defendant who stepped out to the washroom ran the risk of a default judgment, although cases could be "held" for hours if the plaintiff's attorney was busy elsewhere.

Every courtroom on the eleventh floor seemed to operate in continual bedlam. The plaintiffs' attorneys were always huddled and talking to each other. The clerks were always shouting orders to the ill-fated defendants. The judges were always barking out their judgments—seven days to move, thirty days to pay, add on the attorney's fees, and do not ask any questions. To me, the noise represented the character of the entire place; I thought of it as the din of injustice.

Legal services lawyers were seen as interlopers, people who wanted to ruin everyone else's easy time. We were tolerated, but just barely. I think that the judges considered us to occupy a position about half a step higher than the indigent defendants. These were courtrooms badly in need of reform.

Then one day, when I was sitting in one of the worst courtrooms waiting for my daily portion of judicial abuse, it happened. A pinstriped, downtown lawyer walked up to the bench and said, "Your Honor, I would like to present Mr. Albert Jenner." In 1975, the late Albert Jenner was probably the most well known and widely respected lawyer in Chicago. A name partner in Jenner & Block, he was most famous as the Republican counsel to the Senate Watergate Committee. Many believed that Mr. Jenner was the man most responsible for the eventual committee vote to impeach President Nixon. His visage—stern countenance, ramrod posture, piercing eyes, and signature bow tie—was well known to every Chicagoan who owned a television set. Albert Jenner was a man of unrivaled prominence, integrity, and power, and he had apparently come to the eleventh floor as a favor to a friend or employee.

Once Mr. Jenner's presence was announced, the entire courtroom suddenly metamorphosed. The muttering plaintiffs' bar fell silent. Clerks began answering inquiries from unrepresented defendants. The judge actually asked questions about the facts and the law. It was as though we were now in a real courtroom where justice, and people, mattered. Furthermore, this effect lasted for the entire day, long after Mr. Jenner left.

More than anything else imaginable, the unexpected presence of an important lawyer recast procedures on the eleventh floor. The judges and court personnel began to worry about how they appeared. Instead of facing only disinterested regulars and perceived no-accounts, they now had to be concerned about the well-to-do and powerful. For the rest of that day it was possible to practice law on the eleventh floor as though we were in a real courtroom.

By the next week, unfortunately, the residual effects of Mr. Jenner's visit had worn off. The clerks and judges were back to their old, short-tempered selves. Occasionally, however, even they seemed to long for the dignity and status that comes with procedural regularity; they bragged, as though it reflected honor upon them, of the time that "Bert Jenner handled a case in our courtroom."

There is a lesson in this digression. The presence of a prominent lawyer can have a transformative effect on a courtroom. And there are many courtrooms that are in serious need of transformation. While the eleventh floor of the 1970s might have been unique in its combination of clerical squall and juridic torpor, there are numerous others today that differ only as a matter of degree. Eviction courts, collection courts, traffic courts, juvenile courts, and misdemeanor courts everywhere would all no doubt benefit from a healthy dose of public exposure.

Imagine the effect, then, if on any given day some contemporary equivalent of Albert Jenner were likely to walk into any given courtroom. Best behavior would become a constant, rather than an aberrant, occurrence. The norms of process would change for the better. There could be no more dirty little secrets or comfortable procedural shortcuts, since missteps would now run the risk of offending someone capable of requital.

Again, it is not "politically biased" to say that justice is best done in the sunlight. Nor is it political to recognize that certain corners of our judicial system suffer from lack of exposure and public concern. It is all too possible for courts to become bureaucratized to the point that they become concerned with delivering results rather than doing individual justice. Indeed, one of the primary justifications of an independent bar is to ensure that individual rights are respected and not sacrificed in the interest of efficiency or expedience. Eleventh floor type courts are essentially lawless in that they operate without reference to the norms, rules, and procedures that are intended to govern our judicial system. The required presence of important lawyers at all levels of the judicial system would provide a robust corrective against this hazard.

Note that the effect of the Eleventh Floor Principle would go far beyond Terrell's and Wildman's proposed lawyer tax. While taxation of attorneys might raise sufficient funds to fulfill a collective obligation to provide legal services, it would not place influential lawyers in courtrooms generally occupied only by the powerless. The financing of a relatively few legal services or pro bono attorneys is a fine endeavor, but the impact of such an approach is necessarily limited in time and space. No matter how many cases they handle, "do-gooders" will always be regarded as marginal by bureaucrats and case processors. It is "establishment" lawyers who are esteemed, respected, and accommodated.

* * *